Praise for Kay Redfield Jamison's

Robert Lowell, Setting the River on Fire

Kay Redfield Jamison

Robert Lowell, Setting the River on Fire

Kay Redfield Jamison is the Dalio Professor in Mood Disorders and a professor of psychiatry at the Johns Hopkins University School of Medicine, as well as an honorary professor of English at the University of St. Andrews in Scotland. She is the author of the national bestsellers *An Unquiet Mind*, *Night Falls Fast*, and *Touched with Fire*, and is the coauthor of the standard medical text on bipolar disorder, *Manic-Depressive Illness: Bipolar Disorders and Recurrent Depression*. Dr. Jamison is a fellow of the American Academy of Arts and Sciences and the Royal Society of Edinburgh, as well as a recipient of the Lewis Thomas Prize, the Sarnat Prize from the National Academy of Medicine, and a John D. and Catherine T. MacArthur Fellowship. She is married to Thomas Traill, a cardiologist at the Johns Hopkins University School of Medicine.

Robert Lowell

Setting the River on Fire

Robert Lowell

Setting the River on Fire

A STUDY OF GENIUS, MANIA, AND CHARACTER

Kay Redfield Jamison

VINTAGE BOOKS
A Division of Penguin Random House LLC
New York

FIRST VINTAGE BOOKS EDITION, FEBRUARY 2018

Copyright © 2017 by Kay Redfield Jamison

All rights reserved. Published in the United States by Vintage Books, a division of Penguin Random House LLC, New York, and distributed in Canada by Random House of Canada, a division of Penguin Random House Canada Limited, Toronto. Originally published in hardcover in the United States by Alfred A. Knopf, a division of Penguin Random House LLC, New York, in 2017.

Vintage and colophon are registered trademarks of Penguin Random House LLC.

Owing to limitations of space, permissions to reprint previously published material appear beginning on page 529.

The Library of Congress has cataloged the Knopf edition as follows:
Names: Jamison, Kay R., author. | Traill, Thomas A., author.
Title: Robert Lowell, setting the river on fire : a study of genius, mania, and character / Kay Redfield Jamison.
Description: First edition. | New York : Alfred A. Knopf, 2017.
Identifiers: LCCN 2016028281
Subjects: LCSH: Lowell, Robert, 1917–1977—Mental health. | Manic-depressive persons—United States—Biography. | Poets, American—20th century—Biography. | Genius and mental illness. | Creative ability. | BISAC: BIOGRAPHY & AUTOBIOGRAPHY / Literary. | PSYCHOLOGY / Psychopathology / Depression. | PSYCHOLOGY / Creative ability.
Classification: LCC RC537.J356 2017 | DDC 616.89/50092 B—dc23
LC record available at https://lccn.loc.gov/2016028281

Vintage Books Trade Paperback ISBN: 978-0-307-74461-6
eBook ISBN: 978-1-101-94796-8

Author photograph © Thomas Traill
Book design by Soonyoung Kwon

www.vintagebooks.com

Printed in the United States of America
10 9 8 7 6 5 4 3 2 1

For my husband,

Tom Traill

For a week my heart has pointed elsewhere:
it brings us here tonight, and ties our hands—
if we leaned forward, and should dip a finger
into this river's momentary black flow,
infinite small stars would break like fish.

—*From* "The Charles River"

Robert Lowell in Paris, 1963

Reading Myself

Like thousands, I took just pride and more than just,
struck matches that brought my blood to a boil;
I memorized the tricks to set the river on fire—
somehow never wrote something to go back to.
Can I suppose I am finished with wax flowers
and have earned my grass on the minor slopes of Parnassus. . . .
No honeycomb is built without a bee
adding circle to circle, cell to cell,
the wax and honey of a mausoleum—
this round dome proves its maker is alive;
the corpse of the insect lives embalmed in honey,
prays that its perishable work live long
enough for the sweet-tooth bear to desecrate—
this open book . . . my open coffin.

—Robert Lowell

Contents

―――――

VI

MORTALITY

Come; I Bell Thee Home

Prologue

Old Cambridge, Massachusetts
March 19, 1845

No one knew what she was thinking. It was a short carriage ride; perhaps she was not thinking much at all. "In regard to her mind," her husband had said, "I hardly know what to say." No one did. Had she looked from her carriage window the tracks in the snow might have triggered a memory from childhood, helped to ward off the present. More likely, that kind of innocence was past retrieving. The Boston paper had said that today's snow was a "March sugar snow," one that would speed the flow of maple sap in the New England sugar orchards. As a child she might have found pleasure in such an image; she had been known for her lively mind. Now she was impenetrable. In her son's words, only as much of her remained as the "hum outliving the hushed bell."

The carriage took her from Old Cambridge to Somerville, a neighboring town on the banks of the Mystic River. It took her away from her husband, children, and their home with its great elms and long view of the Charles River. The house, built for a colonial loyalist, had in its time been a field hospital for Washington's troops and then home to a vice president of the United States. Later it would become the official residence for the presidents of Harvard. But for the passenger it was the house in which she had lived with her family for nearly thirty years and where her youngest child had been born. She was about to exchange one grand house for yet a grander one, one view of the Charles River for another. It was not an exchange anyone would willingly make.

Had the passenger cared, and had she kept an eye open for such things, she would have noticed that a street in the town of Somerville was named for her husband's family; so too was one of its railroad lines. Beyond the town limits an entire city bore his name. Her husband's name could be found in many places, it seemed, but it was of little help. It could not make right what was wrong in her head. And it was what was wrong in her head that brought her to Somerville.

The carriage drove up Cobble Hill and stopped at the large mansion built in the eighteenth century for a Boston merchant. The two-hundred-acre estate of gardens and fishponds, fruit orchards, and a rose-covered summerhouse had been described by a visitor to Boston in 1792 as "infinitely the most elegant dwelling house ever yet built in New England." When the original owner died, the wealthy of Boston, the "treasurers of God's bounty," had purchased the residence and a portion of the grounds in order to provide for the "class of sufferers who peculiarly claim all that benevolence can bestow . . . the insane." This "most elegant dwelling house" was now the McLean Asylum for the Insane and it was here that Harriet Brackett Spence Lowell was committed on March 19, 1845.

She arrived at the asylum in a "very irritable state." She would not permit the attendant to help her from her carriage nor would she allow anyone to carry her cloak. She would not converse with the other "boarders" and was "all the while scolding the staff." Her name, entered into the asylum's admission book, joined those of other old New England families—brokers and bankers, university presidents, writers, legislators, and merchants—whose ancestors had sailed on the early ships from England. Others, not so often with *Mayflower* names— the blacksmiths, rope makers, sailmakers, farmers, and whalers who lived and worked in Boston or other towns in New England—were also in the ledger. Insanity then, as now, cut across class and circumstance.

The patient's husband, Dr. Charles Lowell, minister of the West Church in Boston, knew from his own life, as well as the lives of his

McLean Asylum for the Insane, c. 1845, Somerville, Massachusetts

congregants, that madness could come to anyone. His account of his wife's erratic behavior, recorded in the medical ledger of the McLean Asylum, makes this clear. Mrs. Lowell's natural disposition, he said, was "to be particular about things"; each detail of her life had to be carried out with precision. Habit and exactitude had become all. She took long hours at dining and spent longer still at "dressing and undressing for her [corset] strings must be exactly even, & her garters wound round the stockings, at night, in a certain way."

She would not allow her family to touch or come near her. Once fastidious about her personal care, she now was heedless. Reading and the company of her family, even listening to the Bible read to her, no longer pleased her. More concerning was her lack of reason. "It has been her habit when anything seems foolish to her, to say *nonsense*," her husband said. "Now she uses it constantly & applies it to her own thoughts. And her reason seems often to be contending against these thoughts, & she will suddenly burst out, 'Be still! I didn't say so. Why did you put these thoughts into my head—I didn't say so. Why did you make me say so for?'"

Charles Lowell was not the only one to express concern about his wife's behavior. Their children, as well as friends, described her as being at times unmanageable and violent. Her moods swung wildly from "manic fits" to despair. She became reclusive for long periods of time and, on occasion, was indisputably insane. Once high-spirited and charming, she now sat by the fire depressed and unreachable. Occasionally she raved. The wife of Henry Wadsworth Longfellow, their friend and neighbor, wrote to an acquaintance the common view: Mrs. Lowell, she said, is deranged.

Harriet Brackett Spence Lowell had "been insane for many years," according to the admission note made in the asylum ledger at the time of her commitment. Except for a brief period of treatment with Dr. Rufus Wyman, the first superintendent of the McLean Asylum, she had been cared for entirely at home. The first seven months of her confinement at McLean were uneventful. She was quiet and particular and required little of her attendants. She spoke next to not at all. She walked, rode, did needlework, and visited with her husband and children on their weekly trips to the asylum. Things were to "be today as they were yesterday."

In early November 1845 she changed. Her doctor and attendants observed that "she began to be more excited, which was shown in paroxysms of screaming, running about her room disarranging her furniture & not seeming to know what she is about." She "has had scarce any sleep." By January of the following year she was "more comfortable" but far from well: "For the month or more just passed [she] has been more afflicted with false hearing & under that influence frequently screams with great violence. Is the great annoyance of all about her. In other respects she continues on from month to month with scarce any variation." Her obsessive eating rituals continued; she insisted on solitude. "Almost the only communion she has," states her medical record, is "with spirits not of this earth." On a few occasions she allowed "another lady" to stand in her doorway and talk with her about music. Mrs. Lowell "makes herself very interesting in these conversations," her attendant noted, and "expresses herself very understandingly."

It is not known what medicines Harriet Lowell received, nor if her blood was let. We know from the McLean ledger that her children visited her every week and she appeared glad for this. It helped but did not cure. She returned to her family in Old Cambridge after nearly three years in the asylum but was not, in a meaningful way, improved. "The fire is turning clear and blithely," wrote her youngest son, but "there thou sittest in thy wonted corner / Lone and awful in thy darkened mind."

Harriet Brackett Spence Lowell died insane. She passed on to her children, and their children in turn, the instability that her parents had passed on to her. Her great-great-grandson was heir to this mental instability. He was also to write poetry that, in the words of a critic, "will be read as long as men remember English."

"The Trouble with Writing Poetry"

The trouble with writing poetry is that you have readers, and the trouble with readers is that you have to listen to them after they have spent their time reading you. Mine, unless they are young poets or teachers of English, usually say one of three things. If they are relatives, they ask me why I choose such sordid downhill subjects. If they are strangers who want to be cordial yet dislike what they have read of me, they admit that some of the things I have published are over their heads. If they are not sure that they want to be cordial, they overemphasize that they are not intellectuals. They confess that all they can do is run a brokerage, make money, have five children, build a house from their own plans, and run, say, the Boston Museum of Natural Science as a hobby. The final blow is to ask me in a harsh, clear, incredulously polite voice about the Pulitzer Prize. "You won the *Nobel* Prize, didn't you? Everyone can't do that." Now, at the time when I was choosing "Art and Evil" as a title for this talk, I was spending many evenings with a favorite relative, an elderly lady who had recently been through a landslide of sorrows, but yet managed to be more observant, more light-hearted, more full of talk, and more all there than anyone I have known. We would listen to the lavishly anguished music of Schubert's *Winterreise* sequence, a work in which naïve and morbid lyrics are made sublime by the music. My cousin enjoyed every drop of this work, but then she would talk to me about being more positive. "You mustn't mislead younger people," she would say, "with your verses." Though a moderate drinker herself, my cousin believed with A. E. Housman that malt could do more than Milton. She would hold out a huge pale cylinder of martinis. "This will do you good," she would say. She would urge me to take siestas after lunch, knowing that sloth is the safest cure of all vices. Finally she would hand me an armful of fierce whodunits with horrifying covers. Nothing in this line was too rough for her: I still feel wounded when I think of how my cousin found my poems gloomier than the *Winterreise*, more inflammatory than martinis, duller than detective stories, and deader than sleep.

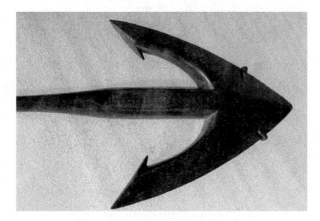

Harpoon, New Bedford Whaling Museum
"All men live enveloped in whale lines."

I

Steel and Fire

Your *Cantos* have re-created what I have imagined to be the blood of Homer. Again I ask you to have me. You shan't be sorry, I will bring the steel and fire, I am not theatric, and my life is sober not sensational.

—Letter to Ezra Pound, 1936

No Tickets for That Altitude

The resident doctor said,
"We are not deep in ideas, imagination or enthusiasm—
how can we help you?"
I asked,
"These days of only poems and depression—
what can I do with them?
Will they help me to notice
what I cannot bear to look at?"

—*From* "Notice"

"Darkness honestly lived through is a place of wonder and life," Robert Lowell wrote. "So much has come from there." It was October 1957 and he was forty, writing poetry "like a house a fire," and taking darkness into "new country." It was, he said, the best writing he had done, "closer to what I know" and "oh how welcome after four silent years." The new poems became the heart of *Life Studies*, "perhaps the most influential book of modern verse since T. S. Eliot's *The Waste Land*." The poems, most written at the boil in a few months' time, left their mark. "They have made a conquest," wrote a reviewer. "They have won . . . a major expansion of the territory of poetry."

In December 1957, after his summer and fall blaze of writing, Lowell was admitted to a mental hospital severely psychotic. It was his fifth psychiatric hospitalization in eight years. He was involuntarily committed to the Boston State Hospital and then transferred to the Massachusetts Mental Health Center (until 1956 known as Boston Psychopathic Hospital). In early 1958 he was transferred yet again, this time to McLean Hospital, where his great-great-grandmother had been institutionalized more than a hundred years earlier. The repetition of circumstance was not lost on Lowell; *Life Studies* had begun with a steeping in his ancestry. Harriet Brackett Spence Lowell, he had come to believe, was the one who had brought poetry into the Lowell line.

Lowell told the doctor who admitted him to the Massachusetts Mental Health Center that the preceding months, September and October 1957, had been "some of his most productive months of writing poetry." It was the pattern he had come to know well: first, the weeks of intense, fiery writing. Then the spike into mania, and finally, as night follows day, the "dust in the blood" of depression. His psychiatrist wrote in Lowell's medical chart what many of his doctors were to observe: "The patient has had a series of breaks," she wrote, "all in the light of unusual literary output." Much had come from the darkness, but not without a cost.

This book is about fire in the blood and darkness; it is about mania and the precarious, deranging altitude to which mania ascends. It is about the poetic imagination and how mania and imagination come together to create great art. But it is as much and more about the vital role of discipline and character in making art from inborn gift. Poetry may come from an unhappy and disordered life, Lowell wrote, "but a huge amount of health has to go into the misery." Without question, Lowell's attacks of mania spurred his work; they also brought pain to him and to those he loved. Things he had done when he was manic haunted him when he was well. They were public and they gave fodder to his detractors. Yet Lowell came back from madness time and again, reentered the fray, and kept intact his friendships. He kept his wit and his capacity to love. He went back to his work.

This faculty for regeneration is uncommon; so too is the courage to face, and to write from, the certainty of impending madness. Creating poetry that expands the territory is rarer still. Lowell's poetic imagination was tethered to an unstable but disciplined mind; it forged his work and branded his life. Mania took his poetry where it would not have gone, to an altitude for which, as he wrote in the first poem of *Life Studies*, "there were no tickets."

"My trouble," Lowell wrote to his friend, the poet Elizabeth Bishop, is "to bring together in me the Puritanical iron hand of constraint and the gushes of pure wildness. One can't survive or write without both but they need to come to terms. Rather narrow walking—." Lowell turned to his use the warring elements of what one doctor described as a "rock crystal" will, "glittering, very hard, and very definite in its formation," and the mania that lay almost beyond its reach; the fight gave a yield in art and a life graced but damaged. No measure of will could prevent madness, any more than it could bring down a storm at sea. It was the contending, the struggle, the effort that marked Lowell's life and set the terms of his writing and ambition. A century earlier, Byron, no stranger to ungovernable moods, had written, "Yet see—he mastereth himself—& makes / His torture tributary to his will." So too did Lowell.

This book is not a biography. I have written a psychological account of the life and mind of Robert Lowell; it is as well a narrative of the illness that so affected him, manic-depressive illness. This disease of the brain bears down on all things that make us human: our moods, the way we see and experience the world, the way we think, our changing capacities of energy and will and imagination, our desires, the gift to create, our determination to live or die, our expectation of the future, our sanity.

My interest lies in the entanglement of art, character, mood, and intellect. My academic and clinical field is psychology and, within that, the study and treatment of manic-depressive (bipolar) illness, the illness from which Robert Lowell suffered most of his life. I have studied as well the beholdenness of creative work to fluctuations in mood and the changes in thinking that attend such fluctuations. Mood disorders, depression and bipolar illness, occur disproportionately often in writers, as well as in visual artists and composers. Studying the influence of both normal and pathological moods on creative work is critical to understanding how the mind imagines.

We know mania and depression to be ancient diseases, described by Hippocrates five hundred years before Christ and intensively studied by physicians and scientists in the centuries since. Mania is an unstable and complex state. It is seductive and blinding to those who are caught up in it, laden with risk and energy. It can bolt the mind into new regions and propel it to act upon ideas. Mania insinuates its way into its hosting brain: intoxicating enough to be dangerous, original enough to be valuable. Narrow walking indeed.

If it were only Robert Lowell afflicted by mania it still would bear thought because mania was a dominant force in the life and work of a major poet. Because it is a part of the lives of so many other writers and creators, however, it is of more general interest. Mania has had a subtle as well as a blunt impact on human history: it has struck those who founded religions and empires, discovered the laws of nature and mapped new lands; it has set fire to the imaginations of those who write, paint, and compose. Mania is important to understanding many who create; it occupies rare real estate in the brain, sharing permeable borders with the normal mind, madness, and imagination.

This book will explore the patterns of Robert Lowell's mania and the mutability of his moods, as well as his long periods of depression, all of which shaped his temperament, character, thinking, and imagination. It will look at the forces Lowell brought to bear against his illness: his character and New England heritage; his discipline, intellect, capacity for friendship, and iron-laced upbringing. Lowell had a severe form of manic depression. He fought to control, fend off, and make sense of his manic attacks and was acutely aware that his control was incomplete. Instability and the relentless recurrence of his illness hardened his discipline while mania impelled and stamped his work. Knowing that his sanity was subject to forces beyond his control marked his poetry and darkened his life philosophy.

"We face the precariousness of keeping alert, of keeping alive in the triple conflict between madness, death and life," Lowell once said. "We must bend, not break." Lowell was dealt a hand of cards high in privilege and poetic imagination but he also received dark cards, impossible to play, that broke him time and again. There are no rules for how to play such cards; no one is provided a map to navigate madness or depression. I will argue that Lowell played his cards with courage and imagination; above all, he did not fold. It would have been easy to do so. Much of his adult life was engaged in a battle against madness or fear that it would come back, contending with the suffering that it caused him, and the pain it caused others.

Nothing about Lowell's mind was simple. The English poet and novelist Alan Brownjohn described spending time in his company: "We left feeling completely kind of drained, shattered, stupefied really . . . literary conversations with him were . . . tiring in the sense that you felt every nerve was stretched. It was partly the man's knowledge, which was encyclopedic, partly the sort of darting perceptions and intuitions on behalf of *you* for what you were going to say next. He made links and connections *for* you in this slightly manic—and paranoid—way."

Any attempt to understand such a mind must be partial and qualified; the usual limits of understanding another's mind are compounded when trying to understand Lowell, a man who thought in metaphor, lived in history, and whose mind was engaged in a restless, stupendously elaborate game of three-dimensional chess. Lowell's mind was of a lurching, revising originality.

"Metaphor was his reality, not the original fact," recounted his friend Esther Brooks. Lowell made her feel, another friend, the literary critic Helen Vendler, said, "like a rather backward evolutionary form confronted by an unknown but superior species. And when one asked what the name of the species was, the answer came unbidden: Poet." Lowell, to the philosopher Isaiah Berlin, was "a man of genius": complex, likable, and bewildering, he added, but a genius.

Lowell's originality and breadth of thinking were matched by prodigious energy. Ideas flew. Brooks, a longtime friend, said that Lowell's way of looking at things was "so completely original that you yourself began to see everything from a different perspective. Hours meant nothing to him when he was interested. Day turned into night and night back into day while he, with his seemingly limitless stamina, worried an idea, rejected it, discovered another, built mental pyramids, tore them down, discoursed on the habits of wolves, the Punic Wars, Dante, Napoleon, Shakespeare, Alexander the Great, politics, his friends, religion, his work, or the great noyade at Nantes. Whatever the subject it all came forth as though it were being pushed at you, helped on its way by that outward prodding palm. Sometimes this incredible energy of his would exhaust you and you would suddenly feel like screaming, or running away in search of some undefined moment, some unexamined fact, some purely sensuous reaction to beauty."

I do not believe, as a psychologist or from my life, that anyone can more than partially understand the mind of another. When I teach psychiatry residents and graduate students about psychotherapy, I stress the respect one must keep for the abyss between what one thinks one knows and what one actually knows about another individual's mental life. That abyss, unless its existence is kept in mind, will stand in the way of empathy and clinical acuity. We have a precarious understanding of our own thoughts and emotions, much less another's. There are limits, but one can hope, within those limits, to create some sense of a life and to bring a fair mixture of compassion and dispassion to the task. Lowell's mind, however many worlded and metaphoric, has a lighted way into it. His autobiographical writings, letters, poetry, and prose contain critical insight into his writing patterns and the evolution of his poetry; they allow a close look into his childhood and family, friendships, marriages, and the ongoing struggle he had with his mental illness. His letters, particularly, give a sense of who he was as a person, poet, father, and friend.

Looking back over thirty years of writing, Lowell said, "My impression is that the thread that strings it together is my autobiography." Yet of course his poetry was spun from his imagination as well as from fact, and fact itself, like memory and mood, is mutable. "From year to year," he wrote, "things remembered from the past change almost more than the present." His "autobiographical poems," he made clear, are "not always factually true. There's a good deal of tinkering with fact. You leave out a lot, and emphasize this and not that. Your actual experience is a complete flux. I've invented facts and changed things, and the whole balance of the poem was something invented." Yet, he said, if the writing is autobiographical, "you want the reader to say, this is true." The memory mattered, certainly, but also imagination. He quoted the poet G. S. Fraser that there is a real sense "in which good poets are, when you meet them, like their works."

Lowell's letters, posted before revising and time could alter them, are particularly helpful in understanding his life. So too are the writings of those who knew him. Most of his friends and lovers, as well as the three women to whom he was married, were writers and described in detail his personality and work, as well as the dramatic changes in his behavior when he was manic. Lowell was interviewed at length by journalists and critics, and his primary biographer, Ian Hamilton, conducted comprehensive interviews with many of those who knew Lowell best. The original tape recordings of these interviews, together with Hamilton's meticulous notes and correspondence, are of significant help in any attempt to understand Lowell. They are archived at the British Library and provide an invaluable portrait of Robert Lowell as a poet, husband, and friend. The interviews reveal the devastating impact of his mania on those who experienced his attacks at close hand, but they also give a good sense of why so many who knew him well loved him deeply.

Hamilton's biography of Lowell, published in 1982, was carefully researched and written; it was widely read in the literary community and its impact on Lowell's reputation as a poet and man was lasting and negative. The Lowell that Hamilton chose to portray is loutish, mad, humorless, a snob, and an overrated poet. There is much detail about Lowell's breakdowns but relatively little about how his illness affected his poetry. Lowell's capacity to live and work in the shadow of his madness is alluded to but not brought out in meaningful detail. His struggles and suffering, except for the suffering he caused to others, are not much in evidence. The cumulative and corrosive toll of Lowell's disease on his personality, most apparent in the last years of his life when he lived in England, receives disproportionate weight over the longer years of his life in America when he was in better psychological health. Negative excerpts from reviews of Lowell's work and interviews conducted by Hamilton predominate over the positive ones, which are given short shrift.

Artists and writers whose lives were spelled with madness and turmoil—Schumann, van Gogh, Woolf—have tended to attract sensationalist press and biography. Their art is crowded out by the drama of insanity or suicide. Irrational or shocking behavior makes better copy than the uses to which the turmoil is put and the discipline that shapes and constrains it. Hamilton's biography of Lowell is no exception to this, perhaps in part because he knew Lowell toward the end of his life when Lowell's mania was either on the simmer or full-blown, pernicious; a time when his behavior was often abrasive and when he lived in the determining light of his fame and madness. Simon Gray, the playwright and a friend of Hamilton, acknowledges this. "Towards the end of the life of Robert Lowell," Gray writes, "you can feel all Ian's unwritten revulsion working its way through the prose." Exactly because Hamilton did know Lowell and was, as well, a poet, his biography has had a lasting impact. Paul Mariani's biography of Lowell, *Lost Puritan*, is more sympathetic—more human, more complex, more appreciative of both the man and his work—but it has been less influential.

"Robert Lowell was notably unlucky in Ian Hamilton's major biography," wrote the poet and critic Richard Tillinghast. "[It was] a damagingly wrong-headed and skewed picture." One could wish, he said, for an account that would give a more rounded picture of the man "his friends put up with, laughed about, became exasperated with, but always admired and deeply loved." Another critic observed that "many readers and critics tend to regard Ian Hamilton's 1982 biography as the book that broke the back of Robert Lowell's reputation or, at the very least, turned his fame into infamy." Jonathan Raban, a writer and friend of Lowell who knew him well, described the book as "pitiless and strangely incomprehending of his illness."

Grey Gowrie, a poet, close friend, and pallbearer at Lowell's funeral, concurs with the criticism of Hamilton's biography. It "missed his humor. It got the snaffle and bit but is missing the horse. Lizzie [Elizabeth Hardwick, Lowell's second wife] said after she read it that one would never know why we all loved and cared about him." Hardwick's point is one reiterated by many who knew Lowell best.

Lowell's daughter, Harriet Winslow Lowell, believes that the relentless portrayal of madness fails to capture the father she knew: "Every serious story ends in buffoonish insanity, a manic affair and poetic reinvention," she states. "The breakdowns did happen, but the real life was full of unknowns and possibilities. . . . The hilarity and fun of being with the man is inadequately conveyed. . . . He had an enormous capacity for regeneration, hard work and a desire to re-connect with his family and friends on a deep level and engage with the world, in the midst of a deeply moving struggle with severe mental illness. Above all he was a poet. . . . He had a terrible disease, but was charming, mischievous and full of fun." His view of the world was dark, she says, but he was not. "I am not trying to say the ill man did not cause real pain and also the well man. It was a messy life in many respects."

I am indebted to Harriet Lowell, not only for talking with me about her father but for giving me permission to obtain and review his medical records. These provide a detailed account of his psychiatric illness and hospitalizations, as well as his thoughts and feelings about his illness and the relation of his mania and depression to his poetry. His fear that his illness would recur is palpable in the notes made by his doctors; so too is the remorse he felt over the hurt he caused his family and friends when manic. This is the first time that Lowell's hospital records have been made available. (See Appendix 1 for details of obtaining and using these records.) It is also the first time that Lowell's daughter has spoken about her father's work, her memories of him as a father, and her parents' marriage.

While I was doing the research for this book, Harriet Lowell asked if I would be interested in looking through the contents of the briefcase her father had been carrying with him at the time of his death in September 1977. It was a deeply moving thing to do. In addition to finding his glasses, his checkbook, a note from Elizabeth Bishop written to him shortly before he died, and a listing of the items he was carrying with him at the time he was pronounced dead at Roosevelt Hospital in New York, I came across a red hardbound appointment book. It contained more than two hundred pages of Lowell's handwritten notes, including fragments and drafts of poems, many of which found their way into his last book, *Day by Day*. The notebook, previously unknown, spans a critical year in Lowell's life, 1973, a year in which he published three volumes of verse, two of them to blistering controversy, one that received the Pulitzer Prize. During 1973, Lowell's poetry changed significantly in tone and focus. The writing in the notebook—marked by themes of wandering and an agitated search for home, for peace; of madness; of love and aging and death—is valedictory and wrenching.

I have drawn upon this notebook, together with Lowell's medical and psychiatric records, interviews I conducted with many of those who knew him well, and the existing literary, biographical, and autobiographical material, to give what I hope is a fresh reading of Lowell's life and work.

I am interested in who Robert Lowell was, how he came to be the man and poet he was, and why his poetry matters; in what we can learn from his work about the ambition of art, the necessity for art; courage, suffering, family; the fragility of sanity, the certainty of death, and the strands that link madness to action and imagination. And, in this promising, scrambling, pelting age of neuroscience, I am particularly interested in why character—courage, hard work, discipline, holding to one's true north—matters so deeply in understanding both art and mental illness.

I believe that mania and genius not uncommonly exist together, that suffering can be brought to some good, that the fast swither of mania can fire ambition, steel the nerve, and give high wind to imagination. If checked by discipline, and made flesh and blood by experience, doubt, and despair, they can forge great art. They did this in the work of Robert Lowell.

The Archangel Loved Heights

Timur said something like: "The drop of water
that fails to become a river is food for the dust.
The eye that cannot size up the Bosphorus
in a single drop is an acorn, not the eye of a man."
                                        —*From* "Fame"

When he was nineteen years old, Robert Lowell wrote to Ezra Pound asking to study with him in Italy. He had ambition and nerve. He went after what he wanted. "All my life I have been eccentric," he wrote. "I had violent passions for various pursuits usually taking the form of collecting: tools; names of birds; marbles; catching butterflies, snakes, turtles etc.; buying books on Napoleon. None of this led anywhere, I was more interested in collecting large numbers than in developing them." He had caught more than thirty turtles, he explained, and "put them in a well where they died of insufficient feeding." His collections of objects had overtaken the available space. Sometimes, "overcome by the collecting mania," he wrote, "I would steal things I wanted." He had never lived in the "usual realities"; he was "proud, somewhat sullen and violent." He chafed against the "insipid blackness of the Episcopalian church" and had turned instead to Zeus and Homer. Zeus's world was enticing, morally complex, and one that "blinked at no realities."

He had spent a summer with two friends on Nantucket, he continued, "dedicating themselves to art." Their hours and habits had been strictly regimented: no smoking, meals of grain, cooked eels, and honey. They wrote and read—Job, Wordsworth, Blake, Shakespeare, Coleridge—and took a high oath to be serious in their work. The insistence on near-monastic order, imposed by Lowell, was perceived by his friends as a seductive form of pale tyranny: "I wasn't really *afraid* of him," said one of his friends, but he was overwhelmed. "I think my picture of our friendship is of Aesop's bronze vessel and clay vessel crossing the stream. The bronze vessel says: 'Come and help me, give me company.' And the clay vessel foolishly does it and is jostled and of course the clay breaks and the bronze goes on. I think I rather saw myself as the clay vessel there." By the end of their time in Nantucket Lowell proclaimed that he had begun to "understand God" and had grown "to love my art, and those who were great in it."

Lowell's novitiate summer in Nantucket, he explained to Pound, had changed the game: "Since then I have been sucking in atmosphere, reading; and dreaming. Writing and trying to help one or two friends have been the only real things in life for me. At college I have yearned after iron and have been choked with cobwebs . . . no one here is really fighting." He ended his entreaty to Pound in passion and a plea to be taken seriously: "Your *Cantos* have re-created what I have imagined to be the blood of Homer. Again I ask you to have me. You shan't be sorry, I will bring the steel and fire, I am not theatric, and my life is sober not sensational."

It would be a remarkable letter coming from anyone, and it was the more so for coming from a first-year college student criticized for a lack of purpose by his parents, teachers, and doctors alike. It has the boldness and directness of his poems and prose; it is infused with the grandiosity and will of someone who knows where he wants to go and is set upon finding out how to get there. He was determined, he wrote to Pound a few months later, "to bring back momentum and move-ment in poetry on a grand scale. . . . [I] will throw myself into the fight and stay there." He was forming himself, certain that he could: creat-ing himself into a serious writer of great ambition who would use the extreme, contrasting forces in his mind to lasting artistic effect. Art was constant, if the mind was not.

Frank Bidart, a poet and friend who later worked closely with Lowell, underscored the seriousness of Lowell's ambition: "He once said to me, 'When I'm dead, I don't care what you write about me; all I ask is that it be *serious*.' This sentence reflects, I think, the relent-less mind that disturbed so many people, even friends and family. In a central way, Robert Lowell was not quite civilized. However courtly or charming, casual or playful, he was by turns, in his art and his personal relationships, Lowell was unfashionably—even, at times, ruthlessly—*serious*." He would not drift or be incidental.

Lowell's seriousness of purpose helped to frame his ambition, a wide capacity that spanned his expansive imagination and the manic illness that now and again would catapult him into delusion. Vaulting ambition had been his since childhood; maddened grandiosities came to him later, first in ecstatic faith and then in mania's "twists of fire." When Lowell had the ruthless conqueror Timur say, "The drop of water / that fails to become a river is food for the dust," it was clear that Lowell aligned with the river, not the dust.

A great canvas was to be necessary for Lowell's work, one that yoked a passion for greatness with the vastness of scale he admired in other writers. Ambition tied the writers together, slung them upward, broke some.

"The Archangel loved heights," Henry Adams wrote in *Mont Saint Michel and Chartres*. "Standing on the summit of the tower that crowned his church, wings upspread, sword uplifted, the devil crawling beneath . . . Saint Michael held a place of his own in heaven and on earth. . . . His place was where the danger was greatest." No one could touch Henry Adams, said Lowell. And like Adams's Archangel, Lowell loved heights and did not turn his back on danger. He would hold a place of his own. He would set the river on fire.

Lowell took faith in his ambition by looking to other writers. Melville and Hawthorne, he said, "pour out more than the measure will hold. What wonderful dangers, errors, condescensions and breathless abundance!" Melville's vastness was of a different order than Lowell's—"Give me a condor's quill!" Melville had proclaimed. "Give me Vesuvius' crater for an inkstand! . . . as if to include . . . all the revolving panoramas of empire on earth, and throughout the whole universe not excluding its suburbs"—but both Lowell and Melville wrote to change the game. Pasternak—whose poetry Lowell admired and translated and whose *Doctor Zhivago* had staggered him by the sweep of its story and sheer ambition—spoke to the role of greatness, and the aspiration to greatness, in art: "Greatness, greatness, above all else. . . . One must be great or learn to achieve greatness. . . . One must have moved mountains—actually moved them, and not merely claimed to have done so; and having moved them, one must move on to new goals."

Pasternak, Lowell, Hawthorne, Melville, Whitman: like Coleridge, all were "habituated *to the Vast*"; they swung for the fences. Lowell was "excited by greatness, by comparing greatness," Alfred Kazin wrote in his journal. "His sense of greatness, his sense of the great work, of the great moment in the great work, made me feel, again, as if I were breathing the unfamiliar, pure air at the mountain peak." Lowell's poetry, said John Berryman, "displays, in high degrees, passion, vista, burden." His ambition, he added, "is limitless."

Lowell's habitation of the vast, his frictionless slides into history, and his comfort in the company of the great meant that he learned from the great writers, historians, and epic heroes in a rare and immediate way; it placed him in an unbounded field under a high canopy. "Immense ambition was always central to his poetic ambition," observes the poet Dana Gioia. "He wanted to be the American Milton." Frank Bidart said that Lowell's poems "don't settle down into the comfortably grand and dead. They always suggest a vastness of feeling—like touching a wire that has electricity in it. He was an audacious maker."

Ambition, an acute sense and longing for a place among the great, widens the imagination and emboldens it. Too little ambition narrows the emotional and imaginative field; it makes it less likely that risks will be taken and new territory seized. But ambition carries risk. It shares space with self-deception; it can cross into grandiosity and, more rarely, into madness. If one punches a hole in the sky there can be no certainty about what is beyond.

Lowell's behavior at the time he was committed to the Massachusetts Mental Health Center in 1957 provides an example of the open boundaries between poetic ambition, obsession, and clinical grandiosity. Two facts were clear at the time of his admission to the hospital. First, Lowell was indisputably psychotic. Second, he had just written many of the poems that would make up *Life Studies*, one of the most influential books of poetry of the twentieth century. The psychiatrist's admission note is particularly interesting in this light: "There is undue preoccupation with greatness," Dr. Marian Woolston wrote about Lowell, "almost a sense of mission in making a new contribution. He has a great need to be not only good but unique among poets—[this] need for greatness was early established." He was obsessed with being among the great, she continued. "He wanted to be a second Dante and actually thought he could be." (Lowell at times not only aspired to be ranked with Dante but thought that he *was* Dante. At different times, in different hospitals, he believed himself to be T. S. Eliot or Shakespeare or Homer and revised their works accordingly.) Ambition, imagination, and delusion reside in close quarters of the mind. Research bears this out: individuals with a history of mania have much higher levels of ambition and expectation of success.

From childhood, Lowell had shown a striking capacity to conjure and live alongside the great figures of history. "History lived in his nerves," said Derek Walcott. Lowell "gossiped about the English poets the way other people gossip about their friends," recalled James Atlas. "He spoke of them as if they were colleagues and contemporaries." Helen Vendler wrote that Lowell gave his poetry students the sense "of a life, a spirit, a mind, and a set of occasions from which writing issues—a real life, a real mind, fixed in historical circumstance and quotidian abrasions." History gave Lowell an intellectual structure, Vendler continued, "a frame into which everything could be put . . . an independent vantage point from which to write as soon as he drew back from the moment and contemplated life and the world more largely." Other poets of his time who also had mental illness, and there were many, were "more deeply locked into the personal."

Almost everyone who knew Lowell remarked on his affinity for the past, his easy transit into historical times, his unrivaled comfort with those long dead. "Surfacing constantly in what Cal says, are touchstones from all levels of history," said the poet Philip Booth. "Cal is like an archeologist at a dig-site; there are ages and ages under him." Another friend observed that "the great past, Revolutionary America, the Renaissance, Rome, is all contemporary to him. He moves among its great figures at ease with his peers." He is "the man who on a very large scale sees more, feels more, and speaks more bravely about it than we ourselves can do."

Like Henry Adams, who lived by "shuttle-like movements of his thought, from present to past, from past to present" and who saw no obvious demarcation between the past and the present, Lowell too "pulled the present age backward into the past, and jammed the past into the present." "He was a survivor from another age," recounts Jonathan Raban. "You felt like you were meeting a seventeenth-century poet at times. His capacity to make himself contemporary to Marvell. To Yeats." He had an unparalleled historical imagination, said Robert Fitzgerald, the translator of Homer and Sophocles. "He could hold the world of archaic Rome and the world of contemporary Washington together in his mind."

Not long ago, a scientist touched the carcass of a baby mammoth that had been preserved in the Siberian ice for thirty thousand years. "I laid my hand on its skin and felt a chill," he said. "I had touched the Stone Age." Lowell laid his hand on history.

The past had always exerted a vivid grip on him, said Lowell. His mother read Hawthorne's *Greek Myths* to him when he was a child, and the stories fixed themselves to his imagination, like limpets to a sea rock. "Sometimes when I am trying to go to sleep," he said years later, "I can almost touch these people and talk to them. If I read some false, modern retelling of the old stories, I say to myself, 'This isn't the way it happened. I was there.' . . . Hawthorne's fables are history to me, and just as much fact as the earth, the water, and the sky." Fables were history for Lowell and history was fact; all were earth and water and sky. He took these imagined worlds into him; he drew upon them when he was sane and fell into them without a map when he was mad.

––––––

The chief charm of New England was harshness of contrasts and extremes of sensibility—a cold that froze the blood, and a heat that boiled it—so that the pleasure of hating—one's self if no better victim offered—was not its rarest amusement; but the charm was a true and natural child of the soil, not a cultivated weed of the ancients. The violence of the contrast was real and made the strongest motive of education.

—HENRY ADAMS, *THE EDUCATION OF HENRY ADAMS*

Henry Adams, believed Robert Lowell, was "our greatest man maybe, certainly the greatest New Englander." No one could touch Adams, he said: he was wonderful on so many things, including "his and our manic-depressive New England character." Like Adams, Lowell was New England to bone and marrow. Both had been "born under the shadow of the Dome of the Boston State House," both carried the weight and privilege of family names—Henry Adams was the grandson and great-grandson of presidents and, like Lowell, traced his ancestry to the *Mayflower*. More important, they had much in common by way of temperament and the way they experienced life. Adams and Lowell were skeptics, marked by the "habit of doubt," and they were natively contrary. Intent on navigating life in ways that made sense to them, if not to others, they took covenant with the idea that to learn best one taught oneself or sought out those able to teach what was needed.

Lowell and Adams, restive members of their tribes, shared minds that were shaped by contrast and ruled by flux; their temperaments were fine wired to light, season, and experience. Mutability in mood and will, cycles of passivity and wildness—integral not only to their temperaments but to the manic-depressive illness Lowell was heir to—these were laid out by Henry Adams in his autobiographical master-piece *The Education of Henry Adams*.

The double nature of "a cold that froze the blood, and a heat that boiled it" gave life its relative value, he wrote: "Winter and summer, cold and heat, town and country, force and freedom, marked two modes of life and thought, balanced like lobes of the brain. Town was winter confinement, school, rule, discipline; straight, gloomy streets, piled with six feet of snow in the middle; frosts that made the snow sing under wheels or runners; thaws when the street became dangerous to cross. . . . Above all else, winter represented the desire to escape and go free."

Summer, on the other hand, "was drunken." The New England boy was wild, like all boys, but he had a "wider range of emotions than boys of more equable climates." To the New England boy, winter was and always would be the "effort to live." Summer in its expansiveness, its long fields and full orchards, its infinite sensation: summer was free-dom, it was "tropical license." It brimmed with life; it gave; it flew. Winter was dead, dangerous; it dragged and discomfited. The con-trast between winter and summer, Adams wrote, was the most decisive force he would ever know: "It ran through life, and made the division between its perplexing, warring, irreconcilable problems, irreducible opposites." From youth he knew that life was double, that the multi-plicity of the self was elemental. The tidal rhythms pulsing in the mar-row of Henry Adams found a responsive place in Lowell's imagination; he held a debt to Adams for giving witness to the nervous forces at the heart of life and to the full-blooded call of memory.

Lowell returned often to Henry Adams. To an extent he mod-eled his autobiographical "91 Revere Street" in *Life Studies* on Adams's

autobiography. In his poem "Henry Adams 1850," written when he
was in his fifties, Lowell, as was his wont, borrowed freely and created
uniquely. He used Adams's words to capture the experiences of childhood that had stamped Adams's "menaced" and "knowingly sensuous
mind":

> Adams' connection with Boston was singularly cool;
> winter and summer were two hostile lives,
> summer was multiplicity, winter was school.
> "We went into the pinewoods, netted crabs,
> boated the saltmarsh in view of the autumn hills.
> Boys are wild animals, I felt nature crudely,
> I was a New England boy—summer was drunken,
> poled through the saltmarsh at low tide."

The summers and winters of Henry Adams's New England stayed
in Lowell. He knew their extremes, he had lived them. The New
England country, wrote Lowell, was "a world I knew mostly from summer and weekend dips into it. It was a boy's world, fresher, granier,
tougher, and freer than the city where I had to live." Antithetical forces,
within and outside the self, metaphoric and literal, became a part of
how his mind wrote the world. The task was to take the wind and sun
when he could, endure the cold, and put his shoulder to the wheel to
make sense of the irreconcilable. One gained will by exerting it.

Later in Lowell's life, after knowing mania and depression, he
would describe opposing factions of a different kind, a war within, to
his friends as well as to his doctors. In 1951 he wrote to the philosopher George Santayana: "What a heavy way of saying that *the* peculiarity I seem to have been born with is a character made up of stiffness
and disorder, or lethargy and passion. These words are not necessarily
the best. The two horses, judgment and emotion perhaps, take many
names; but they go together ill at best, and at bad times, one is lying
down immobile, the other galloping."

Lowell told one of his psychiatrists that there was an uneasy alli-
ance between these two, the visceral and the higher minded; it affected
his work: "I find that I fall into two parts which roughly correspond
to instinct and conscience. . . . Neither one, as far as the single daily
calls of life go, is much of a success. Instinct . . . thinks by means of

images. . . . Conscience is a fine fellow, but it has never written any-thing, not even a thought-out critical essay, and its experience almost entirely derives from what instinct has felt. An angel's abstract mind on a brute's body it talks against everything conceivable, for it cannot conceive of anything that might make its queer centaurish being work like a man." Lowell, like the New England Puritan, knew a "sober pru-dence," but he had as well a "divine recklessness which would make all things new."

"The lightning which explodes and fashions planets, makers of planets and suns, is in him," Emerson had written about force and order in his essay on fate. "On one side, elemental order, sandstone and granite, rock-ledges, peat-bog, forest, sea and shore; and on the other part, thought, the spirit which composes and decomposes nature,—here they are, side by side." Lowell felt Emerson's presence acutely—"the greatest nonfiction writer, the most radiant explorer among our Protestant divines"—as he did so many of the nineteenth-century New England writers. As, too, he experienced the English and French, Roman and Greek, and English writers long before them. Jonathan Miller, who directed Lowell's plays in England and America, said that "he loves the contrast between the uncontrollable rush of the present and those things in the past with their strong, firm outlines coming to take their small clear place in history." Contrast and contention were critical; so too was a measure of continuity.

To Elizabeth Bishop, Lowell had described the contending forces in his mind as "the Puritanical iron hand of constraint and the gushes of pure wildness." If not checked, he added, "I can always go off the beam into hallucinations, or lie aching and depressed for months." Cycles in mood and will, in the capacity to act, coursed through his life. "Maybe it's just my nature, but one seems to see-saw from a sort of rosy blandness to a blank, bare cracking feeling. It's like swimming across a pond littered with pieces of wood; one wonders if one has the energy to push through it all, then one floats gaily and the [current] draws one forward."

Lowell's experience of dueling instinct and conscience, the con-trast between light and dark, was an opposition Miltonic in its inten-sity. This opposition, as Lowell made clear, was more than metaphor. "During this time I have had five manic depressive breakdowns," he wrote when he was forty-two. "Short weeks of a Messianic rather bestial glow, when I have to be in a hospital, then dark months of indecision, emptiness etc. So the dark and light are not mere decoration and poetic imagery, but something altogether lived, inescapable. Even survival had to be fought and fought for."

Nathaniel Hawthorne, with whom Lowell declared a strong temperamental affinity, had said of himself, "Lights and shadows are continually flitting across my inward sky, and I know neither whence they come or whither they go." His friend Herman Melville agreed: "For spite of all the Indian-summer sunlight on the hither side of Hawthorne's soul, the other side—like the dark half of the physical sphere—is shrouded in a blackness, ten times black." Shifting patterns of darkness and light were the heart of truth for Hawthorne and Melville, Adams and Lowell. For good cause, Lowell was drawn to tyrant as well as hero.

Those who knew Lowell knew his contradictory sides: With his courage came fragility, with his darkness a saving wit. Mania brought brutality, even violence, but it stood sharply in contrast to his more usual and often-noted gentleness. "Lowell had the most disconcerting mixture of strength and weakness," wrote Norman Mailer, "a blending so dramatic in its visible sign of conflict that one had to assume he would be sensationally attractive to women. He had something untouchable, all insane in its force; one felt immediately there were any number of causes for which the man would be ready to die. . . . But physical strength or no, his nerves were all too apparently delicate. Obviously spoiled by everyone for years, he seemed nonetheless to need the spoiling. These nerves—the nerves of a consummate poet— were not tuned to any battering."

Lowell's close and lifetime friend from college years, the writer Peter Taylor, recalled that Lowell searched to understand himself by mining his opposite qualities; by doing so he also searched to make meaning of life: "From the time I first knew him in his later teens, he seemed determined that there should be no split in his approach to understanding profound matters. He was searching for a oneness in himself and a oneness in the world. He would not allow that any single kind of experience denied him the right and access to some opposite kind." Access to experience was not a problem for Lowell. It came to him as the air and when he needed more he left to find it elsewhere.

Lowell learned best on his own and chafed under the strictures of traditional education. He was curious, observant, and thought uncommonly about what he saw. He found pleasure in his own imaginings and maintained a saving distance from structure that others might impose. He kept well enough into himself to protect room for growing. He was comfortable with discordant beliefs. He believed writing was a calling, not a profession; he aimed for the stars. His novitiate summers in Nantucket changed him; the religious fervor for ideas and art that streaked those summers would come back to him in cycles of gust or gale force for the rest of his life. He didn't quit. He didn't settle. He worked hard. These qualities—independence, contrariness, ambition, toughness, receptiveness to experience—are the blood supply to a creative mind and temperament; they are wellspring to imagination. The ferocity and peculiarity that shadowed him when he was a boy later made their own contributions to the man and to his poetry.

Lowell recognized that he could be remarkable. When he was eighteen he wrote in a school essay that "the accomplishments of man are unlimited . . . when he places all the strength of his mind and body to the task, a new almost divine power takes possession of him." The enlightened mind is "always questioning itself, always seeking means of self-improvement, and always striving for something higher." While still in school, his friend Frank Parker said, Lowell decided he could do whatever he wanted to do if he worked hard enough at it. "He would be a writer, he said. . . . He would work at it . . . and he would be great."

Another friend, Blair Clark, said that Lowell somehow survived the "quite dreadful tensions" of his childhood and "managed to invent himself. The being he created was a spring coiled by his strong, fumbling hand." Lowell created himself in "an unusually conscious and deliberate way," observed Clark, but that paled when "compared to the way in which he created Robert Lowell the writer. He set about that task even before he had a notion of what it was to 'write,' or what there was for him to write about." Lowell "created himself as an intellect, as a creative spirit, in the most deliberate, self-conscious way. . . . How do you make yourself better? . . . Cal immediately went to the classics—to Homer. . . . The compulsion was moral—it wasn't literary or cultural, it was an entirely priestly thing. It was to do with the improvement of ourselves."

Force, most significantly manic force, was a cardinal element in Lowell's life and work; it was given and lasting, something with which he had to reckon, battle to control, try to contain. He would draw upon literature, myth, and history for his heroes, those who had engaged in epic mental or physical struggles, channeled great wrath and powers—Achilles, Alexander, Napoleon, Jonathan Edwards, Cuchulain—and brought to the struggle his own "rock crystal" will and imagination. He looked to the past to draw down otherwise destructive force to advantage, keep it from surging over the banks; he would start in life as Achilles, bound by his wrath, and end as Odysseus: navigating, wandering, searching for home and a semblance of peace. His poetry would fill with strafing, then shielding images: net and hook; lance, shell, armor, and carapace. The wrath of God, the force of nature—storm and fire, river and sea—surged through Lowell's early years, then his convert years of Catholicism.

Homer and the Old Testament were obvious home waters for Lowell. In a school essay about *The Iliad*, Lowell declared that the "unreasoning hate of Achilles cannot continue. His smoldering anger is actually more harmful to himself than to the Trojans." The hero's punishment, wrote the young Lowell, will be in proportion to his wrath. "This titan must conform to the will of the universe . . . even he can accomplish nothing when he is out of harmony." Years later, Lowell would return to *The Iliad* to describe the "insensate rage" of Achilles, the great blind force of mind that was a "wavering, irresistible force, a great scythe of hubris, lethal to itself." Force and madness share quarters; Lowell knew it well.

Each translator of Homer opens *The Iliad* with his own word for the wrath of Achilles. Robert Fitzgerald starts with "anger": "Anger be now your song, immortal one, / Akhilleus' anger, doomed and ruinous." Richmond Lattimore, too, writes of "anger": "Sing, goddess, the anger of Peleus' son Achilleus / and its devastation." More recently, Robert Fagles called it "rage": "Rage—Goddess, sing the rage of Peleus' son Achilles, / Murderous, doomed." And George Chapman, whose seventeenth-century translation of Homer left John Keats spellbound and thunderstruck, wrote of the "wrath" of Achilles: "Achilles' baneful wrath resound, O Goddess, that impos'd / Infinite sorrows on the Greeks." So too did Alexander Pope.

Lowell, who knew the translations of Homer well, uniquely used the word "mania" in his own translation of Homer. In "The Killing of Lykaon" he writes, "Sing for me, Muse, the mania of Achilles / that cast a thousand sorrows on the Greeks." Lowell, deeply educated in the classics, was certainly aware of and used other translations when he did his own more than a decade after the first time he was hospitalized for mania. "Mania" is in the first line of the first poem, "The Killing of Lykaon," in *Imitations*, his 1961 book of translations; it is also in the last line of the last poem in the book, his translation of Rilke's "Pigeons":

> Over non-existence arches the all-being—
> thence the ball thrown almost out of bounds
> stings the hand with the momentum of its drop—
> body and gravity,
> miraculously multiplied by its mania to return.

Mania and its attendant forces, dangerous and creative, had entered his language, as they had his life.

Robert Lowell in Nantucket, 1935

"I have grown to love my art, and those who were great in it."

Lowell coat of arms, Lowell House, Harvard University
"Ours was an old family."

The Puritanical Iron Hand of Constraint

My trouble seems to be to bring together in me the Puritanical iron hand of constraint and the gushes of pure wildness. One can't survive or write without both but they need to come to terms. Rather narrow walking.

—Letter to Elizabeth Bishop, 1959

3

Sands of the Unknown

Robert Lowell, Poet. Born in Boston, bearer of a name twice honored in the literary history of your country, you have brought the keen moral vision of your Pilgrim ancestors to the understanding of our secular and violent age. Your New England, like theirs, has proved to be a country of the mind.
—Honorary degree citation, Yale University, 1968

Robert Traill Spence Lowell IV was born in his grandfather's house in Boston on March 1, 1917. Sixty years later his requiem Mass would be sung a few hundred yards away. Lowell was New England born, cast, and buried. His character, and the receding line of windmills against which he was to tilt, were formed in the shadow of his New England ancestors and his mind was hallmarked by the New England writers who kept his regard from the beginning of his life to its end. "I wrote about only four places," Lowell said: "Harvard and Boston, New York and Maine. These were the places I lived in and also symbols, conscious and unavoidable." The New England landscape, her history and people, were the Ithaca to which he returned over and again. "I come with signposts in one hand lettered Boston, Beacon Hill, the Atlantic Ocean etc.," he wrote. "In the other I hold a handful of dust picked up somewhere along the road, true stuff, but unsorted, unlabelled."

New England, as understood by Lowell, began with his ancestry, continued with his education and upbringing, and filled out in his imagination. Land and people were experienced through an uncommonly responsive temperament. Early impressions, like later ones, were fluid, mixing time, image, and fact. "If you had come out of the brown pillared doorway of my Grandfather Winslow's house at 18 Chestnut Street," Lowell wrote of his earliest childhood imaginings, "you would have seen house-high brown horses with Norman noses and silver bells" that "pulled down great swags of turning leaves from the poplar trees. I thought of falling green umbrellas." It was Beacon Hill, a sliver of upper-class New England, an era experienced through Lowell's creating eyes and forming mind.

In his will, written in 1938, the year he died, his maternal grandfather Arthur Winslow had written, "To my children and grandchildren I bequeath the gift of life in New England and the heritage of our ancestry dating back to early times. I am proud to be of New England and happy to have completed my life there. Its antecedents I count among the most valuable legacies to my children." It was not a usual thing to include in a will, but it spoke to his beholdenness to New England.

"He was my Father," wrote Robert Lowell of his grandfather. "I was his son." Their relationship, not so simple as Lowell's remark would have it, was enough realized to make all the more painful to Lowell the part that was not. Arthur Winslow's New England was as critical to Lowell's imagination as that of his own father's very different Lowell line. The Boston of his grandfather, and Lowell's childhood visits to the Winslow New Hampshire farm, figure importantly in *Lord Weary's Castle* and *Life Studies*. Arthur Winslow was a domineering figure, edging out Lowell's own father for respect and not infrequently overshadowing the younger Lowell as well.

Forty years after his grandfather's death, Lowell, in the final months of his own life and a patient in the same Boston hospital room in which his grandfather had died, remembered and still compared: "This room was brighter then / when grandfather filled it. . . . / He needed more to live than I, / his foot could catch hold anywhere." He conjured his grandfather's death, mythic, a ride beyond the "Charles River to the Acheron / Where the wide waters and their voyager are one." Arthur Winslow was buried in the cemetery of his New England ancestors, the family cemetery where he and his grandson had years earlier "raked leaves from our dead forebears," the cemetery where Lowell himself would be buried next to his parents and close to his grandfather. In death as in life, Arthur Winslow passed on the "gift of life in New England."

The New England of Arthur Winslow was a less complex, less dark and allegorical New England than Lowell's, but for both men New England was determining. New England was not just a place, it was an idea, the history of a people passed on in a ringing, righteous, rebellious account of action and conscience. "It was in the stars," wrote

Lowell, "for the American Revolution to have flamed first in Boston. Wasn't the Jamaican rum drunk there spiced with gunpowder to burn the tongue? Here debate was hottest, debate changing to riot." In its beginning New England was the story of pilgrims, people of a granite and intolerant faith who sinned and fell from grace often enough to set fire to any child's imagination. Later, it was more complicated.

"We New Englanders," wrote Lowell, "can never get over the idea that simple experience is marked with pointers left here by providence, that all is allegorical and has its clue." The New England spirit was "something of the mind. Intensely of the mind, the naked ideal hidden in vestments of a life-denying drabness, opposed to display and yet expensive, sensual, baroque disclosures of the flesh." A mind such as Lowell's—metaphoric, allegoric, caught in the thickets of history and ancestry, enthralled and appalled by decay and sin, played on by madness and erratic moods—could hardly have had a better home country than New England. The evocative land, Melville had said, "is not down on any map; true places never are."

It would seem an overstatement to assert that New England was a defining influence on Lowell—New England is too much of an abstraction, too easily called up as a symbol, too various, too taken with a history long past, too etched by change and disregard—but it was. New England was critical to how Lowell came to be. New England, and how he construed it, created a context, a net of myth and metaphor, with which to better understand his complex, variable mind and, later, his madness. The molding of his character began in New England, a region of original thinkers and revolutionary leaders. New England provided examples toward which to move, and disenchantments against which to rebel. New England, flawed and full, stood up well to reinterpretation and opposition. It was the home of writers whose work he could learn from and use. New England was a place to leave and come back to. It was the geography of first impressions. New England, as it shaped the life and work of Robert Lowell, was a country of the mind, containing within itself the beginnings of a nation and the myths the nation created as it grew.

Lowell's disciplined, curbing, and creating intellect would be brought to bear on the New England myth and reality, on a disposition that registered life acutely, distributively across mind and senses. Lowell's early grapplings with the instability in his mind and moods would help him later to bring madness to the bit. Or more to the bit than otherwise would have been likely. His close study of the Puritanism of his ancestors, as well as his immersion in Boston's literary and political history, gave him a deep well from which to draw. The North Atlantic coast, the "thousand small town New England greens," Boston, Nantucket entered first into his memory and later his poetry. He took New England's influence seriously. There was in New England, he believed, "a kind of carnal gravity," a longing "so strong for what is not that what is not perhaps exists. Or maybe something still deeper, a peculiar stain or genius that is unkillable, inescapable."

Lowell drew deeply from the work of other writers who shared not only his New England roots but his temperamental disquiet: Nathaniel Hawthorne, Herman Melville, Henry Adams, Jonathan Edwards, Henry David Thoreau. Lowell, who had declared Henry Adams particularly good "on his and our manic-depressive New England character," himself understood this aspect of that character; he inherited not only his manic-depressive illness from his New England ancestors but their legacy for nerve, hard work, and words as well. After a particularly devastating mental breakdown he wrote to Elizabeth Bishop that he would welcome her visit "with open arms, joy, and whatever stability and wisdom my hereditary granite New England morality still retains." Hard work and nerves alone could not keep madness at bay, but they provided tactics and mettle for the fight. The forces that shaped him as a child gave him armor—partial, imperfect, essential—for what he would come up against as an adult.

Shaping forces are all. "Everything in the geologist's mind is a symptom of something happening," wrote Adam Nicolson when describing how islands come into being. "They see the process, the mineralisation, the conductive cooling, the developing faults." To understand the creating forces is to understand what is important. The force of wind and tide, fire and cold, make an island the way it is; one must "think always of how it came to be." We, like islands, come to be. Land, history, and family shaped who Robert Lowell was, how he came to be: his imagination and ambition; his conscience, his moral failures; the bounty and shortfall in his life; his periodic madness, his dominant lucidity. At a more ancient and abiding level, he came into being through the capricious, determining hurl of the genetic dice.

When he was thirty-eight years old, Lowell undertook a sustained exploration of his ancestry. He did this in part at the suggestion of his psychiatrist and in part because of the inescapable interest shown by his family and others in his Lowell and Winslow ancestry. They were prominent New England names, with roots going back to early colonial times. "Ours was an old family," he said once. "It stood-just." The family names of his father and mother represented different things to Lowell at different times in his life. His Lowell and Winslow ancestors were real to him, part of a historic past to which he was drawn and into which he entered easily by way of a vivid imagination. They were a link from times past to the future. "I woke up the other morning with a curious feeling of continuity," he wrote to his cousin Harriet Winslow. "Great falling festoons of loose green vines, trees and white woodwork. One thing dropping, slightly tangling and touching another indefinitely. And a feeling that as we pass through our fairly brief lives, we stay long enough to pass something on that someone else catches by his fingertips. A little bit of my grandfather and that old world seems to touch Harriet." Ancestors were part metaphor, part fate, part explanation; they symbolized values against which to fight, forces to live up to, decay to resist. He would rake through his pedigree for flaw and madness, for poetic gift; he would use it as a portal into the history of his race.

Lowell's ancestors not only entered into, they inhabited his imagination: they were biddable, subject always to fresh interpretation, a mythic or flaw-finding take. Jonathan Miller, who directed Lowell's New England plays in London and New York, said that Lowell's imagination seemed to "feed off history" and that his poetry was "nourished by figures from the past." These ancestral figures were not so much dead as living: When his forebears emerged in his writing, most unforgettably in *Life Studies*, they came with a specificity of name and place and carried with them not only personal but historical and artistic meaning. They came with possibility and regret, a sense of pride, discontent, enmity, and tenderness. "In different hours," wrote Emerson, "a man represents each of several of his ancestors." They are rolled up in his skin and "constitute the variety of notes for that new piece of music which his life is." Lowell's ancestors passed down uncommon sheet music. "What is history?" asked Lowell. "What you cannot touch." Seamus Heaney observed that Lowell spoke with a "dynastic as well as an artistic voice." His "preoccupation with ancestry was a constant one.

From beginning to end, his poems called up and made inquisition of those fathers who had shaped him and the world he inhabited."

Lowell's research into his ancestry was thorough and enthusiastic. "I had a little ancestor worshipping spree the other day," he wrote to his cousin Harriet Winslow. "[I] even worked out on four typewritten pages my family-tree. How quickly it runs into the sands of the unknown." A month later, fully immersed in family records and genealogies, and beginning to see what he could not see, he wrote to her again: "A lot is lost and a lot was never seen and understood. We stand in our own characters, of course, and warp our own knowledge. Still, it's fascinating to see what one can fish up, clear up and write down." It was like going to a chiropractor, he said, "who leaves me with all my original bones jumbled back in a new and sounder structure."

The ancestors return in their own way, he wrote in "Revenants":

> They come back sometimes, I know they do,
> freed like felons on the first of May,
> if there's a healthy bite in the south wind,
> Spring the echo of God's single day.
> They sun like earthworms on the puddly mall,
> they are better equipped for everything than people,
> except perhaps for living. When I meet them
> covertly, I think I know their names:
> Cousin So, Ancestral Mother-in-Law So . . .
> I cannot laugh them into laughing back.
> "Dead we have finally come to realize
> what others must have known from infancy—
> God is not about. We are less scared—
> with misty bounds we scale the starry sheer."

The idea of ancestral sin was seed and crop for many New England writers, Puritan to present. John Calvin had believed that original sin was "an hereditary depravity and corruption of our nature, diffused into all parts of our soul." There was, he added, a "positive energy of this sin." The notion that darkness passed down the bloodlines proved irresistible to writers with impressionable imaginations. Decay and sin had appeal then as now; each generation looks fresh to the past and mines it. Ancestry is preordaining, corrupting, benevolent, benign, damning.

Several of the New England writers most influential on Lowell attached themselves to the idea of ancestral sin; Nathaniel Hawthorne did so with particular genius. "I feel more warmth for Hawthorne than the more exemplary heroes . . . a certain closeness to his temperament," wrote Lowell. His "being was of such intermingled gloom and brightness [that] his mood is hard to find. . . . He was an anti-Puritan, troubled as perhaps no true believer has ever been by the Puritan light, which was darkness." Hawthorne was the great-grandson of a magistrate who presided during the Salem witchcraft trials of 1692. Found guilty of witchcraft by the magistrate, one of his victims hurled a curse upon the judge and his descendants. The curse, enticing in imaginative possibility, fell onto Hawthorne's bleak temperament and paid its dividend in literature.

"How comes it you have such a taste for the morbid anatomy of the human heart?" asked a friend of Hawthorne. "I should fancy from your books that you had some blue chamber in your soul, into which you hardly dared to enter yourself." Hawthorne wrote from the blue chamber. He ruminated on sins and sinners and the role of suffering in life and art. Truth, he believed, came from suffering; redemption and art, were they to come, must begin in despair. "He was earnest as a priest," his daughter said, "for he cared that the world was full of sorrow & sin."

"The spirit of my Puritan ancestors was mighty in me," Hawthorne wrote in his notebook. It was a sentiment he took into his fiction. The sins of the father were his son's, he wrote in *The Scarlet Letter:*

> It is now nearly two centuries and a quarter since the original Briton, the earliest emigrant of my name, made his appearance in the wild and forest-bordered settlement. . . . He had all the Puritanic traits, both good and evil. His son, too, inherited the persecuting spirit, and made himself so conspicuous in the martyrdom of the witches, that their blood may fairly be said to have left a stain upon him. . . . I, the present writer, as their representative, hereby take shame upon myself for their sakes, and pray that any curse incurred by them . . . may be now and henceforth removed.

The theme of sin passing from generation to generation was front and deep in *The House of the Seven Gables:* "The wrong-doing of one generation lives into successive ones," Hawthorne wrote. There "might be drawn a weighty lesson from the little regarded truth, that the act of passing generation is the germ which may and must produce good or evil fruit, in a far distant time; that, together with the seed of the merely temporary crop, which mortals term expediency, they inevitably sow the acorns of a more enduring growth, which may darkly overshadow their posterity." Corruption, blighted ambition, persecution, madness: all pass their way through the family line. Predestined, blighted, unseeing, man travels from birth to death on a course fixed to his ancestors.

"As a man-of-war that sails through the sea, so this earth that sails through the air," wrote Herman Melville. "We mortals are all on board a fast-sailing, never-sinking world-frigate, of which God was the shipwright; and she is but one craft in a Milky-Way fleet, of which God is the Lord High Admiral. The port we sail from is forever astern. And though far out of sight of land, for ages and ages we continue to sail with sealed orders, and our last destination remains a secret to ourselves and our officers; yet our final haven was predestinated ere we slipped from the stocks at Creation."

That sin and culpability might pass down through the generations—as we would have it in our time, like the helical strands of DNA—is an intensely attractive metaphor, and it is not surprising that the New England writers, brought up in the shadow of their Puritan past, would make good use of it. Lowell's great-great uncle, James Russell Lowell, a pallbearer at Hawthorne's funeral, wrote after Hawthorne's death, "I never thought it an abatement of Hawthorne's genius that he came lineally from one who sat in judgment on the witches in 1692; it was interesting rather to trace something hereditary in the sombre character of his imagination, continually vexing itself to account for the origin of evil, and baffled for want of that simple solution in a personal Devil." The minister who spoke at Hawthorne's graveside said simply, "I know of no other thinker or writer who had so much sympathy with the dark shadow, that shadow which the theologian calls sin. . . . He seemed to be the friend of all sinners."

Robert Lowell, drawn to Hawthorne and his dark original work, took him as a subject in both his poetry and prose and adapted two of Hawthorne's short stories for his play *The Old Glory*. He saw Hawthorne as a kindred spirit who, with Thoreau, Emerson, Melville, and other nineteenth-century writers, shaped the myth of New England.

"It was then," said Lowell, "that the great imaginative minds first clearly saw their heritage as something both to admire and fear."

"Hawthorne died depressed," wrote Lowell. "Like Mallarmé and many another, he found life too long for comfort and too brief for perfection." In a poem about Hawthorne, written a century after his death, Lowell wrote that Hawthorne's "hard / survivor's smile is touched with fire":

> Even this shy distrustful ego
>   sometimes walked on top of the blazing roof,
> and felt those flashes
> that char the discharged cells of the brain.
> .   .   .   .
> Leave him alone for a moment or two,
> and you'll see him with his head
> bent down, brooding, brooding,
> eyes fixed on some chip,
> some stone, some common plant,
> the commonest thing,
> as if it were the clue.
> The disturbed eyes rise,
> furtive, foiled, dissatisfied
> from meditation on the true
> and insignificant.

Ancestry, like all in life, was a source both of darkness and light. In "91 Revere Street," Lowell contrasted the Puritan legacy left him by the early Lowells and Winslows with the lighter, more recent one of his great-great-grandfather Myers, someone who "had never frowned down in judgment on a Salem witch. There was no allegory in his eyes, no *Mayflower*. Instead he looked peacefully at his sideboard, his cut-glass decanters, his cellaret—."

Norman Mailer, who Lowell, his daughter, and numerous of Lowell's friends believe captured Lowell's personality and character uncannily well, better than anyone, wrote that one could see in Lowell the weight of family blood. And its privilege:

> The hollows in his cheeks give a hint of the hanging judge. . . .
> The hollows speak of the great Puritan gloom in which the

Nathaniel Hawthorne, daguerreotype, c. 1850
"I cannot resilver the smudged plate."

country was founded—man was simply not good enough for God. . . . Lowell's shoulders had a slump. . . . One did not achieve the languid grandeurs of that slouch in one generation—the grandsons of the first sons had best go through the best troughs in the best eating clubs at Harvard before anyone in the family could try for such elegant note.

Robert Lowell gave off at times the unwilling haunted saintliness of a man who was repaying the moral debts of ten generations of ancestors. So his guilt must have been a tyrant of a chemical in his blood always ready to obliterate the best of his

moods. . . . Lowell was at the mercy of anyone he considered
of value, for only they might judge his guilt, and so relieve the
intolerable dread which accompanies this excessive assumption
of the old moral debts of his ancestors.

In 1850, the year that Robert Lowell's great-great-grandmother Harriet Brackett Spence Lowell died insane in Boston, a violent storm
swept across the Orkney Islands. Orkney, an archipelago of seventy
islands and skerries off the northeastern coast of Scotland, was the
birthplace of her father and her mother's father and the home ground
for her imagination. Now, in the year of her death, wild winds ripped
the grass off the top of sand dunes above the bay on the main island
of Orkney. Exposed beneath the dunes was a long-buried Neolithic
village, a small grouping of stone houses. Five thousand years earlier
the inhabitants of the village of Skara Brae had raised sheep and cattle,
farmed, fished, and harvested seaweed. Their furniture was cut from
local stone and included cupboards, storage chests, and dressers; there
were indoor water tanks to keep limpets alive, perhaps for food or bait.
The people of Skara Brae had lived in their small prehistoric village for
six hundred years. When they abandoned Skara Brae—no one knows
why—they left behind them pottery, ornamental beads and awls made
from walrus and whale ivory, and intricately carved stone balls, used
perhaps as gaming pieces or ritual items for worship. They left behind
pieces of a small seaside world; they left behind questions, provoking
and unanswerable.

Skara Brae is a place that invites myth, one where imagination
takes over. The Orkney poet George Mackay Brown wrote that all one
knows of Skara Brae is "a few ambiguous scratches on a wall—a scattered string of beads." It is a world with all things left unsaid, unwritten. It seems even now a place somehow beyond path or sail, beyond
understanding. Where did the first people of Skara Brae come from?
Why did they leave? Perhaps they were in danger, perhaps disease had
come or invaders threatened. They left behind jewelry and pottery that
must have been of value to them. They left the trace of art.

Had there been music as well at Skara Brae? Had there been a
poet? Why had they left? Had the sea invaded their freshwater loch,

spoiling what they needed to survive? Did they leave because they had to, or because someone imagined a better life somewhere beyond? Did they go inland or to sea? We don't know. There are limits to knowledge, but none to imagination. We weave worlds, we fill in the comings and goings of left places. We fill in why some stay, others leave.

Harriet Brackett Spence Lowell spoke often of her Orkney blood, conjured for her family the land of their Traill and Spence ancestors. In 1837 she traveled with her husband to see Orkney for herself. (Her great-great-grandson would do this more than a century later to see, as he put it, his "ancestral islands." It was to the Traill-Spence bloodline, his Orkney ancestors, that Robert Lowell believed he owed a not inconsiderable part of his gift for poetry.) No one knew for certain why the Traills and Spences had left Orkney, or why they had come to New England. But Harriet Lowell kept close to her the island music and poetry that her parents and grandparents had sung and read aloud. She wove her own ancestry. She was descended, she said, from Sir Patrick Spens, the greatest of Scots sailors, whose final resting place was in Orkney. Or, if one believed the ballad, he lay fifty fathoms deep, drowned in a winter storm at sea. If in fact he had ever lived. What Lowell's great-great-grandmother could not know, she imagined. Literature and music were always a part of this; they were in her blood. This she inherited from her parents and this, along with her mercurial moods and precarious grasp on reality, she passed on to her children.

Harriet Brackett Spence Lowell's father, Keith Spence, was born in Orkney in 1735. Little is known about his parents, only that his father's occupation is listed as "writer" on the baptismal record in Kirkwall. Spence immigrated to New England just before the Revolutionary War and served as an officer on the USS *Constellation* and USS *Philadelphia*. His wife, Mary Traill Spence, had strong New England roots, but her father, like her husband, was also born in Orkney. (Harriet Brackett Spence Lowell gave her father's and mother's surnames to her second son, Robert Traill Spence Lowell, a name that would be passed down for another three generations.) Like Charles Darwin's tangled root bank, the dominant branches of Robert Lowell's family tree—the Traills, Spences, Lowells, and Winslows—came together to create a dense thicket of temperament and talent, gift and blight.

Medical record of Harriet Brackett Spence Lowell, 1845,
McLean Asylum for the Insane

Keith Spence's letters to his wife lay open not only their respective struggles with depression and mental instability, they also reveal his gift for writing about people and ships and the downward drag of melancholy. He is direct in his description of his low spirits, lethargy, and confusion but, when well, writes vividly about the places he has sailed— Palermo, Gibraltar, Malta, Syracuse, the Bay of Tunis; about painting, architecture, and history; storms at sea, ship riggings, sea duty. Dark moods passed down through his blood—dark moods, we know, carry a strong debt to inheritance—but so too did a turn for language.

In a letter to his wife written in 1804, Spence told her of his dismal state of mind: "Time, that used to drive on the happy moments of my existence with lightning velocity, as if he envy'd me my enjoyment; now, as if he took pleasure in my suffering, limps and lags behind like a weary traveler; and if I murmur or complain of his tardiness, he lifts his ugly [scythe] and threatens to cut me down." The sun, he said, "stands still at noon day; at night the Stars seem stationary; for watch after watch I look up to them but they move not." Sleep, "that silent soother of human sorrow," had almost entirely forsaken him, "or, if he sometimes deigns to pay me a visit, is soon drawn away, by the fantastic figures, and dreary prospects, which fancy, thro' her magic lantern of dreams and visions, plays before my imagination."

Despondency and a gnawing indolence come up in many of his letters. He writes on repeated occasions about "a lowness of spirits" and a prolonged fatigue when nothing but "the absolute force of necessity rouse[s] me to action." "There are circumstances and situations in life," he tells his wife, "in which people may be placed, where silence alone enables them to support it; and when they dare not give their afflictions the form of words, for making them too hideous."

At the same time that Spence was sending bleak letters to his wife, he was also responding to disturbing ones from her. He writes, in light of her "Sickness," that she "must support Serenity and Cheerfulness." Later he tells her, "I shudder at your past Indisposition . . . I am much concerned for the state of your health, and the more so as the seat of it seems to be in your mind. . . . Keep up your Spirits."

She writes to him of the "perturbations" of her nerves, which "destroy the whole system" and reduce her "corporal strength to a state converging to the grave." To her daughter Harriet Lowell she confides that her "distress" is increasing "each year, each month, each week, each day and hour." Her suffering, now the severest she has known, "sinks me to the grave." Her "diseased mind," she writes, "renders me totally incapable of deciding upon anything of importance."

Later, in a letter with a large section since cut out of it, she confides: "This must not be seen by any body but yourself. . . . It is a long time since I have been able to write a coherent letter; such has been the malady of my mind, to which the complication of sickness, affliction of mind, and great perplexities have conspired. . . . My head [is] not competent to the dictates of my heart; indeed, that is too often the case, and of the former derangement and torpor makes me fear that my reason will forsake me, or be broken down."

The disposition to "derangement and torpor" seems to have passed in a particularly strong way through Mary Traill Spence's maternal line. Her mother had had psychological troubles. Her physician wrote to her husband, Robert Traill, "She is I think quite recovered of the indisposition she laboured under last summer," but, he added, "her nerves are yet weak." A petition to the New Hampshire General Court in 1781 indicates that her health had "for a long time past been much impaired." A bill for medical services presented to her husband lists, among other things, medications "for your lady" such as "Nervous drops" and sudorific drugs, among them scarlet pimpernel, often used in treating melancholy and other mental diseases. Certainly Mary Traill's daughter and granddaughter suffered from disorders severe enough to warrant the designation of mental illness.

The son of Keith and Mary Traill Spence, Robert Traill Spence, seems to have had a milder form of his parents' difficulties. Keith Spence expressed concern to his wife that their son had an "extreme volatility of Temper" and that he was "ungovernable." A few years later he wrote that his son's "extraordinary state of mind" was "truly alarming." He had done all he could do as a father "to rouse him from his poetic Dreams, and from that stupor and inactivity which seems to have taken possession of him. . . . He seems much in the same way that he was when he was in the Mediterranean, a despondency and lowness of spirits." Of his son's literary passion, he wrote, "What could put Poetry in his head? . . . I cannot conceive." Despite his parents' concern that he would come to naught, Robert Traill Spence became a successful naval officer and was cited for bravery by the American naval hero Commodore Stephen Decatur. He also continued to write, to experience occasional bouts of melancholy, and to have "poetry in his head." An obituary noted that he had been "a good writer in both prose and poetry," another that he had been "an elegant scholar . . . [and] a good poet."

A link between volatile moods and the determination and ability to write, to be a poet, was an emerging one in the bloodline. Keith and Mary Spence's other child, Harriet Brackett Spence, later institutionalized at the McLean Asylum, like her parents and brother loved poetry and music and was, as well, an accomplished watercolorist. In 1806 she married Charles Lowell, the minister of the West Church in Boston. Her new family, the Lowells, long a part of New England history, was not without its share of excitable and brooding minds.

The early Lowells, the first of whom settled north of Boston, appear to have been a steady lot. Percival Lowle (1571–1664), the first of the Lowell family to immigrate to America, sailed from London in 1639 and went to lands near Plum Island Sound, north of Boston. A prosperous merchant, he was also well schooled in English poetry, educated in Latin, and enough well-thought-of as a poet to write the elegy for Governor Winthrop. There is no indication of significant mental instability in the Lowell line until the late eighteenth century. John "The Old Judge" Lowell (1743–1802), delegate to the Continental Congress, eminent jurist, and great-great-great grandfather of Robert Lowell, had three sons. "All three were high-strung delicate men, prone to overwork and periods of nervous exhaustion," states Ferris Greenslet, the biographer of the Lowell family. "Perhaps each, like his father, had a streak of the *malade imaginaire* in him."

The eldest son, John "The Rebel" Lowell (1769–1840), graduated with distinction in classics from Harvard and became a prominent Boston attorney and activist in the Federalist Party. Throughout his life he had intermittent periods of "overwork," followed by months of depression and exhaustion. In 1804 he described his mental state to his family: "I have in a very considerable degree restored the tone of my nervous system. . . . The least deviation, the least anxiety, disturbs my nerves and makes me dread a relapse—I hope however that time will fortify me against this most terrible of all maladies." Years later, when he resigned his position on the Harvard Board of Overseers, he explained to the board that his indisposition was one that "perfectly incapacitates the subjects of it . . . as [from] a [paralytic] shock. There is an apparent physical vigour and health, but such a morbid state of the nervous system, as deprives the patient of all power over his faculties, and volition."

The second son of "Old Judge" Lowell, Francis Cabot Lowell, graduated with highest honors in mathematics from Harvard and became one of the most successful businessmen in the history of New England. (It is Francis Cabot Lowell for whom the city of Lowell, Massachusetts, is named.) He, like his older brother, had periods of ferocious energy and "overwork," followed by an incapacitating stagnancy. When on the verge or in the midst of a nervous breakdown, he, like other members of the Lowell family, went abroad to recuperate. It was an expensive way to heal but money was not a major consideration for the now and again nervously afflicted Lowells.

Charles Lowell, the third son of the Old Judge, was the husband of Harriet Brackett Spence and great-great-grandfather of Robert Lowell; he was minister of the historic West Church, a fiery congregation before and during the Revolutionary War, and a socially activist one after the war's conclusion. (An early West Church minister is credited with railing from his pulpit against British rule, shouting out the inflammatory words of his friend James Otis, "No taxation without representation.") There Charles Lowell taught Louisa May Alcott and Charles Eliot, the future president of Harvard and cousin of T. S. Eliot, in the church Sunday school and there he preached passionately against slavery.

There is some suggestion that Charles Lowell had a trace of the Lowell instability. He was said to share his brothers' "high-strung" ways, excitable periods followed by weeks or months of "nervous exhaustion." During his ministry at the West Church he moved to the country rather than continue living in Boston, which some congregants and family believed to be too stressful for him. His father-in-law, Keith Spence, not the ideal person to question someone else's mental stability, wondered whether Charles Lowell, "like all Lowell men," was perhaps too passionately inclined. Toward the end of his life, Charles Lowell was said by his family to be "alarmingly excitable." Lowell's youngest son, James Russell Lowell, believed that he had inherited his father's "indolence (I know not whether to call it intellectual or physical)."

Two clusters of descendants particularly distinguished by creativity and literary gifts followed the "high-strung delicate" generation of John, Francis, and Charles Lowell. They too were mercurial by temperament, and by any account, their achievements stand out. Abbott Lawrence Lowell became president of Harvard and his sister Elizabeth Lowell (Putnam), the author of six books, pioneered reform in child and maternal health. Their sister, Amy Lowell (1874–1925), was a renowned poet. Like her distant cousin Robert Lowell, who was eight years old when she died, she was awarded the Pulitzer Prize for Poetry and she, like him, was the cover subject for *Time* magazine (as was her brother Abbott Lawrence Lowell). Amy, a leader of the Imagist movement in poetry, intermittently suffered from "nervous prostration" and protracted "fits of depression."

Percival Lowell (1855–1916), Amy's older brother, graduated from Harvard with distinction in mathematics. He was a businessman, Orientalist, and astronomer who was most famous for his belief that canals existed on Mars, which, he speculated, had been built by a dying civilization. His writings about Mars influenced generations of science fiction writers, including H. G. Wells, Ray Bradbury, and Robert A. Heinlein. He founded the Lowell Observatory in Flagstaff, Arizona, and contributed significantly to the early scientific efforts that led to the discovery of Pluto (whose name, which includes Percival Lowell's initials, was given in part to recognize Lowell's contribution).

Percival Lowell had repeated nervous breakdowns, described by his associates as "nervous weakness" or "nervous exhaustion" and by himself as a "complete breakdown of the machine." These episodes lasted from months to years at a time and usually came after periods of "frenzied over-work": weeks of high enthusiasm, an outpouring of creative scientific work and writing, and little sleep. This pattern of excited work, peaking in a fevered mental state, and followed by depression, is strikingly similar to the one experienced by his cousin, the poet Robert Lowell.

This debilitating pattern of Percival Lowell's nervous condition repeated itself throughout his life. In September 1897 one of his colleagues wrote, "I am quite anxious about his condition; his [nervous] weakness seems to continue, and he will need *absolute rest* in order to recuperate. It would be well if he would give up work entirely." The following month the same colleague noted that Lowell was worse than ever, and that his attorney had had to take over his correspondence. He required, it was said, "absolute rest." Two months later Lowell had improved but his "nervous weakness still continues."

A similar extended period of nervous illness occurred again in 1912. His secretary and companion wrote to one of his colleagues: "Dr. Lowell has not been in the office for seven weeks. It is nervous exhaustion and he is up and down. Some days he cannot even telephone. He gets nervous about the work and is impatient." Three weeks later she asked, "Is it not too bad that his nerves are so long in getting strong?"

Although Robert Lowell wrote little about his distant cousin Percival—"I hadn't realized his errors were so fruitful, I suppose that's the rule in science," he wrote to his second wife, Elizabeth Hardwick, toward the end of his life. "In the family, we always doubted his Mars, but swore by the accuracy and orthodoxy of his Pluto"—they had in common a pursuit of things on a great scale, questing minds, conspicuous ambition, restless imagination, and a sense of the dark grandeur of life. They also were inclined to long periods of intense creative work followed by months of "nervous exhaustion." It is more usual to place Robert Lowell's artistic ancestry in the context of his fellow poets James

Russell Lowell and Amy Lowell, but in many ways his mind was more kindred to that of the astronomer.

Percival Lowell wrote poetically as well as scientifically; indeed, several of his colleagues at the Lowell Observatory remarked that his work was excellent as literature but considerably less impressive as science. In his book *Mars as the Abode of Life*, published in 1908, he wrote about the types of discovery. There is discovery of a factual nature, he said, one that adds to what is known. Then there is original thought: "Breadth of mind must match breadth of subject. For to plodders along prescribed paths a far view fails of appeal; conservative settlers in a land differ in a quality from pioneers." There were no Martian-created canals on Mars, no Martians, but Lowell's imagination primed our curiosity about the planet and made it a more imaginable, unimaginable place.

Percival Lowell was an adventurer, indefatigable, an enthusiast who swept up others in his vitality and lived by the belief he often shared with others: "Not the possible, but the impossible." He was an explorer and took risks; he was a pioneer as Willa Cather meant it. "A pioneer should have imagination," she wrote, "should be able to enjoy the idea of things more than the things themselves." Despite his essentially exuberant temperament, Percival Lowell had a bleak view of the probable fate of the universe, a view not unusual in those who watch the skies and spend their lives thinking in unthinkably large numbers and distances and contemplating the births and deaths of stars.

Of the interwoven, complicated Lowell bloodlines it is the Traill-Spence-Lowell line that is most directly related to Robert Lowell. His great-great grandparents, Charles Lowell and Harriet Brackett Spence Lowell, had six children, five of whom survived to adulthood. Three were writers, and at least two had serious illnesses of mood. James Russell Lowell (1819–91), born in the same year as Herman Melville and Walt Whitman, was a prominent nineteenth-century poet and essayist, and cofounder—with Ralph Waldo Emerson, Harriet Beecher Stowe, Henry Wadsworth Longfellow, and Oliver Wendell Holmes—of the *Atlantic Monthly*. He was as well a professor at Harvard, the United States minister to Spain, minister to the Court of St. James, and godfather of Virginia Woolf.

James Russell Lowell, indebted he said to his mother for the gift of language, was stricken with grief and horror when she became insane. It was he, her youngest son, who had written about her that only as much remained as the "hum outliving the hushed bell." He dedicated many of his poems to her, saying that she was "the patron and encourager of my youthful muse," but he was heir to her wild mood swings as well, instabilities that he described as his "morbid excitements." He told friends that he had inherited more than a trace of "my dear Mother's malady." There were many times, he said, when "everything is dreary, and time ceases to exist. . . . Tis as if I had taken of the insane root."

As a young man, suicidal, he had put a pistol to his head; on two other occasions, he admitted, he would have killed himself had he had a revolver nearby. If strychnine had been available, he said, he would have taken it. "The drop of black blood I inherited from my dear mother," he wrote, "is apt to spread itself over the pupil of my eye and darken everything." He thought "of my razors and my throat and that I am a fool and a coward not to end it all at once."

"How shall a man escape from his ancestors," asked his friend Emerson. "Or draw off from his veins the black drop which he drew from his father's or his mother's life?"

New England was in the bones and blood of James Russell Lowell and he wrote often about it in his poetry and essays. "We had some toughness in our grain," he wrote in a poem about early New England and his Pilgrim ancestors. "They talk about their Pilgrim blood, / Their birthright high and holy! / A mountain-stream that ends in mud / Me thinks is melancholy." In the Chapter House at Westminster Abbey there is a stained-glass window that commemorates the life of James Russell Lowell. One of the panels depicts the Pilgrim Fathers and the *Mayflower*. The harkening back is telling. "In one sense it matters very little who our ancestors were," Lowell had written. "Though in another it is of enormous import to us, for they make us what we are; but we can't do anything about it. There they were, and here they are, all the while dominant in our lives and fates, whether we will or no." A century later his great-grandnephew would acknowledge this ancestral influence: "I envy his strenuous grace," wrote Robert Lowell about James Russell Lowell. "And fear affinities with the cold, gone-out fire."

James Russell Lowell's sister Rebecca inherited a more severe form of their mother's illness. A neighbor and friend in Cambridge, the wife of Henry Wadsworth Longfellow, referred to her as "mad," a description given by several who knew her. Rebecca Lowell grew more violent as she grew older and, like her mother, intermittently remained silent for weeks on end. James Russell Lowell believed, as did many, that his sister had inherited their mother's deranged mind and dark moods.

The first Robert Traill Spence Lowell, born in 1816, was the brother of James Russell, Rebecca, and the writer and translator Mary Traill Spence. Educated as a physician and a priest, he served for a while as a missionary in Newfoundland. Then, he said, "I broke down." He accepted the headmastership of St. Mark's School in Massachusetts, where, sixty years later, during the 1930s, his great-grandson, Robert Lowell, would attend boarding school. Robert Traill Spence Lowell was an educator, classicist, and writer as well as a priest and a doctor. Although his literary reputation hovered in the shadow of his younger brother, James Russell Lowell, his first novel was widely acclaimed at the time of its publication and sold well. It was a book the poet Robert Lowell knew well, and in 1969 he visited Newfoundland, "the setting of my Grandfather's [sic] longest and best loved novel, *Priest of Conception Bay.*" (It was a time in Lowell's life for ancestral pilgrimage. Two years later, in 1971, he traveled to Orkney to visit the home of the Traills and Spences.)

The first Robert Lowell also wrote two volumes of poems, a second novel, short stories, and hymns (including a Harvard commemoration hymn). None has come down through the years in association with anything but a gentle mediocrity, although his poem "The Relief of Lucknow" still makes its way into the occasional anthology, as does a short story, "A Raft That No Man Made." "His poetry is forgotten," wrote a critic, "and justly so." But the same critic also said that "he was unquestionably a man of genuine, though minor, literary originality, a poet and a novelist who wrote to please himself and in so doing earned his own position in American literary history."

Little is known about the son of the first Robert Lowell, Robert Traill Spence Lowell II, except that he was born in Boston, died young at the age of twenty-six, and was a naval officer. He married the granddaughter of Mordecai Myers, a man whose "tame and honorable" life opens *Life Studies*, and they had one child, Robert Lowell III. He too was a naval officer. Born two months after his father's death, he was, as his son the poet wrote, "at each stage of his life . . . forlornly father-less." Like his father, he had but one child, Robert Traill Spence Lowell IV, who was born in 1917 in the Boston house of his grandfather Winslow. The Lowell men had numbers after their names, but more often than not they were alone as they grew into them.

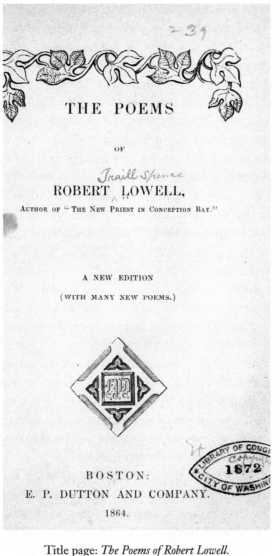

Title page: *The Poems of Robert Lowell.*
Published by Lowell's great-grandfather in 1864.

Robert Lowell's dominant maternal line, the Winslows, dated to the origins of New England. Through his mother he was a direct descendant of Mary Chilton, a young passenger on the *Mayflower*, who arrived twenty years before Percival Lowle settled to the north of Plymouth in the marsh and meadowlands near Plum Island Sound. She married John Winslow, who became one of Boston's most prominent and wealthy men. His brother Edward Winslow had the more lasting influence on the history of New England, however. He was three times governor of Plymouth Colony, represented the interests of the colony in London, and became an active link between the colonists and the local Native American tribes.

Edward Winslow was also a lucent writer. Together with William Bradford he wrote *Mourt's Relation: A Journal of the Pilgrims at Plymouth*, an account of the Puritan settlement at Plymouth. Edward Winslow would come to know Plymouth in a way few would ever know it: he mapped and governed it, negotiated on behalf of its Puritan people, and put into words its starkness and beauty, its possibility.

Bradford wrote of the founding of Plymouth during a time of peril in *Of Plymouth Plantation: 1620–1647*. His book, written in the beautiful language of the seventeenth century, left its mark on many New England writers including, three hundred years later, Robert Lowell. Bradford's description of the seasons and tides of Cape Cod, the earth and sea cycles of want and abundance, fill his pages as with the song of Ecclesiastes. He describes the *Mayflower*'s sail into Cape Cod Bay and the hard welcome given to the Pilgrims: "They fell amongst dangerous shoals and roaring breakers, and they were so far entangled therewith as they conceived themselves in great danger; and the wind shrinking upon them withal, they resolved to bear up again for the Cape and thought themselves happy to get out of those dangers before night overtook them, as by God's good providence they did. And the next day they got into the Cape Harbor where they rid in safety." It is the language of Tyndale, anciently rooted and wrought in beauty.

God gave them danger, then deliverance. The cycles of New England life pursued their relentless course: peril, then a measure of safe harbor; ice and gale-force storms, then "fair, sunshining days." Fields and crops, "parched like withered hay," seemingly dead, were brought back by rain in such abundance "as to revive and quicken the decayed corn and other fruits." Death, renewal, resurrection—terror

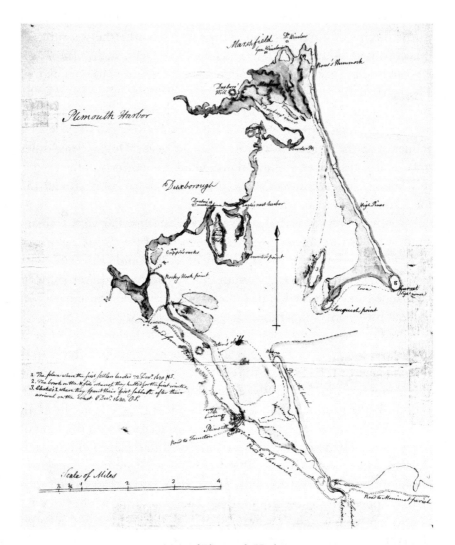

Map of Plymouth Harbor
"So uncertain are the mutable things of this unstable world."

made bearable by the solace of faith: these were the rhythms of the
natural world. They are as well the cycles of moods and imagination.

The ancient cycle of death, birth, death; the determining rhythms
of season, tide, and crop; the killing winters and days fair, then foul: all
come fresh in the writings of Bradford and Winslow. The peril was all-
present—hurricane, disease, earthquake, starvation—but the bounty of

New England was overflowing, a gift from God, a promise to those who might come. There are great oaks, they wrote, and pines, walnuts, beech, ash, birch, hazel, holly, aspen, sassafras in abundance and vines everywhere, cherry trees, plum trees, and many others that "we know not." The water was the best they had known, and the brooks full of fish. They had cast their die, England was behind them, and Bradford could in all truth declare, "We are well weaned from the delicate milk of our mother country." The small Plymouth colony had kept its faith in God but increased its wariness in the ways of nature.

The historian Perry Miller believes that this "cry of the heart," the recognition of the weaning of the colonists from England, "signals a point at which the English Puritan had, hardly with conscious knowledge, become an American, rooted in the American soil." In "The Gift Outright," a poem admired and anthologized by Robert Lowell, Robert Frost described this complex, evolving bond with the land:

> The land was ours before we were the land's.
> She was our land more than a hundred years
> Before we were her people. She was ours
> In Massachusetts, in Virginia,
> But we were England's, still colonials,
> Possessing what we still were unpossessed by,
> Possessed by what we now no more possessed.

The spiritual commitment to place, to possession, specifically to New England, is of much weight. New England had been conceived as a chosen land and settled by a chosen people unshakeably beholden to God. Now they, and the settlers who came in later ships, were making a commitment to place as an idea, a covenant, a future. The land and the people had been chosen by Providence but, in making that choice, through the teachings of their faith, there was an account to be rendered. The accounting, the recurrent betrayal of origin and ideal, was a subject that found its way into Robert Lowell's writing more than three hundred years later.

New England would be a light, a beacon, a spirit, and an exemplar. It was to shine, as Bradford had said: "One small candle may light a thousand, so the light here kindled hath shone unto many, yea in

some sort to our whole nation." John Winthrop, later the governor of
the Massachusetts Bay Colony, spoke of this to his shipmates on their
crossing from England to New England: "We shall find that the God
of Israel is among us, when ten of us shall be able to resist a thousand of
our enemies; when He shall make us a praise and glory that men shall
say of succeeding plantations, 'may the Lord make it like that of New
England.' For we must consider that we shall be as a city upon a hill.
The eyes of all people are upon us."

New England, although assumed by the Puritans to be a place of
privilege in the scheme of God, would be held to harsh, high standards
as well. Privilege would not come without cost, nor failure without
shame. The Puritan minister Peter Bulkeley, a founder of Concord and
ancestor of Emerson, warned of this as early as 1646. New England
had been given much but "no people's account will be heavier than
thine if thou do not walk worthy. . . . The Lord looks for more from
thee than from other people. . . . Thou shouldst be a special people, an
only people—none like thee in all the earth." The Puritans had gouged
out a life from the wilderness and established commerce and education
in a land lashed by a harsh climate and disease. Their first years in the
unknown world could not help but give rise to a myth that encouraged
high dreams and rewarded risk. It guaranteed an unrealizable moral
standard.

As early as 1642, William Bradford decried the decay that had
entered the life of Plymouth Plantation. "Wickedness did grow and
break forth," he wrote. For Bradford, the sinfulness among the Pilgrims was a betrayal of the Christian life and the promise of Plymouth
Plantation. "It is now a part of my misery in old age, to find and feel the
decay," he wrote late in life. The Pilgrims had fled a corrupt faith only
to risk corrupting their own. The force of the early Pilgrim ideal was
drifting, diluting. So, too, the abundance of New England's streams
and rivers was being squandered. Bass and other fish that had once
packed the waters of Cape Cod were becoming scarce. Few countries
had had such an advantage, wrote an observer; more than fifteen hundred bass were known to have been taken in a single tide. Now, fish
were fewer and game more scarce.

The success of New England commerce and the growing population led to the corrosion of some values and an embalming or enshrin-
ing of others. "What had been a wondrous and intimate experience of
the soul, a flash into the very crypt and basis of man's nature from the

fire of trial," wrote James Russell Lowell in 1865, "had become ritual and tradition. In prosperous times the faith of one generation becomes the formality of the next." The Puritans, he stated, "could not renew the fiery gush of enthusiasm when once the molten metal had begun to stiffen in the mould of policy and precedent." His friend Henry David Thoreau said it as emphatically: "It is time we had done referring to our ancestors. We have used up all of our inherited freedom, like a young bird and the albumen in the egg. It is not an era of repose. If we would save our lives, we must fight for them."

The Puritan candle and beacon were less constant, less bright, but Puritanism, according to James Russell Lowell, had already done what it had set out to do: "As there are certain creatures whose whole being seems occupied with an egg-laying errand they are sent upon, incarnate ovipositors, their bodies but bags to hold this precious deposit, their legs of use only to carry them where they may most safely be rid of it, so sometimes a generation seems to have no other end than the conception and ripening of certain germs." Puritanism, Lowell said, "believing itself quick with the seed of religious liberty laid, without knowing it, the egg of democracy."

Robert Lowell, more than a hundred years later, acknowledged the debt owed by democracy to the Puritans but added a darker tone when he addressed the particular reprehensibility of the abuse of moral authority by the educated and powerful against those less fortunate. "A century passes," he wrote, and the Pilgrim "has grown twisted with subtlety, like the dark, learned, well-connected Cotton Mather . . . the Salem witch hanger [and] professional man of letters employed to moralize and subdue. His truer self was a power-crazed mind bent on destroying darkness with darkness, on applying his cruel, high-minded, obsessed intellect to the extermination of witch and neurotic. His soft, bookish hands are indelibly stained with blood."

The Winslows settled across New England; they cleared the land and killed in large numbers those whose land it had been. They governed and traded; they planted, defended, and profited. They wrote about their God and their pilgrimage. Their descendants were many and influential; so too were others of Lowell's maternal ancestors, including Jonathan Edwards, the great eighteenth-century theologian whose work held such sway over Lowell's imagination and poetry; Anne Hutchinson, the Puritan preacher, heretic, firebrand, and healer, was another.

In 1668 Anne Hutchinson's granddaughter married the son of John and Mary Chilton Winslow. Nearly two hundred and fifty years later, their descendant Charlotte Winslow married Robert Traill Spence Lowell III. In 1917, their son was born. The blood of Edward Winslow, Jonathan Edwards, and Anne Hutchinson joined that of the Lowells.

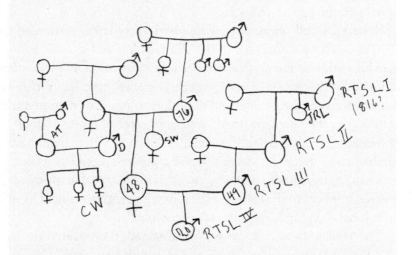

Pedigree of the Winslow-Lowell families,
drawn by Merrill Moore, M.D.

4

This Dynamited Brook

Resistance to something was the law of New England nature; the boy looked out on the world with the instinct of resistance; for numberless generations his predecessors had viewed the world chiefly as a thing to be reformed, filled with evil forces to be abolished, and they saw no reason to suppose that they had wholly succeeded in the abolition; the duty was unchanged. That duty implied not only resistance to evil, but hatred of it. . . . The New Englander . . . had learned also to love the pleasure of hating.

—Henry Adams, *The Education of Henry Adams*

"I grew up as an only child," Lowell told a psychiatrist when he was nearly forty, "one that was always fighting off his parents and yet rejoiced at holding the center of the stage. I became stubborn, dreamy, silent, gauche, cold, furious, charming for brief moments, impenetrable." He was awkward, he said, an albatross on land. He rebelled whenever and however he could, was harsh on his parents, harsh on himself. "I was girl-shy. Thick-witted, narcissistic, thuggish." As young as four he consciously rebelled against his mother's demands that he behave in ways he was not willing to: "I already felt the stirrings of revolt against my mother's judgment; I already felt an attraction to what she rebuked or condemned; in her enemies, or at least in her castoffs, I always saw a possible ally of my own."

Lowell was disposed to resist force and disposed to use it. He was of a temperament to query and defy, to blast. His parents held to their certainty that emotion should be kept on a short lead and private; this made a collision of wills inevitable. The clash led to twenty years of conflict and showdown; it also tutored him in the art of wile and words. He learned early to spar and to defend his ground, to put his imagination to combative and restorative use.

"Is there no way to cast my hook / Out of this dynamited brook?" Lowell asked in a poem written when he was in his twenties. Words and art were his way to recast, to throw a line into stiller, imagined waters. From the discord and his originality came *Life Studies*, a jolting portrayal of the pain, the quiet terror of disillusionment, the simmering rage and disenchantments of childhood. Dynamite, a word that finds its way into many of Lowell's poems, has its uses. It provokes change, gives notice.

Lowell's mother kept a judgmental watch over him as long as she lived. She disapproved of much of what he did and how he did it. She held back her approval and seeded his life with her own discontent. When family tension approached the unbearable she brought all back to her bidding with bursts of hysteria. She had a will of iron, Lowell said, and a "haughtiness and chilliness" that "came from apprehension." Boston was home in every way to her: "There was iron in the air for her will, taste in the drawing rooms," wrote Lowell. "Wherever she turned in Boston, she met herself." The toughness of Boston was tonic for all that was wrong, including the "misbegotten" years the Lowells spent in Washington when Lowell was a child. "What Bobby needs are bracing winters," Charlotte Lowell declared of their navy-ordered years in exile, "and a daily walk around the Basin in Boston."

She resented her husband, any place that was not Boston, and being pregnant with her only child. In the months before he was born, Lowell wrote, the only thing his mother enjoyed while his father was away at sea was "taking brisk walks and grieving over the fact that she was pregnant. She took pride in looking into the gray Atlantic and saying, without a trace of fear or illusion, 'I wish I could die.'" His mother's antipathy toward her unborn child sent Lowell, when he learned of it, on a journey of incomprehension. He came back to it time and again, in hospital after hospital, with psychiatrist after psychiatrist.

"The patient states that when the mother first learned she was pregnant she said she wanted to die," his Boston doctor wrote in 1957 in Lowell's medical chart. A statement of like meaning can be found written in nearly every psychiatric history taken of Lowell. Indeed, when he was seen by a psychiatrist for the first time at the age of fifteen, there is a simple, unelaborated sentence in the doctor's report: "He was an unwanted child."

Nearly fifty years later, Lowell was still thinking about, writing, and rewriting his mother's words. In "Unwanted," published a few months before he died, the psychiatrist asks:

> "You know
>
> you were an unwanted child?"

He knew:

> Mother,
> I must not blame you for carrying me in you
> on your brisk winter lunges . . .
> for yearning seaward, far from any home, and saying,
> "I wish I were dead, I wish I were dead."
> Unforgivable for a mother to tell her child.

That he had been unwanted cut Lowell. His mother's grinding disapproval and her assault not only on his but his father's will fueled defiance. When Lowell was hospitalized for depression at the Payne Whitney Clinic in 1949, his doctor wrote that Lowell had "all his life consciously rebelled against the mother for being disappointed in her ineffectual husband." He had fought as well against his mother's attempts to make him into a "conventional human being." He had refused to learn to dance, Lowell told his doctor; likewise, he rejected her pleas to play cards or tennis, to dress well, or to cultivate the kind of socially prominent friends she thought suitable.

Years later, during one of his many hospital admissions for mania, the psychological issues were the same. His basic issue with his mother, wrote his psychiatrist, "was not to be mastered by her." This, the doctor believed, had extended into "a general fear of not being mastered by anyone." His determination to escape his mother's rule and to live life on his own terms motivated Lowell into near-monastic discipline and, in his psychiatrist's words, put him on the course to "mastering learning." And, it is clear, to mastering his own emotions. Mania, he told his doctor, allowed him to shatter the control. Rebellion flared, anger boiled over. When he was manic, he said, he could relive his battles with his mother and win them. It allowed him to vent his rage at being "fixed in society," bound to the expectations of his social class; it allowed him to escape the "dreariness of being a Lowell."

Those who knew Charlotte Winslow Lowell said that she was incapable of accepting her husband and son as they were: one bland, the other raging. Lowell's friends found her judgmental, cold, and controlling: "Charlotte was a Snow Queen who flirted coldly and shamelessly with her son," wrote one. Another, a close friend of Lowell from boarding school, recalled her as "a monstrous woman, clinically monstrous." Lowell's wives agreed. His first wife, the writer Jean Stafford, referred to Charlotte Lowell as "Mrs. Hideous." Elizabeth Hardwick, who knew Charlotte Lowell best and longer, said that in her presence "all the joy goes out of existence—there is not even a little corner left which you can fill up with affection or humor or respect or pleasure."

But Hardwick was kinder in her judgment of Charlotte Lowell than most who knew her, more circumspect in her overall assessment, perhaps because she knew Lowell's mother when Lowell was older and less pulled into her grasping orbit. "In general Mrs. L. was much more insecure, hysterical, frightened than she has been made to appear," she said at one point. "She was a thorn, but not a formidable thorn, if there is such a thing, rather a neurotically scratching presence." She was "instinctively conventional." "The thing about the Lowells," Hardwick said, "was their unwavering gentility in conversation, manner of life. This gross, arguing couple [as portrayed by others], this domineering Clytemnestra is the most painful invention."

Charlotte Lowell was subject to hysteria, as her son noted in an autobiographical piece he wrote describing the time in 1924 when he, seven years old, and his parents lived in Washington. "Mother had lately been having dizzy spells. New naval people, a new city, and new child-problems made her hysterical." In 1957 he told his doctor that his mother had been subject to "hysterical fainting spells" when he was young and that she had been "very unstable." Low-grade hysteria occasionally flared into a full-blown attack. Her psychiatrist in Boston, Merrill Moore, described to a medical colleague an attack Charlotte Lowell experienced in 1937 when Lowell was twenty years old: "She went into a hypnotic trance. She was in a complete state of hysterical dissociation and as far as the world was concerned was unconscious." She could not be awakened, despite loud noises and painful stimuli. It was, he said, "just like a demonstration from Charcot." A few days later Moore wrote to another colleague, "I think that she can become so disturbed that she herself may go into a mild hysterical semi-psychotic state and may need to have a nurse or go to a mental hospital." Lowell's father was sufficiently concerned to contact several psychiatric and neurological specialists at Harvard about his wife's condition.

Ten years earlier, Moore said, when Lowell was ten years old, she had had a similar episode following an emotional family scene. After fainting and an extended period of unconsciousness, "she came to with a complete amnesia for the entire episode." She was, he added, "as interesting and simply dissociated a personality as anybody Dr. Janet could ever have described." It does not appear that Moore ever formally diagnosed Charlotte Lowell, although he wrote in her medical records, two weeks prior to her hysterical episode in 1937, that she was "slightly manic."

Charlotte Lowell wrote poetry on occasion, especially after her son's writing moved into the public eye. She appears to have written most of her poems for her psychiatrist, whose opinion of their quality and psychological meaning is not discernible. Her poetry does not stun the reader with its originality or beauty, but its content—the importance of art, the ubiquity of suffering, suicide, the sense of being alienated and misunderstood, is of interest. Lowell's mother, who was referred to as Lady Macbeth by more than one who knew her, was well known for her preoccupation with social class and power. Her cutting ambition—however much an overlay to her insecurity and acknowledged incapacity to love—was a subject of conversation for Lowell's friends and for Lowell himself. At one point Charlotte Lowell wrote a poem for Dr. Moore based on Macbeth's speech to his wife's doctor. Shakespeare had written:

Macbeth
How does your patient, doctor?
Doctor
Not so sick, my lord,
As she is troubled with thick-coming fancies
That keep her from her rest.
Macbeth
Cure her of that.
Canst thou not minister to a mind diseased,
Pluck from the memory a rooted sorrow,

> Raze out the written troubles of the brain,
> And with some sweet oblivious antidote
> Cleanse the stuffed bosom of that perilous stuff
> Which weighs upon the heart?
> *Doctor*
>   Therein the patient
> Must minister to himself.

Charlotte Lowell was concerned with the healing of the mind—she read deeply in psychology and psychiatry and assisted Moore with his psychiatric practice—albeit more with what the doctor could do than what the patient must. She rendered her own *Macbeth:*

> Has Byrnam Woods then come to Dusmane Hill?
> Do witches with black magic try to kill?
> Ah no; Tis but a poets [*sic*] pretty thought
> To light a darkness, cheer a mind distraught.
>
> Be lyon mettled proud and take your share
> For he who frets[,] psychiatry will care
> And even though life be a scorching flame
> We thank the ones who help us play the game.

It is not surprising that mother and son alike, fascinated as they were by power and control, by the kings and tyrants of Shakespeare, were drawn to the life of Napoleon. For an entire year Charlotte Lowell took on the habits of the French emperor: she insisted on sleeping on an army cot, took cold plunges in the morning, and, in behavior not without psychoanalytic interest, began calling her father "Napoleon." Once she threw a hairbrush at a maid for turning on the bedroom radiator before noon. Through this and other means, observed Lowell, she "learned how to lead her father: she only pretended to let him dominate."

As a young boy Lowell, too, was fixated on Napoleon. He compiled an extensive library of books about him and put together a collection of notebooks, crammed tight with troop strengths, the names of the French commander's marshals and subordinate officers, battles won and lost, and the capture and surrender of regimental eagles. The psychiatrist who saw Lowell when he was fifteen years old wrote that Lowell had "a mania about Napoleon" and that he had insisted upon taking twenty-one books about Napoleon with him when the family went away on summer vacation.

When he was a boy, Lowell said, his mother had read to him about their hero:

> And I, bristling and manic,
> skulked in the attic,
> and got two hundred French generals by name,
> from *A* to *V*—from Augereau to Vandamme.
> I used to dope myself asleep,
> naming those unpronounceables like sheep.

Lowell's interest in Napoleon persisted; years later, when he was manic, Lowell identified delusionally with Napoleon. His attraction to force and military genius, especially during periods of manic excitement, was not uncomplicated, and the implications of the attraction were to prove disturbing not only to Lowell but to some of those who knew him. Years after his youthful fixation on Napoleon had come and gone Lowell would reflect on the dangers of unchecked power:

> for uprooting races, lineages, Jacobins—
> the price was paltry . . . three million soldiers dead,
> grand opera fixed like morphine in their veins.
> Dare we say, he had no moral center?
> All gone like the smoke of his own artillery?

Lowell's fascination with Napoleon continued until the late years of his life, at times reassuming a manic obsessiveness. Jonathan Raban described Lowell, well into his fifties, providing a nearly real-time reenactment of Napoleon's battles: "Cal came down and sat on my carpet and traced out the battles. I have had almost every major battle that Napoleon ever conducted demonstrated to me in detail on the carpet . . . with Cal taking all the parts. And they were incredibly boring, and you just *ached* for him to show some semblance of normalcy."

Lowell's ties to his father were differently fraught from those to his mother. He rose up against his mother to preserve his identity and battled his father, whom he believed had capitulated to his mother. He wrote of his father, whose own father had died before he was born, that he "was half orphaned . . . such a son / as the stork seldom flings to ambition." Lowell's father, decidedly not flung to ambition, was a naval officer and an engineer educated at Annapolis, Harvard, and the Massachusetts Institute of Technology. His military career was no Napoleonic calling: "His ivory slide rule," wrote his son, "protruded from a pigeonhole of the desk, where it rested in its leather case, as handy as some more warlike householder's holstered revolver." He was subject not only to the orders of his commanding officer but to those of his wife. She was clear that she was neither born nor bred to be a navy wife, nor was she transportable. Naval barracks were not Beacon Hill and postings away from Boston were postings away from civilization. She did not take well to the life she had agreed to. Her husband yielded, her son watched. Both simmered.

Lowell watched his mother hollow out his father's will, cringed as she demanded that he leave the navy. His father became, as his son later would describe himself, an albatross on land: city bound, a stranger to the sea, a stockbroker with few clients and fewer assets. As a promising young naval officer his "life had opened out utterly to him," Lowell said of his father; he had possessed a "buccaneer imagination." Now, drifting in the civilian world, his employers "were afraid of his heart condition and quite astonished by a certain beaming inattentive languor."

"Why doesn't he fight back?" his son asked. "*Why doesn't he fight back?*" There was no good answer. "In his forties," Lowell wrote, his father's soul "went underground: as a civilian he kept his high sense of form, his humor, his accuracy, but this accuracy was henceforth unimportant, recreational, *hors de combat.* . . . In the twenty-two years Father lived after he resigned from the Navy, he never again deserted Boston and never became Bostonian."

"Mrs. Lowell," her daughter-in-law Elizabeth Hardwick said, "got Mr. Lowell to retire—and I think [his son] found this unforgivable. There was nothing for him to do . . . he began to draw into himself . . . he'd lost his nerve, so to speak." Hardwick, like most who knew him, spoke of Mr. Lowell's affability and intelligence, his emptiness, his surrender. His son, she said, thought that his father "didn't know who he was" and there was in this something that he "minded terribly." "Mr. Lowell," she added, was also "a bit frightened" of his son. "Having this large, somewhat bumbling young man around the house was quite bewildering to him."

To his psychiatrists, Lowell described his father as "constantly belittled" by his mother. He was an "affectionate, but distant and ineffectual man—shy, uncertain, and inadequate." Yet, Lowell always added, his father was also "gentle and considerate." He was "quiet and humorous, a man of good tastes but completely overpowered by my mother." He disdained his father's passivity but extended to him an affection and pity he could not to his mother. (Throughout his life, when corresponding to his parents, he would address them as "Mother" and "Daddy," respectively.) "I was like Father, but not so marked and tried to be just the opposite."

"We were all born with hardening arteries." Lowell wrote about himself and his parents: "Our drives ran in grooves. Mother wanted to live in Boston, and be a daughter. Father wanted to live on his battleship, and be a bachelor just about to announce his engagement. I wanted to live at Rock [his grandfather's farm] twelve months of the year. I wanted to be the Napoleon of my daydreams, an orphan who lived on a trust fund, a fisherman who lived on fish that cooked themselves."

Lowell told his doctors that his father seemed to him to be depressed—there was, as he wrote in "Near the Unbalanced Aquarium," an "inattentive languor that had been growing on him for years"—and that his mother had been sufficiently concerned to consult a psychiatrist about his depression. After his father died, Lowell wrote to Elizabeth Bishop that his father had not been a "suffering or heroic man." But, he said, there was "at least one great might-have-been—a first-rate Naval career. The death seems almost meaningless, as is perhaps always the case when the life has long resigned itself to a terrible dim, diffused pathos." The border between demoralization and depression is a porous one.

Lowell's father wrote to him with less obvious emotion than his mother did, but he injected into his letters the details of places and people he had seen. Specificity, not expressiveness, marks his writing. He described the Peabody Museum in Salem: "I think you would like the Museum, it houses the East India Marine Society . . . they brought back archeological & marine exhibits, and perfectly fascinating ship models." The Natural History of the Essex Institute, he continued, "with all the fish & birds & snakes & other stuffed animals—you would thoroughly love it."

He looked forward, he said, to showing his son the museum and taking him to lunch. It is a dry and literal letter, but considerable affection comes through. At Christmas, he thanked his son for a knife: "I liked the way it was done up, with the interesting Xmas paper, & the stars you pasted on, like the Southern Cross—which incidentally is about the only constellation you can see in the Southern hemisphere." Unlike his wife, for whom emotional expression was paramount, if problematic, and abstractions such as "Boston" were all, Lowell's father kept his words and ideas more grounded. "Talking with Daddy before bed was different," observed his son. "There was no magic phrase, like let's go back to Boston, that would have made my Father happy."

His father wrote about the sea and the natural world better than he did about people and emotions, but his eye for the specific in the world made its way into his son's writing. If his father's words lack complexity or stay too long in the light, if they are at variance with his mother's more emotion-rich language, then that is not inconsistent with Lowell's own contradictory nature. "Somehow it's hard to write very fully, or interestingly or honestly about personal matters," he wrote to Elizabeth Bishop. "I always feel my Mother's moralizing wrestling with my father's optimism. Almost from birth I decided they were both wrong and the truth lay elsewhere. Then from time [to time] I talk like both of them at once."

Lowell's views of his father, like those he had of his mother, gentled over time; perhaps he was more aware of human frailty—theirs and his—and the limits of personality and character. In "Middle Age" he looked to his own life in the light of his father's:

> At forty-five,
> what next, what next?
> At every corner,
> I meet my Father,
> my age, still alive.
>
> .   .   .   .
>
> You never climbed
> Mount Sion, yet left
> dinosaur
> death-steps on the crust,
> where I must walk.

Twenty-five years after his father's death, Lowell wrote a short recognizance, "To Daddy." Life was more complicated, his father more complicated and protecting, than he had thought when young:

> I think, though I didn't believe it, you were my airhole,
> and resigned perhaps from the Navy to be an airhole—
> that Mother not warn me to put my socks on before my shoes.

From childhood, Lowell felt himself to be of a different tribe from his parents. He began in their world, took it in sparingly, fought it, and re-formed it into something neither conventional nor quiet. It was as if a goose had been born to a mallard pair, the ducks ill-suited to each other but of like look, common expectation, and uncritical respect for the boundaries laid down by others. Lowell did not fit; he was ungainly, restless, wild, thrashing, brash, irritable, contrary, and discontented with the boundaries of his home waters. He grew, his wings scraped. He was clumsy, broody. Boundaries were not inviolable, he knew this instinctively; they were to be crossed and renavigated. Routes were anything but set; they needed to be found, redrawn, renamed. Flight itself was different, its dangers were his, his destination different: "There were no tickets for that altitude," he would write. His parents, knowing no subtler way, pressed hood and fetter; he shook his way out. He would write throughout his life of free flight and sailing, bubbles and balloons, stairs, mania, and all things leading out of restraint and darkness. Here, from "My Last Afternoon with Uncle Devereux Winslow":

> I picked with a clean finger nail at the blue anchor
> on my sailor blouse washed white as a spinnaker.
> What in the world was I wishing?
> . . . A sail-colored horse browsing in the bulrushes . . .
> A fluff of the west wind puffing
> my blouse, kiting me over our seven chimneys,
> troubling the waters. . . .
> As small as sapphires were the ponds: *Quittacus, Snippituit,*
> and *Assawompset,* halved by "the Island,"
> where my Uncle's duck blind
> floated in a barrage of smoke-clouds.
> Double-barrelled shotguns
> stuck out like bundles of baby crow-bars.

In December 1932, when Lowell was fifteen and in his third year at St. Mark's School, a private Episcopal preparatory school in Massachusetts, his parents took him to see a psychiatrist at the Judge Baker Guidance Center in Boston. His mother reported to the doctor that Lowell was "doing very poor work," as well as having "personality difficulties." He was "always against things," she said, "disagreeable at home, uncommunicative, and did as much as possible outside the family circle." She reported that when young he had, for hours, repetitively rocked himself back and forth in bed, obsessively collected junk, and showed little competitive interest.

"On the top floor of our house, in a room that was dark but always germ-free because the windows were open, I used to lie on my back, and hold my knees, and vibrate," Lowell wrote later. " '*Stop rocking*': my nurse or Mother would say. I remember this trembling fury."

The extensive psychological evaluation done on Lowell when he was fifteen revealed, not surprisingly, that he possessed a very good vocabulary. His reasoning powers were assessed as "variable," however, and his motor control as "poor average." His IQ, recorded as 121, was in the superior but far from highest range, a seemingly unexpected finding in someone later widely acknowledged as a genius. Inattention may have contributed to the relatively low score, although the person who administered the intelligence test noted that Lowell was "quite cooperative during the test period"; the score is, however, consistent with research demonstrating that creativity and intelligence often diverge above an IQ of 120. (Nobel laureates James Watson, the codiscoverer of the structure of DNA, and Richard Feynman, the theoretical physicist, both tested with IQs of approximately 120.) The gap between Lowell's verbal intelligence and his other abilities is consistent with the neuropsychological profile common in those who go on to develop manic-depressive (bipolar) illness; that is, a marked discrepancy between high verbal skills and significantly lower motor and spatial skills.

The psychiatrist who saw Lowell at the clinic found him "reticent, unwilling to face his situation." He was without goals and easily bored but said he liked jazz. He seemed "a little confused, a little obstinate, weakly argumentative." Lowell, when asked to describe himself, said that he was "lazy" and read only what he wanted to read. He said he was sorry when his father left the navy; he thought he would himself end up in business. It was clear to the doctor that "the boy badly needed a father." He ended his psychiatric evaluation with the hope that "the young gentleman will face it all." Two years later, Lowell's father reported to the psychiatrist that Lowell's behavior at home had not changed significantly but that he was on the school football team and had received honors in three of his six college examinations. Things were changing, although not as rapidly as Lowell's parents wished.

In November of 1936, when Lowell was nineteen years old and a sophomore at Harvard, his parents consulted with the Boston psychiatrist Dr. Merrill Moore. Moore was a poet as well as a doctor, and a member of the Fugitives, a Vanderbilt-based group of poets and literary scholars that included Robert Penn Warren, Allen Tate, and John Crowe Ransom. His professional relationship with Charlotte Lowell was to prove unorthodox by any standards. He may have had an affair with her; certainly Lowell and others thought he had. He asked her for money and social introductions and encouraged her to counsel his patients, despite her lack of educational qualifications.

"We are having trouble with our boy," Lowell's parents told Moore. "We don't know what to do. We want to see if psychiatry can help us." His chief difficulties, they said, were his attitudes toward his parents, life in general, and Harvard. He was living at Lowell House at Harvard, they said. "We tried to explain to him what we thought he should be like in order to live up to the expectations of what would be demanded of a member of our family, but he paid no attention." His mother elaborated: "He is so uncooperative and antagonistic to all reasonable arguments and demands." His parents did not tell Lowell that they were seeking psychiatric advice about him.

It is hard not to sympathize with Lowell's parents, who appear to have been at the end of their tether in making sense of, much less influencing, their son's behavior. Yet it is clear that for them he had become as much of a problem as a person, not an ideal situation for any child. In the eleven pages of typed notes that Lowell's mother gave to Dr. Moore she does not mention a single positive thing about her son's personality, character, or abilities. Instead, she begins her long litany with "I always thought that Bobby was a peculiar child." He was a terrible crier, she continues, he rocked ceaselessly in his bed, was uncooperative; he was always a problem. It was hard to get anyone to look after him, "A nurse would come in one door and go out the other."

He collected screwdrivers, nails, and hammers rather than playing like "normal" children. He took his bed to bits. "He gave us a miserable time most of the time. He never was a natural child." He was irritable and would break things, was defiant and oppositional in the extreme.

"He was very hard to manage from the start," his mother told Dr. Moore. "He would have awful tantrums and scream and howl." He "goes off his head," she explained. "He bangs doors and slams windows. He has scenes and leaves suddenly." He collected everything around him, "like a mouse." His parents and nurse "could hardly get him past an ash or trash can. He wanted to stop, investigate, and get things out." It took Lowell's parents most of his youth to recognize that oppositional behavior is, in fact, in opposition to someone or something, and that the more tightly they tried to control him the more defiant he became.

Some light drifted in after Lowell and his mother had a prolonged battle over his obsession with snakes. Lowell had been sent to a summer camp for "difficult children" and, not surprisingly, had proven to be difficult; after an initial period of trial and resistance, however, the camp counselor was able to interest Lowell in nature, particularly in snakes. His mother recounted to Dr. Moore what happened next:

> He returned home at the end of the summer with a large box of small snakes. He was a very nervous, highly strung child. . . . That started the snake craze. He never let up on the snakes for several years but cultivated them, and got them from everywhere and kept them all over the house. He frightened the servants to death. This lasted a long time. He would bring them into the house, and if I opened a bureau draw[er] there would be a snake, if I opened the closet there would be another snake, and one day he came in with a very large one, he had gotten from somewhere. He was argumentative and troublesome about it. He looked up passages in the Bible about snakes and argued with his father and me saying that they were God's creatures, and that they deserved affection and attention like anything else. I have noticed that he gets through with things about the time the opposition stops. We decided we would accept the snakes and him, but when we did this he lost his interest in them. Then he went in for fishing.

The defiance; the wile, stubbornness, and perverse mischief in fighting against those who tried to control him; the intense energy and monomaniacal interests; the letting up of resistance as another's control lessened: all of these things were there when he was young and they continued for the rest of his life. There was a slight shift in his mother's appreciation for what his control and will might entail, however. Charlotte Lowell's preliminary eleven-page accounting of the difficulties brought into her life by her unwanted son was supplemented not long afterward by another two pages of things done and left undone by Lowell. She describes his "terrible temper tantrums which he tries to overcome, white and dangerous" but, for the first time, mentions a positive quality. He has, she writes, "great strength of character—controls himself when [he] wants to, [has] great control over suffering." "He has a very strong will," she told Dr. Moore. "He can make himself do what he wants to do. He can stand pain, and once when bitten by a muskrat the doctor cauterized the wound without any anesthetic and Bobby did not flinch."

"Mentally or verbally, it was hardiness which was always praised," Lowell was to write. "When, later, I simply would not be sick, hardiness was fine and yet somehow associated in my mind with perverse stubbornness, with an assertion of my will against my mother's." Imagination would allow him to escape, vanquish.

Merrill Moore concluded, on the basis of the mother's reports, that Lowell, whom he had not met, had "considerable unconscious conflict" and might be in the "early stage of a psychosis." Three months later Moore, who still had not actually met Lowell, wrote that he was also "something of a genius" and that "there were moments when he was probably not responsible for some of his emotional reactions." He was sullen, short fused, and curt to his parents, less often but not infrequently to his friends.

The battle of wills in the Lowell family continued, each participant adamant and unbudging. A diagram drawn up by Dr. Moore and Lowell's parents captures the struggle. It shows the "ideal" trajectory Lowell's parents thought Lowell's life should take over the next few years; that is, that he should graduate from Harvard with the rest of his class. They drafted a "failure course," as well, one portraying the possibility that Lowell would drop out of Harvard and end up like his friend Frank Parker, who had left Harvard prematurely (Parker became an artist and did the cover art for Lowell's books), and an unspecified "compromise" life course. Lowell was not present for the mapping out of his life.

The conflict came to blows in December 1936, a month after Lowell's parents first consulted Dr. Moore. It was inevitable. His parents were attempting to control someone who had fought control in all ways from the youngest of ages and who now was far less controllable: he was older and freer to act independently and, at the same time, his moods and behavior were less under his own control, much less the control of anyone else. The accelerant for the conflict was Lowell's "unsuitable" engagement to a woman older than he was and "not of his class." Lowell's father wrote a formal letter to the young woman's father disapproving of her visits to Lowell's rooms at Harvard and calling into question her "good reputation." Lowell, gored and raging, went to his parents' house, confronted his father with what he had

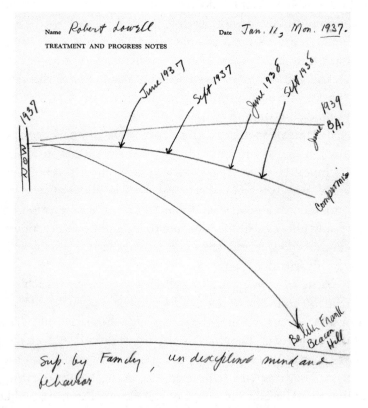

Parents' plans for Lowell, 1937–39

done, and knocked him to the ground. "He glowered apelike," his father recounted to Moore. "He's sick and dangerous and ought to be put away." He is "so awfully wild when he gets wild," his father said. "He is an extremist even for a wild person."

It was an act that Lowell was to regret for the rest of his life, one that would make its way time and again into his poetry and letters. Like dynamite, it shook the settled. It was an act that his father, a gentle man whatever else, found inexplicable but stark and undeniable; it also forced father and son to restructure what had been a frayed and superficial relationship. It forced Lowell to face the gravity of what he had done; it pressed him to rethink, build, and create. A few months later, in March 1937, he apologized to his father, asking that they both look to themselves for a reasonable division of blame and to make better what had not been good:

Dear Daddy:

I have been churning about and turning things over for the last two months or so, and have at last come to realize I have been very foolish, very weak, aside from the fact that what I did might have had far more disastrous results; one can not get away with striking his father or for that matter using violence to anyone. I am sorry and wish to be forgiven.

Things in the past have been very wrong, and of course the blame must be divided. Relations were not cordial, but cold, distrustful, and deceptive, and if I am allowed to re-enter the family I hope we can establish a condition of mutual confidence. I believe that many of the provisions you have made for me have proven sound, but I do not believe they were made with sympathy and understanding. My objections have not been to *what* you have done but to *how* you have done it. Our aims and desires, I think will turn out to be much less opposed than they have appeared, if discussed openly without prejudice. I think that given a fair chance I can work with and not against you, and hope if you will permit it to have a much more intimate relationship than was ever possible in the past. I will be glad to apologize whenever you find it convenient.

Affectionately,

Cal

Lowell's violence against his father reflected not only the friction in their relationship but his steadily developing manic illness. He would need to come to terms with rash acts not always under his control, acts for which there would be, and he would feel, moral culpability.

The act of bringing down a father was an ancient and fit subject for poetry. Ten years after the incident, in "Rebellion," Lowell described what had happened:

> There was rebellion, father, when the mock
> French windows slammed and you hove backward, rammed
> Into your heirlooms, screens, a glass-cased clock,
> The highboy quaking to its toes. You damned
> My arm that cast your house upon your head
> And broke the chimney flintlock on your skull.

More than two decades after the publication of "Rebellion" in *Lord Weary's Castle*, years after his father had died of a heart attack, Lowell returned to the primal act, to the festering violence and his mind's "hot nerves":

> myself brooding in fire and a dark quiet
> on the abandoned steps of the Harvard Fieldhouse,
> nomad quicksilver by saying *Lycidas*—
> Then punctiliously handing the letter to my father.
> I knocked him down.

"I struck my father," wrote Lowell, in a continuation of memory and remorse; "later my apology / hardly scratched the surface of his invisible / coronary . . . never to be effaced." He took the complex relationship between remorse and forgiveness, the tangled feelings of those who obligate forgiveness and those who must forgive, into "Middle Age":

> Father, forgive me
> my injuries,
> as I forgive
> those I
> have injured!

His father was a "gentle, faithful, and dim man," Lowell wrote in "Near the Unbalanced Aquarium." He didn't really know why he was against his father: "I hope there will be peace."

———

Lowell's erratic moods and behaviors escalated alongside his growing discipline and his determination to be a poet. These parallel threads, a relentless Puritan work ethic together with the exertion of will against his more destructive energies—energies that could headwater his imagination or drown him—are threads that run together throughout his creative life. He re-created himself from the "thuggish" schoolboy, who had been nicknamed "Cal" for the Roman emperor Caligula (or, some said, for Caliban from *The Tempest*), into an introspective adolescent determined to be a writer. Something could come from imagining, inhabiting the life of the mad, pained, and brutal emperor to whom Lowell had become bound by name. Something might be hooked from the identification with degradation.

"Tell me what I saw / to make me like you," wrote Lowell in "Caligula," thirty years after his school days at St. Mark's. "I took your name":

> Your true face sneers at me, mean, thin, agonized,
> the rusty Roman medal where I see
> my lowest depths of possibility.
>
> What can be salvaged from your life? A pain
> that gently darkens over heart and brain,
> a fairy's touch, a cobweb's weight of pain,
> now makes me tremble at your right to live.

Lowell wrangled his ferocious energy into writing. He wrote his first poem in 1934 when he was seventeen years old and by the fall of that year had written more than thirty. "I have come to realize more and more the spiritual side of being a poet . . . of breathing the same air as Shakespeare," he wrote to one of his teachers. The following month he wrote about God "that he always forgives, suffers when we suffer, and that he seeks only to serve, and never punishes. This is the highest, and only duty of art, for here only is truth."

He continued to write poetry at school and during his years at Harvard. His subjects were death and decay, God and art. Lowell wrote a raw, free-associative account—surreal, morbid, and hypersensitive—of life rotting into shadow and spoil. "Sometimes, when we are in disorder, every pinprick and scraping blade of grass magnifies," his essay begins. The gardener spills a bag of mown grass in a pond; its smell is "wet and lifeless, floating and stifling." Then, a "grass green sea," with shark fins and water "toothed" with tusks, a nether world with submerged, submerging shadows. "The underneath was dank. Maggots crawled and crawled, searching after a putrifying [sic] rat, buried under grass. Fermentation had set in. . . . And the maggots seethed and seethed, searching for the rats. . . . Earth devours her offspring. . . . Earth, I am able to momentarily retard your dinner." All rots, all decays. Lowell ended his essay as he began it, speculating that the fever in his brain was linked to his dark perception of the world: "When I woke up and lay for months in bed, the membranes of my brain sprained, I wondered if the coincidence existed between noon, the putrifying [sic] rat, and my sunstroke."

Others were beginning to acknowledge his work. His advisor at Harvard said that there was "a sense of grandeur in his verse which can stand alone." And Lowell made it clear that he meant to write: "The honor of earning one's own living," he wrote to his parents, "is a very small thing when set against the honor of writing lasting literature." To his mother, when he was twenty, he wrote, "My vocation is writing and . . . if I should fail at that I should certainly fail in anything else: fail to make good and fail to gain happiness." He was in no hurry for recognition, he wrote to a teacher: "I have no doubt in my ability to produce in the end."

Lowell set his course, but Harvard was not a part of it. It was not able to give him what he wanted; indeed, it gave him a great deal he did not want. His conflict with his parents and with their expectations for the correct Boston life he felt would keep him bogged and bound. (These expectations were held beyond his family; Lowell's decision to leave Harvard was written up in the Boston newspapers.) Merrill Moore, who had finally gotten together with Lowell, was perceptive enough to see that his best choice was to leave Harvard and, at least for a while, to move away from New England. "We are dealing with a boy who has a personality like rock crystal, glittering, very hard, and very definite in its formation," wrote Moore. "The longer I know Cal," he said, "the greater respect for his personality I have." In 1937 Moore wrote to his friend, the poet John Crowe Ransom, and asked him to take Lowell under his tutelage at Vanderbilt. "It is my opinion that Harvard is a very bad place for him on account of his family associations which irritate him and do not particularly help him," he wrote to Ransom. Lowell, he said, was an extreme individual, a bit odd and ornery, but someone who had a gift for poetry. Ransom agreed to take Lowell on as a student, a tribute to Moore's intuition and Ransom's kindness.

A year later, Moore wrote to Charlotte Lowell that her son's poetry was "tight, compact, difficult but full of meaning and originality and psychologically subtle, very subtle." He had become more and more convinced, he said, that Lowell was "a man of genius and that we will just have to adjust to him as he is." Moore had gone from doctor to admirer and advocate, a long journey over a not-too-long period of time. "It looks as if our future job is going to be nursemaid for a famous poet," Moore wrote to Lowell's mother in January 1938. "If I am correct in this, then it behooves us to learn all we can about neurotic geniuses and their patterns of behavior and their difficulties just like one has to learn all about diabetes if one has to live with a diabetic." The psychiatrist who a year earlier had met with Lowell's parents to chart their wayward son's future was now counseling them to give him a long lead. They did this, to an extent. Lowell, for his part, tried as well. Things were less fractious, but not intimate.

Time gentled Lowell's view of his mother, although in a complicated and incomplete way. His letters to her moved from a combative tone to a gentler one, as if agreeing to look away from the things he knew had not worked or had been poisonous, as if recognizing she was still and after all his mother. She, in turn, extended more tenderness to him in the aftermath of his breakdowns. After his first hospitalization in 1949 she wrote, "I can well understand how you must feel, and admire your courage and wisdom. . . . We have undoubtedly made many mistakes in your upbringing but we have always loved you and tried to help you and we always will. . . . Our thoughts are often with you and I feel that when this is all over you will be much better than ever before."

She wrote to him with pride as his work gained recognition, and her pleasure in his dedication of an early book to her and in memory of his father is clear. "Nothing could have given me more pleasure than receiving your beautiful book 'The Mills of the Kavanaughs,'" she wrote. "I feel greatly touched and honored by its dedication to me and in memory of Daddy. Your affection and thoughtfulness in doing this I shall always appreciate. I am really so pleased to have the book that I hardly know what to say."

In time Charlotte Winslow Lowell came to consider the possibility of her own culpability in their earlier, fraught relationship: "Time is so final, relentless and unforgiving," she wrote to her son three years before she died. "If we could only have it over again, how much better we might do." There had been "plenty of time for memories, regrets." Acknowledging the pain her son had been through, she added, "Your own life has not been easy."

When his father died, Lowell slipped into his place, if partially, and in a less conflicted way. It was a slow circling around to a relationship with his mother that had less edge and more compassion, one sealed with the inescapable recognition of shared traits. "Most of our lives were weighed on each other like stones," he wrote to Ezra Pound after his mother died. "But at the end [in the last ten months] we were in a funny way, speaking different languages, very close—the same metabolism, the same humor, the same boldness, and slowness." In a late poem, "To Mother," published more than twenty years after her death and in the year of his own, he wrote:

> It has taken me the time since you died
> to discover you are as human as I am . . .
> if I am.

Lowell would return to New England at different times throughout his life to reroot and teach, to write, to marry and become a father, and to spend long summers with his wife and daughter. He would choose to be buried there, next to his father and mother; he would choose and select their epitaphs. Carved into his father's gravestone, under the eagle and anchors of the United States Navy, are the last lines of "Where the Rainbow Ends," the final poem in *Lord Weary's Castle*. "Stand and live," it reads. "The dove has brought an olive branch to eat." "Where the

Rainbow Ends" was the only poem read at Lowell's own funeral nearly thirty years later.

Lowell's mother died in Italy in 1954, less than an hour before Lowell arrived to be with her. Her nurse told him of her final days: "She kept trying to heal the hemorrhage in her brain by calling for her twenty little jars and bottles with their pink plastic covers, and kept dabbing her temples with creams and washes." "And always," he added, in a nod to her now and again spartan ways, "her quick cold bath in the morning."

Lowell arranged an Episcopal service for his mother in Rapallo and picked out a "black and gold baroque casket . . . suitable for burying her hero Napoleon at Les Invalides." It "was regal but flawed," he wrote later. "The spelling of her name on the casket was incorrect, *Lovel* not *Lowell*." She was still and sealed; he accompanied her body home.

The day of their sailing the shoreline "was breaking into fiery flower," a sight at far remove from the frozen ground and firs of New England. Lowell had a long time to think as he kept vigil over his mother's coffin. "Mother, permanently sealed in her coffin, lay in the hold," he wrote. "She was solitary, just as formerly, when she took her long walks by the Atlantic." She had walked a lifetime; in more recent years during her September holidays in Mattapoisett and, thirty-seven years earlier, pregnant with her son, wishing that she were dead. Now, Charlotte Winslow Lowell "shone in her bridal tinfoil, and hurried homeward with open arms to her husband lying under the White Mountains." It is a stunning and curious image.

Lowell wrote about his mother's death, as he did his father's, in *Life Studies*. Traveling "first-class in the hold," sealed in death and with her son in attendance, she sailed past the fiery banks and through the Mediterranean waters. She was on her way home to New England:

> While the passengers were tanning
> on the Mediterranean in deck-chairs,
> our family cemetery in Dunbarton
> lay under the White Mountains
> in the sub-zero weather.
> The graveyard's soil was changing to stone—
> so many of its deaths had been midwinter.

Dour and dark against the blinding snowdrifts,
its black brook and fir trunks were as smooth as masts.
A fence of iron spear-hafts
black-bordered its mostly Colonial grave-slates.

. . . .

Frost had given their names a diamond edge. . . .

In the grandiloquent lettering on Mother's coffin,
Lowell had been misspelled *LOVEL.*
The corpse
was wrapped like *panettone* in Italian tinfoil.

On Charlotte Winslow Lowell's gravestone, carved below the
Winslow family crest, there is an epitaph chosen from another poem
he had written: "Reserved and bracing lady," the granite reads. "Buoy-
ant now where time is love."

—————

"The wheel is broken at the well," the eighteen-year-old Lowell wrote
in his poem "New England." In the spring of 1937, he left that New
England, and what he thought to be its brokenness, long enough to
study and come into his own. But he did not leave it for long. Like
Henry Adams, he had honed his instinct for resistance and reform; he
had learned to fight for what he wanted and to write from what chafed
him. He was twenty years old when he left New England. By the age of
thirty he had exchanged Protestantism for Catholicism, anonymity for
literary acclaim, and sanity for madness.

5

A Brackish Reach

the bough
Cracks with the unpicked apples, and at dawn
The small-mouth bass breaks water, gorged with spawn.
—*From* "After the Surprising Conversions"

Lowell left Boston for Nashville in order to study with the poets John Crowe Ransom and Allen Tate. It was more than clear, he wrote of his train ride south, that he was no longer in New England. The village greens and the North Atlantic, Boston and Cape Cod and Nantucket slid into a Tennessee countryside that was "plains of treeless farmland." The pulverizing heat that "gushered" up over the concrete highway and "bombard[ed] the horizon." It was like watching a Western, he said, "waiting for a wayside steer's skull and the bleaching ribs of a covered wagon." He was wearing "last summer's mothballish, already soiled white linens, and moccasins, knotted so that they never had to be tied or untied." His head was full of "Miltonic ambitions" and his suitcase "heavy with bad poetry."

The South to which he came was attuned to its own culture. Lowell became newly and differently aware that he was a New Englander: "I was Northern, disembodied, a Platonist, a Puritan, an abolitionist." He was far from averse to finding himself in an opposing world, but more important, he was provided examples of how a poet and person ought to be. Allen Tate and John Crowe Ransom tutored him in art and life. "Like a torn cat," he would write later, "I was taken in when I needed help."

John Crowe Ransom, whose work and character early on commanded Lowell's respect, gave him a long lead to pursue his poetry. Lowell would be judged by his writing and academic studies, not by the parental judgments he had found grating and impossible to live with. Given freedom to create, and literary standards to match his ambition, he opened up as a writer and person. Lowell found in Ransom the father and teacher he had desired but not had. Ransom understood where Lowell's imagination could go and he was able to give him the structure, freedom, and affection that allowed his originality free yet disciplined movement. The affection went in both directions. "Lowell is more than a student," Ransom wrote in a letter of recommendation, "he's more like a son to me." Twenty-five years after first meeting him, Lowell made his debt clear: "I often doubt if I would have survived without you. I was so abristle and untamed, nor would any discipline less inspired and kind than yours have held me."

Lowell spent the late spring and summer of 1937 in Tennessee and then enrolled in Kenyon College in Ohio, where Ransom had taken a faculty position. While at Kenyon he studied deeply in the classics, published several of his poems, and talked through the night with other students likewise in earnest about their work. Several of them, the short-story writer Peter Taylor, the poet Randall Jarrell, literary critic and poet John Thompson, and novelist and critic Robie Macauley, became friends for life. "How sad and serious we were," said Taylor. "We wanted to be writers."

In April 1940 Lowell completed his undergraduate studies at Kenyon; he wrote to his parents what neither would have predicted from his flailing youth: "Dear Mother and Daddy," he wrote. "Monday I graduated summa cum laude, phi beta kappa, highest honors in classics, first man in my class and valedictorian."

———

From the brashness of his adolescence, Lowell moved into a period of important writing, marriage, and the onset of severe manic illness. In 1940, shortly after he graduated from college, Lowell married the novelist Jean Stafford. Stafford, who became an acclaimed writer and received a Pulitzer Prize for her work, suffered repeated depressive breakdowns, attempted suicide, and was on several occasions hospitalized for implacable alcoholism. Lowell and Stafford fueled each other's worst tendencies and in the process provoked corrosive mistrust and jealousy.

Jean Stafford described Lowell as a man whose rages—more fierce than those he had experienced as a child and adolescent—terrified her. When she initially refused to marry him, she said, "he kept saying if I didn't marry him he would just run the car off the road etc., so I said he could go to hell . . . and he got savage and I got scared, so I said well I will see you once more but only in the company of other people." There is no question that Lowell could be frightening when he was manic, and Stafford was not alone in her fear of him when he was ill. He was powerful and tall, six foot one; when he was psychotic, it was hard for the police to constrain him; a smaller, unarmed woman had cause for fright. Stafford was no minimalist in putting her words together, however. "I had the tongue of an adder," she wrote in an autobiographical short story about her relationship with Lowell; her heart, she said, was "black with rage and hate."

Lowell, Stafford wrote to a friend shortly before she decided to marry him, was "an uncouth, neurotic, psychopathic murderer-poet." Lowell, writing later about their relationship as it drew to an end, spoke of its ill health: "Jean is mysterious and contradictory. We had an excruciatingly unpleasant meeting in which she said that she loved me and her one desire was to drive me wild." The truth of any marriage is not fully given, even to those bound by its vows; certainly it is beyond the understanding of those who are not. But no one who knew them spoke to amity in the Lowell-Stafford marriage.

The years between Lowell's graduation from Kenyon College in 1940 and his first hospitalization for mania in 1949 were shot through with unrest. The fitful rages that punctuated his childhood and adolescence uncoiled into something more dangerous, although at times they came together into eruptively brilliant poetry. In December 1938 Lowell crashed his car into the wall of a cul-de-sac in Cambridge, Massachusetts. Stafford, who was in the passenger seat, was seriously injured and required repeated operations to repair her injuries, including a badly broken nose. She would suffer the physical and emotional aftermath of the accident for years. Although physically unhurt, Lowell was "thrown almost into a psychosis." His moods swung wildly, continued his mother's psychiatrist, ricocheting between inappropriate "hypomanic happiness," "despair," and a "state of hysteria."

There would be more violence associated with Lowell's mental instability, usually in short-lasting, impulsive, seizure-like rages, most notably in the years before he was treated with lithium. In 1940, Lowell rebroke Stafford's nose in an argument, and in December 1945, jealous, enraged, almost certainly manic, although not yet formally diagnosed as such, he tried to strangle her. This reportedly happened with two other women as well; he was to both of them "unrecognizable" in his manic rage. According to Stafford and to Lowell's friend Frank Parker, she was dreaming of a former lover and spoke his name when Lowell woke her to make love. Lowell, in his long poem "The Mills of the Kavanaughs," reimagined the incident:

> "Then I was wide
> Awake, and turning over. 'Who, who, who?'
> You asked me, 'tell me who.' Then everything
> Was roaring, Harry. Harry, I could feel
> Nothing—it was so black—except your seal,
> The stump with green shoots on your signet ring.
>
> "I couldn't tell you; but you shook the bed,
> And struck me, Harry. 'I will shake you dead
> As earth,' you chattered, 'you, you, you, you, you. . . .
> Who are you keeping, Anne?'
> . . . .
> "'Harry, I am glad
> You tried to kill me; it is out, you know;
> I'll shout it from the housetops of the Mills;
> I'll tell you, so remember, you are mad.'"

In an earlier version of "The Mills of the Kavanaughs," the husband spends the rest of the night rocking back and forth, much as Lowell's mother had described him doing as a child, hours on end, waiting for "the blue of morning." Lowell wrote his memory and remorse into verse of careful specificity. The signet ring was engraved with the "stump with green shoots," the crest of the Winslows, his mother's family. Its motto, "Cut down we flourish," was carved deep into his grandfather's ring; it was the seal of his Pilgrim fathers.

Lowell's manic illness simmered in his youth, with outbursts of consuming anger and obsession, then progressed to manic psychosis in his early thirties. The pattern in his twenties was marked by focused zeal, dotted by fits of rage, diverted into an extended period of religious fervor. Lowell's spiritual pilgrimage was neither surprising nor without benefit. He was by temperament inclined to impose a monastic structuring on his enthusiasms; he had done this with his childhood obsessions and during the novitiate summers in Nantucket. Cycles of excitement, disciplined pursuit, and enervation marked his life. It was no great surprise that he threw himself into Catholicism and, when incipiently mad, took his Catholicism to a psychotic extreme.

Religious conviction was at times a sedating influence on Lowell; at others, it was a symptom of his mania or a propellant to it. Religious images and devotional practice were natural metaphors for Lowell, a way to make sense of his intense ecstasies and put them to use; the Church provided a rich, ancient, and complex language. Catholicism lived in history; its coinage was sin and redemption, the promise of rebirth. It was a metaphysical system uniquely able to hold and give language to Lowell's imagination and the involutions of his mind. As Elizabeth Hardwick put it, religion was a "vast, valuable museum."

The Episcopal Church in which Lowell had been raised, and the Calvinist heritage of his Puritan ancestors, had been his settled fare; the latter, Lowell would argue later, was not so distant from Catholicism. "I was born a non-believing Protestant New Englander," he told Ian Hamilton. "My parents and everyone I saw were non-believing Protestant New Englanders. They went to church, but faith was absurd. In college, I began reading Hawthorne, Jonathan Edwards, English seventeenth-century preachers, Calvin himself, Gilson, and others, some of them Catholics—Catholics and Calvinists I don't think opposites; they are rather alike compared to us in our secular sprawl. From zealous, atheist Calvinist to a believing Catholic is no great leap."

A friend who was introduced to Lowell at the time of his conversion to Catholicism agreed that Lowell's leap from Protestantism to Catholicism was not as great as it might have seemed: "Though his immediate ancestors were either agnostic or pale and proper Episcopalian, he had in his bones the Yankee Calvinistic sense of original sin, of the iniquity of man and of himself. His literary ancestors were Hawthorne and Melville, not Emerson or Whitman; his Catholicism was Augustinian and Pascalian, not any of the softer Counter-Reformation varieties." Calvinism and Catholicism were to be a generative mix for Lowell and for his writing.

In the late fall of 1940 Lowell took instruction in Catholicism. It was a critical time in his life, one that he remembered more than thirty-five years later in a letter to the priest who had shepherded him through. "I remember well your long patient explanations to me of catechism," he wrote. "The books we discussed, I still have. You were a road over a dark stream. . . . I turned out to be a poet, and so it continued." Lowell read deeply and broadly in Catholic theology—Aquinas, Newman, Hopkins, Étienne Gilson—and for an extended period in Lowell's twenties the Roman Church became the axis upon which turned his work and relationships. It offered an inner world of principle, certainty, and order; it contained enough complexity to accommodate the subtlety and ferocity of his thinking.

Lowell described to his psychiatrist what he saw as the links between his religious beliefs, his life, and his poetry: "When I first married, I had some of the usual dreams: house, children, career etc.; but mostly I thought of setting myself to read and write works that would astonish. Society would be a little group of sympathizers and masters. This wasn't enough. I discovered the Catholic Church, for me another mobile inner world, one that connected with the real world and was pleasantly critical of it. I tried to convert my wife. I read more books. After a while religion and poetry came together, and after a lapse of two years I started writing again and with more power and coherence. In my life religion was largely reading polemic, going to mass, but things had more order, or in a more orderly fashion I was even fiercer against the world. In the third year of my marriage I boiled over."

Lowell was received into the Catholic Church in March 1941. He was ardent and insistent, not to say fanatical in the practice of his new religion. He declared that his earlier marriage to Stafford was invalid and that they must remarry in the Catholic Church, which they did. He insisted on Mass at six thirty each morning, grace before and after meals, two rosaries a day, benediction in the evening, and confession. He told Stafford that they could no longer read newspapers, nor could they read any novels except those by Proust, James, Tolstoy, and Dostoyevsky. Otherwise, these two omnivorous readers and intellectuals were to read only books of faith. They would go to no movies unless approved by the Church censor.

"It's what he's been destined for from the start," wrote Peter Taylor to a mutual friend. "He's literally hunted down the most complete sort of orthodoxy; and once he found it, I must say, he gobbled it up as only Cal can gobble—day and night in an earnestness that approaches perversion."

Six months after Lowell's conversion to Catholicism he and Stafford moved to New York to work at a publishing house specializing in Catholic writers. There he pursued a life of monastic purity and poverty, becoming in the process a "veritable messiah." He was determined to "lead us all out of the paths of sin and war," said the publisher's business manager. His asceticism and zeal continued apace; his writing followed at a distance. In the winter of 1942 Lowell and Stafford moved from New York to Tennessee to share a house with Allen Tate and his wife, the writer Caroline Gordon. There Lowell wrote many of the poems that would go into his first book, *Land of Unlikeness*, which would be published in 1944.

Catholicism was constituent to his writing. "I think becoming a Catholic convert had a good deal to do with writing again," Lowell told the poet Frederick Seidel. "I was much more interested in being a Catholic than in being a writer. I read Catholic writers but had no intention of writing myself. But somehow, when I started again, I won't say the Catholicism gave me subject matter, but it gave me some sort of form, and I could begin a poem and build it to a climax. It was quite different from what I'd been doing earlier." Lowell's pattern of work—a driven, high-enthusiasm state, characterized by a rush of ideas and a mass of fragmentary writing that led, on occasion, to a shift in poetic form, followed by exhaustive revision—was to be a thread throughout his life.

Land of Unlikeness was widely and well reviewed. The poet and critic Randall Jarrell predicted that Lowell would write some of the best poems in the years to come. "In a day when poets aspire to be irresistible forces," he wrote, Lowell had become "an immovable object." He was "a rock in the stream that would have to be reckoned with."

The United States was at war during the time that Lowell and Stafford were living and writing in Tennessee. Lowell volunteered on several occasions for military service but was rejected because of his poor eyesight. After the United States demanded Germany's unconditional surrender, and following the Allied bombings of Hamburg in 1943 that razed the city and killed tens of thousands of civilians, Lowell stated that he no longer supported the American war effort. He sent a "Declaration of Personal Responsibility" to President Roosevelt; he also mailed copies of his statement to major newspapers, friends, and family members. Lowell gave his reasons for refusing military service: "Members of my family had served in all our wars since the Declaration of Independence," he wrote to the president. "Our tradition of service is sensible and noble; if its occasional exploitation by Money, Politics and Imperialism is allowed to seriously discredit it, we are doomed. . . . By demanding unconditional surrender we . . . [declare] that we are prepared to wage a war without quarter or principles, to the permanent destruction of Germany and Japan.

"No matter how expedient I might find it to entrust my moral responsibility to the State," he continued, "I realize that it is not permissible under a form of government which derives its sanctions from the rational assent of the governed." He could not "honorably participate in a war whose prosecution, as far as I can judge, constitutes a betrayal of my country."

It was a statement of conscience, one offered as a Catholic conscientious objector, not as a pacifist, and, as he knew it would, the declaration made newspaper headlines across the country. He was arraigned and sentenced to a year and a day at the Federal Correctional Institution in Danbury, Connecticut. He served a shortened sentence of five months and was released on parole, a convicted felon.

While awaiting transfer to Danbury, Lowell was incarcerated for ten days at the West Street Jail in New York. His poem "Memories of West Street and Lepke" was published in *Life Studies* in 1959. In it he alludes to his letter to President Roosevelt and to his own mental state:

> These are the tranquillized *Fifties*,
> and I am forty. Ought I to regret my seedtime?
> I was a fire-breathing Catholic C.O.,
> and made my manic statement,
> telling off the state and president.

If it was a manic statement, and certainly there were signs of early mania at the time, it was not past the bounds of reason.

Refusing to serve in World War II was the first of several high-profile political actions that Lowell took during his lifetime, most notably his protests against the Vietnam War. Being a conscientious objector during World War II went against the grain of public opinion, but Lowell's decision was generally seen as a matter of principle. "No one," he wrote to Peter Taylor, "has questioned my sincerity."

Lowell's Catholicism took on a deepening manic tint. While jailed at Danbury he attempted to organize the inmates into a strict Catho-

lic community; as in the novitiate Nantucket summers of his earlier
devising, they were to follow monastic rules. Not surprisingly, his
calling lacked appeal. His letters to Stafford were filled with religious
obsession. He had become "so fanatical," she wrote to Peter Taylor,
"so insanely illogical that our conversations and his letters could be
written into a case history of religious mania." Lowell, she said, bore
no resemblance to the person she had met. After her husband's release
from Danbury, Stafford wrote to Taylor again, concerned about what
appears to have been a hysterical seizure she had witnessed in Lowell.
"He had a terrifying seizure of some sort in church last Sunday and I
thought he was going to faint at the communion rail."

Lowell, still obsessed with Catholicism, began writing poetry
again, including many of the poems for *Lord Weary's Castle* (1946), a
book dominated by themes of a fallen New England, moral decay, ret-
ribution, and the unforgiving Puritanism of his ancestors. He wrote of
the complex burden of heritage and of the dark, ambiguous grace of
God. The battle raged between Calvinism—the New England Protes-

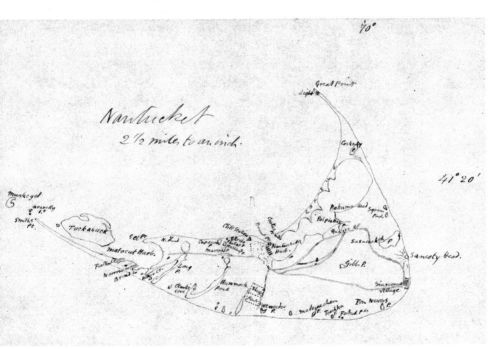

Nantucket survey map by Henry David Thoreau
"A brackish reach of shoal off Madaket,—
The sea was still breaking violently."

tantism that he had known longest and breathed most deeply—and the Catholicism that as an adult he had taken to heart and mind. That clash entered into his work violently and unforgettably in the poems of *Lord Weary's Castle*, poems, said John Crowe Ransom, that were "written"; that is, written to stay. Poems of ambition.

"The Quaker Graveyard in Nantucket," a long poem at the heart of *Lord Weary's Castle*, is an elegy of blood force written by Lowell for his cousin who died at sea in World War II. The energy of the poem is coiled, unstable, and manic in its fury. It is beholden to "Lycidas," Milton's great lament for a young man drowned at sea, and to Melville's *Moby-Dick;* an early version of the poem is titled "To Herman Melville." But it owes a debt as well to the Old Testament, Henry David Thoreau, Gerard Manley Hopkins, and a life's immersion in literature. The poem is Homeric in force, mythic in scale, and spelled by the violence of God and North Atlantic waters. It is the battleground for the contrasting forces that defined Lowell's mind as a young poet.

The North Atlantic fleet of Lowell's poem merges with the whaleboats of Ahab, man and men in blind, maddened pursuit. "The Quaker Graveyard in Nantucket" offers little consolation; there is ambiguity in God's plans and limits on man's will. Dense, vehement, driven by a manic rhythm, the poem is suffused with an impenetrable, dark ecstasy. The raw force of killed whale and killing whaler, death-lance, and harpoon, bones crying out for blood; rage and slaughter against sanctuary and singing stars; its violent, rhythmic power packs his verse:

> The bones cry for the blood of the white whale,
> The fat flukes arch and whack about its ears,
> The death-lance churns into the sanctuary, tears
> The gun-blue swingle, heaving like a flail,
> And hacks the coiling life out: it works and drags
> And rips the sperm-whale's midriff into rags,
> Gobbets of blubber spill to wind and weather,
> Sailor, and gulls go round the stoven timbers
> Where the morning stars sing out together
> And thunder shakes the white surf.

The poem, as Seamus Heaney said, is one where "the percussion and brass section of the language orchestra is driven hard and . . . the string section hardly gets a look in." ("I got drunker and drunker with the sea," wrote Lowell. "I put all my chips on rhythm, more than I have ever done since.") Energies and images are flung upward and downward. "Their boats were tossed / Sky-high"; "sea wings, beating landward, fall / Headlong"; "upward angel, downward fish": all is perturbed and heaving. Lowell's poem draws upon specific images from Henry David Thoreau, a fellow New Englander with whom Lowell shared a pull toward opposition, a draw toward the easeful writing moods of summer, and a beholdenness to the cycles of the natural world. They wrote books structured around the seasons and revised unendingly. They were steeped in the classics, at ease in imagining across history. They aimed high. "My desire," said Thoreau, is "to bear my head through atmospheres and heights unknown to my feet." The desire was "perennial and constant." They were willing to go to jail for their political beliefs. Renewal, as sewn into the cycles of the natural world, was more than metaphor to Lowell and Thoreau; it sang in their nerves.

In "The Quaker Graveyard in Nantucket," Lowell drew upon Thoreau's observations of the carnage from a shipwreck on Cape Cod that had drowned more than 140 people. Thoreau described the scene:

> I saw many marble feet and matted heads as the cloths were raised, and one livid, swollen, and mangled body of a drowned girl,—who probably had intended to go out to service in some American family,—to which some rags still adhered, with a string, half concealed by the flesh, about its swollen neck; the coiled-up wreck of a human hulk, gashed by the rocks or fishes, so that the bone and muscle were exposed, but quite bloodless,—merely red and white,—with wide-open and staring eyes, yet lustreless, dead-lights; or the cabin windows of a stranded vessel, filled with sand.

"The Quaker Graveyard in Nantucket" begins:

> A brackish reach of shoal off Madaket,—
> The sea was still breaking violently and night
> Had steamed into our North Atlantic Fleet,
> When the drowned sailor clutched the drag-net. Light

Flashed from his matted head and marble feet,
He grappled at the net
With the coiled, hurdling muscles of his thighs:
The corpse was bloodless, a botch of reds and whites,
Its open, staring eyes
Were lustreless dead-lights
Or cabin-windows on a stranded hulk
Heavy with sand. We weight the body, close
Its eyes and heave it seaward whence it came.

There is a debt to content and image, but the poetry lives in the changes.

Thoreau, looking at the wreckage on the beach and in the sea, had found it more disquieting to imagine the death of one individual than many. "If I had found one body cast upon the beach in some lonely place, it would have affected me more," he wrote. Instead, "I saw that corpses might be multiplied, as on the field of battle, till they no longer affected us in any degree, as exceptions to the common lot of humanity." It is, Thoreau concluded, "the individual and private that demands our sympathy." Although death—of man and beast, of good, of innocence—scores Lowell's poem, the death of one man, his cousin Warren Winslow, is the subject of the elegy. The individual would continue to be at the center of his work.

"The Quaker Graveyard in Nantucket" ends as it begins, with apocalyptic winds and high seas; there is violence in the forming of life as well as in its taking, beauty in the intimation of hope, although the beauty is uncertain. In Genesis, God had placed the rainbow in the sky as his compact with man. "I do set my bow in the cloud," declared the Lord. "And it shall be for a token of a covenant between me and the earth." It is the promise of God: "The waters shall no more become a flood to destroy all flesh."

Lowell's God is more ambiguous, the covenant darker:

You could cut the brackish winds with a knife
Here in Nantucket, and cast up the time
When the Lord God formed man from the sea's slime
And breathed into his face the breath of life,
And blue-lung'd combers lumbered to the kill.
The Lord survives the rainbow of His will.

Robert Lowell in 1946

"The voice is vibrant enough to be heard, learned enough to speak with authority, and savage enough to wake the dead."

PATIENT: Robert Lowell				
DATE:	TIME:	MEDICATION: (NOTE REASON IF OMITTED)	B. P.	NURSE:

Medication records for Robert Lowell, 1957
"My round-the-clock injections . . . left shoulder, right shoulder, right buttock, left buttock.
My blood became like melted lead."

The Kingdom of the Mad

At last the trees are green on Marlborough Street,
blossoms on our magnolia ignite
the morning with their murderous five days' white.
All night I've held your hand,
as if you had
a fourth time faced the kingdom of the mad—
its hackneyed speech, its homicidal eye—
and dragged me home alive.

—*From* "Man and Wife"

6

In Flight, Without a Ledge

Getting out of the flats after a manic leap is like our old crew races at school. When the course is half-finished, you know and so does everyone else in the boat, that not another stroke can be taken. Yet everyone goes on, and the observer on the wharf notices nothing.

—Letter to Theodore Roethke, 1958

Mania is a high-voltage, tense, and unstable state. The mind leaps; speech rushes: words ribbon out fast, unbidden, cutting. Ideas and schemes proliferate; alliances shift. Mania calls the plays. Robert Lowell, who was subject to attacks of mania throughout his adult life, knew all of this. For the thirty years that he was in and out of mental hospitals, his diagnosis, manic-depressive illness, was consistent. This is not surprising. His life was laden with instability; mental illness ran deep in his family. Incendiary enthusiasms marked his youth; later they accelerated into the religious zealotry of his twenties. His mind was high velocity. As a child he had been moody, volatile, and often beyond his parents' control. His defiant childhood gave way to the late adolescent summers in Nantucket he had described to Ezra Pound: a fevered immersion in literature that took place in the midst of a self-imposed monastic discipline just shy of the hair shirt and whip. After college came his conversion to Catholicism, an embrace so sudden and extreme as to seem like madness to many who knew him. He left the Church and then, when he again became manic, he rejoined it.

When Lowell first left the Church, he did it gradually but emphatically. Jean Stafford believed that he had simply "used up" Catholicism, gotten from it what he could artistically and emotionally and then, as with their marriage, moved on. Allen Tate suggested that Lowell, psychotic, had "merely used the Church . . . to establish his mania in religious terms." Lowell viewed his decision differently. "When I came on the Catholic Church," he wrote to the philosopher George Santayana in 1951, "it was a museum to contemplate, of course; but what I was after was a way of life." He had hoped, he said, that "I could respect and feel at peace and at home with that lived life. I never got very deep. There was discipline, gentleness and understanding, but not at the heart, or rather, not at my heart, or if at the heart it never circulated from there into the fingers." The Church and he had remained strangers, at heart's length, despite his attempt to become one with it.

Santayana wrote back: "I recognize that your center, as in Protestant religion, is in yourself, not in the cosmos or history or even society. If it had been in natural science or history you would never have thought of taking refuge in Catholicism. No doubt, it was not a refuge for you but an adventure—a voyage and a love-affair in a new dimension." Santayana, perhaps uniquely, understood Lowell's Protestant roots and his complicated wending toward and away from Catholicism, saw the appeal of adventure and the gaps in his experience to date. Importantly, he intuited the mutability of Lowell's religious passion into the secular passion of love. This was prescient. Lowell's first mania came in the wake of his wranglings with God and the Devil; virtually all of his remaining attacks of madness would be prefigured by intense love affairs. These romantic obsessions, like his earlier ruling passion for the Church, would be forsaken once sanity returned.

Lowell left the Catholic Church for the first time in 1946, the year *Lord Weary's Castle* was published. The following year he divorced Jean Stafford. Between 1946 and his first hospitalization for mania in 1949 Lowell lived in Massachusetts, Maine, Washington, D.C., and New York; had a few tense love affairs; met Elizabeth Hardwick, whom he would marry in a few years' time; and met and became friends with the poets Elizabeth Bishop, William Carlos Williams, Ezra Pound, Delmore Schwartz, Theodore Roethke, and John Berryman.

He was awarded the Pulitzer Prize for *Lord Weary's Castle* in 1947 and acclaimed by critics as the poet of his generation.

In October 1948 Lowell went to Yaddo writers' colony in Saratoga Springs, New York, to work on a long poem, "The Mills of the Kavanaughs." For many years a residence for writers, Yaddo was described by John Cheever as the home to "more distinguished activity in the arts than any other piece of ground in the English-speaking community and perhaps the world." Lowell described Yaddo to Elizabeth Bishop in less acclamatory terms: It has "run down rose gardens, rotting cantaloupes, fountains, a bust of Dante with a hole in the head, sets called *Gems of Ancient Literature, Masterpieces of the World,* cracking dried up sets of Shakespeare, Ruskin, Balzac." There were "pseudo Titians, pseudo Reynolds, pseudo and real English wood, portraits of the patroness, her husband, her lover." There was, in short, everything to recommend it. "I'm delighted," he ended his letter. "Why don't you come?"

Lowell was "winding up," a phrase he and his friends would come to use to describe his ascents into mania. As was its wont, his mania smoldered before it ignited. He drank heavily. His mind sped. The poem he was working on was running with the wind; there were nine hundred lines altogether, five hundred written in October and November alone. He was writing flat out, in great "messy spurts," and, throughout it all, his personal experiences kept "flooding up." He was beginning to lose control over his writing.

In February 1949, "wound to the breaking point," he became obsessed with what he felt was a growing Communist influence at Yaddo. This fixation grew to delusional proportions, and the subsequent unwarranted charges made by Lowell were damaging to the director of Yaddo, Elizabeth Ames, although she eventually was exonerated; they were also damaging to Lowell's reputation. Most who were directly involved in the scandal, including the writers who publicly denounced him, came to realize that Lowell had been mentally ill when he made his allegations, but the consequences of his accusations remained. Early stages of mania are not always recognized as derangement, and the capacity to injure is that much the greater.

Exalted, excited, filled with a sense of bestowed grace and the divine, Lowell again sought out the Catholic Church. On Ash Wednesday he attended Mass for the first time in a year, accompanied by the writer Flannery O'Connor, herself a devout Catholic. She, like most of those who knew him during his breakdown at Yaddo, had no experience to aid her in understanding Lowell's escalating madness. "I just thought that was the way poets acted," she said. "Poor Cal was about three steps from the asylum," O'Connor would write years later. "He had the delusion that he had been called on some kind of mission of purification and he was canonizing everybody." Lowell's mind and behavior rocketed out of control, she recalled, "until I guess the shock table took care of it. [Lowell was given electroshock therapy when he was hospitalized a few months later.] It was a grief for me as if he had died. When he came out of it, he was no longer a Catholic."

Lowell told the other residents at Yaddo that he had received an "incredible outpouring of grace" and that God was "speaking through him." He fell in love with the writer Elizabeth Hardwick and declared his determination to marry her. He sent an urgent telegram to Allen Tate enlisting him in the Fight against Evil. He slept little, "canonized" those he met, and then retreated to a Trappist monastery for a week. When he returned to Yaddo he was yet more consumed with the notion of evil, as well as with its obverse side, the grace and bidding of God.

In early March, Lowell called his friend the classicist and translator Robert Fitzgerald. On Ash Wednesday, he disclosed to Fitzgerald, the "day of the Word made Flesh," he had "received the shock of the eternal word." Fitzgerald was instructed to transcribe Lowell's actions and thoughts, which he did:

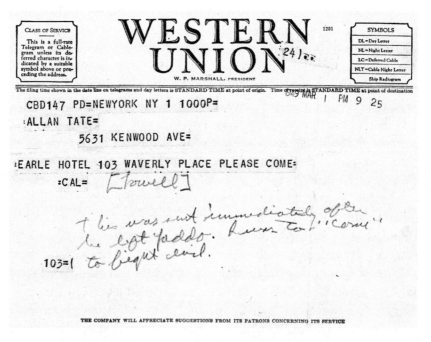

Telegram to Allen Tate, March 1949
"Come fight evil."

March 3 was the day of humors; I [i.e., Lowell] prayed to
St. Anthony of Padua, who himself held the child (and prayed
God to spare me His humor) and Elizabeth was miraculously
purged of the pollution caused by her evasions. I prayed over
her, and had to call on all the heavenly host, St. Michael and
others, and prayed over her using the psalm (?) beginning
"God said to the prophet, Even if the mother should forsake
the child . . ." She was purged and became like that music of
Haydn's.

Today is the day of Flannery O'Connor, whose patron
saint is St. Therese [sic] of Lisieux.

Also: you are to take St. Luke the physician and historian
as your patron saint.

That morning, he said afterward, he filled his bathtub with
cold water and went in first on his hands and knees, then arch-
ing on his back, and prayed thus to Therese [sic] of Lisieux in
gasps. All his motions that morning were "lapidary," and he
felt a steel coming into him that made him walk very erect. It
came to him that he should fast all day and give up cigarettes.
After mass and communion he walked, going in to a Protestant
Church to observe and think about the emptiness and specu-
late as to how it could be filled—also the "nimbleness" there
(for Protestants have some good things that Catholics don't)
and then up to the Jesuit Church on 14th Street and then to
the Church of St. Francis in the 30s feeling how in both love
radiated from the altars.

Lowell was very sick, and things hurtled out of control from there.
He set off for Chicago to visit his friend and former teacher Allen Tate.
It was a disaster. He revealed to Tate's wife that he had discovered the
secret of the universe; he also told her the names of her husband's lovers over the years. Then, reputedly, he held Tate out of a second-story
window while reciting Tate's poem "Ode to the Confederate Dead."
There was a scene at a restaurant. Later, Lowell opened the window
in his hotel room and shouted obscenities to the world beyond. It took
four policemen to overpower and handcuff him.

Lowell was taken to a psychiatrist at the University of Chicago, who diagnosed him as having had a "psychotic reaction," a nonspecific term generally indicating a profound mental removal from reality. Tate called Peter Taylor and told him that Lowell was "deranged"; then, with trepidation, anger, and relief, he saw him onto the train to Bloomington. Lowell, persuaded that there was a plot against him orchestrated by "the forces of evil," was terrified that there was dangerous gas in the air in the train; he, however, was "indestructible." Taylor met him at the station; it was soon apparent that Tate had not overstated the disarray in Lowell's mind.

"As soon as Cal stepped off the train," said Taylor, "I could see he was out of his head. He wasn't the Lowell I knew." During lunch at the Indiana University faculty club, Lowell sniffed the air and asked, "Do you smell that?" It was brimstone, he said, and the Devil was hiding behind one of the potted plants. Chaos unfurled after that. Lowell darted from the faculty club into the street, assaulted a police officer, and was put into a straitjacket. Then he was jailed.

Years later Lowell described what had been going on in his mind during that time. "I had an attack of pathological enthusiasm," he said. "The night before I was locked up I ran about the streets of Bloomington Indiana crying out against devils and homosexuals. I believed I could stop cars and paralyze their forces by merely standing in the middle of the highway with my arms outspread." He was convinced that he possessed special powers and that he alone could decipher the delusions and hallucinations fixing him in their grip. "Each car," Lowell explained, "carried a long rod above its tail-light, and the rods were adorned with diabolic Indian or Voodoo signs. Bloomington stood for Joyce's hero and Christian regeneration. Indiana stood for the evil, unexorcised, aboriginal Indians. I suspected I was a reincarnation of the Holy Ghost, and had become homicidally hallucinated. To have known the glory, violence and banality of such an experience is corrupting." Glory, violence, banality: it is an apt and killing description.

After a night in the Bloomington jail, Lowell was taken to the airport to return to the East Coast. During a holdover at LaGuardia in New York he talked exuberantly about Italian opera with the police officers assigned to guard him. The flight to Boston was a nightmare. When he arrived he was driven thirty miles north to a small New England town that, in a twist of coincidence and continuity, was but a few miles from where his ancestor Percival Lowle had first settled in 1639. Lowell was admitted to Baldpate Hospital, a small private psychiatric institute surrounded by acres of woods. The beauty of the hospital grounds gave the lie to the pain that was housed within, but this reality was one that escaped Lowell during the early days of his stay at Baldpate. The hospital, he said with some jocularity soon after he arrived, was "a combination of boarding school, jail, and Yaddo." He had not yet come down from the bubbling irreverence of his high mental state. The screams from the locked wards registered more acutely a few weeks later.

Lowell was admitted to Baldpate Hospital in early April 1949 and received a diagnosis of acute mania; he remained at the hospital for three months. When he arrived he was euphoric, overexcited, overactive, exalted, and talked "without cease." He told his doctors that he was "indestructible," a messenger from heaven. He had been Christ not long before, he said; he had walked upon the waters. He was in regular communication with God and had defeated the massing forces of evil. He was the reincarnation of the Holy Ghost. But not everything had been glorious in the past weeks, he acknowledged. He had had hallucinations of people with green skin, which had terrified him. He had seen a rooster that wasn't there. He had seen things he ought not to have seen. He had been assaultive, verbally abusive, and had slept next to not at all. He was, in short, manic.

It was a particularly frightening time for Elizabeth Hardwick, who was engaged to marry Lowell in a few months' time. "It went on for months," she said about the confusion leading up to his hospitalization. "He was in terrible shape and I was petrified. . . . It shouldn't have been allowed to go on so long—and, of course, it wouldn't be again." Once he was in the hospital he was still "raving" but "glad to be in there in a way . . . he felt protected in some way."

Lowell's first letters from the hospital billowed with high spirits, a tone at variance with his circumstance but not with his mania. Palm Sunday seemed a propitious time for Lowell to send out a stream of ebullient messages. He sent many. "I'm in grand shape," he wrote to Elizabeth Bishop. "The world is full of wonders," he confided to George Santayana. "I've been having rather tremendous experiences."

"I hope some one told you why I couldn't spend the week-end with you," he wrote to William Carlos Williams. "I'm taking sort of a rest. . . . The doctors are learning about as much as I am." They probably were. He wrote to Hardwick, his wife-to-be, to a former girlfriend, and to his former wife, Jean Stafford. To Stafford he said, cryptically, "I'm going through another Yaddo, but with flying colors. I think we're still married in a sense, but not meant to be together."

Lowell's early correspondence from Baldpate reflects a mind in denial, a mind intoxicated by mania. His behavior, however, made it increasingly difficult for those who knew him to continue their own denial. Frank Parker, his friend from boarding school and Harvard, acknowledged this: "My trouble was that I didn't believe he really was mad until I saw him in Baldpate . . . he was in the maximum [locked ward]. . . . People wandered in and out, these nuts. He of course was right in his element, lecturing and haranguing and instructing them."

By this time the unequivocal nature of Lowell's illness—his bizarre delusions and hallucinations, his religious mania and uncontainable energy, the assaultiveness and verbal attacks so inconsistent with who he was when sane—made the diagnosis of mania reasonably straightforward. His doctors briefly considered a diagnosis of schizophrenia, another early onset psychotic illness but with a generally poorer prognosis; they dismissed it within a few days, however, and mania was, with only brief, quickly abandoned consideration of schizophrenia, the diagnosis he received for the rest of his life.

The only meaningful treatment for mania in 1949 was electroconvulsive therapy (ECT). Also known as electroshock therapy, ECT is effective in treating both severe depression and mania. It was first used in the late 1930s and is still often employed as a treatment for severe depression; it is used less often for acute mania because modern medications generally work quickly and well. Small electrical currents are passed through the brain to induce a seizure. It is thought to work by, among other things, altering the chemical messengers in the brain and adjusting stress hormones that regulate mood, sleep, energy, and appetite. The use of ECT has been controversial, not because of its efficacy or safety, but because it was overused and misused, leading to sensationalist portrayals of it in films and books. Too, before the introduction of safe muscle relaxants and short-lasting anesthesia, there were more medical complications from the procedure.

Lowell received six ECT treatments in June 1949, fewer than would be typical in modern psychiatric practice. His delusions and manic behavior stopped almost immediately, and he was moved from the locked ward to the convalescent area of the hospital. Within a week of his final ECT treatment, however, Lowell plummeted into a deep depression. He was unable to concentrate or write and he talked about killing himself. He told his doctors he felt hopeless and wished to die. His speech was slow, his energy nonexistent, and he avoided being with other people.

Lowell left the hospital better than when he had arrived, but he was far from well. He was left to piece together his mind, which had been shattered; it was a hard and unsettling business. He had, as well, to make right the damage he had done to others when he had been manic. He felt humiliated and was overcome with remorse; he was not clear what he had done or why. The "whole thing," he said, "seemed like a prolonged dream."

"I'm well and about to leave," he wrote to Peter Taylor, "feeling rather gravelled and grim and dull." He was out of his "delirium" and "sorry for all the foolishness and trouble of my stay in Bloomington." Public spectacle, "pathological enthusiasm," depression, remorse, humiliation: these would milepost each attack of madness. Dread of future attacks would weigh upon him. Mania not only blasted apart Lowell's dealings with God, it shredded his belief in what he might expect of his mind.

Lowell's illness abraded his expectations of the future, to a point, but he kept the capacity after each attack to reconstruct his life, to rebuild his relationships with his family and friends. It was a painstaking atonement for things done and left undone. He returned to his work. This—the determination to move forward and to imagine a future, the work itself—remains the lasting thing.

He was, he made clear to his friends, indebted to them for their kindness to him when he had been ill. "The hospital is still too near a memory for me to find much amusement or pleasure in describing it," he wrote to T. S. Eliot shortly after having left the hospital. "But all my friends and even my mother and father were wonderfully helpful." He was deeply moved by Eliot's support, he said. "I feel that you have vicariously suffered my vicissitudes with me. Now I am taking to heart your comment on Huxley's comment on Lawrence—about the foolishness of a spectacular life—I mean mine, not Lawrence's, of course."

The reaction from Lowell's parents during his illness and hospitalization was well-meant but mixed. They wrote to him sending their love and concern. But Lowell's father also wrote him a blunt letter shortly after he had returned home from the hospital, just two weeks before he was to marry Elizabeth Hardwick. "I think it is much too soon to marry anybody," he wrote. "Just after you have been discharged from a mental hospital, after shock treatment." Both Lowell and Hardwick "should clearly understand that if she does marry you, that *she* is responsible for you." At the present time, he continued, "I do not feel that you are in any position to take care of yourself let alone to . . . provide for a wife." He and Lowell's mother, he made clear, "cannot assume any financial obligations for either you or your wife."

It was a harsh, practical letter and not entirely out of line given the reality and uncertainties attending Lowell's illness. No one knew what the future would bring; no one knew how his sanity would fare a year or ten years out. The psychiatrist who treated Lowell at Baldpate told Hardwick he didn't envy her. She was taking a terrible risk, he said: Lowell's mania would almost certainly return.

Everything was unpredictable, a muddle of uncertainty and shame. The psychotherapist and writer Eileen Simpson, married for a time to John Berryman, recalled a dramatically discordant view during the same painful period. After Lowell was released from the hospital, Simpson wrote, "All he could remember (this John found heartbreaking) was that he had never been happier than during those manic weeks."

———

Lowell married Elizabeth Hardwick in July 1949, two weeks after his release from Baldpate Hospital. Hardwick was from a family as filled with children, eleven, as his was not, and from a state, Kentucky, as different as imaginable from Massachussetts in politics, history, land, accent, and custom. She would become a noted essayist and a novelist of impact and originality, a writing teacher at Barnard College, and cofounder of the *New York Review of Books*; she earned along the way a reputation as a great, if on occasion acerbic, wit.

"The curls, the infectious chuckles," Derek Walcott said of her. "The drawl like poured-on honey, the privilege of sharing her astute delight, and the benign devastation of her wit." She was, he said, "more fun than any American writer I have known."

Lowell first met Hardwick in Greenwich Village in the summer of 1946, a time and mood he captured in "Man and Wife":

> Oh my *Petite*,
> clearest of all God's creatures, still all air and nerve:
> you were in your twenties, and I,
> once hand on glass
> and heart in mouth,
> outdrank the Rahvs in the heat
> of Greenwich Village, fainting at your feet—
> too boiled and shy
> and poker-faced to make a pass,
> while the shrill verve
> of your invective scorched the traditional South.

Hardwick was in many ways the ideal wife, friend, and critic to Lowell. Theirs was a complex marriage, one that lasted more than twenty years despite the kind of uncertainty and pain known only to those who have or live with someone who has severe manic illness. She was, importantly, a writer he respected. "He liked women writers," Hardwick said. "I don't think he ever had a true interest in a woman who wasn't a writer—an odd turn-on indeed, and one I've noticed not greatly shared. Women writers don't tend to be passive vessels or wives, saying, 'Oh, that's good, dear.'"

Their life was to be a Nantucket sleigh ride, tumultuous and uncharted. Hardwick's introduction to her husband's madness—his religious mania in Yaddo and his psychotic behavior in Bloomington; the long hospitalization at Baldpate—was not for the faint of heart. It pointed to the years of instability to come.

"I didn't know what I was getting into," Hardwick said, "but even if I had, I still would have married him. He was not crazy all the time—most of the time he was wonderful. The breakdowns were not the whole story. I feel lucky to have had the time—everything I know I learned from him. I very much feel it was the best thing that ever happened to me."

Hardwick maintained a lasting admiration for Lowell's intellect and work. "Certainly Cal had a great influence on every aspect of my life," she told an interviewer. "In literary matters, his immense learning and love of literature were a constant magic to me." The quality of his mind, she stated, was "quite the most thrilling I've known." Given this, and Hardwick's own intellect and strength of mind, it is difficult to fathom that she has on occasion been characterized as long-suffering or a "martyr" for staying with Lowell. It is a restricted view of a difficult, rich, long, pained, productive marriage and of a lasting friendship.

Lowell and Hardwick both had constitutive toughness, a quality critical to his survival and to the endurance of their relationship. She had as well a practical and empathetic view of his mental illness. She was not so much given to castigating or romanticizing his manic behavior as she was to getting him to a hospital. His aberrant behavior was seen by her as that: aberrant. Hurtful and threatening at times, certainly, but first and foremost she saw in the early signs of his mania—his precipitate romantic entanglements followed by demands for a divorce; his increased drinking, abusive behavior, and domineering argumentativeness—an illness that needed medical treatment.

Lowell was aware of the toll that his manic-depressive illness might take. Soon after Hardwick first visited him at Baldpate, he wrote to her: "*Gosh*, your visit was wonderful and *saning*. Hope you can stand me still." He was high on mania but rational enough to recognize the distress he had brought to the woman he planned to marry.

During their first summer together the newness of their married life was overshadowed by his illness. "Somehow, quite soon, he was in a very depressed state about what had happened, saying, 'No one can care for me. I've ruined my life. I'll always be mad,'" Hardwick remembered later. "As the weeks went on I felt Cal wasn't well at all, but depressed. Very self-critical, very tortured about himself, his future. . . . My heart was just breaking for him."

Then, once again, Lowell started hallucinating and became delusional. During a visit to friends he came downstairs one morning to tell them he had just seen the Holy Ghost; he asked them to smell the brimstone on his pajamas. He was getting sick again, even as he was trying to understand what had happened to him.

He tried to describe to his friends and family how and why his mind had gone off the rails. In August he wrote to Peter Taylor about some of what he had been through. "Before receiving electric shocks," he said, "I had a comical mad period singing ballads (very badly and baldly with made up tunes) and destroying furniture." He asked Taylor's forgiveness for not having wanted to see him. "It's been tough," he admitted. "Shaking all the unease, torpor, desire to do nothing."

In a letter to Ezra Pound's wife he said, "My 'experiences' that led to the hospital now seem like a prolonged dream—and so they were, then almost unbearably dull and depressing." He had thought often, he said, of the similarity between Pound's experience of madness and his own, "the astonishing jolt of having things happen to you, being put somewhere, the surprises you never planned."

In August, a month after leaving the hospital, Lowell wrote a letter of explanation and regret to a former lover, Gertrude Buckman:

> Nothing I can say will really do to tell you everything that happened, or why. By the time I reached the hospital I was completely out of my head—strange physical sensations— I was a prophet and everything was a symbol; then in the hospital: shouting, singing, tearing things up—religion and antics. Then depression (extreme) aching, self-enclosed, fearful of everyone and everything anyone could do, feeling I was nothing and could do nothing.
>
> I'm sorry about the mix-up on writing to Bald-Pate, that you heard about our marriage the way you did—sorry because of all my ill, inconsistent, selfish and so on actions toward you. . . . I try to accept myself and hold on to the joyful.
>
> . . . I want to be forgiven and to stay friends. No harm or coldness was ever meant.

Lowell's depression got worse over the summer; in mid-September 1949 he was admitted to the Payne Whitney Psychiatric Clinic of New York Hospital. His psychiatrist there, Dr. John Blitzer, wrote in his admitting note that Lowell was "sloppily dressed, unshaven, appeared and was sad and tense"; despite this he made "a considerable effort to appear friendly." His speech was slow, with long pauses. Lowell told Dr. Blitzer that he was unable to concentrate or write and that he had withdrawn completely into himself. Before coming into the hospital he had spent entire days in bed, had had nothing to say to anyone, and had been thinking of suicide. He felt empty, he told the doctor. Empty and discouraged. He had been working on a poem begun at the onset of his elated phase but was now "very depressed by how confused he had been when writing it."

Dr. Blitzer's psychiatric history concluded that Lowell had experienced several periods of intense elation as an adult, times during which he had been "overactive, over confident, over talkative, occasionally rude and domineering." These elated periods had lasted approximately eight months and "their onset had usually coincided with [the] patient's beginning some new [literary] project." Each mild to moderate mania had been followed by an extended period of depression, during which Lowell reported that he felt "wrapped up in himself," "empty," and "self-depreciatory"; believed that he had "used others"; and had been "unable to work efficiently." Dr. Blitzer diagnosed Lowell, as had the doctors at Baldpate Hospital, as having manic-depressive illness.

During the initial weeks of Lowell's hospital stay, Blitzer noted that Lowell was "extremely dependent" and sometimes followed Blitzer down the hallway, seeking "constant reassurance that he would get well." For the first month he was too depressed and confused to engage in meaningful psychotherapy. No antidepressants, in the modern sense of the word, were available in 1949 (amphetamine and methamphetamine, although occasionally prescribed for depression, were addictive and problematic), so Lowell received only psychotherapy during the nearly four months of his hospitalization at Payne Whitney.

In addition to his own distress, Lowell was struggling once again with the pain he had caused others. He wrote to Hardwick on his first night: "Dearest, dearest, dearest Lizzie I think of you all the time; and worry so much about all I have dumped on you. We are going to work it all out, dear. . . ." His desire to convince her, and himself, that he was better is apparent in a letter written a few days later: "O Lord, how empty I am. However, this letter is just to tell you that the depression that I am well. Please don't worry. When you come on Saturday, you will see improvement."

Two weeks later he wrote, "After I'd told all the sordid and awful things about myself I could think of, he [Dr. Blitzer] said it was 95 percent due to my condition." The doctor's reassurance went only so far. "Things are much the same," he continued. "Mornings, the unbearable; afternoons, the numb—both dumb and diminishing fast. I guess all's well."

Dr. Blitzer noted in Lowell's chart at the end of six weeks in the hospital that he was "somewhat less depressed." His sense of humor was beginning to return, he was more assertive and independent, and he was able to participate in psychoanalytically oriented psychotherapy. Lowell told his friends and family that the therapy was helpful. He was "beginning to really learn something from the psycho-therapy," he wrote to his mother. "For many fairly obvious reasons," he said, "I have not wanted to write about coming here." He was "ashamed and puzzled by it . . . shut up like a clam."

In two pages of notes he wrote for himself while he was in the hospital, Lowell jotted down his observations about his illness and what he must do to go forward. His thinking, he noted, was scattered and vulnerable. He was concerned about his "physical nervousness, stiffness, hesitancy" and worried about his memory. "I remember so much," he wrote, "then memory stops (on *100s* of things). I do so much, then action stops." The best things he had done in his life, he observed, had been "done against hardest competition, with great effort." He thought this would continue to be true. He missed "healthy summer life" and knew he needed to "get back in normal society." He was concerned that his stay at Payne Whitney would increase his reputation for "oddness." He resolved he must try harder with everyone.

At the top of his list, as always, was his writing. "My profession [is] writing," he scribbled in his near-illegible hand. This declaration was followed by three compressed phrases: "a) whole personality, b) competition, c) mania phases figure." That Lowell had begun to link his writing to his "phases" of mania is interesting. Dr. Blitzer had written in Lowell's chart during the same time period that "patient's strong emotional ties with his manic phase were very evident. Besides the feeling of well-being which was present at that time, patient felt that, 'my senses were more keen than they had ever been before, and that's what a writer needs.'" A complex relationship between his illness and his poetry was beginning to be apparent not only to Lowell but to the first of several doctors who would comment on it.

Lowell came to believe that his prolonged religious "enthusiasm" had been a symptom of his illness rather than rightful revelation. "The *mystical* experiences and explosions turned out to be pathological," he wrote to George Santayana toward the end of his stay at Payne Whitney. Sacred gave way to secular. "Much against my will," he would write in the first poem of *Life Studies*, "I left the city of God where it belongs." Lowell characterized his religious zeal as a mania. "I'm out of my dumps (the religious mania seems to necessitate a kind of hangover of melancholia) and feel much as always," he wrote to Santayana. Depression had left him "inert, gloomy, aimless, vacant, self-locked." He had been unable to write during the depression that came on the heels of his mania, he said. "During all that blind mole's time—the fascinated spirit watching the holocaust of irrationality[,] apathy tormenting apathy . . . forgive me for my involuntary foolishness."

Lowell described his depression in the evocative, simple words that many patients use to convey their mental confusion: the fog and wit-lessness and chaos. But he chose the words of a poet as well—the "blind mole's time," the "holocaust of irrationality." He wrote about the "long, burdensome dull period" of his mind and the months of "wad-ing in the muck and weeds and backwash of a depression." Lowell's many and original images of his stagnant, self-locked mind expanded the language of suffering.

At the end of December 1949, a few days before he left Payne Whitney, Lowell was offered a teaching position at the University of Iowa for the spring and another one at Kenyon College for the sum-mer. Dr. Blitzer wrote in his notes that Lowell was extremely relieved to be offered a job given what he had been through. His behavior toward the end of his hospital stay was "more cheerful and outgoing" and, although he was unable to write poetry, he was working "con-structively" in preparation for his teaching.

Lowell was released from the hospital in early January 1950. His condition on discharge was listed as "improved" and his prognosis as "good." He had lost a year of his life to illness. It was the first of many and not the worst.

Robert Lowell Hospitalizations
1949–1977

Date	Hospital	Clinical State on Admission	Diagnosis
April 6, 1949– July 12, 1949	Baldpate Hospital Georgetown, MA	Mania	Manic-Depressive Psychosis
September 13, 1949– January 3, 1950	Payne Whitney Clinic New York	Depression	Manic-Depressive Illness
August– mid-September 1952	American Army Hospital (Salzburg) / U.S. Army Hospital (Munich) / Binswanger Sanitorium (Switzerland)	Mania	[Manic-Depressive Illness]
April 8– September 15, 1954	Jewish Hospital in Cincinnati / Transferred to Payne Whitney Clinic, New York, on May 21	Mania	Manic-Depressive Illness
December 12–17, 1957	Boston State Hospital Boston	Mania	Manic-Depressive Illness
December 17, 1957– January 14, 1958	Massachusetts Mental Health Center (Boston Psychopathic Hospital) Boston	Mania	Manic-Depressive Illness
January 30/31– May 22, 1958	McLean Hospital Boston	Mania	[Manic-Depressive Psychosis]

Date	Hospital	Clinical State on Admission	Diagnosis
April 28– July 22, 1959	McLean Hospital Boston	Mania	[Manic-Depressive Psychosis]
March 4– end of March 1961	Columbia-Presbyterian Hospital New York	Mania	[Manic-Depressive Psychosis]
September 10– October 1, 1962	Clinica Bethlehem Buenos Aires	Mania	
October 1– November 7, 1962	Institute of Living Hartford, CT	Mania	Manic-Depressive Illness
Early December 1963– mid-January 1964	Institute of Living Hartford, CT	Mania	Manic-Depressive Illness
Early January– February 1965	Institute of Living Hartford, CT	Mania	Manic-Depressive Illness
December 6, 1965– February 2, 1966	McLean Hospital Boston	Mania	[Manic-Depressive Psychosis]
December 24, 1966– March 8, 1967	McLean Hospital Boston	Mania	[Manic-Depressive Psychosis]
July 9– August 13, 1970	Greenways Nursing Home London	Mania	
November– early December 1975	Priory Hospital London	Mania	
December 1975– January 4, 1976	Greenways Nursing Home London	Mania	
January 5–20, 1976	24-hour private nursing care London	Mania	
End of January– mid-February 1976	St. Andrews Hospital Northampton	Mania	
September 15– October 27, 1976	Greenways Nursing Home London	Mania	
February 1–9, 1977	Massachusetts General Hospital Boston	Pulmonary Congestion	Cardiac Failure Manic-Depressive Illness

Robert Lowell: Hospitalizations, clinical state on admission, and diagnosis

The course of Lowell's manic illness was unrelenting following his first hospitalization in 1949. This progression, as well as the consistency in his diagnosis, manic-depressive illness, and the clinical state, mania, for which he was hospitalized, is clear. It is not clear exactly how many manic episodes Lowell had. Before 1949 his manic behavior was not generally recognized as symptomatic of a psychiatric illness.

Later, some of Lowell's manic episodes, while serious, were not severe enough to warrant hospitalization. On a few occasions, for example, he was able to stay out of the hospital by taking antipsychotic medications during the early stages of an attack. At other times he was hospitalized twice for the same episode of mania, either because he was transferred to a different hospital for treatment or because he was released too soon and then had to be readmitted. Once, when acutely manic, he received twenty-four-hour private nursing care instead of being hospitalized. Hospitalization is an imperfect marker for the occurrence of mania.

Lowell had a three-year respite between his first hospitalization for mania in 1949 and his second in 1952, a respite not uncommon for those with his illness. It was a time of travel and teaching but not a great deal of writing. It was also a time of loss. His father died suddenly but not unexpectedly in 1950. *The Mills of the Kavanaughs* was published to mixed reviews. He and Hardwick traveled in Europe and lived for extended periods in Florence and Amsterdam. In Hardwick's autobiographical novel *Sleepless Nights*, the main character describes living in Holland as one of the happiest periods of her life:

> With what gratitude I look back on Europe for the first time. . . . Antwerp and Ghent: what wonderful names, he said, hard as the heavy cobbles in the square. Amsterdam, a city of readers. All night long you seemed to hear the turning of pages. . . . Those fair heads remembered Ovid, Yeats, Baudelaire and remembered suffering, hiding, freezing. The weight of books and wars.

Lowell had been insistent they settle in Amsterdam: "It is quiet and still—as far as the outer world goes, I guess it has been still since the seventeenth century, when it was at the full tide, a baroque, worldly, presbyterian, canal-and-brick, glorious Boston." He read "gobs of Italian, German, French and Latin poetry, Greek, French and Turkish history, and art books, till my head rocks, as though it held the lantern-slides of the world."

In the summer of 1952, Lowell and Hardwick went to Salzburg, where he taught in a conference on American studies. By most accounts he taught dazzlingly well, and then too dazzlingly well. He "got very wound up," in Hardwick's words: he was euphoric, voluble, goading, impulsive. He fell in love with an Italian music student. He disappeared from the castle where the conference was being held and had to be tracked down to the German border, where he had wandered off alone. He talked excitedly and ceaselessly from evening into the early morning hours. He wore out those whose company he kept.

The director of the seminar, Shepherd Brooks, described the scene at the castle after Lowell had become overtly manic. Police cars swarmed everywhere; it was chaos. "All the faculty were at one end of the castle," said Brooks. "At the other Professor Lowell was on the top floor surrounded by police . . . barricaded in his room and wouldn't come out." When Brooks went into Lowell's room, "Cal [was] wearing just a pair of shorts, looking wild and terribly strong, and charged with adrenaline."

Lowell was taken, talking fast, furious, incessantly, incoherently, to the American Army Hospital in Salzburg; from there he was transferred to the U.S. Army Hospital in Munich. It was a harrowing, exhausting experience for those in the car with him. Reality is an early casualty of mania. "It was extraordinary," recounted Brooks. "He was creating his own reality and then responding to it, and everyone else had to go along with it." Sleep is another casualty of mania, not only for those who are manic but for those who find themselves in their fellowship. Depression, Lowell once said, is an illness for oneself, mania an illness for one's friends. His friends came to know this well.

Hardwick, distraught by the recurrence of Lowell's mania and by being on the receiving end of the sharp-tongued, cruel remarks that so often spewed out during it, wrote to friends during Lowell's stay in the Army Hospital in Munich: "I pity Cal from the bottom of my heart, and I fear for him in every way. Even though he's still in a closed ward, they let me see him. . . . I don't dare to tell them that I can hardly bear it for more than five minutes. I find responding extremely difficult and he sees that. He torments me, apparently so far as I can tell trying to provoke tears or an argument. . . . I don't know how to respond for his own good." She added the fear that would come to haunt them both: "What tomorrow holds no one knows."

Lowell's stays in the U.S. Army Hospital in Munich and the Bellevue Sanatorium in Switzerland, where he was transferred, were relatively short, less than a month. The doctors attributed this to the sudden onset of his mania, generally more treatable than one with a more insidious course, as well as his willingness to go into the hospital sooner rather than later. The mania was nonetheless crushing for them both. Lowell was "terrified of such a thing ever happening again," said Hardwick. He was "*utterly heart-broken* . . . shattered and ashamed." Her hopes for him and their marriage lay in "how much courage he has."

Lowell was given a course of six or seven electroshock treatments in the U.S. Army Hospital in Munich; as it had in Baldpate Hospital, the electroshock therapy stopped his mania. With the passing of not much time, his stay in the hospital and the electroshock treatment moved from experience into verse:

> "Oh mama, mama, like a trolley-pole
> sparking at contact, her electric shock—
> the power-house! . . . The doctor calls our roll—
> no knives, no forks. We file before the clock,
>
> and fancy minnows, slaves of habit, shoot
> like starlight through their air-conditioned bowl.
> It's time for feeding. Each subnormal boot-
> black heart is pulsing to its ant-egg dole."

In a letter to his mother after his Salzburg breakdown, Lowell gave credit to Hardwick for helping avert a more serious attack. She had an informed insight into the nature of his illness, the kind of insight that disappears for most patients when they are manic. Due to her alertness, he said, it was a "very mild repetition of the trouble" that had led up to his 1949 hospitalization. He minimized the severity of his recent attack and projected an optimism about the future that must have been hard to summon. "In a period of twenty days," he wrote, "I went through the three stages of exuberance, confusion and depression, and can now safely say it's all definitely over, without any likelihood of relapse or return." He was eager to keep rumors about his illness at bay. "I'm not anxious to build up a reputation for poetic instability," he ended his letter. He was whistling past a grave.

Generally Lowell was able to get back into life uncannily well. "Cal's recuperative powers were almost as much of a jolt as his breakdowns," wrote Elizabeth Hardwick. "Knowing him in the chains of illness you could, for a time, not imagine him otherwise. And when he was well, it seemed so miraculous that the old gifts of person and art were still there, as if they had been stored in some serene, safe box somewhere. Then it did not seem possible that the dread assault could return to hammer him into bits once more."

Lowell and Hardwick returned to the United States in 1953, where Lowell took up a short-term teaching appointment at the Iowa Writers' Workshop. He then accepted a visiting professorship at the University of Cincinnati, meant to last from January through June 1954. Cincinnati was to be the backdrop for one of Lowell's most severe attacks of mania. It also continued a remarkable exposition of madness and its toll by two of America's great writers, Robert Lowell and Elizabeth Hardwick Lowell. Their letters, and the prose writings and poetry that came from that time, give an extraordinary portrayal of madness, art, love, and navigation through suffering.

Hardwick's descriptions of mania, and the pernicious effect it has on those flailing, drowning in its wake, are among the best I know. She is astute and direct in her account of being married to someone with manic illness, of being married to a famous poet with manic illness. Madness is easy to overdramatize and thereby underestimate; it is less easy to convey its capacity to erode identity, disfigure love, and violate trust. The real horror of madness is more subtle and corrosive than its caricature.

Lowell wrote brilliantly about his illness, and that is, in part, the subject of this book. But Hardwick had the contemporaneous view. She wrote as she tried to get Lowell into the hospital, as she met with lawyers and talked to the police, as she visited him in the ward. She wrote as he shot into mania, fell into depression. And she wrote time and again as they rebuilt their life. Hardwick and Lowell left a written legacy of madness, imagination, and determination that is unmatched. The two writers struggled not only with Lowell's manic illness but with its moral, psychological, and legal reverberations; they fought for the survival of their marriage, for their writing, and for their friendship. Together and separately, they contended with fundamentals. What is madness? Is it beyond one's control or not? How does madness cross into work, into art and imagination? What is character? What are its limits? How does a marriage of two strong wills and intellects survive madness and infidelity? Is art worth the pain it causes? What lasts? What sustains?

Silhouettes of Robert Lowell and
Elizabeth Hardwick Lowell, 1953

After the 1952 manic recurrence in Salzburg, Lowell and Hard-wick lived with heightened uncertainty about what would happen to his mind—would he stay sane, how long would it be before his next manic attack? They had their answer sooner rather than later. Two years after Salzburg it all happened again. In February 1954, Lowell's mother, touring in Italy, had a severe stroke. On his way to be with her Lowell stopped in Paris to have dinner with his friend Blair Clark, who recognized the signs of incipient mania straightaway. "He was in the early stages," he recalled. "I knew the symptoms by that time—he couldn't sleep, sat up all night talking and drinking and so on. Everything was racing."

Lowell, concerned about his health in the wake of his mother's death, wrote to Hardwick from Europe, "I know you worry about me.

But I am taking great care to sleep. The nine days [*sic*] voyage [accompanying his mother's body back to America] will be a great easing." As a precaution he asked a doctor to give him a box of sedatives. Despite his efforts, Lowell's mania took off after his mother's funeral. (Funeral mania has been observed since ancient times. Psychoanalysts have attributed it to the individual's conflicted feelings toward the dead, more biologically inclined psychiatrists to the stress and the accompanying lack of sleep that may set off mania in those susceptible to it.) By March he was "completely deranged," observed Hardwick, "but still in the extremely 'happy' stage." He fell in love again with the Italian music student he had fallen for in Salzburg and declared his intention to divorce Hardwick. The sudden obsession with Giovanna Madonia, while humiliating and painful to Hardwick, was also a clear sign to her of his mania. "The blow will always fall upon me," she wrote to friends in April. "When Cal gets a little manic the first desire is to be away from the person who represents reality, responsibility, skepticism, and to make new connections." She was in a difficult position, she admitted. "I can't say, 'Cal wants to leave me, therefore he's crazy.'"

The early stages of Lowell's mania were difficult for many of his colleagues and friends to recognize, or to recognize quickly enough to act. Randall Jarrell, who saw him in April 1954 and noted his eccentric behavior, grew impatient and angry with Lowell's preoccupation with himself and his "tactless Yankee comments about Southerners." Only later, when Lowell telephoned to say he was in the hospital, did he realize that Lowell had been ill. According to Jarrell's wife, when he got off the telephone after talking with Lowell he shook his head from side to side and said, "So that's what it was. He was manic. . . . As any fool could plainly see . . . but me. . . . Oh, Randall, you're so dumb. . . . How really stupid of me. . . . Poor old Cal."

Not only Jarrell was slow to recognize Lowell's illness. In the early stages of his mania Lowell was seductive, flush with words and ideas and confidence. If his thinking did not always flow in a coherent way, it was tantalizing and it came from a renowned poet. His ideas and behavior fitted the stereotype of the brilliant and disturbed artist. Other professors and poets were taken in more often than not. "Cal is definitely out of his senses," said Hardwick. But, she wrote later, "if he asked for a knife one of these dumb 'professors' would take it to him."

Mania is extraverting, disinhibiting, and infectious; its early, mild effects can be captivating. "One of the difficulties with inexperienced observers," noted Hardwick, "is that these states of Cal's do seem fine, partly because he's so friendly, so available—that's one of the signs. The man in our house said he'd been seeing a lot of Cal, they had long talks." Had he been well, she made clear, the long talks with a stranger would have been very unlike him.

Many of Lowell's friends and colleagues confused early mania with mere eccentricity. Jonathan Raban, the editor of Lowell's *Selected Poems*, a friend and companion fisherman, described first meeting him in London. Lowell was becoming manic, but Raban did not recognize the signs. "His manic passion then was dolphins, especially stone dolphins—and then buying a large number of stone dolphins on the King's Road." They visited the London Dolphinarium together; stone dolphins began to dot the Lowell gardens and the steps leading up to his house. Raban saw Lowell's exuberance for all things dolphin as "poetic and eccentric, how you might have found Yeats. It took a good long while for a rather callow 28 year-old to understand mania." The difficulty that some colleagues and friends had in recognizing his manic behavior continued through his lifetime. His publisher, Robert Giroux, remarked that Lowell was "encouraged by people who have no suspicion of the boiling volcano beneath the apparently controlled and sometimes even sweet exterior"; then, "the fireworks begin."

It is one thing to dismiss early mania as eccentricity or as a manifestation of the artistic temperament but quite another to ignore or make excuses for distinctly pathological behavior. John Thompson, a friend from college days and the person who had taken Lowell to Baldpate Hospital in 1949, had few illusions when he observed Lowell's mental state in Cincinnati in 1954. He, like Hardwick, was unhappy with the denial of Lowell's illness by his colleagues in Cincinnati and with their failure to see his erratic behavior as part of an illness rather than as poetic sensibility: "Literary people would rather be murdered than call the police," Thompson said caustically. The "sentimental saps" found it hard to make tough decisions. "The President of the University—he didn't want any scandal, of course—he didn't want to have his star lecturer hauled off to the loony bin. He was very upset. He said, 'But he's supposed to deliver his lecture. We've sold all the tickets.' I said, 'Believe me, you don't want this man to get up there and deliver a public lecture.'"

Lowell when manic was not the person described by those who knew him when he was well. "In his manic states," said George Ford, an English professor at the University of Cincinnati, "he was a frightening fellow, very powerful physically, and not the traditional willowy poet at all." When he was well, the contrast was total. "He was gentle . . . kind and considerate, interested in other people, and altogether excellent company." He had charmed Ford's young daughter, Ford said, and had gotten her to talk when no one else could.

Lowell was not at all well when he lectured in Cincinnati in 1954. His lectures progressed from tensely brilliant to indisputably psychotic. His lecture on Ezra Pound and madness, "a tricky subject for Cal at that time," was "full of tensions," according to Ford. Another lecture, on Robert Frost, which focused on Frost's depression and dark view of life, was thought by the faculty to be excellent, but things went from cusp to beyond when he returned to Cincinnati after his mother's funeral.

"He came back to Cincinnati [from Italy] in an alarmingly manic state, talking like a machine gun with blazing eyes and even more tense than ever," said Ford. One evening Lowell talked brilliantly and without stop about the Roman poets through drinks, through dinner, and then long after dinner. "It was dazzling, but also alarming," Ford recalled. "One felt he might be on the edge of a breakdown." It got worse, to the point that the chairman of the English Department, once dismissive of Hardwick's warnings about Lowell's illness, prepared for Lowell's lectures by putting "the strongest and biggest members of the department . . . in the front row in case anything violent developed." Flannery O'Connor, who had been slow to see the signs of Lowell's madness when they were together at Yaddo, said drolly, "It seems [Lowell] convinced everyone it was Elizabeth who was going crazy. . . . Toward the end he gave a lecture at the university that was almost pure gibberish. I guess nobody noticed, thinking it was the new criticism."

It had been noticed. In early April, Hardwick initiated a court order to commit Lowell involuntarily to Jewish Hospital in Cincinnati. The weeks leading up to his admission had been a pinwheeling scramble of disruption, insults, and public spectacle, prodigious drinking, and increasingly bizarre behavior. His "seizure," wrote Hardwick, had been building up slowly like the Yaddo attack; this, she had been told by the doctors, "is much more dangerous than going completely berserk quickly." She described Lowell's mania as a "brain fever," a brain "literally hot, whirling . . . fevered, askew and shaken out of shape."

Hardwick, the symbolic hindrance to unrestrained manic freedom, was again the focus of Lowell's manic vitriol; he humiliated her with cutting words and disparaging comments about her background and appearance, all the while openly pursuing his Italian girlfriend. Verbal lashings and a relentless pursuit of love affairs are common signs of mania, but this clinical observation, for all that it dates back two thousand years, gives little solace to those devastated by the manic behavior of a husband or a wife. Knowing that Lowell was manic and unable to control his behavior was a weak reed toward which to swim. Hardwick pitied him, and recognized that he was sick, but she was also exhausted and furious.

"Cal is badly deranged," Hardwick wrote shortly before Lowell was committed to the hospital, but "I feel at the moment something near hatred for this horrible idiot talking such insulting nonsense, but then of course he is ill and is not all that sort of moral monster when he is himself." Her awareness of the cause of his behavior was of limited consolation. "I am shocked and repelled by what Cal has done to me this time . . . he has been of course indescribably cruel. I simply cannot face a life of this."

What she had been through, she said, was impossible for anyone to understand who had not experienced what she had:

No one has the slightest idea of what I have been through with Cal. In 4½ years, counting the present break-up, he has had four collapses! Three manic and one depression. These things take time to come and long after he is out of the hospital there is a period which can only be called "nursing." The long, difficult pull-back—which does not show always to others. I knew the possibility of this when I married him, and I have always felt that the joy of his "normal" periods, the lovely time we had, all I've learned from him, the immeasurable things I've derived from our marriage made up for the bad periods. I consider it a gain of the most precious kind. But he has torn down this time everything we've built up—he has completely exposed to the world all of our sorrows which should have been kept secret; how difficult these break-ups are for both of us. I've put on a show to some extent. But he has opened the curtain and let everyone look in.

Lowell was admitted to the Cincinnati hospital in early April 1954. His doctor wrote in Lowell's chart that he was extremely elated, his speech was pressured, and he exhibited flight of ideas, which is characterized by a rapid flow of speech and a leapfrogging of loosely linked words and images. His thinking was meandering, indirect, circumstantial. He had been buying things, especially clothes, indiscriminately and had had both visual and auditory hallucinations. He was diagnosed with manic-depressive illness, heavily sedated, and prescribed a regimen of "relaxing baths" and psychotherapy. Lowell's physician, Dr. Philip Piker, a professor at the College of Medicine, University of Cincinnati, used and studied electroconvulsive therapy extensively. When a combination of sedation, hydrotherapy, and psychotherapy failed to check Lowell's mania, he was given nearly twenty electroshock treatments; they worked quickly and "quieted him down considerably." He became temporarily depressed after the ECT, however, as he had at Baldpate Hospital.

The recovery from mania was incomplete. Within days of stopping the ECT Lowell became "more and more unruly, restless, strange, less and less serious about the illness." He was "agitated and scattered." There were a few signs of improvement, however. He was still manic, but for the first time in months, Hardwick wrote, "I enjoyed him . . . we laughed and everything was just as it used to be." The electroshock treatment had brought him "to be partly his delightful self." Still, there was "tremendous chaos beneath the superficial control."

Hardwick wrote to Lowell's cousin Harriet Winslow about the pleasure of seeing Lowell reemerge, however fitfully, into sanity. "His wit, subtlety, variety" had returned, she said, but "one of the great difficulties of this present breakdown was that he was in greater control than during the others." Because of this he was still wreaking havoc. Addressing the particularly close relationship Lowell had with his cousin, as well as his inability to judge himself when ill, she continued: "I know how much he means to you and how deeply he cares for you. What is so heart-breaking about these breakdowns is that during them Bobby thinks he is exceeding himself, but actually is much less than his normal self. I can't bear to find him dull, repetitive, aggressive, obvious—all the things he isn't when well." Hers is an excellent description of the gap between manic certainty and its reality.

Lowell was in a severe hypomanic, if not overtly manic state. Hypomania, mania's less extreme relation, occupies hazy ground between mania and normal moods and behavior, can be hard to recognize and harder still to live with. It can exist in its own right or it can be a transitional state between mania and normal moods, or between mania and depression. It is, as Hardwick described it, a state "in which the patient has a lot of control, a lot of ability to function, while being at the same time extremely unwise, deranged." Dr. Piker had told Hardwick that "such a state is the most difficult one in psychiatry—usually even the family thinks the patient is all right and friends nearly always resent any restraints being put upon a man who has so much of his powers left." Hardwick added her own experience. "You are so afraid of accusing a person of being ill simply because he is acting in an inconvenient way."

Hardwick's discouragement with Lowell's condition was palpable. "I do not see any future: this half-sane, half-mad condition is truly defeating to my spirit." Sheer obstinacy, she said, kept her going. "Like a grim missionary I will save him if it kills him." Given his irrationality and manic impulsiveness, she added, "he may be in Paris before I know it. But it will be over the corpse of one dead Hardwick, not because of love but because of my relentless pursuit of poor Cal's sanity. I'm afraid I've become a sinister Goddess of Reason."

Dr. Piker recommended that Lowell be transferred from Cincinnati to another hospital for "convalescence." His condition was improved, but it was not possible to predict how much further treatment he would need. In a paternalistic aside not uncommon for medical practice in that era, he added, "I suppose that Mr. Lowell's wife should be consulted concerning the next move." Hardwick, for her part, was developing an understandably jaundiced view toward doctors. "One of the great troubles with psychiatrists," she wrote to friends, "is that they do not have to take responsibility; they don't advise or discourage nearly enough in my opinion, having all kinds of possible evasions ready at hand. They won't do what a doctor does for a person with a bad heart, simply tell him the facts of life; on the contrary they sit back looking wise, letting you go to your doom." The one exception, she said, had been the bluntly pessimistic Dr. Watson at Baldpate Hospital, who had warned her about the likely recurrence of Lowell's illness. Delivering a bad prognosis, she said, "is not a pleasant thing to do, but it ought to be their duty."

Lowell was transferred to an interim hospital for a week and then admitted to the Payne Whitney Clinic of the New York Hospital in New York toward the end of May 1954. His new psychiatrist, Dr. James Masterson, examined Lowell on admission and found him to be "neat, cooperative, extremely tense, anxious, preoccupied, and some-what depressed." His speech was "vague, rambling, halting, and indeci-sive." When Lowell was asked to describe his mood, he said it was one of "nervous intensity." He appeared to be in "a mixed phase with some evidence of depression which is covered over by superficial affect of ela-tion." Lowell had been preoccupied with suicide, wrote Dr. Masterson, but was not currently thinking seriously about killing himself. There were no delusions or hallucinations, no obsessions, compulsions, sus-piciousness, or excessive difficulty in thinking. His remote and recent memory was good. When asked what he hoped for his future, Lowell said, "I intend to go on writing and teaching." Lowell's mania of the preceding months had cleared and left only the charring from its high-voltage path. He was depressed but not morbidly so.

Dr. Masterson asked Lowell about the circumstances leading up to his manic attack in Cincinnati. Lowell told him that he had arrived too late in Italy to be with his mother when she died and that he had brought her body by ship back to the United States. He reported that during the trip he had been "over-exuberant and light-headed," over-active, slept too little, spoken too much, spoken too fast. He had found it difficult to control his behavior: "I felt like a drunk person with sober people."

During his mother's funeral, he told the psychiatrist, he had "main-tained himself well," but once back in Cincinnati he had again become elated, talked too much, and written too many letters. He had been "extremely over-active," aggressive, out of control, and had made "sav-age verbal attacks at various social affairs." He had announced to all who would listen that he was divorcing Hardwick and marrying his Italian lover; he had spent his money loosely and had taught "unreal-istic seminars" far too fast. He had been delusional, had hallucinated, and now was suffering from a "terrible, unpleasant inner and outer distractibility." He was living a nightmare.

Dr. Masterson diagnosed Lowell as having manic-depressive illness. There was no evidence Lowell had a personality disorder, he said, a clinical opinion of significance in light of Masterson's later international recognition as a psychoanalyst and authority on personality disorders, specifically narcissism. He conceptualized Lowell's psychiatric problems as a manifestation of a psychotic mood disorder, not as a disorder of personality or character. Lowell told Masterson that his illness was "something deep in my character." The doctor disagreed.

Masterson described Lowell's behavior during his first ten days in the hospital as "restless, preoccupied, aloof, indecisive, dependent on others, anxious, tense and depressed," a clinical description not unlike the one given by Dr. Blitzer, who five years earlier had treated him at Payne Whitney. Then, two weeks into his hospitalization, Lowell switched into mania. He became "aggressive, over-talkative, overactive, elated, anxious, tense, hostile with much sexual talk and much rumination about a romance with Giovanna, and the need to divorce his wife." He slept poorly, refused to cooperate with the nursing staff, was easily annoyed, impulsive, and exceedingly irritable.

Lowell was transferred to a ward for more severely ill patients. He told the nursing staff and his doctor that he was Christ. His conversation was hard to follow; he spoke in "analogies" and was, at times, "incomprehensible." He sparred with the nurses and doctors, chain-smoked in his room against hospital rules, spoke incessantly on the telephone, and "needled" other patients. He was tense, coiled, and defiant. He sang at the top of his voice in the lounge. Once, jealous of the attentions another patient was paying to a woman patient, he grabbed him by the feet and yanked him off a couch. He had profuse night sweats. He deliberately broke his glasses by dropping them from the window and drank great quantities of milk and buttermilk. He had dreams and daydreams in "bright colors," during which he talked with Ezra Pound and walked through the bombed-out city ruins of Italy. In one particularly frightening dream he found himself alone with his dead mother; in another, he was called out to a firing squad. The bright colors of his dreams lay over dark waters.

Three weeks after Lowell switched into mania he was given chlorpromazine (Thorazine) for the first time, a new antipsychotic drug that had been found to be of striking benefit to patients with severe psychotic illnesses. The first psychiatric patient to be given chlorpromazine, two and a half years before it was prescribed for Lowell, had been acutely manic and had responded dramatically well to it. As did Lowell. Within twenty-four hours of his first injection he showed "a marked and dramatic improvement." The overactivity, elation, pressured speech, flight of ideas, irritability, and sexual talk "disappeared." His sleep improved markedly. "Thank heaven [chlorpromazine] seems to be working," Hardwick observed. "The results are quite astounding. Cal is rational, the first time in five months." Within a few years chlorpromazine would largely replace electroconvulsive therapy as the treatment of choice for mania and would be the primary reason for the decreasing number of patients institutionalized in state mental hospitals and asylums. It worked well in acute mania but, unlike lithium, which Lowell would be prescribed more than a decade later, chlorpromazine did not prove effective in preventing recurrence of his illness.

Lowell's striking improvement was a relief, but it came at a cost. He suffered from the common side effects of chlorpromazine; he told his doctor that he felt "restless and weighed down" by the drug and had a "desire for more activity but [felt] less able to do it." He felt "slow witted and helpless intellectually," "as though I'm carrying 150 lbs. of concrete in a race." When Lowell's clinical condition improved, his medication was decreased and then stopped altogether.

As Lowell's mania cleared he was better able to discuss other psychological issues with Dr. Masterson: his imperfect but cornerstone marriage; his tendency toward "vagueness and withdrawal"; his intense, at times contradictory needs for solitude and affection. Once Lowell's mania resolved, he immediately retracted his plans to marry Giovanna and wrote to her to that effect. "I see more and more clearly that I will never be over my disturbance and back to my health and work again without Elizabeth," he explained to her. Hardwick "understood my disease far better than I myself." He had made a commitment to be in psychotherapy for several years: "I've really been quite sick and this time I want to get to the bottom of it all . . . I need [Hardwick's] knowledge of me and encouragement to get well. . . . She loves me, I love her."

Blair Clark told Hardwick during this period that Lowell was committed to the idea of treatment and had been for some time: "He told me sitting in Venice and, I think, long before that in the Public Garden in Boston, that he knew he ought to take psychiatric treatment and that there was something in psychiatry which was both useful and interesting."

Lowell made it clear to his doctor that above everything he wanted to preserve his marriage. He recognized that his attacks of mania "started with falling in love," with a restless discontent and an irritable desire to slip the collar. When he was well, he said, he knew he had a "perfectly good marriage" and didn't want it to end. It had "bare spots" but it was good: he and Hardwick had the same values, liked the same people, trusted each other, and were used to each other. "I can't get well without Elizabeth," he said. "She doesn't go crazy." She was earth to his fire, lived in a comforting reality not his own. He went "into a stupor" when practical matters came up; she didn't. She loved him. He loved her.

Many of Lowell's sessions with Dr. Masterson focused on his marriage and his parents, but always in the room was his shame about what he had done while he was manic, a shame attended by a mounting alarm that he would "go mad again." As early as Lowell's first day in the hospital, Dr. Masterson wrote that Lowell was "preoccupied" with his "fear of manic attacks and a desire to control them." Lowell told the doctor, "Manic attacks terrify me"; it was "humiliating to be here because of mania." He had had three attacks in five years, didn't know when the madness would come back, and it was frightening beyond words. (John Haslam, apothecary to Bethlem Hospital, quoted Dr. Johnson for the epigraph to his 1809 textbook on madness and melancholy: "Of the uncertainties of our present state, the most dreadful and alarming is the uncertain continuance of reason.")

But mania was complicated to Lowell, as it is to most who experience it; it had some attraction. Even if "having manic episodes control me [was] terrifying, I like to have these feelings but under my control—feelings of speed, instantaneous reaction to people, environment." Force brought under control had meaning to Lowell; the exertion of will over adversity was an identifying part of his character and what he admired in others. He told Dr. Masterson that he knew he would have to invoke "more manhood to control these episodes." The psychiatrist noted simply that Lowell felt "humiliated and frightened by the attacks."

By June, having come down from his mania, Lowell was again depressed and filled with remorse. He told Dr. Masterson that he was "ashamed about myself. I feel I've made an awful fool of myself." The best he thought he could hope for was "to know when symptoms are coming so I can do something about them." "Mania always is in the background," he said. It could be "pleasant," he acknowledged, but only "until it gets out of control." Then it annihilated everything he valued in himself.

Dr. Masterson recorded time and again Lowell's horror of madness: "his feelings of terror, his inability to control these attacks, and his shame at some of the things he does during these attacks." In Masterson's last clinical note, written the day that Lowell was discharged from the hospital, his final sentence is simple: Lowell, he wrote, "dreads depression and elation."

Hardwick more than anyone was aware of Lowell's suffering. "I feel so sorry for Cal I can hardly bear to think of him," she wrote to Peter Taylor. "This is simply going to break his heart when he comes to and learns he had another of these things. . . . I so fear he will have a depression afterwards because of his anguish about this latest episode." People would never understand, she said. "They understand that a person is deranged, but at the same time they cannot help but hold such a person responsible for his actions, or some of them." Time and again she expressed the same concern. "Underneath, Cal feels dreadfully ashamed of this last illness, filled with fear of the future, utterly shattered in his self-esteem. All of this was more than he could endure. . . . I wonder if he will ever be himself again, with the need to escape the pain of this."

Lowell left Payne Whitney in September 1954. After his first admission to Payne Whitney in 1949, Dr. Blitzer had written in Lowell's chart that his prognosis was "good." This time Dr. Masterson wrote that it was "fair." Hardwick had been reading about prognosis in manic-depressive illness and was shaken by what she read. "Cal will recover from his attacks when they come," she wrote to a friend. "But they will probably come. I was up at Brentano's recently reading a large big new book about mental illness; it said about the manic-depressives: as they get older the attacks become more frequent, more prolonged, more difficult to treat. My heart nearly stopped beating."

Once again Lowell had to sift through the embers to make sense of what he had been through, contend with what might come, and atone for things done and left undone. "According to Paine-Whitney [*sic*],

I have made remarkable progress and the whole business is curable," he wrote to a friend. "It's also been imbecilic, inhuman, dangerous, embarrassing, and hell on Elizabeth. Now the world is beginning again for us." A few months later, Lowell wrote to Elizabeth Bishop about his most recent illness: "I have been sick again, and somehow even with you I shrink both from mentioning and not mentioning. These things come on with a gruesome, vulgar, blasting surge of 'enthusiasm,' one becomes a kind of man-aping balloon in a parade—then you subside and eat bitter coffee-grounds of dullness, guilt etc."

Lowell's release from Payne Whitney came a long seven months after his tense dinner with Blair Clark in Paris. The look back was dark, the look forward not much better. He wanted peace and the safety of what he had known. "He just wanted to go back to New England," said Hardwick.

7

Snow-Sugared, Unraveling

> We feel the machine slipping from our hands,
> as if someone else were steering;
> if we see a light at the end of the tunnel,
> it's the light of an oncoming train.
>
> —*From* "Since 1939"

The Lowells moved back to Boston in September 1954 and a year later settled at 239 Marlborough Street, not far from his parents' old house, "a block down Marlboro [*sic*] and almost visible when there are no leaves." The neighborhood had changed little in thirty years. Marlborough Street itself was much the same, and even their dining room, said Lowell, was a bond with the past, "a fraying reconstruction of my parents' dining room at 170 Marlborough Street." If mental quiet could be secured by reentering the geography of childhood, Lowell had purchased it with their new home. Elizabeth Hardwick, in *Sleepless Nights*, described their new existence:

> Here I am in Boston, on Marlborough Street, number 239. I am looking out on a snowstorm. It fell like a great armistice, bringing all simple struggles to an end. . . . Under the yellow glow of the streetlights you begin to imagine what it was like forty or fifty years ago. The stillness, the open whiteness—nostalgia and romance in the clear, quiet, white air . . .
>
> Climbing up and down the four floors gives you a sense of ownership—perhaps. It may be yours, but the house, the furniture, strain toward the universal and it will soon read like a stage direction: Setting—Boston. The law will be obeyed. Chests, tables, dishes, domestic habits fall into line.

Lowell started psychotherapy with the psychiatrist Dr. Vernon Williams not long after he returned to Boston and saw him three to five times a week for the first two years and then once or twice a week after that. "His doctor is very, very sensible," wrote Hardwick. "He tells one the truth in a simple, fatherly way and we are all above board at least." The doctor recommended a routine of regular sleep, walking, and writing that Lowell took to "gladly." The occasional downswing in mood was surmountable. "Together we have managed so far to keep the depression from becoming incapacitating," Hardwick said. "It comes down upon us like a cloud, but always lifts in a day or two." She spent so much of her time reassuring Lowell when he was depressed, she said, that she found it difficult to remember the devastating mania, the "other side of the coin."

Lowell began work on a prose autobiography, in part at the suggestion of his psychiatrist as a way to help him reconstruct his childhood. By February 1955, five months after Lowell had left Payne Whitney, Hardwick was writing to Peter Taylor that "Cal is fine. He's been steadily improving week by week and now seems his old self again . . . he's been at the desk for the last 3 days 16 hours or so and I've very nearly been feeding him through a tube. He is writing some remarkable prose things. . . . They are reminiscences of childhood—that is the closest I can come—and I think of extraordinary beauty and interest."

Lowell kept to his determination for a calmer life; he gave up smoking and drinking and rejoined the Episcopal Church, the faith of his family. His return, to the Church of the Advent on Beacon Hill, only a few minutes' walk from his grandfather Winslow's house, was beholden more to liturgy and tradition than to any belief in doctrine.

In April he wrote to Ezra Pound that his return to Boston had exposed the vulnerability of being without the colored cloths and dreams of his youth:

> This has been a funny, eye-opening winter i.e., living in the Boston I left when I was seventeen, full of passion and without words. I suppose all young men get up the nerve to start moving by wrapping themselves like mummies from nose to toe in colored cloths, veils, dreams etc. After a while shedding one's costume, one's fancy dress, is like being flayed. I've just been doing a little piece on *Why I live in Boston*. I made it impersonal

and said nothing about what I was looking for here—the pain
and jolt of seeing things as they are.

It was an icy spring day in Boston, he added. The "magnolia blossoms
are freezing as they decay."

At the end of the year, in December 1955, Hardwick wrote
to friends that "Cal is feeling very well—calm, energetic and con-
tented. . . . A few weeks ago he read his poems at Harvard and put on
the most superb show, very witty, very relaxed. This winter has been
the best in some time." Lowell concurred. Two weeks later he wrote to
his cousin Harriet Winslow about the happiness of his Christmas Eve
and Christmas and the peace that came from staying put in Boston:
"It's soothing to be stopped in one place—it's like suddenly discovering, after running for twenty years that one can move just as fast by
standing still on some sort of escalator—maybe I've been on one all
along, only running against the mechanism."

Throughout 1956 Lowell was immersed in the study of his ancestors and began to write about his parents, grandfather, and childhood,
work that was to be central to *Life Studies*. He also wrote "Near the
Unbalanced Aquarium," an autobiographical piece about his 1954 stay
at the Payne Whitney Clinic. Hardwick wrote to Harriet Winslow,
"Cal is fine, still deep in his genealogical studies. He seems very happy
up on the top floor, with his long writing table, his books, and his
beloved FM radio which goes all day with the finest music. His book is
coming along day by day. . . . That makes him happy above all." In late
February 1956 she wrote that Lowell had not had a drink for a year,
was "well and happy," writing steadily, and eating an improbable pound
of honey every day—a nice touch for a man who identified with bears
and did bear imitations throughout his life.

It was a time of calm, steady but not frenzied writing, and a long-
hoped-for but, because they were nearing their forties, unexpected ven-
ture into parenthood. In June 1956 Lowell wrote to Elizabeth Bishop
that he and Hardwick were expecting a child in January; his droll
delight is clear in the many letters he dashed off to friends. "Already
we are exhausted," he wrote Bishop. "We lie about on sofas all day
eating cornflakes, no-calorie ginger-ale and yoghurt. Elizabeth never
moves except to turn the page of an English newspaper or buy a dress.
I never move except to turn on my high-fi radio or go on expeditions

for second-hand books." "We hear of women," he continued, "who ski all through pregnancy, give birth in bomb shelters without doctors etc. But we don't approve, and are timid, delicate and ante-bellum." To another friend he wrote, "It's terrible discovering that your one moral plank, i.e. an undiluted horror of babies, has crumbled! We're so excited we can hardly speak."

Harriet Winslow Lowell was born in January 1957; she became a source of gentle wonderment to Lowell, a constant in his inconstant life. Over the next twenty years, until his death, he dedicated many of his poems to her, openly delighted in her precocity, and wrote often about her in his poetry and in his letters to his friends. His late-born daughter was an answer to the question he had posed in "Mr. Edwards and the Spider": How will the heart endure?

Lowell kept free of severe mania for more than three years, from the fall of 1954 to December 1957. It was a long time but not unlimited. Not unusually, there is an extended period of normal health in the

Western Union Storkgram
"We're so excited we can hardly speak."

early stages of manic-depressive illness; later, if untreated, the disease
becomes more unforgiving. The relative stability of Lowell's moods
was due as well to the protective net he and Hardwick had woven
together to maintain routine and fend off excessive excitement. They
kept a quiet way of life. He saw his doctor often, they saw friends. He
followed ordered days of reading and writing in their Boston house on
"hardly passionate Marlborough Street." He taught poetry at Boston
University. He drank less, for long periods not at all. The rheostat was
set to Slower.

But mania, like the seasons and the sea, has its own force and keeps
to its own rhythm. Restraint could not hold back the madness. It was as
with the great sailor Sir Patrick Spens, claimed as kin by Lowell's imaginative but unstable great-great-grandmother Harriet Brackett Spence
Lowell. Spens had drowned. His sailors' efforts were to no avail; twine
and "silken claith" were no match for the sea: "they wrapp'd them
round that gude ship's side, / But still the sea came in."

The sea came in. In early 1957, Lowell traveled to the West Coast
for a reading tour; it was the start of a jagged escalation into full-blown
mania. He slept less and drank more than his brain could stay quiet
by. He took low doses of chlorpromazine to settle himself but soon
"wound up"; in the bubblings of mania, he started writing poetry again.
This time, however, he wrote in the loosened, more simplified language that was to distinguish the work of *Life Studies*.

The same enthusiasm that sped his imagination frayed his nerves.
The previously forsaken whiskey sours and martinis went down quickly
again; his mind flew. During his family summer in Maine he made
unwanted advances to his close friend Elizabeth Bishop. This was ill-
advised. He was married and his wife and Bishop were friends; Bishop
was in a long-standing lesbian relationship. Bishop's friendship with
Lowell was of great meaning to them both; they were supporters and
astute critics of each other's work and frequent correspondents. Lowell
wrote openly to Bishop about his illness in a way he did to few others. Fortunately both Lowell and Hardwick recognized the symptoms
of early mania—the frenetic pace and heavy drinking, the pursuit of
women—and he was able to ward off a psychotic attack by taking pro-
mazine, a drug closely related to chlorpromazine. The medication took
hold; judgment returned. So too did remorse.

"I see clearly now that for the last few days I have been living in a state of increasing mania—almost off the rails at the end," he wrote to Bishop in early August. "It almost seems as if I couldn't be with you any length of time without acting with abysmal myopia and lack of consideration. My disease, alas, gives one (during its seizures) a headless heart. . . . I *am* at last in reverse." The effect of the medication was "like the slowing and ache of a medium fever. One's thoughts are not directly changed and healed, but the terrible, over-riding restlessness of one's system is halted so that the mind can see life as it is. I want you to know . . . Oh dear, I wanted you to know so many things."

The return to health was not easy. "Today I feel certain that I am not going off the deep end," he wrote. "Gracelessly, like a standing child trying to sit down, like a cat or a coon coming down a tree, I'm getting down my ladder to the moon." Bishop, for her part, wrote back with a deflecting grace: "Dear Cal, do please please take care of yourself and be an ornament to the world (you're already that) and a comfort to your friends."

Lowell continued to work on the poems that collectively became *Life Studies.* His behavior settled down to the point that Hardwick could write to their friend Susan Sontag, "Cal is better than he has been for three years! . . . He is quite happy, devoted, sober. . . . When all is going well, I find it difficult to remember the other states. . . . The new well-being is now a month old and I believe it will last throughout the winter."

It did not. Lowell's mania erupted again. In December, without telling Hardwick, he invited more than forty friends to a party. The night was chaos. He insulted his guests, in the deft and awful way that only those who are manic can. He pitted guest against guest, sent the wine and cocktail glasses flying off a coffee table with a dramatic sweep of his foot. Alcohol flowed. Once again, as a guest observed, "nobody seemed to realize he was mad."

At the end of three sleepless days and nights he was much worse. Lowell's close friend, William Alfred, the playwright, described the wrenching scene after the police arrived at Lowell's home: "So the police arrived at Marlborough Street to take him away. Before he left, he wanted to sit for a few moments in Harriet's room and watch her sleep. He did this, with me telling the cops: 'He won't be long.' Then we left in the police wagon. And I remember the look on Cal's face—it was as if the real Cal, the Cal I knew, were looking out at me from within the mania. It was very moving. I'd never seen him crazy."

The police took Lowell to Boston State Hospital in early December 1957. The papers that authorized his involuntary commitment stated that for the week prior to admission he had been excited, violent, overactive, and at times suicidal. His Boston psychiatrist, Dr. Vernon Williams, told the Boston State doctors that Lowell had been free of symptoms until three weeks prior to the involuntary commitment; at that time he had become "overly active," "threatening," and had made an excessive number of unrealistic plans.

Boston State Hospital, which opened as the Boston Lunatic Asylum in 1839, was far from the elegant sitting rooms of Payne Whitney, where he had been twice before, and from McLean Hospital, where he was to be admitted in six weeks' time. Lowell's psychiatrist at the state hospital, Dr. Robert Spitzer, noted that "the patient refused transfer to a private hospital stating that he wanted to 'experience life.'" Most of Lowell's psychiatric care was in private hospitals, but this would not be the last time that Lowell stated a preference for learning about life from the "less elite."

Dr. Spitzer wrote in Lowell's chart when he was admitted that he was a "large, approximately 6'1", well-built, attractive white male demonstrating hyperactivity and flight of ideas and push of speech in spite of drowsiness produced by tranquilizers." Lowell, notwithstanding his mental state, had retained some of his sense of humor. When asked by the psychiatrist why he thought he was in a psychiatric hospital, Lowell replied, "My wife thought I needed a rest." Then he added, "She was right."

Spitzer examined Lowell and found that he was oriented (that is, he knew when it was, who and where he was, and his circumstance) and that he was neither delusional nor hallucinating. He had no preoccupations of thought or obsessions, although he did exhibit a "moderate flight of ideas." His memory was intact and he had "superior intelligence." He was hyperactive and elated, neither of which was significantly changed by administering sedating medication. His admitting diagnosis was manic-depressive reaction, manic type, with paranoid trends.

Lowell told Dr. Spitzer that he had slept very little in the week leading up to his hospitalization and that he had become increasingly irritable. He "thought that he might be having another manic episode because he [had] been writing with increased facility for the past several months." The presentation of his illness was essentially the same as that recorded during earlier hospitalizations; when asked when he had had his first breakdown, he said that it had been when he was a student at Harvard, an earlier time frame than he had given before. He also said that he had "become involved" with a student six weeks before being admitted to the hospital.

Lowell was given chlorpromazine and intramuscular sodium amytal, a sedative-hypnotic. At the end of a week Hardwick and his private psychiatrist, Dr. Williams, arranged for Lowell to be transferred, while still on an involuntary commitment, to Massachusetts Mental Health Center (formerly known as the Boston Psychopathic Hospital), a teaching hospital affiliated with Harvard Medical School. He was discharged from Boston State Hospital as "unimproved."

Lowell's psychiatrist at Mass Mental, as the psychiatric facility is known by most, was Dr. Marian Woolston, a second-year resident at the time of Lowell's admission. Her examination and medical notes for Lowell are thorough and informative. She noted that during Lowell's stay at Boston State Hospital he had been described by the doctors as "grandiose, hyperactive, occasionally assaultive and destructive." He also had exhibited flight of ideas and insomnia. At the time Dr. Woolston first evaluated him he had begun to come down from his mania; he was "in contact, ingratiating, talking easily but without great pressure of speech. He is extremely intelligent, eager to receive help." She added, with the skepticism that can come with treating mania, "or says so at present."

Lowell told Dr. Woolston that he had stopped seeing his psychiatrist in the fall because he was "too busy writing." It was during this time, in September and October 1957, that Lowell had been working at full bore on his *Life Studies* poems, a period he described as his "most productive months of writing poetry." In November, as he became overtly manic, he had "ceased his great spurt of writing." Following this intense period of literary output, Hardwick told Dr. Woolston, Lowell had become increasingly active, "making too many phone calls and writing too many letters." This intensification of mania, she said, was "characteristic of his behavior following a heavy spurt of writing." He had been "grossly hyperactive and inappropriate in behavior," reciting his poetry everywhere and to anyone. He had been talking far more than usual and was verbally hurtful to others; this, Hardwick told Dr. Woolston, was "very atypical behavior for the patient who is usually much more quiet and reserved."

Dr. Woolston recorded in her initial examination of Lowell that he was a "tall, well-built, attractive, very overactive man." He was "ingratiating" and "seductive." He exhibited a "dramatic flight of ideas, covering everything from Shakespeare to Sec. 79 [the legal basis for his involuntary psychiatric commitment]" and had "the most eloquent use of the English language." He also had an "undue preoccupation with greatness, almost a sense of mission in making a new contribution." Lowell had no delusions or hallucinations at the time he was admitted to the hospital, although he did say that he "thought in hallucinations." He had little insight into the nature of his current condition but told Woolston that in the preceding three years, when he felt he was becoming manic, he had used chlorpromazine on several occasions.

Lowell also told the psychiatrist that new love affairs and intermittent extreme outbursts of writing poetry tended to excite him into mania. His "prevailing tone," wrote Dr. Woolston, seemed to "suggest the desirability of psychosis as a qualification for great artistry." His preoccupation was with "success, energy and creativity. . . . Complete engrossment in his writings has always been accompanied by verbal hyperactivity sometimes to the point of an acute breakdown."

More than fifty years later Dr. Woolston still remembers Lowell well: he was "unforgettable," she says. "When he was in the hospital everyone knew." She describes him as dramatic, flirtatious, and intrusive when manic, and "a romantic." She liked him very much, found him charming and engaging. His insight into his manic illness, however, was limited; he was "on top of the bubble and didn't have much perspective."

During Lowell's hospitalization he was given chlorpromazine at much higher doses than when he had been at the state hospital. His "extreme hyperactivity," which included throwing furniture around the ward, ratcheted down. He became progressively calmer and was allowed out of the hospital for brief periods of time so that he could teach his graduate seminar. Lowell, according to a note in his chart written by a nurse two days before he was discharged from the hospital, was busy with correcting school papers and had many visitors. He was quiet, friendly, and cooperative. The note ends, without apparent irony, "Appears to do a great deal of deep thinking?"

His prognosis at the end of his first hospitalization at Payne Whitney had been "good"; after his second stay it had been downgraded to

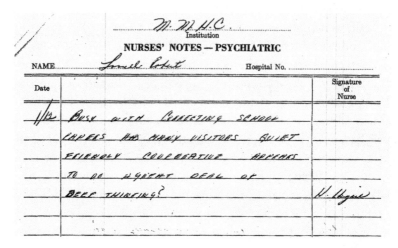

Nurse's note, Massachusetts Mental Health Center, January 12, 1958

"fair." Now, more ominously, Dr. Woolston listed his prognosis as "guarded."

Lowell was better at the time he left the hospital but he remained "as active as electricity," said Hardwick. Certainly he was far from well. The details of his attacks, Hardwick wrote to Elizabeth Bishop, "are always like a Russian novel because of the immense *activity* of these states, the fact that things are happening, wildly, even from the hospital. The activity urge is greater than the confinement and is never fully confined." Hardwick was again at wit's end, "very much discouraged and very fearful of the future." Lowell had "begged to come home to his study, his routine, etc., and of course I agreed." He told her he wanted to come home, stay married forever. He was heavily drugged; if he stopped taking his medication, she predicted, "he would climb right back up to an overexcitement again."

Lowell, at about the same time, wrote to William Carlos Williams, "I've just passed through another of my periodic crack-ups. . . . I'm fine now." Some of this was "keeping up a front," which he had told Dr. Vernon Williams was his "great need of the moment." Hardwick, for her part, while noting that Lowell was "quieting down gradually," wrote to his cousin, "I suppose underneath it has been harder for him to come back to the world than we know. There is a great deal of uncertainty, shame, regret and bravado, fierce self-assertion may be the only way of handling it at first."

Lowell's core of peace, observed Hardwick, was their home at 239 Marlborough Street. "He has always loved the house, loved his study with his books, his records. And loved the beauty of the house. . . . His commitment to the 'things' is complete—they belonged to his family." She and Lowell needed "just to sit tight, with our routine, making the best of things until they right themselves."

Two weeks after leaving Mass Mental, Lowell was once again floridly manic; he was admitted to McLean Hospital in Belmont, Massachusetts. Formerly the McLean Asylum for the Insane, where Lowell's great-great-grandmother had been a patient more than a hundred years earlier, the hospital had been founded in 1811 in affiliation with Harvard's Massachusetts General Hospital. Although McLean has famously treated the well-placed in society, the hospital cares for people from all walks of life. It has provided and continues to provide some of the best clinical care in the country; it has also contributed significantly to our understanding of the causes and treatment of mental illness. Still, the McLean Hospital that treated Lowell in the 1950s and 1960s was far removed from Boston State Hospital. Activities for McLean patients at the time of Lowell's hospitalization in 1958 included poetry evenings, an excursion to Boston Common to view the Christmas lights, a James Thurber reading, and a dinner party at the Colonial Country Club.

These activities are far from the patient activities prescribed in most mental hospitals, but no patient, however wealthy, and however elite the hospital, can escape the pain of mental illness. "I myself am hell," Lowell wrote in "Skunk Hour," echoing Milton, who had said, "within him Hell / He brings." Milton's Satan, for whom Lowell kept an admiring affection, spoke for him: "Which way I fly is Hell; myself am Hell." Lowell could not escape his illness by change of place. Terror was within; gracious surroundings, although they made a difference, did not rid him of the rack and bale of mania.

Lowell was admitted as a voluntary patient to McLean Hospital at the end of January 1958, following what the admitting physician described as "an episode of excitement" and a "general disorganization of ideas." The day before he entered the hospital he had written to the poet and critic William Empson; excerpts from his letter give a sense of the loosely linked thoughts so typical of manic flight of ideas, as well as Lowell's delusional identification with Christ:

> The Christ was killed by the Jews under Caiphas [*sic*] and the Romans under Pontius Pilate. He was manic (just as I—four times—and hundreds of others have been) shortly before his capture. At the time of his capture h[e] was in the depth of a depression. Sweating blood, all but speechless. He didn't quite die but was smuggled by Nicodemus and Joseph of Arimathea from the tomb, and kept reappearing on the margins of activity, at least up [to] the time when he met and commissioned Paul as his Captain general. Did you ever notice what [a] superior job Paul did to the Christ's when he too had to appear in Jerusalem before Lysisas [*sic*], Festus, Felix and King Agrippa? . . .

> 4. The Mass. The composers, Palestrina, Bach, Beethoven[,] Hayden [*sic*], Schubert, Verdi, Berlioz, Stravinsky, made a garden even here, i.e.: in the ~~dreary lit~~ crumby liturgical desert of the R. C. Mass. It's not human sacrifice and sadistic torture that is being celebrated, rather it's Christ climbing to his feet after the cruelest of all electric shock treatments.

Lowell's 1958 hospitalization at McLean continued the painful course of reckoning for himself and Hardwick. She had had little letup in dealing with his illness; he continued to live with the fear of what might happen to his mind and writing in the years to come. In mid-February, Hardwick wrote to Harriet Winslow: "For the future, the unimaginable, frightening future which seems awful no matter what happens about the present: the [McLean] doctors think Bobby can be cured, but that it would be hard, take years of serious working out with a doctor of his profound problems and fears. I spoke quite frankly to them and said, 'It is all very well to talk about cures, coping with problems, working it out, and so on. But do you really believe it? Do you really get these cures when someone is middle aged, has had countless breakdowns, etc.?" They assured her that they did.

The doctors told Hardwick that Lowell's psychological health required him to believe that if he divorced her he would gain a new and stable life. The illusion that a fresh start was possible, they said, kept "knowledge, fear and insecurity from coming to his full consciousness." In short, his doctors said that it was necessary for Lowell to delude himself in order for his sanity to return. "There is in these manic things a kind of flight," Hardwick told Ian Hamilton many years later. "I'm here and I'll go there, and everything will be all right." The illusion faded as his mania faded, but the fear of illness remained. "He becomes furious if you use the word 'sick,'" Hardwick wrote to friends. "He is profoundly aware that depressive symptoms—fear, remorse, uncertainty, anxiety, chaos—are always threatening him and he would truly rather wreck his whole life than have these symptoms for a moment. The doctors think he is scared to death and so do I."

In mid-March Lowell wrote to Harriet Winslow, "My mania has broken." He wrote similarly to Peter Taylor: "It's not much fun writing about these breakdowns after they themselves have broken and one stands stickily splattered with patches of the momentary bubble. Health; but not the kind that encourages the backward look." The backward look discomfited but it also gave a glimpse into the effect he felt mania could have upon his writing: "What can you do after having been Henry VIII or even a cock of the walk weekly sheriff? You get beautifully your character's living for the moment he is seen or heard. All life for the flashes! Everyone has a lot of that, and we writers more than most, only the words, the structure, the tune come out of us, are us."

On the same day, Lowell gave Bishop a vivid account of his fellow patients at McLean:

> The man next to me is a Harvard Law professor. One day, he is all happiness, giving the plots of Trollope novels, distinguishing delicately between the philosophies of Holmes and Brandeis, reminiscing wittily about Frankfurter. But on another day, his depression blankets him. Early in the morning, I hear cooing pigeon sounds, and if I listen carefully, the words: "Oh terror, TERROR!" Our other male, assembles microscopically exact models of clippers and three masted schooners. Both men, and I too, shrink before a garrulous Mrs. Churchill. . . . Sometimes with a big paper napkin stuck like an escaping bra on her throat, she will dance a little jig and talk about being presented to Queen Victoria. She was.

Lowell had been writing poetry intermittently while in the hospital, including two of his most regarded poems about madness, "Waking in the Blue" and "Home After Three Months Away." "I like the language of my new poems," he wrote to Elizabeth Bishop, "but feel fatigued by their fierceness." He enclosed in his letter a copy of "Home After Three Months Away," its last verses telling of time lost, as man and father, bone-weariness, and the elusiveness of cure:

> they tell me nothing's gone.
> Though I am forty-one,
> not forty now, the time I put away
> was child's-play. . . .
> .   .   .   .
> Recuperating, I neither spin nor toil.
> Three stories down below,
> a choreman tends our coffin's length of soil,
> and seven horizontal tulips blow.
> Just twelve months ago,
> these flowers were pedigreed
> imported Dutchmen; now no one need
> distinguish them from weed.
> Bushed by the late spring snow,
> they cannot meet
> another year's snowballing enervation.
>
> I keep no rank nor station.
> Cured, I am frizzled, stale and small.

The frizzled, stale state that comes after mania, the depressive letdown, is one of consuming fatigue, doubt, and fragility. F. Scott Fitzgerald, in his 1936 autobiographical essays, *The Crack-Up*, wrote that his depressive breakdown left him feeling like a cracked plate, "the kind that one wonders whether it is worth preserving." He and the dish were one, he said, and it was not the dish he had ordered. The plate had lost its strength and carrying capacity: "It can never again be warmed on the stove nor shuffled with the other plates in the dishpan; it will not be brought out for company, but it will do to hold crackers late at night." The plate, like Lowell's horizontal tulips, could not bear further weight; it could only "go into the ice box under left-overs."

Lowell had written earlier of holding place, feeling purposeless: "I feel rather like a character in one of Allen Tate's poems that ends I believe, 'The wall-paper, imperishably old / Uncurls and flutters, it will never fall.'" It was the same again.

By the end of April both Lowell and Hardwick had reentered the swing of the world. "We are both fine and so is the baby," Hardwick wrote to Harriet Winslow. "The weather is glorious, our magnolia is in bloom, the swan-boats are gliding along in the garden." But, as a practical matter, Hardwick sought out legal advice to remove some of the burden of having to commit her husband if he again became manic. She was beginning to acknowledge the independent life of his disease: "The thing comes or goes in its own way," she conceded.

A few months later Lowell looked back on his writing of *Life Studies;* it had been a dangerous time but he had written new and well. "My own things rise out of great stylistic and logical helplessness, days of staring at ugly fragments," he told Theodore Roethke. "I leave armfuls of waste paper behind me—exercises, confessions, confusion. Now a new book is almost done, and it seems at times as though I'd discovered a way of getting something new and felt said. A pioneering effort, but worth doing."

Lowell continued in psychotherapy but he had lost faith that it could help; it was dutiful, said Hardwick, rather like going to Mass in the hopes of being saved from his illness. He and Hardwick were correct: psychotherapy could not prevent mania. A year passed; then at the end of April 1959, just before the American publication of *Life Studies*, Lowell was readmitted to McLean, initially as a voluntary patient. The admission form stated that he had been feeling "increasingly anxious over recent events." Aware that past manic attacks had caused him "great embarrassment and inconvenience," the examining doctor wrote, "he voluntarily places himself in hospital at this time to receive treatment and to protect himself."

By mid-June, while still in the hospital, Lowell had to be committed involuntarily by a justice of the district court. Two physicians confirmed for the court that he had a repeated history of psychiatric hospitalizations for manic-depressive psychosis and that, during his current McLean admission, he had been overactive, excited, argumentative,

D.M.H. Form 11 Revised 1955
Please mention this number when requesting blanks.

VOLUNTARY

(PRIVATE)

The Commonwealth of Massachusetts

_____

April 28, 1959

To THE DEPARTMENT OF MENTAL HEALTH,
15 ASHBURTON PLACE, BOSTON.

The Department of Mental Health is hereby notified, as required by law, of the admission of _____
_____ Robert Lowell _____residing at 239 Marlboro Street _____
(name)   (street)
in the city of Boston, Mass. _____County of Suffolk _____
_____ to McLean Hospital _____
as a voluntary patient, on _____ April 28, 1959, under the provisions of sections 81 and 86,
chapter 123, General Laws, as amended, and is furnished herewith a *copy* of the patient's *written application* for
such admission and the following particulars of the case:

1. Sex, M. ; age, 42 years; birth date, March 1, 1917 birthplace
of patient, Boston, Mass. ; color, W. occupation, Writer-teacher-poet
Religion, Unknown ; Social Security number, unknown ; Is patient a
citizen? Yes If not, alien registration number, - - - ; How long a
resident of Massachusetts? Life ; single, married, widowed, divorced

2. Name and post-office address of husband, wife, guardian, nearest relative or friend _____
Wife: Elizabeth H. Lowell, 239 Marlboro Street, Boston, Mass.
(designate relationship)

3. Father:- Name Robert Traill Spence Lowell Place of his Birth Schenectady,
New York Mother:- Maiden Name Charlotte Winston
Place of her birth Raleigh, N. C.

4. Has he ever been a patient in a hospital for mental illness Yes In a hospital for
epilepsy No ; in a hospital school for mental deficiency? No
If yes, state when, where, and for what length of time McLean Hospital, Belmont, Mass.,
Jan. 30, 1958 - May 22, 1958

5. Has the patient been physically injured? No If yes, when, and to what extent?
_____

6. Has the applicant knowledge that the subject has been violent, dangerous, destructive, excited, depressed, homicidal, or suicidal excited
_____

7. The patient presents the following symptoms:- Patient had been feeling increasingly
anxious over recent events in personal life and because of awareness of fact that
he had experienced attacks of mania in past causing him great embarrasement and
inconvenience, he voluntarily places himself in hospital at this time to receive
treatment and to protect himself.

I am satisfied that the above patient is in need of immediate treatment.
_____ M. D.
Psychiatrist in Chief

Admission form, McLean Hospital, April 1959
*"He voluntarily places himself in hospital at this time to receive treatment and to
protect himself."*

and had flight of ideas; he had also been impulsive and, among other things, had thrown furniture around the ward. Medications had helped somewhat, but the doctors stated it would be unwise for him to leave the hospital.

The worsening of Lowell's illness was mirrored in Hardwick's increasing discouragement. She wrote to their friend Mary McCarthy that "it is distressing beyond words." Hardwick found his doctors frustrating although well-intentioned. They talked to her about his "flight into illness" (a psychoanalytic concept that construes mania in part as a flight of escape from depression and reality); she was skeptical and questioned whether it was not "just an illness that comes." She confided, "I feel particularly discouraged because this latest flare-up came after a very happy year for both of us."

Lowell, too, was weary of the lost hopes, the illusions burst. In July he wrote to Elizabeth Bishop: "I feel rather creepy and paltry writing now to announce that I am all healed and stable again. So it is. Five attacks in ten years make you feel rather a basket-case. . . . In the hospital I spent a mad month or more re-writing *everything* in my three books. I arranged my poems chronologically, starting in Greek and Roman times and finally rose to air and the present with *Life Studies*. I felt I had hit the skies, that all cohered. I[t] was mostly waste." The period following a manic attack, he explained to Bishop, was "an incredible formless time of irresolution, forgetfulness, inertia, all the Baudelairean vices plus what he must never have known, stupidity."

To John Berryman, who had been through so much pain of his own—mania, alcoholism, depression, the suicides of his father and an aunt—and who would himself commit suicide in a few years' time, Lowell wrote a letter of compassion:

> I have been thinking much about you all summer, and how we have gone through the same troubles, visiting the bottom of the world. I have wanted to stretch out a hand, and tell you that I have been there too, and how it all lightens and life swims back. . . . There's been so much fellow feeling between us, and for so long now. . . .
>
> Well what is there to say? The night is now passed, and I feel certain that your fire and loyalty, and all-outedness carry you buoyantly on. The dark moment comes, it goes.

By the end of the 1950s Boston had worn thin for Lowell and Hardwick. It had failed as a shield against madness, or as substantive balm. It was, they had come to believe, a place of lost vitality. In December 1958 Lowell wrote to Bishop, "Boston's a pleasant place, but the home product is all dandification and jelly. The woodiness of the old caution, now these 50 years no longer sprouting, the jelly of *Vogue* and *Literary Digest* literary tastes." Intellectual women didn't seem to exist in Boston, he told her, and "our new friends all seem to drift on trust funds or hold Harvard University chairs." To Randall Jarrell he wrote more bluntly. "We are awfully sick of Boston," he said. "The only unconventional people here are charming screwballs, who never finish a picture or publish a line. Then there are Cousins and Harvard professors. All very pleasant, but . . ."

Henry Adams, Lowell's exemplar New Englander, had said that "Boston had solved the universe; or had offered and realized the best solution yet tried. The problem was worked out." For Adams and Lowell, creatures of flux and uncertainty, the assumption of a worked-out solution was repellent. Years later Lowell told V. S. Naipaul that he and Hardwick had moved to New York because Boston "had lost its seriousness, its imagination, and if you wanted to be a writer you couldn't be a conventional New Englander."

Hardwick was more scathing and public in her views on Boston, perhaps because it was her nature, and perhaps because she had not been heir to Lowell's social upbringing in Boston. Nor had she had the imprinting advantages of Boston's intellectual history, an essential nutrient of Lowell's imaginative growth. In December 1959, *Harper's* published her "Boston: The Lost Ideal," a full-throated attack on what she saw as the moral and intellectual depletion and implacable social conservatism of Boston. She started, "With Boston and its mysteriously enduring reputation, 'the reverberation is longer than the thunderclap,' as Emerson observed about the tenacious fame of certain artists. Boston—wrinkled, spindly-legged, depleted of nearly all her spiritual and cutaneous oils, provincial, self-esteeming—has gone on spending her inflated bills of pure reputation, decade after decade."

Her perspective on Boston did not gentle down over the course of the essay. She quoted Henry Adams on Boston, who had said, "A simpler manner of life and thought could hardly exist, short of cave-dwelling"; she decried the decline in Boston's intellectual contributions to the country. "The importance of Boston was intellectual," she wrote. If its intellectual life was dying, Boston most certainly was. She compared Boston to New York, brilliantly, and not to Boston's advantage. If she and Lowell had not already thought about moving to New York she was leaving them little choice:

> Boston is not a small New York, as they say a child is not a small adult but is, rather, a specially organized small-creature with its small-creature's temperature, balance, and distribution of fat. In Boston there is an utter absence of that wild, electric beauty of New York, of the marvelous, excited rush of people in taxicabs at twilight, of the great Avenues and Streets, the restaurants, theatres, bars, hotels, delicatessens, shops. In Boston the night comes down with an incredibly heavy, small-town finality. The cows come home; the chickens go to roost; the meadow is dark.

Yet she circled back to the Boston of tradition, quiet, habit, and winter stillness that she and Lowell had sought out after his 1954 breakdown, a world of retreat and unjangled sensibilities:

> Boston is a winter city. Every apartment has a fireplace. In the town houses, old persons climb steps without complaint, four or five floors of them, cope with the maintenance of roof and gutter, and survive the impractical kitchen and resign themselves to the useless parlors. This is life: the house, the dinner party, the charming gardens, one's high ceilings, fine windows, lacy grillings, magnolia trees, inside shutters, glassed-in studios on the top of what were once stables, outlook on the "river side." Setting is serious.

Their young daughter was the exception to the dead, fine life of the city, and Lowell took obvious pleasure in watching her take in the world and take in her parents. To his cousin Harriet Winslow, her namesake, he wrote in October 1959, "What stands out this fall though is Harriet leaving three times a week at nine for nursery school. Like an artist, she brings back huge colored scrolls of paper covered with her first abstract expressionist paintings. She drives a tricycle, catches a big rubber ball, gulps observations like a vacuum cleaner. Or rather, her foot is on the ladder." To Elizabeth Bishop he said, "Harriet is terrific, like living with the new forces. I don't think she knows how frail we are, but being a child, she is heavy on her feet and we can almost keep up with her by cheating and using cunning and withdrawing into the shadows she can't understand."

In 1961, when Harriet was three years old, Lowell and Hardwick bought an apartment on West Sixty-Seventh Street in New York City. They hoped to set a distance between themselves and the illness that had come to dominate their lives. They could not. The shifts from light to dark, steady to stretched nerve, were to be much the same for him in New York as they had been in Boston; the magic of the city was not magic enough:

> Home from you, and through the trodden tangle,
> the corny birdwalks, the pubescent knoll,
> rowboats three deep on the landing, tundra
> from Eighty-First Street to my 15 Sixty-Seventh,
> snow going from pepper and salt to brain-cell dull,
> winter throwing off its Christmas decorations.
> The afternoon has darkened in twenty minutes
> from light to night—
> .   .   .   .
> I in a Dickensian muffler, snow-sugared, unraveling.

Lowell's cycles of illness and health continued. Hardwick distilled it down for Mary McCarthy: "He leaves home, rushes off to another girl, announces that he's in love, and has this manic affair and then he's carted off to the hospital until he is well and then he comes back home. Everything goes along well for a year or so and this thing begins to mount again." And it did.

Early in 1961, not long into their new life in New York, Lowell started an affair with a young New York poet, declared he was divorcing Hardwick and that he would start life anew.

Lowell was admitted to a locked ward at Columbia-Presbyterian Hospital in New York; his friend William Meredith described his con-

dition: "No one predicts how long it will be before the drugs take hold
& Cal begins to be himself," he wrote to Adrienne Rich and Philip
Booth. "Meanwhile he writes and revises translations furiously and
with a kind [of] crooked brilliance, and talks about himself in connection with Achilles, Alexander, Hart Crane, Hitler and Christ, and
breaks your heart."

He recovered, but the following year, in August 1962 on a trip
to Argentina sponsored by the American Cultural Council, Lowell
became manic yet again: he started to drink heavily, double vodka martinis before lunch, talked too fast and too much, and made advances to
women he had just met. He was "electric" once more and sent an elated
telegram to Elizabeth Bishop: "COME HERE AND JOIN ME ITS PARADISE!"
He couldn't sleep. He threw away his medication and publicly insulted
the general who was about to be sworn in as president. Keith Botsford,
the American representative in Argentina who was shepherding Lowell
from reading to reading, kept a record of his charge's behavior. Lowell, he wrote, was grandiose, irritable, and pulsing with near-inhuman
energy. He insisted on buying everyone expensive presents and sent
cables to the pope and to the former president, Dwight Eisenhower,
expressing his conviction that America was the new Roman Empire.
He believed himself to be the Caesar of Argentina. He took off his
clothes, climbed up onto the military equestrian statues, and "rode next
to the generals"; he did this throughout Buenos Aires, a city not without equestrian statues.

Lowell's conversation sparked in all directions: he talked about the
genius of Boris Pasternak and *Doctor Zhivago*, expressed his ardent wish
that his daughter not have to experience the kind of unhappy childhood he had had, declared Thomas Hardy a great poet for his profound
experience of human life, and praised Yeats for his rhetoric. He rank-
ordered the world's poets, military leaders, and novelists with what he
said was complete objectivity. His conversation, according to Botsford,
"became very fragmentary and disconnected. I used to think of it as a
great knot which would twist and twist and twist and then a sentence
would come out of it, pushed by a sort of breathing impulse, and it
was always in a totally unexpected direction."

The outcome was inevitable. It took six men to force Lowell into
a straitjacket and admit him to the Clinica Bethlehem in Buenos Aires,
where he was restrained with leather straps and heavily medicated with

chlorpromazine. Blair Clark flew to Buenos Aires to bring him back to the United States. On the flight to New York Lowell "fell in love" with one of the stewardesses, told Clark he wanted to marry her and that they were going to start a new life together in South America. He was taken to the Institute of Living in Hartford, Connecticut, where he was a patient for six weeks in October and November 1962; he would be admitted there twice more, first in December 1963 and then in January 1965.

Dr. Erik Linnolt, the psychiatrist who treated Lowell during his inpatient stays at the Institute of Living, recalls that he was assigned to the Whitehall Unit, the "fancy" unit, and that he was "very warm, reserved, polite, and accepting of his situation." He was, Linnolt continued, "physically robust, attractive, and strong; basically he was a rebel but a polite rebel." Lowell had a tremendous sense of humor, Linnolt remembers, and did not complain about his illness or circumstances. He made it clear that he was frightened because his illness had come back and more frightened that it would return. Lowell told Dr. Linnolt, who saw him in psychotherapy once a day at the beginning of his stay in the hospital and later three times a week, that his manic-depressive illness was "part of him and his work." The early stages of his mania, he said, "came with increased creativity and a flow of words." Dr. Linnolt treated Lowell for what everyone knew was a very bad disease that was getting worse. "Mr. Lowell," Dr. Linnolt told me, "was a kind but complicated man who had a bad illness."

The attacks continued. Lowell was a patient at the Institute of Living for a second time in December 1963 and stayed there until mid-January 1964. Hardwick wrote to Allen Tate about Lowell's discouragement and their struggle to understand why his attacks kept coming back. "This thing just came on him and it is most discouraging because he tried awfully hard to push it away," Hardwick wrote to Tate. "He hasn't had a drink for a year; he goes to the doctor and does whatever is suggested. It doesn't seem to be under the control of the will at all, not even a little bit. . . . He's very *triste*, utterly bewildered. They tell him at the hospital that they think it is an organic affliction and it doesn't have to do except in the most indirect way, with what one does."

The causes were fugitive, the pain was what they lived with.

Hardwick wrote to Lowell at Christmas when he was on the psychiatric ward: "How we miss you. The tree is up, the cards are all around, presents everywhere for Harriet." Their daughter, she said, "has begun to worry about you and I am trying to reassure her, as I will be able to of course." Harriet was older when her father explained to her about his mental illness one morning in the lobby of their New York apartment building as they sat waiting for her school bus. "He said he had these periods of 'enthusiasms' and used the term 'manic-depressive,'" she remembers. "He explained it was a disease. He'd stop sleeping, get very 'keyed up' (my mother's word), hallucinated even and ended up hospitalized. In the hospital, they would give him drugs and shock treatments (which he did not remember) and hosed him down with water, which strangely helped. . . . I hated to think of him locked up, drugged and going through all this, but he seemed to accept it." At some point he told her he was taking lithium for a "salt deficiency." Harriet Lowell recalls that she "wasn't hyper aware of his mental illness, though I knew he had these breakdowns. I was influenced by his resignation and my mother's sympathy for it. He was always very gentle with me. I was never afraid of him and neither was my mother."

Lowell's illness continued in its foreseeable way, laced in with writing, friends, and life with his wife and young daughter: mania, near-unforgivable breaches of friendship, shame, depression, greater shame. Then, when the fever had run its course, hope and life and work came back and slowly reassembled. These attacks that threw him into "the kingdom of the mad" came with the seasons and brought with them horror and doubt about his life to come. The form of the disease remained constant; only the details varied of the mania and the social affronts, ever grist for gossip, and the wreckage they left. Lowell's remorse was profound; so too was the increasing awareness that he had little power to affect his illness. "It's a little painful prodding the formless, embarrassed mind to pick up the pieces," he wrote to Mary McCarthy after a winter breakdown in 1964. "These things can come from the air. The stir of a feather can start them, though no doubt I would be immune if I had a different soul."

Lowell's 1964 breakdown had been exacerbated by his increasingly frenzied work on a new play. Jonathan Miller, at about the same time, was directing Lowell's trilogy *The Old Glory*, based on works by Hawthorne and Melville. Two days before opening night Lowell burst into the theater and exclaimed that he had written a new, fourth play that had to be added. It featured the severed head of Sir Walter Raleigh, streaming blood. The blood, Lowell suggested helpfully, "could be done very nicely with ribbons." The dark Raleigh images were not lost; they made their way into a poem a few years later: Raleigh's head, "still dangling in its scarlet, tangled twine, / as if beseeching voyage. Voyage? / Down and down; the compass needle dead on terror."

Lowell wrote to Hardwick in 1965 apologizing for "what a mess I've made of my human ties." He was "full of irrational turbulence. . . . Surely, there's some terrible flaw in my life that blows a bubble into my head every year or so. It mustn't continue, though I suppose that's only partly up to me and partly [up] to fate, nature, God and whatever."

Lowell also wrote to Elizabeth Bishop, not long before his forty-eighth birthday: "I am back from a month in the sanitarium. . . . These attacks seem now almost like something woven in my nervous system and one of the ingredients of my blood-stream, and I blame them less on some fatal personal psychotic flaw. . . . Life and work go on." Bishop wrote back straightaway. "I have a feeling there will soon come a time when the bloodstream you refer to will just refuse to carry the poison one more time and throw it out forever. You will then look back and wonder that it ever happened at all."

But the poison did carry. The tempo quickened, the banal quatrain played out. Lowell was admitted to McLean Hospital for the third time in early December 1965; by the end of 1966, he was manic again. He purchased an expensive bust of Tecumseh, the leader of the Shawnees; became romantically obsessed with his friend Jacqueline Kennedy; believed himself to be King James IV, Napoleon, Hitler. He stood up at the Metropolitan Opera and tried to conduct the orchestra. Xandra Gowrie, Lowell's close friend, described how direful it had become. "The cyclical beginning of his crack-up" began in September, she said. He would start to "look chaotic—hair wild—hand shaking—stopped wine, started in on vodka and milk—staying up later and later—started saying awful things about people he liked." The next morning she would find him "shattered by what he had done. . . . Shattered by his own cruelty."

Lowell's teaching at Harvard became jangled and disconnected as he accelerated into mania, and colleagues had to take over his classes. Each attack of mania added to the mad, brilliant poet myth. He was

generally well liked by his Harvard students, and held in awe by many
of them, but his mania frightened more than a few. "I had never witnessed one of these breakdowns," remembers the writer James Atlas.
"But I had heard about them in grim detail: Lowell showing up at William Alfred's house and declaring he was the Virgin Mary; Lowell talking for two hours straight in class, revising a student's poem in the
style of Milton, Tennyson, or Frost; Lowell wandering around Harvard
Square without a coat in the middle of January, shivering, wild-eyed,
incoherent."

On Christmas Eve 1966, a day Xandra Gowrie described as snowy
and piercingly cold, "eight massive police officers with guns" arrived
to take Lowell away. "Cal was leaning back against the sink, picked
up a milk bottle and threw it at one of the policemen, an agonizingly
sad gesture." Her husband, Grey Gowrie, remembers Lowell as a
tormented-looking man. "I said, 'You should go, you must go,' and
he said, 'Well, I'll make a deal with you. I'll go if they will sit down
and listen to a poem' and I remember very well getting all these heavy
Boston cops to sit down and listen to a poem ["Waking in the Blue"]
he wrote about McLean, where they were just about to take him." "My
heart grows tense," Lowell recited to the police officers and his friends,
"as though a harpoon were sparring for the kill. / (This is the house for
the 'mentally ill.')" It was then, said Gowrie, "not the mad scene at all,
it was rather moving."

The police took Lowell to McLean, where he was put on an involuntary hold. The hospital and court documents stated that he was "in
need of immediate care and treatment because of mental derangement." He was described by the doctors as excited, argumentative,
assaultive, and delusional; he believed that he was the "Jewish Messiah," was "impulsive, unwise in his judgments, threatening, and sleepless." He stayed at McLean for two months.

The McLean Hospital keeps copies of the magazines with pieces
written by patients who have been hospitalized there. One issue from
1965 contains a poem contributed by a patient, "Robert L," and
"reprinted by permission of the author." The poem, "Christmas in
Black Rock" from *Lord Weary's Castle*, ends: "and what is man? We tear
our rags / To hang the Furies."

The Furies would slip the noose.

8

Writing Takes the Ache Away

My great need of the moment is to keep up a front. . . . I see very well that I need to find a middle path and that ecstasy and despair will always be problems. . . . I think therapy can help me not to give up or run away, I think I can learn to use my head and eyes together. I want to be able to see my faults, do something about them, be a good husband, a writer who can grow, and a steady, capable teacher.

—To Vernon Williams, M.D.

The illness from which Robert Lowell suffered, manic-depressive illness (or bipolar disorder), was well-known to the doctors of antiquity. Its scarlet thread, said one medical historian, is discernible throughout the "twisted strands" of history. The priests and physicians of ancient China, Egypt, Persia, India, and Greece described mania and depression in detail. The manic patients they treated were excited, agitated, lacked reason, slept little, and were easily provoked into paroxysms of rage. They talked, ran, sang, and danced without inhibition, declared themselves to be a god or a descendant of the gods, decorated themselves with oils and flowers. Melancholic patients, in contrast, were downcast, slept fitfully, and ruminated on their misery and unworthiness. They had no hope, no will, and often wished to die.

The derangements of the mad, the ancient physicians believed, came from demonic possession or a misalignment of natural forces; ill-sweeping winds, bile, or poison; passions too violent to allow sanity. Five hundred years before Christ, Hippocrates and his followers taught that these were diseases of the brain; they attributed madness to natural rather than supernatural causes. It was the brain that went awry; madness did not come from action of the gods. The brain, Hippocrates said, governed emotion, perception, sleep, and incited madness; from it arose everything that makes us human, "our pleasures, joys, laughter and jests, as well as our sorrows, pains, griefs and tears." From the brain came imagination, madness, and despair. The brain was the discerner, the interpreter of the world, the governor of sleep and mood and the senses, and the determiner of consciousness. If the brain turned too hot, too cold, too moist, or too dry, madness took residence. If fire was ascendant in the blood the brain shifted its moorings, lost its stillness. With stillness gone, reason itself went.

"Mania," used by the early Greek physicians to connote insanity or mental frenzy, was then, as now, a word that could mean different things, describe many states. It could exist with or without fever; it was a furor of the mind and body, a cauldron of agitation, delusion, wrath, and threat. It came and went, often with the seasons. Those who were deranged by mania were consumed by religious fanaticism; their ideas were grandiose, their actions impulsive and intrusive. Mania was a disruptive force that could not be ignored by the doctor, priest, or community.

Melancholia, on the other hand, was a burnt-out state, one that looked much like our modern concept of depressive illness. Its sufferers, then as now, were without hope, despondent, sleepless, anxious, irritable, and confused. They ruminated ceaselessly, asked to die, and sought to be alone. Mania was a soaring of the vital senses, melancholia a sinking, a great tiredness.

Five hundred years after Hippocrates, another Greek physician, Aretaeus of Cappadocia, wrote that "the modes of mania are infinite in species, but one alone in genus," an observation that anticipated by two thousand years the clinical observations of modern psychiatry. The manifestations of manic insanity varied, Aretaeus observed, but they were kin. Some patients had a madness dominated by joy. They, Aretaeus said, "laugh, play, dance night and day, and sometimes go openly to the market crowned, as if victors in some contest of skill; this form is inoffensive to those around." Others, more susceptible to rage, "have madness attended with anger; and these sometimes rend their clothes and kill their keepers, and lay violent hands upon themselves." Yet both types of madness were manifestations of mania, a derangement of the mind that occurred in the absence of fever, one that was "hot and dry in cause, and tumultuous in its acts." Those prone to mania tended to be "naturally passionate, irritable, of active habits, of an easy disposition, joyous."

Although mania was attended by danger, Aretaeus noted that some of his patients displayed a mental edge during their excited states. They learned astronomy and philosophy and created poetry that was "truly from the muses"; their senses were peculiarly astute. His observation that mania might confer advantage even in the midst of its perniciousness was one that had been made centuries earlier by Greek philosophers; it would be repeated time and again in the centuries to follow. The mind could benefit from some mania, but risk was there. The mind needed protecting if it was not to burn. (Marsilio Ficino, writing thirteen hundred years after Aretaeus about the causes of frenzied mental states in scholars, concurred. Madness and perturbed minds in scholars were due to negligence, he argued. "The painter keeps his brushes clean, the smith will look to his hammer, anvil and forge . . . the falconer or huntsman will have a special care of his hawks, hounds, horses." Scholars, on the other hand, "neglect that instrument—their brain and spirits—which they daily use.") Mania might inspire the scholar and poet, but too much inspiration fuels the mania.

Aretaeus made the essential observation that mania and depression are lashed together. "Melancholia is the commencement and a part of mania," he said. Mania reflected a worsening of illness, "rather than a change into another disease." "Dull or stern, dejected or unreasonably torpid," depressed patients were seized by unreasonable fear and the desire to die. Sleep "does not brace their limbs," noted Aretaeus, and "watchfulness diffuses and determines them outwardly." Mania and melancholia did not keep separate company so much as they moved into and out of each other. He intuited then what clinical science has since established: manic-depressive illness is at its heart a cyclic disease of fluctuating moods, energy, sleep, and thinking. Mania and depression, Ovid-like, constitute an illness of mutability, of changing form; they are plaited together in action and fate.

The centuries that followed Aretaeus's clinical studies saw considerable clinical and academic interest in mania and melancholia. Many dissertations in European medical schools, more than sixty before 1750, described the defining features of mania—*excandescentia*, a burning passion or fury; audacity; ferocity; absence of fever—as well as its clinical course and treatment. Similar symptoms, but accompanied by fever or another underlying medical cause, would today be considered a manifestation of delirium or infection.

"These Distempers often change, and pass from one into the other," the English physician and anatomist Thomas Willis wrote in 1683. "For the *Melancholick* disposition growing worse, brings on *Fury*; and *Fury* or *Madness* growing less hot, oftentimes ends in a *Melancholick* disposition. These two, like smoke and flame, mutually receive and give place one to another." In mania, the brain was "an open burning or flame." In melancholia, the brain darkened over with fumes, covered with "a thick obscurity." The manic-depressive mind burned and then grew dark, revived, lightened, articulated. The mind was hostage to a cycle of dark and light, formlessness and then form.

The observation that manic-depressive illness was a single disease was most clearly set forth in the mid-nineteenth century by the French alienists Jean-Pierre Falret and Jules Baillarger. They introduced the concepts of "circular insanity," *la folie circulaire*, and "double insanity," *la folie à double forme*. Cyclicity, with or without remission, was integral to their and to all subsequent conceptualizations of manic-depressive illness.

Falret, like Aretaeus and Willis, was an astute clinical observer. He vividly described the progression of manic illness from its mild beginnings of high spirits to acute mania: "The profusion of ideas is prodigious, the feelings are exalted," he wrote. "Great affection is expressed for people toward whom the patient had previously felt indifferent, and hatred flows against those persons who had before been loved the most." Activity is electric, seemingly without stop. Manic patients create art, they create chaos. They "turn over their furniture, change apartments, dig up their garden, become mischievous, malicious." They carry out impulsively generated plans, they "compose and write prose and verse; and this prodigious activity, flowing forth in all directions, is present at night as well as during the daytime. . . . The senses acquire considerable acuity." Mania is active, alert, and destructive. It is, in the words of the doctors of old, an open burning, a fury.

For most of us who study mania and depression it is to the German psychiatrist Emil Kraepelin (1856–1926) that we owe our deepest clinical and intellectual debt. His 1921 monograph *Manic-Depressive Insanity and Paranoia* remains the clinical cornerstone for understanding the illness. Kraepelin, like Hippocrates more than two thousand years before him, based his notion of psychiatric disease on the patterning of symptoms and the natural course of the illness (that is, the circumstances of its onset, how it progresses, and its outcome). He divided psychosis into two major forms, manic-depressive insanity and dementia praecox (now known as schizophrenia). In distinguishing them he emphasized the periodic course of manic-depressive insanity, as well as its strong genetic component and relatively more benign outcome. Manic-depressive insanity was a broadly conceptualized illness, according to Kraepelin; it included not only the periodic and circular insanities but recurrent depression as well. He and his students further described mixed forms of the illness in which symptoms of mania and depression combined in important and potentially dangerous and perturbing states, including agitated depression, manic stupor, and depressive mania.

In the first half of the twentieth century, European and American psychiatrists formulated more specific diagnostic criteria for mental illness. In 1949, the year Robert Lowell was first hospitalized for mania, his diagnosis, manic-depressive reaction, was defined in very much the same way as it would be three years later in the first edition of the *Diagnostic and Statistical Manual for Mental Disorders*, the *DSM-I*, as a psychotic condition "marked by severe mood swings and a tendency to remission and recurrence." The symptoms for mania included elation or irritability, overtalkativeness, flight of ideas, and increased activity. Accessory symptoms included delusions and hallucinations. The diagnostic criteria were succinct, if broadly interpretable.

"Manic-depressive illness" was the diagnostic term used throughout Robert Lowell's lifetime, and it is the one that appears in his medical records. It is the term used by Lowell and his doctors, as well as by his friends and family. Today he would be diagnosed as having bipolar I disorder, terminology first formally incorporated into the *DSM-III* in 1980, three years after Lowell's death. The current diagnostic criteria for mania and depression are discussed in Appendix 2.

———

Treatments for mania and depression are as ancient as their first description. Hippocrates stressed the natural cures for madness—time and rest, bathing in spring or mineral waters, diet, exercise—but he and his followers also dispensed a wide variety of natural balms and excitants such as myrtle, laurel, incense and myrrh, lotus and hellebore. That doctors and priests would turn to roots and flowers to calm their patients' nerves, to sedate the frenzied and vitalize the dulled, was not new. The Chinese and Egyptian healers used herbs and other plants long before the Greeks. Herodotus, in his travels to Babylon in 300 BC, wrote that the local treatments for madness and sleeplessness included mulberry, iris rubbed into the head, poppy, mandrake, apples, and saffron. Pliny the Elder recorded in his *Naturalis Historia*, published circa AD 77, that there were thirty-two medicinal uses for the rose, including as a treatment for the mentally ill.

Caelius Aurelianus described the treatment of mania in fifth-century Rome: "The patient should be kept in bed (tied up, if necessary for safety reasons), in a warm and peaceful room. . . . He is massaged, fomented, phlebotomized, cupped and medicated (helleborized, if need be); he is prescribed fasting, then light food, physical exercise." Words, said Aurelianus, could help in treating the mentally distraught as well, since they "alleviate fear, sorrow, and anger." The Roman physicians emphasized that manic patients should not be beaten, forced to listen to music, kept in the dark, or permanently tied up. Nor should their delusions be encouraged. Sea voyages and baths were recommended.

Paul of Aegina (c. 625–c. 690), a Greek physician and the author of an important compendium of Western medicine, argued that mania could best be treated by leeches, fennel, and applying oil of roses to the head. Manic patients were to be secured in their beds to keep from hurting themselves or others, or they were to swing in a wicker basket hanging from the ceiling. The Anglo-Saxons, a few centuries later, were not inclined to rose and fennel. They advised whipping. But treatment of the insane in Saxon times was complicated. According to Daniel Hack Tuke, it was a "curious compound of pharmacy, superstition, and castigation." Herbs and ale were "to be drunk out of a church-bell, while seven masses were to be sung over the herbs, and the lunatic was to sing psalms, the priest saying over him the *Domine, sancte pater omnipotens*." Peony and periwinkle were prescribed in early Britain, and wolf flesh given for hallucinations. There were wells and pools in Scotland to heal the insane.

Medieval Persian treatments for mania were gentle, until they were not: damask rose, lavender, cinnamon, white lily, balsam apple, and pomegranate. The Persian doctors also recommended milk and honey—centuries later Lowell was to consume these in legendary quantities—and for depression, clove and cinnamon. Ibn Síná, the great eleventh-century Persian physician and philosopher, wrote that when the north wind blew, those inclined to mania got restless and perturbed. He prescribed bloodletting and bathing in water in which poppies had brewed; advised the use of pomegranate and pear juice, barley water, and lavender and honey. If these did not work, the manic patient was to be tied and put into a cage suspended from the ceiling.

Priest and remedy were inseparable from cure. Faith in the healer transformed herbs and the laying on of hands into relief from suffering. John Guy, in *Thomas Becket,* describes the murder of Becket at Canterbury in 1170 and how the blood that flowed from his death became a balm to pilgrims who streamed to the archbishop's tomb in search of cure. After the coup de grâce, Becket's brains had been scraped out from his skull and smeared together with his blood and bone. Many of the pilgrims who were treated with the "water of Canterbury," the potion made from Becket's blood and brain diluted in water, were the insane and the melancholic. One of the "miracle windows" at Canterbury Cathedral portrays an insane man, beaten with sticks and tied with ropes by his caretakers, dragged to the tomb of Becket. Cured overnight, he is shown in the stained-glass window together with the ropes that had bound him and the sticks that had beat him, left in faith at the base of Becket's tomb. Together, saint and potion effected the impossible.

Robert Burton, in his 1621 *Anatomy of Melancholy,* described remedies from the natural world: marigold is "much approved against melancholy," he wrote, as was "a ram's head that never meddled with a ewe." The brain of the unsullied ram once removed from the skull and spiced with cinnamon, ginger, nutmeg, and cloves would act powerfully against depression, Burton wrote. Many of the flowers and plants thought by the ancients to be effective against mania and melancholia were still of use: dandelion, ash, willow, tamarisk, roses, violets, sweet apples, syrup of poppy, and sassafras. More lyrical than effective perhaps.

The New England Puritans also turned to powders and elixirs to treat madness. Mania could be cured by an "elixir made of dew," John Winthrop the Younger, son of the founding governor of Massachusetts Bay Colony and a physician as well as governor of Connecticut Colony, was advised in 1656. The elixir was to be purified until it became a powder "black as ink, then green, then gray." After two years, when it was "white & lustrous as any oriental pearl," it was guaranteed to "cure mania at 15 months end." This was a guarantee with little risk; mania left to run its own course resolves more quickly. Time alone will cure many who are ill in mind or body, Sir William Osler taught his medical students and house staff at Johns Hopkins 250 years later. Prescribe time, he said. Time in divided doses.

The nineteenth-century asylum physicians treated manic patients with enforced quiet, darkened rooms, and sedating medicines such as digitalis, camphor, rhubarb, tincture of ginger, salts of morphia, and other preparations of opium. Patients soaked in hot baths, water mixed with hemlock and cherry laurel leaves, for hours at a time and were fed diets of milk, peaches, and lemonade to further calm them. Melancholic patients were treated with stimulants—iron bitters, quinine, malt liquors—as well as long baths, and tinctures of camphor or opium for sleeplessness, agitation, and suicidal depression.

Remedies that were uncertain in their effects were common in times when the causes of insanity were uncertain. In the nineteenth-century asylums little was known about the etiology of mental disease, although heredity and dissipation were not uncommonly cited. Indeed, Dr. Rufus Wyman, the physician who first treated Harriet Brackett Spence Lowell, wrote that the most prominent causes of insanity in the patients admitted to the McLean Asylum were intemperance, insane ancestors, and madness associated with pregnancy. "Unknown" was often listed as the cause of insanity in the asylum ledgers, as was "insane ancestry." Insanity, said Wyman in 1835, was transmitted from generation to generation, "a medical fact everywhere admitted."

At the time that Robert Lowell was first hospitalized in 1949, the primary treatments for mania were hospital care, sedative medications, hydrotherapy, and electroconvulsive therapy. The hospital was meant itself to be therapeutic, designed as a safer, quieter, less stressful place than life outside its walls. Lowell generally found that being in a hospital, however demoralizing, was a respite and protection. His expectations of what he would get done while he was in hospital were often unrealistic: "I went off to the hospital armed with a suitcase of classics," Lowell wrote to Adrienne Rich in 1964. "Freud, the complete Aristotle, Dante, etc. and then spent most of my time looking at popular television, even waiting breathlessly for the next Thursday's Dr.

Causes of insanity, patient ledger, McLean Asylum, 1845

Kildare." Later came the poignant aftermath. "Then at last the books were brought back home," said Elizabeth Hardwick. "The socks, with their name-tapes as if for a summer camp, were gathered up. And there it was, with only the sadness, actually the unfairness of the fate, remaining."

Hospitals by their nature sap dignity. Privacy, privilege, and freedom are in short supply. Doctors and nurses determine the flow of hours and activity. Writing to Hardwick from the Institute of Living in Hartford in 1965, Lowell said, "I won't go into the boredom of 'leather appreciation' and ceramics appreciation, of watching basketball games for an hour without smoking, or of trying to converse with the oldster reading Francis Bacon sentence by sentence." In "Near the Unbalanced Aquarium," he drew a particular arrow against the lost cause and embarrassment of occupational therapy: "It was a sunny, improving world; and here, unable to 'think' with my hands, I spent a daily hour of embarrassed anguish. Here for weeks I saw my abandoned pine-cone basket lying on the pile for waste materials. And as it sank under sawdust and shavings, it seemed to protest the pains Mr. Kemper, our instructor, had once taken to warp, to soak, to reweave, to rescue it." Reweaving was the difficult thing. Many who knew Lowell agreed that despite his dread and shame of having to be in a hospital, he was relieved once admitted. It shielded his mania from the eyes of others and limited the damage he could inflict.

Lowell received electroconvulsive therapy for mania in 1949, 1952, and 1954. It worked quickly and well, but it did not prevent him from getting sick again. In May 1954, while hospitalized at Payne Whitney, he was given the antipsychotic chlorpromazine for the first time; he was prescribed it during several subsequent hospital stays and, on occasion, when he felt himself speeding up, he took it when he was out of the hospital as well. It was an effective drug against acute illness but, like electroconvulsive therapy, it did not successfully prevent recurrence of his mania.

It was inevitable that Lowell, introspective and beholden to words, would want to understand what he had been through. "All the late froth and delirium have blown away," he wrote to Elizabeth Bishop. "One is left strangely dumb, and talking about the past is like a cat's trying to explain climbing down a ladder. One would like to look at it all without moodiness or bravado." Consistent with the era, Lowell was in and out of psychotherapy, starting with his first hospital stay in 1949. His therapy was often with psychoanalysts, although he was not in formal psychoanalysis. At times he was enthusiastic about what he was learning from therapy. He wrote to Elizabeth Bishop in 1949, early in the long years of his illness: "Psycho-therapy is rather amazing—something like stirring up the bottom of an aquarium—chunks of the past coming up at unfamiliar angles, distinct and then indistinct." In early 1950 he wrote to his parents, "I have been seeing a psychiatrist here about once a week, and we agree that I am well out of my extreme troubles. There is a stiffness, many old scars, the toil of building up new habits."

He was fascinated and impressed by Freud. "I've been gulping

Freud," he wrote to Hardwick in 1953, "and am a confused and slavish convert." In later years he retained his respect for Freud's humanity and writing but became disenchanted with psychoanalytic theory and techniques, especially the extremes to which Freud's work had been taken by his followers. Lowell told the English critic Al Alvarez in 1965, "I get a funny thing from psycho-analysis. I mean Freud is the man who moves me most: and his case histories, and the book on dreams, read almost like a late Russian novel to me—with a scientific rather than a novelist's mind. They have a sort of marvelous old-order quality to them, though he is the father of the new order, almost the opposite of what psycho-analysis has been since."

Lowell was drawn to Freud's affinity for the past and his portrayal of the intricacies of the human condition. "All that human sort of color and sadness, that long German-Austrian and Jewish culture that Freud had, seems something in the past; but it was still real to him. There is something rather beautiful and sad and intricate about Freud that seems to have gone out of psycho-analysis; it's become a way of looking at things." Freud and Lowell had important interests in common. They both grappled with the hard truths of the mind: irrational forces that drive behavior and belief, madness, war, and death. In his 1918 "Reflections on War and Death," Freud wrote that the truth of death should be given its due: "Were it not better to give death the place to which it is entitled both in reality and in our thoughts?" he argued. It was a critical question for Lowell as well. If you wish to have life, argued Freud, prepare for death. *Si vis pacem, para bellum. Si vis vitam, para mortem.* Death is always there, the irrefragable and last place toward which we move. But it is to life that one owes toughness and commitment. "To bear life," Freud wrote, is "the first duty of the living."

Lowell believed that Freud was an original thinker, a religious teacher and prophet, and someone who spoke for both the Jewish and Christian traditions. Freudian orthodoxy, on the other hand, with answers to be presented "like the Catechism," put him off. Freud "is not like Freudians," Lowell wrote. He is "marvelous, like Proust, the most revealing mind of our age." Lowell did not believe that psychoanalysis could treat the madness that broke in him. But, he said, Freud "provides the conditions that one must think in."

Lowell was treated by many psychiatrists over the years, some well-known in the medical communities of New York and Boston. In 1958 he wrote to Bishop (and it was almost always to Bishop he wrote when discussing his psychotherapy) that he was seeing his doctor three times a week. "He does me a lot of good, and I am learning not to throw my weight around the household every minute to prove I am not like my Father. Oh, and much else." A year later, he reiterated that seeing his doctor three times a week was "really doing great things, and I begin to hope that by this time next year the knot inside me will be unsnarled."

Lowell scaled back his expectations of psychotherapy as his illness progressed. His dramatic response to lithium made him skeptical of the therapy that had failed to treat his manic depression, an illness that he had begun to conceptualize as a "salt deficiency." A friend who saw Lowell at the end of 1967, less than a year after he started taking lithium, said, "This was the first year in eighteen he hadn't had an attack. There had been fourteen or fifteen over the past eighteen years. Frightful humiliation and waste. He'd been all set up to taxi up to Riverdale five times a week at $50 a session, plus (of course) taxi fare. Now it was a capsule a day and once-a-week therapy. His face seemed smoother, the weight of distress-attacks and anticipation both gone."

Lowell regretted the time he had spent in psychotherapy, according to his friend Peter Taylor. He also took offense at the things he had been encouraged to believe. "He felt very strongly in his later years that [his madness] was a chemical imbalance and he would tell me that he resented having been made to feel that he hated his father and wanted to marry his mother, all of these. He said, I was made to feel all these things and all the while it was just—it was just a physiological thing."

Whatever truth there was in Lowell's skepticism about psychotherapy, his relationship with his psychiatrists was more complicated than he acknowledged. Lowell's life was one of words and metaphor; his work came out of observations about human relationships; his mental life was of nuance in meaning and mood. His life, family, and childhood were bloodstream to his poetry. "Once he was on lithium," observed Helen Vendler, "he joked retrospectively about all the hours he had spent in therapists' offices, which never cured him. But I think he recognized that he would never have written *Life Studies* without those hours."

Certainly Lowell looked to psychotherapy to help him exert control over his mania and the depression that came in its wake. He told Dr. Vernon Williams, his Boston psychiatrist in the 1950s, "Now coming back to the question of what I would like to get from my therapy. I must say that I find it difficult to be sensible, concrete and sustained on this subject. I am tempted to use empty clichés, rhetoric, irrelevances, unexplained images—then feeling none of these will do, I face a blank and want to avoid answering." He said he knew that life had gone "fairly well for long stretches in the past" and that he "felt drawn to ask impossible things of myself and then do nothing." He stated he hoped to be a better husband, writer, and teacher.

But the "largest thing I hope for from my psycho-therapy," he said to his doctor, was to "put an end to my recurrent wild manic outbreaks and the hangovers of formless self-pity that follow. If a total cure is impossible, I feel sure that both extremes can be moderated, and that I will always have the foresight and self-knowledge." He added that he also hoped that in the future he could take "quick preventive measures and never again lose control."

It is in the nature of manic illness to recur and with recurrence to progress; from this comes a fear that is hard to grasp for those who are not affected. The relatively long periods of health during the early years after the first or second breakdown can lead to unwarranted optimism about the years to come. Thus Hardwick wrote to Lowell when he was in the hospital for depression in 1949, "I know you're all right, dear one. Don't be depressed about being in the hospital. Remember we both know it's for a permanent relief for you."

A month later she wrote to Peter Taylor that the doctors had told her "there should not be an incapacitating attack either of elation or depression again." She and Lowell, like Palinurus, trusted too much to a calm sea and were "betrayed so often by calm, deceptive skies." It is a necessary and human thing. Hardwick's optimism did not mean that she thought others would look at his illness in the same way. Later that year, when she and Lowell had not heard from the University of Iowa about his application for a teaching position there, she wrote to Allen Tate: "I can't quite take it upon myself to tell him what the true difficulty at Iowa is, although I feel sure he's thought of the procrastination in a realistic way. I'm afraid, if he is finally turned down, he'll feel all teaching jobs are closed to him for the same reason."

Hardwick and Lowell dipped into and out of denial about the chances that his madness would come back. In 1952, after his breakdown in Salzburg, Lowell wrote to his mother that "it's all definitely over, without any likelihood of relapse or return." At the same time, however, Hardwick was writing to friends, "Cal takes this all with dead seriousness, of course, and is terrified of such a thing ever happening again."

The writer and psychotherapist Eileen Simpson, who was at the time married to John Berryman, described an evening after the opera during the Christmas season following Lowell's second breakdown. They were dancing, although he was so depressed that he was oblivious to the music. "Over the noise of the band," Simpson wrote, "he asked me the question which was tormenting him: Would it happen again? He knew, as he knew I knew, that, the nature of his illness being cyclical, there was every chance of a recurrence. What haunted him was not simply the idea of another period of mania, during which he would do God knew what, nor even the incarceration in an institution and the horrors of electroshock therapy. It was the fear that the next time, or the time after, he would not recover. Or, if he did, that he would be released with the part of his brain he used for writing poetry burned out by the high voltages of the shock machine. Would his illness finish him as a writer?"

In January 1964, Hardwick wrote to Allen Tate that Lowell's attacks were now "out of the control of the will" and that he was "utterly bewildered." The artist Sidney Nolan observed, much later in the course of Lowell's illness, "Of course, he feared the breakdowns. He said to me in Central Park, 'I've been sixteen times on my knees. I've got up sixteen times.' Then he added, 'But if one day I don't get up, I don't mind.'" Near the end of his life, in "The Downlook," Lowell wrote of the downward, now and again resurrecting cycle:

> How often have my antics
> and insupportable, trespassing tongue
> gone astray and led me to prison . . .
> to lying . . . kneeling . . . standing.

At times he seemed resigned to his fate. "I am back from a month in the sanitarium," he wrote to Elizabeth Bishop in 1965. "These attacks seem now almost like something woven in my nervous system and one of the ingredients of my blood-stream, and I blame them less on some fatal personal psychotic flaw."

In his letters and discussions with his doctors, as well as in his poetry, Lowell expressed dread that his mania would come back. "'Remarkable breakdown, remarkable recovery'—," he wrote, "but the breakage can go on repeating / once too often." In "Waking in the Blue," he described being a patient in McLean Hospital and standing "before the metal shaving mirrors," watching "the shaky future grow familiar." In "Home After Three Months Away," recovering from a breakdown, he watched the tulips in the garden, "pedigreed" just twelve months earlier and "now no one need / distinguish them from weed." "Bushed by the late spring snow," he observed, "they cannot meet / another year's snowballing enervation." Life kept to its cycle of possibility, then it dashed hope. Relief was fleeting:

> "Waiting out the rain,
> but what are you waiting for?
> The storm can only stop
> to get breath to begin again."

Robert Fitzgerald described Lowell's fear and how it led to a new caution: "After his first grave manic attack in 1949, after his first hospitalization, all concerned grew wary on his behalf, as indeed he did himself, of excitements religious, political, or poetic. He could no longer be a Catholic because, as he told me, it set him on fire. He had to govern his greatness with his illness in mind." Years later Mary McCarthy said that Lowell had spoken "with horror of his old mania, like someone who has been through a searing fire."

Fire is a central image in Lowell's work. Destruction is the obverse side of fire that is excitement, creation, and power. His faith, an intoxicating enthusiasm, had set him on fire during his high Catholic days, and he never again saw the Church in an entirely benign way. He wrote to George Santayana in 1950, "I am back where I was in my faith—fallen or standing in disillusionment. Only the bull who has been burned out of a barn looks at the sunset and trembles. Often I long to walk in the great house of the Church, but the candles would set my clothes on fire long before I reached the altar."

Lowell returned time and again to the image of cattle, once burned out of their barns, trembling in terror at the fire of the sunset. In "The Puritan," a prose piece written in the mid-1940s, before his first manic break, he wrote, "Even now I feel as though I were sitting on dynamite. They say a cow who has been burnt out of her barn always looks at the sunset and trembles." Twenty years later, in "Cattle," published in *Notebook 1967–68*, Lowell brought the image back: "Cattle have guts, but after the barn is burned, / they will look at the sunset and tremble." The image repeats in "Cow," a poem revised when he was in his fifties and included in his 1973 *History*.

Fire and mania break erratic and fast into danger and need to be taken with a heed not always possible. There is temptation to push the boundaries of what fire can do. "We do not burn to survive," said Lowell of the Russian poet Andrei Voznesensky, "but to step on the gas." Fire balloons may climb the mountain height, wrote Elizabeth Bishop in a poem dedicated to Robert Lowell. "If it's still they steer between / the kite sticks of the Southern Cross." But "in the downdraft from a peak," they "suddenly [turn] dangerous." Fire gives life, brings death, gives power; it creates, welds, and scorches; it seduces. "I made men look into the fire," Lowell had Prometheus declare in his translation of Aeschylus's *Prometheus Bound*. "Alone and bemused in the slothful dark, they studied the fire's whirling and consuming colors, and believed they would some day taste the breath of life. No one knows, I haven't told anyone, the many wonders I have invented. I was out of my mind, my hand was everywhere."

Fire used well, Lowell's Prometheus says, "can remake, or destroy the earth." Before he stole fire from the gods and gave it to man, "men had eyes and saw nothing. . . . They had ears and heard nothing: a splatter, a splash, fizzings, buzzings, hissings, mazes of muddled vibration, sounds without the cutting edge of words." Fire gave and it took, as mania does. "Before I made men talk and write with words," said Prometheus, "knowledge dropped like a dry stick into the fire of their memories, fed that fading blaze an instant, then died without leaving an ash behind." Lowell's thinking about mania, about fire, was complicated; any healing that would take place—through doctor or writing—would have to contend with this complexity. Mania demanded engagement; it was a war to be fought, if usually lost. It might be harnessed but only at terrible risk.

Lowell had several good doctors over the nearly thirty years he was treated for his illness. Healing is different from treatment, however, and healing from the damage inflicted by psychosis demands a particular kind of understanding. What he does not seem to have had was the kind of healing relationship exemplified by the poet Siegfried Sassoon's with his psychiatrist, W. H. R. Rivers. In Craiglockhart, the shell-shock hospital near Edinburgh where Sassoon was a patient during World War I, madness and the horror of war were at the heart of the therapeutic relationship. The war-damaged mind needed healing. Words used well and memories brought to mind in a way gradual and tolerable could tamp down the horrors of war and madness. Rivers, a British army psychiatrist as well as an acclaimed anthropologist and experimental psychologist, uniquely understood the scars created by the trauma of war.

The scars of madness, Lowell observed, are like those of war. This common territory of war and madness is true and underappreciated. Both madness and war upend habit and incite behavior beyond the moral code. They create dread and uncertainty. For good reason, episodes of mania are referred to as "attacks." Mania is an assault on the mind that is traumatic in every clinical and human sense of the word. The damage from mania cannot be set aside, forgotten, or exiled into the mind's back chamber. It will be remembered. If it is not, it will take a greater toll.

War and madness were powerfully linked in Lowell's life and writing. When he was young, he had been obsessed by Napoleon and his military campaigns. He wrote about the Greek and Roman wars, King Philip's War, the American Revolution, the Civil War, and the long centuries of European wars. He wrote about military heroes and despots. He volunteered several times to serve in World War II; after the Allied razing of Hamburg, he became a conscientious objector and refused to serve. The brutality and senselessness of war were critical to several of his most important poems. He prominently denounced the Vietnam War. Throughout his life he grappled with the question of the just and unjust uses of military power. He was attracted to and repelled by dangerous force. When he was manic, his delusions often centered on military figures. He spoke to his doctors and friends of the damage caused by his attacks of madness, of the warring forces in his head, the fiery sieges that overtook his mind. Mania broke alliances, bred mistrust, sowed destruction.

Mania shatters the mind and principle; it begets guilt. Things done in mania are inexplicable and unjustifiable; the mind during mania, like war, is a pitched battlefield. From it arises chaos, as well as opportunity. War, said Henry Adams, breeds life because it breeds chaos. Within the broken world of war, out of its chaos, courage could emerge. Lowell recognized this early. In his schoolboy analysis of *The Iliad*, he had written that war gives "a chance to gain self-respect and honor." One could learn, act, lead. Likewise with madness. If one was unable to control the attacks, one could exhibit courage in dealing with them. Mania compelled a counteraction and revision; it set the ground for reconstruction and reinvention. But the mind needed to heal.

The healing of war-torn minds was what W. H. R. Rivers practiced, studied, and taught; it was the legendary healing he gave to the shell-shocked officers he treated. It was the kind of psychotherapy that can begin to heal the ravages of mania. Rivers was interested in how he could use the controlled recollection of horror to bring his patients to understand what they had been through, to "face the facts" of their trauma, and to allow them to meet the horror "in their own strength." In lectures given at the University of Cambridge in 1919 and at the Phipps Clinic at the Johns Hopkins Hospital in 1920, Rivers laid out his observations about undertaking psychotherapy in those who had experienced war trauma, or shell shock.

The doctor should make intolerable memories tolerable, Rivers told his colleagues. He should assist his patients in replacing horror with the more bearable emotion of grief. Between them, doctor and patient, they should find a balance between dwelling on the traumatic experience of war and "banishing such experiences from their minds altogether." The problem, Rivers said, "was to find some aspect of the painful experience which would allow the patient to dwell upon it in such a way as to relieve its horrible and terrifying character." "It's bad to think of war," wrote Sassoon in a poem named for Rivers's lecture "Repression of War Experience": "When thoughts you've gagged all day come back to scare you; / And it's been proved that soldiers don't go mad / Unless they lose control of ugly thoughts / That drive them out to jabber among the trees."

Madness and the memories of war go, return, stay:

> You're quiet and peaceful, summering safe at home;
> You'd never think there was a bloody war on! . . .
> O yes, you would . . . why, you can hear the guns.

Hark! Thud, thud, thud,—quite soft . . . they never cease—
Those whispering guns—O Christ, I want to go out
And screech at them to stop—I'm going crazy;
I'm going stark, staring mad because of the guns.

T. E. Lawrence, who knew the horror of war well and had been instructed in the ancient Arab remedies for healing through recollection, sometimes in hard memory, wrote in *Seven Pillars of Wisdom* about Arab reckoning of their animals:

> I was on my Ghazala, the old grandmother camel, now again magnificently fit. Her foal had lately died, and Abdulla, who rode next me, had skinned the little carcase, and carried the dry pelt behind his saddle, like a crupper piece. We started well, thanks to the Zaagi's chanting, but after an hour Ghazala lifted her head high, and began to pace uneasily, picking up her feet like a sword-dancer.
>
> I tried to urge her; but Abdulla dashed alongside me, swept his cloak about him, and sprang from his saddle, calf's skin in hand. He lighted with a splash of gravel in front of Ghazala, who had come to a standstill, gently moaning. On the ground before her he spread the little hide, and drew her head down to it. She stopped crying, shuffled its dryness thrice with her lips; then again lifted her head and, with a whimper, strode forward. Several times in the day this happened; but afterwards she seemed to forget.

A healing forgetfulness could follow sharp remembrance, but not by averting or tamping down pain and loss.

For a poet such as Lowell, who did much of his healing through his writing, and who by character returned to, rather than retreated from, the front lines of life, Rivers's psychotherapeutic philosophy would have been compassionate and practical. Standing back from or skirting the trauma of madness would not work. Repression would not work. "If imagination is active and powerful," Rivers insisted, "it is probably far better to allow it to play around the trials and dangers of warfare than to carry out a prolonged system of repression." This encouragement of limited but direct engagement, although it carried risk, suited Lowell's character and temperament. The human part of war, wrote Lowell, may help the poet through "war's sordor, heroism, the death and adventures of friends, the blow brought home to one's whole being." So too the human part of madness.

Rivers repeatedly made the point that men of courage could and did fall to madness. Siegfried Sassoon, whose courage in battle was renowned throughout the British Army and who had received the Military Cross for "conspicuous valour," gave to Rivers, as did his fellow poets Wilfred Owen and Robert Graves, who knew but were not treated by him, the kind of respect that makes healing possible. Rivers, by all accounts tough, sympathetic, and deeply intelligent, saw a significant part of his role as a doctor, as a healer, as someone who could accompany his patients through their terrors.

"My definite approach to mental maturity began with my contact with the mind of Rivers," wrote Sassoon. "He exists [now] only in vigilant and undiminished memories, continuously surviving in what he taught me. It is that intense survival of his human integrity." When everything had "fallen to pieces and one's mind was in a muddle and one's nerves were all on edge . . . ," said Sassoon, "unexpected and unannounced, Rivers came in and closed the door behind him. Quiet and alert, purposeful and unhesitating, he seemed to empty the room of everything that had needed exorcising."

It was the kind of healing, of exorcising, that seems to have eluded Lowell, perhaps because such doctors are impossibly rare or perhaps because the ravages of Lowell's illness did not allow it. It is a pity. The laying on of hands and binding up of wounds is ancient, biblical, and continues still. "I undo the clotted lint, remove the slough, wash off the matter and blood," wrote Walt Whitman, who nursed dying soldiers during the Civil War. "I thread my way through the hospitals, / The hurt and wounded I pacify with soothing hand, / I sit by the restless all the dark night."

Lithium curbed the relentlessness of Lowell's manic attacks until, toward the end of his life, when he took it only erratically, and sometimes not at all, his mania came back. His anxiety in the wake of recur-

rence was palpable. In February 1976, a year and a half before he
died, Lowell wrote to Frank Bidart, "I am weighed down by the new
frequency of attacks. How can one function, if one is regularly sick.
Shades of the future prison." He made the point again to Blair Clark
the following month. "I can't really function against two manic attacks
in one year," he said. It was untenable. He expressed the same fear to
Elizabeth Bishop: "I had a longish though not violently troubled stay
in the hospital, and have been out a month—mildly depressed as the
cheerful doctors insist. Mildly is bad enough. Though I can't make too
much of it. I fear the frequency of these things, fear becoming something that must be categorized as a burden."

Lowell's third wife, Caroline Blackwood, reiterated Lowell's fear
of becoming manic again. He was "terrified of being mad alone," she
said. "I don't think people generally realized the terror he was in that
he might lose his mind minute by minute. In fact, his last lines were
about that: 'Christ, may I die at night with a semblance of my senses.'"
The regret for lost time, the grinding cycle of hope and despair, the
dread of madness find their way into Lowell's last book, *Day by Day*,
which was published just months before he died; hope is shown to be
fool's gold: "if we see a light at the end of the tunnel, / it's the light of
an oncoming train."

―――――――――

In 1949, the same year that Lowell was first admitted to a hospital for
mania, John Cade, an Australian psychiatrist, published in the *Medical
Journal of Australia* an article titled "Lithium Salts in the Treatment
of Psychotic Excitement." The impact of Cade's discovery—or, more
accurately, rediscovery; it had been used briefly by Danish physicians
in the 1890s to treat depressive illnesses—is difficult to overstate. Lithium was the first drug that not only treated but prevented mania and
depression. His work, often described as serendipitous because it took
a rather higgledy-piggledy path of scientific reasoning, was intuitive,
odd, risky, and utterly changed clinical practice and research in psychiatric medicine.

G. P. Hartigan, an English psychiatrist who did early clinical work
with lithium, and whose paper "Experiences of Treatment with Lithium Salts" I occasionally give to residents as an example of excellent

clinical writing, put Cade's work, which spanned a line of reasoning from speculation about toxins in the urine of manic patients to lethargy in excitable guinea pigs, thus: "Some Australian physiologists, working on some recondite project whose exact nature I regret I am unable to recall, found it expedient to introduce a lithium salt into the peritoneal cavities of guinea-pigs. It was observed that for some hours after this outrage the animals became thoughtful and preoccupied."

Cade's guinea pigs, thoughtful and preoccupied though they may have seemed, more likely were acutely ill from the lithium, which at too high a dose can be toxic. Cade made excellent use of his observation of passivity in his experimental animals and speculated that the effect might be transferable to the very sick manic patients he was treating on the wards. He gave lithium to ten severely ill patients with mania and in all of them there was a significant reduction in psychotic excitement. When the lithium was discontinued, the psychosis returned. There were problems: the first patient who received lithium stopped taking it after having become "overcome with confidence" at being well. When he restarted his lithium, however, he again showed a dramatic recovery. He later died of lithium toxicity, an outcome far more common in the early days of treatment and research than it is now.

Cade, in his landmark paper, speculated that lithium might be an essential trace element. "It is widely distributed," he wrote, and "has been detected in sea-water and in many spring and river waters, in the ash of many plants, and in animal ash." Soranus of Ephesus in the second century, and physicians long before him, had recommended the use of mineral well waters, some of which had high concentrations of lithium, for patients who were manic. The concentration of lithium in these waters doesn't approach the level necessary for a clinical response, but speculation about lithium concentrations in ancient wells and modern water supplies remains a part of the drug's lore.

Lithium spewed out in the first minutes of the creation of the universe. Fifteen billion years later it was discovered by a chemist analyzing minerals in an island cave off the coast of Sweden. The element, which exists in mineral springs and igneous rocks, was named *lithos*, the Greek word for stone. In the two decades after Cade's clinical findings were published in 1949, Danish researchers demonstrated that lithium was effective in preventing both mania and depression. They also worked out the dosages and preparations of lithium that were effective

Lithium salt reserves

"All I've suffered, and all the suffering I've caused, might have arisen from the lack of a little salt in my brain."

and safe. The drug was then used in Britain and continental Europe and eventually found its way over the Atlantic into American medical practice.

Lithium is light—only hydrogen and helium are more so—flammable, and as ancient as is possible. Better than anything we know, it treats and prevents mania and depression; better than anything we have, it acts to prevent suicide. It also appears to protect and heal the brain from the damaging effects of repeated attacks of mania and depression. Recent studies suggest that lithium prescribed to bipolar patients increases gray matter volume and density, increases cortical thickness and hippocampal volume, and may reduce the risk of dementia. There are other drugs now available to treat manic-depressive illness, primarily anticonvulsant medications used for seizure disorders and antipsychotic drugs, but lithium remains the gold standard for treatment. Lithium, as Hartigan wrote, possesses "certain modest magical qualities."

Lowell was first given lithium in 1967 and, early in his treatment, he felt Cade's wonder toward the drug. In February 1967 he wrote to Elizabeth Bishop, "Nothing new worth writing about, except that I have another doctor now, and there seems to be real hope that my manic seizures can be handled by a new drug, Lithium, and that all my giddy reelings come from a kind of periodic salt deficiency in some lower part of the brain. At least, this drug is now working with many."

That June he wrote to another friend, "I'm in terrific shape! I even have pills that are supposed to prevent manic attacks . . . which supplies some salt lack in some obscure part of the brain." A year after first taking lithium he wrote to Bishop again: "Yes, I'm well. The pills I am taking really seem to prevent mania. Two or three years will be necessary, but already critical months have passed. Ordinarily I would certainly have been in a hospital by now. The great thing is that even my well life is much changed, as tho I'd once been in danger of falling with every step I took. All the psychiatry and therapy I've had, almost 19 years, was as irrelevant as it would have been for a broken leg. Well, some of it was interesting, tho most was jargon."

Lowell made the same point again in May 1968: "These pills for my manic seizures seem to have made a cure, tho I will take them to

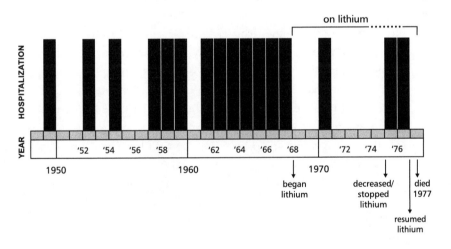

Robert Lowell: Hospitalizations and lithium treatment
"No attacks, no hospitalizations, but even, and perhaps most, health itself is different, freer and out of the shadow."

my dying. This has changed my life, not only no attacks, no hospitals, but even, and perhaps most, health itself is different, freer and out of the shadow." For many years lithium, though an imperfect drug, gave him relative health and stability; it untied him from the killing cycle of manic-depressive illness to which he had been bound.

Some of Lowell's friends found lithium to be a problematic treatment, in part because of its side effects—he was kept at a higher dosage than he would be now, which appears to have somewhat flattened his moods (clinical practice has changed significantly in this regard)—and in part because his illness still was not entirely under control. Although Lowell fit the clinical profile of someone likely to respond to lithium— his manias were "classic," that is, characterized by elation, flight of ideas, and grandiosity; he had a family history of mood disorders; and his attacks of mania preceded his depressions, rather than the other way around—he was put on lithium late in his illness, and stability is harder to achieve after repeated episodes of mania. Lowell also drank heavily at times, most notably when he was manic, which almost certainly affected his response to lithium as well as disrupting his sleep. Other medications that he took for his heart disease, including methyldopa and digitalis, may have had an impact on his moods as well.

Mary McCarthy, in a letter to Hannah Arendt in the fall of 1967, gave her usual unvarnished opinion of Lowell and his treatment:

> He is taking some new drug, a kind of salt [lithium carbonate], that is supposed to guarantee that he'll never have another manic seizure. But what it has disclosed, by keeping him "normal," is how mad he is all the time, even when on his good behavior. It is as we said last December. And this, we hear from Lizzie, is the view of the new doctor, who is more a physiologist than a psychiatrist: "The salts," he told her, "will prevent manic outbreaks, but they can't change the fact that he is crazy." He's very tense and, when he's drinking, quite grandiose; he oughtn't to drink and has stopped for the moment, but I don't think he can keep it up. It's as though the drug were depriving him of his annual spree and he compensates for the deprivation rather cunningly by using the license given to drunkards. My opinion is that it would be better to let him be crazy once a year, be locked up, then emerge penitent, etc.

Jonathan Miller, who trained as a physician before his work in the theater, observed that Lowell "became much more frazzled. I've got a feeling that the episodes of lunacy, instead of being concentrated in acute, easily manageable episodes at the beginning or the end of the year—the drugs had somehow squashed it out and spread it evenly throughout the year."

Grey Gowrie described the advantage and cost to Lowell of taking lithium. "Lithium had made a terrible difference to him. I don't think it was very good for him physically, but he seemed to be on a much more even keel. He was unhealthy, Cal. He smoked all the time and he liked to drink, and this drug was blowing him up a bit. And he was puffier. He'd lost his fitness in a way." Another friend, Esther Brooks, stated that she thought lithium worked for a while and that "he appeared to be released from the terrible ordeal of more and more frequent break-downs." As the years passed, however, "he became more and more careless about its use and the consequent effects were subtly noticeable to those who knew him well. The well person and the unwell person seemed to rub together in a strange kind of muted euphoria. One no longer feared that he would go mad but one kept waiting for the delicate and exquisite side of his mind to assert itself once again."

It is difficult to gauge the effect of lithium on Lowell's work. There is little available about his blood levels, which are critical in any discussion of the drug's effects on thinking and writing. His stepdaughter Ivana states that Lowell felt lithium flattened him out and had a negative effect on his creativity; his friend the poet Kathleen Spivack agreed, and said he complained that lithium "flattened him out, all his moods; there was a creative price to be paid for medicine." The painter Sidney Nolan said that lithium stopped him going to the hospital but "I think it was a dampener at both ends. It stopped the mania and it stopped the depression and left him somewhere in between. From the point of view of the artist, I don't know that it was necessarily a good thing. I think he sometimes realized this and didn't take it."

Lithium appears to have checked the extremes of Lowell's mania, but his mind continued to create at a fast, submanic pace. He was first prescribed lithium in March or April 1967 and began writing the *Notebook 1967–68* poems in July 1967. "I never wrote more," Lowell said about his productivity during this time. By Christmas of that year he had written more than seventy sonnets. He told Elizabeth Bishop in

July 1968, "I guess the summer goes, because I write so much. I must average six days a week nine to three-thirty. . . . 19 new sections added. It must end, but impulse keeps pushing up something new." "This beautiful summer," he wrote to Adrienne Rich, was "the best, the most productive I've had." Later he commented, "Words came rapidly, almost four hundred sonnets in four years. . . . I did nothing but write."

When he was taking lithium, Lowell was rarely overtly manic but on occasion mildly to moderately so. During those periods his mind was a simmering, mixed state of moods and thoughts, one that threw out more ideas and generated more poetry. Esther Brooks described his mood during this period as often being one of "muted euphoria," which is consistent with what is known about elated mood states driving productivity and creativity, as we shall see later. It is possible that the lithium capped his mania well enough to allow him to write with some of the productive advantage of mild mania.

"He had a massive drive to write," Helen Vendler observed. "Perhaps one of the consequences of having his extreme ups and downs was his interesting pendulum-swings between counted and free-verse, in both of which he could be masterful. I think one unfortunate result of his initially exhilarating freedom from hospitalization after he was put on lithium was the unrelenting drive—once he had started on his blank-verse sonnets in *Notebook 1967–68*—to continue in that form." Ian Hamilton suggested that Lowell's post-lithium writing was "different from the more pointed articulation of the earlier books; his poetic intelligence is on the rampage, swooping into all kinds of biblical, classical, and historical sources for analogies and omens, and deliberately shunning the old, orchestral melodiousness."

There is not much known about lithium's specific impact on productivity and creativity. Two small studies during the 1970s found that three-quarters of artists and writers reported an increase in productivity, or no change, while on lithium. A study of the impact of short-term lithium use on creativity in normal individuals found no effect. Other studies of patients with bipolar illness, however, found that measures of creativity increased as the level of lithium decreased. All of these investigations have been problematic; they studied only a small number of individuals, the patients had different durations and severities of illness, and they varied in their blood levels of lithium. None of the studies looked at the effects of altering dose or discontinuing lithium in writers or artists.

Lithium gave Lowell a relative mental stability that led to greater productivity; this may or may not have come at the expense of originality. Although many, but by no means all, critics believe that Lowell's work declined during the last decade of his life, which was when he was being treated with lithium, it is as likely that his progressing illness would have taken a far greater toll on his work had he not been taking the drug. Lithium's well-established efficacy in preventing the recurrence of illness resulted in Lowell spending less time in the hospital, less time ill with mania and depression. The accumulating evidence that lithium has neuroprotective and neurogenerative effects on the brain suggests that lithium may have decreased some of Lowell's vulnerability to an otherwise progressive, neurodamaging disease.

In May 1975, during a trip to New York, Lowell suffered from lithium toxicity and had to be hospitalized. During lunch with his editor, Robert Giroux, Lowell's head fell forward onto the table and he appeared heavily sedated. Robert Silvers, a friend and the editor of the *New York Review of Books*, described what happened some time later that evening: "We'd all been to the opera, and at the restaurant afterwards Cal seemed in terrible shape—exhausted, excited, incoherent. He slumped at the table drinking glass after glass of orange juice." The next day in the hospital, "he talked in a wandering way about Alexander the Great—how Philip of Macedon had been a canny politician but Alexander had been able to cut through Asia." Lowell was treated for lithium intoxication and possible delirium at Mount Sinai Hospital; the experience left him and his friends shaken.

Some of Lowell's medical difficulties stemmed from his being treated by different doctors in different cities, including Boston, New York, and London. Dr. Curtis Prout, one of Lowell's Boston doctors, wrote to him on May 13, 1975. "A week ago, you called me because you were feeling lethargic and sleepy. You felt unwell and thought, perhaps, you needed to take more Lithium to prevent a manic attack." Lowell, he said, appeared to have increased his lithium from five tablets a day to eight and his lithium blood level was 1.5 milliequivalents per liter (mEq/L), which is in the toxic range. Dr. Prout continued, "Because I was overly concerned with the overdose, I overestimated the time it would take to reduce the Lithium in your blood." This, he explained, had resulted in too low a blood level, 0.2 mEq/L, well below the therapeutic level. The toxicity and the lowering of his lithium level almost certainly played a role in Lowell's subsequent unstable psychiatric course. If lithium is sharply decreased or stopped, it can be difficult to restabilize the illness and recapture the previous effectiveness of the drug. Mania often comes back quickly after lithium has been discontinued, and the risk of suicide increases. These things are better understood now than they were forty years ago.

From the time Lowell started taking lithium in early 1967 until his lithium toxicity in May 1975, he was hospitalized for mania only once, briefly, in 1970. After 1975 his moods were unstable and, by many accounts, he was fitful in taking his lithium. His manic attacks returned with a vengeance and he had to be admitted to the hospital several times in 1975 and 1976. In January 1976 Hardwick wrote to Mary McCarthy, "I suppose it is back to the lithium. It is a lifeline, but somehow we are all depressed about it." He was taking lithium at the time he was hospitalized for heart failure at Massachusetts General Hospital in January 1977.

Lowell died in September 1977; it is not clear what would have happened to his manic illness had he lived. What we do know is that lithium worked well for him, if problematically, for nearly ten years. He gained hope and relative stability from it. "Of all our conversations," Robert Giroux wrote after Lowell died, "I remember most vividly Cal's words about the new drug, lithium carbonate, which had such good results and gave him reason to believe he was cured: 'It's terrible, Bob, to think that all I've suffered, and all the suffering I've caused, might have arisen from the lack of a little salt in my brain.'"

Lowell had the advantage of good doctors, a good salt, and caring friends and family. But it was to his writing he turned for healing. Writing could restring the beads, mend the rent. It would require and provide the discipline and excitement of creating poetry, and it would give some solace, albeit limited, once the madness returned.

———

I am at the end of something. Up till now I've felt I was all blue spots and blotches inside, more than I could bear really, if I looked at myself, and of course I wanted to do nothing else. So day after day, I wrote. . . . I look back on the last months with disgust and gratitude. Disgust because they seem so monstrous, gratitude, because I have lived through the unintelligible, have written against collapse and come out more or less healed.

—LETTER TO ELIZABETH BISHOP, 1963

"I have a formidable new doctor," Lowell wrote to Bishop in 1965. "Maybe I'll get well, this doctor is the first I've had who is really much like an artist, though it took several days for us to speak a language intelligible to the other." The doctor, Kurt Eissler, a psychoanalyst who emigrated from Vienna to the United States in 1938 to escape Hitler, was the author of twelve books and the director of the Sigmund Freud Archives. In his two-volume study of Goethe, Eissler concluded his examination of the relationship between psychosis and artistic creativity by quoting Heinrich Heine:

> Sickness, methinks, has been the final cause
> Of the whole urge to create;
> By creating was I able to recover
> By creating I became well.

Lowell agreed with Heine, to a point. He wrote because he was a poet, not because he was ill. But, like other writers, Lowell described the solace he found in his work and the meaning it gave to him when he was depressed. Writing could keep black moods at bay; it could allow escape from pain, give purpose. It could heal. "Sometimes nothing is so solid to me as writing," Lowell wrote to Elizabeth Bishop when he was thirty-one years old. "I suppose that's what vocation means—at times a torment, a bad conscience, but all in all, purpose and direction." "If I don't write I am a blank," he told Hannah Arendt twenty years later. This is a view reminiscent of Virginia Woolf. "Directly I am not working, or see the end in sight," she wrote in her diary, "nothingness begins." She kept afloat by writing: "Directly I stop working I feel that I am sinking down, down."

Repeated attacks of mania left deep scars on both Lowell and Woolf. Time helped them to heal, but work helped more. "For the last four months I have been writing every day," Lowell wrote to his cousin shortly after being released from a hospital. "It seemed the best way to live through the slump that usually follows my attacks. . . . Now that I begin to look back, I feel as though I had been wrestling with some giant, and I say to myself, 'you've somehow survived.'" Many writers have expressed their indebtedness to writing. "I *fight* depression by work," wrote the Orkney poet George Mackay Brown. After countering darkness with new poems, he said, "I inflicted 2 bright wounds on the dragon by writing." Isak Dinesen, the author of *Out of Africa* and someone subject to debilitating depressions, said that art could bind the wounds of the mind: "All sorrows can be borne if you put them into a story or tell a story about them."

The Antarctic explorer Apsley Cherry-Garrard, a writer subject to paralyzing and, on occasion, psychotic depression, observed, "To go through a terrible time of mental and physical stress and to write it down as honestly as possible is a good way of getting some of it off your nerves. I write from personal experience." His friend, T. E. Lawrence, likewise subject to depression, had written his masterpiece *Seven Pillars of Wisdom* in the midst of "morbid self-introspection and distortions and weaknesses and fears." The fights he had with himself "were worse than anything he had with the Turks abroad, or the Foreign Office at home." He won relief to his "tortured mind" through writing, self-discipline, and self-forgetfulness, maintained Cherry-Garrard. Writing, as Lowell would put it, takes the ache away.

Writing imposes order and demands discipline. To draw down pain through meter and discipline is to tame grief, wrote John Donne:

> Then as th'earth's inward narrow crooked lanes
>   Do purge sea water's fretful salt away,
> I thought, if I could draw my pains
>   Through rhyme's vexation, I should them allay.
> Grief brought to numbers cannot be so fierce,
> For, he tames it, that fetters it in verse.

Writing also compels mental concentration. "Dejection of spirits," wrote the poet William Cowper in 1795, "which, I suppose, may have prevented many a man from becoming an author, made me one. I find constant employment necessary. . . . Manual occupations do not engage the mind sufficiently, as I know by experience, having tried many. But composition, especially of verse, absorbs it wholly."

Lowell expressed a similar view a century later. "Writing," he said, had been his "indissoluble bride for forty years":

Working, I sit groping,
monomaniacal,
jealous of even a shadow's intrusion,
a nettle
impossible to divert, deflect.

"Writing fell to me like a life-preserver," Lowell told his psychiatrist. It gave him a place to channel his excitable blood, to exert control, mount a defense against the world without, and the world within. "At last I could dominate, despise, say nothing mattered except the great works of art. I think I really cared for these, but I enjoyed using them as a battering-ram against everything and everybody who puzzled me or seemed indifferent or critical." Writing was two edged, cutting even as it gave life:

The onionskin typing paper I bought by mistake
in Bucksport Maine last August? The last sheet
creasing cuts my finger and seems to scream
as if *Fortuna* bled in the white wood
and felt the bloody gash that brought me life.

Tennyson argued that the exercise and discipline of poetry offered relief from despair. "But, for the unquiet heart and brain," he wrote in *In Memoriam*, "A use in measured language lies; / The sad mechanic exercise, / Like dull narcotics, numbing pain." Structure and purpose are required for art, but it is the gift of art to provide structure, purpose, and escape. "No one has ever written, painted, sculpted, modeled, built, or invented except literally to get out of hell," declared the French playwright and poet Antonin Artaud. The novelist Graham Greene concurred: "Sometimes I wonder how all those who do not write, compose, or paint can manage to escape the madness, the melancholia, the panic fear which is inherent in the human situation." In Lowell's 1973 appointment book, which is filled with fragments and sketches of poems, there is a single line written for February 19: "The cheer of writing that cures no physical hurt."

Transformation can heal and art can transform. There is a connection, Lowell believed, between how the world is and what the imagination comes to rest upon, what it works to transform. "What it usually

FEBRUARY 1973

19 Monday   Week 8 (50-315)

FEBRUARY
S   4 11 18 25
M   5 12 19 26
T   6 13 20 27
W   7 14 21 28
T   1   8 15 22
F   2   9 16 23
S   3 10 17 24

THe CHeen of whiThing ThaT cunos no

physical HeaT .

Excerpt from 1973 notebook
"The cheer of writing that cures no physical hurt."

lights on now is some grueling murk or release at all costs. Well, why not? It has always been so. Nothing could be more terrible than *Lear* and the *Oresteia*, both of which I have been reading. And there is no more harmless way for the elemental and black to come out than in words, paint and notes, where nothing ever can be hurt."

Lowell wrote, "I think I am escaping my destiny by writing, much, much too much my habit and even now inescapable," he observed to a friend. "At least it was absorbing. Often three or four hours would go by before I looked up, and saw low tide changed to high." Ten years later, not long before he died, he wrote in like vein to another friend. Writing salves, he said. The ambition of art gives glory, exhausts, and frays. It saves. He offered the consolation of writing, and the reality of its limits, to the poet Frank Bidart:

I gather from your phone calls the summer has had some very hard moments for you. It's miraculous, as you told me about yourself, how often writing takes the ache away, takes time away. You start in the morning, and look up to see the windows darkening. I'm sure anything done steadily, obsessively, eyes closed to everything besides the page, the spot of garden . . . makes returning a jolt. The world you've been saved from grasps you roughly. Even sleep and dreams do this. I have no answer. I think the ambition of art, the feeding on one's soul, memory, mind etc. gives a mixture of glory and exhaustion. I think in the end, there is no end, the thread frays rather than

Hydrotherapy room, Payne Whitney Clinic
"Why don't I die, die?"

is cut, or if it is cut suddenly, it usually hurtingly frays before being cut. No perfected end, but a lot of meat and drink along the way.

In a poem published a few months later, Lowell put forward the question at the heart of it all: the ambition of art, the tending of the soul, the healing of the mind. "Is getting well ever an art," he asked, "or art a way to get well?"

In September 1954, after a four-month hospital stay in the Payne Whitney Clinic, Robert Lowell went home to Boston. Within weeks he began work on an autobiography, in part at the suggestion of his psychiatrist, Dr. Vernon Williams, who believed that writing down his early memories would help him piece together and make sense of his childhood. There were other reasons. Lowell was finding it difficult to write poetry, and both he and Hardwick had come to believe, as had his mother ten years earlier, that writing prose was less likely than writing poetry to set off the kind of excited state, the enthusiasm, that led to mania. (The relationship between writing and mania was more complicated than this. Lowell was also more likely to write poetry when he started to become manic.) The border between enthusiasm and mania was permeable for Lowell; he crossed it with abandon. The words "enthusiasm" and "pathological enthusiasm" held heavier meaning for Lowell than for most; they were words he often used to describe his manic attacks.

Lowell dredged his memory in the belief that it would lead him somewhere he wanted to go. It did, but not without frustration. Prose was more difficult than he had imagined. "I've just started messing around with my autobiographical monster," he wrote to John Berryman in October 1954. "Prose is hell. I want to change every two words, but while I toy with revisions, the subject stinks like a dead whale and lies in the mud of the mind's bottom." He found it difficult to keep from veering into "intolerable poetic darknesses." To Flannery O'Connor, whom he regarded as a master of prose, he lamented, "I find it hard to be neither sugary nor acid; and Oh the effort to keep one's eyes open and see what one describes!" His struggle between poetic and prose expression did not go away. He wrote to Elizabeth Bishop years later, "How different prose is; sometimes the two mediums refuse to say the same things." Without verse, he said, and without philosophy, "I found it hard, I was naked without my line-ends."

Lowell's criticism of his prose was misplaced; "91 Revere Street," "New England and Further," and "Near the Unbalanced Aquarium" are remarkable works. If they were fitfully created—drafted, redrafted, and revised yet again—then so too was his poetry. His writing came first from the creating, then from revising, chiseling; from reworking shards that he set together, ripped apart, rearranged, reimagined, and changed, at times beyond recognition.

"Near the Unbalanced Aquarium," an account of Lowell's 1954 stay in Payne Whitney, is an unmatched portrayal of madness and life on a psychiatric ward. Threaded through his recollections of mania are memories of his childhood and descriptions of his parents, many of which he took later into the poems and prose of *Life Studies*. Even the title of his essay was unsettled: in the first six drafts the title object was a "balanced" aquarium; by the final version, published after his death and considerably altered in content and style from the drafts, it had shifted to "unbalanced." Lowell liked the aquarium metaphor. Five years earlier, during his first stay in Payne Whitney, he had likened psychotherapy to "stirring up the bottom of an aquarium." The ward's aquarium, Lowell wrote, was "a huge affair with snails, sanitary plants, little fish with seven tails, midget sunfish and midget silver tarpon." The day nurse complained that none of the other nurses "understood 'balance' but were always casting breadcrumbs and dead flies on the waters, so that the fish and snails didn't know whether they were coming or going. I made my worn-out joke about the aquarium being a sanitarium within a sanitarium, 'only I'm not on display.'"

Later, in "For the Union Dead," the aquarium would take on a different meaning: the old South Boston Aquarium would be an image of decay with its broken, boarded windows, a child's tracing hand, scaling weather vane, and dry tanks filled with the memory of "cowed compliant fish." Memories of his madness and childhood floated up from the bottom of his mind, mixed in with recollections of his agitated days as a patient in a psychiatric hospital. The chips of memory move restlessly within the frame of "Near the Unbalanced Aquarium." The movement of the separate yet meshing parts is fluid, perturbed. His mind, he said, "remained in its recollections, weightless, floating."

Lowell was admitted to the hospital "trying as usual to get my picture of myself straight." Once again he had known "the yeasty manic lift of my illness"; once again he had been struck by "a violent manic seizure, an attack of pathological enthusiasm." Everything—his mind, his marriage, his work—was in flux. Even the walls of the Payne Whitney Clinic, like the workings of his mind, "seemed to change shape like limp white clouds." He likened the hospital to "that island in the Seine, a little Manhattan with river water on both sides, the island of King Louis's Sainte-Chapelle, all heraldry and color and all innocent, built to house a thorn!" The associative path his ill mind took was to suffering and beauty. The medieval chapel, it is said, houses the crown of thorns worn by Christ. I have been Christ, Lowell had told his doctor. I have walked on the Sea of Galilee; I have known Christ's suffering, the thorns he wore. Had Christ borne toward the lee shore as he walked on the Galilee? Lowell surely had.

The hospital in its own way was like Sainte-Chapelle, "purely and

puritanically confined to its office of cures." Lowell was in no doubt
that his mind was in need of curing. He had become unhinged after his
mother's death and had fast-edged into mania. "Tireless, madly sanguine, menaced, and menacing," he had entered the Payne Whitney
Clinic "for all those afflicted in mind." He seesawed from deranged to
torpid, watched as his mind chased "its own shuffle down the empty
ward."

Dr. James Masterson, Lowell's doctor during his 1954 Payne Whitney admission, recorded in Lowell's medical chart the changes in his
clinical condition. ("Was I paying Dr. Masterson to talk to me or to listen?" asked Lowell. He "sat in his white smock, like the Snow Queen.")
Later, in "Near the Unbalanced Aquarium," Lowell gave his own version of his mental state and behavior during that time. The contrast
between the sparse language of clinical observation and the writing
of a poet is striking, if not unexpected. Most of the events that Lowell
describes in "Near the Unbalanced Aquarium" are documented in Dr.
Masterson's medical notes. Tellingly, Lowell does not write about the
subject he broached most often with his doctor: his unshakeable fear
that he would go mad again.

Dr. Masterson:

*The patient began showing signs of going into another manic attack.
He became aggressive, over-talkative, over-active, tense, hostile with
much sexual talk. . . . Another patient was reading F. S. Fitzgerald
to Miss A. Patient grabbed him off the couch by his feet. Singing at
the top of his voice in the lounge. Breaking rules on the floor. Transferred to the 7S floor.*

Lowell:

Suddenly I felt I could clear the air by taking hold of Roger's
ankles and pulling him off his chair. . . . Without warning, but
without lowering my eyes from Anna's splendid breastplate
blouse, I seized Roger's yellow ankles and pulled. Roger sat on
the floor with tears in his eyes. A sigh of surprised revulsion
went round the room. . . .

Next morning, while I was weighing in and "purifying"
myself in the cold shower, I sang

Rex tremendae majestatis
qui salvandos salvas gratis

at the top of my lungs and to a melody of my own devising. Like the catbird, who will sometimes "interrupt its sweetest song by a perfect imitation of some harsh cry such as that of the great crested flycatcher, the squawk of a hen, the cry of a lost chicken, or the spitting of a cat," I blended the lonely tenor of some fourteenth-century Flemish monk to bars of "Yankee Doodle," and the *mmm-mmm* of the padlocked Papageno. I was then transferred to a new floor, where the patients were deprived of their belts, pajama cords, and shoestrings. We were not allowed to carry matches, and had to request the attendants to light our cigarettes.

Dr. Masterson:

He was started on Chlorpromazine treatment. The dose was started at 15 mg. qid [four times a day] and gradually worked up to 200 mg. qid. The patient's subjective response was "feeling restless and weighed down." "I feel as though I'm carrying 150 lbs. of concrete in a race." "I feel slow witted and helpless." Likes to play badminton but tires easily.

Lowell:

For holding up my trousers, I invented an inefficient, stringless method which I considered picturesque and called Malayan. Each morning before breakfast, I lay naked to the waist in my knotted Malayan pajamas and received the first of my round-the-clock injections of chloropromazene [*sic*]: left shoulder, right shoulder, right buttock, left buttock. My blood became like melted lead. I could hardly swallow my breakfast, because I so dreaded the weighted bending down that would be necessary for making my bed. And the rational exigencies of bed-making were more upsetting than the physical. I wallowed through badminton doubles, as though I were a diver in the full billowings of his equipment on the bottom of the sea. I sat gaping through Scrabble games, unable to form the simplest word; I had to be prompted by a nurse, and even then couldn't make any sense of the words the nurse had formed for me.

Dr. Masterson:

Patient desires peace. Patient discussed his drab feelings of hollowness and withdrawal. Blankness, fatigue, despondent.

Lowell:

"Why don't I die, die?" I quizzed myself of suicide in the mirror. . . . I suspected that my whole soul and its thousands of spiritual fibers, immaterial ganglia, apprehensive antennae, psychic radar, and so on, had been bruised by a rubber hose.

The concise language of the physician stands in distinction to the words of the poet, words that are inward, direct, dense, and hopeful of healing. Lowell's words are vivid; he describes a world as though it is important that we *see* the place. Important for its writer, important for the reader. "Near the Unbalanced Aquarium" bears witness to that hope, to the promise of art and the possibility of solace. "I am writing my autobiography literally to 'pass the time,'" Lowell wrote at the end of his essay. "I almost doubt if the time would pass at all otherwise. However, I also hope the result will supply me with swaddling clothes, with a sort of immense bandage of grace and ambergris for my hurt nerves."

This book is in part about mania and depression and how, at times, they serve art. What Lowell knew, as did many writers before and since, is that art also serves the writer who is ill. Not perfectly, seldom lastingly, but essentially. Words heal, provide a bandage of grace, give meaning and moment to awful things. The Gettysburg Address, Lowell said, was a "symbolic and sacramental act"; it gave meaning to what the war had wrought. Through his words Lincoln had given the field of battle "a symbolic significance that it had lacked." Words give meaning to the battle.

Robert Lowell in Boston, 1959
"These are the tranquillized Fifties,
and I am forty."

Rowan tree with berries

"Into its emptiness, there grew a solitary, beautiful, rusty-red-leafed rowan tree."

How Will the Heart Endure?

Your lacerations tell the losing game
You play against a sickness past your cure.
How will the hands be strong? How will the heart endure?

—*From* "Mr. Edwards and the Spider"

9

With All My Love, Cal

Bringing ice out from the kitchen, Cal stops in the warm gloom of the unpainted passageway, puts the ice-bucket down on the plank floor, and scootches to the fruit-crate level inhabited by Harriet's pets. As Harriet tends them, Cal tends her. . . . He hugs her to his shoulder with total gentleness. Then, with no perceptible transition, he picks up the ice-bucket, and lugs his whole grizzly-bear frame back over the transom into the adult barn.
—Philip Booth, "Summers in Castine"

Robert Lowell had a severe form of manic-depressive illness. When mania came, it was brutal; when it left there remained depression, remorse, and the certainty it would be back. Yet Lowell endured the kind of suffering that brings most to their knees or to suicide. And, more remarkably, he did it without irredeemably ceding his work, dignity, or friendships. Courage, which he had in measure, could not change the course of his illness, but it was determinative in how he dealt with the pain and fear that came with mania and depression. He studied the actions of courageous men with the kind of care he studied other poets.

Lowell's character, upbringing, and intellect were central to his survival. He was disciplined and had a stone will, a mind that learned from adversity, and character and imagination that put the learning to good use. He believed he could shape his fate and, to an unlikely extent, he did. Like Thoreau, he believed that man could elevate his life by conscious endeavor; he believed he could choose what to resist, what to worship, what to pursue. And he worked remarkably hard. He loved his work, drew from it. He didn't give up. He had the capacity to regrow, regenerate, and heal.

Robert Lowell survived his repeated attacks of mania through courage and discipline, definingly; work, most sustainingly; family and friends, essentially. But it was complicated. He was among the sanest of men, his friends said, except when he was ill; during those times they scarcely recognized him. He became then everything he was not when he was well: unkind, arrogant, and incomprehending. Those closest to him came to understand the madness that twisted him from Jekyll into Hyde. Mania lay dormant most of the time. Now and again it broke out, and when it did, it seared everyone. His family, friends, and colleagues had to learn to disentangle his personality and character from his disease, had somehow to reconcile the wrenching contrast between Lowell when sane and Lowell when ill.

Lowell for his part had each time to grapple his way back from madness, face embarrassment and worse among his family and friends, students and colleagues, and return to writing. He had to make sense of what mania had done to him and what his manic cruelty had done to others. It was one thing to regret the hurt he had caused, another to heal a bruised marriage or friendship. Repairing the damage done by mania was made more difficult by the depression that came in its wake. Lowell felt lasting remorse for things he had done—he made this particularly clear to the doctors who treated him—but more than anyone he knew the limits of apology, the limits to which wrongs could be righted. In addition to confronting the pain his illness caused others, and the shame he felt from his often public behavior, he had to face the certainty that his madness would come back.

Getting well, repairing that which had been damaged, facing the inevitability of another attack: each required courage and time. Each required underlying psychological health, however eroded, on which he could draw and which he needed to replenish. Lowell wrote of erosion and rebuilding in a letter to Elizabeth Bishop in 1964: "I think of my life with its recovery from steps into disintegration. There must be a huge hunk of health that has survived and somehow increased through all these breakdown[s], eight or nine, I think, in about fifteen years. Pray god there'll be no more." It was as if, as Henry Adams put it, his identity remained but "his life was once more broken into separate pieces." As the spider did, he had to "spin a new web in some new place with a new attachment."

Lowell brought a complex and uniquely observant mind to understanding the effects of his madness on his friends and family. Toward the end of his life, when his illness had come back full force and he knew that his mind would not hold, he wrote about it without self-pity. When he was a young man he had described the fear and uncertainty he faced: "You play against a sickness past your cure," he had written. "How will the hands be strong? How will the heart endure?" The questioning proved elemental from youth to death.

Lowell sustained himself with books and ideas, of course. In addition to literature—Dante, Milton, Hardy, Homer, Virgil, Hawthorne, Melville, so many—he drew upon his passion for history, paintings, the late music of Schubert and Beethoven. He looked to the lives of other poets, to history and myth, and to the ancient exemplars for a path through uncertainty. He availed himself of the strength of his Protestantism and recognized its weaknesses; then, for a while, he turned to the theology and rites of Catholicism. He found peace in fishing, albeit in a distracted, falling in the water sort of way, holding on to the pleasure he had taken casting for bass in New England ponds when he was a child. He looked to figures such as John Crowe Ransom and his cousin Harriet Winslow for the acceptance and affection he had not received from his parents as a child.

Like Henry Adams, Lowell sought out those who could teach him. His decision as a young man to leave Harvard, his parents, and New England was one of the most important he made. He chose possibility over predictability and the exertion of will over hopelessness, choices he would make in one form or another for the rest of his life. He made decisions when he was well that secured against the damage he did when he was ill.

Lowell learned early how to take advantage of the sea when it was fair. When he was well he headed under his own sail to ports of his own determining; when he could not make harbor on his own, he rode in tow as best he could. As a young man, he had written of the choice he was to make time and again throughout his life:

> The channel gripped our hull, we could not veer,
> the boat swam shoreward flying our wet shirts,
> like a birchlog shaking off loose bark and shooting:
> *And the surf thundered fireworks on the dunes.*
> This was the moment to choose, as school warned us,
> whether to wreck or ride in tow to port.

Lowell endured because he was tough, because when he was well he made good decisions, and because his work gave him reason to live. He also endured because he had an unusual capacity for friendship. He was a good friend and someone who elicited loyalty in others. His friends described him as deeply loyal, generous, principled, witty, and quick to recognize and encourage the ability of other poets. He was known as a gentle and kind man when he was well. That he was well most of the time is underappreciated; the shadow cast by his illness was long.

"Cal was a big man in bulk but an extremely gentle, poignant person, and very funny," said the poet Derek Walcott. "I don't think any of the biographies have caught the sort of gentle, amused, benign beauty of him when he was calm." Lowell's gentleness was intrinsic to who he was, Walcott added. So too was the immediacy of his person and his openness to new experience. People who met Lowell tended to remember him, in part because he was one of the most famous poets of his time, of course, but also because of the strength of his personality, his distinctive appearance, and his disheveled dignity and wit.

Lowell was "attractive, rather feverish-faced," observed Joyce Carol Oates. "He carried himself with an air of ironic dignity." He was "achingly well-mannered," James Atlas said. He was tall, had arrestingly blue eyes—"troubled blue eyes, intense and roving behind the thick glasses, rarely [coming] to rest," according to Stanley Kunitz—an energetic way of jabbing his hands in the air to make a point, and a patrician disarray; he was said to drop shirt buttons, manuscripts, cigarette ash, and magazines in his wake and to lose his way as often as he found it. He was a relentless chain-smoker. "The ashtray was heaped with bent and broken half-smoked cigarettes," remembers Atlas. "Lowell wasn't one of those smokers who exhale in vigorous plumes; he smoked as if it made him ill. His skin had a mushroom-like pallor; his tie was streaked with ash."

His accent was notable, as much for what it was not, patrician Boston, as for what it was: a bit southern, a bit Boston, a bit unplaceable. His voice, said the poet Robert Shaw, was "a drawl, quizzical and wavering, dipping into throatiness, it was Tennessee with some of the softness taken out, given a tough New England edge." Words and ideas flew. "At submanic velocity the man was truly amazing," Dudley Young recalled of Lowell's days in England. The range of his conversation was "dazzling, the anecdotes endless and funny and fine." Jason Epstein added that Lowell's words "seemed to come out all in a heap as though they were dumped from a suitcase."

"Lowell was the most engaging man, very kind," Peter Levi, the Oxford Professor of Poetry, recalled at the time of Lowell's death. "He was a man one actually loved." "I feel almost too much about him to be able to get to the heart of it," Flannery O'Connor said of Lowell. "He is one of the people I love." Donald Jenkins, a student in Lowell's writing seminar, described Lowell as "really a kind, intimately friendly man." In addition to helping him with his writing, he said, Lowell had offered to pay for an operation that his wife needed. Isaiah Berlin commented, as did many, on his simultaneously civilized and engaging nature. "Everyone likes him," he wrote.

Not everyone, but most. A cloud of rumor and drama, not untinged by envy, tended to precede and follow Lowell. Poets, students, and friends described the contrast between the literary gossip and how they actually found him. The poet W. D. Snodgrass, who studied with Lowell, wrote about the discrepancy between Lowell's reputation for erratic behavior and who he turned out to be upon getting to know him: "Until his arrival he was the one topic of conversation: The time he'd done as a conscientious objector, his periods of madness, his past violence. We were surprised to find that, though tall and powerfully built, he seemed the gentlest of mortals, clumsily anxious to please." Likewise, William Phillips, the editor of the *Partisan Review*, wrote: "In the name of his art and his psychological needs, Lowell has been said to have done many reprehensible things. But I always found him gentle, sweet, and considerate—if somewhat wild."

Lowell's daughter, Harriet Lowell, and his stepdaughters, Evgenia Citkowitz and Ivana Lowell, describe him as a parent who was tender and sympathetic, unusually attuned to their emotional needs as children and adolescents. Evgenia recollects that although she never saw Lowell when he was manic (her mother sent her to the Hebrides when he was hospitalized in 1970; she was away at school at other times when he was ill), she could sense his psychological frailty. Ivana states that she "adored" him. When she was burned over most of her body in an accident as a young child—still in "the last madness of child-gaiety," he wrote in a poem for her, "before the trouble of the world shall hit"— Lowell spread a towel on the floor of her hospital room and slept by her bed. The words used time and again by his daughter and step-daughters are "kind," "gentle," and "sensitive."

Elizabeth Bishop, one of Lowell's closest friends, said, "I loved him at first sight." He was "rumpled," in need of a haircut, and "handsome in an almost old-fashioned poetic way. I took to him at once." She remembers that Lowell, aware that she was somewhat intimidated by him, tried hard to put her at ease. "Kindness has always been the dominant note in his attitude to me, over many years, and shown in many ways." They respected each other's poetry and were sympathetic to the tumultuous circumstances of each other's lives. Each was a great poet; each had more than his or her share of psychological problems and complicated relationships. Each had a brilliance that the other understood and encouraged; they were competitive but neither felt substantially threatened by the other.

"There's no one else I can quite talk to with confidence and abandon

Robert Lowell and Elizabeth Bishop, Rio de Janeiro, 1962
"I always feel a great blytheness and easiness with you."

and delicacy," Lowell wrote. "I think of you daily and feel anxious lest we lose our old backward and forward flow that always seems to open me up and bring color and peace." Bishop expressed a similar indebtedness: "Dearest Cal," she wrote. "Please never stop writing me letters—they always manage to make me feel like my higher self." During a dark time in her life, she wrote to him, she had felt "just the faintest glimmer" that she would "get out of this somehow, alive. Meanwhile—your letter has helped tremendously—like being handed a lantern, or a spiked walking stick." They handed off lanterns for twenty-five years.

Lowell and Bishop dedicated poems to each other (Bishop's "Armadillo" to Lowell, Lowell's "Skunk Hour" to Bishop); each was a sharp but generous critic of the other's work. They wrote poems about their friendship and common ties: New England, other poets and poetry, the depression that both were heir to. "Water," a poem written by Lowell about their relationship, began, he told her, "from thinking about your letter, how indispensable you are to me, and how ideally we've really kept things, better than life allows really." The mood, the gray-green rocks and movement of the sea, her physical form, and the shape of their relationship, were mutable; his caring was not:

> It was a Maine lobster town—
> each morning boatloads of hands
> pushed off for granite
> quarries on the islands,
>
> and left dozens of bleak
> white frame houses stuck
> like oyster shells
> on a hill of rock,
>
> and below us, the sea lapped
> the raw little match-stick
> mazes of a weir,
> where the fish for bait were trapped.
>
> Remember? We sat on a slab of rock.
> From this distance in time,
> it seems the color
> of iris, rotting and turning purpler,

but it was only
the usual gray rock
turning the usual green
when drenched by the sea.

The sea drenched the rock
at our feet all day,
and kept tearing away
flake after flake.

One night you dreamed
you were a mermaid clinging to a wharf-pile,
and trying to pull
off the barnacles with your hands.

We wished our two souls
might return like gulls
to the rock. In the end,
the water was too cold for us.

Bishop had her own memories of Lowell, her sense of what was constant; she left them in an unfinished manuscript:

Swimming, or rather standing, numb to the waist in the freezing cold water, but continuing to talk. If I were to think of any Saint in his connection then it is St. Sebastian—he stood in a rocky basin of the freezing water, sloshing it over his handsome youthful body and I could almost see the arrows sticking out of him.

His courage—kindness—increasing good manners—gentleness with his daughter—capacity for work—

Her manuscript ends abruptly, tellingly, on his gentleness and work.

Lowell took an "inexhaustible pleasure" in being with his friends, said Alan Williamson, spending "whole day[s] together, reading each other's new work, taking walks, drinking white wine through dinner, and long after. He showed affection easily and without embarrassment. . . . willingly used his own prestige to 'throw a lifeline' to others." Elizabeth Bishop was one of those on the receiving end of such a lifeline. In a statement read at his memorial service in London, she said, "I know that he used his influence to be helpful to me personally in more than one difficult period of my life—acts of kindness I learned of only later and by chance." Others took a different kind of lifeline from how he dealt with his suffering. "In my middle age, haunted by fears and hints that I have lost my way," wrote Donald Davie to Lowell, "I hold by the thought of you and the image of you." At social gatherings Lowell often gravitated toward those who looked in a bad state and tried to pull them out of their depression. "There was a kind of litmus quality about his sensibility," said William Alfred. "I suppose it was the suffering that he, that he himself went through."

Lowell's oldest friends, Frank Parker and Blair Clark, said that Lowell, an intensely loyal person, put a particularly high value on loyalty. "I have never had a more loyal friend, ever," said Frank Parker. Clark agreed. "One of the most extraordinary things about Cal was something you had to call loyalty. In our little cabal at St. Mark's [School] loyalty was the first principle, imposed by Cal." "It wasn't a fearful, defensive loyalty," he explained. "It was something that Cal felt essential to his own peculiar ideas of human relations and what was worth doing in life." Loyalty was part of a code of conduct that Lowell established for himself when he was young; it strengthened his ability to survive as life became harder. "I think he never really ever lost a friend," observed William Alfred. "His heart was as large as his mind." Lowell, recounts Parker's daughter, the reporter and producer Diantha Parker, "was a supremely challenging and demanding friend, but he was a loyal and grateful one to the end. This constancy was part of Lowell's lightness, the side of him my father wished more people understood."

Lowell was a complicated man, made more complicated by an illness that periodically and radically changed his personality and behavior. He was a study in contradiction. His manic-depressive illness gave an aura of tragedy to his life, said a friend, but it was a darkness that fiercely contrasted with "his gaiety, his love of life, and his extraordinary intelligence." The contrast in Lowell's behavior when he was well and ill was stark. Stanley Kunitz said that Lowell was someone who could be "modest and arrogant, tender and mean, generous and indifferent, masterful and helpless, depressed and manic." He was "knowing about fame and power, but no less knowing about his weaknesses." There could be an edge, acknowledged Seamus Heaney. "You never felt quite safe with him but neither did you ever feel sold short." The health of his mind and moods determined everything. Most who knew him acknowledged his frightening, disturbing behavior but put it in the context of a wider caring. "All flaws considered," wrote Norman Mailer, "Lowell was still a fine, good, and honorable man."

Lowell's student and friend Kathleen Spivack has described the contrasting sides of his personality. Lowell, she wrote, was "complex, tortured, and difficult, with multiple breakdowns, a horror of them, and a lot of ambition and dark streaks mixed in." At the same time, she continued, "his darting sudden insights, humor, kindness, and generosity prevailed, despite and beyond the illness and difficult part of his character." Lowell also exuded a potentially dangerous sexuality, she added. "If pulled into the sexual orbit of this extremely attractive person, one would be burnt to cinders." But, first and foremost, she said, he was a man "I deeply loved." He was "a great friend and a great poet."

Lowell was larger than life, said William Alfred. It was an observation made by many. "He was great fun," Alfred said. "He loved to laugh." His wives Elizabeth Hardwick and Caroline Blackwood, as well as many of his friends, said that Lowell enhanced the world around him, gave an added depth to life, and made it more exciting. Frank Parker, his childhood friend, remarked that Lowell made life difficult, at times very difficult, but he also made it more vivid: "The world became larger," Parker said. "Somehow, things glowed. . . . Everything became *more.*" Caroline Blackwood said much the same thing. "He had that quality, that he could make the dullest thing, like going to pick up the laundry, seem exciting." He had such intensity "that if he read something aloud you felt: you won't hear this again." His artistic vision was often dark and desperate, she acknowledged, but as a person "he wasn't dark at all."

Lowell was "very sociable, curious, fond of a large number of people," Elizabeth Hardwick said. He never seemed to have enough of life, seemed never to tire. The capacity for joy was not that far from the capacity for despair. "Everything about him was outsized: his learning, his patience with his work, his dedication, and the pattern of his troubled life. I think it is true, as he said, that he knew a lot of happiness in each of his decades, happiness that is when he was fortunately for such long creative and private periods 'himself.'" Lowell "took up all the air in a room," Hardwick told the writer and editor Wendy Lesser. It was not meant as a criticism; rather, "it was meant to suggest what a substantial and attractive if difficult person he was—that he was essentially the only person you could pay attention to when he was around."

Jonathan Raban, who for a while lived in Blackwood and Lowell's downstairs flat in London, said, "There was no point at which he was not more vividly alive, and thinking, and feeling and playing with words and inventive than anyone I've ever met. To the point at which there is an awful flatness left in the world after his death; one has absolutely no conviction that one is going to meet anyone who is as vivid to one as Cal was vivid."

Such intensity was not for everyone. Even Raban had a limit. Lowell staged a reenactment of Napoleon's war against Russia—using full ashtrays and empty wineglasses as soldiers—taking much of a day. He exhausted friends and students with his nonstop manic and submanic dialogues about poets and poetry. "There were times toward the end [when Lowell was increasingly ill] when I got tired out by Cal. One was drawn into a [manic] labyrinth of somebody else's total egotism. . . . I was used up by it," Raban wrote. Stephen Spender, although he too liked and admired Lowell, said, "I felt that I couldn't bear to be with him for hours on end. I felt this kind of pressure of his personality." Jonathan Miller found Lowell overwhelming, dominating, and draining and felt the need to pull himself out of the Lowell orbit. Intensity, especially when it takes on a manic hue, is often oppressive.

Lowell could be great fun and fill the room with his personality; when he was manic, he could horrify and humiliate those he most loved. But laughter was much more a part of him than were his manic springs for the jugular. The poet Alan Brownjohn described a raucous, laughter-filled dinner at one of Lowell's favorite restaurants in London. They had drunk their full share of wine and whiskey and were several sheets to the wind. "I can remember being unable to find my avocado with my spoon," recalled Brownjohn. Lowell, for his part, was "shooting escargots out of the nutcracker thing that you crack them with and two of these things hit me in the chest." The evening flew on from there.

Shooting snails across a table to great hoots of laughter is not the image people have of Robert Lowell. But laughter is a defining memory held by those who knew him best. Laughter, and an appreciation for the things in life that bind: summer evenings with friends and family, martinis, rescuing a turtle lost on the road. Normal times and fellowship. Lowell caught the hours: "We gossiped on the rocks of the millpond," he wrote of a summer evening, and "baked things in shells on the sand, and drank, as was the appetite of our age." Perhaps life was deeper, simpler for its drops into desperation.

Lowell was a teacher as well as a friend. He was anything but conventional in his approach to teaching—untidy and distractible, an idiosyncratic wanderer in words and chains of ideas who, now and again, had to be taken off to a psychiatric hospital—but he made a difference in the lives of many of his students. Anne Sexton was a student in his poetry class at Boston University, which was taught in a room she described as "a bleak spot, as if it had been forgotten for years, like the spinning room in Sleeping Beauty's castle." Lowell worked "with a cold chisel" on her poems, she wrote, and "showed no more mercy than a dentist. He gets out the decay." But, she added, "if he is never kind to the poem, he is kind to the poet." He taught his students what to leave out of their poems, she said. He taught taste. He taught them to set higher hurdles for themselves, then run the course.

Lowell's preternatural, scholarly knowledge of poetry and history, along with his infectious excitement for writing and ideas, had a lasting effect on many of his students, as did his expectation of seriousness and excellence. His mind, naturally wide flung and associative, brought to life long-dead writers and their worlds and made connections between eras and ideas that students might come to understand only days or months after leaving his seminar. "Week after week," said W. D. Snodgrass, "we came away staggered under a bombardment of ideas, ideas, ideas. None of these works would ever look the same again." When Lowell took on a student's poem for analysis, "it was as if a muscle-bound octopus sat down over it. Then, deliberately, it stretched out one tentacle to haul in Mythology, a second for Sociology, a third for Classical Literature, others for Religion, History, Psychology. Meantime, you sat there thinking, 'This man *is* as mad as they said; none of this has anything to do with my poor, little poem!' Then he began to tie these disciplines, one by one, into your text; you saw that it *did* have to do, had almost everything to do, with your poem." Lowell set out a vast canvas before his students, the one upon which he himself drew. If it was at times incomprehensible, it was yet one of erudition and covenant. Lowell, Snodgrass said, hauled his students with him, "through uncharted galaxies of idea and association. Who could feel less than grateful for a mind so unpredictable, so massive, so concerned?"

With unusual exception, Lowell's students admired and liked him, but the possibility that he would become ill while he was teaching was disturbing for more than a few. This was particularly true in his last years at Harvard when his precarious sanity and overshadowing reputation as a poet made the anticipation of his presence in the classroom at times charged and uncomfortable. Students competed and scrambled to be accepted into his seminars, but, once there, they were uncertain about what to expect. "I was disquieted, as I think many others were, by apprehensions of his vulnerability," said the poet Robert Shaw, "of what seemed a perilously delicate equilibrium that he was effortfully maintaining. Everyone knew his history of manic-depressive episodes; several times during his years of teaching at Harvard his courses were interrupted when he withdrew for treatment." Students, he said, were deferential to Lowell because he was a great poet, but the deference was "laced with a fear of inadvertently saying *the wrong thing*, abrading nerves that were already rubbed raw." Kathleen Spivack recalled that "once during class he was pushing on the window ledge, had one leg over, students thought he was going to jump out the window. He went into the hospital right after that."

It is hard to imagine what it was like for students to witness the transformation of their professor from famed poet into psychotic stranger. It is likewise hard to imagine how difficult it must have been for Lowell to face his students after he was released from the hospital, knowing how aberrantly he had behaved. Anne Sexton, who often acknowledged Lowell's kindness and support for her work, and like him received a Pulitzer Prize for poetry, also like him spent time as a patient at McLean Hospital. In "Elegy in the Classroom" she wrote:

> In the thin classroom, where your face
> was noble and your words were all things,
> I find this boily creature in your place;
>
> find you disarranged, squatting on the window sill,
> irrefutably placed up there,
> like a hunk of some big frog

watching us through the V
of your woolen legs.

Even so, I must admire your skill.
You are so gracefully insane.
We fidget in our plain chairs
and pretend to catalogue
our facts for your burly sorcery

or ignore your fat blind eyes
or the prince you ate yesterday
who was wise, wise, wise.

Less to the gut but powerful, Derek Walcott drew the contrast between Lowell's gentleness and the lingering presence of his madness:

Cal's bulk haunts my classes. The shaggy, square head tilted,
the mist of heated affection blurring his glasses,
slumped, but the hands repeatedly bracketing vases
of air, the petal-soft voice that has never wilted—
its flowers of illness carpet the lanes of Cambridge,
and the germ of madness is here.

Not everyone was able to accept or live through Lowell's attacks of mania; some had to distance themselves until he was well again. Staying away was understandable. Lowell experienced full-bore madness, not the pastel version of mental illness portrayed in drug company advertisements as containable, acceptable, simplistically treatable. Kathleen Spivack, a young woman at the time she first met Lowell, said that she was "incapable of dealing with Lowell's breakdowns, so I stood outside his inner circle in that respect. . . . I never was able to shake a slight fear of his unpredictability, the flashes of cruelty that could and did emerge." William Meredith wrote to Lowell in similar vein. His silence, he explained, was not "altogether cowardice, but a sense of my being necessarily in exile when that part of you is in power. But you know, too, it is not unconcern." Lowell, for his part, understood the difficulty. "There was no point in getting in touch with me," he wrote to Meredith. "I know all too much about the uninstructed heart, and it is wearisome and quite fruitless for human ears to try and catch its clamorous babble."

Some colleagues found it difficult to understand Lowell's mania; it was not so much that they withdrew until the storm had blown through, it was that they attributed his madness to weakness in character or self-indulgence. This is not an uncommon reaction to mental illness even now, although there is more public awareness about mania and depression. The critic and poet William Empson, who had received at least one profoundly delusional letter from Lowell comparing himself to an electroshock-treated Christ, told Jonathan Raban, "There's nothing wrong with the man at all. Just one of those things that Americans invent." Empson was one of several who never grasped the extent of Lowell's illness and who failed to recognize, in Elizabeth Hardwick's words, the "incredible flow of energy, the streams of incredible madness." (Empson did go forward during a poetry reading to embrace Lowell, who, just recovering from a breakdown, was shaking violently.) W. H. Auden too was left unmoved by Lowell's suffering. Anthony Hecht recalls telling Auden about Lowell's breakdown in Salzburg in 1952, expecting from him "some grunt of commiseration, at least." There was none. "He regarded Lowell's whole tortured history of crack-ups as pure self-indulgence and undeserving of any sympathy." Auden, it was said, had joked that John Berryman had written in his suicide note: "Your move, Cal." There was no note.

William James, perhaps because he knew mental suffering so well himself, had given a broader berth of explanation to illnesses of the mind. In 1901, after Henry Adams's brother-in-law killed himself, James wrote a letter of consolation to his daughter. "Not only death but all forms of decay knock at our gate," he wrote to her. "We must house it and suffer it and take whatever it brings for sake of the ends that are certainly being fulfilled by its means, behind the screen." Her father's death proved the separation of character and disease, how "purely extraneous" and disconnected they were. The cause, he continued, was "probably an internally generated poison in the blood which 'science' any day may learn how to eliminate or neutralize, and so make all of these afflictions so many nightmares of the past."

No one understood better or went through more of the best and the most difficult of Robert Lowell than did Elizabeth Hardwick. She has been portrayed as a martyr to Lowell's illness, infidelities, and verbal cruelty, yet those who knew her well disagree. Even a cursory look at her work, letters, and interviews makes clear that she was more than able to sort through and live with their complex marriage and friendship. It was not an easy relationship but it was a lasting one that both took meaning in. In substantial ways she provided the love, respect, and constancy that many other writers' husbands and wives, such as Leonard Woolf and Sophia Hawthorne, have provided over the years. Sophia Hawthorne, for one, understood that her husband, brooding and difficult and a genius, needed long periods of time to himself if he was to write and keep psychologically afloat; he also needed a highly regimented lifestyle, a tight routine of meals, sleep, writing, and friends. Hawthorne's prickly and frail temperament required tending: "He cannot bear anything," she wrote. "He must be handled like the airiest

Elizabeth Hardwick, 1983
"my wife . . . your lightness alters everything,
and tears the black web from the spider's sack."

venetian glass." His dark moods took their toll. "I have been weighed to the earth by my sense of thy depressed energies and spirits in a way from which I tried in vain to rally," she wrote to him. "This wrenching off thy wings and hanging dead upon thy arrowy feet." Her frustration would be familiar to anyone who has lived with a depressed spouse: "So apathetic, so indifferent, so hopeless, so unstrung."

Yet exasperation not uncommonly exists alongside love, in the midst of relationships of great caring. It is in the nature of depression and mania to be complicated, hard, and insinuating. Moods are contagious—depressive, joyous, infuriating. They change, damage, and enrich. Husbands and wives have understood this, and poets have written about it, for centuries. Little is straightforward for spouses who come to know mania. Lowell's parents had advised their son against his marriage to Hardwick in large measure because of his mental illness and the toll it would take. Four days before his own death, Lowell's father acknowledged they had been wrong. "We think it is nice to do well in your poems," he wrote, "but it is equally advisable to do well in a wife, & we think that you did."

Robert Lowell and Elizabeth Hardwick had a complicated marriage and a hard divorce; importantly, they also had a lasting friendship. At different times, and in many ways—in his letters, conversations with his friends, and writing—Lowell made clear his debt to her. He was acutely aware that his illness had burst into her life and their marriage. In "Man and Wife," published in *Life Studies* in 1959, the wife yet again faced the "kingdom of the mad," once more dragged her husband home alive:

> All night I've held your hand,
> as if you had
> a fourth time faced the kingdom of the mad—
> its hackneyed speech, its homicidal eye—
> and dragged me home alive.

In "Night Sweat," a poem that Elizabeth Bishop particularly loved—it is "very beautiful, musical, spontaneous . . . wonderful"—Lowell wrote of his life's fever and the cost of art; of the debt to the dawn by the night forces; a lightness that altered everything; a wife's absolution and salvaging, the heavy cost:

Work-table, litter, books and standing lamp,
plain things, my stalled equipment, the old broom—
but I am living in a tidied room,
for ten nights now I've felt the creeping damp
float over my pajamas' wilted white . . .
Sweet salt embalms me and my head is wet,
everything streams and tells me this is right;
my life's fever is soaking in night sweat—
one life, one writing! But the downward glide
and bias of existing wrings us dry—
always inside me is the child who died,
always inside me is his will to die—
one universe, one body . . . in this urn
the animal night sweats of the spirit burn.

Behind me! You! Again I feel the light
lighten my leaded eyelids, while the gray
skulled horses whinny for the soot of night.
I dabble in the dapple of the day,
a heap of wet clothes, seamy, shivering,
I see my flesh and bedding washed with light,
my child exploding into dynamite,
my wife . . . your lightness alters everything,
and tears the black web from the spider's sack,
as your heart hops and flutters like a hare.
Poor turtle, tortoise, if I cannot clear
the surface of these troubled waters here,
absolve me, help me, Dear Heart, as you bear
this world's dead weight and cycle on your back.

"Your lightness alters everything, / and tears the black web from
the spider's sack," he wrote. It is tribute and supplication—from husband to wife, and drowning man to lifeline.

Hardwick recognized the good beyond the ill in their marriage. It
was worth it, she said: "He was the most extraordinary person I have
ever known, like no one else—unplaceable, unaccountable." But Hardwick, more than anyone in his life, was also aware of how destructive
Lowell could be when he was manic. The harm was real; she did not

pretend otherwise. In a letter to Allen Tate, she raised the moral questions that she knew close at hand. "If only these things of Cal's were simply distressing," she wrote. But "they cause me and other people real suffering. And for what? I do not know the answer to the moral problems posed by the conduct of a deranged person, but the dreadful fact is that in purely human terms this deranged person does a lot of harm." He was, she continued, "terribly demanding and devouring. I feel a deep loyalty and commitment to him, and yet at the same time I don't know exactly what sort of bearable status quo I can establish with him."

"I tire of my turmoil," Lowell wrote, "and feel everyone else has, and long for a Horatian calm." Indeed. It was not only Hardwick who took the brunt of Lowell's manic attacks; it was not only Lowell who suffered. It was his friends and colleagues as well. Those in his life had different capacities to tolerate his illness depending upon their own mental vulnerabilities, how many of his manic attacks they had witnessed, and the extent to which their blood had been drawn by Lowell's lacerating remarks. Lowell's illness was, for everyone, exhausting. He knew this:

> Nothing! No oil
> for the eye, nothing to pour
> on those waters or flames.
> I am tired. Everyone's tired of my turmoil.

No one said otherwise, yet what is striking is that he kept his friendships. His daughter, Harriet, describes this capacity and the loyalty and love he commanded when he was himself:

No doubt people did tire of the repeated breakdowns and were saddened and unnerved by them and tired of taking turns rescuing him, but what is missing is why the man commanded such loyalty. The originality and depth and warmth of his company and the real pain of the descents and strange humor in them made us love him. . . . We weren't casualties to art,

but witnesses to it, enriched by our contact with this unusually tender and intelligent man. We loved him and he loved
us almost more, as his need for love was so great, but not in
a pulverizing way. He felt things deeply though he could be
careless and dismissive and even arrogant. It's a complex legacy.
Mostly he wasn't arrogant and came off nervous and wanting
everyone's opinion. He was the most collaborative of writers
and livers, wanting and needing to share it all and take it all
in. . . . He seemed so vulnerable, almost heartbreakingly so,
yet was full of fun. He was happiest, surrounded by his friends
and family, and when he was working. These are the things
that saved him.

Harriet Lowell, firstborn, hoped for and not expected, disagrees
with the stereotypic portrayal of her father that emerged after his
death: unstintingly mad, lacking in humor, and thoughtless. "He'd
become a cartoonish version of himself," she says, "a mad Caligula, who
destroyed his art as carelessly as he seemed to destroy lives." The father
she knew was a "very present and loving father, whatever his mental
state, and wonderfully odd." He took her to museums, zoos, and ice
skating, carried her on his shoulders in Central Park, taught her how to
ride a bike and swim. They took late-night summer drives in Maine to
spot deer, porcupines, foxes, and skunks. He was an "interested father,
who would ask me all kinds of questions as a child and really wanted to
know what I was thinking." He was not in the least patronizing, unlike
most of the adults she knew, and was "very empathetic about what it
was like to be an only child and awkward at school."

He read *Charlotte's Web* to her, Kipling's *Just So Stories*, and *The
Hound of the Baskervilles*. He read his own poetry and asked for her
opinion, as he asked for everyone's. (Being read to aloud was "the
lament of the poet's wife," said Elizabeth Hardwick.) Mostly, Harriet
says, "I remember the sound of his voice, his breathing. It sounded like
waves crashing to me as a child." Her father, she adds, "was unusually
tender and open, for a man." They had quiet family evenings at home
listening to opera or songs from the American Civil War. Her parents
scarcely had a "debauched lifestyle," she notes. "They were not liber-
tines, but rather stodgy WASPs." Her parents also entertained friends,
intellectuals, artists, and poets, evenings she describes as brilliant:

Robert Lowell and Harriet Lowell, Castine, 1960
"I'll love you at eleven, twenty, fifty,
young when the century mislays my name—"

"There is no way to recreate or even describe these conversations. Part of the attraction was the sharing of ideas. He had a terrible disease, but was charming, mischievous and full of fun."

Lowell, for his part, delighted in his daughter from before she was born to her visits to him in England as a young woman. In a poem he dedicated to her he recalled a summer evening in Maine that started in darkness and ended on a father's love:

> I wake to your cookout and Charles Ives
> lulling my terror, lifting my fell of hair,
> as David calmed the dark nucleus of Saul.
> I'll love you at eleven, twenty, fifty,
> young when the century mislays my name—
> no date I can name you can be long enough,
> the impossible is allied to fact.

Like most children born to older parents, Harriet brought her parents a particular sense of wonder. And change. "Chaos grows like a snowball in our house," Lowell wrote to a friend shortly after Harriet's birth. She was a "handful," yet delicate, and frighteningly so: "The world would stop for us," he said, if anything should happen to her. Harriet's birth put a different slant on Lowell's and Hardwick's world. "I've always suspected that Lizzie and I were curiously unlike other families," he wrote drolly to Peter Taylor. "My multiple absent-mindednesses, Lizzie's way of executing small, domestic acts with the splendor of an early Verdi heroine—now against the background of a normal child, I see we are very strange. However, we now have our own flower garden, play doubles daily and have a faint glimmer of how people live."

Months before his daughter's twenty-first birthday, in September 1977, Lowell died suddenly. At the memorial service Seamus Heaney read two of Lowell's poems. The first was "Home After Three Months Away" from *Life Studies*, which told of a father who returns home from the mental hospital and laments the time he has missed with his young daughter; grieves the time and hope that he has lost to madness; fears his darkening, uncertain future. Heaney then read a poem that Lowell had written years later. It spoke differently to the rush of time and the certainty of decay, the switch from mouse-brown hair to the white lion's mane; the hurry of spring into summer. It spoke of the ripening of youth and a father's love. Like "Home After Three Months Away," it spoke as well of the uncertainty of what might come:

Summer: 5. Harriet

> Spring moved to summer—the rude cold rain
> hurries the ambitious, flowers and youth;

our flash-tones crackle for an hour, and then
we too follow nature, imperceptibly
change our mouse-brown to white lion's mane,
thin white fading to a freckled, knuckled skull,
bronzed by decay, by many, many suns. . . .
Child of ten, three-quarters animal,
three years from Juliet, half Juliet,
already ripened for the night on stage—
beautiful petals, what shall we hope for,
knowing one choice not two is all you're given,
health beyond the measure, dangerous
to yourself, more dangerous to others?

———

Their sentiments and instincts are wholly transformed by the
disease; men, formerly kind and benevolent, become violent,
passionate, vindictive. . . . They acquire faults and vices foreign
to their former nature, and which render it impossible to live
with them.

—DANIEL HACK TUKE, "CIRCULAR INSANITY," 1892

Mania, Robert Lowell had said, was an illness, extremity, for one's
friends, depression an illness for oneself. There is truth in this, and
Lowell was aware of it. Certainly, mania wreaks havoc in those who are
psychologically and physically in its path. Manic psychosis is peculiarly
social and personal in its impact, a fact noted by the ancient physicians
as well as contemporary ones. Intense, irrational, and abrasive behavior toward others is, in many ways, as characteristic of mania as the
more classical symptoms such as grandiosity, flight of ideas, relentless
energy, and pressured speech. Manic behaviors—verbal attacks; boor-
ishness; outbursts of rage punctuated by seductiveness; sexual infidelity; excessive spending and impulsive financial investments; physical
violence—seem more willful than they are. There are convincing, but
illusory, islands of reasonableness during mania.

Thus manic behavior can at times seem less part of a psychiatric
illness than a manifestation of flawed character: self-indulgence, irre-
sponsibility, narcissism. This pattern has been described for centuries,

and modern diagnostic criteria incorporate it as a significant part of manic illness. The *DSM-5*, for example, lists as a criterion for mania "excessive involvement in activities that have a high potential for painful consequences (e.g., engaging in unrestrained buying sprees, sexual indiscretions, or foolish investments)." Still, it is understandably difficult for people who have been hurt to see the harmful behavior as part of an illness, rather than as a reflection of the true intent of a friend, spouse, or child. It may be clinically accurate to conclude that an impulsive love affair was a result of mania, but it stretches the credulity and understanding of the person wronged.

Nevertheless, clinical studies of thousands of manic patients confirm that impulsive love affairs are far more common in mania; there is, relatedly, a marked increase in sexual desire and behavior during mania. This was described two thousand years ago by Aretaeus of Cappadocia— his manic patients, he wrote, were unrestrained and notable for their "lewdness and shamelessness"—and by clinicians since. "Manic patients are very susceptible to quick courtship and sudden marriage," wrote John D. Campbell in his 1953 text on manic-depressive illness. Mania, he observed, alienates husbands from their wives and increases the demand for divorce; it leads to the often public pursuit of new romantic involvements. The sexual symptoms of mania are "the most powerful and important of all," wrote John Custance of his own experience. One lusts, one acts on lust; lust becomes a part of love, then a part of urgent, universal love. "The normal inhibitions disappear." One acts. Mania brings passion, depression brings apathy. Hope lies in moods and seasons that pass; it lies in love and in "things that spring."

———

Chaucer's old January made hay with May.
In this ever more enlightened bedroom,
I wake under the early rising sun,
sex indelible flowers on the air—
shouldn't I ask to hold to you forever,
body of a dolphin, breast of cloud?
You rival the renewal of the day,
clearing the puddles with your green sack of books.
— *FROM* "HARVARD: 3. MORNING"

When Lowell was in his late forties, he translated Horace's "Spring's Lesson." Life is short, Horace wrote. Death waits, but not for long, and time does not wait at all. The only hope against the night was to grasp pleasure and pursue beauty; Lowell translated: "Now, now, / the time to tear the blossoms from the bough, / to gather wild flowers from the thawing field." Lowell gathered life from the ruins as best he could. "Cal's recuperative powers were almost as much of a jolt as his breakdowns," Elizabeth Hardwick said. "Knowing him in the chains of illness you could, for a time, not imagine him otherwise. And when he was well, it seemed so miraculous that the old gifts of person and art were still there, as if they had been stored in some serene, safe box somewhere. Then it did not seem possible that the dread assault could return to hammer him into bits once more." Work and doctors, friends and family, helped preserve his gifts of person and art. But sometimes, as he wrote to John Berryman, "it's only love that lets air in our lungs."

Lowell read Boris Pasternak's *Doctor Zhivago* not long after it was published in 1957. He was stunned by its ambition and its novelistic vision of the human condition; its sweeping world of revolution, history, and disillusion; the love story that gave life back to those who had been broken. In a way that Lowell felt could not be expressed in poetry, *Zhivago* consciously took on the deepest things: death and resurrection; life that emerges from love, that brings sensation to the numb. "The last pages of Pasternak's *Zhivago* are still reeling through my mind," Lowell wrote to his cousin in September 1958. "It covers most of our century with a tragic weary hero who loathes the stereotyped and has a Graham Greene–like willessness and worlds besides. For a moment the stone facades of the new Russia blow away like gauze, much of our own too."

"You must read the Pasternak *Dr. Zhivago*," he wrote to Elizabeth Bishop two days later. "Everyone says it's great but too lyrical to be a novel. I feel shaken and haunted by the main character." It "dwarfed" all postwar novels, he thought, except Thomas Mann's *Doctor Faustus*. He saw in Zhivago, doctor and poet, more than a glimpse of himself. A month later he wrote to Bishop again. "Did I write you about Pasternak—really an earthquake—bigger perhaps than anything by Turgenev and something that alters both the old Russia and the new for us—alters our own world too." To Peter Taylor he wrote simply, "I'm shatteringly impressed by Pasternak."

Pasternak and Lowell had much in common. They were public poets, highly critical of the state yet with unseverable emotional ties to their respective countries. Their writing—dense, complex, original— was bred in the personal, especially *Life Studies* and *Doctor Zhivago*. Lapsed convert and Jew, they both used Christian imagery and ritual to effect. Both poets were attractive to women, and attracted to them. Each had affairs and married three times; both turned to passion for escape and solace, and muse. Both were translators, and their voices were strong and idiosyncratic, elliptical. Lowell, who translated Pasternak's poetry—Peter Levi wrote in his biography of Pasternak that Lowell's translations were "the best by far that have ever been done of Pasternak"—acknowledged his difficulty in translating the Russian poet (he had to rely upon others' translations), but his respect for Pasternak was constant. "I have come to feel that he is a very great poet," he wrote. Only a few months before he died, Lowell visited Pasternak's grave in Russia and raised a glass of vodka in respect.

"The Frosted Rowan," a pivotal chapter in *Doctor Zhivago*, is an ice-fire depiction of Lowell's most important subjects: death and renewal; the restorative, then killing, cycle of nature; the entangled roots of love and art: violence, upheaval; the history of a race. In the "dense, impassable forest," Zhivago comes upon a "solitary, beautiful, rusty-red-leafed rowan tree, the only one of all the trees to keep its foliage. It grew on a mound above a low, hummocky bog, and reached right up to the sky, into the dark lead of the prewinter inclemency, the flatly widening corymbs of its hard brightly glowing berries."

The first woman, according to Nordic myth, was made from the rowan tree, and Lara Antipova, Zhivago's lover and muse, seems to him as the rowan: life in the midst of death, comfort in mid-winter. The rowan tree, Pasternak writes, was "half covered with snow, half with frozen leaves and berries, and it stretched out two snowy branches to meet him. He remembered Lara's big white arms, rounded, generous, and taking hold of the branches, he pulled the tree towards him. As if in a conscious answering movement, the rowan showered him with snow from head to foot." The rowan—its berries the blood force of nature, its wood a balm againt suffering—gave hope against time's passing. The Russian song of the rowan tree was, in Pasternak's words, "a mad attempt to stop time with words," a force against the unspeakable, against the atrocities of the Revolution.

———

The rain falls, and the soil swims up to breathe;
a squatter sumac shafted in cement
flirts wet leaves skyward like the Firebird.
Two girls clasp hands in a clamshell courtyard, watch
the weed of the sumac failing visibly;
the girls age not, are always last year's girls
waiting for tomorrow's storm to wash
the fallen leaf, turned scarlet, back to green.

— *FROM* "THE HEAVENLY RAIN"

Lowell, too, tried to stop time with words and women. He had many affairs, most of them in the early stages of his manic attacks. They were hallmarked by an intense, impulsive involvement, usually with someone young. He was reckless: declared that his marriage was over, pledged his future to the woman involved, set up new living arrangements, and spent rashly. Then, when the mania cooled, he or his lawyers disassembled the commitments. This pattern is not rare in mania. Less frequently, Lowell had romantic and sexual involvements with women when he was not manic. Most of these affairs were with writers, a few of them students, and generally they were characterized by respect and affection. For the most part the women were more emotionally involved with Lowell than he was with them. When he was not ill, he made it clear that he did not plan to leave his marriage and, until he fell in love with Caroline Blackwood in 1970, he did not.

Lowell often described his lovers in terms of healing and renewal. "I was in a hospital for five weeks or so," Lowell wrote to Elizabeth Bishop in 1961. "Once more there was a girl, a rather foolish girl but full of a kind of life and earth force." To someone he had fallen in love with when he was manic in 1954, he wrote, "It has been as though there were deep inside me some great festering wound, as if I had rolled some great stone over it (to pretend it wasn't there) and thus I went on half alive. And now that I know you still love me and are waiting, the wound is purifying and draining. I am alive again." A few months later he wrote to her, "Away from you I dry up like grass." (Later, after Lowell's mania had cleared and he had broken off from her, Elizabeth Hardwick wrote, "Poor Giovanna—Cal leaves the bones all over the world.")

Several of Lowell's affairs were associated with not only renewal of body and mind but the inspiration of poems, including, "Waking in the Blue" and the poem sequences "The Charles River," "Harvard," and "Mexico." For Lowell, like Pasternak's rowan tree in the snow, love affairs were the representation of life, the possibility of regeneration. "Love is resurrection," Lowell wrote. "Woman wants man, man woman, as naturally / as the thirsty frog desires the rain." Love, or the illusion of love, set one free. "O to break loose," he wrote. "All life's grandeur / is something with a girl in summer." Love, he wrote elsewhere, is "all that kept off death at any time."

Renewal, "dying into rebirth," were critical themes in his work. But renewal was a complicated, messy thing; it was not simple and was often mixed with pain for himself and others. Rot was proximate to renewal. After William Carlos William died, Lowell wrote, "Our town was blanketed in the rain of rot and the rain of renewal. New life was muscling in, everything growing moved on its one-way trip to the ground." Life came from death and returned to it. Lowell knew this. He knew the New England seasons as Thoreau and Henry Adams did, the seasons of love as a poet does, the seasons of moods and madness as those who have suffered greatly. Childhood, desire, and suffering: each kept its own season. Imagination did as well. Words spun frictionless or they went dry—"a slack of eternity," Lowell said of these times. It was as he had written of the ice in Maine: it goes "in season to the tropical, / then the mash freezes back to ice, and then / the ice is broken by another wave." Our hope, he wrote, is in things that change, that spring:

> Tannish buds and green buds,
> hidden yesterday, pioneers today.
> The Georgian thirties' Harvard houses
> have shed their brashness in forty years;
> architecture suffers decline with dignity
> and requisitions its atmosphere—
> our hope is in things that spring.

Tonight in the middle of melting Boston,
a brick chimney tapers, and points a ladder
of white smoke into the blue black sky.
    —"RETURN IN MARCH"

When Lowell was fifty, he had a brief but intense affair with a young woman. From it came some of Lowell's most directly sensuous, voluptuous, and tender writing. "I, fifty . . . / dead laurel grizzling my back," he wrote in "Mexico"; "you, some sweet, uncertain age, say twenty-seven, / untempted, unseared by honors or deception." Their differences in experience, age, and position were set out by him from the start. But within these limits he found a kind of amulet against passing time. "I have lived without / sense so long the loss no longer hurts," he wrote. Life seeped in. His young lover wrote to him as he returned to New York: "I wanted to run over and give you the blue flower I was wearing," she said. "But then I thought how it would begin to die and wither in your hands on the way home, and I didn't want you to have anything but a sense of life, not withering. . . . Let us clasp and not grasp what's life and fragile." She thought of him, she said, had twined jasmine flowers in her hair. Lowell kept the blue flower alive: "Poor Child, you were kissed so much you thought you were walked on; / yet you wait in my doorway with bluebells in your hair." Words kept memory, if unable to hold off time.

In "Eight Months Later" he looked back on what remained:

> The flower I took away and wither and fear—
> to clasp, not grasp the life, the light and fragile. . . .
> It's certain we burned the grass, the grass still fumes,
> the girl stands in the doorway . . .
>
> .   .   .   .
>
> I see the country where the lemon blossoms,
> and the pig-gold orange glows on its dark branch,
> and the south wind stutters from the blue hustings;
> I see it; it's behind us, love, behind us—
> the bluebell is brown . . .

Lowell's affairs brought him distraction, pleasure, discomfort, and poems. To others, certainly Elizabeth Hardwick, they brought pain. She was almost always aware of the women he was involved with when he was manic; he made little effort to conceal those relationships and, indeed, was humiliatingly public about them. Hardwick seems not to have been so aware of his nonmanic affairs. His impulsive alliances undertaken while manic, made easier by mania's accompanying extraversion and disinhibited charm, could be understood by Hardwick on a clinical level. The human level was harder. What gave hope to Lowell and helped sustain him gave her nothing but pain.

———

When mild, the disinhibiting qualities of mania can charm others, ease conversation, and loosen imaginative thought. As the mania progresses and the disinhibition accelerates, however, little charm remains for others, only hurt, anger, fear, betrayal, and embarrassment. Satan, it has been said, "loves to fish in roiled waters." Mania roils. It damages, and often destroys, marriages and friendships in obvious and not so obvious ways. Infidelity and physical violence are among the most devastating and difficult to forgive. But verbal cruelty is also hard for many spouses and friends. The psychoanalyst Frieda Fromm-Reichmann wrote that manic-depressive patients "are uniquely able" to find and exploit vulnerable emotional spots in other people. This has been documented in the clinical research literature. Cutting remarks made during mania are often stinging in their perceptiveness. When they are made in front of other people, which is often the case, they are yet more crushing. The manic verbal cut or enraged diatribe is hard to forget and hard to forgive, even after the mania has resolved. Mania is a brutal thing.

Lowell, when manic, injured others, himself, and his reputation. He was unfaithful. He took up quite publicly with young women. He went on relentlessly about Christ and extolled Hitler and other tyrants. He accused others unfairly and made cruel remarks. As his illness got worse, and his delusions became more darkly tainted, tyranny took on a disproportionate weight. He was on several occasions physically violent. He had a virulent illness.

Lowell was a public person, in sickness as in health, and accounts of his illness took on a semi-mythic quality, relayed from person to person, colleague to colleague, student to student. The things he did when he was manic were viewed by some with compassion, by others with bewilderment, outrage, or malice. His illness gave confirmation to those who disliked or envied him; it confused and frightened those who cared about him. It is one of the unfairnesses of manic-depressive illness that it causes suffering not only to those who have it but to the people they love and that it places the responsibility for an unsought disease onto the person who has it. It makes those who become ill feel responsible for doing things that are beyond their control and against their values.

Yet while it is in force, for the patient, mania is a compelling state that confers certainty and power. If, as John Custance said, "I am God. I see the future, plan the universe," or if, like Lowell, you believe that you are the Holy Ghost or Achilles or Alexander the Great, the moral constraints of the world do not seem applicable. Sexual drive is commanding; cruelty is less apparent and seems less awful than it would in the light of a normal day. Violent force seems a more justified response to threat. Christopher Ricks has argued that violence and family were Lowell's essential subjects, an apt perspective on his life and work. The violence, Ricks said, is "terrible in its variety (of time, of place, of motive, of nature) and terrible in not changing."

The amoral force at the heart of mania has always raised philosophical, moral, and medical questions. Is mania a failure of character or is it a disease? What control does a person have over an inherited illness, one whose impact on brain structure and functioning is demonstrated by modern neuroimaging techniques? How do we understand what is said or done in mania? Is the behavior willed or is it beyond the will, like delirium or a seizure? If the breakdowns repeat, and the pathological periods blur more and more into the norm, does the moral disturbance remain separable from character?

From his childhood until he died, Lowell struggled to impose his will on forces that were beyond his control. Whether reason can hold any meaningful sway over insanity is a debate that dates back to the ancient philosophers and physicians and remains today at the center of discussions by doctors, ethicists, jurists, patients, and their families. Eli Todd, the first superintendent of the Hartford Retreat for the Insane, which opened in 1824 and where Lowell was a patient at three different times during the 1960s, knew madness close at hand. His father was mentally ill and his sister killed herself. "The great design of moral management," Todd wrote, "is to bring those faculties which yet remain sound to bear upon those which are diseased, and by their operation to modify, to counteract, or to suspend their morbid actions. This constitutes the process of self-control, the groundwork of cure, the grand tactical principle which is to decide the issue of the contest between reason and insanity." This he knew was easier said than done.

Lowell did what he could do to control his illness. With unusual exception he took the medications he was prescribed, undertook extensive psychotherapy, and submitted to hospital admission time and again. He expressed remorse for his behavior after each attack of mania. It was not enough. He was jailed; he alienated friends and family; he suffered the kind of psychological pain that often leads to suicide; he lost the regard of more than a few people he liked and respected. Some who disagreed with him for other reasons used his illness to undermine his writing and personal convictions. When, for example, Lowell refused an invitation from President Lyndon Johnson to the White House in 1965 in protest against the Vietnam War, members of Johnson's staff said that Lowell was a "troubled man" and an "unstable poet," rather than that he differed on principle and objected vehemently to what he considered an immoral war. His mental illness affected his reputation while he was alive; it affects it still.

"Cal was perfectly analytic about when he had been manic," said Grey Gowrie. "The worst thing was that he didn't forget a thing from his manias. He was consumed by guilt and remorse. By the awfulness of what he had done. He was a very gentle and sweet man. These things were quite out of character for him." Gowrie's former wife, who also knew Lowell well, said that after a manic evening, having said awful things about the people he most liked, he would be overcome with remorse, "shattered by what he had done . . . shattered by his own cruelty."

After Lowell had been released from the hospital, said William Alfred, "he was blue, which happens after these breakdowns. And what you do is go for a walk with him. . . . His chin began to drag. I said, well, why do you get blue like this? He said, I remember all the mean things I said and did while I was sick. One by one . . . I just shrivel with shame." Lowell's friend Esther Brooks said that Lowell had told her that "he could remember all he had said and done when he was ill. . . .

Everything. And that is the worst part of it." He felt himself "responsible for everything he was, regardless of his state, sane or deranged,
manic or depressed, or on the thin edge of illness." Lowell made a
particularly chilling remark to Caroline Blackwood toward the end of
his life: "It's the most awful feeling—I never know when I'm going to
hurt the people I love most. And I simply can't stand it, and in a way I
would rather be dead."

Madness and remorse; the grace and hard limits of love; the expediencies of art—he put these at the heart of the last poem in the book
he dedicated to Blackwood:

> My Dolphin, you only guide me by surprise,
> captive as Racine, the man of craft,
> drawn through his maze of iron composition
> by the incomparable wandering voice of Phèdre.
> When I was troubled in mind, you made for my body
> caught in its hangman's-knot of sinking lines,
> the glassy bowing and scraping of my will. . . .
> I have sat and listened to too many
> words of the collaborating muse,
> and plotted perhaps too freely with my life,
> not avoiding injury to others,
> not avoiding injury to myself—
> to ask compassion . . . this book, half fiction,
> an eelnet made by man for the eel fighting—
>
> my eyes have seen what my hand did.

The final line echoes words he had written many years earlier. In "The
Mills of the Kavanaughs," the wife confronts her husband after he has
tried to strangle her. "I saw your eyes," she said. "Looking in wonder
at your bloody hand."

Remorse came after madness subsided. Lowell had at times when
manic thought that he was Alexander the Great, sometimes wore a
golden coin stamped with the likeness of Alexander on a chain around
his neck. Not by chance he wrote in "Death of Alexander," "we know
this, of all the kings of old, / he alone had the greatness of heart to
repent."

Compassion was the note of grace. In June 1968, a few days after

the assassination of Robert Kennedy, Lowell spoke to a gathering of
Yale students about the capacity for gentleness that can reside within a
predestined, driving force. "His doom seemed almost woven into his
inheritance, into his nervous system," Lowell said about Kennedy. He
had used these words three years earlier to describe his own madness
to Elizabeth Bishop. "These attacks seem now almost like something
woven in my nervous system," he had written to her after a recurrence
of his mania. He urged the students to take a compassionate view of
the person beholden to disturbing forces. The most important thing,
he said, is that the "impetuous driving force that was sometimes rather
scary really was governed by gentleness, a good merciful heart."

Frank Sinatra once said that being a manic-depressive meant living
a life of violent contradictions. It meant having an "overacute capacity" for feeling. Whatever his critics threw at him for the way he lived
his life, he said, his music was honest. A moral sense might be com-
promised in the effort to stay alive; often surviving madness becomes
a pragmatic thing. In Sinatra's words, "I'm for anything that gets you
through the night."

10

And Will Not Scare

The struck oak that lost
a limb that weighed a ton
still shakes green leaves
and takes the daylight,
as if alive.
—*From* "We Took Our Paradise"

Contending with his madness and its attendant uncertainties was to Robert Lowell a matter of courage. From childhood, he had studied the lives and actions of courageous leaders, observed and emulated those whose bravery he admired. He took what he could from history, religion, and literature to provide him with the "battle array for the fire." To act with courage was the thing. When he was nineteen years old, Lowell had written to the woman with whom he was involved:

All law, morals, and rewards are based by necessity on the black and white of action. No notice can be taken of the individual's utter depravity or suffering. For some warfare is a lark, they are incapable of being terrified. They are dull amiable cows, munching buttercups. There is also the man whose heart's blood flows consciously to his fingers and the bottoms of his feet, whose every nerve is a glowing filament, and whose soul flounders in his mouth. Both receive the same reward. In the staggering zig-zag to a machine gun nest, one endure[s] little more annoyance than the keeper of the beehives caught without his gloves, the other goes through the darkest horrors of hell.

Lowell was intensely interested in what it meant to overcome fear, just as he was drawn to study the use and abuse of power. Courage is usually discussed in the context of nerve on the field of battle or equa-nimity facing death. But the courage to live with madness and with the knowledge that it will return is as real as zigzagging to a machine gun nest. Courage was to serve Lowell well, if not always sufficiently.

"A man should stop his ears against paralyzing terror," wrote Rob-ert Louis Stevenson, "and run the race that is set before him with a single mind. . . . As courage and intelligence are the two qualities best worth a man's cultivation, so it is the first part of intelligence to recog-nize our precarious estate in life, and the first part of courage to be not at all abashed before the fact." Lowell ran the race set before him aware of the precariousness of his mind and uncertain about when it next would break. He kept in the race, uncertain after each break whether he would write again, love again, teach again. Or whether he could regain the edge to write poetry that would "change the game."

"What—beyond his poetry, even—made him a hero to a great many people," wrote the critic Alan Williamson, who had been Low-ell's student at Harvard, "was the fact that, living in the imminence of an internal chaos that would have wrecked many lives, he so often seemed stronger and not weaker than the normal person: in his steady and enormously ambitious work, which even illness could not inter-rupt; in his political courage; in the importance he gave to friendship; and in his ability to synthesize harsh truths with deeply felt values."

———

"Courage," Lord Moran said in his classic study of the psychological effects of war, is a "moral quality; it is not a chance gift of nature like the aptitude for games. It is a cold choice between two alternatives, the fixed resolve not to quit; an act of renunciation which must be made not once but many times by the power of will. Courage is will power." Moran, Winston Churchill's personal physician during World War II, was himself the recipient of the Military Cross for valor during the Battle of the Somme. Courage, he believed, was the individual's "exer-cise of mind over fear through self-discipline." Some individuals had deeper wells of willpower from which to draw courage, but all had lim-its on how often the well could be tapped. War drew deep. Courage was necessary to make it through the worst and most extreme conditions in life: war, madness, exploration of the unknown, proximity to death.

Apsley Cherry-Garrard, the youngest member of Captain Robert

Falcon Scott's last Antarctic expedition, made the famous, horrifically cold, five-week winter journey to collect emperor penguin eggs for scientific study. He was keenly interested in physical and mental courage, endurance, and in their limits. Like Scott, Cherry-Garrard was subject to dark moods. He had severe depressions and, ultimately, a debilitating psychotic break. Scott and Cherry-Garrard were explorers legendary not only for their attempt to be the first to reach the South Pole, but for undertaking an ambitious and successful scientific expedition to collect rocks and fossils, make magnetic observations, and bring back thousands of geological and zoological specimens. They mapped a new territory, measured the winds and temperatures of the Antarctic, and contributed hundreds of articles to the scientific literature. They sought the primacy of discovering the South Pole, which they did not obtain, but they sought knowledge as well. "There are many reasons which send men to the Poles," wrote Cherry-Garrard in his classic book, *The Worst Journey in the World*. "But the desire for knowledge for its own sake is the one which really counts."

The primacy of discovery matters, of course, as does the journey itself and the response to risks taken, the need for impossibility denied. But what one learns from the struggle counts as much or more. "Much of that risk and racking toil had been undertaken," Cherry-Garrard wrote, "so that men might learn what the world is like at the spot where the sun does not decline in the heavens, where a man loses his orbit and turns like a joint on a spit and where his face, however he turns, is always to the North." They traveled for Science, he said, "in wind and drift, darkness and cold . . . that the world may have a little more knowledge, that it may build on what it knows instead of on what it thinks." They sang hymns against night and ice. A poet might say a similar thing about the journey to understand the human condition, the search for words and images that will make a difference, the confrontation with the bleak and the final. "Oak and three layers of brass were wrapped round the heart of that man who first entrusted a fragile craft to the savage sea," proclaimed Horace. Land led to sea; the sea became its own hard crossing.

Throughout his Antarctic journey and for the rest of his life Cherry-Garrard was intrigued with why some survive great stress, setback, terrifying circumstances of mind and body, and others do not. "The man with the nerves goes farthest," he wrote. "What is the ratio between nervous and physical energy? What is vitality? Why do some things terrify you at one time and not at others? What is this early morning courage? What is the influence of imagination? How far can a man draw upon his capital?" He believed, as did Lord Moran, that deliberate willpower was the basis of courage, and that it was not limitless. Some were courageous beyond reckoning and endured what only a few could. But always there was a price. In his own case, he said, there had been "an overdraft on my vital capital which I shall never quite pay off." In the case of five other men, including Scott, the price was death.

Character, "sheer good grain" character, pulled Scott through not only the extremes of polar exploration but also his black moods, concluded Cherry-Garrard. Courage, grit, a sense of responsibility toward others: the words he applied to Scott were as applicable to himself. "The man with nerves," he said, "gets things done, but sometimes he has a terrible time in doing them." Scott would go down as the Englishman who conquered the South Pole, though he did not reach it first. But Scott oversaw a great expedition that brought a new understanding of the Antarctic: its rocks and penguin eggs, its sea flow, the patterns of its ice and winds. An excellent observer and writer, he gave words to an unknown continent. Scott would be remembered in history for his character, for how he died, "as fine a death as any man." But the South Pole, said Cherry-Garrard, was not Scott's greatest triumph: "Surely the greatest was that by which he conquered his weaker self, and became the strong leader whom we went to follow and came to love." Their journey ended differently than they had hoped—it became instead "a first-rate tragedy"—but they completed it on terms they believed to be moral ones. "We took risks, we knew we took them," Scott wrote. "Things have come out against us [but] we have no cause for complaint."

Robert Lowell's character was the mix of nerve and risk and ice that Cherry-Garrard and Lord Moran described. Few can prevail against mental illness as severe as Lowell's; still less can they reenter the mix of life, as he did time after time. Insanity can be a stress as extreme as being under fire or surviving brutal temperatures, and it demands energy and psychological reserves most do not have; it entails exposure to the world most neither want nor feel they can tolerate. They redraw their borders and lower their expectations of life. To anyone who knows the pain of mania and severe depression, this is the human and natural response to assault and suffering.

Lowell did not do this. He had a virulent disease but his determination and discipline, together with his ability to form and keep relationships, made it possible for him to continue to work and love, imagine ways to survive, and to take what he learned from adversity into his poetry. A disease is not just a constellation of symptoms with a natural course; it is something that occurs to an individual who has strengths and liabilities of character; these, in turn, determine how the disease is perceived, fought, and handled. Most diseases change over time and manic-depressive illness particularly so. Early in its course strong character and discipline may make survival more likely, life fuller, and allow the rendering of good from pain. But this may change as the illness progresses. The power of character to affect circumstance can erode under the repeated battering of mania; disillusion and hopelessness may come to dominate. Toughness of character is important, but it may not be enough.

From childhood on, Lowell knew and lived with dark swings in moods and attacks of violent irrationality. He was used to difficulty and he learned from it. His imagination allowed him to create his way to a new poetry and fresh chances at life. Stability and conventional sanity never came easily to him, and he did not have the expectation that he should have a straight shot at the meaningful things in life or art. Even his mother, reluctant though she was, had acknowledged her young son's "great control over suffering." When he had been bitten by a muskrat as a child, she had told her psychiatrist, he "did not flinch." He knew young that art and life were difficult and that he would need courage. It was a deliberate approach to life. In that lay the iron and haleness of his life, the restoration of his mind after each attack of madness.

It fares, indeed, with the patient after an attack of Mania, as with a city or garrison after the horrors of an assault. The milder but more permanent supremacy of the enemy may succeed; or the whole may present but a heap of smouldering ruins; or the reaction of native strength having repelled the foe, there may be more or less of obvious dilapidation to mark the fierceness of the conflict.

—J. C. BUCKNILL AND D. H. TUKE, "MANIA," 1858

Lowell often used military images in his poetry—armor and shield—as he did images of exposed flesh and flayed or missing skin. Exposure to the physical and psychological elements was fundamental to him; fighting it was a given. Armor was not a simple idea; it was necessary for protection but it slowed and was cumbersome; it was a barrier to direct sensation and contact. It allowed its wearer a safer passage, but it made for less nimble, less imaginative navigation of battle and life. Armor pulled its wearer down; it was the opposite of the ballooning lightness and high, free flight of mania, although a balloon was bound, in its own way, to a fragile, enclosing, death-guaranteeing skin.

Lowell needed but derided the armor he had put on as a young poet. His early poems, he said, seemed to him "like prehistoric monsters dragged down into the bog and death by their ponderous armor." Courage in art, as life, meant exposure and risk. The breakthrough in style that led to *Life Studies* required getting rid of his "medieval armor's undermining." Too much elaboration and too baroque a style had left chunks of the human experience behind. They made him less vulnerable but stagnant. His work, he wrote, had been "alive maybe, if anything can breathe under the formidable armor of its rhetoric and stance."

Courage was necessary to break down the standing order, to create something new. The courage that allowed him to survive madness was a helpful, if costly, education for his art. Survival in life and art came from staring danger down and looking ahead, creating a new world on the ruins of the old. In his "Afterthought" to *Notebook*, Lowell wrote, "A poet can be intelligent and on to what he does; yet he walks, half-balmy and over-armored—caught by his amnesia, ignorance and education. For the poet without direction, poetry is a way of not saying what he has to say." But in order to say it he must be close joined to life. Armor conceals flaw, vulnerability, and paralyzing terror. "I too wore armor, strode riveted in cloth," Lowell wrote, "stiff, a broken clamshell labeled man."

Seamus Heaney believed that Lowell's repeated use of the word "net" in his poetry reflected a tactical maneuver of sorts; far from being just a fisher's net, it was the net thrown by the retiarius in the gladiator's arena. Poetry was a way of dealing with the world. "Lowell's poetry didn't attack the world," Heaney said, "but it was aware that the world was an enemy of sorts, a certain kind of public world was at enmity with certain kinds of attitudes and so the poetry was at once a net that dragged things out of himself, but it was a style of net waving that warded off and was—was a weapon almost, you know, for certain values."

"Flayed" and "flesh" and "exposed" were words that came naturally to Lowell. Part biblical, part *Iliad*, they were chinks in armor that he consciously set about to fill. Lowell was vulnerable, but he was also determined not to let it keep him from going where he wanted to go as a man and a poet. "Don't keep me waiting," he wrote to a lover when he was manic. "It's like hanging on a meat-hook, going through a vegetable grinder, like being one of those pictures of flayed men—all purple and nerves—on an anatomical chart!" "Flayed" was a good word. He told Ezra Pound that "shedding one's costume, one's fancy dress, is like being flayed." Three months later he wrote to Elizabeth Bishop, "The thought of going back to Boston sometimes makes me feel like a flayed man, who stands quivering and shivering in his flesh, while holding out a hand for his old sheet of skin."

A man might stand against the night, Lowell said, but then "the shell breaks and the cold air tortures the exposed flesh." The protection, the "great callousness," lasts for a while; then the world or madness or too close an encounter with danger breaks through it. One must put on the shield again, don again the "battle array against the fire." Throughout his life's work—from *Lord Weary's Castle* to *Day by Day*—Lowell wrote about exposure and the attraction and danger of fire; he wrote about the courage to live boldly in spite of seeing and feeling too much "*with one skin-layer missing.*"

Not only man had courage. Lowell gave it also to the occasional animal in his poetry, the creature who faced the dark and who stood, not ran. In one of his last poems, an old turtle—the armored animal he wrote into several of his poems—wades out into life and illusory hope. It wears its useless shield, its "foolsdream of armor." Still, it wades out.

> I pray for memory—
>
> an old turtle,
> absentminded, inelastic,
> kept afloat by losing touch . . .
> no longer able to hiss or lift
> a useless shield against the killer.

> Turtles age, but wade out amorously,
> half-frozen fossils, yet knight-errant
> in a foolsdream of armor.

In "Words for Muffin, a Guinea-Pig," Mrs. Muffin—the "small mop," the "short pound God threw on the scales"—denies fearing the dark and the brevity of life; she will not scare:

> "Of late they leave the light on in my entry,
> so I won't scare, though I never scare in the dark;
> I bless this arrow that flies from wall to window . . .
> five years and a nightlight given me to breathe—
> Heidegger said spare time is ecstasy . . . .
> I am not scared, although my life was short."

In "Skunk Hour," Lowell's most often quoted and anthologized poem, his account of the dark night of the soul, the cracking of his mind—"I hear / my ill-spirit sob in each blood cell, / as if my hand were at its throat. . . . / I myself am hell; / nobody's here"—is followed immediately by the image of skunks marching "on their soles up Main Street":

> white stripes, moonstruck eyes' red fire
> under the chalk-dry and spar spire
> of the Trinitarian Church.
>
> I stand on top
> of our back steps and breathe the rich air—
> a mother skunk with her column of kittens swills the garbage pail.
> She jabs her wedge-head in a cup
> of sour cream, drops her ostrich tail,
> and will not scare.

"This is the dark night," Lowell said about the poem. "I hoped my readers would remember John of the Cross's poem. My night is not gracious, but secular, puritan, and agnostic. An existential night. Somewhere in my mind was a passage from Sartre or Camus about reaching some final darkness where the one free act is suicide. Out of this comes the march and affirmation, an ambiguous one, of my skunks in the last two stanzas." Elsewhere he described the skunks as "indomitable," symbols of "horrible blind energy," "quixotic" and "absurd." They were defiant. From darkness and emptiness a new style of poetry, the soul of *Life Studies*, had come to him, he wrote. It was "freedom and an accomplishment after more or less staring into the wall. I meant the skunks at the end to move with their thud of triumph. My whole sad, hesitating journey to their walk is perhaps no less so—tactics of survival stopping so as not to stop." The last line of "Skunk Hour," the final poem in *Life Studies*—a work of courage and originality written during, and in the aftermath of, a particularly terrible attack of mania, months of depression and personal upheaval; a work of psychological and imaginative genius—is, notably and unforgettably, "and will not scare."

To create great art requires toughness, eyes that do not avert their gaze, and intellect that does not back away from the great, hard subjects: love, betrayal, suffering, madness, war, death. Truth is not always an uplifting thing; human nature is flawed. Madness often kills that which matters most. To continue to live and work, to keep faith in love and words, friends and work and music, requires stopping one's ears to paralyzing terror. It is not for the faint of heart. Art is the "ruthless cutting edge that records and celebrates and prophesies on the stone tablets of time," wrote the Scottish poet George Mackay Brown. He knew this, as he knew depression and the myths of his Orkney race: "A too-refined sensibility could not do that stern work."

Lowell, who spent time with George Mackay Brown on his late-life trip to Orkney to trace the ancestral roots of his poetry and madness, put it plainly. "We must all live by taking a few uncontrolled screams—in our stride."

Mr. Edwards and the Spider

I saw the spiders marching through the air,
Swimming from tree to tree that mildewed day
   In latter August when the hay
   Came creaking to the barn. But where
     The wind is westerly,

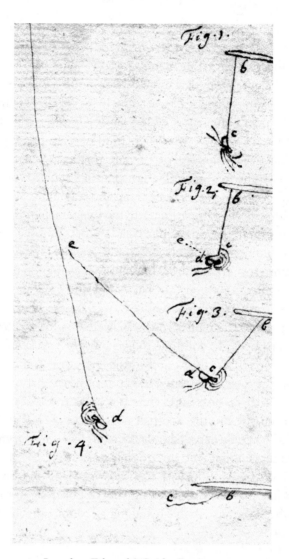

Jonathan Edwards's Spider Letter, 1723

Where gnarled November makes the spiders fly
Into the apparitions of the sky,
  They purpose nothing but their ease and die
Urgently beating east to sunrise and the sea;

What are we in the hands of the great God?
It was in vain you set up thorn and briar
  In battle array against the fire

And treason crackling in your blood;
 For the wild thorns grow tame
And will do nothing to oppose the flame;
Your lacerations tell the losing game
You play against a sickness past your cure.
How will the hands be strong? How will the heart endure?

A very little thing, a little worm,
Or hourglass-blazoned spider, it is said,
 Can kill a tiger. Will the dead
 Hold up his mirror and affirm
  To the four winds the smell
And flash of his authority? It's well
If God who holds you to the pit of hell,
 Much as one holds a spider, will destroy,
Baffle and dissipate your soul. As a small boy

On Windsor Marsh, I saw the spider die
When thrown into the bowels of fierce fire:
 There's no long struggle, no desire
 To get up on its feet and fly—
  It stretches out its feet
And dies. This is the sinner's last retreat;
Yes, and no strength exerted on the heat
 Then sinews the abolished will, when sick
And full of burning, it will whistle on a brick.

But who can plumb the sinking of that soul?
Josiah Hawley, picture yourself cast
 Into a brick-kiln where the blast
 Fans your quick vitals to a coal—
  If measured by a glass,
How long would it seem burning! Let there pass
A minute, ten, ten trillion; but the blaze
 Is infinite, eternal: this is death,
To die and know it. This is the Black Widow, death.

As a young man Lowell had read deeply in the life and writings of
his mother's ancestor, the eighteenth-century New England theolo-

gian Jonathan Edwards. "He was an ancestor," Lowell said, "but this doesn't make our relation exactly personal—another grandfather." Perhaps, but early on in Lowell's life, Edwards's work impressed upon him a belief in the hardness of life and the need to summon the courage to face what the pain of the world would deliver him. Edwards's writings stamped Lowell's religious and historical thinking, as well his early poetry. Lowell abandoned his initial plan to write a biography of Edwards, but he returned to his life and work as the inspiration for four poems, including one of his greatest, "Mr. Edwards and the Spider," which was published in *Lord Weary's Castle* in 1946. Thirty years later, a few months before he died, it was one of the poems Lowell read during his last public reading at Harvard.

Lowell and Edwards shared more than blood. Both took language in original directions and both were decisively shaped by New England Puritanism, although its hold was more fierce and lasting upon Edwards. They felt the weight of ancestral madness. (Edwards's grandmother was insane—her husband stated in their divorce proceedings that she "often threaten[ed] my Life to Cut my Throat when I was asleep"—and one of her brothers and a sister were declared by the court to be *non compos mentis,* one a "lunatic," the other "mad." Another brother was convicted of murder and executed.)

Both Lowell and Edwards knew the persuasive power of ecstatic states and drew from them. They knew, too, the downward lure of melancholy. Edwards wrote repeatedly in his diary and letters that he was shadowed and often overwhelmed by unshakeable depression. "I have a constitution peculiarly unhappy," he said, "a low tide of spirits." Both lived captive to the cycles of their moods, the "dull-decay-revising" cycles, as Edwards put it. They were close observers of the natural world and saw no contradiction to charting its beauty and decay in the same mental tract of land. Lowell and Edwards took in a full measure of the earth's beauty; as much, or more so, they took in its brute darkness. They exerted their preternatural wills to master their suffering. Neither extended an easy consolation to those for whom they wrote.

Edwards, like Lowell, moved with ease in vast intellectual and psychological spaces, whether they were in the natural world or in the world of ideas and experience. "The immense magnificence of the visible world is inconceivable vastness," wrote Edwards in 1728, "the incomprehensible height of the heavens, etc. is but a type of the infinite magnificence, height and glory of God's work in the spiritual world: the most incomprehensible expression of his power, wisdom, holiness and love, in what is wrought and brought to pass in that world." Glory was mutable; a mood of light or ecstasy could and did tip to its counter pole. In Edwards's mind, as in Lowell's, the "exuberant goodness of the creator" sat in the same hard pew with the annihilating wrath of God. Glory and damnation were in the hands of the Creator; man of necessity could be nothing next to this.

In a sermon whose title left little to the imagination, and spurred it to blood, "The Future Punishment of the Wicked Unavoidable and Intolerable," Jonathan Edwards spoke to his congregation of God's force and dark intentions toward sinful man: "What art thou in the hands of the great God, who made heaven and earth by speaking a word?" he asked. "What art thou, when dealt with by that strength, which manages all this vast universe, holds the globe of the earth, directs all the motions of the heavenly bodies from age to age, and, when the fixed time shall come, will shake all to pieces?" Christ, who keeps the key of hell, "shuts and no man opens." It was the will of God made manifest through the word of Edwards. The fixed time will come, the earth will shake to pieces. Sinners will have no rest; there will be not so much as a drop of water to cool their tongues. They will burn in fire and brimstone. Forever, beyond forever.

In "Mr. Edwards and the Spider," Lowell wrote, he was "trying to get a little prose piece and two Edwards's sermons into Donne's St. Lucy stanza. I thought it was odd that Edwards liked real spiders as a boy and figure of speech spiders as a preacher. There were several years when he seriously thought through morbidity that he was the worst man who ever lived; but he was really a modest, rational, mystical sort of man—not all the terror and brimstone one I picture."

Lowell's portrayal of Edwards in his poetry is complex. He took words and phrases from Edwards's writings, as he did from Thoreau and would in the future from others, and put the words to his own use. He gave full portrait to Edwards as a young man who, entranced, watched spiders with awe and carefulness near his boyhood home. Young, less worn by life and moods, his spiders then were free, ballooning creatures of the air. They sailed, moved on by a calm wind, marched in the air from tree to tree. They were dangling creatures of heaven: "I have seen vast multitudes of little shining webs and glistening strings," he observed, "brightly reflecting the sunbeams, and some of them of a great length, and at such a height that one would think that they were tacked to the vault of the heavens."

In "Jonathan Edwards in Western Massachusetts," Lowell re-created the quiet exuberance of the young Edwards, vital with God's presence in the world:

> As a boy, you built a booth
> in a swamp for prayer;
> lying on your back,
> you saw the spiders fly,
>
> basking at their ease,
> swimming from tree to tree—
> so high, they seemed tacked to the sky.
> You knew they would die.
>
> .   .   .   .
>
> Then God's love shone in sun, moon and stars,
> on earth, in the waters,
> in the air, in the loose winds,
> which used to greatly fix your mind.

In "Mr. Edwards and the Spider," however, Lowell turned to the older, darker Edwards for words. The Jonathan Edwards who as a youth had described the beauty of the marching, flying, swimming spiders was now the preacher of hell. Mood had darkened, mildewed. The once billowing spider had spun into an agent of hopelessness: "They purpose nothing but their ease and die / Urgently beating east to sunrise and the sea."

The spider dies, thrown into "the bowels of fierce fire" where "full of burning, it will whistle on a brick." The "incomprehensible height of the heavens" had become the fire of incomprehensible suffering, a pit of slow and lingering death, one that would exact a brutal justice past the end of time. The Old Testament wrath of the Almighty was bent on rooting out the decay in man and his makings; like the Achillian wrath that seared Lowell's early poetry, it would later sear his mind when he was mad.

The epigraph to Edwards's sermon about God's punishment of the wicked was taken from Ezekiel 22:14: "Can thine heart endure, or can thine hands be strong in the days that I shall deal with thee?" Edwards renders this in his sermon: "How then will thine hands be strong, or thine heart endure? . . . What then canst thou do in the hands of God? It is vain to set the briars and thorns in battle array against glowing flames; the points of thorns, though sharp, do nothing to withstand the fire."

Lowell thrusts man's struggle into the heart of "Mr. Edwards and the Spider." We know the ravages from insanity that will come to Lowell, and two lines stop the pulse:

> Your lacerations tell the losing game
> You play against a sickness past your cure.

It would not be in vain to set the battle array against the fire, to play with all stops out against a disease past a cure. But it was to be hard tackling.

Robert Lowell in Boston, 1959

"I've got my book off at last. . . . I'm in the fine mood of an author with a new style and feel nothing else I've ever done counts."

LIFE STUDIES
ROBERT LOWELL

NEW POEMS
and an Autobiographical Fragment
by the author of LORD WEARY'S CASTLE

Life Studies, 1959
"*After* Life Studies, *as after* The Waste Land, *nothing has quite been the same.*"

ILLNESS AND ART

Something Altogether Lived

During this time I have had five manic depressive breakdowns: short weeks of Messianic rather bestial glow, when I have to be in a hospital, then dark months of indecision, emptiness etc. So the dark and light are not mere decoration and poetic imagery, but something altogether lived, inescapable. Even survival has had to be fought and fought for.

—Letter to Chard Powers Smith,
October 3, 1959

A Magical Orange Grove in a Nightmare

There is personal anguish everywhere. We can't dodge it, shouldn't worry that we are uniquely marked and fretted, and must somehow keep even-tempered, amused and in control. John B. [Berryman] in his mad way keeps talking about something evil stalking us poets. That's a bad way to talk, but there's truth in it.

—Letter to Philip Booth, 1966

Robert Lowell, Randall Jarrell, and John Berryman were "brilliant, mordant, and lighthearted young men," recalled the classicist Robert Fitzgerald at Lowell's memorial service in 1978. In the late 1940s, they were poets in a class by themselves. "They faced the age of anxiety with nerve and love, and they had hard lives." Indisputably they had nerve and hard lives. Berryman killed himself and Jarrell almost certainly did as well. They were of a generation of writers whose madness, stints in mental hospitals, and public acts of self-destruction became front-page news; at times they were more written about than read. Death comes sooner or later, said Lowell. "These made it sooner."

It seemed a uniquely blighted era of writers; manic breakdowns, depression, addiction, alcoholism, or suicide struck, among others, Hart Crane, Vachel Lindsay, Sara Teasdale, Edna St. Vincent Millay, Ezra Pound, Robert Frost, Sylvia Plath, Anne Sexton, Delmore Schwartz, Theodore Roethke, Randall Jarrell, Robert Lowell, Jane Kenyon, Boris Pasternak, Dylan Thomas, F. Scott Fitzgerald, Ernest Hemingway, William Styron, Jean Stafford, James Schuyler, James Wright, Thom Gunn, Geoffrey Hill, Mary McCarthy, F. O. Matthiessen, Elizabeth Bishop, Edward Thomas, Virginia Woolf, Graham Greene, Eugene O'Neill, Tennessee Williams, John Berryman, Anthony Hecht, William Carlos Williams, Walker Percy, Moss Hart,

William Inge, George Mackay Brown, Louis MacNeice, Paul Laurence Dunbar, Edmund Wilson, Robert Penn Warren, Franz Wright,
James Dickey, and William Meredith.

Allen Ginsberg, himself no stranger to instability, began "Howl"
with words that would be repeated by a river of followers: "I saw the
best minds of my generation destroyed by madness." They "bared their
brains to Heaven . . . passed through universities with radiant cool eyes
hallucinating." They jumped to their deaths from city rooftops, fire
escapes, and bridges. John Berryman, one of these best minds, who
leapt to his death from a bridge, had written of the tax levied on his
contemporaries:

> I'm cross with god who has wrecked this generation.
> First he seized Ted, then Richard, Randall, and now Delmore.
> In between he gorged on Sylvia Plath.
> That was a first rate haul. He left alive
> fools I could number like a kitchen knife
> but Lowell he did not touch.

Lowell he did touch, of course. In a tribute to Berryman after his
suicide in 1972, Lowell described their common anguish: "I feel the
jagged gash with which my contemporaries died, with which we were
to die." Later he added his name to the marked and mad:

> Ah the swift vanishing of my older
> generation—the deaths, suicide, madness
> of Roethke, Berryman, Jarrell and Lowell.

Berryman, wildly brilliant, was bound to literature as poet, Shakespeare scholar, critic, and teacher. He mixed his madness with alcohol to deadly effect. "He seemed to throb with a singular rhythm and
pitch," Lowell wrote. "One felt the fierce charge of electricity and
feared that it might burn out the wires." Berryman's intensity made
him difficult for others to bear at times. "Hyper-enthusiasms made him
a hot friend," Lowell said, and could "make him wearing to friends—
one of his dearest, Delmore Schwartz, used to say no one had John's
loyalty, but you liked him to live in another city."

Lowell, whose own attacks of mania upended lives around him,

recognized the chaos wrought by others of like mind and temperament. "I felt frightened to be with him," Lowell wrote about Delmore
Schwartz. "I was sure it would lead to confusion and pain." The "dark
rays of his paranoia" scorched those nearest to him and he became "unbearable." Schwartz, whose literary destiny Lowell described as "the
most hopeful of any young poet in 1940," disintegrated into the "most
dismal story of our generation." It was due, in Lowell's way of putting it, to "some germ in the mind."

Lowell was acutely aware of the mental instability that haunted him
and many of his contemporaries. In March 1959 he wrote to Berryman, "It seems there's been something curious twisted and against the
grain about the world of poets of our generation have had to live in.
What troubles you and I, Ted Roethke, Elizabeth Bishop, Delmore,
Randall—even Karl Shapiro—have had." Three years later he wrote
again to Berryman, in similar vein: "What you said about the other
poets of our generation is something I've brooded much on. What
queer lives we've had even for poets! There seems something generic
about it, and determined beyond anything we could do. You and I have
had so many of the same tumbles and leaps. We must have a green old
age. We both have drunk the downward drag as deeply as is perhaps
bearable."

The downward drag would come in the wake of a dizzying upward
current; it came as ash from fire, backwash to the fierce writing life led
by their generation. It came coiled within a mania for words, as Lowell
wrote in a poem for Berryman:

> all the best of life . . .
> then daydreaming to drink at six,
> waiting for the iced fire,
> even the feel of the frosted glass,
> like waiting for a girl . . .
> if you had waited.
> We asked to be obsessed with writing,
> and we were.

They, and other poets of their age, had been obsessed with words.
"I feel I know what you have worked through," Lowell wrote; "you /
know what I have worked through—we are words; / John, we used the

language as if we made it." Mania, Lowell had said, was "a magical orange grove in a nightmare." It began in incandescence, lighting them and the sky against which they stood. In time, the darkness was more the reality than the incandescence. The shifts in light were beyond metaphoric to Lowell.

Lowell corresponded with many writers, but his closest correspondent was Elizabeth Bishop, to whom he wrote often about his life and especially about poetry. He confided in her about his breakdowns and treatment, yet it was to his male friends, also poets—Ezra Pound, Theodore Roethke, John Berryman, and Randall Jarrell—that he confided the raw details of his attacks of mania and the depression that followed. Perhaps he wanted to spare Bishop and their relationship how he had felt and what he had done while he was manic; perhaps he believed that Bishop, who unlike Lowell, Pound, Jarrell, and Roethke had never been manic, would not understand the particular terrors of mania. From her own experience, Bishop knew depression and alcoholism well. But she did not know full-bore madness, a very different thing. Her spells, she wrote to Lowell, "are a lot like yours, on a modest scale, I think. . . . But you have to do everything on the grand scale!" The proportion was not one in which he took pride or pleasure.

In April 1965 Lowell wrote sympathetically to Randall Jarrell, who had been manic and medicated, attempted suicide, and was at last in the hospital. He extended hand and heart from his own life:

> I have thought twice about intruding on you, but I must say that I am heart-broken to hear that you have been sick. Your courage, brilliance and generosity should have saved you from this, but of course all good qualities are unavailing. I have been through this sort of thing so often myself that I suppose there's little in your experience that I haven't had over and over. What's worst, I think, is the grovelling, low as dirt purgatorial feelings with which one emerges. If you have such feelings, let me promise you that they are temporary. What looks as though it were simply you, and therefore would never pass does turn out to be not you and will pass.
>
> Please let me tell you how much I admire you and your work and thank you for the many times when you have given me the strength to continue. Let me know if there's anything I can do. And *courage*, old Friend!

Six months later Jarrell lunged in front of an oncoming car and was killed. Lowell, like most, believed that Jarrell's death was a suicide and was devastated. Jarrell had been brilliant in a rare way, Lowell said, "the most heartbreaking" poet of his generation.

Lowell had written with understanding to Ezra Pound two years earlier: "It was sad to hear that you have been suffering greatly in the last two years. There's no reason. But I think it does no good to say this. I think there are times that cannot be softened or explained off, but which can only be lived through—that blank sense of failing. Now I gather it has lifted and you are reviving. Don't let me intrude. I sympathize and suppose I've lived in the same cellar for moments."

It was to Theodore Roethke, however, that Lowell wrote at greatest length and with most feeling about mania and the toll it and depression had taken on both of their lives. "I feel a great kinship with you," Lowell wrote to Roethke in 1958. "We are at times almost one another's shadows passing through the same jungle." He and Roethke were very different poets, Lowell once told an interviewer. "What we share, I think, is the exultant moment, the blazing out." Their manic-depressive illness was a shared affliction that they wrote about with droll understanding. "Well, it's happened again," Roethke wrote to Lowell in 1957 after yet another manic attack. "Same old routine: 4 or 5 city police . . . dragging me off to the same old nut-bin, the same old commitment routine—what a bore."

Lowell wrote to Roethke about experiences that came with "our dizzy explosions." "Our troubles are a bond. I, too, am just getting over a manic attack. Everything seemed to be going swimmingly, then suddenly I was in the hospital—thorazine, windy utterances, domestic chaos . . . the old story. Now it's passed; I'm back typing in my study; my feet are on the floor. When you come we can spill out to each other." A few months later Lowell observed that Roethke appeared to have passed through the worst of his attack. Still, he predicted, there would be darkness to come: "For months (perhaps always) there are black twinges, the spirit aches, yet remarkably less as time passes. I feel almost in a thanksgiving mood—so much of life is bearable. I've quite stopped wanting to turn the clock back or look for a snug hole."

Lowell wrote his last letter to Roethke in 1963, a month before Roethke died of a heart attack at the age of fifty-five. He spoke again of their common bond, rued the forces that were wrecking the poets of their time:

We couldn't be more different, and yet how weirdly our lives have often gone the same way. Let's say we are brothers, have gone the same journey and know far more about each other than we have ever said or will say. There's a strange fact about the poets of roughly our age, and one that doesn't exactly seem to have always been true. It's this, that to write we seem to have to go at it with such single-minded intensity that we are always on the point of drowning. I've seen this so many times, and year after year with students, that I feel it's something almost unavoidable, some flaw in the motor. There must be a kind of glory to it all that people coming later will wonder at. I can see us all being written up in some huge book of the age. But under what title?

In 1976, the year before he died, Lowell became manic again and had to be committed to a hospital. Roethke, Jarrell, and Berryman were dead. Threads that had connected him to a shared kind of understanding were cut or fraying. It was left to another poet, Philip Larkin, to allude to the painful company Lowell's poetic mind had kept. He was sorry to hear that Lowell was not well, he wrote to Caroline Blackwood, but perhaps it was "the price one pays for being such a rich, inventive and variegated writer. I only wish I had one-eighth of his creativeness." It was a high price.

Lowell and his contemporaries were far from being the first to observe that a germ in the mind, some flaw in the motor, rocks the lives of poets. The early Greek philosophers had described the "divine madness" that touched the minds of poets and taught that melancholia was a determining element in the minds of artists. This Aristotelian conception of "divine madness" was broad. Over the centuries the suggested link between "madness" and genius narrowed to a more clinical notion of madness, usually the excitable mental state we know as mania. Mania, whose clinical description has scarcely changed over the centuries, was believed by the philosophers and doctors of antiquity to make minds and senses keener; it heightened the power of observation, they believed, and it yoked passion to discovery and imagination.

The body and mind were unearthly alive, freed from the mundane. Mania intensified and sped the mind, forced it into places it would not otherwise go. "Their senses are acute," Aretaeus of Cappadocia wrote about his manic patients in the second century AD. They learned that which they could not when they were well—astronomy, philosophy, and other previously unknowables. There were "advantages in disease," Aretaeus concluded; his patients not only learned new material uncannily well but they "wrote poetry truly from the muses."

The clinical observation that intellectual and imaginative advantage might accompany mania, especially a conspicuous fluidity of language, was reported time and again. During mania, it was thought, the senses could perceive what normal senses could not; memory, the tributary to imagination, could be preternaturally tapped. The manic mind flooded with original associations. For more than a thousand years—in clinical papers, asylum records, correspondence to other physicians— doctors made note of instances of enhanced memory and originality in their manic patients.

The nineteenth- and early twentieth-century physicians left a long chronicle of these observations. Benjamin Rush, the "father of American psychiatry," was a signer of the Declaration of Independence, surgeon general in the Continental Army, and Thomas Jefferson's pick to tutor Meriwether Lewis in medicine before he set out on his westward exploration. He was also a keen observer of aberrant mental states, particularly mania. He wrote in his widely used 1812 text on the diseases of the mind that when patients are manic "the senses of hearing and seeing are uncommonly acute." Knowledge long buried could be "resuscitated," new talents could emerge:

> Where is the hospital for mad people, in which elegant and completely rigged ships, and curious pieces of machinery, have not been exhibited, by persons who never discovered the least turn for a mechanical art previously to their derangement? Sometimes we observe in mad people an unexpected resuscitation of knowledge; hence we hear them describe past events, and speak in ancient or modern languages, or repeat long and interesting passages from books, none of which we are sure they were capable of recollecting, in the natural and healthy state of their minds.

Jean-Pierre Falret, the nineteenth-century French alienist who delineated the symptoms and course of "*la folie circulaire*," wrote that manic patients "cause surprise by the activity and fertility of their ideas, by their esprit and by their vivid imagination. . . . Their intellect is, as it were, in fermentation, and suggests a thousand undertakings and plans." Their memory, inflamed and overexcited, is able to call to mind that which ordinarily was inaccessible. They are "astonished with their remembering a great number of often insignificant facts, which they believed to have faded out of their memory a long time ago. They remember long phrases from classical authors, which they learned in their childhood and of which they were able to remember only isolated fragments before their illness." They compose poems and "speak and write incessantly, and often with a variety of terms and aptness of expression which they did not possess in the normal condition." Falret's countryman Jean-Étienne Esquirol had written in 1838 that the manic patient "associates the ideas most unlike; forms images most whimsical; holds the conversations most strange."

Emil Kraepelin, the German psychiatrist and author of the seminal text *Manic-Depressive Insanity*, noted the fluency of mental associations during mania and the increase in writing and rhyming. Ideas "become unbridled," he wrote, and "associations with external impressions and rhyming frequently occur in the conversation of the patients. . . . Many patients develop a veritable passion for *writing* [Kraepelin's emphasis], cover innumerable sheets." They are also "very fond of composing poems, letters, petitions to highly placed personages." A prominent early twentieth-century British text on insanity described similar behavior. During mania, its author wrote, patients are "often able to recall at will whole pages of poetry, to quote extensively from standard prose works . . . all of which would be impossible in the sane state." They display, he continued, an unexpected "mental brilliancy" and a "wonderful facility" in expressing ideas. Their command of language "appears inexhaustible" and, while manic, they have "solved problems, and written even brilliant works." John Campbell, whose excellent clinical textbook on manic-depressive illness was published in 1953, observed that the intense pressure of thoughts during mania often led to a propulsive drive to write. "Urged on by the pressure of ideas as well as an excess of physical energy the manic patient has an inner drive which will not allow him to rest." Ideas rush from mind to paper.

None of these physicians, ancient or modern, would have argued that manic-depressive illness was anything but a dangerous, corrosive disease. Yet they and many of their colleagues were piqued by the occasional brilliant surge of ideas; the urgent pressure to write, especially poetry; and the fluid access to memory that they observed in their manic patients. Such clinical anecdotes cannot form a scientific case that mania has a role in bringing art into being. They have, however, encouraged more systematic study of the cognitive and mood changes that occur during mania, and of the characteristics of temperament shared by those who become manic and those who create. In its own right, anecdotal observation offers a vivid glimpse into why a link between creativity and madness has been posited for so many hundreds of years.

Is there, contemporary psychologists and neuroscientists have asked, a fundamental link between "madness" and creativity, or is this old belief just a cultural myth, a naïve romanticization of mental illness and a clichéd caricature of the tormented artist? If there is such a link, if those who have been manic, or otherwise mentally perturbed, are more likely to write lasting poetry or music, or to be more imaginative in mathematics and the sciences, may they also be disproportionately innovative in business, the law, or in the acts of everyday life? And, if so, why? The question is not whether the majority of great artists and writers have been mentally ill, nor is it whether most of those who have been mentally ill have been unusually creative. Neither is true. The question is whether there is a higher rate of mental disorder, especially bipolar illness, in those who are unusually creative and, if so, why?

What once was a field of speculation, case study, and biographical research has splayed out into a teeming field of cognitive and affective psychologists, linguists, neuroscientists, psychiatrists, geneticists, neurobiologists, and epidemiologists. Many studies have been published in recent years, and the number is rising sharply. Not everyone regards this as a good thing. Some have an aesthetic or intellectual aversion to scientific study of the artistic mind, or to work that suggests an association between psychopathology and creativity. It may appear to be reductionist in the highest degree to investigate the relationship of brain circuitry to something so importantly complex as creativity, or setting off on a fool's journey to study the association between mental illness and creativity across populations of hundreds of thousands of people—but the ship has sailed. Scientists have been doing exactly this, and their research is narrowing in on increasingly specific questions about brain and mind. Such questions are of elemental and broad human importance.

Skepticism about neuropsychological research and studies that use neuroimaging or genetic techniques remains appropriate; research findings are early, tentative, and inconsistently replicated. But existing methods, and the incrementally more sophisticated methods that will evolve from them, promise a different kind of insight into ancient questions. Skepticism about psychological science is essential and well directed toward the quality of the questions asked, how the findings are interpreted, and what the research means in the broader human context. At the moment, the scientific study of creativity and psychopathology is in an early stage, but the accumulating evidence for a connection between creativity and mood disorders, especially with manic-depressive (bipolar) illness, is proving to be even stronger than previously thought. And Robert Lowell was right: poets *are* uniquely marked and fretted.

Five lines of evidence make an increasingly persuasive case for a link between mental illness, especially bipolar disorders, and creativity: biographical studies of individuals that examine the rates of mental disorders in people distinguished by their creative eminence; diagnostic studies of mental disorders in living artists and writers; large population studies that look at the association between psychiatric diagnosis and intelligence, academic performance, and creative occupation; experimental studies that investigate the effect on creativity of cognitive and mood states associated with mania and depression; and, most recently, genetic and brain imaging studies that look at the biological mechanisms common to both creativity and psychopathology.

Biographical studies investigate mental disorders in eminent writers, composers, and artists by reviewing autobiographical writings, accounts given by contemporaries, correspondence, medical records, journals, and court records. Studies done in this way are, of course, more subjective and involve far fewer individuals than is ideal. Diagnostic accuracy is affected not only by the availability and comprehensiveness of medical records but by the clinical experience and skill of the investigator. There may be bias in determining who is chosen to be included or excluded for study. By its nature, posthumous diagnosis is difficult: evidence of high energy during periods of sleeplessness, exalted mood, and increased productivity may reflect perfectly normal periods of creative excitement or they may be indicative of mania. They may overlap as the illness takes hold. Alcoholism, drug addiction, and medical conditions such as thyroid disease or seizure disorders may present as symptoms of mania or depression. If mildly elevated mood states have not been severe enough to be observed by other people, then major depression rather than bipolar illness may be incorrectly diagnosed. Still, enough is known about specific and defining characteristics of mania and depression—their symptoms; their course (the age at the onset of illness, a worsening of illness over time, seasonal patterns); a family history of mania, depression, or suicide; their close association with alcohol and drug abuse; the implication of a mood disorder in most suicides—to make it possible for experts to do meaningful biographical research. The caveats are many, but it is important to note the results.

The first biographical studies, carried out in the late 1800s, found improbably high rates of insanity in those defined as artistic geniuses. By the middle of the twentieth century, studies of mental illness in eminent artists and writers had become more refined in their diagnostic techniques and clearer about the criteria they used to select the artists and writers to be studied. The studies remained problematic but less so than they had been.

Despite the difficulties in research design and the wide variety of methods used, the findings are surprisingly consistent. They find a much higher rate of psychosis, usually mania, psychiatric hospitalization, depression, and suicide in writers and artists than in the general population. (Epidemiologic studies of the more severe form of bipolar illness, bipolar I, find rates of 0.6 percent in the general population and 0.4 percent for the less severe form, bipolar II. An estimated one person in a hundred, then, has bipolar illness. Individuals with milder forms of the disorder, those who do not reach the threshold for a diagnosis of bipolar illness, make up another 1 to 2 percent of the population.) This is true whether the research is conducted in the United States, Hungary, England, or France and whether the artists are painters, poets, or jazz musicians. Among types of artists, there is consistency: poets are the most likely to have a history of mania and the most likely to kill themselves. None were diagnosed with schizophrenia.

High rates of mood disorders have been found not only in biographical studies but in investigations of living artists and writers as

Biographical Studies of Depression, Mania, and Suicide in Eminent Writers, Composers, and Artists

Study	Sample	Findings
Juda, 1949	113 German artists and writers	Two-thirds were "psychically normal"; more suicides and "insane and neurotic" individuals in artistic group than general population. Highest rates of psychiatric abnormalities in poets (50%), musicians (38%), painters (18%), and architects (17%). First-degree relatives of artists and writers were more likely to be cyclothymic, commit suicide, or have manic-depressive illness. Psychosis was much more common in grandchildren of the artists and writers.
Martindale, 1972	21 eminent English poets (born 1670–1809); 21 eminent French poets (born 1770–1909)	55% of English poets and 40% of French poets had significant psychopathology ("nervous breakdown," suicide, and/or alcoholism). One in 7 had been placed in asylum or had suffered from severe "recurring and unmistakable symptoms," such as hallucinations or delusions.
Trethowan, 1977	60 eminent composers	Mood disorders "easily the commonest and most important of psychiatric illnesses" in composers; approximately 50% had a "melancholic temperament."
Jamison, 1993	36 most anthologized British and Irish poets (born 1705–1805)	17% had been committed to insane asylum; 22% had a history of psychosis; 39% had a strong family history of psychosis, suicide, and/or melancholia; 6% committed suicide.
Schildkraut et al., 1994	15 abstract expressionist artists (New York School)	More than 50% had a depressive illness; 40% received treatment; 20% hospitalized; 13% committed suicide; 2 paternal suicides.

Study	Sample	Findings
Ludwig, 1995	1,005 eminent individuals across all fields of accomplishment	Compared with other professions (business, science, public life), artistic group had 2–3 times the rate of psychosis, suicide attempts, mood disorders, and substance abuse. They were 6–7 times more likely to have been involuntarily hospitalized. Poets were the most likely to have committed suicide (20%), had mania (13%), been depressed (77%), and/or been psychotic (17%).
Post, 1996	100 eminent American and British writers	5% had history of bipolar psychosis; 16% severely disabled by depression; 8% committed suicide, most of them poets. Total of 82% with "affective abnormalities."
Preti and Miotto, 1999	3,093 artists and writers	Suicide highest in poets (2.6%) and other writers (2.3%); lowest in painters (0.7%) and architects (0.4%).
Czeizel, 2001	21 eminent Hungarian poets (born 1554–1925)	Bipolar I (14%); bipolar II (53%); major depression (9%); committed suicide (9%).
Wills, 2003	40 eminent American modern jazz musicians	Psychotic illness (7.5%); major mood disorder (28.5%); inpatient treatment for depression (10%); committed suicide (2.5%).
Kaufman, 2005	826 Eastern European writers	Diagnosis not specified. Mental illness designated on basis of suicide, breakdown, or psychiatric hospitalization. Poets had by far the highest rate of mental illness, fiction writers the lowest.

Adapted from K. R. Jamison, "Creativity in Manic-Depressive illness," in F. K. Goodwin and K. R. Jamison, *Manic-Depressive Illness: Bipolar Disorders and Recurrent Depression* (New York: Oxford University Press, 2007).

well. In 1987, Nancy Andreasen, a psychiatrist at the University of Iowa, used standardized diagnostic interviews to study thirty writers and thirty control subjects (individuals who were matched for education, gender, and age but whose professional work was not in the arts). The writers were participants in the Iowa Writers' Workshop, some but not most of whom were nationally acclaimed. Dr. Andreasen's primary research specialization is schizophrenia, a disease characterized by psychotic breaks but not by mania or bipolar ranges in mood. She expected that she would find a correlation between schizophrenia and creativity; that is, that the writers would have relatively high rates of schizophrenia. She found instead that fully 80 percent of the writers met the diagnostic criteria for a mood disorder; most strikingly, nearly one-half of the writers met the criteria for bipolar disorder. Indeed, writers were more than ten times as likely as the general population to be diagnosed with bipolar I disorder, the more severe form of the illness. They were also more likely to kill themselves. None were diagnosed with schizophrenia.

A few years after Andreasen's study of writers, I published a paper on forty-seven eminent British artists and writers I had studied while on sabbatical leave in England. They were selected on the basis of having won at least one of several major awards in their fields; for example, the painters and sculptors were Royal Academicians or Associates of the Royal Academy, an institution established by King George III in 1768 to honor a limited number of British artists and architects. Literary prizes used as criteria included the Queen's Gold Medal for Poetry and other prestigious British awards in fiction, nonfiction, and poetry. At the time of my study, one-half of the poets had already been anthologized in *The Oxford Book of Twentieth-Century English Verse*; since then, most of the remaining poets have been included as well. The playwrights who participated in my study were recipients of the major awards in their field; for example, the New York Drama Critics' Circle Award, the Tony Award, or the London Evening Standard Theatre Award.

My research focused not so much on mental illness in these artists and writers as on the influence of mood and seasonal changes on their creative work, but I also inquired whether they had been treated for depression or mania. A significant percentage, more than one-third, reported that they had. Because most people who meet the diagnostic criteria for mood disorders never seek treatment, this is likely a low estimate of the true rate of depression and mania in this group. Of artists and writers who had been treated for a mood disorder, three-quarters of them had been prescribed lithium or antidepressants and/or admitted to a hospital for psychiatric care. All of those who had been treated for mania were poets. One-half of the poets had been treated for bipolar illness or depression and, of the artistic groups, it was poets who most often reported that they had experienced extended periods of elated mood states. Most of them reported that their intense moods were essential to their creative work.

Arnold Ludwig, a psychiatrist who had conducted a large biographical study of psychopathology in eminent scientists, artists, writers, and military and civic leaders, then turned to the study of living writers. He compared fifty-nine women writers with fifty-nine women nonwriters who had been matched for age, educational level, and their fathers' occupational status. He found that the writers in his study were four times more likely than the nonwriters to meet diagnostic criteria for depression, five times more likely to have attempted suicide, and six times more likely to meet diagnostic criteria for mania; these findings were consistent with those from his own earlier biographical research and the studies by Dr. Andreasen and me. These studies, like the biographical ones, are hampered by methodological problems, such as possible inclusion bias and small sample size. They are illustrative and suggestive but far from definitive.

More recent investigations of creativity, intelligence, leadership, entrepreneurship, and mental disorders have used more sophisticated research designs applied to very large numbers of individuals. Six population studies have been carried out in Sweden and one in Denmark, where the governments maintain comprehensive medical and psychiatric records, as well as information on occupation, intelligence, military service, and educational attainment. Three studies were conducted elsewhere, one each in New Zealand, the United States, and the United Kingdom.

In the case of studies linking mental disorders to intelligence and other measures of cognitive ability, it emerges that lower childhood

Population Studies of Intelligence, Achievement, and Creativity in Individuals with Bipolar Disorder

Study	Sample	Findings
Zammit et al., 2004	N=50,087 27-year longitudinal study of IQ and hospital admissions for mental disorders (Sweden)	Lower IQ was associated with subsequent risk of schizophrenia, severe depression, and other nonaffective psychoses. No association between IQ and development of bipolar disorder.
Koenen et al., 2009	N=1,037 20-year study of association between childhood IQ and adult mental disorders (New Zealand)	Higher childhood IQ was significantly associated with hospitalization for bipolar disorder later in life. Lower childhood IQ was associated with schizophrenia and major depression.
MacCabe et al., 2010	N=713,876 9.5-year study of school performance at age 16 and adult bipolar disorder (Sweden)	Individuals with excellent school performance, especially in music and language, were four times more likely to later be hospitalized for bipolar disorder than those with average grades. Poor performance also was associated with an increased risk of bipolar disorder.
Tremblay et al., 2010	N=20,861 Epidemiologic Catchment Area Study (USA)	Individuals with bipolar disorder were disproportionately concentrated in creative occupations (artists, musicians, writers).
Kyaga et al., 2011	N=300,000 Patients with severe mental disorders and their first-degree relatives compared with normal controls (Sweden)	Individuals with bipolar disorder were overrepresented in creative professions. This was not true for individuals with schizophrenia or depression. First-degree relatives of individuals with bipolar disorder or schizophrenia were more likely than controls to hold creative jobs.

Study	Sample	Findings
Gale et al., 2013	N=1,049,607 20-year prospective study of men followed from military conscription (Sweden)	Men with highest IQ, especially those with highest verbal scores, had 41% increased risk of hospitalization for bipolar disorder. Men with lowest IQ were also at increased risk for bipolar disorder.
Kyaga et al., 2013	N=1,173,763 40-year total population study of creative occupations and mental disorders (Sweden)	Individuals with bipolar disorder were more likely to be in creative (artistic and scientific) professions. Not true for individuals with schizophrenia, depression, alcohol/drug abuse, ADHD, or anorexia nervosa. First-degree relatives of individuals with schizophrenia, bipolar disorder, anorexia nervosa, and autism were more likely to be in creative occupations. Very elevated risk of suicide in writers.
Biasi et al., 2015	N=3,400,000 Prescription, wages, and employment data (Denmark)	Individuals with bipolar disorder earned 43 percent less on average than the Danish labor force, but were 8 percent more likely to enter the 90th percentile of the wage distribution. Lithium treatment eliminated the wage penalty for those at risk for bipolar disorder and increased the chances of a very high income. It also decreased the rates of entrepreneurship.
Smith et al., 2015	N=1,881 14-year longitudinal study of childhood IQ and manic symptoms at age 22–23 (UK)	Better performance on IQ tests at age 8 was predictive of higher scores on a measure of manic features. This was particularly true for verbal IQ.

intelligence is associated with a higher risk of developing schizophrenia or major depression, but that the relationship is more complicated for bipolar disorder. A study of fifty thousand individuals, published in 2004, found no association between childhood intelligence and the development of bipolar disorder. Two others, one of more than one million men, found that high measured IQ in childhood was significantly associated with subsequent hospitalization for bipolar disorder. At the other extreme, individuals with the lowest IQ were also more likely to develop bipolar illness.

In a study of academic performance, as opposed to simple IQ, in more than seven hundred thousand individuals, those sixteen-year-olds who excelled at school, especially in music and language, were four times more likely to be hospitalized later for bipolar disorder than were those who performed at an average level. As was the case for intelligence, not only were those with excellent school performance more likely to develop bipolar disorder but so too were those with the lowest IQ and worst school performance.

A recent study from Stanford University and Aalborg University in Denmark found a similar split distribution in those with bipolar disorder, between those who exceeded the population performance—in this case, in wages and being an entrepreneur—and those who fell far below it. The researchers, who used Danish registry data from more than 3.4 million individuals, found, on the one hand, that individuals with bipolar disorder earned 43 percent less in wages; on the other hand, they were more likely to be entrepreneurs (for example, they were 33 percent more likely to be incorporated, one measure of entrepreneurial willingness to take risk) and 8 percent more likely to enter the ninetieth percentile of the wage distribution. Access to lithium treatment eliminated the difference between the population wage level and that earned by those with bipolar disorder; it also increased the chances that those with bipolar disorder would enter the ninetieth percentile of the wage distribution. Access to lithium treatment decreased the probability of becoming an entrepreneur, however; the investigators suggest that this may be due to lithium's effect of decreasing the willingness of individuals with bipolar disorder to take risks in the same way that they would if they were unmedicated. A recent Swedish total population study of leadership found that bipolar patients without comorbidity (that is, without any additional psychiatric diagnosis), and their healthy siblings, demonstrated superior leadership traits. Bipolar patients, but not their healthy siblings, were overrepresented in the lower strata of leadership as well. Healthy siblings of the bipolar patients were more likely to hold executive positions than the general population (particularly in political professions).

The brain vulnerable to mania and depression, it would seem, can veer to illness from origins of unusual strength or weakness. This is consistent with what we know from clinical experience. Some people become ill with almost no warning, their lives to that point characterized by good academic performance, by good relationships and psychological stability. In others, the onset of illness is more insidious and clinical symptoms develop earlier. Life even before the first manic or depressive break is more troubled, the personal and academic toll more lasting.

Patients with bipolar illness often show marked deficits in specific types of intellectual functioning, some much more than others. Neuropsychologists have found, for example, that the cognitive abilities most dependent on language are the ones least affected by bipolar disorder. Thus, verbal intelligence—language and verbal skills—tends to be normal or increased in bipolar patients. However, many if not most patients with bipolar illness display deficits in performance intelligence when tested on measures of visuospatial ability, perceptual reasoning, attention, and concentration. Often the deficits in attention and concentration, usually measurable before the first manic attack or depressive episode, are severe.

Additional characteristics interact with bipolar disorder to determine a patient's life story. Temperamental, genetic, and environmental factors may protect some patients more than others. Alcohol and drug use and too little sleep make the illness worse. A young developing brain assailed by mania or severe depression is usually more adversely affected than a brain that is older and has a longer history of stability.

The interplay between an individual's illness and temperament exerts a decisive role in how those with bipolar disorder ultimately do. It is clear that the prevailing mood during mania—whether paranoid and irritable or expansive and elated—influences the flow and the use of ideas during mania. This is important in creative work. But the difference in an individual's predominant mood may color the capacity for friendship and marriage as well; exuberance is more attracting and binding than suspiciousness and a short fuse. Certainly the age at which the illness begins and the number, duration, and severity of episodes of mania and depression are critical. Those who become ill when young or who remain untreated are less likely to enter successfully into the stress and scramble of life. And, after an attack of illness, they are less able to reenter life and regenerate what they need to thrive. Bipolar disorder is by no means a unitary diagnostic category. Hippocrates, Aretaeus, and Kraepelin knew this from their patients; modern scientists who study mania and depression provide evidence to buttress their observations. The variability of mania and depression remains constant.

In addition to the large population studies of the association between bipolar disorder, intelligence, leadership, and academic and entrepreneurial performance, three studies have looked more specifically at the association of bipolar disorder with creativity. In each, the researchers examined the association of the disorder with creative occupation rather than with creativity itself. They are not the same, but occupation is a pragmatic measure to use when studying very large numbers of individuals. Studies of eminent creators necessarily must involve relatively small numbers of individuals. Each kind of research, whether biographical or population-based, has its limitations and assets. An American study of more than twenty thousand individuals published in 2010 found that those with bipolar illness were disproportionately concentrated in the most creative occupations such as writing, the visual arts, and music. This finding is consistent with two much larger Swedish studies that were published shortly after. The first looked at three hundred thousand patients, their first-degree relatives, and controls, and the second at more than one million individuals; both investigations found that those who had been hospitalized for bipolar illness were overrepresented in the creative professions. This was not true for those who had been hospitalized for schizophrenia or depression. The first-degree relatives of individuals with bipolar disorder or schizophrenia were also more likely than controls to hold creative jobs. In the larger of the studies, the researchers found that writers had a greatly elevated rate of suicide.

The fact that the first-degree relatives of individuals who suffer from bipolar illness, and to a lesser degree those with schizophrenia, were more likely to be in creative occupations is given further strength by a recent study from Yale University. Co-twins of bipolar patients had higher scores on tests of verbal learning and verbal fluency than did control subjects. Earlier, less rigorously designed studies had found much the same thing. An investigation conducted in Iceland in 1970, for example, found that first-degree relatives of psychotic patients, as well as the patients themselves (many of whom initially were diagnosed as having schizophrenia but were later characterized by researchers as having had mood disorders, most often bipolar illness), were far more likely than the general population to be distinguished in the arts and intellectual pursuits. Nancy Andreasen, in her study of writers in the Iowa Writers' Workshop, found that there was a significantly higher rate of bipolar disorder and depression in the relatives of the writers than in the relatives of the controls. In addition, more first-degree relatives of the writers had histories of creative accomplishment than those of the controls.

In the late 1980s, Ruth Richards and her colleagues at Harvard University studied "everyday" creativity (which they defined as originality demonstrated in a wide range of ordinary endeavors, rather than societally recognized accomplishment in the arts or sciences) in a group of patients, their relatives, and control subjects. They found that the patients with bipolar illness, or mild variants of it, and their unaffected first-degree relatives had significantly higher creativity scores than the control subjects. In this study, the relatives of the patients with bipolar illness scored higher on creativity measures than the patients.

These studies confirm much earlier biographical work done in the 1890s and the 1930s that showed that creativity and psychopathology threaded their way through the families of eminent composers, artists, and writers. More recently, I found the same. I studied the family histories of eminent writers, artists, and composers and found extensive histories of mania, suicide, depression, and psychosis in their pedigrees, including those of George Gordon, Lord Byron; Virginia Woolf; Eugene O'Neill; Alfred, Lord Tennyson; Robert Schumann; William and Henry James; Herman Melville; Samuel Taylor Coleridge; James Boswell; Samuel Johnson; Vincent van Gogh; Gustav Mahler; John Berryman; Anne Sexton; Tennessee Williams; August Strindberg; Théodore Géricault; and many others. Creativity and instability ran together through the bloodlines. These families had heavy burdens of mania, depression, and suicide. It is reasonable to wonder why disease genes with such dire consequences persist in our species and what evolutionary pressure might protect them.

Many clinicians, geneticists, and evolutionary biologists have suggested that the answer may lie with the adaptive traits or states associated with the manic spectrum: greater reactivity to the environment; positive and expansive moods; increased energy and confidence; more tendency to take risks and to explore; greater ambition and curiosity; heightened aggression and increased sexual drive; more original and diverse cognitive styles; and a decreased need for sleep. Increased creativity may be part of this evolutionary advantage conferred to both the individuals who have bipolar illness and to their relatives, whose subtler manifestations of bipolar traits may benefit not only themselves and their families but society at large.

Manic-depressive illness is not like hemophilia, color blindness, or sickle-cell disease, caused by a well-characterized mutation in a single gene and traced through families in a Mendelian dominant or recessive pattern. The genetic contributions for manic depression and schizophrenia certainly come from variations in multiple genes on diverse chromosomes. Genome-wide association studies now allow us to begin looking for these patterns by studying the entire complement of genes in tens, indeed hundreds of thousands, of individuals. Using these powerful methods, a study of nearly ninety thousand Icelandic, Dutch, and Swedish subjects, published in 2015, found that certain patterns involving multiple genes were associated with bipolar disorder and schizophrenia. The same patterns were also significantly associated with measures of creativity. The researchers concluded that "creativity, conferred, at least in part, by common genetic variants, comes with an increased risk of psychiatric disorders conferred by the same genetic variants." The study is the first major one of its kind and has significant flaws in its design; it requires replication. But it is of scientific interest as a step toward defining biologically the link between psychopathology and creativity. To date, most scientists, for good cause, have focused more on the clinical implications of a genetic basis for mania and depression, less on its possible advantage. But it is clear that scientists will be looking more and more at the genetic underpinnings of both mental disease and creativity.

This is not a new concept. In 1920, Bronislaw Onuf, an American neurologist whose research had led him to conclude that the temperaments of great composers were strikingly similar to those who suffered from manic-depressive illness, published a paper in the *New York Medical Journal*. He asked provocative questions of "eugenic interest": "May it be beneficial to mankind to propagate the manic depressive temperament?" If so, "[c]an this be done safely, i.e., without bringing actual psychoses in the trail? Can this temperament be transmitted in combination with qualities of a superior order, fitting the individual for accomplishments of a high order?"

Two decades later, in 1941, during an era of intense interest in eugenics not only in Germany but also in the United States, the *American Journal of Psychiatry* published the results of a study undertaken by the Committee on Heredity and Eugenics of the American Neurological Association. There had been "justified horror," wrote the authors, that "mental disease appears generation after generation, causes untold social expense, and is an increasing burden of civilized society." But, they noted, there also had been many books and papers that suggested a "relationship between mental disease and genius or, at least, high ability." The purpose of the paper was to consider what might be the consequences of sterilizing patients with hereditary mental illnesses. Their subjects were patients and family members who, for generations, had been hospitalized at McLean Hospital in Boston.

The authors examined the records of twenty socially important families, by which they meant families whose members included presidents of the United States, secretaries of state, chief justices, governors of Massachusetts, founders of universities and railroads, eminent poets, "medical men galore," philosophers, and scientists. "One could not write a history of the United States without giving an important place to the individuals in these families," they wrote.

The "socially important" families, the researchers concluded, were saturated with manic-depressive psychosis; there would have been a high cost to sterilization:

It does not necessarily follow that the individuals who appear in these records were great because they had mental disease, although that proposition might be maintained with considerable cogency and relevance. It may be that the situation is more aptly expressed as follows. The manic drive in its controlled

form and phase is of value *only* if joined to ability. [If] the hypomanic temperament is joined to high ability, an independent
characteristic, then the combination may well be more effective
than the union of high ability with normal temperament and
drive might be. The indefatigability, the pitch of enthusiasm,
the geniality and warmth which one so often sees in the hypomanic state may well be a fortunate combination and socially
and historically valuable. . . . Sterilization procedures would
have deprived America of some of its most notable figures.

A study published in Germany in 1933—a few years before the
Nazis undertook their systematic program of killing tens of thousands of the mentally ill, who were, Hitler maintained, "unworthy
of life" and should not perpetuate themselves (doctors were ordered
to starve, poison, or gas their patients)—concluded much the same as
the New England researchers. The author of the German study, which
had found that manic-depressive illness was greatly overrepresented in
the professional and higher occupational classes, recommended that
patients with manic-depressive illness should not be sterilized, "especially if the patient does not have siblings who could transmit the positive aspects of the genetic inheritance."

There are consequences for any type of population selection
and control—in our time more likely to be tied to preimplantation
genetic diagnosis, or newly evolving genetic manipulation techniques
that include, most controversially, methods to edit genes in the germ
line and thus alter the DNA of all cells so that "dysfunctional" genes
would no longer be passed on generation to generation. The ethical
and societal implications of manipulating the inheritance of any trait
are potentially monumental; altering the inheritance of a complex,
treatable disease that manifests itself in variegated patterns of thinking, behavior, temperament, and energy—and one that may be linked
to creativity and ambition and distributed adaptively across healthy
relatives—is profound.

There are related issues associated with the recent development
of psychosis prevention programs that, laudably, attempt to identify
young people at risk for psychotic illnesses in order to slow or stop
progression in diseases such as schizophrenia and mania. It is important research and holds clinical potential for preventing devastating

conditions. But there should be discussion of possible unintended consequences. What if the prevention of psychosis or idiosyncratic cognitive styles or extreme mood states has a dampening effect on creativity or ambition? What if clinical decisions that benefit individuals are disadvantageous to society as a whole? It is not to suggest that these interventions should not progress; they should. It just means that the societal implications of the interventions should be discussed. There has been some discussion of these issues but not enough. Not nearly enough. If we purify, Lowell asked, do the water lilies die?

———

I think that your friends must not only sympathise with you but also thank you for going into terrible places of experience to bring back such poetry.
—LETTER FROM STEPHEN SPENDER TO LOWELL, 1965

It is not obvious that pathological mental states, especially those so aberrant as mania, should themselves aid imagination and art. It is possible that the studies reporting high rates of mania and depression in artists and writers are flawed, biased by the influence of a shared but not contributive association. Perhaps it is temperament alone, not manic thinking or moods, that artists and writers share with those who have manic-depressive illness. But, more likely, there are changes in thinking and mood that occur during mania and depression that act upon individuals who are already creative. These may catalyze art, affect its form, change its content, or determine the timing of its coming into being.

Mania and depression each contribute, but by nearly opposite pathways. Mania is generative; it speeds the mind and fills it with words, images, and possibility. It ties together distant thoughts and blasts buried recollection into consciousness; it brings to awareness that which otherwise would pass unregistered, unfelt, unwritten. Mania infects with the certainty that newly generated ideas are important and must be shared. Mania provokes the appalling and the violent and, now and again, partakes in creating that which is beautiful. The elated mood that usually accompanies mania disinhibits, makes the taking of risks and exploration more likely and creative combination of ideas more probable. To be in the grip of mania is to experience the unimaginable, try the unthinkable, do the unforgivable. The depressed mind is entirely different; it surveys darkly. It ruminates on the raw, generally unusable work that spills out during manic fertility. The depressed mind criticizes, revises, prunes, censors, improves. It shapes chaos, or tries to.

This is borne out by studies of the syntactical elements in speech samples taken from manic and depressed patients. Manic speech is more pressured, distractible, and colorful. Manic patients use more adjectives and action verbs and more words that reflect power and achievement; they also express themselves more vibrantly, with more color, and greater urgency. Depressed patients, on the other hand, use more qualifying adverbs; their speech is more impoverished and predictable than that of manic patients or normal individuals. Manic patients tend to talk more about things, depressed patients about themselves and other people.

Mania and depression are first and foremost diseases of the brain; too often this is overlooked. The brain is in all ways complex; it is who we are, how we think. It determines that which makes us human: our moods, affinities, imagination; our memories and capacities. Mania originates in this brain and, when active, it transforms it. If manic depression can abet creativity, the reason must lie substantially in the mood and thinking changes that take place when individuals are manic. The fluidity and force of ideas, and the original, if often bizarre, associations that occur during mania are critical to understanding the link between mood disorders and creativity. The symptom of mania referred to as flight of ideas, so defining of mania, was described by the ancients and has long been a part of formal diagnostic criteria. It lies central to manic thought. Flight of ideas is clinically unmistakable, characterized by a torrent of near-unstoppable speech; thoughts brachiate from topic to topic, held only by a thin thread of discernible association. Ideas fly out, and as they do, they rhyme, pun, and assemble in unexampled ways. The mind is alive, electric. "Bizarre associations sprang into his mind like enchanted crickets," said Vereen Bell about Robert Lowell. It is the perfect description.

Virginia Woolf was another whose mind sped into genius and madness. She "talked almost without stopping for two or three days," said her husband, "paying no attention to anyone in the room or anything said to her. For about a day she was coherent; the sentences meant something, though it was nearly all wildly insane. Then gradually it became completely incoherent, a mere jumble of dissociated words." Virginia Woolf wrote succinctly, "Once the mind gets hot it can't stop."

Emil Kraepelin observed that manic speech was a type to itself and that its characteristic pacing and sounds tied it to rhyme and free associative speech. "Apparently the only disorder in which the associations show a characteristic change is the *manic* excitement. In these cases for the most part the tendency to clang associations comes out very distinctly, especially rhymes, citations, and word completions, which may finally surpass all other forms." Flight of ideas often shows itself in rhyming or repeated vowel sounds, wordplay, or grouping of words by some common element. Clang associations, words that are associated to one another by sound rather than by idea or perception, are of obvious importance to poetic composition and are particularly common during mania. It is a fecund state: "My thoughts bustle along like a Surinam toad," said Coleridge of his overflowing mind, "with little toads sprouting out of back, side, and belly, vegetating while it crawls." So it is with manic flight of ideas: sprouting, bustling. For most individuals, words link in a reasonably straight line. For those who are manic, or those who have a history of mania, words move about in all directions possible, in a three-dimensional "soup," making retrieval more fluid, less predictable.

The abnormal flow of mental associations during flight of ideas is shown in an illustration from a textbook of psychopathology. The original thought can be traced, just, through the associations it sends scattering. The mind skips ahead, darts back and sideways. The brain is engaged in knight's move thinking.

John Custance, a Royal Navy officer who studied modern languages, theology, and psychology at Oxford, Cambridge, and the Sorbonne, wrote about mania in his 1952 memoir *Wisdom, Madness and Folly*. His flight of ideas sped from the Devil's colors to Satanic cats, from Julius Caesar to a king's coin. Although his ideas flew, mad, from topic to topic, there was a connecting strand. His account gives a vivid sense of the racing manic mind, a squash ball ricocheting wall to wall at angles sharp and unpredictable:

Blue was the heavenly colour; I was in Heaven, so that blue was appropriate and could be regarded as on my side. Black, on the

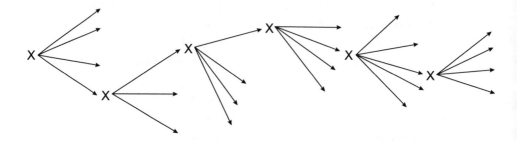

Flight of ideas during mania
"Bizarre associations sprung into his mind like enchanted crickets."

other hand, was another of the Devil's colours. Was he going to get me after all? What had grey to say about it? At night all cats are grey, so perhaps grey was a feline colour. I like the cat tribe, particularly when in the manic state. They are, I know, slightly Satanic, but it is the kind of Satanism I prefer; it reminds me of a favourite delusion—that I am Satan, the Servant of All, the Scientific Snake who told the truth in the Garden of Eden. . . . So I need not fear the Devil or his sable colour. As for the purple, well in those circumstances I could reasonably look upon it as the imperial purple, a sign that I was Emperor of colours, if of nothing else. I asked the spirit of Julius Caesar by the simple process of tossing a coin with the image and superscription of his successor, King George. Julius was good enough to give me confirmation. The coin fell heads.

To a point, the manic flight of ideas is such a natural part of manic excitement that patients wear it lightly. This changes. The mind moves too fast, to too many places. There is no reining it in and no familiar thinking to go back to. Sanity edges into madness. "In my mental or nervous fever or madness," wrote Vincent van Gogh, "my thoughts sailed over many seas." The magic, the brilliance, splinters into confusion, and then into terror. Flight of ideas gives pleasure at first, but that gives way to panic. Manic excitement disinhibits as surely and more vehemently than alcohol. This may abet artistic activity, observed Kraepelin, "especially poetical activity by the facilitation of linguistic expression." The president of the New York Psychoanalytic Society said much the same thing in 1918. The increased verbosity observed in mania, he said, gives rise to "rhyming, playing on words," to the "grouping and successive enumeration of things. . . . Objects just coming into their line of vision or sounds just heard or other sense-impressions of the moment are at once drawn into their talk by a quick illusion."

Ideas fly, often into madness; mania switches from the rapturous and clever into the baffling and bizarre. Lowell, in a letter to William Empson written the day before being committed to McLean Hospital in 1958, showed this loose-strung flying of ideas. The Garden of Eden unspooled into God's "pre-verbal" ways, into Christ's mania, into Lowell's mania. From there, his mental associations shot to Christ's/Lowell's depression, to the machines set up by Christ and Saint Paul, to the Mass and its composers, to Christ climbing to his feet after having undergone electric shock treatment. And there it stopped, at least on the page.

In "Visitors," a poem from Lowell's last book, *Day by Day*, an ambulance arrives to take the writer to the mental hospital. His mind skips; then it doesn't. Words stop. Virgil's journey winds back upon itself, paradise falls hellward:

> "Come on, sir." "Easy, sir."
> "Dr. Brown will be here in ten minutes, sir."
> Instead, a metal chair unfolds into a stretcher.
> I lie secured there, but for my skipping mind.
> They keep bustling.
> "Where you are going, Professor,
> you won't need your Dante."
> What will I need there?
> Is that a handcuff rattling in a pocket?
>
> I follow my own removal,
> stiffly, gratefully even, but without feeling.
> Why has my talkative
> teasing tongue stopped talking?
> My detachment must be paid for,
> tomorrow will be worse than today,
> heaven and hell will be the same.

The Swiss psychiatrist Eugen Bleuler, while acknowledging that the pelting stream of ideas may be unpleasant to patients, suggested that there may be advantage to those artistically talented. "Because of the more rapid flow of ideas, and especially because of the falling off of inhibitions," he wrote, "artistic activities are facilitated even though something worth while is produced only in very mild cases and when the patient is otherwise talented in this direction." It is this facilitation that commands attention. As does the caveat that carries the deepest weight: otherwise talented.

When mania swept through Robert Lowell's brain it did not enter unoccupied space. It came into dense territory, thick with learning, metaphor, and history; filled with the language and images of Virgil and Homer, the violent rhythms of Nantucket whaling; a decaying Puritan burial ground stacked with ancestors and ambiguity; the words and moods of New England writers, Hawthorne and Melville, Emerson, Thoreau, and Henry Adams, Jonathan Edwards; and the thicket of memories kept by a sensitive and observant child reeling within his family. The words of Dante, Shakespeare, Pasternak, Hardy, and Milton were not just in his mind but *were* his mind, kept alongside the place he kept for Dutch paintings and Beethoven's late quartets. Lowell's mind had been stamped by words and shaped by shifting moods; always, it had been beholden to words. Mania, when it came, shook his memory as a child shakes a snow globe.

When Lowell was well, which was most of the time, his mind was fast, compound, legendary. The depth of his knowledge and the relentless seriousness with which he acquired and used it were spoken to by virtually all who knew or studied with him. His was a retentive and elaborating mind; brilliant, all encompassing; a labyrinth of myth and language and experience. When mania attacked it advanced on a well-used and comprehended library of history and life, a field of ideas that could not be crossed. Mania attacked in the way characteristic of mania, a stereotypic assault, but the brain it set afire was rare in its capacity, seriousness, and discipline.

Seamus Heaney, in his memorial address for Lowell, spoke of Lowell's "amphibious" mind and iron discipline. "The molten stuff of the psyche ran hot and unstanched," he said, "but its final form was as much beaten as poured, the cooling ingot was assiduously hammered." Lowell went "into the downward reptilian welter of the individual self and yet [was able to] raise himself with whatever knowledge he gained there out on the hard ledges of the historical present."

Lowell's mind, said his friend Esther Brooks, was "so original, so perceptive, so finely wrought, that it seemed to intuit sensory experience without reacting directly to it." It was a mind that reached out and retained. And then wrought. The poet Stephen Spender wrote, "I more than envy the wonderful freedom with which you call in diverse experiences and references, like birds from the air, so that even the wildest things eat out of your hand." Wild things came into his mind, stayed until they found their place to go.

Lowell believed that poetry demanded "not just a technical mastery but also a human suppleness and range of response," wrote the critic Al Alvarez, qualities that were "everywhere in his nervous, flexible line, his sudden electric connections between literature and politics, history and sex, painting and marriage." Each year, mania set the range on fire.

Mania did not make Lowell a great poet; he was that before he was ever recognizably manic. But it was a determining force at times, driving rhythm and content. And, after long-drawn-out periods of no writing, it disturbed the embers and breathed back the life into his poetry. As he said to doctor after doctor, if he could control the mania rather than the mania controlling him, he would welcome it for his poetry's sake.

Why mania and milder states of excitement influence creativity is becoming better understood. The increase in speed of thinking so typical of mania, for example, may affect creativity in several ways. The increased number of ideas and associations is important in its own right. But this increase in quantity can influence the quality of thought as well; that is, the speed may so increase the volume of thinking as to change the nature of the thoughts themselves. From this may stem yet more originality of ideas and associations.

Some studies—the biographical ones discussed earlier, for example—use artists and writers whose designation as highly creative would not come into question. Most recent research, however, involves students or patients in laboratory situations. For these, scientists require more specific and universal criteria for creativity; the definition most widely used by psychologists is that creativity is the generation of ideas that are both novel and useful. The ideas can be of such an impact that they have a major influence on history, or they can be solutions to problems that arise in everyday living and affect only a few. There are many questions that arise in defining and measuring creativity, and, not surprisingly, an extensive research literature addresses these issues.

There are divers tests of creativity. The Torrance Tests of Creative Thinking, for example, are well validated and have been used for more than fifty years. They assess, among other things, fluency of thinking, originality, abstraction, richness and colorfulness of imagery, and fantasy. The Torrance Tests use a variety of tasks, including asking those being tested to come up with as many uses as possible for an object, such as a book or a tin can; to list as many "impossibilities" as possible (a nod perhaps to the Red Queen in *Through the Looking-Glass:* "Sometimes I've believed as many as six impossible things before breakfast"); to write "exciting and interesting" stories; to list all the things that might have happened when the cow jumped over the moon; to elaborate on physical representations or incomplete figures. Other frequently used measures of creativity are tests of word association or word fluency in which the individual is asked to give as many responses as he or she can produce to a test word, for example, to "moth" or "snowflake." The total number of responses, as well as the originality of the responses, is one gauge of creative thought.

Creativity and intelligence share characteristics and correlate with each other, but only to a point. An IQ in the general range of 120 seems to be the necessary minimum for moderate to high creativity, but after that point IQ and creativity go somewhat separate ways. Many people who are highly intelligent are not creative and many creative individuals do not score in the highest ranges of intelligence. Intelligence and creativity alike have a strong genetic base; the genetic contributions are estimated to be at least 50 percent.

Recently, neuroscientists have been attempting to study creative thought through neuroimaging, or brain scanning techniques. The methods are promising, but at this early stage of research they are difficult to interpret and inconsistent in their findings. A review of forty-five brain-imaging studies of creative thinking, for example, found that the wide diversity of measures of creativity and variability in neuroimaging methods made it impossible to draw definite conclusions. But it is clear from the recent history of scanning in medicine and neuroscience that the technology improves rapidly. Not too far into the future we will know a great deal more about the circuitry of the creative brain and the manic brain; we will know where they overlap and where they diverge.

Other scientific approaches used in studies of psychopathology, elated mood, and creativity have been quite consistent, however. There is a significant link among several pathological traits, especially those associated with mania, and measures of creativity. Early studies, including those done by Emil Kraepelin and his contemporaries, found that rhymes, punning, and sound associations increase during flight of ideas; many manic patients were observed to spontaneously start writing poetry. Psychologists have shown since that symptoms associated with mania, particularly flight of ideas, contribute to performance on tests measuring creativity. In studies of word fluency and association, researchers have found that the total number of responses given on a word association task increases threefold during mania; the number of predictable, that is, statistically common, responses falls by one-third. Lithium, presumably through its effect on manic thinking such as flight of ideas, has the reverse effect. Although the short-term use of lithium does not appear to affect creativity in normal individuals, in those who have a history of mania lithium decreases associational fluency and the originality of responses. The higher the lithium blood level the greater the dampening effect on verbal fluency.

In mania and excited states, elated mood contributes to creative thought. The evidence for this is strong and comes from many directions. Early clinical observers noted that manic patients who were elated were especially likely to exhibit flight of ideas. In 1858, Franz Richarz, the German psychiatrist who treated Robert Schumann during his final years in an asylum, described the importance of euphoric mood in the linking of thoughts. Sound, rhythm, and content were key and, he thought, closely tied to elation. In euphoric mania, Richarz wrote, "thoughts tend to form strings of ideas . . . that link together by their content, alliteration, or assonance." Euphoria encouraged association and rhythm. When euphoria was absent, and the manic patient's mood was one of unease and irritability, ideas sped, but differently: "The ideas come and go rapidly as if they were hunting each other, or continuously overlapping without any link between them." Thoughts crowded the mind but did not tie together in a pattern. The imaginative links were significantly beholden to elated mood.

A more recent study of one hundred acutely manic patients found, as had Richarz, that euphoric manic patients were more likely than those who were predominantly irritable to show flight of ideas. The patients with elated mania were also more likely to be expansive and grandiose. In 1946, researchers at the Payne Whitney Clinic in New York studied associational fluency in different groups of patients—manic-depressive, depressive, schizophrenic—and found that the patients with manic-depressive illness scored the highest on verbal fluency. Across all patient groups, patients scored higher when their mood was elated than when it was not.

During their attacks, manic patients generate many more word associations than normal individuals or patients with major depression or schizophrenia; they also use broader conceptual categories, a tendency they share with creative individuals. Some of this is due to the expansive mood and grandiosity that are so often a part of mania. Some of it may be due to the distractibility and attentional problems that many patients with bipolar illness experience, both while they are well and far more so when they are manic. Difficulty in maintaining attention generally has a negative effect on personal and professional success, but many studies show that it can be of some advantage in noticing things that others do not and combining observations in an original way. Psychologists studying latent inhibition, the capacity of the brain to screen objects or events that have been determined by experience to be "irrelevant," find that both highly creative individuals and individuals prone to psychosis tend not to screen out these "irrelevant details." This lack of filtering thus casts the net of attention over a wider range of objects; more ideas or objects are taken into awareness, then are available to be combined in original ways.

Lowell, in his essay "Hawthorne's Pegasus," writes to this point, the importance of indirection and glide in imagination. The child who will become a poet or storyteller knows that he cannot see "the marvelous winged" Pegasus by "trying to look directly at it, by gaping at the sky, or by hiking over the hot Greek hills. Only by letting his thoughts wander and wonder over the water's surface will he snatch up a reflection—it is just a common white gull's wing at first—and this will be the horse." Focus takes a toll on vision.

It is possible that once captivated by an idea or observation the scattered manic mind, paradoxically calmed by the enthusiasm that attends it, can settle into sustained concentration. Elated mood may act on diffuse bipolar thinking in a way analogous to how stimulants act in attention deficit disorder. In exuberant play, children and young animals display a similar pattern. They are distractible and far-flung over the field until their diffuse attention secures a point of interest. Then they focus their thinking and way of exploration. When Lowell was tested by psychologists as a young adolescent, he showed a striking inability to pay attention to the task at hand. Yet at the right time, when held by the beauty or complexity of the problem in front of him, he was formidable in his ability to focus intently on his work, hold his focus until a problem was solved, until the next high tide.

Artists and writers often report that elevated mood precedes periods of intense creative work. The majority of the British writers and artists in my study, for example, reported that during the preceding thirty-six months, sharp increases in their mood came just prior to periods of highly creative work. Researchers at Harvard University found that the great majority of their manic-depressive patients reported a greatly elevated mood when they were most creative. Both the British writers and artists and the American patients reported that these elevated mood states were characterized by ease and speed of thinking, expansiveness, and the effortless generation of new ideas. It is natural to expect that increased creativity should lead to a high or elevated mood. It is as, or more, likely that high mood leads to greater creativity.

Periods of high mood drive creativity; intense creative work may escalate mood yet higher. For those prone to mania the risk grows dramatically, particularly if the excitement of writing or composing leads to less sleep and more drinking. Lowell's mother, Lowell, and Elizabeth Hardwick all believed writing poetry could excite Lowell into mania. As early as 1943, Lowell's mother blamed his poet friends for pushing him over the edge with the "emotional excitement of poetry." When he was first hospitalized in 1949 she wrote that the doctors felt his illness was due in large part to overwork, overstimulation, and mental strain. Elizabeth Hardwick was glad for the respite that prose writing brought him since prose, unlike poetry, "need not thrive . . . on bouts of enthusiasm." This overheating of the poetic brain has long been a topic for physicians and philosophers. "Men of genius," declared Thomas Middleton Stuart in an 1819 essay, "Genius and Its Diseases," are like "some noble bird of heaven, stretching its flight towards ethereal regions, which soars and soars, unconscious of fatigue and reckless of danger, till it dies in the clouds." The man of genius, Dr. Stuart said, should "divert his mind" and "break in upon those strong associations which else might lead to evil consequences." He must take care. He must be tended. He must sleep. The brain was hot, Virginia Woolf had said less floridly.

The findings from studies that temporarily induce elevated mood in experimental subjects—through music, for example—also support the idea that positive mood enhances verbal fluency, more flexible thought, and a greater ability to solve problems in original ways; makes the subject see more relationships among ideas that at first appear to be unrelated; and encourages active exploration. Most of these studies use university students, not writers or artists of unquestioned creativity. Most do not use individuals who have a history of mania. The induced mood is generally mild, not comparable even to the earliest stages of mania; the subjects have been given champagne, in effect, not cocaine. Yet the results are quite consistent and provide a different perspective on elevated mood and creativity.

That positive mood increases creative thinking seems not unexpected, but how it does so, and why, is less obvious. Perhaps positive mood is incompatible with anxiety and other emotional states that interfere with generative thinking. There is evidence to support this; for example, scientists recently showed that when they stimulated areas in the brains of mice that usually are activated by pleasurable experiences, they protected them from the depressive consequences of stress. Perhaps we have evolved a specificity of mood to task; for example, researchers find that individuals in whom a positive mood has been induced do well on verbal tasks but less well on visual ones. The opposite is true when an anxious state has been induced. Since detecting physical danger is largely based on visual cues, the primitive emotion of anxiety may be wired better to serve visual perception. Language, on the other hand, newer to the brain, may be more linked to those parts that regulate dopamine and thereby connected to pleasure.

Dopamine, a neurotransmitter that long predates our mammalian ancestors, was a regulator of brain function in species that lived more than half a billion years ago. It controls mood, attention, movement and is central to reward; it strongly influences exploratory behavior as well. Dopamine is also strongly implicated in mania. Clinical research shows that drugs that decrease dopamine levels also decrease symptoms of mania. Some patients with Parkinson's disease, an illness characterized by a depletion of dopamine, given dopamine-enhancing drugs, have shown unexpected spurts of creativity. The same drugs not uncommonly induce mild expressions of mania. Certainly positive mood is associated with increased dopamine levels in the brain and abrupt release of dopamine may stimulate an individual to chase, explore, or advantageously notice.

Euphoric mania is an intoxicating state of mind: exuberant, exalted, and inclined toward a sense of cosmic relatedness. Anything is possible; all relates to all. But mood during mania is also fluctuating and volatile. Mania, observed Emil Kraepelin, "is predominantly exalted and cheerful, influenced by the feeling of heightened capacity for work. The patient is in imperturbable good temper, sure of success, 'courageous,' feels happy and merry, not rarely over flowingly so." But, he continued, there often exists a "great emotional irritability."

Among adolescents suffering early in their lives from mania, scientists can distinguish two subforms of the condition, one that is predominantly irritable and another that is predominantly exuberant. This is consistent with studies of mania in adults. These patterns appear to be genetically determined. The exuberant manic patients are more likely than the irritable ones to score high on measures of verbal intelligence and to show better psychological and social adjustment.

Mania is more than fevered mood and pelting thoughts. It is a disinhibiting force to act on ideas, fearlessly and however rashly; put ambition to action; scald the earth, splash color against the gray; to harm, to create. The seventeenth-century English physician Thomas Willis wrote that "Madmen are not as Melancholicks, sad and fearful, but audacious and very confident, so that they shun almost no dangers, and attempt all the most difficult things there are." Mania is tied as well to temperament—the largely hereditary characteristics of personality—and, specifically, to many of the characteristics of temperament associated with creativity. Stanford researchers have found, for example, that bipolar patients and highly creative individuals have more personality traits in common than do healthy controls and creative individuals. Patients with bipolar illness, in general, show more emotional responsiveness to people and events in their lives; they are, as Emerson put it, "of a fibre irritable and delicate, like iodine to light." Patients with the more severe form of bipolar illness, or those who have a predominantly manic course, are more likely to have an underlying hyperthymic temperament; that is, to be warm, extraverted, uninhibited, independent, energetic, and self-assured. They are also more likely to take risks others would not and to vigorously explore the environment around them. Their disease may be virulent when it is active, but their temperaments allow for greater reengagement with the world, more resilience. Many of these traits of temperament are closely associated with creativity as well.

Most patients say that they feel good, exquisitely good, in the early stages of mania, on the way up. They feel they can do anything, charm anyone, write rings around Dante and Shakespeare. One of John Campbell's manic patients summed it up as many do. When told by his doctor that he was ill he replied, "If I'm ill, this is the most wonderful illness I ever had."

———

Patient says he "thinks in hallucinations." This is representative of the entire tone of the patient which almost suggests the desirability of psychosis as a qualification for great artistry. Apparently the whole thought process is unrealistic although the actual phrases are very comprehensible and make good enough sense.
— HOSPITAL ADMISSION NOTE FOR ROBERT LOWELL, DECEMBER 1957

Mania, whatever its relation to art, is a serious illness; the delusions and hallucinations that often accompany it make this particularly clear. Delusions—fixed, false, idiosyncratic beliefs—marked Lowell's attacks of mania from the time he was first ill until his final episodes in the year before he died. This is more common than not in mania; half of those who have been manic have been delusional at one time or another. Of those who have been delusional, half have had grandiose delusions and half have had paranoid delusions. Lowell's delusions were overwhelmingly of the grandiose type. (In children with bipolar I disorder the rate of delusions is even higher than in adults, and grandiose delusions are far more common than persecutory ones.) Delusions during mania are often religious, expansive, and infused with the experience of special journeys and identification or intimate communication with the great.

The manic patient is a prophet, observed Kraepelin; he has to "fulfill a divine mission, hides the world-soul in himself." Delusionally manic patients take journeys that only they can take, participate in special adventures that no one else is privy to. Manic delusions intensify the external and internal worlds; the fear and ecstasy of the psychotic mind are projected inwardly and outwardly.

Psychosis, in the form of delusions, hallucinations, want of reason—madness, in short—have implications for creative work that go beyond those of exuberance and elated mood states. What is the impact of even a single psychotic break, much less repeated ones, on the inventing brain? At a biological level, psychosis—manic insanity—almost certainly changes the chemistry of the brain, and perhaps even its structure as well. It is likely that a single attack increases the chances of future attacks of mania. There are progressive changes in the brain—decreases in gray matter volume in the prefrontal region, for example—related to the number of manic episodes. These, it has been hypothesized, may be due to decreased levels of neuroprotective factors, stress-induced elevation in cortisol, or neuroinflammatory factors. The psychological effects of psychosis on the brain, as well as on the person who has been psychotic, are pernicious. To lose one's mind and to have to live with the emotional and professional consequences of having done so are among the most terrifying experiences anyone can have. To be haunted by the fear of going mad again, to lose faith in the reliability of one's mind: these are fears not knowable to anyone but those who have been psychotic. The life that follows the breakdown is the broken plate that F. Scott Fitzgerald described. One can enter into life again; less well can one reenter the fray of life.

And yet, in some minds that have been attacked by mania, under some circumstances, a psychosis may expose imagined worlds that are so intense, so believable, so wonderful, so terrifying, so inhabited that the mental landscape is scorched and also broadened in a way that changes not only the content of thinking but its form. Like the Australian *banksia* flower that needs fire to release its seeds, mania sets loose dormant thoughts and emotions. Once escaped, they take root in unexpected ways and places. The mind must then expand and create to comprehend what has happened. Psychosis compels that a bridge be built, that the mind invent a way from madness back to sanity.

The grandiose delusions of identity to which Lowell fell captive so often—he was at times Christ, the Holy Spirit, Achilles, Aeneas, Saint Paul, Alexander the Great, Napoleon, King James IV, Hitler, Henry VIII, the Messiah, John the Baptist, Dante, Milton, Julius Caesar, T. S. Eliot—reflected the imaginative history in which he moved easily. He knew these figures well, their work better. They were creators and destroyers: gods, heroes, tyrants, and saints. When he was manic, Lowell entered their world; he assumed their rage and took on their charms, saw the Devil and smelled the brimstone: felt keenly the danger in which the world hung, hacked his way through the walls of his house looking for the Etruscan treasures he knew had been hidden there. He entered into history—world, personal, psychotic—with sympathy and wisdom; provided detail from a teeming, informed mind. At times, the Devil and brimstone were metaphoric; when he was mad they were real; when he was well again, they were metaphoric but differently known and expressed. Poetry called upon life. "It is hard to say what you can put into poetry," he told an interviewer in Maine. "It has to be something you've lived."

With distance from his illness came the opportunity to use slivers of his delusional experience for poetry; the backward look discomfited. "What can you do after having been Henry VIII or even a cock of the walk weekly sheriff?" he wrote to Peter Taylor. "You get beautifully your character's living for the moment he is seen or heard. All life for the flashes! Everyone has a lot of that, and we writers more than most, only the words, the structure, the tune come out of us, are us." Lowell's delusions came from the dangerous, as well as the extraordinary, elements within himself. He could uniquely hurt with his command of language; he could uniquely captivate by the same power. He drew upon his discipline, imagination, and courage to write.

Lowell's delusions came in part from the random stirrings of memory, shredded and rearranged, in many ways apropos of nothing. Delusions are like the bits of recollection and perception that push to the surface during delirium or dreams. But unlike delirium, they usually coalesce into a story. Lowell's delusions came as well from his personally registered history of the world; his loves and his convictions; his deep reading of poetry, classics, and history. His psychosis, although beyond his control, was beholden to the specifics of his life and to the intricate minuet and genius of his brain; when he recovered, he would change and chisel the poetry he had written when he was manic. Parts were unsalvageable, others radically original.

Mania gives rise to "new and wonderful talents and operations of the mind," wrote Benjamin Rush in 1812. It can be compared to an earthquake, "which by convulsing the upper strata of our globe, throws upon its surface precious and splendid fossils, the existence of which was unknown to the proprietors of the soil in which they were buried."

"The foundations of the earth do shake," it says in Isaiah. "Earth breaks to pieces, / Earth is split in pieces, / Earth shakes to pieces." Mania shook Lowell's brain from its moorings; assailed his identity and certainties. There were hard ways back to sanity—imagination, work, grit, love, and medicine—and he made use of them.

Art in the early twentieth century, Lowell said, was a remarkable thing. The creative world was on fire. Foundations broke. "Life seemed to be there," he said. "It seemed to be one of those periods when the lid was still being blown. The great period of blowing the lid was the time of Schönberg and Picasso and Joyce and the early Eliot, where a power came into the arts which we perhaps haven't had since. . . . They were stifled by what was being done, and they almost wrecked things to do their great works."

Lowell's imagination moved as on tectonic plates; during mania, the plates shifted and clashed. His mind and poetry did not rest; they grew, innovated, transformed. "He could have settled into a fix," Derek Walcott wrote. "But every new book was an upheaval that had his critics scuttling. . . . Then his mind heaved again, with deliberate, wide cracks in his technique." Any attempt to understand Lowell's work must necessarily be "more seismographic than aesthetic." Upheaval was beyond the will; the discipline to shape it was not. Imagination was somewhere in between.

12

Words Meat-Hooked from the Living Steer

The needle that prods into what really happened may be the same needle that writes a good line, I think. There's some sort of technical connection; there must be at best. Inspiration's such a tricky word, but we all know poetry isn't a craft that you can just turn on and off. It has to strike fire somewhere, and truth, maybe unpleasant truth about yourself, may be the thing that does that.

—Interview with Al Alvarez, 1963

Inspiration, like his moods, came fitfully to Robert Lowell. Poems fueled by it, he said, "somehow lift the great sail and catch the wind." It was a wind Lowell had known since childhood, when his mother read to him from Hawthorne's retelling of the Greek myths. Pegasus, the winged horse who lived in the wind, was imagination, Lowell said; Pegasus was the sky flyer. He had taught Lowell to "travel in the sky." Day after day, "we walk the same sidewalks, go into the same rooms, see the same people." Then, the shift: "Imagination catches us and carries us off on the winds of invention. Dragons smoke, gold blazes in rock holes, we stare at the dull old carpet and see a kingdom."

Some, said Lowell, even great writers like Horace, set limits on what they allow into their imagination. They insist that horses cannot have wings. Horace, who like most Romans "wanted to see things straight and as they are," may have believed that horses can't fly and are meant for plowing, wrote Lowell. He might in our modern times have told Bellerophon, who rode and mastered Pegasus, "to go to a hospital." But perhaps Horace was right, Lowell added. Perhaps "even people of imagination must learn to walk on the ground."

The boundary between vivid imagination and madness is porous. It is notably so for those inclined to mania. Percival Lowell, astronomer, writer, and distant cousin, more than once slipped across the border from the fever of imagination into breakdown. He wrote about life on Mars and sketched canals built by Martians yet also warned that there should be a balance between shackle and unreined forces. "Let me warn you to beware of two opposite errors," he said. "Of letting your imagination soar unballasted by fact, and, on the other hand, of shackling it so stolidly that it loses all incentive to rise. You may come to grief through the first process; you will never get anywhere by the second."

Imagination needs a bridle—Pegasus had a golden one—but it needs as well an open field in which to run. How best then to balance the bit and the spur is the question for any imaginative writer. It was a struggle Lowell knew well: how to master natural forces, how to use them artfully. Mania, of all the forces, was uncontrolled, kept a capricious schedule, brought destruction. But, now and again, it brought inspiration as well. And shook the foundations.

Neither life nor poetry moved in a line. "The arts do not progress," said Lowell; they "move along by surges and sags." Inspiration was part of it, certainly, but so too was hard work. Jonathan Miller once asked Lowell about the traditional impression that poets lay in wait for inspiration and then wrote "in some sort of transport." Lowell disagreed. Inspiration may be needed but it was not enough. "There is something inside [that you] have to catch," he said. "It's not a feeling usually, it's some sort of image or even abstract image or sequence—and then it's days and different moods tinkering with it." At some point in the creative process, he argued, mood ceases to be as important as the ideas being worked on and the effort put into shaping them. "I think it must be sort of rough dirt that can be formed into something . . . but it's not valuable until that's done."

The wind of inspiration was an image that Lowell returned to often. Wind was a natural force: fickle, undivinable, part of the long history of the race. Wind dispersed seeds, scattered life, moved the still. He saw it—on the ponds and ocean, moving its way across the fields, and in the shaking of the leaves and branches. The wind, Lowell said during a reading at the Library of Congress, was at times inspiration; at others, it was nothing but nothingness. In the summer of 1968, he wrote to his eleven-year-old daughter, Harriet, from their summer home in Castine, Maine: "While you were playing your music, I was lying on my bed in the bedroom, watching the tops of the elms, tossing high in the wind and sunshine—by themselves, if you could imagine them somehow not part of their trees, the tree-tops were no taller than bushes on the ground. I wrote a poem about it all: you playing your own work, the trees tossing in the wind, and that other wind, what I might call the wind of inspiration, what blows in your mind when you compose or just think." The poem begins:

> I see these winds, these are the tops of trees,
> these are no heavier than green alder bushes;
> touched by a light wind, they begin to mingle
> and race for instability—too high placed
> to stoop to the strife of the brush, these are the winds.

It ends on crosswinds and mystery, on the uncertainty of imagination: "how often / winds have crossed the wind of inspiration— / in these too, the unreliable touch of the all."

Toward the end of his life, after mental illness had taken a greater toll, Lowell wrote more darkly about the wind's way through the trees. "Tops of the midnight trees move helter-skelter / to ruin," he wrote when he was living in London in the 1970s. "We stand and hear the pummeling unpurged, / almost uneducated by the world— / the tops of the moving trees move helter-skelter."

Lowell's poetry is thick with images of winds and tides, nature's forces that ebb back, and flow. Rivers. The poet is a fisherman: "groping for trout in the private river, / wherever it opens, wherever it happens to open." He writes too of flight, escape, and navigating high places; of balloons and bubbles, transients that float "jobless" in the air, only to burst pricked or too high; to die. Beholden to time, wind, caprice, they are slave to the forces that make them rise, pull them moonward, skyward, sunward. A balloon once blithe now is snagged "high in an elm." Bubbles and balloons, like hope, rise, swell, burst; they are given, like Achilles, a short, glorious life before an early dying. The bubble's beginning, like the balloon's, edges into its end. Colonel Shaw riding on his bubble in "For the Union Dead" waits for the "blessèd break." The bubble, not the rose or skull, is Lowell's chosen symbol for mortality, *memento mori*.

Like balloons and bubbles, mania rises and expands: insistent, illusory, precarious. Seductive. Lowell took his epigraph for " 'To Speak of

Elms in Castine, Maine
"I was lying on my bed . . . watching the tops of the elms."

Woe That Is in Marriage'" from Schopenhauer: "It is the future generation that presses into being by means of these exuberant feelings and
supersensible soap bubbles of ours." Illusion is necessary. Mania bursts
after its early, inebriating days. "It's not much fun writing about these
breakdowns after they themselves have broken and one stands stickily
splattered with patches of the momentary bubble," Lowell wrote to a
friend in the wake of a manic attack. Mania was glorious but transient,
and its damage lasted. So too did the knowledge that it would return,
rise, swell, and break again. "Surely, there's some terrible flaw in my
life that blows a bubble into my head every year or so," Lowell wrote
to Elizabeth Hardwick.

The patient has had a series of breaks, all in the light of unusual literary output.

—HOSPITAL ADMISSION NOTE, DECEMBER 1957

A connection between Robert Lowell's manic-depressive illness and his poetry was readily apparent to Lowell's psychiatrists as well as to most of his friends and colleagues. Lowell and his doctors observed a clear link between the onset of mania and a marked increase in the fluency of his words and the amount he wrote. Dr. Erik Linnolt, Lowell's psychiatrist during his stays at the Hartford Institute of Living in 1962, 1963, and 1965, stated that "Lowell felt that the early stages of his mania came with increasing creativity and flow of words. He felt his illness was part of him and his work." Dr. John Blitzer, Lowell's psychiatrist at Payne Whitney in 1949, recorded in his medical notes that Lowell had experienced repeated periods of elation and mania that were characterized by greatly increased creativity and "coincided with the patient's beginning some new [literary] project." Lowell's "strong emotional ties with his manic phase were very evident," he observed. "Besides the feeling of well-being," Lowell told his doctor, his "senses were more keen than they had ever been before, and that's what a writer needs." Five years later, during his second stay in Payne Whitney, Lowell told his psychiatrist that he wrote best when he was "a little too excited." When manic and "elated of being Christ," he said, "confidence was all-present" and he was certain that "everything will work out. There is an order of things." Lowell explained that he took the images and ideas he had when he was manic and, after he was no longer psychotic, he assembled the bits; he carved his poems from them.

Throughout the intensely creative months of 1957, during which Lowell wrote most of the poems for *Life Studies*, he told his doctors that his pattern of illness and writing was the same as it always had been: his mood had been elated, his mind raced, he spoke too much, did too much, and he slept too little. Most important, he said, when he was manic, poetry came far more easily to him than when he was well; it was fresher, radical, more original. When he was admitted to Boston State Hospital in December, he told the admitting psychiatrist that he "might be having another manic episode because he had been writing with increased facility for the past several months." He had begun or completed "Skunk Hour," "Man and Wife," " 'To Speak of Woe That Is in Marriage,' " "Beyond the Alps," and several of the other poems that were to be in *Life Studies*.

As time went by, writing fast, furious, and near ceaselessly became a warning symptom of impending mania, along with falling in love and beginning a new affair or grandiose delusions when he declared himself to be Dante or Alexander the Great. When Lowell was transferred to the Massachusetts Mental Health Center in December 1957, Dr. Marian Woolston drew up a summary of Lowell's writing patterns and his manic illness:

> From February until April 1949 the patient's literature included no productive writing.
>
> In September and October 1957 the patient enjoyed some of his most productive months of writing poetry.
>
> About one month prior to admission, this being sometime in November [1957], the patient ceased his great spurt of writing.
>
> The patient has consistently been almost explosive in his outputs of energy. His life history is characterized by temporary complete engrossment in his writings which has always been accompanied by verbal hyperactivity sometimes to the point of an acute breakdown.

Many of the friends and colleagues who knew him best agreed with the psychiatrists who treated him that Lowell wrote much more poetry during the time leading up to mania. He then extensively revised the raw poems, or fragments of poems, when he was depressed or recovering from mania. They did not all agree about the quality. In 1975 Lowell told his London doctor, "I write my best poetry when I'm manic." The doctor had his doubts. Raving was not the same as creating, he said.

The painter Sidney Nolan, a friend of Lowell, was asked what he thought the effect of Lowell's mania was on his writing. "I noticed that at a certain point—from when he was dead sane to when he started to bubble a bit—he would get witty and write very good poetry. Then it would go further and further and then he'd get the poems a bit confused. And then he'd go further and it was all completely confused. But for that period of, well, *fizz*—he was writing good poetry. He tended to spoil early poems when he was ill. I came to the conclusion, though, that there was a connection between the dead-on syntax and him being a bit goofy."

Ten years earlier, Allen Ginsberg had talked with Lowell, who was, at the time, on the way to the hospital for a "rest cure." Lowell told him that "the particular hopped-up state of mind in which he found himself was precisely the state of mind in which his best ideas for poetry occurred." The manic attacks that put Lowell in the hospital, said the classicist Robert Fitzgerald, were brought on by his having been "overborne by the fever that one felt to be just beyond some of his poems from the beginning." The fever that brought his mind alive was the same fever that could destroy it.

The writer Jonathan Raban, as a friend of Lowell and editor of his selected poems, was in a particularly good position to observe the relationship between Lowell's mania and his poetry. He told Ian Hamilton that Lowell's manic-depressive illness was closely aligned to his work: "The affliction was so like the poetry—the way the metaphors got released, the way that all the teasing and verbal games that he'd play ordinarily would become totally consuming activities in this affliction." Raban said that Lowell often wrote bad first drafts of poems, drafts he would not tolerate when sane, but that they gave him the raw material for his poetry. He then assiduously revised the drafts when he was depressed. Lowell, Raban told me, had said to him on many occasions, "I write in mania and revise in depression." When he was in the hospital, Raban visited and found him with "sheets and sheets of paper—writing at a furious rate."

"In many ways," Raban recalled, "the delusion of mania was so close to the mischievousness of invention which was his sanest side. The peak was a very narrow one." Lowell, he continued, "was the most continuously metaphoric person I've ever met. Somebody who was incapable of seeing one object without wanting to fantasize it into another kind of object. His whole habit of thinking and feeling was metaphoric. In mania the metaphors took over."

Lowell's mind as one of constant metaphor was widely observed. "I have always felt that Cal stood at a different angle to experience than most people I've known," said Esther Brooks. "Most of us, I believe, encounter something, then we feel it, and then we think about it. With Cal it would seem that whatever he encountered he thought about first, then he turned it into metaphor, and then he reached with feeling to that abstraction." Brooks recounted the time that one of his stepchildren came to him shouting that her friend was stuck in a bog. "Cal didn't move. Instead he looked around the room in anguish and said, with his outward prodding palm jabbing at the air, 'We are all stuck in the bog. Nobody can help us. It's impossible to help someone out of their bog when we can't get out of our own bog.'" It took further screams and passing time before Lowell grasped the fact that the bog was real, not metaphor.

The great ambition that is so much a part of mania is also impervious to the usual checks on language; mania vaults over the rules of syntax and grammar. Much of what Lowell generated during mania was unusable; some of it, however, became the rough material for later and great poems.

Lowell wrote little poetry when he was depressed. He told psychiatrists that during his depression he was "unable to concentrate, was only interested in himself, and completely unable to write." In 1949, when he was a patient at Payne Whitney, he told Dr. John Blitzer that he had renewed work on a poem that he had begun at the onset of his elated phase but was now "very depressed by how confused he had been writing the poetry." He could write, he said, but he could not concentrate nor make the kind of connections that came so easily to him when he was manic. If, however, he was only mildly depressed, he wrote to Peter Taylor, his "periodic *de profundis*" was "a spur to writing."

When he was depressed, Lowell said, he went over his work, painstakingly, trying to understand it and trying to salvage what he could. Melancholic reflection could add something to art, he said; suffering was a muse of sorts. "Only out of pain is the art that can hide art," he had said about the poetry of John Crowe Ransom. "Art demands the intelligent pain or care behind each speck of brick, each spot of paint." Mood combines with memory in odd, contrary ways. Lowell ended *Notebook* (1970) by saying, "In truth I seem to have felt mostly the joys of living; in remembering, in recording, thanks to the gift of the Muse, it is the pain." Memory was mutable; joy moved into pain, pain changed into joy. "On the great day, when the eyelid of life lifts— / why hide it? Joy has had the lion's share."

Depression did not transform Lowell's work in the way that mania did. "Depression's no gift from the Muse," he once said. "At worst, I do nothing. But often I've written, and wrote one whole book—*For the Union Dead*—about witheredness. It wasn't acute depression, and I felt quite able to work for hours, write and rewrite. Most of the best poems, the most personal, are gathered crumbs from the lost cake. I had better moods, but the book is lemony, soured and dry, the drouth I had touched with my own hands. That too may be poetry—on sufferance." Depression isn't danger, Lowell continued. "It's not an accomplishment. I don't think it a visitation of the angels but a weakening in the blood."

Lowell rewrote ceaselessly, on occasion radically altering the meaning of individual words and entire poems. John Berryman recalled one poem that Lowell had first titled "To Jean," which ended up as "To a Whore at the Brooklyn Navy Yard." Charles Mingus ripped apart his jazz compositions and rebuilt them into something new. Lowell did likewise with his poems. Mutability in his language was as fundamental as the mutability in his moods. When Frank Bidart pointed out contradictory meanings in different versions of a poem, Lowell said, "But they both exist." The draft of one poem, for example, read "the mania for phrases dried his heart." In a subsequent version, it became "the mania for phrases enlarged his heart." Contradictory, but they both exist. Most of the time he felt his poetry benefited from the reworking; occasionally he believed he had lost some of the original intensity of his writing in the process. "I took 14 poems from *Notebook* called 'Long Summer,'" he said, which had been written about a summer in Maine with Elizabeth Hardwick and their daughter. The original poems were "dense, symbolic, almost hallucinated," a "mixture of the style and mood behind it." In his subsequent book *History*, he continued, "I calm them up, make them poems about boyhood in Maine. But the first version is much better."

"I don't believe I've ever written a poem in meter where I've kept a single one of the original lines," Lowell said. He revised "endlessly"; sometimes there were as many as thirty versions of one poem. He "was revising something from the moment he got up until the moment he went to sleep," observed Elizabeth Hardwick. Depression is a ruminative, highly self-critical state, ideal in its way for revising work generated in a spewing, generative, less self-censoring manic state. Depression prunes and edits. "I have observed that one mood is the natural critic of the other," wrote Henry David Thoreau. This is true. Depression also corrects. Lowell's passion for accuracy came in part from the corrective of depressive self-criticism; it came as well, Helen Vendler has suggested, from his understanding that "madness does not give an accurate sense of life."

The extent and complexity of Lowell's revising were legend. His friend Peter Taylor described the process in an interview: "One of the first things I noticed was his revision, his revision and revision and revision and you would see the poem written over in this sort of printed handwriting, over and over the same point with slight changes and then on each piece of paper, arrows and asterisks and changes—endless

Draft manuscript of "Epilogue"

Draft manuscript of "Epilogue"

changes till finally the poem didn't have the same, wasn't the same poem at all, didn't mean the same thing at all. I think that was the beginning of my learning that all things are equal in poetry, all the elements that go into making a poem and that including the theme, the theme is no more important than the form."

The drafts here of "Epilogue," only a few of the many that went into the final poem in Lowell's final book, show how to the end he painstakingly revised his work. The meaning, language, and form of the poem changed across its many drafts, not least in upending its title from "Preface" to "Epilogue." The published version of the poem is given on page 371. He brought, as one critic put it, a "grinding labor" to his raw genius.

───────

Not a great deal of Lowell's poetry is specifically about his mental illness; his work would not be of lasting literary importance if it were. But he wrote extraordinarily well about mania and depression, about madness. And his imagery—winds and tides that open this chapter, balloons and bubbles—reflect his preoccupation with moods and mutability. His poetic genius, together with his dispassion, his capacity to stand back and reimagine, make his poetry so powerful.

Bubbles, in Lowell's language, foreshadow death and madness but they also bring hope, at times magic. "Lately, I've felt I was waking from a long dream," Lowell wrote to Elizabeth Bishop. "Fearful, hopeful, thrilled, a great weight pulling me backwards, a great air-bubble floating me upward, and somewhere a kind of birth in the substantial." After Lowell died, a manuscript poem titled "Balloon" was found among his papers in England. It tells of the pull to rise, the illusion of freedom, a cold and final journey, and the debt owed for the flight:

> It takes just a moment
> for the string of the gas balloon
> to tug itself loose from the hand.
>
> If its string could only be caught in time
> it could still be brought down
> become once more a gay toy
> safely tethered in the warm nursery world
> of games, and tears, and routine.
>
> But once let loose out of doors
> being gas-filled the balloon can do nothing but rise
> although the children who are left on the ground may cry
> seeing it bobbing out of human reach.

On its long cold journey up to the sky
the lost balloon might seem to have the freedom of a bird.
But it can fly only as a slave
obeying the pull to rise which it cannot feel.

Having flown too high to have any more use as a plaything
who will care if it pays back its debt and explodes
returning its useless little pocket of air
to an uncaring air it has never been able to breathe.

Flight is precarious, whether it is the flight of a balloon, the imagination, or mania. Being suspended in air, with no assurance of ledge or foothold, is a central image in Lowell's work. The toe is "skating the sheet for bedrock." He writes in a poem, "I hang by a kitetail"; in another of awakening on the "window's sloping ledge." Lost in flight, he searches for a foothold but is left "in flight without a ledge." In "Dropping South: Brazil," he loses his "foothold on the map, / now falling, falling, bent, intense, my feet / breaking my clap of thunder on the street." Ambition and defiance are like flight. "There is no foothold on your heights," Prometheus warns, and is warned, in Lowell's translation of Aeschylus. "You are already on your way down. Your fall will be hard, your fall will be soon." And, at play's end: "We've reached the end of the road, the topmost stone on the rooftop of the world. Beyond here, everything is downhill." The ladder leads first to the moon, then down from it to earth and hell.

The possibility of falling, plummeting from a life of high mood and ideas, is integral to creative work. If there is enough imagination, forcing together ideas and words and feeling may create something new. More usually it does not. Lowell knew this risk better than most. Innovation is uncertain. "When I finished *Life Studies*," he said when he accepted the National Book Award in 1960, "I was left hanging on a question mark. I am still hanging there. I don't know whether it is a death-rope or a life-line." In a poem for Elizabeth Bishop about words suspended in air, he described the wait for the "unerring Muse":

Have you seen an inchworm crawl on a leaf,
cling to the very end, revolve in air,
feeling for something to reach to something? Do

you still hang your words in air, ten years
unfinished, glued to your notice board, with gaps
or empties for the unimaginable phrase—
unerring Muse who makes the casual perfect?

Like Georges Cuvier and Henry Adams, Lowell believed that upheaval, the overthrow of the existing form and arrangement, changes
earth and life forms in ways that gradual forces, the slow deposit of
sediment, the steady flow of rivers, cannot. Upheavals in blood and
brain were not so different in the life of man.

The psychological upheaval and intense infusions of high mood
that preceded many of Lowell's most innovative times of writing were
usually associated with mania or the rise into mania. They were important; they stripped away stale ideas, generated new ones, and allowed
him to create anew. Old lands need to be retilled, he wrote in an essay
about Robert Frost. "Excellence had left the old poetry. Like the New
England countryside, it had run through its soil and had been dead a
long time." Frost, he said, "rebuilt both the soil and the poetry." So too
did Wallace Stevens: "The subject throughout Stevens's poems is the
imagination, and its search for forms, myths, or metaphors. . . . This
is a threefold process: the stripping away of dead forms, the observation of naked reality, and the construction of new and more adequate
forms." New imaginative life for Lowell, new ordering of words and
ideas, often came from upheaval and disturbance; imagination came
from subterranean movement, storm, and hard action taken against
established ways.

The man who believes his life should be hazarded, wrote Robert
Louis Stevenson, "makes a very different acquaintance of the world,
keeps all his pulses going true and fast, and gathers impetus as he runs."
Such a man "may shoot up and become a constellation in the end."

Fire like upheaval cleared the path to new ways of thinking; Lowell used the image often, from his first book of poems to his last. Fire
could obliterate the dead brush and rot. But it could obliterate life as
well. He had taken, he said in "Reading Myself," "just pride and more
than just, / struck matches that brought my blood to a boil; / . . . memorized the tricks to set the river on fire." "The fires men build live after
them," he wrote elsewhere; "this night, this night, I elfin, I stonefoot, /
walking the wildfire." "Fire will be the first absolute power," said Pro-

metheus, the fire bringer. "It will be the last to rule. I am burning in my own fire." When a whale is rendered, its blubber is used to feed the flame. "Like a plethoric burning martyr, or a self-consuming misanthrope," wrote Herman Melville, "once ignited, the whale supplies its own fuel and burns by its own body." Its smoke, wild and hellish, "smells like the left wing of the day of judgment."

Fire and fever were forces that Lowell knew well; he recognized and respected them in the incendiary states of his mind, recognized their danger and believed in their possibilities. Fever and madness scorch, clear, and incite the brains they inhabit. "For aught we know to the contrary," William James had written in *The Varieties of Religious Experience*, "103° or 104° Fahrenheit might be a much more favorable temperature for truths to germinate and sprout in, than the more ordinary blood-heat of 97 or 98 degrees." Lowell's imagination was testament to this; he described his ill blood, high blood, and fire blood and wrote about the fever that convulsed his mind. In literature "it is only the wild that attracts us," wrote Thoreau. It is not the polished and refined, it is the untamed and uncivilized that pierce our armor, find the heart. It is the "wild thinking in Hamlet, in the Iliad, and all the scriptures and mythologies that delight us." Lowell, more than a hundred years later, would contrast "cooked" poetry—"marvelously expert" and "laboriously concocted to be tasted and digested by a graduate seminar"—with "raw" poetry, "huge blood-dripping gobbets of unseasoned experience . . . dished up for midnight listeners."

Blood brought life at its highest energy; it brought it at its most diseased. "My mind's not right . . . ," he says in "Skunk Hour," in his great description of despair. "I hear / my ill-spirit sob in each blood cell, / as if my hand were at its throat. . . . / I myself am hell; / nobody's here."

In "High Blood," Lowell describes his exultant days of mania, the mad pounding of his blood's live flow, the high blood that fires up the tyrant and the tyrannized:

> I watch my blood pumped into crystal pipes,
> red sticks like ladycrackers for a child—
> nine-tenths of me, and yet it's lousy stuff.
> Touched, it stains, slips, drips, sticks; and it's lukewarm.
> All else—the brains, the bones, the stones, the soul—

is peripheral flotsam on this live flow.
On my great days of sickness, I was God;
and now I might be. I catpad on my blood,
and the universe moves beneath me when I move.
It's the aorta and heartbeat of my life;
hard rock turned high, chosen record purring,
as if the sapphire in the cat were stuck—
cry of high blood for blood that gives both tyrant
and tyrannized their short half-holiday.

A revised version of the poem, "For Ann Adden 4. Coda," carries the same lines of high blood and life blood, tyrants and tyrannized, but in it Lowell also describes his nightmare days as God, the "great days of sickness." Even on the steadiest day, he wrote, "I have to brace my hand against a wall / to keep myself from swaying—swaying wall, / straitjacket, hypodermic, helmeted / doctors, one crowd, white-smocked, in panic, hit, / and bury me running on the cleated field." Yet he longs to hold on to the gentler side of high blood. In "While Hearing the Archduke Trio," he writes of the mood he hopes to keep, the one he felt listening to Beethoven, evocative, beautiful: "I so pray this pretty sky to stay: / my high blood, fireclouds, the first dew, / elms black on the moon."

───────

"Stable equilibrium is death," proclaimed Henry Adams. This was bedrock for Lowell. "Life by definition breeds on change," he wrote. After each new book of poems he was driven to move on from it, try a different way; forge a new style; grow. This desire and capacity to innovate created a greatly varied body of work, a life arc of work, one that changed from the baroque, knotted, violent intensity of *Lord Weary's Castle* to the more personal, direct language of *Life Studies* and then beyond. Lowell's innovations in poetic style define periods or epochs of his work; this capacity to change has been remarked upon time and again by critics and by other poets.

Al Alvarez wrote in 1965 that "each book of Lowell's seems, to an extraordinary degree, complete and resolved in itself. Then the next one appears and goes so unexpectedly far beyond the last that you have to revise your demands. He has, in short, a genius for constantly setting and then raising the standards by which his own work is to be judged." The poet Donald Hall wrote that Lowell was "not the first poet to undertake great change in midcareer, but he was the *best* poet to change so *much*." Randall Jarrell believed that Lowell was "a poet of great originality and power who has, extraordinarily, developed instead of repeating himself."

More recently, the critic A. O. Scott tied Lowell's art to the sweep of his artistic ambition and to his capacity to write and think in epic terms. "To read Lowell in sequence," he wrote, "is to discover that he was indeed a supreme maker—not just of individual lyrics, but of sequences, of books . . . and, above all, of his own biography. . . . [Lowell's *Collected Poems*] is a big, sprawling novel, the narrative of a career, an epic story of literary ambition. Which means, given the poet and the times, that it is a story about both the eclipse and the apotheosis of such ambition." Adam Kirsch also speaks of Lowell's sweep of imagination and creative boldness: "There is an art of restraint and witness," he writes in *The Wounded Surgeon*, "which many poets of the late twentieth century found to be the appropriate response to their time. But Lowell's art is one of power and grandeur, assertion and transformation. It is this that makes him the natural heir and companion to the classic English poets, starting with his beloved Milton; it is this that gave him the confidence to write so magnificently in so many different styles."

When Lowell wrote about audacity in *Prometheus Bound* he could have been speaking of himself. "I was guided by the great gods of that day, their most powerful flashes, and later by the steady light of my own mind. That mind was in no way walled in or useless. Each thought was like a finger touching, tampering, testing, and trying to give things a little of my bias to alter and advance. I never felt bound to keep anything to its original custom, place or purpose. I turned the creatures on their heads, and lifted the doors from the hinges of determination."

From the start of his creative life to its end, Lowell lifted the doors from the hinges of determination. It would have been easier to stay with the way he had written before, and what he knew he could do. As early as 1951, just a few years after he had won the Pulitzer Prize for *Lord Weary's Castle*, he said, "It's been tough getting down to writing." He wavered, he said, "between a desire not to repeat, and the void and formlessness of what I haven't tried." A year later he felt he had made progress. "I think I am going into new country, and will not be repeating my old tricks; at least I'm full of stuff I had no notion of saying before." Still, it was difficult to come up with a new way to write. "It's hell finding a new style, or rather finding that your old style won't say any of the things you want to, and that you can't write it if you try, and yet that petrified flotsam-bits of it are always bobbing up when you don't want them."

Lowell's discontent with his work; his determination to change it, to expand the territory; his will to keep at it until he did define artists who change the face of art for those who follow. "It's only possible by being usually impossible. I want to do all the things I can't do now," he wrote during his run-up to the historic break in style he developed for *Life Studies*. "The game is to push and not be carried by this old jungle of used equipment."

His new poems, he wrote to Robert Frost, "seem to me a gift of the muse . . . for me they breathe, seem engagingly put together. And yet, and yet!" Already he was dissatisfied. His new work was too fierce, he said, too personal. "The direction rather appalls me," he continued. "Such a narrow fierceness, so many barbed quills hung with bits of skin." He was set on taking his work in a new direction. He had replaced the "old stuff" (*Lord Weary's Castle*), which now seemed to him "like something from the ancient extinct age of the reptiles, cumbersome creatures, bogged down and destroyed by their protective hide," with the autobiographical poems of *Life Studies*. It wasn't enough. "Now the need to be impersonal has come again, with it a need for some third style, still unfound."

As he had in the years leading up to *Life Studies*, Lowell went through extended fallow times, searching for new ways to shape form and content. "One wants a whole new deck of cards to play with, or at least new rules for the old ones," he wrote to Randall Jarrell at the beginning of 1960. He needed to strip away the old to allow in the new: "Time to grub up and junk the year's / output, a dead wood of dry verse: / dim confession, coy revelation, / liftings, listless self-imitation." As a child, Lowell had kept snakes; like them, he shed and grew and shed again. In 1970 he wrote to Elizabeth Hardwick that he had been writing new poems at a furious rate; it was, again, "a new tune, a new meter, a new me." The world "owes all its onward impulses to men ill at ease," wrote Nathaniel Hawthorne. "The happy man inevitably confines himself within ancient limits."

Readers exert a pull on writers to stay within a different kind of limit. The history of literature, Pasternak said, "shows that every poet has different generations of readers who accept one but not another period in his work." A writer must "have the courage to disregard the tasks of his admirers, to fly in the face of their instinctive desire to force him to go on repeating himself."

The pattern of restlessness and discontent, the determination to innovate and not to rest on past accomplishment continued to Lowell's death. In 1976, not long before he sent off his final volume of poems to his publisher, he wrote again to Elizabeth Hardwick. He expressed his dissatisfaction with his new poems but said that his mind simmered yet. "Man is never happy," he wrote. "I have been chronically complaining about overconcentration on work, both because of what it does to one, how it distracts one, and because I feel afraid of a certain stylistic callousness, plough-pushing if there's such archaic idiom. Now on the verge of mailing off my new book . . . I feel in this ebb of the European heatwave, as if all the grass has been burned off the view. Pause and be wise; but the machine goes on clanking in the head." When he died a year later he was carrying a briefcase; within it was a notebook filled with poems and fragments of poems. He was creating to the end.

At a literary symposium dedicated to his work, Lowell summed up the living, evolving quality of creative work. He said he believed his poetry to be a "continuing story—still wayfaring. A story of what? Not the 'growth of a poet's mind.' Not a lesson and example to be handed to the student. Yet the mind must eventually age and grow, or the story would be a still life, the pilgrimage of a zombie." "My journey," he told the audience, "is always stumbling on the unforeseen and even unforeseeable." It was also, and always, about ambition and his place in history, about breaking free. Frank Bidart quotes Lowell's opening line, "O to break loose," that opens "Waking Early Sunday Morning"; it is, as he says, a line filled with promise, energy, desire, and limit. It is a line of ambition, a poem of ambition. It is a poem that goes from life-spewing, ecstatic leap—

> O to break loose, like the Chinook
> salmon jumping and falling back,
> nosing up to the impossible

—to the depleted, to a "[f]ierce, fireless mind, running downhill." It ends with desolate lines about war and corruption of the state, lines that knell man and planet. "Waking Early," Lowell wrote to a reader, is a poem "about energy," "too much and too little energy." "Both conditions were dangerous," he continued. A "sort of non-clinical manic-depressive state, resembling the world and the American national character, mine too."

> Only man thinning out his kind
> sounds through the Sabbath noon, the blind
> swipe of the pruner and his knife
> busy about the tree of life . . .
>
> Pity the planet, all joy gone
> from this sweet volcanic cone;
> peace to our children when they fall
> in small war on the heels of small
> war—until the end of time
> to police the earth, a ghost
> orbiting forever lost
> in our monotonous sublime.

"In the years I knew Lowell," writes Frank Bidart, "the growing, live enterprise of his work seemed itself to be a breaking loose from the past, to be part of an arc that no one—perhaps not even Lowell himself—could change or deflect. He said to me a number of times that he couldn't write in the styles he had used in the past. . . . What I have always found hard to talk about is the constant sense I had, in the years Lowell was producing new poem after new poem, of the enormous fundamental seriousness, the range and intellectual ambition animating his enterprise. That it *was* an enterprise."

———

Lowell's legacy is to poetry, but through his writing he also made the experience of madness and depression more real, more human; he made the suffering that comes with them less easy to close one's eyes to. He wrote about what he knew and he put his blood and genius into it.

Lowell's view of mental illness was not a romantic one. It was clear-eyed and understated. The best poems, he said, have compassion and are made of iron. This is how he wrote about mania and depression and about the experience of being committed to mental hospitals. His poems do not dramatize; rather, they reflect Graham Greene's view that "when one is dealing with horrors one should write very coldly." Much of what has been written about mental illness has been written too close to the throes of breakdown, too close to the bone to carry the full horror of experience; it has given idiosyncratic accounts rather than art. Raw experience, unless incubated in memory and coupled with great gift, may be heartfelt but does not necessarily lend itself to the kind of portrayal to render it part of the greater human condition.

"Memory is not an end but an invaluable means for selecting and accumulating," wrote Lowell, "for holding an experience as in a pair of tongs so that the intellect many intuit from many angles, distort, refine, invent and develop etc." Lowell, in his poetry, prose, and letters, gave lucid, often wrenching accounts of mania, depression, and his mental illness. But he held his experiences in a pair of tongs before he published his work. He wrote frequently about mania, what he often referred to as pathological enthusiasm. Mania was variously "a ladder to the moon," "a magical orange grove in a nightmare," a "fine puff of madness," "a gruesome, vulgar, blasting surge of enthusiasm," a "holocaust of irrationality," a "violent seizure." It was a "rage monstrous, causeless," a time when one was "tireless, madly sanguine, menaced, and menacing."

Lowell described the euphoria and confidence that the early stages of mania gave him and, like most who have been manic, he delighted in it. The world was "full of wonders" and "rather tremendous experiences." It was "PARADISE!," a time of throbbing "hyperenthusiasm." He knew, however, that soon the tide would go out; wariness was required. Too much happiness was the harbinger of madness. "The state of happiness is wrong," he said. "We are dangerously happy." "I grow too merry." "No voice outsings the serpent's / flawed, euphoric hiss," he wrote in "Paradise Regained: June at McLean's Hospital." The glory of mania veered into violence and banality; pathological enthusiasm flipped into madness. Mania corrupted and disabled. "I can't see myself," he said. "I have stood too long on a chair or ladder, / branch-lightning forking through my thought and veins."

The rising madness was dangerous, isolating, inhuman:

Sometimes, my mind is a rocked and dangerous bell;
I climb the spiral stairs to my own music,
each step more poignantly oracular,
something inhuman always rising in me.

After the fever of mania had run its course, bringing with it infidelity, mayhem, the police, and straitjacket, he climbed down his ladder from the moon: "our hallucinator, the disenchantress"; the "gadabout with heart of chalk, unnamable / void and cold thing in the universe, / lunatic's pill with poisonous side-effects." Climbing up, backing down the ladder to the moon, was Lowell's common metaphor for his ascent and plummets from mania. Always he knew the damage he had done, the toll taken on his relationships and his reputation. He told Elizabeth Bishop that he had acted with "abysmal myopia and lack of consideration"; his disease had given him "a headless heart." Mania was "bluster and antics," "windy utterances, domestic chaos." How often, he wrote, "have my antics / and insupportable, trespassing tongue / gone astray."

Lowell viewed his illness as unavoidable, described it as "some flaw in the motor," "some germ in the mind." The depression that followed mania was a "formless time of irresolution, forgetfulness, inertia"; "the bottom of the world"; a "long, burdensome dull period"; "that blind mole's time"; "dust in the blood." He was, when depressed, "inert, gloomy, aimless, vacant, self-locked"; "graveled and grim and dull"; he was "empty." Once well again, he looked back on his depression as "muck and weeds and backwash." He had to shake off "all the unease, torpor, desire to do nothing," the "grovelling, low as dirt purgatorial feelings," the "blank sense of failing." After mania the "somberness" set in, "the jaundice of the spirit," the "pathological self-abasement."

Helen Vendler gives an excellent analysis of how Lowell transformed his depression into art, into the "naming work of poetry." She describes the forms that depression takes—its incoherence, repetitiveness, hopelessness, blotting out of memory, its stifled rhythm and imagination—and shows how Lowell persisted beyond the suffering and inhibition of his depression to transcend its stifling influence. Lowell's depressive style and language, Vendler points out, are quite beautiful in their own way. He was able to declare simultaneously, "I am depressed" and "I am inventive in finding equivalents for depression." His poetry was an artistic and moral victory over despair.

During his prolonged stay in McLean Hospital in 1958, Lowell drafted and then began revising the poem that would become "Waking in the Blue." Originally addressed to Ann Adden, a young woman he had fallen in love with when he was manic, the final version maintains much of the imagery of the first draft—the harpoon to the heart, the mad of Harvard, the dark daybreak at Bowditch Hall, the Roman Catholic attendants, and the "Boston screwballs" that will become "Mayflower screwballs." The early drafts are filled with descriptions of Adden and details of their affair. The revised version, published in *Life Studies*, omits Adden entirely (as Lowell did in his life once he recovered). It tightens into a brilliant, controlled poem about madness, about the illusion that class or education protects against insanity. There is a trace of "Richard Cory," "envied" and "admirably schooled in every grace," who "one calm summer night, / Went home and put a bullet through his head." Being a thoroughbred, of *Mayflower* stock,

Bowditch Hall, McLean Hospital

carries little meaning. Madness is now, it lies in the future: he stands
"before the metal shaving mirrors, / and see[s] the shaky future grow
familiar." The asylum levels all: "each of us holds a locked razor."

Waking in the Blue

The night attendant, a B.U. sophomore,
rouses from the mare's-nest of his drowsy head
propped on *The Meaning of Meaning.*
He catwalks down our corridor.
Azure day
makes my agonized blue window bleaker.
Crows maunder on the petrified fairway.
Absence! My heart grows tense
as though a harpoon were sparring for the kill.
(This is the house for the "mentally ill.")

What use is my sense of humor?
I grin at Stanley, now sunk in his sixties,
once a Harvard all-American fullback,
(if such were possible!)
still hoarding the build of a boy in his twenties,
as he soaks, a ramrod
with the muscle of a seal
in his long tub,
vaguely urinous from the Victorian plumbing.
A kingly granite profile in a crimson golf-cap,
worn all day, all night,
he thinks only of his figure,
of slimming on sherbet and ginger ale—
more cut off from words than a seal.

This is the way day breaks in Bowditch Hall at McLean's;
the hooded night lights bring out "Bobbie,"
Porcellian '29,
a replica of Louis XVI
without the wig—
redolent and roly-poly as a sperm whale,

as he swashbuckles about in his birthday suit
and horses at chairs.
These victorious figures of bravado ossified young.

In between the limits of day,
hours and hours go by under the crew haircuts
and slightly too little nonsensical bachelor twinkle
of the Roman Catholic attendants.
(There are no Mayflower
screwballs in the Catholic Church.)

After a hearty New England breakfast,
I weigh two hundred pounds
this morning. Cock of the walk,
I strut in my turtle-necked French sailor's jersey
before the metal shaving mirrors,
and see the shaky future grow familiar
in the pinched, indigenous faces
of these thoroughbred mental cases,
twice my age and half my weight.
We are all old-timers,
each of us holds a locked razor.

Robert Lowell reading at Harvard, 1977
"We too follow nature, imperceptibly,
change our mouse-brown to white lion's mane."

King's Chapel bell, Boston

The bell—inscribed, "The sweetest bell we ever made. Paul Revere & Son. 1817"—
tolls over the graveyard where Lowell's ancestor Mary Winslow (1607–1679) lies.

Come; I Bell Thee Home

Nothing will go again. The bells cry: "Come,
Come home," the babbling Chapel belfry cries:
"Come, Mary Winslow, come; I bell thee home."

—*From* "Mary Winslow"

13

Life Blown Towards Evening

What shall I do with my stormy life blown towards evening?
No fervor helps without the favor of heaven,
no permissive law of nature picks up the bill.

—*From* "New York Again"

In the spring of 1970, when he was fifty-three, Robert Lowell took up a visiting fellowship at All Souls College, Oxford. It was "a bachelor world," he wrote to Elizabeth Hardwick, "but very beautiful." By the end of his first day, the "half lost soul in All Souls" had "eaten in gown, handled a 14ᵗʰ century psalm book," and enjoyed a hailstorm with its "crystal peas bouncing off mouldy parapets." He was to remain in England for more than seven years, until shortly before he died in September 1977.

There was little at the time to suggest that Lowell's visit to England would be other than brief. He and Elizabeth Hardwick were still married, and their daughter was a thirteen-year-old student in Manhattan. They lived in New York during an exhilarating, churned-up time, the explosive decade of the 1960s. They flourished as writers in a writers' city. Lithium had given Lowell more than three years free of mania, an Indian summer that lasted longer than he or his doctors had hoped or thought possible. His work was full. He was teaching at Harvard and, with Hardwick, Robert Silvers, and Barbara Epstein, he helped found the *New York Review of Books.* He published several plays and volumes of verse, most to acclaim and award, some not. He was a prominent public figure opposed to the Vietnam War, actively involved in the antiwar movement. He worked for the 1968 presidential campaign of Senator Eugene McCarthy and he witnessed the violence at the Democratic National Convention in Chicago. He wrote "For the Union Dead"—his great poem of America at the height of her moral and civic strength, and of the counterpoint, her downward turning—and read it

to a crowd of thousands on Boston Common; he adapted the work of
Hawthorne and Melville for the theater. He wrote as an American, he
said, as a twentieth-century American: "For all the horrors of this age,
and for all the attractions of others such as antiquity and 19th Century
New England, I'd rather be alive now than at any time I know of. This
age is mine, and I very much want to be part of it."

All the odder, then, that Lowell left America at such a time in his
life and in the life of his country. It was through no lack of belief in
America. Although he shared with many other artists and citizens a
dark view of his country's midcentury soul, he made it clear that he was
not in flight from the land of his ancestors. "I'll go back to America and
be American," he told an interviewer, but he was glad, for a while, "to
dull the glare" after ten years of living on the "front lines." The front
lines of protest and disillusionment, the New York atmosphere, sometimes bristled, he continued, "as if with bits of steel in the rain when it
falls." It struck the mind and agitated; it showed in New York edginess.
He would stay just awhile in England, he said. Perhaps he would find
a kind of peace.

Mostly, Lowell said, he had chosen to live in England for personal reasons. He had fallen in love. And for once he had been sane,
or predominantly sane, not manic at the time that he fell. The poetry
of Lowell's years in England would be marked by that love, and by
the joy and the awakening, the despair, and finally the unsurvivable
turmoil that came with it. His work would also be marked by the madness he had hoped to leave behind him, madness that came galing back
like a nor'easter. His poetry would be touched by a sharp sense of time
passing and the limits to love, by the nonnegotiability of death. He
would write what he lived: a restless odyssey, his broken way back to
Ithaca, his hard way back home. He would write again about New
England, his parents, and his madness. He had no expectation that it
would be less than difficult. Life, like his art, was no easy thing.

Art, unlike craft, drew upon life. The latter, Lowell said, was "hard
to learn and not for everyone, but once mastered always available."
Art was different, tougher: "You went to the well every time." When
he asked of himself in his fifties, "What shall I do with my stormy life
blown towards evening?," the answer was no different from the one
he gave as a young man. He would draw upon it and use it for his art.

Lowell fell in love with the Anglo-Irish writer Lady Caroline

Blackwood not long after he arrived in England in 1970. They had much in common: they were writers; they shared determining bits of temperament, social class, a tenebrous wit; and each was drawn to fellow artists. Blackwood had been married to the painter Lucian Freud, then to the composer Israel Citkowitz, and last to Lowell; all of Lowell's wives—Jean Stafford, Elizabeth Hardwick, and Caroline Blackwood—and most of his lovers were writers. Both he and Blackwood came from socially privileged but comfortless childhoods. They had fraught heredities. Blackwood's Guinness and Sheridan ancestries rivaled those of Lowell. She had "reckless blood," she said, "which seethed and tingled like Champagne."

Kathleen Spivack, who came to know Caroline Blackwood well when Lowell was teaching at Harvard, regarded Lowell and Blackwood as "twins" who "thought alike, looked and moved alike, were open and vulnerable alike." They had the "same wide, high forehead; eyes straining to understand; the same way of staring without blinking." They both "shambled and lurched, rather than walked: a long, hunched, stumbling stride." Xandra Gowrie, who also knew Blackwood and Lowell, agreed that they were a matched pair. "They were both drinkers, and clever, and had tons to talk about. They loved jokes. And both lived very near the cliff edge. As Cal said at some point, near the end, 'We're like two eggs cracking.'"

They cracked to dangerous effect. Blackwood was addicted to alcohol. Lowell's mania was notably destructive to his friends and family. Much brought them close; later, their reverberating instability broke them. "Sufferer, how can you help me," Lowell asked in a late poem, "if I use your sickness / to increase my own?":

> Will we always be
> one up, the other down,
> one hitting bottom, the other
> flying through the trees—
> seesaw inseparables?

When their relationship began, Blackwood did not know how hard Lowell's attacks of madness had been on him or those close to him. His friends believed this was part of her appeal to him, that he wanted to escape from a life where his illness was known and a source of gossip

Caroline Blackwood in the 1950s
"When I was troubled in mind, you made for my body
caught in its hangman's-knot of sinking lines."

and pain. He was newly in England; people had not yet seen him at his most disturbed. Blackwood, Spivack states, "had not seen him mad and she did not act as a reminder of his madness." Elizabeth Hardwick, on the other hand, was "someone he knew he had hurt, for whom he felt much guilt, and someone who had seen him sick many times." Mania had burned through their love and hopes, left them with too many bad memories.

Helen Vendler agrees. Lowell, she said, "dealt with consequences of his madness by taking a new wife." After starting on lithium he wanted "a new life with someone who would not think of him as a potential madman, who had not lived through the awful scenes that Hardwick had coped with for many years." Caroline Blackwood and his new life in England, Vendler suggests, gave Lowell the heart of his book *The Dolphin*, just as the "undoing" of their relationship gave him his final book, *Day by Day*. Blackwood, first a muse of life and creation, became the muse who tutored him in heartbreak. This hard tutoring, Elizabeth

Hardwick wrote, made him, at the end of his life, more human and "more like the rest of us."

Lowell's early vision of Blackwood, from the myths of antiquity, was as an Ovidian dolphin, free-swimming, a savior of the shipwrecked; guide and escort for the lost and wandering; conveyor of the dead. She brought him joy and an interlude of peace. She excited his imagination, gave him a son. She cut the nets that yanked him upward into world beholdenness, severed those that drew him downward into dying. Lowell wrote of her: "I am a woman or I am a dolphin, / the only animal man really loves, / I spout the smarting waters of joy in your face— / rough-weather fish, who cuts your nets and chains." She brought surprise and danger.

Lowell was a spur to Blackwood's writing as she was to his. He encouraged her, reiterated his conviction that she was a "first-class" writer. He "spotted the genius in Caroline," said Jonathan Raban. "She was surrounded by Lowell's belief in her ability to write." They were close collaborators, recalls Blackwood's daughter Evgenia Citkowitz; they worked side by side, in psychological as well as physical space. "I always showed him everything I wrote," Blackwood said. He was not threatened by her writing or by her commitment to writing. "Nobody gives me any credit for taking on three clever writers," he once joked to her. "Most men choose to marry their secretary or somebody weaker. I think I should be given honor for my bravery." He had a point, Blackwood said. "Writers can retaliate."

Evgenia Citkowitz, Blackwood's daughter with the composer Israel Citkowitz, first met Lowell when he and Caroline told her they were planning to marry. They were holding hands in the corridor of Blackwood's London flat, she remembers. "They were shy and nervous to share the news, which gave them the appearance of young lovers, although to a child of 9, a man of 52 also looks a lot like Father Time. Cal, as he was known, seemed sympathetic and gentle; an impression that was borne out throughout the years." He was also, she says, humorous and brilliant. He and her mother "took happiness where they could and tried to make sense of it." "The golden summers and shadowed beauty" of *The Dolphin* and *Day by Day*, she says, were "a true evocation of the period."

Citkowitz never saw her stepfather when he was ill; her mother protected her and her two sisters, Natalya and Ivana, from the ravages

Robert Lowell with his stepdaughter Evgenia Citkowitz, 1972
"Our hope is in things that spring."

of his mania. Still his depression weighed on them, especially on her mother, "who had her own afflictions" and was "temperamental, unable to cope." Blackwood was terrified by Lowell's manic delusions and the possibility that he might attack her or her children. "She spoke of the dread of wondering when the next episode would come," remembers Citkowitz. Lowell, for his part, was "likewise unequipped to deal with [Blackwood's] difficulties."

Lowell and Blackwood were together seven years. Their early relationship—passionate, artistically vibrant—in time was corroded by his mania and by her drinking. The mania came quickly. They had become lovers by late April 1970; in July he was manic and, for the first time in more than three years, he was admitted to a hospital. It was a grim reminder that his illness lay dormant, like a virus embedded in tissue and blood, quiet until awakened. It was a disturbing glimpse of what was to come. Always it was to be, as Lear had implored: Let me not be mad.

Lowell's mania in the late spring and early summer of 1970 followed the familiar course of his earlier attacks. In Oxford, dining at All Souls High Table, he was domineering, incoherent, arrogant, and rude; he made sexual advances to a don's wife. He drank too much. He proclaimed himself the Messiah. He locked Blackwood into her London flat and kept her from telephoning anyone, including her children. Terrified not only for her own safety but that of her young daughters, she had him admitted in early July to Greenways Nursing Home, a London hospital. "I didn't want him in the same flat as the children in the state that he was in," Blackwood said. "Neither did I want to be locked in with him. It was the longest three days of my life." It was a nightmare for both of them. Having exhausted her emotional resources, she announced to Lowell that she too was in the midst of a nervous breakdown, then left.

As much as anyone, Lowell knew how frightening and destructive his madness could be; and he understood Blackwood's fear. He understood in July 1970 why she left him when he was sick, but loathed that she did. A few years later, when he was confined to yet another ward, under the care of yet another doctor, he understood, more acutely, why she had left him and taken her daughters with her to the Hebrides until he was well. But it was a hard understanding. Like all patients in a mental hospital, he waited. He waited for the doctor; he waited for medication; he waited for sanity; he waited for his wife to return:

> Since you went, our stainless steelware ages,
> like the young doctor writing my prescription:
> *The hospital.* My twentieth in twenty years . . . .
> Seatrout run past you in the Hebrides.

He waited for the sea trout beyond his casting.

Lowell's mania in the summer of 1970 could have been predicted. He was far from his own country, family, and friends; he was newly in love: heart and nerve exposed, high wired, vulnerable. His nights were late, his sleep was fractured, and he drank more than his brain could overlook. "He seemed a poor crazed creature," said Philip Larkin at the time. Most of all, he was torn apart by the breakup of his twenty-year marriage to Elizabeth Hardwick. The affair with Blackwood was devastating to Hardwick, who recognized that this was not just another impulsive romance incited by mania. It was a serious relationship that promised the end of their marriage. "I draw a card I wished to leave unchosen," wrote Lowell, "and discard the one card I had sworn to hold."

Guilty and torn, Lowell wrote infrequently and ambiguously to Hardwick. Transatlantic telephone calls were expensive and unsatisfactory. Left in the dark, she was anxious about their marriage and distraught about the hurt and confusion his absence was causing their daughter—"All is as it was," he wrote to Harriet in late August. "Tho not quite." She was also concerned about money, Harriet's schooling, and where they would live; she had major writing and teaching obligations of her own, in addition to the practical responsibility she had for Lowell's papers, correspondence, and finances. As Harriet Lowell describes it, her mother had been "left to make all the arrangements for renting an apartment full of Lowell family furniture and a studio full of his papers. She had left her job and taken me out of school. She needed his input on all these decisions. She was used to talking about everything with him. Until he knew whether he wanted us to come to England or it was over, she could not move forward or backward." And as always, Hardwick was worried about how his mind was bearing up.

Hardwick had good cause to worry. Lithium had held Lowell's illness in check for nearly three years, but things began to unravel soon after he moved to England. Blackwood, who disliked doctors, particularly psychiatrists, had doubts about whether he should be taking lithium at all—she doubted that it worked and disliked the side effects—and it was left to Hardwick to encourage him to continue to take the drug. In April 1970 she mailed him an article about lithium; in June she wrote to him asking whether she should try to get a prescription for lithium from one of his New York doctors. She told a friend that although she thought Lowell was "more or less under control with the pills, but he should be taking more." She reassured him about lithium even after he had been hospitalized. "Don't feel that the lithium has let you down because of this setback," she wrote. "It will work, it does work."

Concerned about Lowell's mental state, Elizabeth Hardwick flew from New York to London in late July to visit him in the hospital. She was aghast to find that he was allowed to walk around the neighborhood in his pajamas, disheveled, drugged, and ill, even free to go to the local pub. The hospital staff, she felt at least initially, allowed him to make a spectacle of himself. He was a "brilliant, proud, dignified man," she protested, "not an ape."

Despite her misgivings about the future—"I realized when I got here that I had no wish to start over again," she wrote to Mary McCarthy, although this determination was to change and then change again—she had "cut Cal's shoulder length hair, had his shirts washed, his trousers cleaned." He was "very weak & trembling & rather frail & needs help even to get around & is quite exhausted after an hour or so." She was frustrated and upset. "Sometimes a look of unutterable depression crosses his face for a moment and I want to weep," she wrote to McCarthy shortly before she returned to New York in early August. "Then he pushes it back with a careless joke."

Blackwood, despite her love for Lowell, was reluctant to be with him when he was sick. The letter she wrote while he was in the hospital is one written by a strained, wary lover:

> Darling Cal—I think about you every minute of the day, and I love you every minute of the day. Have just got your letter. You are right to object to me calling it "your" sickness. It is mine. Or ours. That is the trouble. I know it is better if I don't see you or speak to you until your attack is over even though I really long to and without you everything seems hollow, boring, unbearable. I still feel as if I am under some kind of emotional anaesthetic and can't plan or think. But that will change. I feel in an odd way and against obvious appearances that everything is going to be alright. But not immediately. As you say we got across the Godstow Marsh and manipulated that endless Military Road, and we reached Hadrian's wall. . . . At the moment I feel really sub-humanly low.
>   Love Caroline

Her words, as was not infrequently the case, found their way, literal yet transformed, into Lowell's work. Three years later in his book *The Dolphin*, dedicated to Blackwood, Lowell included the poem "Caroline." The fourth section is titled "Marriage?":

> "I think of you every minute of the day,
> I love you every minute of the day;

you gone is *hollow, bored, unbearable.*
I feel under some emotional anaesthetic,
unable to plan or think or write or feel;
mais ça ira, these things will go, I feel
in an odd way against appearances,
things will come out right with us, perhaps.
As you say, we got across the Godstow Marsh,
reached Cumberland and its hairbreadth Roman roads,
climbed Hadrian's Wall, and scared the stinking Pict.
Marriage? That's another story. We saw
the diamond glare of morning on the tar.
For a minute had the road as if we owned it."

Lowell struggled to convince Blackwood he could set things right and start anew. "I love you with all my heart and mind, what can I do, if you give me nothing to go on?" he pleaded from the hospital in July 1970. "I can't crowd in on you. Let's for God's sake try again, cool and try. So much love should go on to something. P.S. If I were with you I'd do all within my defects. Can you pretend to be the same? O try!"

After leaving the hospital, Lowell, not yet well and "terrified of being mad alone," moved into a place not far from Blackwood's London flat. Within a few months they were again doing "most things" together and he had recovered enough to write that he was "well and not depressed." He stayed out of the hospital, remained relatively stable for more than four years.

In mid-October, three months after Hardwick visited him in the hospital in London, Lowell sent her a long letter giving the reasons why it was unlikely that he would return. It was a valedictory to their marriage, a testament to the spine and governance she had given to his life, and a recognition that their shared, yet separate, pain was in the end insurmountable:

I don't know whether I've said or written ~~that~~ I feel like a man walking on two ever more widely splitting roads at once, as if I were pulled apart and thinning into mist, or rather being torn apart and still preferring that state to making a decision. Is there any decision still for me to make? After all I have done, and all that seven months have done, can I go back to you and Harriet? Too many cuts.

Time has changed things somewhat since we met at Greenways, I am soberer, cooler. More displeasing to myself in many little ways, but mostly about you. A copy of my new book [*Notebook*] came the other day, and I read through all the new and more heavily revised poems. A sense of the meaning of the whole came to me, and it seemed to be about us and our family, its endurance being the spine which despite many bendings and blows finally held. Just held. Many reviewers saw this; though it was something I thought pretentious and offensive if claimed to push in my preface, I saw it too. I have felt as if a governing part of my organism were gone, and as if the familiar grass and air were gone.

I don't think I can go back to you. Thought does no good. I cannot weigh the dear, troubled past, so many illnesses, which weren't due to you, in which you saved everything, our wondering, changing, growing years with Harriet, so many places, such rivers of talk and staring—I can't compare this memory with the future, unseen and beyond recollection with Caroline. I love her very much, but I can't see that. I am sure many people have looked back on a less marvelous marriage than ours on the point of breaking, and felt this pain and indecision—at first insoluble, then when the decision has been made, incurable.

I don't think I can come back to you, but allow me this short space before I arrive in New York to wobble in my mind. I will be turning from the longest realest and most loved fragment of my life.

Three days later he wrote that he had been depressed. His "once annual depression" was lighter than usual but it was enough to make him "peculiarly indecisive and useless." No matter what choice he made, he wrote, "I am walking off the third story of an unfinished building to the ground. . . . My useless, depressed will, does nothing well. Just the usual somberness after mania, jaundice of the spirit, and yet it has so many absolutely actual objects to pick up—a marriage that was both rib and spine for us these many years." By early November, less than a month later, there was a wobble in his certainty to end the

marriage. "I wonder if we couldn't make it up?" he wrote to Hardwick. He acknowledged he had "done great harm" and that even if he
returned to her much would stay unresolved.

"Our love will not come back on fortune's wheel," he wrote in
"Obit," the final poem in *For Lizzie and Harriet:* "After loving you so
much, can I forget / you for eternity, and have no other choice?" In
another poem in the same book, he set his grief for their lost marriage
in coastal Maine, the place of their shared summers; times of friends
and writing, of a stillness in the surrounding waters:

> White clapboards, black window, white clapboards, black window,
>   white clapboards—
> my house is empty. In our yard, the grass straggles. . . .
> I stand face to face with lost Love—my breath
> is life, the rough, the smooth, the bright, the drear.

Not long before going into the hospital in 1970 Lowell had written to
Hardwick, "This is almost the first time since lithium that I am mostly
unemployed—take leisure to be wise. I'm not ~~quite~~ what I was when
one groping and reaching summer I began *Notebook*." (Lowell's first
version, *Notebook 1967–68*, was revised, expanded, and then published
as *Notebook* in 1970.) He told Ian Hamilton that during that time he
"never wrote more, or used more ink in changes. Words came rapidly,
almost four hundred sonnets in four years—a calendar of work days. I
did nothing but write; I was thinking lines even when teaching or playing tennis." He wrote five or six sonnets a day. "Ideas sprang from the
bushes and from my head," he said.

It had been a period, not long after starting on lithium and still
"simmering," of unparalleled productivity. He wrote in those early
years of lithium treatment about seasons passing, the making of art
from life; about the discontents and solace of marriage; about pernicious power. "The time is a summer, an autumn, a winter, a spring,
another summer," Lowell wrote about his *Notebook* sonnets. "I began
working sometime in June 1967 and finished in June 1970. My plot
rolls with the seasons, but one year is confused with another. I have
flashbacks to what I remember, and fables inspired by impulse. Accident threw up subjects, and the plot swallowed them."

Notebook, which was dedicated to Harriet and Hardwick, received mixed reviews. It was a "beautiful and major work," wrote one critic; for another, it was "the response of a racked but magnanimous mind." The poet Howard Nemerov said that the *Notebook* poems were "so outrageously beautiful as quite to overcome my natural envy at another writer's success." Douglas Dunn noted that Randall Jarrell had predicted Lowell would write the best poems of the age. "The prophecy has long been fulfilled," wrote Dunn. "*Notebook* is the major endeavor so far, both as regards scale and innovation. As a record of life it is incomparable." The writing in *Notebook*, he said, is "consistently brilliant." While critical of Lowell for incorporating his ancestors into the mythic patterns of history, Dunn praised Lowell's ambition, his "preference for the large canvas," his aim for grandeur. *Notebook*, he wrote, revealed a "nervous subtlety of feeling and statement that represents a major innovation in poetry."

Some disagreed. *Notebook* was "erratic," "self-indulgent," "self-important," and punctuated by archaic references and "private allusions." Lowell's portrayal of his life was seen as idiosyncratic, if not desperate. The writing, said some, treaded old waters. No one, least of all Lowell, could say whether lithium had made *Notebook* possible and remarkable, or if it had kept better work from emerging.

———

In November 1970 Lowell wrote to Peter Taylor that he had fallen in love while "part manic." He had been "sick in hospital a good part of the summer, got well, stayed in love. There was great joy in it all, great harm to everyone." A week later, with "baffling vacillation . . . the jerky graph of the heart," he wrote to Blair Clark that he thought he and Hardwick would get back together. Hardwick, for her part, had written to Clark two weeks earlier, "I do not want Cal back under any circumstances." The end of a marriage tends not to bring out consistency in those involved. Lowell described Hardwick as veering from "frantic affection to frantic abuse," while he himself tacked from "perfect happiness" with Caroline to anguish at the loss of his marriage and the hurt he was causing Harriet. This time the remorse he felt was not for manic behavior beyond his control; it was for the pain inflicted by wrenching duplicities and expediencies in his marriage; by the betrayal, infidelity, the pain and sadness of divorce. "I increasingly fear for the blood I'll have to pay for what I have done," he said. "For being me."

Lowell returned to New York for Christmas, carrying with him a note written by Caroline. He took lines from it into "With Caroline at the Air-Terminal," part of the sequence of poems "Flight to New York" that was published a few years later in *The Dolphin*: "'If I have had hysterical drunken seizures, / it's from loving you too much. It makes me wild, / I fear. . . . / I feel unsafe, uncertain you'll get back.'" The future was less uncertain to Hardwick, however. When she saw Lowell at Christmas it was clear to her that he had made the decision to go back to Blackwood. He had. When he returned to England he moved in with her; two months later they learned she was pregnant. The months of her pregnancy and after were ones of unusual happiness and calm for Lowell. It was an interlude that he wrote about to friends.

"Caroline and I are having a child," he wrote to William Alfred in March 1971. "Many problems, but somehow a calm has come for the last month and a half that is quite surprising. Like walking through some gauze screen that allowed one to see real things without touching them; but what we see is different. Anyway, for me and Caroline a peace we haven't known, perhaps ever." Whatever came his way in the future, he said, would be easier to face because of what they had together. In May 1971 he wrote in like vein to Peter Taylor. "I think I am happier than I've been," he said. "Caroline and I haven't quarreled for four months, an absolute record for me with anyone." "Not a fight for seven months," he wrote to Taylor again a few months later. It was an "unnatural and happy calm" and "unnatural to be reborn and find yourself fifty-four." He asked another friend, "Will the hailstones of the gods fall on me, if I say I've never been so happy, nor knew I could be?" The peace was soothing, stilling, primitive: "We breathe now as the cattle breathe," he said.

Lowell's new life with Caroline was, for a while, like the rowan berries of winter had been to Pasternak's Zhivago: new life; scarlet against white; a promise. But the pain he knew he was causing Hardwick and Harriet made his life with Caroline a darker thing. "We are never born again I think, nor would want to be," he wrote to the poet Adrienne Rich in the summer of 1971. "A marriage ends, and nothing stays unchanged. We face the freshness and fears and release of looking at what we really are." Rich, a friend of Hardwick, saw things differently;

her disapproval was visceral. (Rich never forgave him for leaving Hardwick and two years later wrote a blistering, often-quoted review of *The Dolphin*, damning him for his explicit poems—some based on private correspondence—about Blackwood and Hardwick.) "The only important thing wrong with marriage with Lizzie was our unending nervous strife," Lowell remarked, "as tho a bear had married a greyhound. We were always deeply together and constantly fascinated and happy together, and constantly sadly vexed." He wrote to another friend, "I think of Lizzie and Harriet hourly, yet the strain of the motor was shaking us all screwloose."

In the spring of 1971, recalls Jonathan Raban, Lowell was on the brink of mania. He was "massively enthusiastic, schoolboyish, frantically playful." He became obsessed with dolphins, living and inanimate, staying to watch performance after performance of the dolphins in the London Dolphinarium and purchasing stone dolphins, some outrageously expensive, in the antique shops in the King's Road. For a while, Raban said, stone dolphins arrived at Lowell's and Blackwood's house in almost daily British Road Services delivery vans. Dolphins were on either side of the front door, in the garden, in the hallways; there were dolphins as hat stands. Dolphins were everywhere; they were in poetry in the making. Yet somehow Lowell was able, just, to fend off a full-blown manic attack. "Lowell and Blackwood were both treating each other with a sense of each other's fragility," observed Raban. Lowell held himself back because "he saw the panic in Caroline, and Caroline in a way [held] herself back from her thing, from her fear of Cal. They treated each other with an almost drunken delicacy, and you could feel a massive amount of self-restraint on both sides, and terror—terror that if one of them flipped, the whole thing would crash." Lowell said on more than one occasion, "I am manic. Caroline is panic." It was gasoline to tinder.

That summer Lowell and Raban went to Orkney, in part to trace Lowell's Traill and Spence bloodlines, which he believed to be the headwater of both his poetry and his instability. He was, recalls Raban, "terrifically excited," repeatedly asking their driver, *"Where are the Spences, where are the Traills?"* He did not get far in his ancestral search, but he and Raban— "pretty bad fishermen"—fished the Scottish islands for trout. Lowell, distractible as ever, fell into a loch. (It was neither the first nor the last time when, mind elsewhere, he had to be pulled out of a river or lake. Lowell's distractibility was well-known to friends and colleagues alike, as was his striking inability to negotiate three-dimensional space. He had an "eccentric sense of geography," according to Raban, one of many who commented on Lowell's palpable geographic shortcomings. He lacked compass to discern north from south, right from left. Whether he was trying to find his way to his office at Harvard or navigate Central Park, the direction he found was at best indirect. England was yet worse, said Raban. It was like Mars.)

While they were in Orkney, Lowell met George Mackay Brown, another poet of dark moods and religious conversion. Lowell was charmed by Brown, Raban recalls. They drank together and discussed the poetry and myths of Orkney. As someone with his own profound and deeply carved sense of his native New England, Lowell recognized in Brown a like personal and poetic tie to the land and sea, a like beholdenness to history and legend. Brown was, he said, "an animal in its own territory."

———————

Robert Sheridan Lowell was born in September 1971. "After 12 hours of labor pains," his father wrote to Harriet, "Robert was born in thirty seconds." He looked like "a lobster-red stiff gingerbread man, in crimson mud. . . . like a bartender who imbibes as well as sells." Two years after Sheridan's birth he took the images into "Robert Sheridan Lowell":

> too much blood is seeping . . .
> after twelve hours of labor to come out right,
> in less than thirty seconds swimming the blood-flood:
> Little Gingersnap Man, homoform,
> flat and sore and alcoholic red.

Lowell's young son brought energy, the chaos of a child, and a sharpening of Lowell's already sharp sense of mortality. "I have a doctor's and psychiatrist's statement exempting me from ever throwing a football," he wrote jokingly to Peter Taylor not long after Sheridan's birth. In two poems for Sheridan published shortly before his death, Lowell spoke to the half-century gap between father and son. In "Sheridan" he described the green growth of childhood and the mortality that edged the lives of those older and less changeable:

> How unretentive we become,
> yet weirdly naked like you. Today
> only the eternal midday separates
> you from our unchangeably sunset
> and liver-invigorated faces. High-hung,
> the period scythe silvers in the sun,
> a cutting edge, a bounding line,
> between the child's world and the earth—
>
> Our early discovery that only children grow.

Later, in the same volume, in "For Sheridan," Lowell makes clear the gap between intention and deed, makes clear the regret that the years bring:

> Past fifty, we learn with surprise and a sense
> of suicidal absolution
> that what we intended and failed
> could never have happened—
> and must be done better.

———

In 1973 Lowell published three volumes of verse. Two, *History* and *For Lizzie and Harriet*, were revised and expanded versions of *Notebook*. *History*, a book that begins with early time—antiquity, biblical, before—carries through the millennia and ends with the mid-twentieth century. The poems center on the rupturing ambiguities of power; the mutability of individual lives and empires; the cold sanity and hot madness of tyrants; the courage of a few; the fragile psychologies of artists; the steel, the backward glancing and dark imagination of the New England writers. The subjects of *History* spread out over a wide and untidy field: Ulysses and Alexander, Achilles; Beethoven, Lincoln, Schubert; the writers and thinkers who so influenced him: Henry Adams, Hawthorne, Dante, Thoreau, Emerson; the moon landing, Israel; Attila and Hitler; ancestors; his poet contemporaries, including Frost, Plath, Eliot, MacNeice, Berryman, Roethke, and Bishop.

For Lizzie and Harriet, a book that centers on his life with Elizabeth Hardwick and their daughter, Harriet, is steeped in regret and tenderness. It renders the conflict and human need that Lowell locates at the heart of marriage, the renewal he sought in his love affairs and the betrayal that they entailed. The long days of family summers in Maine—friends and children; writing, always; bay sailing and clambakes; martinis, talking into the morning—long days distilled into eternal, repeating, summer days. Like Henry Adams's contrast between his boyhood days of summers in Quincy and the cold constricted winters in Boston, Lowell's summer poems set children in nature against the passing of seasons and the intimation of mortality; regeneration against ending, fresh impression against irony and pain. Earlier, in "Soft Wood," he had written of these things and more: that which lasts, and the constancy of mutability; the shedding of the worn; the layers

Lowell's writing barn in Castine, Maine
"It's right on the bay . . . rocky islands with pine trees ease off into birches and meadows."

of appearance; death; the reach of pain. He dedicated the poem to his
cousin Harriet Winslow:

Soft Wood
(For Harriet Winslow)

Sometimes I have supposed seals
must live as long as the Scholar Gypsy.
Even in their barred pond at the zoo they are happy,
and no sunflower turns
more delicately to the sun
without a wincing of the will.

Here too in Maine things bend to the wind forever.
After two years away, one must get used
to the painted soft wood staying bright and clean,
to the air blasting an all-white wall whiter,
as it blows through curtain and screen
touched with salt and evergreen.

The green juniper berry spills crystal-clear gin,
and even the hot water in the bathtub
is more than water,
and rich with the scouring effervescence
of something healing,
the illimitable salt.

Things last, but sometimes for days here
only children seem fit to handle children,
and there is no utility or inspiration
in the wind smashing without direction.
The fresh paint
on the captains' houses hides softer wood.

Their square-riggers used to whiten
the four corners of the globe,
but it's no consolation to know
the possessors seldom outlast the possessions,

once warped and mothered by their touch.
Shed skin will never fit another wearer.

Yet the seal pack will bark past my window
summer after summer.
This is the season
when our friends may and will die daily.
Surely the lives of the old
are briefer than the young.

Harriet Winslow, who owned this house,
was more to me than my mother.
I think of you far off in Washington,
breathing in the heat wave
and air-conditioning, knowing
each drug that numbs alerts another nerve to pain.

The third of Lowell's 1973 books, *The Dolphin*, is a novelistic
sequence of poems that focuses on the disintegration of his marriage to
Hardwick and his courtship, marriage, and finally unliveable relationship with Blackwood. Lowell's portrayal of love, and its limitations, is
raw: There is gratitude for the renewal of life and for a second chance,
for a quickening of the senses, for awakening the imagination. There
is gratitude for the peace, however short-lived. "After fifty so much
joy has come, / I hardly want to hide my nakedness— / the shine and
stiffness of a new suit, a feeling, / not wholly happy, of having been
reborn," he writes in "Flight to New York." Many of the poems exult
with a sense of new, faster blood in the veins. And, at times, a quiet joy.
He describes "a happiness so slow burning, it is lasting": "when I open
the window, the black rose-leaves, / return to inconstant greenness. A
good morning, as often."

It is love, he makes clear, not madness:

My hand
sleeps in the bosom of your sleeping hands,
firm in the power of your impartial heat.
I'm not mad and hold to you with reason,
you carry our burden to the narrow strait,

this sleepless night that will not move, yet moves
unless by sleeping we think back yesterday.

Lowell conjures the image of cattle, for him a symbol of scarred innocence and primal terror. He describes in "Overhanging Cloud" the quiet breaths of an animal peace:

it's enough to wake without old fears,
and watch the needle-fire of the first light
bombarding off your eyelids harmlessly.
By ten the bedroom is sultry. You have double-breathed;
we are many, our bed smells of hay.

The peace does not last. Blackwood—dolphin, whale, mermaid— twists into a darker muse: damaged, damaging, hard bound to alcohol and chaos. "None swims with her and breathes the air," Lowell writes:

A mermaid flattens soles and picks a trout,
knife and fork in chainsong at the spine,
weeps white rum undetectable from tears.
She kills more bottles than the ocean sinks,
and serves her winded lovers' bones in brine.

"I see you as a baby killer whale," he writes, "free to walk the seven seas for game, / warm-hearted with an undercoat of ice." The mermaid, muse to others before him, might move on: "One wondered who would see and date you next, / and grapple for the danger of your hand." Lowell's language becomes one of chaos, danger, hazard, and storm:

I've searched the rough black ocean for you,
and saw the turbulence drop dead for you,
always lovely, even for those who had you,
Rough Slitherer in your grotto of haphazard.
I lack manhood to finish the fishing trip.
Glad to escape beguilement and the storm,
I thank the ocean that hides the fearful mermaid—
like God, I almost doubt if you exist.

The depiction of marital bleakness in *The Dolphin* is, in its way, a poetic parallel to Albee's *Who's Afraid of Virginia Woolf?* The play and the poems are deeply bound to memory and dead or dying hopes, deluded dreams. Both are fueled with ice and alcohol. "[W]e totter off the strewn stage," Lowell writes, "knowing tomorrow's migraine will remind us / how drink heightened the brutal flow of elocution." . . .

> It's over, my clothes fly into your borrowed suitcase,
> the good day is gone, the broken champagne glass
> crashes in the ashcan.

Lowell won the 1974 Pulitzer Prize for *The Dolphin*, and many critics acclaimed its originality, ferocity, and beauty. Others described it as the work of a poet who had turned too inward, become too self-bound, too obscure. The reviews were mixed, as they were for *Notebook*; some were damning, some enthusiastic. The issue for some critics, based on the source of material in many of the poems, became as much a moral as a literary one: Was it acceptable to incorporate, and in some instances change, portions of letters that Elizabeth Hardwick had written to Lowell during a time of emotional distress in their marriage and for which she might reasonably have assumed privacy?

It has been more than forty years since the publication of *The Dolphin*, and the indignation over Lowell's taking lines from Hardwick's letters has lessened but not disappeared. Time has a blanketing effect on outrage. In many respects, as literary and historical controversies go, the appropriation is not particularly egregious. The issue was an important one to many of those most involved, however, including critics, friends, and, of course, Elizabeth Hardwick, Caroline Blackwood, and Lowell himself. Elizabeth Bishop's burning words to Lowell on first reading the *Dolphin* poems—*"Art just isn't worth that much"*— are repeated still. They raise general questions about the use of private observation in art; they also raise questions of hypocrisy.

Lowell's culpability for his behavior during mania, behavior that was beyond his control, is a different moral issue from his use of Hardwick's letters, which he deliberated at length while sane. Throughout his life, Lowell, like most writers, incorporated into his art observations and words from others. He freely acknowledged this in the introductions to his books, as well as in his letters and in interviews.

The essence of his work was personal; it would have been odd had he not drawn upon what he saw around him. For years he had taken bits of conversation and correspondence from his friends, including from T. S. Eliot, Ezra Pound, Robert Frost, Delmore Schwartz, Robert Penn Warren, Elizabeth Bishop, George Santayana, William Carlos Williams, Mary McCarthy, several of his lovers, and each of his three wives. He had folded into his work the words of earlier writers, as well: the Greek dramatists, the Greek and Roman poets, Thoreau, Emerson, Hawthorne, Melville, Henry Adams, and Jonathan Edwards. Lowell had a poet's magpie eye and an imprinting ear: he spotted, snatched, rejected, revised, incorporated. Words of others became part of his available stock. But it was his imagination that picked, sorted, and built. That created poetry.

Lowell is scarcely the first writer to use privately communicated material of others in his work. It is as old as poetry; writers use what they see and hear. This does not make a moral case, only a human and artistic one. "The writer's only responsibility is to his art," said William Faulkner. "He will be completely ruthless if he is a good one. He has a dream. It anguishes him so much he must get rid of it. He has no peace until then. Everything goes by the board: honor, pride, decency, security, happiness, all, to get the book written." Lowell, who lived with an acute sense of his place in history, felt that history would judge his art the most important thing. For Elizabeth Bishop, art just wasn't worth that much. For Lowell, art was indeed worth it. Art was the most important thing. "I couldn't bear to have my book (my life) wait ~~hidden~~ inside me like a dead child," he told her.

Although Bishop was clear in her admiration for the poetry, she was unequivocal in her disapproval of Lowell's determination to publish *The Dolphin*. She wrote to him that she thought the poetry was "wonderful," "magnificent," "marvelous." But she vehemently decried his use of Hardwick's letters. "Lizzie is not dead," she said. Worse, Lowell had changed Hardwick's letters so that they had become a "mixture of fact & fiction." Such a mixture would not be the truth, but others would take it to be so. A gentleman, she said, would not do what he had done. "It is not being 'gentle' to use personal, tragic, anguished letters that way," she wrote. "It's cruel."

Bishop was not alone in her excoriation. Stanley Kunitz thought that Lowell's inclusion of Hardwick's letters in the *Dolphin* poems was a "cruel invasion" of privacy, "morally and esthetically objection-able." Lowell's friend William Alfred wrote that he thought the poems would "tear Elizabeth apart, important though I agree they are to the wholeness of the book." He had met W. H. Auden, Alfred continued, who told him that because of the book he would no longer speak to Lowell. In reply, Alfred had told Auden that he "sounded like God the Father." He "gave me a tight smile," Alfred wrote. Lowell, who seldom expressed anger in his letters, was outraged that Auden, who had not read the book (and was not perhaps the best person to be chastising anyone), would take such a moralistic stance. He cabled Auden: "DEAR WYSTAN—ASTOUNDED BY YOUR INSULT TO ME." Lowell was angry and cut by the criticism, but he did not pull his decision to publish.

Other poets concurred with the criticism that had been leveled against Lowell. Donald Hall described Lowell as a "cannibal-poet . . . dining off portions of his own body and the bodies of his family." Adrienne Rich was yet more scathing. In a widely cited review she wrote, "What does one say about a poet who, having left his wife and daughter for another marriage, then titles a book with their names [*For Lizzie and Harriet*], and goes on to appropriate his ex-wife's letters written under the stress and pain of desertion, into a book of poems nominally addressed to the new wife?" The book, she said, was "cruel and shallow," and the "inclusion of the letter poems stands as one of the most vindictive and mean-spirited acts in the history of poetry." This is a stretch. Whatever legitimate criticism there may be of Lowell's including excerpts from Hardwick's letters, it is far from one of the most vindictive acts in the history of poetry. There is too much competition. And, however hurtful was Lowell's decision to publish the letter poems, there is no evidence that mean-spiritedness was the reason he did it.

Lowell defended his use of Hardwick's letters. "I did not see them as slander, but as sympathetic, tho necessarily awful for her to read," he wrote to Bishop in March 1972. "She is the poignance of the book. . . . The trouble is the letters make the book, I think, at least they make Lizzie real beyond my invention. . . . How can the story be told at all without the letters?" He discussed with Bishop, as he did with others, rearranging the poems to make the overall effect less painful. "The problem of making the poem unwounding is impossible," he continued a week later; "still I think it can be made noticeably milder without losing its life." The struggle between not using the letters and compromising the poems—between protecting his family and protecting his art—obsessed him: "How can I want to hurt? Hurt Lizzie and Harriet, their loving memory? Working on my poem is a must somehow, not avoidable even though I fail—as I must partially."

In July 1973, in the wake of a few particularly savage reviews of *The Dolphin*, Lowell wrote to his publisher, defending having published fragments of Hardwick's letters—"a mixture of quotes, improvisation, paraphrase"—which appeared to have been "shocking" to some critics. "The portrait is very careful and affectionate," he maintained. "The essence of her charm and bravery, her own words humor and sharpness" remained intact. Caroline Blackwood, although she had been portrayed in a much harsher light in several of the *Dolphin* poems, nonetheless told an interviewer, "Lizzie didn't come out badly. . . . And when he did it with me, I didn't care. Once it's turned into a poem, I don't think it has anything to do with one. When he called me a 'baby killer whale' or wrote that I was 'warm-hearted with an undercoat of ice' or a mermaid who 'serves her winded lover's bones in brine,' I didn't mind."

Elizabeth Hardwick did mind. They were different women and in different circumstances. Before she actually saw the poems, Hardwick's view on Lowell's publishing them was open, even philosophical. In April 1972 she wrote to Lowell, "I don't know what you should or should not do, but it seems to me that you have been writing for thirty years and publishing for nearly the same number. The matter of your work is yours entirely and I don't think you have it in your power to 'hurt me.' I suppose that is something I control since the feelings are mine and perhaps my feelings are not as simple as my friends think. I mean that I cannot see what harm can come to me from a poem by you. Why should I care? The credit or discredit is entirely yours. I don't see any of this as having anything to do with me in the long run. I just wanted to 'go on record' in this." She added, "I feel strongly that you should do what you wish." To a point, Lowell could be forgiven for assuming some permission to go on writing the *Dolphin* poems.

Hardwick's openness to publication stopped dead when she read the poems a year later. She was angry and humiliated. She wrote to Lowell's publishers, aghast that they had published the poems without obtaining her permission. When she received the book, she told them, "the reality was disturbing far beyond anything I could have imagined. Had I seen the poems, the letters of mine, those using my name, I do not know what I would have done." It should not have been left up to Lowell's discretion, she continued. It was the publisher's job to advise and to tend to the "indiscretions of authors." She particularly resented the inaccuracy of Lowell's portrayal of key facts. There was, she wrote, "nothing about my willingness to divorce, my acceptance of the separation, the good spirits of myself and the utterly gratifying contentment of my daughter."

"He used and misquoted her letters," acknowledges Harriet Lowell many years after the deaths of both her parents. "It seemed out of character. . . . It was so vituperative to my mother. The quotes did not sound much like her, but then she wasn't writing him sonnets and he did change them. She resented the bad lines he gave her as a writer with her own unique voice and that the story was changed so that her anger was taken out of context." Hardwick did not change her mind about the *Dolphin* poems. "She minded his use of the letters always. In general, she did not object to him writing about his life (which meant her). This was different. She resented that he took the worst of her reactions, out of context, and excised all the many acts of generosity. She felt he misrepresented her. He made it all about two women fighting over him. . . . They made up, clearly, so she forgave him, but she did not change her mind. It wasn't so much that it was revealing and embarrassing, but it was ungenerous." For Hardwick, it was not enough to hear from Lowell, "I'm sorry I brought this on you, the ghastly transient voices, the lights." The transient voices, the lights, the public scrutiny were not transient at all; they were there, indelible, and painful.

Scandals blaze; they die down. Art lasts or it doesn't. Douglas Dunn put the question of Lowell's responsibility into the context of his art: "On the evidence, Lowell seems to have cared deeply about the pain his behaviour and literary revelations caused others. His private Court of Appeal was Poetry, which said that he must do what Poetry must have—the device is rhetorical and sentimental, and I think it was to Lowell, too."

Two years after Lowell died, Elizabeth Hardwick told an interviewer that Lowell was "like no one else—unplaceable, unaccountable." Unplaceable, unaccountable. Perfect words: wife to husband, writer to writer.

Madness—misarranging to art and love, monstrous, capricious—was the subject of many poems in the three books Lowell published in 1973. Lowell had dreaded that his madness would return. When it did, it was a devastating and extended attack. Other than the brief recurrence of mania in summer 1970, lithium had kept him out of hospitals from spring 1967 until late autumn 1975. This sharply contrasted with his life before he began lithium; his attacks of mania had occurred at least once a year, required hospital admission, and were followed by months of depression. His recurrence of mania in November 1975 can be traced in all likelihood to lithium toxicity he experienced in May 1975 and the instability in his blood levels that followed.

Predictably, only a few months after Lowell's toxic reaction to lithium he was once again manic. He was treated in late autumn 1975 for mania, first at Priory Hospital in London, then at Greenways Nursing Home, and, at the end, at St. Andrews Hospital in Northampton. For more than two weeks after he left Greenways and before he was admitted to St. Andrews Hospital, he received twenty-four-hour private nursing care at home. He was severely manic. At first, Blackwood was hopeful that Lowell's London doctor would be able to intercede quickly enough to keep his mania from escalating. This did not happen. "We had one hope," Blackwood said, "that if he had a massive valium injection it might stop—you know, that thing where they do it right into the vein. . . . Dr. Brass came round and gave him the massive valium. Dr. Brass was here all night giving him more valium." The physician told Blackwood that patients had their legs amputated under the same dose he had given Lowell. "Cal was still walking around, talking and waving his arms." Dr. Brass "had never seen anything like it."

Lowell was "mad as the vexed sea." He dug for Etruscan treasures he believed to be hidden in the walls of their house and carved into an electric light socket with a nail file until he reached the exposed wires. He drank disinfectant and ate detergent. He stripped off wallpaper with a bread knife. He was incoherent, delusional, and overpowering. Remembering that T. S. Eliot had told him he "adored English hardware stores," he went to the local ironmonger and shoplifted domestic appliances. (The psychiatrist asked Blackwood, "Why do you think the professor loves hardware so much? Is he a man of the kitchen?") He read *Mein Kampf* aloud to Blackwood and, with tears streaming down his face, proclaimed that Hitler was a better writer than Melville. This was a declaration Blackwood found so far from anything Lowell believed when sane, so at variance with his political liberalism, not to say with his reverence for Melville, that she was horrified, repelled, and terrified. She feared that he would never regain his sanity.

When Jonathan Raban visited Lowell at the Priory he found Lowell deeply mad, "wandering out on the lawn, carrying what looked like a piece of motor car engine, or part of a central heating system, and Cal was standing there holding it up and saying, 'The Chief Engineer gave me this. This is a present from the Chief Engineer.' I said, 'Oh yes.' And he said, 'You know what this is. This is the Totentanz. This is the instrument they used to eliminate the Jews.' I said, 'Cal, it's not. It's a piece of steel. It's nothing to do with the Jews.' And then this awful sad look in his eyes, full of sorrow, as if he were hearing what his mouth was saying and was appalled, and he said something like, 'It's just my way. It's only a joke.'" For Lowell, like many patients with manic delusions, the tyrants and conquerors in history, such as Hitler, Napoleon, Caesar, Mussolini, Achilles, and Alexander, came easily to mind as subjects of identification or persecution. An insatiable passion for conquest and power and the drive to reap some cosmic good or sow unmatched destruction get fueled by the grandiose mood of mania and its paranoid bent of mind. Vitriol and bigotry often emerge. Once mania has passed, the delusional identity is abhorred, disavowed, or forgotten.

Blackwood grew skeptical about the value of traditional medical care in treating Lowell's mental illness. She arranged for homeopathic treatment as well as acupuncture. Seamus Heaney accompanied Lowell to his acupuncturists in Harley Street in January 1976. "They called him Professor. They spoke calmingly to him and he became calm. He answered their questions about what they called his tension with an unexpected childlike candor. He allowed them to palp along the line of his neck and over his temples and down the back of his skull. He took off his shirt. He bowed a little and accepted the needles, one by one, in a delicate gleaming line, from the point of his shoulder to the back of his ear. I had a great feeling of intimacy and honour and heartbreak as I watched it all from behind, yet I could not stop myself from turning that accidental moment into an image, there and then, as it was happening. Gulliver in Lilliput, disabled, pinned down, yet essentially magnificent. The bull weakened by the pics of the picador. St. Sebastian. At any rate, it remains with me as an emblem of his afflicted life, his great native strength and his sorrowful, invigilated helplessness."

Heaney, who was to receive the Duff Cooper Prize for literature in early 1976, asked Lowell to present the award. John Julius Norwich, the son of Duff Cooper, recalls the nightmare that unfolded. Caroline Blackwood, an old friend of his, called to tell him that Lowell was in the hospital and could not attend the award ceremony; later in the afternoon she telephoned to say he had checked himself out of the hospital and might turn up after all. He was "drugged up to the gills," Blackwood told Norwich, and on no account was anyone to let him have anything to drink. Norwich warned his mother, Lady Diana Cooper, who was known for her aplomb as well as her wit and beauty. "She was thrilled," he recounts, "as I knew she would be; this was just the sort of situation she loved."

Norwich dropped his mother off and parked his car. By the time he arrived at the award celebration, Lowell was standing with "a brimming champagne glass in each hand" talking to Lady Diana. He looked as if he had "been pulled through a hedge—tousled hair on end, a sweat-sodden white shirt open to the navel and, it seemed to me, a wild, wild look in his eye. 'Oh darling,' my mother said. 'You must meet this delightful gentleman. I'm afraid I didn't catch his name, but I've just been telling him all about this loony who's going to try and present the Prize.'"

"Then came the anguish," Norwich remembers. "Cal took up Seamus's book and read aloud the first four lines, which he settled down to analyse, unfavourably and at length." He did the same with the second four lines and then the third. "The audience grew restive. Mercifully he stopped in midsentence. 'So here's your prize,' he said—and handed it over." At that moment, Caroline Blackwood arrived "accompanied by two men in white coats." "Cal went quietly," Norwich observed. Seamus Heaney remembers the evening as a "sad, mad event, Lowell going about with a jacket over his pyjama tops." He was drinking champagne and "looking absolutely wild," recalls Lowell's British publisher. He gave an "odd rambling speech and now and again 'crowed' with a sort of 'wild manic laughter.'" Most in the audience, he said, "simply assumed he was drunk. Of course, he was. Mad and drunk."

Lowell was taken to St. Andrews Hospital in Northampton. It was, he wrote in "Home," a place where "[o]ur ears put us in touch with things unheard of," a place where "a thorazined fixture" such as himself "might envy museum pieces / that can be pasted together or disfigured / and feel no panic of indignity." It was a way station to death, a place where visitors came only to leave, and where desertion was felt by visitor and visited alike:

> At visiting hours, you could experience
> my sickness only as desertion . . .
> Dr. Berners compliments you again,
> "A model guest . . . we would welcome
> Robert back to Northampton any time,
> the place suits him . . . he is so strong."
> When you shuttle back chilled to London,
> I am on the wrong end of a dividing train—
> it is my failure with our fragility.
>
> *If he has gone mad with her,*
> *the poor man can't have been very happy,*
> *seeing too much and feeling it*
> *with one skin-layer missing.*

> The immovable chairs have swallowed up the patients,
> and speak with the eloquence of emptiness.
> By each the same morning paper lies unread:
> *January 10, 1976.*
> I cannot sit or stand two minutes,
> yet walk imagining a dialogue
> between the devil and myself,
> not knowing which is which or worse,
> saying,
> as one would instinctively say Hail Mary,
> *I wish I could die.*
> Less than ever I expect to be alive
> six months from now—
> *1976,*
> a date I dare not affix to my grave.

"I wish I could die," Lowell wrote in 1976; twenty years earlier, pacing and despondent in the Payne Whitney Clinic, he had "quizzed" his "face to suicide in the mirror" and asked, "Why don't I die, die?" He told more than one of his doctors that he "wished only to die," and in several of his hospital charts the attending physician recorded that Lowell was "potentially suicidal." Often Lowell's expressed desire to die was in the context of depressive bone weariness. At other times he believed he had irrevocably destroyed his ties with his friends and family, or humiliated himself in front of his colleagues or students. He repeatedly told his psychiatrists that he could not face the prospect of his madness coming back. Lowell, recalled one friend, said he wanted to die because he had "absolutely no future, that he would just wreck all the people I love." He had expressed the same despair to Blackwood. "I never know when I'm going to hurt the people I love most," he told her. "And I simply can't stand it, and in a way I would rather be dead." Blackwood, although she told Ian Hamilton that Lowell had not been suicidal during their time together, said in the same interview, "I did always worry that he was going to jump out of a window." The concern that Lowell would jump out the window was expressed by more than one of his students at Harvard.

After leaving St. Andrews Hospital in Northampton, Lowell wrote to Frank Bidart, "I am weighed down by the new frequency of attacks. How can one function, if one is regularly sick. Shades of the future prison." He had lost much of his earlier hopefulness that lithium would keep his mania at bay, although he was now having regular tests to monitor his blood level. He repeated his fear to Blair Clark: "I can't really function against two manic attacks in one year." Lowell was look-ing behind him at the damage he had done and forward to the damage he was certain to do. The reality of his future was that his illness would come back, peace would elude him, he would humiliate himself, wound people he loved, and he would be unable to write as he wished and needed. It took sheer will to live and continue to create.

At times Lowell expressed not so much an active desire to die as passive submission to an accumulating tide of despair. His mind was less willing and able to engage the fight. "I've been sixteen times on my knees," he had told Sidney Nolan. "I've got up sixteen times. But if one day I don't get up, I don't mind." Jill Neville, in her roman à clef about her brief affair with Lowell, quotes the Lowell character as saying—

after having talked about his repeated breakdowns—"I'd never drown myself. But if I had a button I'd switch myself off. The show's been going on too long."

Lowell seldom mentioned suicide to his family or friends. We know no details about intent or plans he might have had. He wrote about suicide in his poetry, but so have many poets who were not suicidal. He did discuss suicide with his doctors on several occasions. All but one of Lowell's hospital admissions were for mania, so suicide was not the major clinical concern during those periods.

Still, manic-depressive illness carries a very high rate of suicide, and a constellation of factors put Lowell at particular risk: being male; his history of impulsive and violent behavior when he was manic; his heavy use of alcohol. Many of his contemporaries similarly affected by manic-depressive illness did go on to kill themselves. What stopped Lowell? A few reasons are likely. There is a genetic tendency to suicide, and Lowell did not have a significant history of suicide in his family. His impulsiveness, a risk factor for suicide, was largely confined to his manic periods. He was less impulsive during times when he was depressed. He received good psychiatric care and, unlike many, he largely followed the treatment recommendations of his physicians. For more than twenty years, Elizabeth Hardwick provided as stable a life as possible and, by seeing to the practical things to which he was oblivious, kept him grounded. He had strong friendships. He had a will of granite and a compact with his work. He had no expectation that life would be without suffering. He had contended throughout his life with madness and had known violence and depression since childhood. He knew as best one could how to live with them. Critically, for many years when he was at high risk for suicide he was taking lithium, a drug that is impressively effective in preventing suicide.

Lowell wrote about suicide at different points in his life, beginning with early poems, such as "A Suicidal Fantasy," which he wrote when he was twenty, revised, and then published as "A Suicidal Nightmare" in *Land of Unlikeness*. "After the Surprising Conversions," published in *Lord Weary's Castle* in 1946, took as its starting point a letter written by Jonathan Edwards and included a graphic description of suicide. A few years later, in *The Mills of the Kavanaughs*, Harry Kavanaugh, who wears a Winslow family ring and in a jealous rage tries, as Lowell had, to strangle his wife, kills himself. In other poems, Lowell wrote sympathetically and perceptively about friends who had died by suicide. Finally, in *Day by Day*, published a few months before his death, he wrote "Suicide," which ends:

> Do I deserve credit
> for not having tried suicide—
> or am I afraid
> the exotic act
> will make me blunder,
>
> not knowing error
> is remedied by practice,
> as our first home-photographs,
> headless, half-headed, tilting
> extinguished by a flashbulb?

In "Suicide," as in his earlier poem "Home," not only does he express the wish for death but also his piercing fear of being abandoned. "One light, two lights, three—" Lowell writes in "Suicide." "Your car I watch for never comes, / you will not see me peeping for you / behind my furtively ajar front door." In "Home," the imagery of departure is palpable. "At visiting hours, you could experience / my sickness only as desertion," Lowell wrote. "When you shuttle back chilled to London, / I am on the wrong end of a dividing train— / it is my failure with our fragility."

Lowell's relationship with Blackwood had become one of love withdrawn and promised, love needed. He missed what they had known:

> I don't need conversation, but you to laugh with—
> you and a room and a fire,
> cold starlight blowing through an open window—
> whither?

The things that attracted Lowell and Blackwood to each other— their passion and shared aspects of mind—made the turmoil and pain all the worse when he was manic and her drinking was out of control. Blackwood had been clear at the time of Lowell's breakdown in 1970, only a few months into their affair, that she could not provide him with what he needed when he was sick. Her instinct was to leave him until his illness cleared. "I always felt it was my fault in some way, that I must have sent him mad," she said after his death. "I should have been nicer about his mania. But I couldn't be. I hadn't got that stamina."

Blackwood worried about having to make hospital arrangements for him when he was manic and about getting trapped together in their house with its "terrifying" balcony. She was anxious that Sheridan would be damaged by "seeing his father mad." The situation was not survivable, she said. "It's like someone becoming an animal, or someone possessed by the devil. And that's what tears you apart. You think, I love this person, but I hate him. So where are you?" Lowell felt abandoned at these times; she knew it but could not be otherwise. "He'd say, 'Supposing I go mad—you won't be able to bear it, will you?' And I'd say, 'Perhaps you won't go mad.' I couldn't say I could bear it, because I couldn't."

Lowell, for his part, found it increasingly difficult to hold on to his sanity in the presence of Blackwood's heavy drinking and depression. They made each other worse. His breakdowns made her "more wild, more destructive, more out of control," observed Frank Bidart. "And he was afraid of how destructive she could be when she drank. She was always a very vivid talker, but she got to be much more flamboyant, and there was a kind of vehemence, an apocalyptic, destructive coloration, and one never knew how much would remain only talk, or somehow would get acted out in her life. Cal said to me, 'I feel I make her sick.'" "At the sick times," Lowell wrote, "our slashing, / drastic decisions made us runaways."

It is difficult to read Lowell's last letters to Blackwood, to watch the disintegration of a marriage that had begun in hope and passion and sympathy. It is pointless to assign responsibility. Madness and alcoholism destroy love indiscriminately, without intent. Love is not enough.

In April 1977, five months before he died, Lowell wrote to Blackwood from America of his increasing pessimism about their relationship: "And us? I really feel too weak and battered by it all. I fear I do you more harm than good. I think your blackness would pass if you didn't live in fear of [my] manic attacks. And they don't seem curable—almost thirty years. How's that for persistence? I miss you sorely."

Lowell's view to the future was dark, its contrast with his earlier happiness almost entire. "I don't know what to say, our problems have become so many-headed and insuperable. Nothing like the sunshine of the years we had together—when it shone, as so often—so blindingly." And, a few days later, "Us? Aren't we too heady and dangerous for each other?" Lowell's letters to Blackwood during the last months of his life make it clear that he was still in love with her but that their marriage could not be salvaged. The damage they had done to each other— inadvertent, devastating—made it impossible.

"I am afraid of your visit," Lowell wrote to Blackwood in early May 1977. "I am afraid nothing will be done except causing pain. How many lovely moments, weeks, months, we had." But, he continued, "the last two years have been terrifying for us both—and neither of us have made it any better for the other. It hasn't been a quarrel, but two eruptions, two earthquakes crashing." There was no way to go back, Lowell ended the letter. "I have had so much dread—the worst in my life—that I would do something, by my mere presence I would do something to hurt you, to drive you to despair. Who knows cause."

Lowell wanted peace, he told Blair Clark in November 1976. He wanted to return to America and to Elizabeth Hardwick. He told Grey Gowrie the same, that he was going to leave Blackwood and go back to Hardwick. He was tired. The first symptoms that his heart was failing were apparent, and years of smoking and drinking, as well as the physical ravages of his manias, were obvious in his energy and appearance. "He was very clear, very un-high, very agonized," Gowrie recalled. "He said, 'You know, I'm not going to live long. I just must have some peace.'" Not long before he died he talked with Helen Vendler about leaving Blackwood. He said he was still in love with her but that "life with her was impossible, because of what they were like together. He didn't blame her. There weren't any recriminations or ill-speaking of her." But, he said, "there was no way he could live in the turbulence of their mutual life. He had to have something quieter."

When Lowell returned in late 1976 to teach at Harvard he had stayed for a while with Frank Bidart in Cambridge. He was "unbelievably grateful and relieved" to be in an environment where there wasn't "enormous turmoil, anger, drama, tension," Bidart said. It was clear that Lowell needed a haven. He wanted to return to a life with Hardwick because "he needed security, needed a home, needed someone who could deal with his illness."

Hardwick had no illusions about taking Lowell back. In June 1977, she wrote to Mary McCarthy, "There is no great renewed romance, but a kind of friendship, and listening to his grief. His intention is to stay here with me, staying mostly in the studio, but sharing the life here, the books, the records, his family setting (Boston), which is pretty much as he left it. He went up to Maine with me for part of the week I spent there opening up. It could be said we 'are back together,' but the phrase is not really meaningful.

"We are trying to work out a sort of survival for both of us, and both are sixty," she continued to McCarthy. "We, together, are having a perfectly nice time, both quite independent and yet I guess dependent." She was, as ever, practical about his illness. "I know that Cal can get sick again and will talk to the McLean doctor on the way up to Maine. Cal has been very much in touch with him, working out what could be most sensibly done if he becomes 'keyed up.'"

Harriet Lowell remembers going into her mother's office at Barnard, where Hardwick taught and Harriet was a student, the day they were expecting him home, the day her father died. "She said she was unsure what would happen, but for now he was frail, and she did not expect him to 'learn to cook after all these years or live like a bachelor'

Inscription to Elizabeth Hardwick in *Day by Day*

and 'it was his house too and I have always been aware of that.' Despite all that had happened, she felt great affection for him and that 'he gave me everything, including you, and all that I learned from him those years in Europe and all the years we spent together.'" Harriet adds, "They had made their peace clearly enough."

Nearly twenty years earlier Lowell had written in *Life Studies* about the wife who yet again had "faced the kingdom of the mad," who once again had "dragged her husband home alive." A few weeks before his death he gave Hardwick an inscribed copy of his just-published *Day by Day* and inscribed it. "For Lizzie," he wrote, "who snatched me out of chaos."

Lowell knew that peace was impossible with Blackwood. "I feel broken by all conversation, and a voice inside me says all might be well if I could be with you. And another voice says all would be ruin, and that I would be drowned in the confusion I made worse. If I were to

Caroline Blackwood

"Out of your wreckage . . . came your book."

get sick in Ireland? But here it all can be handled. But it's the effect my troubles have on you. It's like a nightmare we all have in which each motion of foot or hand troubles the torment it tries to calm."

Lowell carried with him a photograph of Caroline Blackwood taken when she was "bright as the morning star":

> in the photo of you arranged as figurehead
> or mermaid on the prow of a Roman dory,
> bright as the morning star or a blond starlet.
> Our twin black and tin Ronson butane lighters
> knock on the sheet, are what they are,
> too many, and burned too many cigarettes. . . .
> Night darkens without your necessary call,
> it's time to turn your pictures to the wall.

In the end, Lowell did turn her pictures. The personal cost went deep, but it perhaps changed him for the better. Elizabeth Hardwick believed that Lowell's suffering and vulnerability to Caroline changed him in a fundamental way. "The passion and grief he knew from Caroline and from his feeling for her have made him more like the rest of us," she said. His fear "made Cal a better person, more in touch with the terror of this kind of turmoil than he had ever been before." "I think there *was* more openness in him," Frank Bidart observed. It opened him to the suffering of others. There was "a little more kindness, a little more empathy, a little more pity. I did feel that happened in that last year. The thing that in a sense broke something in him also gave him something."

Lowell's hopelessness at the return of his madness, his broadening awareness of his mortality, and his newfound vulnerability to heartbreak all went into *Day by Day*. In this, his final book, he wrote for Caroline Blackwood what he could have written for himself: "Out of your wreckage, beauty, wealth, / gallantries, wildness, came your book."

14

Bleak-Boned with Survival

The line must terminate.
Yet my heart rises, I know I've gladdened a lifetime
knotting, undoing a fishnet of tarred rope;
the net will hang on the wall when the fish are eaten,
nailed like illegible bronze on the futureless future.

—*From* "Fishnet"

There was, Lowell said, a single main theme coursing through the poetry of Robert Frost, "that of a man moving through the formless, the lawless, and the free, of moving into snow, air, ocean, waste, despair, death, and madness. When the limits are reached, and sometimes almost passed, the man returns." It was the journey Lowell knew. It was the epic journey, Homeric: the voyage out, the seeking and longing for home; the return of Odysseus to Ithaca.

"Sing to me of the man," *The Odyssey* begins: "the man of twists and turns / driven time and again off course. . . . / Many cities of men he saw and learned their minds, / many pains he suffered, heartsick on the open sea." Odysseus had read the minds of men as keenly as he read the swells of the sea. For ten years after the fall of Troy, he sailed in search of Ithaca and home. Storm-wrecked, time and again blown off the map, he willed and reckoned his way home to Ithaca. His supple mind and eloquence—words that "came piling on like a driving winter blizzard," a language of grace and sense—gave him means, the stars, to navigate his way home.

Homer's epic of journey and trial, of finding one's way, had captured Lowell's imagination as a schoolboy and young man. Odysseus, wrote Lowell when he was eighteen years old, was a man of hardship and war, who radiated "life, energy, and enthusiasm." Only by going through hell could Odysseus "reach aesthetic perfection." By the end of his life Lowell knew the truth of that hell. He knew art; he knew the futility of its perfection; he knew hell. The Odysseus described by Lowell in his final years had "grown bleak-boned with survival." Lost at sea, he grasped for peace.

As an undergraduate, Lowell had written to Ezra Pound that Homer's world "contained a God higher than anything I had ever known." When young he had reveled in the energy and savagery of Homer's heroes, took to heart their valor. He knew *The Odyssey* first from the early days of his childhood; later, in college, he majored in classics. He translated and on occasion taught Homer and Virgil and the Greek tragedians. "It is hard for me to imagine a poet not interested in the classics," he once said.

Lowell's great-grandfather, the first Robert Traill Spence Lowell, a priest, poet, and novelist, was a classicist as well, a professor of Latin studies. In 1862 he wrote a short story, "A Raft That No Man Made," about an Odysseus-like character who had "grown wise in seafaring" and "visited the far countries," who had "learned the story of the King of Ithaca." He had kept "words and things from crowded streets and fairs and shows and wave-washed quays," seen the "great wonders of land and sea," and been with those who had "gone forth and forward into a dim and shadowed land." Like the Greek warrior, he had been "borne along a perilous path," learning "something of men and something of God" during his long years of exile.

His great-grandson wrote about exile nearly one hundred years later. The title of the first poem in *Lord Weary's Castle*, "The Exile's Return," is a phrase that recurs in *The Odyssey*. "Odysseus journeys home," writes Homer. "The exile must return." The exile would not remain innocent, said the Greek poet, nor would he return in the "convoy of the gods or mortal men." Instead he would come back on "a lashed, makeshift raft and wrung with pains."

In "Ulysses and Circe," the first and establishing poem of *Day by Day*, Lowell writes explicitly of Odysseus's/Ulysses's wrenching search for home. He must break the spell of the witch-goddess, Circe, the chaotic enchantress reminiscent of Blackwood, before he can sail for Ithaca:

> She is a snipper-off'er—
> her discards lie about the floors,
> the unused, the misused,

seacoats and insignia,
the beheaded beast.

She wants her house askew—
kept keys to lost locks,
unidentifiable portraits, dead things
wrapped in paper the color of dust . . .

the surge of the wine before the quarrel.

Exhausted, wrung out, Odysseus starts once again for home. Life has dealt him what it will; Odysseus will die like any other, beholden to the gods, seeking the world beyond the sun:

Young,
he made strategic choices;
in middle age he accepts
his unlikely life to come;
he will die like others as the gods will,
drowning his last crew
in uncharted ocean,
seeking the unpeopled world beyond the sun,
lost in the uproarious rudeness of a great wind.

Always Lowell came back to Homer. During the last summer of his life, writing in New England about New England, Lowell wrote as well about the craft and resourcefulness of Odysseus, the soaring and rage of the "mercurial and proud" Achilles: a world of valor. He celebrated "the cycle of Greek radiance, barbarism, and doom"; Homer and New England had never left him.

———

Robert Lowell spent his final summer in England in 1976 before returning to America, Elizabeth Hardwick, and Harvard. He returned to what he knew. Everything drew him back to childhood and his country. England was not America, he said. America was different from England in memory and fact.

"England didn't have real summers like my Grandfather's farm," he wrote to Elizabeth Bishop in July 1976. "Sometimes I almost move to set off for the lake with my trolling rod for pickerel." He sought his roots. He was restless, at bay. He was disenchanted with England, did not feel at ease there. His third marriage was unraveling, his mind unstable. The writer's life was different in England; politics and expectations were different. The British literary and social world was removed from what he knew and enjoyed. He wrote in his 1973 notebook about the awkwardness he felt:

A big house in England weedy, fuzzy, unkempt [?] holly-weeds in the drive lush June vegetation [weeds] & garden flowers—

Excerpt from Lowell's notebook, January 1973

trip to meet to [*sic*] queen mother again in her better home—
our laughter at the silliness of it & boldness of it—received by
3 royal figures—are they honoring me or I they? They bow, I
start to bow, humorously realize my error. Startled that these
people are very smart, charming, tough, knowing but gradually
as I go through the house, thru my now casual reception, thru
time, I realize that I am claiming to be in a world, I can't be in,
as in like I can't be part of England—the uneasiness and even
terror of detached roots, of being examined, tried.

By 1976, his friend Esther Brooks observed, "this totally American
man, whose poetic inspiration seemed wrenched from New England
granite, could no longer resist, in all its various meanings, the tug of
home." He had come through much and endured much; as always, he
had taken his experience into words. "I hope," he said, not long before
he died, "there has been increase of beauty, wisdom, tragedy, and all
the blessings of this consuming chance."

Living through pain was necessary; it could not be avoided. Pallas
Athena, the daughter of Zeus, had made this clear to Odysseus:

> I willed it, planned it so
> when you set out for home—and to tell you all
> the trials you must suffer in your palace . . .
> Endure them all. You must. You have no choice.

"In silence," she added, "you must bear a world of pain."

Elizabeth Hardwick, Frank Bidart, and other friends observed an
increasing vulnerability in Lowell toward the end of his life, one that
was accompanied by a growing tenderness. The pain he had known
during madness and from the wreckage of his marriage took its toll but
gave a measure more of compassion. "He suddenly looked so much
older, tired, beaten," said Kathleen Spivack. "There was a tenderness
to him, outspoken, that had not been there before." His "erratic aloofness" was gone, she said. He was "troubled and tired." Peter Levi said
about Lowell's recurring bouts of madness what several did: his suffering had made him more human and open.

Blood smells of iron, wrote Adam Nicolson. The smell from a

broken face of iron-bearing rock has the smell of blood, "one of deep antiquity, a release into the nostrils of elements in the rock which have not been volatile since the rock was made." Sharp-drawn blood, like suffering in the mind, sets loose ancient elements that could be used in art. They could be used in life. Heartbreak was sharp-drawn blood.

The word "heartbreak" was real for Lowell; heartbreak had come to him through his mental suffering and, more recently, the disintegration of his marriage to a woman he deeply loved. It was a critical presence in his late writing. "Heartbreak" was a word he used with sympathy and admiration. He asked Helen Vendler once, "Why don't they ever say what I'd like them to say? . . . That I'm heartbreaking." She and he agreed that he was. Lowell described Randall Jarrell as the "most heartbreaking" poet of his generation, wrote of "broken-hearted lions" in a poem for George Santayana; he characterized John Berryman's poem "Opus Posthumous" as "heartbreaking" in its look on life and death.

Heartbreak was human; it created an opening in the armor to let in others. It made one vulnerable; it taught. Most tellingly, perhaps, heartbreak was the element of a different kind of poetry. Grey Gowrie relates that he asked Lowell who were his favorite poets. "I expected him to choose Eliot, whom he loved and who was his publisher. 'Oh Hardy and Ezra,' he replied, 'because of the heartbreak.'"

Lowell, when he came back to America in October 1976, seemed to be a more compassionate man, said Esther Brooks. "Looking back now one could almost say that his mind had begun to heal itself just as his heart had begun to fail him. Gone was the breezy egotism. He seemed not only in touch with his own feelings but with the feelings of those whom he had caused to suffer so very much. A delicacy of judgment returned along with humility, and compassion replaced once again the rather offhand insensitivity of past years."

Lowell told Brooks that he planned to stay in America. "America and teaching at Harvard are my life's water," he told her. "I don't want to divide what's left of my life between two continents and two cultures." He had been away from America and New England, "the pioneer going into the wilderness." It was clear to everyone who knew him: he wanted to be home.

"Keep Ithaka always in your mind," wrote the Greek poet C. P. Cavafy. "Arriving there is what you are destined for." Know what the journey can give you, he said. The journey is meant for adventure and learning, summer dawns and new ports. It is the gift of experience and imagination. "Ithaka gave you the marvelous journey," Cavafy wrote. "Without her you wouldn't have set out." But at some point Ithaca has nothing left to give.

"In the midst of life we are in death," it says in the Book of Common Prayer. All die. We are given life for a while but not for long. We are given love and desire, words, grief, hope and laughter, music, but not for long. We forfeit our place to others. The *memento mori* of the painters—the rose, the skull, the bubble—the miniature human figures of Regency England, half flesh and fine clothed, half skeleton, were then and remain reminders of the claim of death. Depression, attached as it is to mania, is a *memento mori* of its own kind. It feels of death; at times it creates a longing for it.

Lowell's recurring mania and depression brought with them a dark philosophy and a sharp sense of mortality. His imagination, moving so often and intensely in historical times, made the reality of death inescapable. Death took poet, tyrant, lover, and king alike; Lowell's eyes moved instinctively to the final dates carved into the marble stones of graveyards. He spoke often about age and death. "I miss the long roll of years ahead of me," Lowell wrote to Elizabeth Bishop. Although it had been a lovely summer, he said a few months later, "when I look inside it's sad and acid: age, death of friends, aging of everything in sight." Increasingly the topics of death and decay and his regret for things done and left undone filled his letters to friends. "The things that cannot be done twice!" he wrote to Bishop.

Death and age, subjects that bear down on all, bore down on Lowell harder than most. "I wake up thinking I have perhaps twenty more years, that they are whizzing by," Lowell wrote to Peter Taylor when he was in his early forties. After Theodore Roethke died he said, "It's hard to get used to knowing that it's not just the very remote and old that die, but someone who used to beat you at croquet a few months ago." Not long after, he wrote to Bishop, "Oh, oh, oh, how time whirls us on! Do you realize that we have already outlived more than half the classic English poets." Death is always on your mind once you hit fifty, he said. "Each season we get older—the sky, the ceiling, a little closer." The ceiling, an important image to the poet who wrote so often of chairs and ladders and ascending to the moon, was closing in. "I still feel I can reach up and touch the ceiling of one's end," he wrote to Bishop in 1970.

Death and madness came more into his poetry. "Last Night" was published in 1973:

> Is dying harder than being already dead?
> I came to my first class without a textbook,
> saw the watch I mailed my daughter didn't run;
> I opened an old closet door, and found myself
> covered with quicklime, my face deliquescent . . .
> by oversight still recognizable.
> Thank God, I was the first to find myself.
> Ah the swift vanishing of my older
> generation—the deaths, suicide, madness
> of Roethke, Berryman, Jarrell and Lowell.

In the same year Lowell wrote to Bishop, who expressed her discomfort about his frequent talk of age and death: "It's the twinges of mortality, one's length of life that keeps swimming into eyesight. It seems unbelievable that I've statistically lived so much much the largest division of my life." He quoted a line he had translated from Pasternak, "To live a life is not to cross a field." It was, he said, "poignant, but this is what is comforting. We cannot cross the field, only walk it . . . finishing or not finishing this or that along the way. An image of all this is watching children and stepchildren growing into their futures I cannot see, and all from forty to fifty-five years younger than I even while I live. A rich tangle of the unseen." Thoughts of death and the unknowable future led him to a bleak accounting of his life and work:

> I climb the ladder, knowing my last words,
> no matter how unjust, no longer matter,
> the black marks of my nights erased in blood—
> wondering, "Why was it ever worth my while?"

Robert Schumann observed that a requiem Mass is the "thing one writes for oneself." This is true of Lowell's final book, *Day by Day*, and his final prose essay, "New England and Further." The poems and essay are the endpoint of his thinking and experience, a culmination of his craft and philosophy. The deeper you get into *Day by Day*, believes James Atlas, "the more you realize—and he died just after it was finished—that he has written his own elegy."

Although most critics do not rank *Day by Day* with *Life Studies* or *Lord Weary's Castle*, the collection is an extraordinary poetic summing up, an elegy and reflection over a life and a life's art. "What we want to say," Lowell once said, "is the confusion and sadness and incoherence of the human condition." These are the soul of his last book.

The threads of Lowell's life come together in *Day by Day*: the disturbed childhood scarred by distant, judgmental, and uncomprehending parents; New England's land and politics, her history and writers; friends and fellow poets and teachers; his marriages and love affairs; his daughter and son and stepdaughters; the madness that came, and left, but always came again; the struggle to make art from life; aging, suffering, death; the search for peace, for home.

These threads of his mind and experience were woven into his earlier work, of course, but they became more prominent in the books he wrote during the last ten years of his life. They are evident in a notebook he kept during 1973 that contains drafts and notes for many of the poems of *Day by Day*. This notebook was in Lowell's briefcase at the time of his death, where it has remained. Robert Fitzgerald, who had dinner with Lowell at the Harvard Faculty Club in early 1977, remembers that Lowell opened his briefcase that evening and showed him the new poems that later would be published in his final book. (Elizabeth Hardwick found this notebook too upsetting to remove from Lowell's briefcase even years after his death. "His briefcase which he carried with him always and somehow never lost is still sitting here in my study," she wrote to Mary McCarthy. "Cigarettes, cigarette lighter, nail file, glasses still there. I sent the papers off to the estate long ago, but somehow I can't take the other things out.")

The notebook, dated 1973, is a red hardbound appointment diary that is eight by six inches. There is one page for each day of the year, perhaps a factor in the title of his book, *Day by Day*. (Or, the title may have a more classical basis. In the tenth book of Robert Fitzgerald's translation of *The Odyssey*, the phrase "Day by day we lingered"

appears. The title is in any event appropriate for poems that were written for the day and moment.) Several of the pages of the book are
blank; the rest are partially or entirely filled by Lowell's near-illegible
handwriting. Some entries are simply reminders of appointments for
book readings and lectures, or trips abroad to Holland, Italy, Paris, or
America. The dates correspond to what is known about his schedule
at those times. There are teaching notes for books to be used in his
Harvard classes and entries made for upcoming visits from Harriet,
doctors' appointments, school engagements for his stepdaughters, and
lunch and dinner engagements in London, as well as pages devoted to
a timeline of Caroline Blackwood's life, a listing of the birth and death
dates of friends and family, and a jotting down of Sheridan's words and
expressions. Most pages in the 1973 notebook, however, are fragments
or drafts of poems, many of which were revised and subsequently
included in *Day by Day*. They prefigure poems about ancestry, children, love and death, and madness.

The fragments of these poems, broken phrases and images, show
Lowell looking back over his life and questioning the meaning of nearly
everything. Death is a frequent topic. The fear of dying, he writes in
his scattered impressions, "isn't even that—it's / Knowing that as the
signs say we will die / A few years / The living hair and sinew of the
body is there / To keep us alive—everything functions / Or is broken
function—no tragedy for the / Soul, our purpose is obsolescence." His
notes deal with death, loss, home, and art. The images and mood of
this 1973 notebook find their way into the poems of *Day by Day:* the
melancholy looking back, the regrets, the death and madness ahead.
The desire to return home.

Day by Day is shot through with death: "the hungry future, / the
time when any illness is chronic, / and the years of discretion are spent
on complaint— / until the wristwatch is taken from the wrist." The
poems give testament to Ecclesiastes, to the belief that the house of
mourning is the house of all men. They are written in the shadow of
Lowell's mortality, at the edge of his nerves. They look back in regret
on the damage done by life; on time, youth, and love passing; they
cast back over a life at bay. It is impossible to restore the years that the
locust has eaten, declares the Old Testament. This gets no argument
from Lowell. His final poems are beautiful, heartbreaking, and deeply
human.

Lowell laments in *Day by Day* that he cannot create as he once did,

that he can only depict, only snap a photograph. The maker of patterns and phrases watches as the elements of his imagination fade and
ideas and images elude him. The divide between the imagined and the
literal seems to him impassable, or becoming so. "I've been thinking,"
he wrote a year before he died, "that what happened is all we have to
draw on, yet that isn't art, isn't of course enough for art. . . . its riches
of inharmonious material, its fragmented sharpness—the stuff of life
with its artificial imposed limits." He believed he was drawing from
an empty well. He spoke to this in "Epilogue," the last poem in the
book:

> Those blessèd structures, plot and rhyme—
> why are they no help to me now
> I want to make
> something imagined, not recalled?
> I hear the noise of my own voice:
> *The painter's vision is not a lens,*
> *it trembles to caress the light.*
> But sometimes everything I write
> with the threadbare art of my eye
> seems a snapshot,
> lurid, rapid, garish, grouped,
> heightened from life,
> yet paralyzed by fact.
> All's misalliance.
> Yet why not say what happened?
> Pray for the grace of accuracy
> Vermeer gave to the sun's illumination
> stealing like the tide across a map
> to his girl solid with yearning.
> We are poor passing facts,
> warned by that to give
> each figure in the photograph
> his living name.

The poem gives lie to Lowell's lament. It is no snapshot; it is not para-
lyzed by fact. The yearning for art steals too like a tide across a map;
it is a poem from both mind and heart; it is deeply imagined, not only
recalled.

In Lowell's final book, Helen Vendler writes, he is a poet of "disarming openness, exposing shame and uncertainty." His poems "avoid the histrionic" and "acknowledge exhaustion; they expect death." Lowell had been determined to write about time and age "without hysteria," he wrote to Peter Taylor in 1975. The power would be in understatement and control. It was necessary, he told Bishop, "to hold a shield before one's feelings and the reader."

Day by Day, if less stunningly original than *Life Studies* and *Lord Weary's Castle*, is more haunting and compassionate. It completes the arc of Lowell's life and work in all its toughness, suffering, grandeur, and genius. Darkness, as he had said, was truth. It was not metaphor. His final book, argues Marjorie Perloff, was a renunciation of the "roles he played in his earlier work, judge, preacher, surveyor of history, connoisseur of chaos." Life had been stripped to the bone. "Only when we read *Day by Day* as a *Life Studies* written 20 years later, by a poet who knows his career as a writer and his life as a man are about to end, does its beauty and pathos emerge," observed the critic William Pritchard.

Lowell is valedictory in *Day by Day*. At times there is a sense of the darkly informed Virgil accompanying the reader across deep waters, preparing him for what the poet knows must come, not for what the reader hopes might come. There is solace in not being alone in facing the worst and the final, but there is no backing away from the certainty that the worst and the final will come. Lowell offers no relief from the unavoidable, just a compass and stars for the tragedy that is the human condition. "Ask for no Orphean lute / To pluck life back," he had written as a young poet in "The Quaker Graveyard in Nantucket." One may hope for relief from the pain but there is no answer to death. "I ask for a natural death," he wrote, "no teeth on the ground, / no blood about the place . . . / It's not death I fear, / but unspecified, unlimited pain."

In his translation of *The Oresteia* of Aeschylus, published after his death, Lowell again offered no spell or prayer to keep death at bay: "I have no hope. Crops rise and fall, / and summer follows on the heels of summer, / but when a man dies, and his black / blood falls at his feet, / no spell will sing him back."

"Yet how much we carry away," he wrote in his 1973 journal. "Before we are quiet in the carpenter's vice."

In the fall of 1976, shortly before he was to leave England to teach at Harvard, Lowell once again was hospitalized for mania. It was a damning reminder of the wreckage brought by his illness. He would always be sick, said Caroline Blackwood. His attacks were "destroying her." Nobody could take it on, she told a friend. Life was crashing down on them both. Together and individually they were in dark straits. Blackwood was drinking heavily and depressed. He was desperate that his madness had returned. Their nights were ripped apart by tirades and accusations. Neither could handle the possibility of life continuing as it was. "The great circuit of the stars lies on jewellers' velvet," he wrote in a poem dedicated to Caroline; "be close enough to tell me when I will die— / what will love do not knowing it will die?"

Despite the end now obvious in their marriage, Lowell and Blackwood rented a house in Cambridge for the upcoming Harvard term. Blackwood went ahead of Lowell to America while he remained in the hospital in London. Ten days after leaving the hospital he arrived in Boston; Frank Bidart and Blackwood picked him up at Logan Airport. He was in "awful" shape, said Bidart. "Enormously upset." Blackwood, on edge following Lowell's recent stay in the hospital, was quick wired to any sign that he might be ill. Within minutes of his getting into the car she told Bidart that Lowell was sick again. Bidart disagreed. He was "just nervous," he said. Cal was in "intense distress," but he was not manic.

He had to have peace, Lowell said again and again. He needed quiet, a place apart from Blackwood. He couldn't take the drama anymore, he told Bidart. He couldn't take the anger and tension. His desperation was obvious in everything he said and wrote during this time. Lowell stayed with Bidart for three weeks, grateful to be away from the turmoil. He found relief in the respite, solace in the beauty and familiarity of the Schubert piano trios Bidart played for him the first night he stayed with him. He found a trace of long-elusive peace.

Not long after Lowell returned to America, in late January 1977, he found it increasingly difficult to breathe. He was short-winded, he wrote to Blackwood. Even when sitting he felt he couldn't draw enough breath. Frank Bidart drove him to the Stillman Infirmary at

Harvard; later he was evaluated at McLean Hospital and then transferred to Massachusetts General Hospital in Boston. He described the events later to Blackwood: "After my cardiograph came out irregular, I wavered a long moment, then was practically handcuffed in a sort of sitting up stretcher, bounced down a stairless gangway (all this was in McLean's) then banged in an ambulance to Mass. General. More waits, while I absorbed the imaginable seriousness of my condition. Death? Ivan Ilyich? But there was no pain at all, and it seemed to me that death would be nothing. What gentler thing could one ask for, except, though painless, it had absolutely no meaning, no long private message. Of course, I was soon reassured, when new drugs I had already been given at McLean's removed the drama."

Lowell was admitted to the Phillips House Coronary Care Unit at Massachusetts General Hospital on February 1. He told the attending physician, Dr. Timothy Guiney, that he had found it increasingly difficult to breathe, particularly when climbing stairs. In addition to his cardiac history, the doctor noted Lowell's long history of manic-depressive illness and recorded that his lithium level was elevated. (Lowell told the doctor his lithium level was 1.7 mEq/L, which is in the toxic range, but by the time his blood was drawn at the hospital it was down to 1.2 mEq/L, still high but not remarkably so.) His mood was somewhat slowed and depressed and he seemed to be "anxious and rather shy."

Lowell remained in Phillips House for a week, the same place where as a college student he had visited his dying grandfather Arthur Winslow. In a poem published a few months later in *Day by Day*, "Phillips House Revisited," he described his reaching for breath, as if muffled in snow.

> A weak clamor like ice giving . . .
>
> Something sinister and comforting
> in this return after forty years' arrears
> to death and Phillips House . . .
> this irreverent absence of pain,
> less than the ordinary that daily irks—
> except I cannot entirely get my breath,
> as if I were muffled in snow,
> our winter's inverted gray sky

of frozen slush,
its usual luminous lack of warmth.

The nursing staff noted on admission that Lowell had "very flat affect and falls asleep continually." They were concerned about his history of manic-depressive illness and monitoring his lithium but observed "he reads a great deal and spends a good amount of time in conversation with other 'learned' fellows."

On February 9, 1977, Lowell was discharged "in good spirits" with a diagnosis of congestive heart failure. "Thank you for referring Mr. Lowell to me," Dr. Guiney wrote to Lowell's doctors at McLean Hospital. "He proved to be just as interesting a person and a patient as you suggested he might be."

———

Lowell's marriage to Blackwood was over. He spent Easter with her in March 1977 and returned to Boston distraught and clear in his mind that the relationship must end. Such times of happiness as there were could not stand against the tension, heavy drinking, anger, and threats of leaving and suicide. Lowell appeared to his friends to be resigned to a life without Blackwood; he also seemed to them sadder and less emotionally engaged with the world. Blair Clark, his friend since school, said, "Cal's tone was quite flat, as if he were talking about someone else's life."

Lowell and Hardwick spent a quiet summer in Maine writing and reading and seeing friends. The days followed the predictable pattern of work and friendship that had been the rock-steady rhythm of their family summers in Castine. Hardwick and Lowell "were quite nice to each other—extremely warm and comfortable," said Bidart. "But at the same time he seemed, emotionally, in a kind of suspended animation." In July they went to the Soviet Union for ten days as part of an American delegation of writers that included William Styron and Edward Albee. Lowell looked "tired and melancholy," Styron recalled. "I remember Cal speaking of Boris Pasternak, whose work he admired passionately; he said that he wanted to visit his grave, and spoke of death." He told Styron, "We all have one foot in the grave." There was "so much suffering," Styron said, in Lowell's "brooding, sorrowing Beethovenesque head."

Lowell's last summer in Castine, as in the past, was given to writing. "He lived quietly and most of all wrote an extraordinarily complex essay about a huge number of figures," Hardwick recalled about Lowell's "New England and Further." The essay, which was published after his death, was a sparse, eloquent montage of short pieces about New England thinkers and writers, including Melville, Hawthorne, Emerson, Emily Dickinson, and Thoreau. It was, Hardwick said, done from memory and came from a long life of "saturation in New England texts." This immersion in New England writings "had been his life" and the source of the "originality of his thoughts about American literature." Lowell's mind was well during his last summer, she said, his "free, independent intelligence, still hourly, daily there for him to call upon."

Lowell's writing about New England in the summer of 1977 is epigrammatic, dense, often brilliant. At times it is nostalgic, especially when describing the New England landscape—"so many beautiful villages, one after another. The red maples, ocean, lake, mountain. A twisted seacoast"—at others, blistering in his observations of the corruption of first-held beliefs and fought-for values, the fall from high ideal to indifference and greed. Always there is an appreciation of the questioning, fiery, original minds of New England.

Lowell was writing poetry as well during the final months of his life. He started two new poems in Castine, "Loneliness," which he addressed to Elizabeth Hardwick, and "Summer Tides," his last completed poem, addressed to Caroline Blackwood. These last poems are shot through with summer images of wharf, sea, beach ladders and sail, shore and tides, regret and foreboding. They are of childhood; his own—"I would wish to live forever, / like the small boy on the wharf / marching alone, far ahead of the others"—and the childhoods of his son and daughter and his three young stepdaughters.

In his poem to Hardwick he writes of a separate peace, with all that that implies: "We were / so by ourselves and calm this summer," he writes in "Loneliness." "A stonesthrow off, / seven eider ducks / float and dive in their watery commune . . . / a family, though not a marriage." The summer was a moment of calm and light for Hardwick as well. After Lowell died she wrote to Mary McCarthy, "It has been much more painful than I thought it reasonable to show, much more lonely and sometimes frightening. Having the companionship of Cal this summer and some of the spring before was a wonderful break of lightness and brightness for me."

With the end of his marriage to Blackwood inescapable, death on his mind, his physical and mental health uncertain, Lowell wrote a deeply affecting poem about damaged, damaging love, the precarious present and yet more precarious future. He does not know what his future holds, knows only that there will be a shortfall in what he can give his children. "Last year / our drunken quarrels had no explanation, / except everything, except everything." His bearings tremble. Bolts are missing in the beach ladder; the bulwark rots. The rail is loosened. In every sense, the final lines of his final poem are, as he would have it, heartbreaking:

> My wooden beach-ladder swings by one bolt,
> and repeats its single creaking rhythm—
> I cannot go down to the sea.
> After so much logical interrogation,
> I can do nothing that matters.
> The east wind carries disturbance for leagues—
> I think of my son and daughter,
> and three stepdaughters
> on far-out ledges
> washed by the dreaded clock-clock of the waves . . .
> gradually rotting the bulwark where I stand.
> Their father's unmotherly touch
> trembles on a loosened rail.

In early September 1977, a few days after completing "Summer Tides," Lowell gave Frank Bidart a typed fair copy of it and told him that he was "very proud" of the poem. Bidart agreed; indeed, he said he was "knocked out by it." Lowell had dinner with Bidart and Helen Vendler just before he took the night flight from Boston to Ireland to visit Caroline and Sheridan. "He seemed a very lonely figure," observed Bidart. He was "dreading" seeing Blackwood; it was clear that "this was not a life that could have continued." Lowell talked about death and told Vendler that he wanted to be buried in the family graveyard in Dunbarton. He had specified in his will that his funeral would be a high Mass at the Church of the Advent in Boston. "That's how we're buried," he told her; that was how the Lowells and Winslows were buried.

Lowell's trip to Ireland proved that his decision to leave Blackwood was the only one possible. He was deeply unhappy, as was she. Lowell was extremely restless, Blackwood said. He moved from room to room, discontent to discontent. The electricity went out, the telephone failed, and he had locked himself in the house, unable to get out. He was trapped in every sense, agitated and depressed. He called Hardwick to say he was coming back early to America. Things were "sheer torture" with Blackwood, he said. He changed his ticket to fly into New York rather than Boston so he could stay with her a few days before going back to Harvard.

The stone masons of Winchester Cathedral cement thin pieces of glass across the ancient stones. If the cathedral moves, if the stones shift, the glass breaks to warn of danger.

The glass had broken. He "drifts with the wild ice," he had written: "Ice that ticks seaward like a clock." His heart was failing; his marriage was failing. His mind was unstable; he was near certain to go mad again. He had no peace.

"The east wind carries disturbance for leagues," he had written in his poem for Caroline. They both knew it to be so. After he returned to America she found a fragment of a poem he had been working on:

> Christ,
> may I die at night
> with a semblance of my faculties,
> like the full moon that fails.

Lowell arrived at Kennedy Airport in New York on the afternoon of September 12 and took a taxi to Elizabeth Hardwick's apartment in Manhattan. He had with him his briefcase, containing notes for new poems and, held in his arms, a painting of Caroline Blackwood by her first husband, Lucian Freud. Her picture was not, in the end, turned to the wall. It was a scene of past, present, and a shade of future, thick in symbol and irony. When the taxi arrived at Hardwick's apartment, the driver noticed that Lowell was slumped over and appeared to be asleep. When he did not wake up, the driver rang Hardwick's doorbell; she came down to the taxi and knew immediately that Lowell was dead. She accompanied his body to the hospital, eight blocks away.

"My heart longs to be home," Odysseus told Circe. She said: "Another journey calls. You must travel down to the House of Death." Odysseus replied, "Who can pilot us on that journey? Who has ever / reached the House of Death in a black ship?" And Circe said: "Let no lack of a pilot at the helm concern you, no, / just step your mast and spread your white sail wide— / sit back and the North Wind will speed you on your way / . . . to the moldering House of Death. / And there into Acheron, the Flood of Grief, two rivers flow, / the torrent River of Fire, the wailing River of Tears / that branches off from Styx.

Robert Lowell died suddenly, shortly before 6:00 p.m. on September 12, 1977, at the age of sixty. There was no autopsy, and the death certificate was signed by a doctor at Roosevelt Hospital; at that time and place there was no requirement to identify the cause other than to affirm that death was due to natural causes. Dr. Thomas Traill, a cardiologist at the Johns Hopkins University School of Medicine, reviewed Lowell's available medical records from 1949 to 1977. His summary of Lowell's heart disease and the rest of his medical history is contained in Appendix 3. Sudden death in someone with Lowell's medical history is nearly always due to ventricular fibrillation, the final sequence of severe chronic heart-muscle injury, probably the result of widespread coronary artery disease. In common language, Lowell died suddenly of a heart attack, having suffered for some time from cardiac failure. Death would have been instantaneous and likely came without warning or pain.

"I remember once, a dozen years before he died," Blair Clark recalled, "bringing him back to my house in New York in one of his crazed escapes from home. Watching him breathe in heavy gasps, asleep in the taxi, the tranquillizing drugs fighting the mania, I thought that there were then two dynamos within him, spinning in opposite directions and tearing him apart, and that these forces would kill him at last. No one, strong as he was, could stand that for long. And, finally, the opposing engines of creation and repression did kill him in a taxi in front of his own real home."

CERTIFICATE OF DEATH

Certificate No. 156-77-115323

DATE FILED SEP 12 1977

NAME OF DECEASED (Type or Print)

ROBERT (First Name)   (Middle Name)   LOWELL (Last Name)

MEDICAL CERTIFICATE OF DEATH (To be filled in by the Physician)

2. PLACE OF DEATH
New York City   b. Name of Hospital or Institution. If not in hospital, street address.

a. Borough of MANHATTAN   THE ROOSEVELT HOSPITAL 428 WEST 59TH STREET N.Y.C. 10019

3a. DATE AND HOUR OF DEATH (Month) (Day) (Year) SEPTEMBER 12, 1977   **3b. Hour** 6:00   **AM**   **4. SEX** MALE   **5. APPROXIMATE AGE** 61 YEARS

6. I HEREBY CERTIFY that (I attended the deceased)* (a staff physician of this institution attended the deceased)* (Dr. ____

attended the deceased)* from 9/12 1977 to 9/12 1977 and last saw h IM alive at 5:41 P.M. on 9/12

1977. I further certify that traumatic injury or poisoning DID NOT play any part in causing death, and that death did not occur in any unusual manner and was due entirely to NATURAL CAUSES. * Cross out words that do not apply. † See first instruction on reverse of certificate.

Witness my hand this 12 day of September 19 77 Signature Elizabeth Kantor   D.O. M.D.

Name of Physician ELIZABETH KANTOR (Type or Print)   Address THE ROOSEVELT HOSPITAL

PERSONAL PARTICULARS (To be filled in by Funeral Director)

7. USUAL RESIDENCE
a. State: New York   b. County: New York   c. City or Town: New York   d. Inside city limits of "7C" X Yes ☐ No

e. Street and house number: C/O Eisman 345 Park Avenue   f. Apt.   g. Length of residence or stay in City of New York immediately prior to death: Months

8. SINGLE, MARRIED, WIDOWED or DIVORCED (Write in word) Married

9. NAME OF SURVIVING SPOUSE (If wife, give maiden name) Caroline Blackwood

10. DATE OF BIRTH OF DECEDENT (Month) (Day) (Year) March 1, 1917

11. AGE at last birthday 60 Yrs.   If UNDER 1 year mos. days   If LESS than 1 day hrs. or min.

12a. USUAL OCCUPATION (Kind of work done during most of working life, even if retired.) Writer   b. KIND of BUSINESS or INDUSTRY Poetry

13. SOCIAL SECURITY NO.

14. BIRTHPLACE (State or Foreign Country) Massachusetts

15. OF WHAT COUNTRY WAS DECEASED A CITIZEN AT TIME OF DEATH USA

16. ANY OTHER NAME(S) BY WHICH DECEDENT WAS KNOWN Robert T.S. Lowell

17. NAME OF FATHER OF DECEDENT Robert T.S. Lowell

18. MAIDEN NAME OF MOTHER OF DECEDENT Charlotte Winslow

19a. NAME OF INFORMANT Elizabeth Lowell   b. RELATIONSHIP Friend   c. ADDRESS 15 West 67 Street (City) NYC (State)

20a. NAME OF CEMETERY OR CREMATORY Stark Cemetery   b. LOCATION (City, Town, State and Country) Dumbarton, New Hampshire   c. DATE of Burial or Cremation Sept. 16, 1977

21a. FUNERAL DIRECTOR Frank E. Campbell   b. ADDRESS 1076 Madison Avenue NYC

BUREAU OF VITAL RECORDS   DEPARTMENT OF HEALTH   THE CITY OF NEW YORK

Death certificate of Robert Lowell

From the obituaries for Robert Lowell, September 1977:

The famous American poet died last night in New York. No doubt
the same report had been flashed to Rome, Paris, Berlin,
Madrid, Moscow, Istanbul and beyond. After Eliot and Pound,
had the death of any other American poet been treated as
world news?

—*The New York Times*

Robert Lowell, who died on September 12 at the age of 60,
was fairly generally considered the most distinguished American poet, and indeed the most distinguished poet writing in
English, of his generation. . . . Perhaps no imaginative writer
of our time agonised more over, or turned to more fruitful use
what he himself called "our momentous sublime"; the grandeur and wretchedness of American history.

—*The Times* (London)

He is dead now, and Boston has lost its greatest writer, the poet
who spun magic out of the Public Garden and gave us a brilliant poet's tour of life among the Winslows and the Lowells,
in an area firmly bounded by Revere Street and Beverly Farms,
Marlborough Street and Cambridge, with only occasional side
trips to Belmont for a genteel breakdown at McLean's.

He was a man who could speak with coruscating language,
show a gentle wit, make profound insight seem simple. His
genius was unmatched in his generation. He served Boston
better, by making it seem a magic place, than any paid public
servant has ever served the city.

—*The Boston Herald American*

Robert Lowell followed the [Democratic presidential] campaign of 1968 through the shoe factories and knitting mills
of New Hampshire. . . . He went to the bowling alleys and
to baseball parks, and irritated staff by talking to the candi-
date for an hour about the origin of the word "fungo" . . .

while the press waited. He flew in small planes over the tama-
rack swamps and lakes of Wisconsin, still gray with April ice,
to be introduced to small inland college audiences as "the
poet."

— Eugene McCarthy, *The Washington Star*

A sense of loss, of something now out of reach and foreclosed,
prompts us to measure what remains.

And the sense of loss will be all the greater—for some of
us, anyway—with the passing of this poet, in whose poems we
were obliged to relive so much of the history and so many of
the terrible emotions of our time. These he often stated with a
violence that seared our sensibilities and made the poet seem,
at times, an ally of the very impulses he castigated. . . . Lowell
was never an easy poet.

—*The New York Times*

The Pulitzer Prize judges of 1974 called Robert Lowell "by
common consent of both reader and critic, the most considerable poet since T. S. Eliot." This was a sweeping verdict. From
the beginning of his career, Lowell was recognized as a figure
of eminent stature; he dominated American poetry of the past
30 years. . . . No other American poet of mid-century could
challenge Lowell in the majesty of the total achievement. . . .
Robert Lowell could be uneven, vague and lofty, but he was a
force to be reckoned with, a supreme artist who leaves work
that will endure as long as the American language lives.

—*The Boston Globe*

Robert Lowell's painful and glorious autobiography in verse,
unfolding these many years in more than a dozen books that
brought him fame and honors as the foremost American poet
of his time, was concluded yesterday at a funeral in Boston,
the city where he was born 60 years ago, and in a graveyard in
Dunbarton, N.H., where his forebears rest.

"It was," said a friend, "like a poem by Cal—only he's not
here to write it."

—*The Washington Post*

Robert Lowell's funeral was held in the late morning of September 16, 1977, at the Church of the Advent in Boston, a short walk from where he had been born. The church, antebellum and Anglo-Catholic, is Episcopal but rooted in the nineteenth-century Oxford Movement, which sought a closer alignment between the Church of England and the Catholic Church. For Lowell, the Church of the Advent was a natural choice. He had been born and raised in the Episcopal Church but at times intensely drawn to Catholicism, for a period a convert to it. Like many who have ceased to believe the dogma, he had kept a strong spiritual and cultural tie with the traditions of his church.

Lowell found religious and historical continuity in the hymns and rites of the Episcopal Church. He appreciated and took pleasure in the language of the Book of Common Prayer and the King James Version of the Bible. ("He used to go to Episcopal services," Lowell's doctor wrote in his admitting note at Massachusetts Mental Health Center in 1957; "he didn't actually believe in the doctrine but he enjoyed the ceremony." As recently as his admission to Massachusetts General Hospital a few months before his death, Lowell listed his religion as "Episcopalian.") In response to a letter from Lowell in 1955, the rector of the Church of the Advent replied that he was "happy to report that Bishop Nash has formally restored you to communicant status and does not feel it is necessary for you to be 'received back' by him . . . as you started out in the Episcopal Church."

Lowell was as skeptical about religion as he was about most things, but he was serious. "After much irresolution I became an Episcopalian again (a high one)," he wrote to Elizabeth Bishop. "I used to think one had to be a Catholic or nothing. I guess I've rather rudely expected life to be a matter of harsh clear alternatives. I don't know what to say of my new faith; on the surface I feel eccentric, antiquarian, a superstitious, skeptical fussy old woman, but down under I feel something that makes sober sense and lets my eyes open."

Peter Taylor recalled attending Palm Sunday services with Lowell at the Church of the Advent two years before he died. "He appeared to be elated, even transported by the experience . . . so affected by the beauties of the music and the High Mass inside the church that he had kept up a running conversation on all of it to the companion beside him." Lowell was, Taylor said, "grave and serene . . . responding to his religious environment, trying to embrace it, to comprehend it." It was "a profound contemplation of the great mystery: What does life mean: What is it all about?"

Lowell's funeral and burial, planned by him and specified in his will, were his final public acts. His funeral was held within the walls of his beliefs and the traditions he knew; it was carried out within the ancient structure of his church. It was not only for his family, friends, and colleagues—some of whom found the requiem Mass cold, formal, stiff, unapproachable—but for history. The bodies of poets had been laid out on shields, sent out in long ships, burned on pyres, buried under stones carved with words of their own making. This was to be no different. The words and ritual of the high, solemn requiem Mass—its poetry, its structure, plot, and rhyme—were deep in him and chosen by him for his end.

Behold, I make all things new. And he said unto me, Write: for these words are true and faithful.

———

At the end of the Mass the priest faced Lowell's coffin and recited the ancient consolation:

> Into thy hands, O merciful Savior, we commend thy servant Robert. Acknowledge, we humbly beseech thee, a sheep of thine own fold, a lamb of thine own flock, a sinner of thine own redeeming. Receive him into the arms of thy mercy, into the blessed rest of everlasting peace, and into the glorious company of the saints in light.

There followed the *Nunc Dimittis* that Lowell knew well: "Lord, now lettest thy servant depart in peace." A peace was promised that he had not known.

In his homily, the Reverend G. Harris Collingwood spoke from Genesis. "In the heart of chaos, God made form and order," he said. "Out of the chaos he drew forth a Cosmos." The chaos was maintained, kept at bay, and transformed into form and order, whether by the Creator in Genesis or by the poet in his work. "Robert Lowell knew intimately and painfully those dark chaotic forces forever threatening the firmament," the priest continued. "But let us gather to give thanks for the light he kindled, and to pray for him and for ourselves, knowing that one day we too shall enter into death."

> And the earth was without form, and void; and darkness was upon the face of the deep. And the Spirit of God moved upon the face of the waters. And God said, Let there be light: and there was light. And God saw the light, that it was good: and God divided the light from the darkness.

> —Genesis 1:2–4

Always Lowell's life and work had been about the opposing forces of creation and destruction; about exerting will over forces not easily given to control; about courage and valor arrayed against wrong and darkness. Always it was about shaping, about dark and light.

There was a lone exception to the traditional structure of the requiem Mass. Peter Taylor read "Where the Rainbow Ends," the last poem in *Lord Weary's Castle*; he read the young Lowell's passionate words about things deep to him across his life: God or not. Justice. Boston. Peace. Exile and grace:

> I saw my city in the Scales, the pans
> Of judgment rising and descending. Piles
> Of dead leaves char the air—
> And I am a red arrow on this graph
> Of Revelations. Every dove is sold.
> .   .   .   .

> At the high altar, gold
> And a fair cloth. I kneel and the wings beat
> My cheek. What can the dove of Jesus give
> You now but wisdom, exile? Stand and live,
> The dove has brought an olive branch to eat.

After the funeral family members and close friends drove to Dunbarton in New Hampshire for the burial. The small group included Caroline Blackwood, Harriet Lowell, and Elizabeth Hardwick. "The family graveyard lay under a mist of rain," Hardwick said later, "great trees and a few autumn leaves on the ground and the old gravestones." It is a small graveyard, quiet, removed from the world and packed stone to stone with Winslows and Starks. Lowell, who is buried next to his mother and father, is only the second, and perhaps the last, Lowell to be buried at Dunbarton. Lowell had written often about his family graveyard in his poetry and letters. He associated it with trips he had made with his grandfather; he had keen recollections of the graves and leaves and the looming statue of Christ. He remembered "the black brook, the pruned fir trunks, the iron spear fence, and the memorial slates." "Everything in Dunbarton was an oxymoron, a struggle of good and evil: the sun rose on frozen leaves; all physical and moral color was touched with Caravaggio like emphasis. . . . I used to play about the graves of my ancestors. I dreamed with healthy, burning red cheeks and a mind mossy with the dates on the gravestones."

In "Dunbarton" he had written of his ancestors and those who were to follow:

> Grandfather and I
> raked leaves from our dead forebears,
> defied the dank weather
> with "dragon" bonfires.

As Lowell's coffin was lowered into the ground, Blackwood, Hardwick, and Harriet threw flowers into the grave, and the priest recited the familiar words of Committal from the Book of Common Prayer, laying to rest, calling for peace:

> In sure and certain hope of the resurrection to eternal life through our Lord Jesus Christ, we commend to Almighty God our brother Robert; and we commit his body to the ground; earth to earth, ashes to ashes, dust to dust. The Lord bless him and keep him, the Lord make his face to shine upon him and be gracious unto him, the Lord lift up his countenance upon him and give him peace.

Lowell had chosen from his writing the epitaphs for the gravestones of his parents; his own is taken from "Endings," in *Day by Day*:

ROBERT LOWELL
1917–1977
THE IMMORTAL IS SCRAPED
UNCONSENTING FROM THE MORTAL

A month after Lowell was buried, the Russian poet Andrei Voznesensky visited Dunbarton. It was dark, he recalled, and it was hard to find Lowell's grave. He began his elegy for Lowell, "Family Graveyard," by describing the way Lowell had carried his head at an angle, like a violinist. Now there is no violin, Voznesensky said. "But there is. It is invisible." "The maples in the graveyard now are bare; / And through the dark the violin thinly sounds. / The family graves lie deep within the wood: / Your parents both are there, but where in the dark are you?"

A few months earlier, during his visit to Russia, Lowell had asked Voznesensky to take him to Boris Pasternak's grave. There he saw the rowan tree near where Pasternak lay, whose brilliant berries deep in the winter symbolized for Pasternak life in death. Now Voznesensky laid on Lowell's grave four branches from that rowan tree. "I still hear you," he wrote: "And bring these berries from Pasternak's rowan tree / For all the good that rowanberries do."

Other poets wrote elegies for Lowell, including Derek Walcott, Joseph Brodsky, Seamus Heaney, and Elizabeth Bishop. Heaney wrote of Lowell as Virgil and maker:

> You were our night ferry
> thudding in a big sea,
>
> the whole craft ringing
> with an armourer's music
> the course set wilfully across
> the ungovernable and dangerous.

Elizabeth Bishop's elegy is heartbreaking, a tribute to her friend of so many years, her fellow poet and New Englander, both of them beholden to sea and nature and words, so different in temperament. "Frank [Bidart] read me your beautiful poem over the phone," Elizabeth Hardwick wrote to Bishop in August 1978. "I wept when I went to

Map of North Haven on notecard from Elizabeth Bishop,
which Lowell was carrying when he died

sit outside and think about it. Oh, the magical details of North Haven
and the way you bring them with such naturalness and feeling into a
human landscape, to Cal. Your art is always able to do that—and the
genuineness, the lack of strain, the truth of things. The poem moves
me unbearably."

North Haven
In memoriam: Robert Lowell

I can make out the rigging of a schooner
a mile off; I can count
the new cones on the spruce. It is so still
the pale bay wears a milky skin, the sky
no clouds, except for one long, carded horse's tail.

The islands haven't shifted since last summer,
even if I like to pretend they have
—drifting, in a dreamy sort of way,
a little north, a little south or sidewise,
and that they're free within the blue frontiers of bay.

This month, our favorite one is full of flowers:
Buttercups, Red Clover, Purple Vetch,
Hawkweed still burning, Daisies pied, Eyebright,
the Fragrant Bedstraw's incandescent stars,
and more, returned, to paint the meadows with delight.

The Goldfinches are back, or others like them,
and the White-throated Sparrow's five-note song,
pleading and pleading, brings tears to the eyes.
Nature repeats herself, or almost does:
repeat, repeat, repeat; revise, revise, revise.

Years ago, you told me it was here
(in 1932?) you first "discovered *girls*"
and learned to sail, and learned to kiss.
You had "such fun," you said, that classic summer
("Fun"—it always seemed to leave you at a loss . . .)

You left North Haven, anchored in its rock,
afloat in mystic blue . . . And now—you've left
for good. You can't derange, or re-arrange,
your poems again. (But the Sparrows can their song.)
The words won't change again. Sad friend, you cannot change.

15

He Is Out of Bounds Now

On a thousand small town New England greens,
the old white churches hold their air
of sparse, sincere rebellion.
                    —*From* "For the Union Dead"

Cambridge, Massachusetts
March 2, 1978

"The dead have no need for the living," the minister said. "But the living have great need for the dead." It was an apt comment for the day Harvard marked the death of Robert Lowell. Few drew upon the dead as Lowell had.

After the minister finished his remarks, Walter Jackson Bate, the Lowell Professor of the Humanities and biographer of John Keats, walked to the lectern. He read from the Bible. The seventeenth-century language of Job, Ecclesiastes, and the New Testament had been to Lowell beautiful, much of it surpassingly so. The King James Version of the Psalms, he once said, was the highest expression of free verse. In the beginning was the Word, proclaimed the Gospel of John. It was fundamental. In the beginning was the Word.

The poetry of Homer and Virgil had been as much a part of Lowell as the Bible, perhaps more. Robert Fitzgerald, translator of *The Iliad* and *The Odyssey*, knew the classicist in Lowell better than anyone. He had known Lowell for thirty years, been a pallbearer at his funeral; he had known him during his periods of great poetic originality and the years of drought, through his madness and his sustaining sanity. He had seen Lowell make art from his life. Lowell, he said now in his eulogy, had "exerted a giant's pressure on language and experience." Through "what he wrote and what he *was*," Fitzgerald said, "he had dignified for many people their own metaphysical predicaments in the world of twentieth-century choices that, under great difficulties, he tried bravely to meet." Lowell had exerted pressure on his country and on his students. "Just as in the world at large he embodied the best of social and political protest among the young, so for a generation of students here he embodied, as a Lowell, as a great poet, something intangible but profound in Harvard tradition."

Lowells had been part of Harvard for more than 250 years. They had been students before the American Revolution, had helped finance and administer Harvard. One had been its president. Lowell House was a landmark in Cambridge with its high blue bell tower visible from the Charles River and beyond. At times Robert Lowell had taken pride in his family ties to Harvard; as often he had found them suffocating. He had rebelled against the Lowell tradition of going to Harvard and resented the assumption, preached by his mother, that it was "what Lowells did." After two years he found undergraduate study neither challenging nor enjoyable, and he left. In the end he had come back to Harvard to teach, the goose returning to its home bay. There was a pull, currents. He had written about only four places, Lowell once said. Harvard was one of them.

Robert Gould Shaw and the Massachusetts 54th Regiment Memorial, Boston

David Perkins, professor of English and American literature at Harvard, spoke after Robert Fitzgerald. He had faced a difficult choice, given the broad sweep of Lowell's interests and work, but for his reading he picked "For the Union Dead," which, he told those gathered, "may be the supreme poem of Lowell's career."

For the Union Dead
"Relinquunt Omnia Servare Rem Publicam."

The old South Boston Aquarium stands
in a Sahara of snow now. Its broken windows are boarded.
The bronze weathervane cod has lost half its scales.
The airy tanks are dry.

Once my nose crawled like a snail on the glass;
my hand tingled
to burst the bubbles
drifting from the noses of the cowed, compliant fish.

My hand draws back. I often sigh still
for the dark downward and vegetating kingdom
of the fish and reptile. One morning last March,
I pressed against the new barbed and galvanized

fence on the Boston Common. Behind their cage,
yellow dinosaur steamshovels were grunting
as they cropped up tons of mush and grass
to gouge their underworld garage.

Parking spaces luxuriate like civic
sandpiles in the heart of Boston.
A girdle of orange, Puritan-pumpkin colored girders
braces the tingling Statehouse,

shaking over the excavations, as it faces Colonel Shaw
and his bell-cheeked Negro infantry
on St. Gaudens' shaking Civil War relief,
propped by a plank splint against the garage's earthquake.

Two months after marching through Boston,
half the regiment was dead;
at the dedication,
William James could almost hear the bronze Negroes breathe.

Their monument sticks like a fishbone
in the city's throat.
Its Colonel is as lean
as a compass-needle.

He has an angry wrenlike vigilance,
a greyhound's gentle tautness;
he seems to wince at pleasure,
and suffocate for privacy.

He is out of bounds now. He rejoices in man's lovely,
peculiar power to choose life and die—
when he leads his black soldiers to death,
he cannot bend his back.

On a thousand small town New England greens,
the old white churches hold their air
of sparse, sincere rebellion; frayed flags
quilt the graveyards of the Grand Army of the Republic.

The stone statues of the abstract Union Soldier
grow slimmer and younger each year—
wasp-waisted, they doze over muskets
and muse through their sideburns . . .

Shaw's father wanted no monument
except the ditch,
where his son's body was thrown
and lost with his "niggers."

The ditch is nearer.
There are no statues for the last war here;
on Boylston Street, a commercial photograph
shows Hiroshima boiling

over a Mosler Safe, the "Rock of Ages"
that survived the blast. Space is nearer.
When I crouch to my television set,
the drained faces of Negro school-children rise like balloons.

Colonel Shaw
is riding on his bubble,
he waits
for the blessèd break.

The Aquarium is gone. Everywhere,
giant finned cars nose forward like fish;
a savage servility
slides by on grease.

Lowell, although he was reluctant to describe any poem as his "best," nonetheless had chosen "For the Union Dead" to include in a collection of poems selected by poets as their best work. He read "For the Union Dead" for the first time in June 1960 before a crowd of thousands gathered in Boston Public Garden. The poem, he said, was about "childhood memories, the evisceration of our modern cities, civil rights, nuclear warfare and more particularly Colonel Robert Shaw and his Negro regiment, the Massachusetts 54th." He added that he had brought early personal memories into the poem because he wanted to "avoid the fixed, brazen tone of the set-piece and official ode." The poem, Lowell said later, "may be about a child maturing into courage and terror."

"For the Union Dead" pulls together many strands of Lowell's thinking and experience; it combines his public voice and political conscience with autobiography. Bound in history, it is first and foremost an American poem. It stares into the American character, as the eagle gazes into the sun. It is about a nation born in courage and descending into slack and rust; it is about valor and the corruption of valor. It asks, Which noble acts, which right things done, enter and stay in memory? What remains? What can be preserved? When art memorializes acts of courage and high deeds, can it stand against indifference? Is decay—moral, civic, a "savage servility"—inevitable?

"We're decaying . . . ," Lowell said in 1964. "We're in some great midstream of morality; the old morality doesn't hold, no new one has been born. Genocide has stunned us; we have a curious dread it will be repeated."

Randall Jarrell believed that Lowell's personal experience of dread and terror allowed him to face the horror of twentieth-century wars, racial injustice, and the threat of nuclear annihilation. "Perhaps because his own existence seems to him in some senses as terrible as the public world—his private world hangs over him as the public world hangs over others—he does not forsake the headlined world for the refuge of one's private joys and decencies. He sees all these as the lost paradise of the childish past, the past that knew so much but still didn't *know*." The eyes see, the hand draws back.

Decay was not new. It had been in America's soul since her founding, at times dormant, at times deadly. William Bradford had written about moral decay only a few years after the Pilgrims landed at Plymouth. God had given them danger, he said, then deliverance. Complacency had set in. The cycles of early New England life had followed a relentless course: peril, then safe harbor; uprooting storms, droughts, then once again "fair, sunshining days." Suffering and renewal; madness and healing; death and resurrection: only flux did not change. It was the rhythm of the natural world; it was the rhythm of mood and madness, of imagination; it was the rhythm of the national character.

Lowell saw his ancestors as a part of both the corruption and courage in American history. In an early poem, "At the Indian Killer's Grave," he decried the brutality of his Puritan ancestors, including Josiah Winslow, the governor of Plymouth Colony during King Philip's War (1675–76). Winslow and his men had massacred so many of the Narragansett tribe that they bore a damning responsibility for its ultimate destruction. Their extermination, Lowell said, "was as crisp, bracing, and colorful as pheasant shooting." He described the graveyard of the early Winslows, King's Chapel Burying Ground in Boston, as a "great garden rotten to its roots":

> I ponder on the railing at this park:
> Who was the man who sowed the dragon's teeth,
> That fabulous or fancied patriarch
> Who sowed so ill for his descent, beneath
> King's Chapel in this underworld and dark?

Lowell took his poem's epigraph from "The Gray Champion," a short story by Hawthorne. "Here, also, are the veterans of King Philip's War," Hawthorne had written, "who burned villages and slaughtered young and old, with pious fierceness, while the godly souls throughout the land were helping them with prayer." Hawthorne depicted the degeneration of the Puritan character, once steely with discipline and belief, into a "sluggish despondency," willing to submit to the tyranny of the English king. Only by drawing upon the first spirit, the original character of New England, he said, could Americans prevail in corrupt or perilous times: "His hour is one of darkness, and adversity, and peril. . . . His shadowy march, on the eve of danger, must ever be the pledge, that New-England's sons will vindicate their ancestry." In times of danger in America, Hawthorne wrote, the spirit of New England had prevailed, "on the green, beside the meeting-house, at Lexington." It had been with the colonists at Bunker Hill. It had stayed for a while as the nation broke from the British and created itself; then it ebbed out.

There would be times of valor, times of fire in the American imagination, but there would be longer periods of moral stagnation. If the country's fortune held, an infusion of courage would return often enough to save the depleted state. Plymouth had been exemplar, then it was not. The American Revolution had bred extraordinary thinkers and leaders and the colonies had thrived. They had innovated; pioneers had moved westward, brought life up from the prairies. The country had been again, for a while, John Winthrop's city on the hill. Then rot set in and spread. It was in the nature of things. Fullness of growth pushed life into a false security, drove it into decay and death.

No rot could compare in degree or kind to slavery, the original sin of America. It was the unsurvivable evil for which the nation would be held accountable in ruthless measure. America's civil war would continue, as Lincoln proclaimed, "until every drop of blood drawn with the lash, shall be paid by another drawn with the sword." Not a little of this blood, drawn with the sword, was given by Colonel Robert Gould Shaw and his black regiment as they attacked the Confederate battery at Fort Wagner; it is at the heart of "For the Union Dead."

Lowell's great-great grandfather, the Reverend Charles Lowell, minister of Boston's West Church from 1806 to 1861, was one of New England's earliest and most influential abolitionists. When he was a young man studying in Europe he had sought out the company of the English abolitionist William Wilberforce. They had become friends and correspondents; Wilberforce's portrait hung prominently in the Lowell house in Cambridge. Charles Lowell preached often and persuasively against slavery; his sermons were important in creating the climate in Boston that, among other things, led to the establishment of the first black regiment in the North. The day of redemption will come, John Quincy Adams had declared in 1843. "Let justice be done though the heavens fall."

In July 1862, despite widespread skepticism and resistance, especially in the South, the Congress of the United States authorized President Lincoln to raise and arm black troops to fight for the Union. The first regiment to be called up in the North was the Fifty-Fourth Massachusetts Infantry, led by a young white officer, Robert Gould Shaw. Frederick Douglass, a former slave, orator, and writer, made the impassioned case for the formation of the black regiment. "The arm of the slave was the best defense against the arm of the slaveholder," he said in a recruitment speech in March 1863. "Liberty won by white men would lack half its luster." Massachusetts was the right place to form the regiment: "She was first in the war of Independence; first to break the chains of her slaves; first to make the black man equal before the law; first to admit colored children to her common schools." The white officers, Douglass promised—a promise mainly kept—"will be quick to accord to you all the honor you shall merit by your valor—and see that your rights and feelings are respected by other soldiers. . . . The iron gate of our prison stands half open. One gallant rush from the North will fling it wide open."

"One Gallant Rush" was the original title for a draft of "For the Union Dead." Slavery for Lowell was a subject of profound consequence. America, he believed, had had the "most repressive slavery in history"; the injustice of it was "of the greatest urgency to me as a man and as a writer." The commander of the regiment, Robert Gould Shaw, was related by marriage to the Lowell family. The Shaws, like the Lowells, were a prominent Boston family with strong abolitionist roots. In May 1863 Shaw and his regiment of a thousand men, including two sons of Frederick Douglass and a brother of William and Henry James, marched through one of the largest crowds ever to gather in Boston.

"The more I think of the passage of the Fifty-Fourth through

Boston," wrote Robert Gould Shaw to his bride of a few weeks, "the more wonderful it seems to me. . . . Truly, I ought to be thankful for all my happiness, and my success in life so far; and if the raising of coloured troops prove such a benefit to the country, and to the blacks, as many people think it will, I shall thank God a thousand times that I was led to take my share in it."

"Two months after marching through Boston, / half the regiment was dead," Lowell writes in "For the Union Dead." Shaw, "as lean / as a compass-needle," had "an angry wrenlike vigilance, / a greyhound's gentle tautness." He seemed "to wince at pleasure, / and suffocate for privacy." Colonel Shaw—young, reserved, privileged, principled—was, like his men, pervasively conscious of likely death. As Scott would say of those who accompanied him on his Antarctic expedition, they took risks and they knew they took them. There was no bending of will. Robert Gould Shaw would stay in his country's imagination because he gave up privilege and comfort to die young for what he believed. He "rejoices in man's lovely, / peculiar power to choose life and die."

James Henry Gooding, a private in the Massachusetts Fifty-Fourth, described the resolve of his commanding officer. "Col. Shaw, from the beginning, never evinced any fear of what others thought or said. He believed the work would be done, and he put his hands, his head, and heart to the task." He was not intimate with his men. "He was cold, dis-tant, and even austere. . . . If there was any abolition fanaticism in him, he had a mind well balanced, so that no man in the regiment would ever presume to take advantage of that feeling in their favor."

The day of the assault on Fort Wagner, Shaw's "manner was more unbending than I had ever noticed before in the presence of his men," Gooding recounted. "He told them how the eyes of thousands would look upon the night's work they were about to enter on." He walked along the line of his troops encouraging them on, fully aware that he and most of them might die. "We could see that he was a man who had counted the cost of the undertaking before him, for his words were spoken so ominously, his lips were compressed, and now and again there was visible a slight twitching of the corners of his mouth, like one but bent on accomplishing or dying."

The Fifty-Fourth Massachusetts Infantry led the assault against Fort Wagner in Charleston Harbor near Fort Sumter, where, two years earlier, the first shots of the Civil War had been fired. Clara Barton, a

Union nurse who later would found the American Red Cross, watched Colonel Shaw and his black regiment march along the sea's edge as the Confederate army bombarded them with cannon and gunfire. "A long line of phosphorescent light streamed and shot along the waves ever surging on our right. A little to the left mark[ed] that long, dark line, moving steadily on—pace by pace—across that broad space of glistening sand." The assault began on the evening of July 18, 1863; it ended in the early dawn of the next day.

With Shaw at the front of his troops, sword raised, the Fifty-Fourth Massachusetts charged Fort Wagner. Shaw was killed at the top of the ramparts; two-thirds of his officers and nearly half of his men were killed, missing, or wounded. A Confederate soldier told the horror of what he saw the morning after the battle. "The dead and wounded were piled up in a ditch together sometimes fifteen in a heap, and they were strewn all over the plain for a distance of three-fourths of a mile." It was a massacre. The young Southern soldier added an unusual tribute to what he had witnessed. "The negroes," he said, "fought gallantly, and were headed by as brave a colonel as ever lived." When Clara Barton returned to the field of battle she described it as a charnel house. "The thousand little sand-hills that glitter in the pale moonlight are a thousand headstones, and the restless ocean waves that roll and break upon the whitened beach sing an eternal requiem to the toil-worn, gallant dead who sleep beside."

The Confederate troops stripped Shaw's body and threw it into a ditch with his black soldiers. They thought by doing this to insult Shaw and his regiment; Shaw's father believed otherwise. He declined the offer to have his son's body returned to Boston for burial and insisted instead that he remain buried in the ditch with his soldiers. "We can imagine no holier place than that in which he lies," his father wrote to the regimental surgeon. He could not "wish for him better company.— What a body-guard he has!"

In May 1897 a memorial to commemorate Shaw and the Fifty-Fourth Massachusetts was dedicated on Boston Common. Sixty-five veterans of the attack on Fort Wagner marched past the monument, just a few yards from where the regiment had received its colors thirty-four years earlier; they stopped to place a wreath of lilies of the valley to honor their dead. William James, whose brother had served under Shaw at Fort Wagner, gave the oration. "There on horseback," he said, referring to the newly unveiled memorial by the sculptor Augustus Saint-Gaudens, "sits the blue-eyed child of fortune, upon whose happy youth every divinity had smiled." Why, James asked, were Shaw and his men deserving of a great monument? Why had art been put to the service of commemorating war? The failed action at Fort Wagner did not warrant it. The successful war to save the Union did. Even more than the constitutional questions that the war had resolved, it had "freed the country from the social plague which until then had made political development impossible in the United States." It had freed the country, slave and owner alike. It had preserved the nation.

The Shaw Memorial would stand in memory to something more than "common and gregarious" military courage, William James told those gathered. The poet and orator were needed to keep alive that "lonely kind of valor (civic courage as we call it in peace times)." The kind of courage "to which monuments of nations should most of all be reared," he continued, is not military valor. Of the "five hundred of us who could storm a battery side by side with others, perhaps not one would be found ready to risk his worldly fortunes all alone in resisting an enthroned abuse." It was the day by day civic courage of those who act reasonably, who act swiftly against corruption, resist rabid partisanship. "The lesson that our war ought most of all to teach us is the lesson that evils must be checked in time, before they grow so great. The Almighty cannot love such long-postponed accounts, or such tremendous settlements. And surely He hates all settlements that do such quantities of incidental devils' work."

Booker T. Washington, the voice of freed slaves in America, then principal of Tuskegee Institute, spoke after William James had finished. "Watchman, tell us of the night, what the signs of promise are," he said, echoing the refrain used by slaves in anticipation of Lincoln's signing of the Emancipation Proclamation. "If through me, a humble representative, nearly ten millions of my people might be permitted to send a message to Massachusetts, to the survivors of the 54th Regiment, to the committee whose untiring energy has made this memorial possible, to the family who gave their only boy that we may have life more abundantly, that message would be: Tell them that the sacrifice was not in vain, that up from the depths of ignorance and poverty we are coming, and if we come through oppression, out of the struggle we are gaining strength; by way of the school, the well-cultivated field, the skilled hand, the Christian home, we are coming up; that we propose to invite all who will step up and occupy this position with us."

The Civil War—its slaughter, treason, courage, tragedy—somehow had called from America her best: the complex brilliance of Abraham Lincoln, the rhetoric of Frederick Douglass, the poetry of Walt Whitman, the civic leadership of Booker T. Washington and Clara Barton. The valor of Robert Gould Shaw and the Fifty-Fourth Massachusetts Regiment called out a different kind of genius from the nation's writers and artists. Augustus Saint-Gaudens, the sculptor of the Shaw Memorial, was one of them. "You have immortalized my native city," said Shaw's mother to Saint-Gaudens at the dedication. "You have immortalized my dear son, you have immortalized yourself." The poets James Russell Lowell and Robert Lowell, Ralph Waldo Emerson, Oliver Wendell Holmes, Paul Laurence Dunbar, John Berryman, and scores of other artists created anew in response to the Fifty-Fourth Massachusetts Regiment and to the memorial raised in its honor: a monument to stand for courage and values lost or dying, a monument to "stick like a fishbone in the city's throat." In words, bas relief, or music: artists responded. Robert Lowell's "For the Union Dead" remains a deeply and particularly American work of art.

"You are a great American writer," Elizabeth Hardwick had told Lowell. "You have told us what we are, like Melville, you have brought all the culture of England, and of course even America and other countries have something, to bear on us, on our land, on your past, your people, your family. You are not an English writer, but the most American of souls, the most gifted in finding the symbolic meaning of this strange place." "You drank America," wrote Seamus Heaney in his elegy for Lowell, "like the heart's / iron vodka." "For the Union Dead" is the great tribute of Lowell to his country, like himself a place of the mind, hard to know.

"I love my country, because it's mine, and all I know," Lowell wrote to George Santayana when he was thirty years old, "and [I] think our culture can stand comparison with others of the last 150 years—it's better than most, probably. And, of course, we have Roman virtues—energy, and even clarity of a kind. But there are times . . . oh yes,

Pine cone and evergreen detail, Shaw Memorial

when one trembles, and wonders if a people have ever been so dehu-
manized." America could be a violent godless place, but it was wild and
beautiful and knew rebellion; it was a country that believed in something better. It was ambitious, vast, restless. And it was his. "Where is
America?" he asked. "I've had it about me for fifty remembered years;
it streams through my eyes." The color of his blood was American, he
said.

Over the sculpted relief of the figure of Colonel Shaw and extending
back over the heads of his soldiers, is an angel holding a laurel branch,
symbol of victory, and poppies, symbol of sleep and death. Less obvious, in the bottom corner of the memorial, Saint-Gaudens has placed
a pine cone and evergreen, symbols of eternal life; symbols of the hope
we place in art commemorating valor.

"I see now that the best Colonel of the best black regiment had
to die," wrote Charles Russell Lowell to his fiancée, Robert Gould
Shaw's sister. "It was a sacrifice we owed,—and how could it have been
paid more gloriously?" Colonel Charles Russell Lowell, a Union sol-

dier whose bravery in battle matched Shaw's, was the grandson of Harriet Brackett Spence Lowell—weaver of tales, incurably insane—and of the abolitionist minister Charles Lowell. He was the ancestor Robert Lowell said he'd "most like to have known." His courage during the Shenandoah Valley campaign was legendary, his valor taken into poetry by many, including Herman Melville, who had ridden on scout with him. Robert Lowell, writing about him a hundred years after his death, said, "Twelve horses killed under him. . . . / He had, *gave* . . . everything. . . . / Charles had himself strapped to the saddle . . . bound to death, / his cavalry that scorned the earth it trod on."

William James had spoken of civic courage, individual valor, the kind that resists the forces that corrupt, that stands against the sliding servility of the modern world. It was a subject Lowell returned to time and again; it was critical to his view of society and himself. Character, the struggle to master the difficult, the impossible; the determination to persist, not to squander time or gift; a set course toward a true north: these were what mattered. Robert Lowell admired Charles Russell Lowell for his military valor, for having had "twelve horses killed under him," for having given everything for the Union cause: "He had, *gave* . . . everything."

Robert Lowell knew civic valor. Sixteen times and more he had been down on his knees in madness, he said. Sixteen times and more he had gotten up. He had gone back to his work, entered back into life. He had faced down uncertainty and madness, had created new forms when pushed to stay with the old, had brought back imaginative order from chaos. It was a different kind of courage, this civic courage, and the rules of engagement were unclear. Lowell's life, as his daughter observed, was a messy one, difficult for him and for those who knew him. But it was lived with iron, and often with grace. He kept always in the front of his mind what he thought he ought to be, even when he couldn't be it; believed in what his country could be, even if it wasn't. He worked hard at his art.

A foot of snow lay on the ground outside the church and the wind blew to the bone; it was winter in Cambridge. Had the mourners looked up at the bell tower of the church as they left the service for Robert

Lowell on that March day they would have seen the bell that tolled for him. But they would not have been able to see the words carved into the shoulder of the bell. Words for the dead, they had been chosen by Lowell's cousin nearly fifty years earlier when, as president of Harvard, he donated the bell to the college church. *In Memory of Voices That Are Hushed*, the bell read. In memory of the dead.

The voices of the living could be hushed as well. Lowell's great-great-grandmother had lived a silent death in madness; her son had said that only as much of her remained as "the hum outliving the hushed bell." The poet's voice speaks for the dead, the hushed, the valorous. It signifies the hours, reminds of death. It gives depth and resonance to blithe times, solace in the dark.

"The bells cry: 'Come, / Come home . . . ,'" Robert Lowell wrote. "'Come; I bell thee home.'"

Robert Lowell in Boston, 1965

"He had, gave . . . everything."

It was answered, that all great and honourable actions are accompanied with great difficulties and must be both enterprised and overcome with answerable courages.

—William Bradford, *Of Plymouth Plantation: 1620–1647*

APPENDIX I

Psychiatric Records of Robert Lowell

The executors of Robert Lowell's estate, Harriet Winslow Lowell and Robert Silvers, graciously gave me permission to request and review Robert Lowell's medical and psychiatric records, as well as to interview his surviving physicians. Ms. Lowell and I discussed at length the medical, legal, and privacy issues involved. My clinical, personal, and research background is in the study and treatment of manic-depressive (bipolar) illness and in the relationship between creativity and mood disorders. Her hope, as mine, was that reviewing her father's hospital records would result in a deeper understanding of his mental illness, how his illness affected his life and poetry, and the more general relationship between mania, depression, and imagination.

For unassailable reasons medical records are assumed to be confidential by patients, clinicians, and hospital administrators. They are required to be by law. Medical records remain private until the individual, a legally designated family member, or the executor of the estate gives permission otherwise. Such permission is not given lightly. The hospitals that provided me with Robert Lowell's medical and psychiatric records—including Massachusetts General Hospital, McLean Hospital, Massachusetts Mental Health Center (formerly Boston Psychopathic Hospital), the Institute of Living, and Payne Whitney Clinic—are among the best in the United States. All are committed to the privacy of their patients' medical records. They released Robert Lowell's records because they were legally required to do so. The law is clear that medical records belong to the patient or, if the patient is dead, to the patient's family. Family members often wish to better understand the cause of a parent's or a child's death or desire more details about a specific illness (particularly in the case of a genetic disorder). Some families wish to contribute to medical research, others to provide additional information about a historically, artistically, or scientifically prominent individual that may be of help to historians or of significant interest to the public.

Viola Bernard, M.D., one of Lowell's psychiatrists in New York, made her obligations of confidentiality clear when she wrote to Ian Hamilton in 1980 after he had requested that she send him Lowell's records. "My relationship with Mr. Lowell was that of a psychiatrist," she wrote to him. "It would not therefore be professionally proper, in terms of confidentiality, for me to talk about anything I knew of him in the context of our relationship." She added, "I am aware, of course, that Mr. Lowell himself made no secret, to put it mildly, of his bouts of mental illness; but he had the right to reveal whatever he wished about himself, and I do not."

Much about Lowell's mental illness has been a part of the public record for decades. He was unusually open about his illness, not only in his letters and interviews but in his work and conceptualization of the role mania took in the generation of his poetry. His breakdowns were witnessed by his colleagues, family, students, friends, and strangers. Many of these individuals in turn wrote about or talked to interviewers about his manic attacks and depressions, as did the journalists who wrote about him at great length in national magazines and newspapers.

Most important, Robert Lowell and Elizabeth Hardwick made the deliberate decision to include portions of his medical and psychiatric records in the material they put into his archives at Harvard University and the Harry Ransom Center at the University of Texas at Austin. They turned over letters between Lowell and his friends and correspondence between Lowell and Hardwick that discussed his illness at length; an essay about his illness and treatment that he wrote for his Boston psychiatrist Vernon Williams, M.D.; and the psychiatric files of Merrill Moore, M.D. The latter include Moore's records of his treatment of Charlotte Winslow Lowell, her detailed descriptions of Lowell's psychological difficulties from infancy on, and Moore's diagnostic and clinical impressions of Lowell as a young man. Lowell's archives also include the psychological evaluation that was done at the Judge Baker clinic when he was fifteen years old and the medical and psychiatric correspondence to Lowell from his Boston, New York, and London physicians.

The records I requested from the doctors and hospitals that treated Lowell focused on the many hospital stays he had for mania and included clinical details of his manic-depressive illness, the history of earlier episodes of his illness, admission notes, examinations of his mental state on admission, physical examinations, admitting and discharge diagnoses, laboratory findings, inpatient clinical progress notes, medication records, and nursing notes. I deliberately did not focus my requests on psychotherapy records, although in a few instances brief psychotherapy notes were mixed in with his hospital progress notes. I have limited my clinical description in this book to Lowell's discussions with his psychiatrists about his illness, particularly his fears that his mania would recur and the remorse he felt for things he had done while manic; the effects of his illness on his parents and his marriages; and his observations about the relationship between his mania and his poetry. These issues are of direct relevance to the subject matter of this book; the more intimate psychotherapeutic discussions that were in Lowell's records were not; and I did not use them here.

APPENDIX 2

Mania and Depression:
Clinical Description, Diagnosis,
and Nomenclature

CLINICAL DESCRIPTION

Depression and mania are characterized by significant, often profound disruptions in mood, thinking, sleep, energy, and behavior. Depression is heterogeneous; it has many clinical presentations, widely disparate levels of severity, and different causes. Most depressed individuals are hopeless, irritable, and apathetic; less able to experience pleasure than when well; and unable to stay engaged with the world. A pervasive tiredness is common and the ability to concentrate, learn new things, and remember is impaired. Thinking and movement are slowed and meaningful life appears beyond reach. Ruminative thoughts of guilt, inadequacy, and the desire to die are frequent; sleep is disrupted. The world appears grim, gray, and frightening. Suicide is not uncommon.

Mania is largely the opposite. People engage the world, whether or not the world wishes to be engaged. Manic mood is expansive and elated, but irritable. People with mania have high energy, fast and flighty thoughts that leap from idea to idea; their speech is rapid and they have little need for sleep. They are restless, easily irritated, and often paranoid. They are impulsive, display poor judgment, and impose their enthusiasms and convictions on others. They appear to be indefatigable. They buy things they do not need and cannot afford, become involved in relationships and financial undertakings that are ill-advised and costly. They lash out at those around them. As mania becomes more severe, delusions and hallucinations can occur. Mania is a high-voltage state and often dangerous.

In order to meet the diagnostic criteria for mania or depression, modern psychiatric diagnostic systems require a pattern, severity, and duration of symptoms of mood, thinking, energy, sleep, and behavior. The current diagnostic criteria, published in 2013 in the fifth edition of the *Diagnostic and Statistical Manual of Mental Disorders* (*DSM-5*), form the basis for most of the clinical practice and research in the United States. The *DSM-5* diagnostic criteria for mania and depression are given below:

THE *DSM-5* DIAGNOSTIC CRITERIA FOR MANIA AND MAJOR DEPRESSIVE DISORDER

MANIC EPISODE

A. A distinct period of abnormally and persistently elevated, expansive, or irritable mood and abnormally and persistently increased activity or energy, lasting at least 1 week and present most of the day, nearly every day (or any duration if hospitalization is necessary).

B. During the period of mood disturbance and increased energy or activity, three (or more) of the following symptoms (four if the mood is only irritable) are present to a significant degree and represent a noticeable change from usual behavior:

1. Inflated self-esteem or grandiosity.
2. Decreased need for sleep (e.g., feels rested after only 3 hours of sleep).
3. More talkative than usual or pressure to keep talking.
4. Flight of ideas or subjective experience that thoughts are racing.
5. Distractibility (i.e., attention too easily drawn to unimportant or irrelevant external stimuli), as reported or observed.

6. Increase in goal-directed activity (either socially, at work or school, or sexually) or psychomotor agitation (i.e., purposeless non-goal-directed activity).
7. Excessive involvement in activities that have a high potential for painful consequences (e.g., engaging in unrestrained buying sprees, sexual indiscretions, or foolish business investments).

C. The mood disturbance is sufficiently severe to cause marked impairment in social or occupational functioning or to necessitate hospitalization to prevent harm to self or others, or there are psychotic features.
D. The episode is not attributable to the physiological effects of a substance (e.g., a drug of abuse, a medication, other treatment) or another medical condition.

Note: A full manic episode that emerges during antidepressant treatment (e.g., medication, electroconvulsive therapy) but persists at a fully syndromal level beyond physiological effect of that treatment is sufficient evidence for a manic episode and, therefore, a bipolar I diagnosis.

Note: Criteria A–D constitute a manic episode. At least one lifetime manic episode is required for the diagnosis of bipolar I disorder.

MAJOR DEPRESSIVE EPISODE

A. Five (or more) of the following symptoms have been present during the same 2-week period and represent a change from previous functioning; at least one of the symptoms is either (1) depressed mood or (2) loss of interest or pleasure.

Note: Do not include symptoms that are clearly attributable to another medical condition.

1. Depressed mood most of the day, nearly every day, as indicated by either subjective report (e.g., feels

sad, empty, or hopeless) or observation made by others (e.g., appears tearful). (Note: In children and adolescents, can be irritable mood.)

2. Markedly diminished interest or pleasure in all, or almost all, activities most of the day, nearly every day (as indicated by either subjective account or observation).

3. Significant weight loss when not dieting or weight gain (e.g., a change of more than 5% of body weight in a month), or decrease or increase in appetite nearly every day. (Note: In children, consider failure to make expected weight gain.)

4. Insomnia or hypersomnia nearly every day.

5. Psychomotor agitation or retardation nearly every day (observable by others; not merely subjective feelings of restlessness or being slowed down).

6. Fatigue or loss of energy nearly every day.

7. Feelings of worthlessness or excessive or inappropriate guilt (which may be delusional) nearly every day (not merely self-reproach or guilt about being sick).

8. Diminished ability to think or concentrate, or indecisiveness, nearly every day (either by subjective account or as observed by others).

9. Recurrent thoughts of death (not just fear of dying), recurrent suicidal ideation without a specific plan, or a suicide attempt or a specific plan for committing suicide.

B. The symptoms cause clinically significant distress or impairment in social, occupational, or other important areas of functioning.

C. The episode is not attributable to the physiological effects of a substance or another medical condition.

Note: Criteria A–C constitute a major depressive episode. Major depressive episodes are common in bipolar I disorder but are not required for the diagnosis of bipolar I disorder.

Note: Responses to a significant loss (e.g., bereavement, financial ruin, losses from a natural disaster, a serious medical illness or disability) may include the feelings of intense sadness, rumination about the loss, insomnia, poor appetite, and weight loss noted in Criterion A, which may resemble a depressive episode. Although such symptoms may be understandable or considered appropriate to the loss, the presence of a major depressive episode in addition to the normal response to a significant loss should also be carefully considered. This decision inevitably requires the exercise of clinical judgment based on the individual's history and the cultural norms for the expression of distress in the context of loss.

In response to scientific and clinical criticism of the *Diagnostic and Statistical Manual*, the National Institute of Mental Health has developed a different kind of classification system for use in research, one that takes into account the rapidly accumulating findings from genetics, neuroimaging, molecular biology and neuropsychology. The system, the Research Domain Criteria, seeks to integrate data from patterns of gene expression, epigenetics, protein and signaling data, and brain circuits and physiology into higher-order systems of cognition, motivation, and social behavior. These new criteria, with their emphasis on mechanisms and dimensions, reflect the important reality that the symptoms of mania and depression overlap with other psychiatric syndromes and that they exist on a spectrum of behavioral and cognitive functioning that includes physiological variation in mood, activity, motivation, impulsiveness, and disruptions in circadian rhythm.

Diagnostic and research classification, together with our basic understanding of psychiatric genetics, structural changes in the brains of patients with mood disorders, and how the brain functions during mania and depression, is advancing rapidly. They are the future of clinical practice and an important part of our understanding of the brain. They hold profound implications for treating and understanding not only mania and depression but temperament, thinking, imagination, and many of the most important things that make us human.

NOMENCLATURE

"Manic-depressive illness," the diagnostic term used during Robert Lowell's lifetime, has been largely supplanted by "bipolar disorder," which is the standard term now used in research and clinical practice. The change in nomenclature is a result of attempts by clinicians and scientists to distinguish between those patients who have a history of both mania and depression from those who have a history of depression only. The distinction is an important one in scientific research and it carries significant implications for treatment. There are, however, good reasons not to abandon entirely the term "manic-depressive illness." Recurrent depressive illness, historically included as part of the diagnosis of manic-depressive illness, is in most important ways— family history, course of illness, symptomatic presentation of depression, and response to treatment—more similar to bipolar illness than it is to nonrecurrent major depression. It is premature, until we have better science, to make fixed distinctions between bipolar disorder— a term applied only when there is a history of mild to severe mania—and recurrent depression, where there is no history of mania. In addition, "bipolar disorder" perpetuates the misconception that mood disorders cycle neatly between opposite mental and physical states. Nothing could be further from the truth. Mania and depression combine to form unstable clinical states that are a mixture of manic and depressive mood, behavior, and thinking.

There is a belief that the term "bipolar disorder" is more acceptable—less "stigmatizing"—than "manic-depressive illness." For many people this is true. For others, including myself, it is not. "Bipolar disorder" seems misleading, rather trivializing, and far removed from the clinical reality of depression and mania by those who experience them. The diagnostic language that is used is an individual preference, of course; clinicians and their patients will choose which they prefer for their individual reasons. Yet language has consequences. The pharmaceutical companies, for example, have good cause to use "bipolar disorder" rather than "manic-depressive illness." It is a more benign-sounding term and, as such, can be helpful in marketing medications to physicians and to a broader range of patients. If diagnostic criteria expand and the diagnostic label is more socially and psychologically acceptable, more people will meet criteria for the illness and more doctors will be inclined to prescribe for them.

   This dilution and broadening of diagnostic language can be a good thing if it means that more people who truly need treatment are receiving it, that more research is being funded, and that the general public is better educated and less judgmental about mental illness. But the risks of misrepresentation and trivialization are real. It should be possible to realize that mania and depression are painful and damaging illnesses that need to be treated but also to understand them as broader concepts: to understand them as the important part of human history that they are, and to appreciate mania and depression as illnesses disproportionately associated with great accomplishment in the arts, sciences, and other fields of human endeavor. Replacing ancient, graphic language with euphemistic diagnostic labels risks minimizing the suffering and complexity of an often deadly illness. Losing the historical and social perspective on manic-depressive illness, its contributions as well as its awfulness, is also to risk minimizing the social and ethical implications of our increasing capacity to manipulate the human genome. This is a significant risk. It is not enough to describe and diagnose mania and depression accurately, and it will not be enough to understand them at their basic molecular level. It is necessary to understand moods and their aberrations in the context of individual lives and imaginations; the role they have in shaping societies; and the meaning they assume in the human condition.

APPENDIX 3

Medical History of Robert Lowell

Robert Lowell died suddenly at about 6:00 p.m. on September 12, 1977, at the age of sixty. There was no autopsy and the death certificate was signed by a doctor at Roosevelt Hospital in New York; at that time and place there was no requirement to identify the cause other than to affirm that death was due to natural causes. In light of the rest of Lowell's medical history it is likely that sudden death was from ventricular fibrillation, the final consequence of severe chronic heart-muscle injury. In common parlance he suffered sudden death in the context of chronic cardiac failure. His heart failure was probably the result of widespread coronary artery disease, but one should also consider the possibility that he suffered heart damage from alcohol, or even from his treatment with lithium.

In February, seven months before Lowell died, he had been admitted to Massachusetts General Hospital (MGH) with severe lung congestion resulting from his heart disease. The history he gave is characteristic, and the notes from the time leave no room for speculation about what was happening. For two months he had experienced progressive breathlessness, and his respiratory difficulty was aggravated at night. He was unable to tolerate lying flatter than at an angle of seventy-five degrees and would be woken at night by acute shortness of breath, so-called paroxysmal nocturnal dyspnea. This is unlike breathlessness that might be related to pulmonary complications of his smoking, and he described it in a letter to his wife, Caroline Blackwood: "I sleep sitting up,—good for breathing, bad for sleep."

According to Dr. Timothy Guiney, his attending physician, and Dr. Jerome Groopman, the resident in Phillips House Coronary Care Unit, there was no previous history of pain in the chest. But in his poem "Phillips House Revisited," a seemingly autobiographical account of the hospital admission, Lowell alludes to "this irreverent absence of pain, / less than the ordinary that daily irks." This might refer to a past experience of angina, and it has to be noted that Dr. Brass, his doctor in London, had indeed seen him for pain in the chest. Dr. Brass was generally inclined to optimism and attributed Lowell's thoracic pain, felt as it was in the back and the side, to arthritis of the spine. With hindsight, one cannot be so sure; a cardiologist reading the poem, while recognizing it is a poetic and not a literal account, will be tempted to recognize the story of daily chest pains giving way to breathlessness when coronary heart disease progresses from angina to heart failure. There are other indications that Lowell had heart disease even before 1977: not only the abnormal electrocardiogram (ECG), but the comment in 1974 that he was on digitalis; in September 1975 that his ability to walk and exercise was impaired; and from Dr. Curtis Prout, his physician in Boston, that he undoubtedly had a heart attack of some kind around Christmas 1975.

Other previous medical history included treatment in 1968–69 for hypothyroidism. There was thyroid swelling, and his condition eventually seems to have improved (thyroid hormone was discontinued in March 1969), so one imagines he had thyroiditis. He had an unexplained episode of loss of consciousness in 1974, which seems to have been a simple faint.

The diagnostic studies performed during the admission to MGH were: a chest X-ray, which confirmed lung congestion and cardiac enlargement; electrocardiogram; and a nuclear heart scan. The nuclear scan confirmed the expectation that the left ventricle's contractile function was drastically reduced and is reported as showing that this weakness was distributed unevenly in the heart muscle, as would be expected if it was the result of multiple previous heart attacks, each injuring a separate region of the ventricular muscle. The electrocardiogram is extremely abnormal and fits with the suspicion of multiple previous areas of injury. It shows Q waves in the inferior and ante-rior distributions, consistent with but not necessarily diagnostic of past coronary attacks. The tracing is more pathological than ones that had been described in previous checkups in London and Cambridge, Massachusetts.

At the time he was admitted, his only medication was lithium, with a blood level of 1.1–1.2 mEq/L (Lowell evidently reported to the attending physician that it earlier had been measured at 1.7 mEq/L, a toxic level). His lithium had been reduced or stopped in late 1975, and at some point subsequently the drug had been restarted. He was on no medicines for heart disease and he made a rapid and gratify-ing response to standard measures, namely digitalis (digoxin) and the diuretic furosemide (Lasix). He was discharged from MGH taking 0.25 mg of digoxin daily, 40 mg of furosemide twice a day, and 300 mg of lithium carbonate three times a day. There are no notes extant con-cerning his follow-up, but he was seen in the summer by his physi-cian in Boston and given to understand that he was doing well. We do not know if he had blood testing for electrolytes, or digitalis or lithium levels. During the summer in Castine he worked hard writing, and according to Elizabeth Hardwick he was ostensibly in fairly good health, though still somewhat short of breath. This clinical course, of doing quite well with respect to circulatory function, yet still falling victim to a sudden arrhythmia, is not unusual. It fits well with what has been learned in the last thirty years, that for many patients with severe heart muscle dysfunction, particularly those in whom the cause is coro-nary heart disease (patients with so-called ischemic cardiomyopathy), death comes abruptly, from cardiac arrhythmia, rather than necessarily from continued worsening of the heart's pump strength. It is why today many patients with this diagnosis are given implantable defibrillators.

Even for the times, Lowell was a very heavy smoker, two packs every day for most of his adult life. The deep lining and premature aging of his face betray the extent of his habit, not to mention the presence of cigarettes and overflowing ashtrays in photographs and contemporary descriptions of the poet. Even after the MGH admis-sion with cardiac failure he continued to smoke, claiming that his doc-tors allowed that it was too late to stop. There was a family history of coronary heart disease, but one that is not unusually strong. His father died from a heart attack at the age of sixty-three, his mother from a stroke when she was sixty-five, and both had high blood pressure. He had moderately high cholesterol (in the 1970s doctors had begun to pay serious attention to blood lipids), but, beyond cigarettes, the other significant contributor to his vascular disease was the high blood pressure that ran in his family.

In 1949, when he was thirty-two, Lowell's blood pressure was recorded as 138/90, borderline high, and when he was forty it was recorded as 150/110. In 1967, when at fifty he began treatment with lithium, he was already on medication for blood pressure, probably the methyldopa that he alludes to by name in 1971 and continued to be on through at least 1975, in which year Dr. Brass in London recorded a pressure of 150/100. Considering that a fair number of these medical observations were made at times of psychiatric hospital admissions for mania and that his blood pressure may have been higher then than at times when he was less excited or stressed, one accepts that he had significant hypertension, but not really exceptional.

The other likely potential cause or contributor to his heart muscle weakness is the effect of alcohol. When Lowell was excited or manic he drank very heavily, and even during the calm periods of his life he participated at the high end of the heavy social drinking normal for his era and literary set. The existence of alcohol cardiomyopathy is well accepted by cardiologists, but there is no test to confirm this diagnosis other than to see whether heart function improves after the patient quits drinking. There is no set amount of alcohol required to cause the condition; some people drink prodigious amounts without sustaining heart damage, whereas others develop heart toxicity after years of steadily drinking far less. The arguments against alcohol as the cause of his heart disease and death are that the really heavy drinking was episodic, that the ECG is more suggestive of coronary heart disease than of a diffuse injury, and that the nuclear scan in February reportedly showed discrete patches of heart muscle injury, as would be caused by coronary occlusions, rather than the diffuse pattern of damage caused by a toxin. We cannot know whether alcohol or coronary disease was the main or only culprit in causing Lowell's heart muscle weakness, and indeed Dr. Guiney at MGH was as ready to blame the former as to invoke coronary artery disease, primarily, I believe, because of the purported absence of a history of cardiac pain.

There have been reports that lithium is toxic to the heart, and some cardiologists believe strongly that the drug, even in therapeutic doses, may cause heart damage after years of use. The evidence for this in the medical literature is thin. Lithium treatment affects the appearance of the ECG, as would be expected given that the lithium ion is so similar chemically to the potassium and sodium ions that participate in the electrical activity of the heartbeat. Lithium treatment may also lead to minor forms of cardiac arrhythmia, but there has never been evidence of a consistent effect on the mechanical function of cardiac muscle. The literature contains a scattering of case reports, fewer than ten, of patients taking lithium who had heart failure, and in none of these was lithium the only possible medication or toxin that might have accounted for the illness. On balance, lithium seems vastly less likely than coronary heart disease or alcohol to have contributed to Lowell's heart failure and death.

Patients with manic depression have significantly shorter life expectancy than normal. Even when, despite the odds, sufferers do not succumb to suicide, or die from overdose, accident, or violence—more or less direct consequences of their condition—they are still likely to have diminished access to care; may, on account of their mental instability, find themselves ineligible for complex or demanding treatments; may adhere poorly to medical regimens; and may not be people who naturally follow healthy lifestyles. They suffer from fractured sleep, fatigue, and frequent overexcitement. The physiologic overstimulation that accompanies mania can be acutely lethal and surely takes its own toll in the long term. Lowell's early death at sixty seems to offer some insight into these factors at work, yet with so little available to treat blood pressure effectively, and in a society that readily accepted the volume of his cigarette and alcohol habits, we can be grateful that he could live well and remain so productive even to the end.

Thomas A. Traill, FRCP
Professor of Medicine
The Johns Hopkins University
School of Medicine

Acknowledgments

I am indebted to Harriet Winslow Lowell for her permission to obtain and review her father's psychiatric and medical records, for our many interesting discussions about her father and his work, and for allowing me to look at his unpublished writings and family photographs. It has been a great pleasure to get to know Ms. Lowell, who put no conditions on what I wrote. Her husband, Neal Earhart, was generous with his time and his memories of his mother-in-law, Elizabeth Hardwick.

Robert Lowell's stepdaughters, Evgenia Citkowitz and Ivana Lowell, were kind enough to discuss their memories of their stepfather and to answer additional questions as they came up. Several of Lowell's friends, colleagues, and former students talked with me at length about their relationships with him and about his work. I am particularly grateful to Grey Gowrie, Jonathan Raban, Helen Vendler, Kathleen Spivack, Richard Tillinghast, John Julius Norwich, Jonathan Miller, James Atlas, Christopher Ricks, Dana Gioia, Steven Gould Axelrod, Douglas Dunn, Wendy Lesser, Rose Styron, Polly Kraft, and Cornelia Foss. I am indebted to the poet Saskia Hamilton, editor of *The Letters of Robert Lowell* and co-editor of *Words in Air: The Complete Correspondence Between Elizabeth Bishop and Robert Lowell*. Her scholarship is formidable and she has been singularly encouraging and helpful to me in writing this book. Professor Frank Bidart, the poet and editor of *Robert Lowell's Collected Poems*, read an early version of my manuscript, as did Lowell's publisher at Farrar, Straus and Giroux, Jonathan Galassi. Both were very supportive of what I had written, and I am deeply appreciative.

I am particularly indebted to two of Robert Lowell's psychiatrists, both of whom offered rich insight into his illness and treatment: Erik Linnolt, M.D., who was Lowell's psychiatrist during his three hospitalizations at the Institute of Living in Connecticut during the 1960s, and Dr. Marian Woolston-Catlin, M.D., who treated him at the Massachusetts Mental Health Center during the late 1950s, a critical time for his poetry, as well as for his manic-depressive illness.

It was not easy to find Lowell's psychiatric and medical records, some of which were eighty years old, as hospitals are rarely required to preserve their records for more than ten years. I was helped by the staff and administrators in many of the hospitals that treated Robert Lowell: Jack Barchas, M.D., Chairman of Psychiatry at Weill Cornell Medical College in New York, and Pamela Thrower-Webb, also at Weill Cornell; Elizabeth Simpson, M.D. at Massachusetts Mental Health Center in Boston; Harold Schwartz, M.D., Psychiatrist in-Chief of the Institute of Living in Hartford, Connecticut, and Joanna Fogg-Waberski, M.D., also at the Institute of Living; Shelly Greenfield, M.D., Chief Academic Officer at McLean Hospital in Belmont, Massachusetts, an affiliate of Harvard Medical School, and Terry Alan Bragg, Archivist of the McLean Hospital; Jeffrey Lieberman, M.D., Chair of the Department of Psychiatry, Columbia University Medical Center; John Belknap, Chief Compliance Officer of Massachusetts General Hospital, and Jerrold Rosenbaum, M.D., Chief of Psychiatry at Massachusetts General Hospital.

Several individuals were generous with their time and recollections in showing my husband, Tom Traill, and me around Castine, including the Winslow-Lowell home where Robert Lowell, Elizabeth Hardwick, and Harriet Lowell spent so many family summers. It is easy to see why Lowell loved Maine and wrote so much of his poetry in the converted barn with its lovely view overlooking the bay. Our thanks go to Jack and Julie Burke, Stefanie Scheer Young, Susan Hatch, Peter Davis, and Deborah Joy Corey, as well as to Paige Lilly and Sally Foote at the Castine Historical Society.

I am indebted as well to the Reverend Allan Bevier Warren III, rector of the Church of the Advent in Boston, the Reverend Samuel Lee Wood, and the organist and choirmaster, Mark Dwyer, for their time in telling me about the church where Lowell was a parishioner at the time he died and where his funeral was held. Across the river in

Cambridge, I was fortunate enough to have a highly literate and wonderful tour around "Elmwood," for many years the family home of the Reverend Charles A. Lowell and his wife, Harriet Brackett Spence Lowell, and then their son the poet James Russell Lowell, now the official home of the president of Harvard University. It was from this gracious home that Robert Lowell's great-great-grandmother was taken by carriage to McLean Asylum for the Insane. Professor Charles Rosenberg, who lives there with his wife, Drew Gilpin Faust, the current president of Harvard, showed me around their house, James Russell Lowell's library, and the grounds of Elmwood. He has become a good friend, I am delighted to say. George White and Kimberly Tseko gave me much useful history of the house as it would have been in the eighteenth and nineteenth centuries.

Robert Lowell's papers and those of his colleagues, family, and friends, are held in many libraries. These libraries and their collections were, without exception, welcoming and helpful. Emilie Hardman and the staff of the Houghton Library at Harvard University, where most of Lowell's papers and those of his family are archived, were particularly helpful with my endless stream of requests. I am grateful as well to the staff of the Harry Ransom Collection at the University of Texas at Austin; Helen Melody, curator of Modern Literary Manuscripts at the British Library, where Ian Hamilton's papers and oral history of Robert Lowell are held; the Massachusetts Historical Society; the Huntington Library; Lauren Amundson and the Lowell Observatory Archives in Flagstaff; the London Library; Vassar College Library; James Smith and the staff of the Portsmouth Athenaeum; Princeton University Library; New Hampshire State Archives; Michael Frost and the staff of the Sterling Memorial Library at Yale University; the Library of Congress; Elizabeth Hall Witherell, for her help with manuscripts of Henry David Thoreau, Davidson Library, University of California, Santa Barbara; Westminster Abbey Archives; University of Minnesota Library; New York Public Library; University of Washington Library; Washington University Library; Georgetown University Library; Benjamin Panciera and the staff of the Linda Lear Center for Special Collections & Archives, Connecticut College; Dartmouth College Library; University of Oregon Library; Smith College Library; Tyler Phelps at the Smithsonian Institution Libraries (National Museum of American History); Centre for Research Collections, Edinburgh University Library; Professor Shane Allwright, Trinity College Dublin, University of Dublin; William H. Welch Medical Library, Johns Hopkins University School of Medicine; and the Clinical Center Library of the National Institutes of Health.

I am appreciative as well to Jo Bartholomew, Curator and Librarian of Winchester Cathedral, who verified my husband's boyhood memory of the pieces of glass that are fixed across the stones to detect movement in the walls of the cathedral; it was an image I found heartbreaking as I thought about Robert Lowell's last days. Diana Der-Hovanessian gave me useful information about the New England Poetry Club, Katherine Powers was kind enough to share Lowell's letters to her father, and Christina Ball translated several letters from Italian written by Giovanna Madonia to Robert Lowell. Emily O'Dell introduced me to the works on mania written by the medieval Islamic physicians. Nancy Schoenberger and Alan Tobias were helpful in sharing information relevant to Lowell's life.

I am grateful to many people who helped make this book possible. My editor at Alfred A. Knopf for twenty years, Carol Brown Janeway, died in the summer of 2015. She had taken on my book about Robert Lowell with her usual intelligence, rapier wit, and loyalty; she shepherded me through the first several years of what turned out to be a considerable endeavor. Like all of her friends and authors, I miss her terribly. There was no one like her. Sonny Mehta put my book in the hands of Deborah Garrison, for which I will be forever grateful. She has made the book a better one in so many ways and has done it with deftness and grace. I am also thankful to several other people at Knopf who contributed their talents: Todd Portnowitz, Ellen Feldman, Andrew Ridker, Amy Ryan, Carol Devine Carson, Soonyoung Kwon, Josefine Taylor Kals, and Katherine Burns.

I would not have been able to write this book without the generous support of the Dalio Family Foundation. The friendships of Ray and Barbara Dalio and Paul and Kristina Nikolova Dalio have been of much meaning to me during these past several years. I owe my usual debt to William Collins whose professionalism and flexibility have been invaluable to my work, as has the help of Silas Jones and Ioline Henter.

Professor Guy Goodwin at the University of Oxford and Professor Raymond Depaulo at the Johns Hopkins University School of Medicine, leading authorities on bipolar illness and superb clinicians, read my manuscript for clinical accuracy. Bruce Cuthbert, Ph.D., of the National Institute of Mental Health, was helpful in giving me information about new diagnostic approaches to mania, and the late Lori Altshuler, M.D, a missed and respected colleague, gave me perspective on longitudinal brain scan studies of bipolar patients. Several of my colleagues at the Johns Hopkins University School of Medicine have been particularly supportive professionally and personally: Adam Kaplin, M.D., Ph.D.; Karen Swartz, M.D.; Mary Beth Beaudry, R.N., M.S.N.; Barbara Schweizer, R.N., B.S.; Philip Slavney, M.D.; and Paul McHugh, M.D. Sharon Blackburn, in the Johns Hopkins Department of Pathology, has helped design graphics for my work and Jeffrey Day, M.D., helped with the chart of Robert Lowell's hospitalizations and lithium treatment. Henry Brem, M.D., Chair of Neurosurgery at Johns Hopkins, warmly encouraged my request to attend Neurosurgery Grand Rounds for two years and made me feel welcome. The medical content of the discussions, however fascinating, was of less interest to me than the language used by the surgeons that was new—mapping and naming in the way of poetry. They talked about the geography of the brain in terms of canals and caves and aqueducts and described surgical procedures in fresh and compelling ways. It was helpful to my understanding of poetry, albeit in an oblique way.

Donald Graham read an early version of my manuscript and made very helpful suggestions, most of which I incorporated into the final text. David and Linda Hellman, Duke and Claudia Cameron, Tom and Judy Spencer, and Bill and Pam Schlott read parts of my manuscript and contributed their support, suggestions, and friendship. Erwin and Stephanie Cooper Greenberg invited Tom and me to Nantucket for a marvelous weekend and introduced us to places Lowell had lived and explored as a young man and the North Atlantic about which he wrote unforgettably in "The Quaker Graveyard in Nantucket." The composer Michael Hersch, whose work based on Robert Lowell's poetry was commissioned by the Library of Congress, has been a good friend and we have had many conversations about art and music, and Robert Lowell, over the years.

My family—the Jamisons, Campens, and Traills—have been wonderful throughout the writing of this book. I am indebted to my cousin, James Campen, for photographing the Robert Gould Shaw Monument in Boston and for the many warm family dinners in Cambridge.

As always I am grateful to Daniel Auerbach, M.D., for his excellence as a doctor. I have been and blessed with the caring and company of great friends: Jeremy Waletzky and Susan Clampett, Robert and Mary Jane Gallo, Jeffrey and Kathleen Schlom, Joanne Leslie, and Alain Moreau, who did the drawing of the rowan berries for this book.

There is no one to whom I owe a greater debt than my husband, Tom Traill. This book is in every sense his book. He not only has an unnerving, intuitive understanding of Robert Lowell's work, "not an easy poet," as the *New York Times* wrote in its obituary, but—perhaps because of his distant cousinship with the Traill line of Lowell's ancestry or, more immediately, because he has read his own and the handwriting of other physicians for so many years—he was uncannily able to decipher Lowell's horrific hand. Irreplaceably, he read my manuscript through many times and each time made it clearer; he added precision and eloquence and improved both the clinical and literary discussion. He read through Lowell's medical records, with a focus on his heart disease, and summarized the medical history in Appendix 3. Most important, he made the writing of this book even more pleasurable than it would otherwise have been and gave me the kind of love I could only have dreamed of.

Notes

PROLOGUE

xiii "In regard to her mind": Letter from Charles Lowell to James Russell Lowell, August 8, 1844, James Russell Lowell Papers, Houghton Library, Harvard College Library.

xiii "March sugar snow": (Boston) *Daily Evening Transcript*, March 19, 1845. "In the city the earth was found covered this morning with what the good people in the country would call a March 'Sugar Snow,' which wonderfully promotes the flow of the sap in the giant maples of the sugar orchard." The three Boston newspapers give a lively accounting of that March day in 1845: the schedules for ship sailings and packets to Havana and New Orleans; the comings and goings of whalers; the business happenings of the Boston and Lowell Railroad and the Nashua and Lowell Railroad; Massachusetts politics; reports of the many fires in Boston; lectures in Cambridge; the sale of beeswax and clover seed, cod and hake, tea, white beaver gloves direct from Paris; fine shops in Boston selling parasols and silk bonnet ribbons, sleigh robes, rhubarb and opium, molasses and indigo. The papers also carried accounts of the discussions of the Boston abolitionists like those that filled the church of Reverend Charles Lowell on Sunday mornings.

xiii "hum outliving the hushed bell": James Russell Lowell, "The Darkened Mind," in *The Complete Poetical Works of James Russell Lowell*, ed. Horace Scudder (Boston: Houghton Mifflin, 1896), 427.

xiii their home with its great elms: Martin Duberman, *James Russell Lowell* (Boston: Houghton Mifflin, 1966); Edward Wagenknecht, *James Russell Lowell: Portrait of a Many-Sided Man* (New York: Oxford, 1971); Susan Wilson, *Literary Trail of Greater Boston* (Boston: Houghton Mifflin, 2000).

xiv "infinitely the most elegant dwelling house": Dean A. Fales, Jr., "Joseph Barrell's Pleasant Hill," *Publications of the Colonial Society of Massachusetts*, trans. 43 (1956–1963), 376.

xiv "treasurers of God's bounty": James Jackson and John Collins Warren, "Circular Letter Submitting Proposals for the Establishment in Boston of a 'Hospital for the Reception of Lunatics and Other Sick Persons,'" August 20, 1810.

xiv McLean Asylum for the Insane: Information about the McLean Asylum in 1845 was obtained from the annual reports of the Board of Trustees of the Massachusetts General Hospital for the years 1841 through 1846; discussions with Terence Bragg, archivist for the McLean Hospital; Nina Fletcher Little, *Early Years of the McLean Hospital: Recorded in the Journal of George William Folsom, Apothecary at the Asylum in Charlestown* (Boston: Francis A. Countway Library of Medicine, 1972); S. B. Sutton, *Crossroads in Psychiatry: A History of the McLean Hospital* (Washington, D.C.: American Psychiatric Press, 1986); Alex Beam, *Gracefully Insane: The Rise and Fall of America's Premier Mental Hospital* (New York: Public Affairs, 2001).

xiv She arrived at the asylum: The clinical notes on Harriet Brackett Spence Lowell are from the 1845 admission book of the McLean Asylum for the Insane (now the McLean Hospital). The history of her behavior and mental state provided by her husband, the Reverend Charles Lowell, also are in the 1845 admission book. There is as well a packet of papers in the Scudder Papers at Houghton Library, Harvard, that are abbreviated notes made by Horace Scudder for his 1901 biography of Harriet Brackett Spence Lowell's son James Russell Lowell. Horace E. Scudder, *James Russell Lowell: A Biography* (Boston and New York: Houghton, Mifflin and Company, 1901).

xv "to be particular about things": There is a considerably higher than expected rate of obsessive behaviors and obsessive-compulsive disorder in individuals who suffer from bipolar disorder. For example, see: S. L. Mc Elroy, L. L. Altshuler, T. Suppes, et al., "Axis I Psychiatric Comorbidity and Its Relationship to Historical Illness Variables in 288 Patients with Bipolar Disorder," *American Journal of Psychiatry* 158 (2001): 420–26; F. K. Goodwin and K. R. Jamison, *Manic-Depressive Illness: Bipolar Disorders and Recurrent Depression* (New York: Oxford University Press, 2007), 234–38.

xvi brief period of treatment with Dr. Rufus Wyman: Rufus Wyman was the first full-time medical superintendent of an American mental hospital. His treatment philosophy was based on the so-called moral treatment advocated by the French psychiatrist Philippe Pinel and the doctors at York Retreat in England. Wyman, in addition to his responsibilities at the asylum, usually had a few patients residing with him; Harriet Lowell, before her admission to the asylum, had been one of them. Wyman wrote in medical journals about the diagnosis and treatment of mania and depression and encouraged his patients—as did other asylum doctors at the time—to be actively involved in both work and recreational activities such as chess, backgammon, music, reading, walking, and riding. Rufus Wyman, "A Discourse on Mental Philosophy as Connects with Mental Disease," talk delivered before the Massachusetts Medical Society, June 2, 1830 (Boston: Office of the Daily Advertiser, 1830), 3–21; E. T. Carlson and M. F. Chale, "Historical Notes: Dr. Rufus Wyman of the McLean Asylum," *American Journal of Psychiatry* 116 (1960): 1034–37; S. B. Woodward, "Observations on the Medical Treatment of Insanity," *American Journal of Insanity* 7 (1850): 1–34.

xvi It is not known: No diagnosis or record of treatment for Harriet Lowell can be found in the asylum ledger. She would have been a beneficiary of the "moral treatment" movement in the United States and England, a form of care that stood in compassionate contrast to the chains and bloodletting of earlier times. In 1846, the second year of her stay at McLean, the superintendent of the Massachusetts State Lunatic Hospital gave a talk describing the philosophy underlying the care given in the New England asylums in the middle of the nineteenth century. "The mind must be managed, hope inspired, and confidence secured," he stated. He cited the humane practices of the ancient physicians: insanity was a disease and it required medical remedy, but the mind must be "diverted as well" and the feelings of the mentally afflicted "soothed and assuaged." To these ends, the ancients advised the ill of mind to go to the temple of their gods, to "participate in their religious rites, look upon the beauties of nature from these elevated situations, and, in the temples of Aesculapius, consult the records of experience engraven on the tablets of their walls." S. B. Woodward, "Observations on the Medical Treatment of Insanity."

In a not dissimilar manner, patients at the McLean Asylum in the era of Mrs. Lowell's confinement were encouraged to ride and walk the extensive asylum grounds—at McLean, with its graceful gardens and orchards, this would have reaped a particular bounty in "looking upon the beauties of nature"—and to participate in religious services. Rarely would physical restraints have been used. Instead, the asylum doctors prescribed medicines to soothe the agitated and to restore sleep and volition to the melancholy. Rhubarb, camphor, tincture of ginger, digitalis, and sulphate of morphia were among the many remedies used by the New England physicians. Other treatments—violets and oils of rose to calm and to take down the brain's fever—were part of the apothecary's kit of both the ancient and nineteenth-century doctors. Then, as now, they prescribed what they hoped would work.

xvi "the fire is turning clear and blithely": James Russell Lowell, "The Darkened Mind," 427.

xvii "will be read as long as": Randall Jarrell, "From the Kingdom of Necessity," *Nation* 164 (1947): 74–77.

xviii "The trouble with writing poetry": Robert Lowell, "Art and Evil," in *Collected Prose*, ed. Robert Giroux (New York: Farrar, Straus and Giroux, 1987), 131–32.

I. INTRODUCTION: STEEL AND FIRE

1 "Your *Cantos* have re-created": Robert Lowell to Ezra Pound, May 2, 1936, in *The Letters of Robert Lowell*, ed. S. Hamilton (New York: Farrar, Straus and Giroux, 2005), 3.

I. NO TICKETS FOR THAT ALTITUDE

3 "The resident doctor said": Robert Lowell, "Notice," in *Collected Poems*, ed. F. Bidart and D. Gewanter (New York: Farrar, Straus and Giroux, 2003), 828.

3 "Darkness honestly lived through": Letter from Robert Lowell to Randall Jarrell, October 24, 1957, *Letters*, 298.

3 "like a house a fire": Letter from Robert Lowell to William Carlos Williams, September 30, 1957, *Letters*, 293.

3 into "new country": Letter from Robert Lowell to Allen Tate, November 5, 1952, *Letters*, 194.

3 best writing he had done: Letter from Robert Lowell to J. F. Powers, November 13, 1957, *Letters*, 305.

3 "perhaps the most influential": Stanley Kunitz, *Next-to-Last Things: New Poems and Essays* (Boston: Atlantic Monthly Press, 1985).

3 "They have made a conquest": John Thompson, "Two Poets: *Life Studies* by Robert Lowell; *Heart's Needle* by W. D. Snodgrass," *The Kenyon Review* 21 (1959): 483.

4 brought poetry into the Lowell line: Letter from Robert Lowell to Harriet Winslow, April 10, 1957, Houghton Library.

4 "some of his most productive months": Marian Woolston, M.D., hospital record of Robert Lowell, Massachusetts Mental Health Center, December 21, 1957.

4 "The patient has had a series of breaks": Ibid.

4 "but a huge amount of health": "Poetry can come out of utterly miserable or disorderly lives, as in the case of a Rimbaud or a Hart Crane. But to make the poems possible a huge amount of health has to go into the misery." Stanley Kunitz, "Talk with Robert Lowell," *New York Times Book Review*, October 4, 1964, 34–38.

4 "there were no tickets": Robert Lowell, "Beyond the Alps," *Collected Poems*, 114.

4 "My trouble": Letter from Robert Lowell to Elizabeth Bishop, March 30, 1959, *Letters*, 340.

5 "rock crystal": Letter from Merrill Moore, M.D., to Charlotte Winslow Lowell, February 17, 1938, Robert Lowell Papers, Harry Ransom Center, University of Texas at Austin (hereafter HRC). "We are dealing with a boy who has a personality like a rock crystal, glittering, very hard, and very definite in its formation."

5 "Yet see—he mastereth himself": George Gordon, Lord Byron, "Manfred," act 2, scene 4, in *Lord Byron: The Complete Poetical Works*, vol. 4, ed. Jerome J. McGann (Oxford: Clarendon Press, 1986), 86.

6 "We face the precariousness": Robert Lowell, quoted in Jane Howard, "Applause for a Prize Poet," *Life*, February 19, 1965, 56.

6 "We left feeling completely": Alan Brownjohn, interview with Ian Hamilton, March 1981, Ian Hamilton Papers, British Library.

7 "Metaphor was his reality": Esther Brooks, "Remembering Cal," in *Robert Lowell: A Tribute*, ed. Rolando Anzilotti (Pisa: Nistri-Lischi Edition, 1979), 40.

7 "like a rather backward evolutionary form": Helen Vendler, "Lowell in the Classroom," *The Harvard Advocate* 113 (November 1979): 29.

7 "a man of genius": Letter from Isaiah Berlin to Jacob Herzog, February 18, 1969, in *Isaiah Berlin: Building; Letters 1960–1975*, ed. Henry Hardy and Mark Pottle (London: Chatto & Windus, 2013), 367.

7 "so completely original": Esther Brooks, "Remembering Cal," 37–38.

8 "My impression is": Robert Lowell, "After Enjoying Six or Seven Essays on Me," *Salmagundi* 37 (Spring 1977): 113.

8 "not always factually true": Frederick Seidel, "The Art of Poetry: Robert Lowell," *Paris Review* 7 (Winter–Spring 1961): 56–95.

8 "in which good poets are": Robert Lowell letter to I. A. Richards, April 18, 1959, *Letters*, 346.

9 Hamilton's biography of Lowell: Ian Hamilton, *Robert Lowell: A Biography* (New York: Random House, 1982).

9 "Towards the end of the life": Simon Gray, *The Complete Smoking Diaries* (London: Granta Books, 2013).

9 Paul Mariani's biography: Paul Mariani, *Lost Puritan: A Life of Robert Lowell* (New York: W. W. Norton, 1994).

9 "Robert Lowell was notably unlucky": Richard Tillinghast, "The Achievement of Robert Lowell," *The New Criterion*, January 2004.

10 "the book that broke the back": Stewart Donovan, "Reading Robert Lowell," *Nashwaak Review* 16–17 (Winter 2010).

10 "pitiless and strangely incomprehending": Author interview with Jonathan Raban, June 20, 2012.

10 "missed his humor": Author interview with Grey Gowrie, June 30, 2011, London.

10 Hardwick's point: Others agreed with Hardwick. Derek Walcott, for one, disliked the relentless, negative focus on Lowell's mental illness. Lowell was first and foremost "a great poet who had devastating bouts of mental illness. Clouds covered him, but when they went, he was extraordinarily gentle. He had that masculine sweetness that draws a deep love from men." Derek Walcott, "On Robert Lowell," *New York Review of Books*, March 1, 1984. Daniel Hoffman wrote, "A reader of Ian Hamilton's biography could not imagine how enjoyable was his company, what fun he was to be with: witty, quick, courteous, unaffected. Hamilton's informants told all about Lowell's manic breakdowns but had not much to say of the charm that made writers like Peter Taylor and Randall Jarrell his life long friends." Daniel Hoffman, "Afternoons with Robert Lowell," *London Magazine* 32 (1992): 56.

10 "Every serious story": Correspondence, Harriet Winslow Lowell to the author, April 2012.

2. THE ARCHANGEL LOVED HEIGHTS

12 "Timur saying something like": Robert Lowell, "Fame," *Collected Poems*, 449.

12 "All my life I have been eccentric": Letter from Robert Lowell to Ezra Pound, May 2, 1936, *Letters*, 3–4.

12 "I wasn't really *afraid*": Frank Parker, interview with Ian Hamilton, 1980, Ian Hamilton Papers, British Library.

13 he had begun to "understand God": Letter from Robert Lowell to Richard Eberhart, July 10, 1935, Dartmouth College Library.

13 "Since then I have been": Letter from Robert Lowell to Ezra Pound, May 2, 1936, *Letters*, 4.

13 "to bring back momentum": Letter from Robert Lowell to Ezra Pound, n.d. May 1936, *Letters*, 6.

13 "He once said to me": Frank Bidart, "Robert Lowell," *The Harvard Advocate* 113 (November 1979): 12.

14 "twists of fire": Robert Lowell, "Morning Blue," *Collected Poems*, 657.

14 "The drop of water": Robert Lowell, "Fame," *Collected Poems*, 449.

14 "The Archangel loved heights": Henry Adams, *Mont Saint Michel and Chartres* (1904; New York: Penguin, 1986), 7.

14 "pour out more than the measure": Letter from Robert Lowell to Harriet Winslow, September 17, 1956, Houghton Library.

14 "Give me a condor's quill!": Herman Melville, *Moby-Dick, or The Whale* (1851; Berkeley and Los Angeles: University of California Press, 1979), 465–66.

14 "Greatness, greatness, above all else": Boris Pasternak, quoted in Guy de Mallac, *Boris Pasternak: His Life and Art* (Norman: University of Oklahoma Press, 1981), 336.

14 "habituated *to the Vast*": Letter from Samuel Taylor Coleridge to Thomas Poole, October 16, 1797, in *Collected Letters of Samuel Taylor Coleridge*, vol. 1, 1785–1800, ed. E. L. Briggs (Oxford: Oxford University Press, 1959), 91.

14 "excited by greatness": Alfred Kazin, *Alfred Kazin's Journal*, ed. Richard M. Cook (New Haven: Yale University Press, 2011), 352–53.

15 "displays, in high degrees": John Berryman, "Robert Lowell and Others," in *The Freedom of the Poet* (New York: Farrar, Straus and Giroux, 1976), 286–87.

15 "Immense ambition": Dana Gioia, correspondence with the author, July 2011.

15 "don't settle down into the comfortably grand": Frank Bidart, quoted in "Whatever Happened to Robert Lowell?," *Maine Sunday Telegram*, August 3, 2003.

15 "There is undue preoccupation": Marian Woolston, M.D., hospital record for Robert Lowell, Massachusetts Mental Health Center, December 1957.

16 Research bears this out: C. D. Spielberger, J. B. Parker, and J. Becker, "Conformity and Achievement in Remitted Manic-Depressive Patients," *Journal of Nervous and Mental Diseases* 137 (1963): 162–72; N. J. C. Andreasen and B. Pfohl, "Linguistic Analysis of Speech in Affective Disorders," *Archives of General Psychiatry* 33 (1976): 1361–67; R. L. Leahy, "Decision Making and Mania," *Journal of Cognitive Psychotherapy* 13 (1999): 83–105; D. C. Fowles, "Biological Variables in Psychopathology," in H. E. Adams and P. B. Sutker, eds., *Comprehensive Handbook of Psychopathology*, 3rd ed. (New York: Klumer, 2001), 85–104; B. E. Loranzo and S. L. Johnson, "Can Personality Traits Predict Increases in Manic and Depressive Symptoms?," *Journal of Affective Disorders* 63 (2001): 103–11; S. L. Johnson, "Mania and Dysregulation in Goal Pursuit: A Review," *Clinical Psychology Review* 25 (2005): 241–62; B. Meyer, C. G. Johnson, and E. Simmons, "Unique Association of Approach Motivation and Mania Vulnerability," *Cognition and Emotion* 21 (2007): 1647–68; S. L. Johnson, C. S. Carver,

and I. H. Gotlib, "Elevated Ambitions for Fame Among Persons with Bipolar I Disorder," *Journal of Abnormal Psychology* 121 (2012): 602–9.

16 "History lived in his nerves": Derek Walcott, "On Robert Lowell."

16 "gossiped about the English poets": James Atlas, "Robert Lowell in Cambridge: Lord Weary," *Atlantic Monthly*, July 1982, 56–64.

16 "of a life, a spirit": Helen Vendler, "Lowell in the Classroom," 22–29.

16 "Surfacing constantly in what Cal says": Philip Booth, "Summers in Castine: Contact Prints, 1955–1965," *Salmagundi* 37 (Spring 1977): 37–53.

16 "the great past, Revolutionary America": John Thompson, "Two Poets," 482–90.

16 "shuttle-like movements": Elizabeth Stevenson, *Henry Adams: A Biography* (New Brunswick, NJ: Transaction Publishers, 1997), 160.

16 "He was a survivor from another age": Jonathan Raban, interview with the author, June 20, 2012.

16 "He could hold the world of archaic Rome": Robert Fitzgerald, "Thinking of Robert Lowell: 1917–1977", draft typescript, March 2, 1978, Robert Fitzgerald Papers, Yale University, YCAL mss. 222, box 57, folder 2124.

17 "I laid my hand on its skin": Richard Stone, *Mammoth: The Resurrection of an Ice Age Giant* (London: Fourth Estate, 2003), 15.

17 "Sometimes when I am trying": Robert Lowell, "Hawthorne's Pegasus," *Collected Prose*, 162.

17 "The chief charm of New England": Henry Adams, *The Education of Henry Adams: An Autobiography* (1907; Boston: Houghton Mifflin, 2000), 7.

17 "our greatest man maybe": Letter from Robert Lowell to Blair Clark, March 21, 1954, *Letters*, 225.

17 "born under the shadow of the Dome": Robert Lowell, "Antebellum Boston," *Collected Prose*, 291.

18 "a cold that froze the blood": Henry Adams, *The Education of Henry Adams*, 7.

18 Summer, on the other hand: Ibid., 8.

18 "effort to live": Ibid.

18 "It ran through life": Ibid., 9.

19 "menaced" and "knowingly sensuous mind": Robert Lowell, "New England and Further," *Collected Prose*, 201.

19 "Adams' connection with Boston": Robert Lowell, "Henry Adams 1850," *Collected Poems*, 484.

19 "a world I knew mostly from summer": Robert Lowell, "Robert Frost," *Collected Prose*, 9.

19 "What a heavy way of saying": Letter from Robert Lowell to George Santayana, February 1, 1951, *Letters*, 167.

19 "I find that I fall into two parts": Robert Lowell to Vernon Williams, M.D., n.d. mid-1950s, HRC.

20 "sober prudence": R. H. Tawney, *Religion and the Rise of Capitalism* (London: Harcourt Brace, 1926), 212.

20 "The lightning which explodes": Ralph Waldo Emerson, "Fate," in *The Conduct of Life* (Boston: Ticknor & Fields, 1860).

20 "the greatest nonfiction writer": Robert Lowell, "New England and Further," *Collected Prose*, 186.

20 "he loves the contrast": Jonathan Miller, BBC program, "The Lively Arts: Robert Lowell," March 9, 1965.

20 "the Puritanical iron hand": Letter from Robert Lowell to Elizabeth Bishop, March 30, 1959, *Letters*, 340.

20 "Maybe it's just my nature": Letter from Robert Lowell to Elizabeth Bishop, January 24, 1964, *Letters*, 441.

20 "During this time I have had": Letter to Chard Powers Smith, October 3, 1959, *Letters*, 354.

21 "Lights and shadows": Nathaniel Hawthorne, May 19, 1840, *American Notebooks, Centenary Edition of the Works of Nathaniel Hawthorne*, ed. Claude Simpson, vol. 8 (Columbus: Ohio State University Press, 1972).

21 "For spite of all the Indian-summer sunlight": Herman Melville, "Hawthorne and His Mosses," *The Literary World*, August 17 and 24, 1850.

21 "Lowell had the most disconcerting mixture": Norman Mailer, *The Armies of the Night* (New York: New American Library, 1968), 53–54.

21 "From the time I first knew him": Peter Taylor, "Robert Trail [*sic*] Spence Lowell 1917–1977," *Ploughshares* 5 (1979): 74–81.

22 "the accomplishments of man": Robert Lowell, "*The Iliad*," *Collected Prose*, 150.

22 "He would be a writer": Francis Parker, "Brentwood Camp," *The Harvard Advocate* 113 (November 1979): 8.

22 "quite dreadful tensions": Blair Clark, "On Robert Lowell," *The Harvard Advocate*, 113 (November 1979): 9–10.

23 "unreasoning hate of Achilles cannot continue": Robert Lowell, "*The Iliad*," *Collected Prose*, 150.

23 The hero's punishment: Ibid., 149.

23 "wavering, irresistible force": Robert Lowell, "Epics," *Collected Prose*, 214.

23 "Anger be now your song": Homer, *The Iliad*, trans. Robert Fitzgerald (New York: Farrar, Straus and Giroux, 2004), 5.

23 "Sing, goddess, the anger": Homer, *The Iliad*, trans. Richmond Lattimore (Chicago: University of Chicago Press, 2011), 75.

23 "Rage—Goddess, sing the rage": Homer, *The Iliad*, trans. Robert Fagles (New York: Viking Penguin, 1990), 77.

23 "Achilles' baneful wrath": Homer, *The Iliad*, trans. George Chapman (1614–16; London: J. R. Smith, 1857).

24 "Sing for me, Muse": Robert Lowell, "The Killing of Lykaon," *Collected Poems*, 197.

24 "Over non-existence": Robert Lowell, "Pigeons," *Collected Poems*, 316.

II. ORIGINS: THE PURITANICAL IRON HAND OF CONSTRAINT

27 "My trouble seems": Letter from Robert Lowell to Elizabeth Bishop, March 30, 1959, *Letters*, 340.

3. SANDS OF THE UNKNOWN

29 "Robert Lowell, Poet": Citation for honorary degree, doctor of letters, conferred upon Robert Lowell by Yale University, June 1968.

29 "I wrote about only four places": Ian Hamilton, "A Conversation with Robert Lowell," *The Review* 26 (Summer 1971): 10.

29 "I come with signposts": Robert Lowell, "1916, Manuscript, Antebellum Boston" (ca. 1955), Robert Lowell Papers, Houghton Library, 2209.

29 "If you had come out of": Ibid.

30 "To my children": Quoted in C. R. Hayward, G. A. Packard, and W. H. Coburn, "Arthur Winslow, M.I.T. 1881," tribute of the Alumni Council of the Massachusetts Institute of Technology, n.d., HRC. The passage from Winslow's will was also published in the *Boston Globe*; "Boston Engineer Wills Life in N. E. to Children."

30 "He was my Father": Robert Lowell, "Dunbarton," *Collected Poems*, 168.

30 "This room was brighter then": Robert Lowell, "Phillips House Revisited," *Collected Poems*, 798.

30 "Charles River to the Acheron": Robert Lowell, "In Memory of Arthur Winslow," *Collected Poems*, 23.

30 "raked leaves from our dead forebears": Robert Lowell, "Dunbarton," *Collected Poems*, 169.

30 "It was in the stars": Robert Lowell, "New England and Beyond," *Collected Prose*, 183.

31 "We New Englanders": Letter from Robert Lowell to Anthony Ostroff, August 23, 1957, *Letters*, 290.

31 "something of the mind": Robert Lowell, "New England and Further," *Collected Prose*, 181.

31 "is not down on any map": Herman Melville, *Moby-Dick* (1851; New York: Penguin, 2003), 61.

32 "thousand small town New England": Robert Lowell, "For the Union Dead," *Collected Poems*, 377.

32 "a kind of carnal gravity": Robert Lowell, "New England and Further," *Collected Prose*, 180.

32 "with open arms, joy": Letter from Robert Lowell to Elizabeth Bishop, February 26, 1967, *Letters*, 484.

32 "Everything in the geologist's mind": Adam Nicolson, *Sea Room: An Island Life in the Hebrides* (New York: North Point Press, 2002), 80–81.

32 "think always of how it came to be": Ibid., 81.

33 "Ours was an old family": Ian Hamilton, "A Conversation with Robert Lowell," 10–29.

33 "I woke up the other morning": Letter from Robert Lowell to Harriet Winslow, July 31, 1961, *Letters*, 385.

33 "feed off history": Jonathan Miller, BBC program, "The Lively Arts: Robert Lowell," March 9, 1965.

33 "In different hours": Ralph Waldo Emerson, "Fate," *Nature and Selected Essays* (1860; New York: Penguin, 2003), 366.

33 "What is history?": Robert Lowell, "Mexico," *Collected Poems*, 625.

33 "dynastic as well as an artistic": Seamus Heaney, "On Robert Lowell," a memorial address given at St. Luke's Church, Redcliffe Square, London, October 5, 1977, *New York Review of Books*, February 9, 1978.

34 "I had a little ancestor": Letter from Robert Lowell to Harriet Winslow, February 13, 1956, *Letters*, 254.

34 "A lot is lost": Letter from Robert Lowell to Harriet Winslow, March 8, 1956, Houghton Library.

34 "They come back sometimes": Robert Lowell, "Revenants," *Collected Poems*, 494.

34 "an hereditary depravity": John Calvin, *Institutes of the Christian Religion*, vol. 1, Library of Christian Classics, vol. 20, trans. F. L. Battles (Philadelphia: Westminster, 1960), 251.

34 "positive energy of this sin": Ibid.

35 "I feel more warmth for Hawthorne": Robert Lowell, "New England and Further," *Collected Prose*, 188–91.

35 "How comes it you have": Letter from George Hillard to Nathaniel Hawthorne, March 28, 1850, cited in Edwin Haviland Miller, *Salem Is My Dwelling Place: A Life of Nathaniel Hawthorne* (Iowa City: University of Iowa Press, 1991), 8.

35 "He was earnest as a priest": Rose Hawthorne Lathrop, *Memories of Hawthorne* (Boston: Houghton Mifflin, 1897).

35 "The spirit of my Puritan ancestors": Nathaniel Hawthorne, *The English Notebooks: 1853–1856* (Columbus: Ohio State University Press, 1997), 193.

35 "It is now nearly two centuries": Nathaniel Hawthorne, *The Scarlet Letter* (1850; Oxford: Oxford University Press, 1990), 9–10.

35 "The wrong-doing of one generation": Nathaniel Hawthorne, *The House of the Seven Gables* (1851; New York: Bantam, 1981), vii.

36 "might be drawn": Ibid., 2.

36 "As a man-of-war that sails": Herman Melville, *White-Jacket, or The World in a Man-of-War* (1850; Oxford: Oxford University Press, 1990), 402–3.

36 "I never thought it an abatement": James Russell Lowell, "New England Two Centuries Ago," *The Writings of James Russell Lowell*, vol. 2 (Cambridge, MA: Riverside Press, 1892), 21.

36 "I know of no other thinker": Eulogy for Nathaniel Hawthorne given by the Reverend James Freeman Clarke, March 23, 1864, reported in the Boston *Evening Transcript*, May 24, 1864.

37 "It was then": Robert Lowell, "New England and Further," *Collected Prose*, 190.

37 "Hawthorne died depressed": Ibid.

37 "hard / survivor's smile": Robert Lowell, "Hawthorne," *Collected Poems*, 352.

37 "Even this shy distrustful ego": Ibid., 351. The last verse of "Hawthorne" closely follows the text of Hawthorne's *Septimius Felton*. "Let him alone a moment or two," wrote Hawthorne, "and then they would see him, with his

head bent down, brooding, brooding, his eyes fixed on some chip, some stone, some common plant . . . [in his eyes] a kind of perplexity, a dissatisfied, foiled look in them." Nathaniel Hawthorne, *Septimius Felton*, vol. 11, *The Complete Works of Nathaniel Hawthorne*, ed. George Parsons Lathrop (Boston: Houghton Mifflin, 1883), 232.

37 "had never frowned down": Robert Lowell, "91 Revere Street," *Collected Prose*, 343–44.

37 Norman Mailer: Lowell's friend Robert Fitzgerald said that "by far the best portrait of him" was in Mailer's *The Armies of the Night*. Lowell's daughter, Harriet, described Mailer's portrayal as "capturing the essence somehow, probably better than anything else." Lowell told V. S. Naipaul that Mailer's "description of me is one of the best things ever written about me, and most generous." V. S. Naipaul, "Et in America Ego—The American Poet Robert Lowell Talks to the Novelist V. S. Naipaul," *Listener* 82 (September 4, 1969): 303.

37 "The hollows in his cheeks": Norman Mailer, *The Armies of the Night*, 33.

38 "Lowell's shoulders had a slump": Ibid., 44.

38 "Robert Lowell gave off at times": Ibid., 83.

39 "Lowell was at the mercy": Ibid.

39 long-buried Neolithic village: Evan Mackie, *Science and Society in Prehistoric Britain* (London: Elek, 1977); Colin Renfrew, ed., *The Prehistory of Orkney BC 4000–1000 AD* (Edinburgh: Edinburgh University Press, 1985); William P. L. Thomson, *History of Orkney* (Edinburgh: Mercat Press, 1987); Anna Ritchie, *Prehistoric Orkney* (London: B. T. Batsford/Historic Scotland, 1995).

39 "a few ambiguous scratches": George Mackay Brown, *An Orkney Tapestry* (London: Victor Gollancz, 1969), 18: "There are a few ambiguous scratches on a wall at Skara Brae. We wander clueless through immense tracts of time. Imagination stirs about a scattered string of bone beads found in Skara Brae. Did the girl have no time for adornment when a westerly gale choked the doors with sand; or did sea raiders tear them from her neck?"

40 spoke often of her Orkney blood: Ferris Greenslet in his biography of James Russell Lowell writes, "Mrs. Lowell possessed much of the wild beauty of the people of these windy northern isles, and her mind showed an irresistible tendency toward their poetic occultism. This tendency became irretrievably fixed by a visit which she made to the Orkneys in company with her husband early in their married life. Thenceforward until 1842, when her tense brain became disordered, she was a faerie-seer, credited by some with second sight." Ferris Greenslet, *James Russell Lowell: His Life and Work* (Boston: Houghton Mifflin, 1905), 9.

40 She was descended, she said: Edward Wagenknecht, *James Russell Lowell.*

40 Sir Patrick Spens: "Haf owre, haf owre to Aberdour, / It's fiftie fadom deip, / And their lies guid Sir Patrick Spence, / Wi the Scots lords at his feit." *The Oxford Book of Scottish Verse*, ed. John MacQueen and Tom Scott (Oxford: Oxford University Press, 1975), 284.

41 "Time, that used to drive": Letter from Keith Spence to Mary Traill Spence, January 25, 1804, Spence-Lowell Collection, Huntington Library, box 3.

42 "a lowness of spirits": Letter from Keith Spence to Mary Traill Spence, July 1, 1805, Spence-Lowell Collection, Huntington Library, Box 3. Spence wrote earlier to her of his "indolent lowness of spirits which lands on me," June 26, 1803, Spence-Lowell Collection, Huntington Library, box 3.

42 "the absolute force of necessity": Letter from Keith Spence to Mary Traill Spence, July 26, 1803, Spence-Lowell Collection, Huntington Library, box 3.

42 "There are circumstances and situations": Letter from Keith Spence to Mary Traill Spence, December 23, 1799, Spence-Lowell Collection, Huntington Library, box 2.

42 "must support Serenity": Letter from Keith Spence to Mary Traill Spence, September 18, 1797, Spence-Lowell Collection, Huntington Library, box 1.

42 "I shudder at your past Indisposition": Letter from Keith Spence to Mary Traill Spence, November 21, 1797, Spence-Lowell Collection, Huntington Library, box 1.

42 "perturbations" of her nerves: Letter from Mary Traill Spence to Keith Spence, November 5, 1807, Spence-Lowell Collection, Huntington Library, box 4.

42 "each year, each month": Letter from Mary Traill Spence to Harriet Brackett Spence Lowell, February 21, 1807, James Russell Lowell Papers, Houghton Library.

42 "sinks me to the grave": Ibid.

42 "renders me totally incapable": Ibid.

42 "This must not be seen": Letter from Mary Traill Spence to Harriet Brackett Spence Lowell, March 13, 1807, Spence-Lowell Collection, Huntington Library, box 4.

42 "She is I think quite recovered": Letter from Dr. Joshua Brackett to Robert Traill, July 3, 1781, Spence-Lowell Collection, Huntington Library, box 1.

42 "for a long time past been much impaired": Petition of Mary Traill to New Hampshire General Court, June 12, 1781, New Hampshire State Archives.

43 "Nervous drops": Bill from Dr. Robert Forbes to Robert Traill for medical services, December 22, 1784, Houghton Library, bMS Am 1832.

43 "extreme volatility of Temper": Letter from Keith Spence to Mary Traill Spence, November 21, 1797, Spence-Lowell Papers, Huntington Library, box 1.

43 "extraordinary state of mind": Letter from Keith Spence to Mary Traill Spence, October 17, 1808, Spence-Lowell Papers, Huntington Library, box 4.

43 "to rouse him from his poetic Dreams": Ibid.

43 "What could put Poetry in his head?": Ibid.

43 "a good writer": Obituary of Captain Robert Traill Spence, *The Critic*, October 10, 1891. The paper noted that the commission papers for Robert Traill Spence had been signed by Thomas Jefferson and that he "rose very rapidly in the Navy." Carroll Spence Papers, Georgetown University Library, box 2, folder 11.

43 "an elegant scholar": Obituary for Captain Robert Traill Spence, Carroll Spence Papers, Georgetown University Library, box 2, folder 12.

44 "All three were high-strung": Ferris Greenslet, *The Lowells and Their Seven Worlds* (Boston: Houghton Mifflin, 1946), 87.

44 "I have in a very considerable degree": Ibid., 121.

44 "perfectly incapacitates": Ibid., 176.

44 periods of ferocious energy: Ibid., 125.

45 "like all Lowell men": Letter from Keith Spence to Mary Traill Spence, August 14, 1809, Spence-Lowell Papers, Huntington Library, box 4.

45 "alarmingly excitable": Ferris Greenslet, *The Lowells and Their Seven Worlds*, 265.

46 "complete breakdown of the machine": Percival Lowell to A. E. Douglass, April 21, 1897, Lowell Observatory Archives.

46 "I am quite anxious about his condition": Letter from T. J. J. See to A. E. Douglass, September 13, 1897, Lowell Observatory Archives.

46 "nervous weakness still continues": Letter from T. J. J. See to A. E. Douglass, October 7, 1897, Lowell Observatory Archives.

46 "Dr. Lowell has not been in the office": Letter from W. Louise Leonard to V. M. Slipher, December 31, 1912, Lowell Observatory Archives.

46 "Is it not too bad that his nerves": Letter from W. Louise Leonard to V. M. Slipher, December 31, 1912, Lowell Observatory Archives.

46 "I hadn't realized his errors": Letter from Robert Lowell to Elizabeth Hardwick, July 2, 1976, *Letters*, 652.

46 "nervous exhaustion": Letter from W. Louise Leonard to T. J. J. See, December 19, 1912, Lowell Observatory Archives. "Dr. Lowell has been housed now for two months with nervous exhaustion but is, I am happy to say, well mending now."

47 "Breadth of mind": Percival Lowell, *Mars as the Abode of Life* (New York: Macmillan, 1908), 184.

47 "Not the possible, but the impossible": Louise Leonard, *Percival Lowell: An Afterglow* (Boston: Gorham, 1921), 41.

47 "A pioneer should have imagination": Willa Cather, *O Pioneers!* (1913; New York: Penguin, 1989), 15.

47 a bleak view: Percival Lowell wrote, "But though we cannot as yet review with the mind's eye our past, we can, to an extent, foresee our future. We can with scientific confidence look forward to a time when each of the bodies composing the solar system shall turn an unchanging face in perpetuity to the Sun. Each will then have reached the end of its evolution, set in the unchanging stare of death.

"Then the sun itself will go out, becoming a cold and lifeless mass; and the solar system will circle unseen, ghostlike, in space, awaiting only the resurrection of another cosmic catastrophe." Percival Lowell, *The Solar System: Six Lectures Delivered at the Massachusetts Institute of Technology* (Boston: Houghton Mifflin, 1903), 134.

48 "hum outliving the hushed bell": James Russell Lowell, "The Darkened Mind," in *The Complete Poetical Works of James Russell Lowell*, 427.

48 "the patron and encourager": Quoted in Leon Howard, *Victorian Knight-Errant: A Study of the Early Literary Career of James Russell Lowell* (Berkeley and Los Angeles: University of California Press, 1952), 56.

48 "morbid excitements": Letter from James Russell Lowell to Charles Frederick

Briggs, February 15, 1854, in *Letters of James Russell Lowell*, ed. Charles Eliot Norton (New York: Harper & Brothers, 1893).

48 "my dear Mother's malady": Letter from James Russell Lowell to Lily Norton, quoted in Edward Wagenknecht, *James Russell Lowell*, 50.

48 "everything is dreary": Ibid.

48 As a young man, suicidal: Lowell said he thought "of my razors and my throat and that I am a fool and a coward not to end it all at once." Quoted in Wilson Sullivan, *New England Men of Letters* (New York: Macmillan, 1972), 213.

48 he had put a pistol to his head: Quoted in Edward Wagenknecht, *James Russell Lowell*, 50–51, 192, 206.

48 "The drop of black blood": James Russell Lowell, quoted in Edward Wagenknecht, *James Russell Lowell*, 75.

48 "How shall a man escape": Ralph Waldo Emerson, "Fate," 311.

48 "We had some toughness": James Russell Lowell, "An Interview with Miles Standish," *Collected Poetical Works*, 82.

48 "They talk about their Pilgrim blood": Ibid., 82.

48 "In one sense it matters very little": Letter from James Russell Lowell to Lady Lyttleton, February 20, 1888, *Letters of James Russell Lowell*.

48 "I envy his strenuous grace": Robert Lowell, "New England and Further," *Collected Prose*, 196.

49 referred to her as "mad": Letter from Fanny Longfellow to Thomas Appleton, February 1866, quoted in Martin Duberman, *James Russell Lowell* (New York: Houghton Mifflin, 1966), 436.

49 "I broke down": Robert Traill Spence Lowell, statement for *Memorials of the Class of 1833, Prepared for the Fiftieth Anniversary of Their Graduation*, ed. Waldo Higginson (Cambridge, MA: John Wilson and Son, 1883), 129.

49 "the setting of my Grandfather's": Letter from Robert Lowell to Peter Taylor, n.d. 1969, *Letters*, 512.

49 "His poetry is forgotten": Harold Blodgett, "Robert Traill Spence Lowell," *New England Quarterly* 16 (1943): 589.

49 "he was unquestionably": Ibid., 578.

49 "tame and honorable": Robert Lowell, "91 Revere Street," *Collected Prose*, 310.

50 "at each stage of his life": Ibid., 315.

51 a direct descendant: Tradition, although not historians, has it that the thirteen-year-old Mary Chilton (1607–79) was the first female to wade ashore at Plymouth, following in the slightly quicker footsteps of her fellow passenger John Alden. She married John Winslow, a passenger on the *Fortune*, which had sailed to Plymouth the year after the *Mayflower*; together they had ten children. Winslow, a merchant in the fast-growing town of Boston, was at the time of his death one of Boston's wealthiest men.

  John and Mary Chilton Winslow were active citizens in colonial New England and in 1671 joined the Third Church (Old South), a prominent church in Boston's history. In 1703 Benjamin Franklin was baptized there and, seventy years later, Samuel Adams, a congregant, shouted the signal from the Old South Meeting House to trigger the Boston Tea Party.

From its pulpit in 1677, the only Puritan judge to recant his part in the Salem witch trials stood to bear witness to the "blame and shame" of his actions. The Puritan grip on New England history was a driving force in early Boston and, nearly three hundred years later, in the creative life of Robert Lowell. It was a history rich in metaphoric complexity and stark in the use and abuse of moral authority; Lowell drew upon this from his youth until his death.

When John and Mary Chilton Winslow died they were buried in the Puritan burial ground of King's Chapel in Boston, the first Anglican church in New England, said to have softened "the hard manners and customs of the Puritans." As in many colonial churches the congregation of King's Chapel was deeply divided in the years leading up to the Revolutionary War. Thirty of its seventy-three pews were occupied by Loyalists to the king and forty-three by those of the "Patriotic, or American Party." (Paul Revere cast the bell that to this day summons parishioners to worship. The bell, Revere said, "was the sweetest bell we ever made.") The division within church congregations affected the Winslow family, some of whom were Loyalists and lost their property in the war; other Winslows returned to England rather than support the break from Britain.

51 *Mourt's Relation*: *Mourt's Relation: A Journal of the Pilgrims at Plymouth*, ed. Dwight B. Heath (Bedford, MA: Applewood, 1963). Edited from the original text of 1622. The principal author is assumed to be Edward Winslow, with assistance from William Bradford.

51 *Of Plymouth Plantation*: William Bradford, *Of Plymouth Plantation: 1620–1647*, ed. Samuel Eliot Morison (New York: Knopf, 1996).

51 "They fell amongst dangerous shoals": Ibid., 60.

53 "We are well weaned": Ibid., 33.

53 "cry of the heart": Perry Miller, *The American Puritans: Their Prose and Poetry* (New York: Columbia University Press, 1956), 213.

53 "The land was ours": Robert Frost, "The Gift Outright," *The Poetry of Robert Frost: The Collected Poems*, ed. Edward Connery Lathem (New York: Henry Holt, 1979), 348. For an anthology put together by George Santayana, Lowell recommended two poems by Robert Frost, "The Gift Outright" and "Acquainted with the Night." Letter from Robert Lowell to George Santayana, May 20, 1948, *Letters*, 100.

53 "One small candle": William Bradford, *Of Plymouth Plantation*, 236.

54 "We shall find that the God of Israel": John Winthrop, lay sermon delivered before sailing, or on the deck of the *Arbella* during its crossing to New England, March 1630.

54 "no people's account": Peter Bulkeley, "The Lesson of the Covenant, for England and New England," in Perry Miller, *The American Puritans*, 151.

54 "Wickedness did grow and break forth": William Bradford, *Of Plymouth Plantation*, 316.

54 "It is now a part of my misery": Ibid., 33.

54 Few countries had had such an advantage: Ibid., 123. Bradford quotes William Hubbard's contemporary *History of New England*, which was written before 1683 but not published until 1815.

54 "What had been a wondrous": James Russell Lowell, "New England Two Centuries Ago," 12.

55 "could not renew the fiery gush": Ibid., 7.

55 "It is time we had done": Henry David Thoreau, *The Journal of Henry D. Thoreau*, ed. Bradford Torrey and Francis H. Allen (Boston: Houghton Mifflin, 1906), entry for June 16, 1854.

55 "As there are certain creatures": James Russell Lowell, "New England Two Centuries Ago," 12–13.

55 "A century passes": Robert Lowell, "New England and Further," *Collected Prose*, 182–83.

55 Their descendants were many: One of the direct descendants of Edward Winslow, a member of the branch of the Winslows that lost their property during the Revolutionary War and returned to England, Forbes Benignus Winslow (1810–74), was a physician who wrote one of the first and most influential books in English about suicide. In his *Anatomy of Suicide*, he forcefully argued that suicide was the result of mental disease, not moral or criminal defect. His text discussed the physical and psychological causes of suicide, statistics, suicide's relationship to "the enthusiasm exhibited by men of great genius . . . an unhealthy exercise of the imaginative faculty," seasonal patterns of suicide, and prevention. Winslow brought compassion and rigor to a morally fraught topic. Forbes Benignus Winslow, *The Anatomy of Suicide* (London: Henry Renshaw, 1840), 121. In his lectures as the Lettsonian Professor of Medicine of the Medical Society of London, he stated that he had "carefully, scrupulously, and jealously analyzed no less than 10,000 cases of the various shades and degrees of insanity." He was amazed, he asserted to his medical colleagues, that there "ever could have existed a shadow of a doubt as to the physical origin of insanity." Forbes Benignus Winslow, *Lettsonian Lectures on Insanity* (London: John Churchill, 1854), 53–54.

Forbes Winslow also studied, treated, and wrote about acute mania, a particularly dangerous condition in a time before effective sedating medication was available. He prescribed bloodletting, as was not uncommon in the nineteenth century, but "cautious depletion," not the more extreme bloodletting used in many asylums. He ordered prolonged hot baths, eight to fifteen hours at a time, as well, and tincture of digitalis, hydrochlorate of morphia, and soaking mixtures of henbane, hemlock, and cherry laurel leaves. Throughout his long years of practice with the insane he retained the capacity to observe closely, keep an intelligent sympathy, and write up his findings for science.

4. THIS DYNAMITED BROOK

57 "Resistance to something": Henry Adams, *The Education of Henry Adams*, 7.

57 "I grew up as an only child": Robert Lowell, essay written for Vernon Williams, M.D., n.d. 1950s, Robert Lowell Papers, HRC, box 20.8.

58 "Is there no way to cast": Robert Lowell, "The Drunken Fisherman," *Collected Poems*, 35.

58 Dynamite, a word: For example; "I dwindle . . . dynamite no more" ("Death of a Critic"); "dynamite his way to the gold again" ("Phillips House Revisited"); "Past your gray, sorry and ancestral house / where the dynamited walnut tree" ("The Exile's Return").

58 "haughtiness and chilliness": Robert Lowell, "91 Revere Street," *Collected Prose*, 330.

58 "There was iron in the air": Robert Lowell, "Washington, D.C. 1924," Houghton Library, Robert Lowell Papers, Houghton Library, Ms Am 1905, 2221.

58 "What Bobby needs": Ibid.

58 "taking brisk walks": Robert Lowell, "Antebellum," *Collected Prose*, 300.

58 "The patient states": Robert Lowell's medical record, Massachusetts Mental Health Center, 1957.

58 "He was an unwanted child": Psychological evaluation of Robert Lowell, Judge Baker Clinic, Boston, January 21, 1937, HRC.

59 "'You know'": Robert Lowell, "Unwanted," *Collected Poems*, 832.

59 "Mother, / I must not blame": Ibid., 833.

59 "all his life consciously rebelled": Robert Lowell's medical records, Payne Whitney Clinic, 1949.

59 He had refused to learn: Ibid.

59 "was not to be mastered": Ibid., 1954.

59 Mania, he told his doctor: Ibid.

60 "Charlotte was a Snow Queen": John Thompson, "Robert Lowell, 1917–1977," *New York Review of Books*, October 27, 1977, 14.

60 "a monstrous woman": Blair Clark, interview with Ian Hamilton, 1979, Ian Hamilton Papers, British Library.

60 "Mrs. Hideous": Jean Stafford, letter to Caroline and Allen Tate, n.d., 1943, Princeton.

60 "all the joy goes out of": Elizabeth Hardwick to Robie and Anne Macauley, n.d. February 1953, HRC.

60 "In general Mrs. L.": Letter from Elizabeth Hardwick to Ian Hamilton about his biography of Robert Lowell, Elizabeth Hardwick Papers, HRC.

60 "The thing about the Lowells": Elizabeth Hardwick's notes on C. David Heymann's book *American Aristocracy: The Lives and Times of James Russell, Amy, and Robert Lowell* (New York: Dodd, Mead, 1980), Elizabeth Hardwick Papers, HRC.

60 "Mother had lately been having": Robert Lowell, "Washington, D.C. 1924," Autobiographical Prose, Houghton Library, 2221.

60 In 1957 he told his doctor: Robert Lowell's medical records, Massachusetts Mental Health Center, 1957.

60 "She went into a hypnotic trance": Letter from Merrill Moore, M.D., to Donald Macpherson, M.D., March 23, 1937, Merrill Moore, M.D., files, Robert Lowell Papers, HRC.

60 "I think that she can become": Letter from Merrill Moore, M.D., to Arlie Bock, M.D., April 1, 1937, Merrill Moore, M.D., files, Robert Lowell Papers, HRC.

61 Lowell's father was sufficiently concerned: Notes from Robert Lowell, Sr., to

Merrill Moore, M.D., March 25, 1937, Merrill Moore, M.D., files, Robert Lowell Papers, HRC.

61 "she came to": Letter from Merrill Moore, M.D., to Donald Macpherson, M.D., March 23, 1937, Merrill Moore, M.D., files, Robert Lowell Papers, HRC.

61 "slightly manic": Psychotherapy record of Charlotte Lowell, March 8, 1937, medical records of Merrill Moore, M.D., Robert Lowell Papers, HRC, box 19.1.

61 "How does your patient": Shakespeare, *Macbeth*, act 5, scene 3, Folger edition.

62 "Has Byrnam Woods": Charlotte Lowell, undated manuscript given to Merrill Moore, M.D., Merrill Moore, M.D., files, Robert Lowell Papers, HRC.

62 habits of the French emperor: Robert Lowell, "1916," Autobiographical Prose, Houghton Library, 2209.

62 "learned how to lead her father": Robert Lowell, "Antebellum Boston," *Collected Prose*, 297.

63 "a mania about Napoleon": William Healy, M.D., report on Robert Lowell, Judge Baker Guidance Center, January 21, 1937 (summary of Dr. Healy's earlier observations, made in December 1932), Merrill Moore, M.D., files, Robert Lowell Papers, HRC.

63 "And I, bristling": Robert Lowell, "Commander Lowell: (1887–1950)," *Collected Poems*, 172.

63 "for uprooting races": Robert Lowell, "Napoleon," *Collected Poems*, 474.

63 "Cal came down and sat": Correspondence from Jonathan Raban to author, October 21, 2016.

64 "was half orphaned": Robert Lowell, "Robert T. S. Lowell," *Collected Poems*, 791.

64 "His ivory slide rule": Robert Lowell, "Near the Unbalanced Aquarium," *Collected Prose*, 356.

64 "life had opened out": Robert Lowell, Autobiographical Prose, "The Balanced Aquarium," draft 6, Houghton Library, 2226.

64 "buccaneer imagination": Ibid.

64 "were afraid of his heart condition": Ibid.

64 "Why doesn't he fight back?": Robert Lowell's medical records, Payne Whitney Clinic, 1949.

64 "In his forties": Robert Lowell, "91 Revere Street," *Collected Prose*, 316.

64 "Mrs. Lowell,": Elizabeth Hardwick, interview with Ian Hamilton, November 21, 1979, Ian Hamilton Papers, British Library.

64 "a bit frightened": Ibid.

65 "constantly belittled": Robert Lowell medical records, Payne Whitney Clinic, 1949.

65 "affectionate, but distant": Ibid., 1954.

65 "gentle and considerate": Ibid.

65 "quiet and humorous": Robert Lowell medical records, Massachusetts Mental Health Center, 1957.

65 "I was like Father": Robert Lowell medical records, Payne Whitney Clinic, 1954.

65 "We were all born": Robert Lowell, "Rock," Autobiographical Prose, Houghton Library, 2220.

65 "inattentive languor": Robert Lowell, "The Balanced Aquarium," "At Payne Whitney," Autobiographical Prose, Houghton Library, 2226–28.

65 "suffering or heroic man": Letter from Robert Lowell to Elizabeth Bishop, September 18, 1950, Letters, 159.

65 "I think you would like": Letter from Robert Lowell, Sr., to Robert Lowell, October 16, 1949, Houghton Library.

66 "I liked the way": Letter from Robert Lowell, Sr., to Robert Lowell, December 26, 1949, Houghton Library.

66 "Talking with Daddy": Robert Lowell, "Washington, D.C. 1924," Autobiographical Prose, Houghton Library, 2221.

66 "Somehow it's hard": Letter from Robert Lowell to Elizabeth Bishop, June 27, 1961, Letters, 383.

66 "At forty-five": Robert Lowell, "Middle Age," Collected Poems, 325.

67 "I think, though I didn't": Robert Lowell, "To Daddy," Collected Poems, 513.

67 "There were no tickets for": Robert Lowell, "Beyond the Alps," Collected Poems, 114.

67 "I picked with a clean finger nail": Robert Lowell, "My Last Afternoon with Uncle Devereux Winslow," Collected Poems, 165–66.

68 "doing very poor work": William Healy, M.D., report on Robert Lowell, Judge Baker Guidance Center, January 21, 1937 (summary of Dr. Healy's earlier observations, made in December 1932), Merrill Moore, M.D., files, Robert Lowell Papers, HRC.

68 repetitively rocked himself back and forth: Charlotte Winslow Lowell's descriptions of Lowell's behavior as a young child are contained in several letters and reports to Merrill Moore, M.D., November 24 and 26, 1936, Merrill Moore, M.D., files, Robert Lowell Papers, HRC.

68 "On the top floor": Robert Lowell, "Antebellum Boston," Collected Prose, 300.

68 creativity and intelligence often diverge: For a review of the relationship between intelligence and creativity, see E. Jauk, M. Benedek, B. Dunst, and A. C. Neubauer, "The Relationship Between Intelligence and Creativity: New Support for the Threshold Hypothesis by Means of Empirical Breakdown Detection," Intelligence 41 (July 2013): 212–21.

68 The gap between: For a review of the clinical and scientific literature, see F. K. Goodwin and K. R. Jamison, Manic-Depressive Illness.

68 "reticent, unwilling to face": Judge Baker Guidance Center report, December 1932, HRC.

69 "We are having trouble": Medical files of Merrill Moore, M.D., November 24, 1936, Robert Lowell Papers, HRC.

69 "We tried to explain": Ibid.

69 "I always thought that Bobby": Ibid., 1936.

70 "He returned home": Ibid.

71 "terrible temper tantrums": Ibid.

71 "Mentally or verbally": Robert Lowell, "Antebellum Boston," *Collected Prose*, 304.

71 "early stage of a psychosis": Medical files of Merrill Moore, M.D., November 26, 1936, Robert Lowell Papers, HRC.

71 "something of a genius": Letter from Merrill Moore, M.D., to the Guggenheim Foundation recommending Lowell for a fellowship, February 13, 1937, HRC. On January 13, 1938, Moore wrote to Charlotte Lowell, "More and more I am convinced that he is a man of genius and that we will just have to adjust to him as he is." On December 28, 1938, Moore wrote to Charlotte Lowell, "He has no smile in him. He is sincere, honest, simple, easily influenced. He has poor judgment and doesn't think clearly but with all these things he has in him a spark of genius which must be sheltered from cold blasts . . . . Your charge from now on becomes very clear. It is to protect and nourish a genius . . . . A perfectly normally extroverted male." Medical files of Merrill Moore, M.D., Robert Lowell Papers, HRC.

73 "He glowered apelike": Medical files of Merrill Moore, M.D., December 26, 1936, Robert Lowell Papers, HRC.

73 "I have been churning": Letter from Robert Lowell to Robert T. S. Lowell, March 4, 1937, *Letters*, 13-14.

74 "There was rebellion": Robert Lowell, "Rebellion," *Collected Poems*, 32.

74 "myself brooding": Robert Lowell, "Charles River," *Notebook 1967-68* (New York: Farrar, Straus and Giroux, 1969), 37.

74 "I struck my father": Ibid.

74 "Father, forgive me": Robert Lowell, "Middle Age," *Collected Poems*, 325.

75 "gentle, faithful, and dim man": Robert Lowell, "Near the Unbalanced Aquarium," *Collected Prose*, 363.

75 "I hope there will be peace": Ibid.

75 "Tell me what I saw": Robert Lowell, "Caligula," *Collected Poems*, 360.

75 "I have come to realize": Letter from Robert Lowell to Richard Eberhart, July 10, 1935, Dartmouth College Library.

75 "that he always forgives": Letter from Robert Lowell to Richard Eberhart, August 1935, Dartmouth College Library.

76 "Sometimes, when we are": Robert Lowell, "Grass stroke," ca. 1936, Miscellaneous Prose, Houghton Library, 2790.

76 "When I woke up and lay": Ibid.

76 "a sense of grandeur": Letter from James B. Munn to Robert Lowell, Sr., ca. 1935, Merrill Moore, M.D., files, Robert Lowell Papers, HRC.

76 "The honor of earning": Letter from Robert Lowell to Charlotte Lowell and Robert T. S. Lowell, August 9, 1936, *Letters*, 10.

76 "My vocation is writing": Robert Lowell to Charlotte Lowell, July 5, 1937, Houghton Library.

76 "I have no doubt": Letter from Robert Lowell to Richard Eberhart, n.d. summer 1937, *Letters*, 18.

76 Boston newspapers: *Boston Evening Traveller*, December 21, 1938.

76 "We are dealing with a boy who has": Letter from Merrill Moore, M.D., to

Charlotte Lowell, February 17, 1938, Merrill Moore, M.D., files, Robert Lowell Papers, HRC.

77 "The longer I know Cal": Ibid.

77 "It is my opinion": Letter from Merrill Moore, M.D., to John Crowe Ransom, April 21, 1937, files, Robert Lowell Papers, HRC.

77 "tight, compact, difficult": Letter from Merrill Moore, M.D., to Charlotte Winslow Lowell, January 13, 1938, Merrill Moore, M.D., files, Robert Lowell Papers, HRC.

77 "It looks as if our future job": Letter from Merrill Moore to Charlotte Lowell, January 24, 1938, Merrill Moore, M.D., files, Robert Lowell Papers, HRC.

77 "I can well understand": Letter from Charlotte Lowell to Robert Lowell, October 22, 1949, Houghton Library. Lowell was at the time hospitalized at the Payne Whitney Clinic.

78 "Nothing could have given": Letter from Charlotte Winslow Lowell to Robert Lowell, March 25, 1951, Houghton Library.

78 "Time is so final": Letter from Charlotte Winslow Lowell to Robert Lowell, March 1, 1951, Houghton Library.

78 "Most of our lives were weighed": Letter from Robert Lowell to Ezra Pound, March 20, 1954, *Letters*, 222.

78 "It has taken me": Robert Lowell, "To Mother," *Collected Poems*, 790.

78 "Stand and live": Robert Lowell, "Where the Rainbow Ends," *Collected Poems*, 69.

79 "She kept trying": Robert Lowell, "Near the Unbalanced Aquarium," *Collected Prose*, 349.

79 "black and gold baroque casket": Ibid., 350.

79 "was breaking into fiery flower": Ibid.

79 "Mother, permanently sealed": Ibid.

79 "shone in her bridal tinfoil": Ibid.

79 "While the passengers": Robert Lowell, "Sailing Home from Rapallo (February 1954)," *Collected Poems*, 179–80.

80 "The wheel is broken": Robert Lowell, "New England," Poems 1935, Houghton Library, 2042. It is written in Ecclesiastes 12:6–7, "Or ever the silver cord be loosed, or the golden bowl be broken, or the pitcher be broken at the foundation, or the wheel broken at the cistern. Then shall dust return to the earth as it was: and the spirit shall return unto God who gave it."

5. A BRACKISH REACH

81 "the bough": Robert Lowell, "After the Surprising Conversions," *Collected Poems*, 62.

81 "plains of treeless farmland": Robert Lowell, "Visiting the Tates," *Collected Prose*, 58.

81 "I was Northern": Ibid., 59.

81 "Like a torn cat": Ibid., 60.

82 "Lowell is more than a student": Cited in Ian Hamilton, *Robert Lowell*, 72. Hamilton gives his source as Hamilton's interview with Peter Taylor, 1980.

82 "I often doubt": Robert Lowell to John Crowe Ransom, December 8, 1961, Chalmers Memorial Library, Kenyon College.

82 "How sad and serious": Peter Taylor, "1939," *The Collected Stories of Peter Taylor* (New York: Farrar, Straus and Giroux, 1969), 336–37.

82 "Monday I graduated": Letter from Robert Lowell to Charlotte and Robert Lowell, Sr., n.d. June 1940, *Letters*, 29.

82 "he kept saying": Letter from Jean Stafford to William Mock, November 27, 1938, Dartmouth College Library.

83 "I had the tongue of an adder": Jean Stafford, "An Influx of Poets," *The New Yorker*, November 6, 1978.

83 "an uncouth, neurotic": Letter from Jean Stafford to William Mock, November 27, 1938, Dartmouth College Library.

83 "Jean is mysterious": Letter from Robert Lowell to Peter Taylor, December 4, 1946, *Letters*, 59.

83 "thrown almost into a psychosis": January 1, 1939, Merrill Moore, M.D., files, Robert Lowell Papers, HRC.

83 "hypomanic happiness": Ibid.

84 "'Then I was wide'": Robert Lowell, "The Mills of the Kavanaughs," *Collected Poems*, 83.

84 "the blue of morning": Robert Lowell, "The Mills of the Kavanaughs," *Kenyon Review* 12 (1951); 1–39.

85 "vast, valuable museum": Elizabeth Hardwick, interview with Darryl Pinckney, "The Art of Fiction No. 87," *Paris Review* 96 (Summer 1985).

85 "I was born a non-believing Protestant": Robert Lowell, "A Conversation with Ian Hamilton," *Collected Prose*, 277.

85 "Though his immediate ancestors": "Robert Lowell: 1917–1977," no author, n.d., 5-page typed manuscript, HRC.

85 "I remember well": Letter from Robert Lowell to Bishop Maurice Schexnayder, February 13, 1977, *Letters*, 664.

86 "When I first married": Robert Lowell to Vernon Williams, M.D., n.d. 1950s, Robert Lowell Papers, HRC.

86 "It's what he's been destined for": Letter from Peter Taylor to Robie Macaulay, March 1941, Vanderbilt.

87 "veritable messiah": Letter from Jean Stafford to James Hightower, September 9, 1941, University of Colorado.

87 "I think becoming a Catholic": Robert Lowell, "An Interview with Frederick Seidel," *Collected Prose*, 258.

87 "In a day when poets aspire": Randall Jarrell, "Poetry in War and Peace," *Partisan Review* 12 (Winter 1945): 125.

87 "Members of my family": Robert Lowell, public letter to President Roosevelt, September 7, 1943, *Collected Prose*, 367–70.

88 "These are the tranquillized *Fifties*": Robert Lowell, "Memories of West Street and Lepke," *Collected Poems*, 187.

88 "No one," he wrote: Letter from Robert Lowell to Peter Taylor, October 11, 1943, *Letters*, 42.

89 "so fanatical": Letter from Jean Stafford to Peter Taylor, February 11, 1944, Vanderbilt.

89 "He had a terrifying seizure": Letter from Jean Stafford to Peter Taylor, July 12, 1944, Vanderbilt.

90 that were "written": Quoted in Robert Fitzgerald, "The Things of the Eye," eulogy for Robert Lowell, Harvard University, March 2, 1978, *Poetry* 132 (1978): 107.

90 "The bones cry for the blood": Robert Lowell, "The Quaker Graveyard in Nantucket," *Collected Poems*, 17.

90 "the percussion and brass section": Seamus Heaney, *The Government of the Tongue* (London: Faber & Faber, 1988), 94.

91 "I got drunker": Letter from Robert Lowell to Babette Deutsch, February 24, 1955, *Letters*, 245.

91 "Their boats were tossed": Robert Lowell, "The Quaker Graveyard in Nantucket," *Collected Poems*, 15.

91 "sea wings, beating landward": Ibid.

91 "upward angel": Ibid., 18.

91 "My desire": Henry David Thoreau, *Journal 2: 1842–1848*, ed. Robert Sattelmeyer (Princeton, NJ: Princeton University Press, 1984), 150–51.

91 "I saw many marble feet": Henry David Thoreau, *Cape Cod* (1865; New York: Penguin, 1987), 7.

91 "A brackish reach": Robert Lowell, "The Quaker Graveyard in Nantucket," *Collected Poems*, 14.

92 "If I had found one body": Henry David Thoreau, *Cape Cod*, 13.

92 "I do set my bow": Genesis 9:13.

92 "The waters shall no more become": Genesis 9:15.

92 "You could cut the brackish winds": Robert Lowell, "The Quaker Graveyard in Nantucket," *Collected Poems*, 18.

III. ILLNESS: THE KINGDOM OF THE MAD

95 "At last the trees": Robert Lowell, "Man and Wife," *Collected Poems*, 189.

6. IN FLIGHT, WITHOUT A LEDGE

97 "Getting out of the flats": Letter from Robert Lowell to Theodore Roethke, June 6, 1958, University of Washington Libraries.

97 "used up": Jean Stafford, quoted in Ian Hamilton, *Robert Lowell*, 121.

97 "merely used the Church": Letter from Allen Tate to Peter Taylor, April 10, 1949, Vanderbilt.

97 "When I came on": Letter from Robert Lowell to George Santayana, February 1, 1951, *Letters*, 167.

98 "I recognize that your center": Letter from George Santayana to Robert Lowell, March 1, 1951, Houghton Library.

98 "more distinguished activity": John Cheever, quoted in Ben Alexander, "The Yaddo Records: How an Institutional Archive Reveals Creative Insights," *English Studies in America* 30 (March 2004).

99 "run down rose gardens": Letter from Robert Lowell to Elizabeth Bishop, October 1, 1948, *Letters*, 112.

99 nine hundred lines altogether: Letter from Robert Lowell to George Santayana, November 14, 1948, *Letters*, 115.

99 "flooding up": Ibid.

99 "wound to the breaking point": Elizabeth Hardwick, interview with Ian Hamilton, 1979, Ian Hamilton Papers, British Library.

99 "I just thought": Flannery O'Connor to "A," December 16, 1955, in *The Habit of Being: Letters of Flannery O'Connor*, ed. Sally Fitzgerald (New York: Random House, 1980), 124–25.

100 "day of the Word made Flesh": Robert Fitzgerald journal, March 4, 1949, Robert Fitzgerald Papers, Beinecke Rare Book and Manuscript Library, Yale University.

102 "As soon as Cal stepped off the train": Peter Taylor, "The Art of Fiction No. 99," *Paris Review* (Fall 1987).

102 "Do you smell that?": Ibid.

102 "I had an attack of pathological enthusiasm": Robert Lowell, draft manuscript for *Life Studies*, Houghton Library.

103 "a combination of boarding school": Letter from Robert Lowell to John Thompson, [April ?] 1949, 137.

103 Baldpate Hospital: Robert Lowell was hospitalized at Baldpate Hospital in Georgetown, Massachusetts, in early April 1949 and discharged July 12, 1949. The clinical observations in the text are from the hospital summary of his stay.

103 "It went on for months": Elizabeth Hardwick, interview with Ian Hamilton, 1979, Ian Hamilton Papers, British Library.

103 "I'm in grand shape": Letter from Robert Lowell to Elizabeth Bishop, April 10, 1949, *Letters*, 135.

103 "I've been having rather tremendous": Letter from Robert Lowell to George Santayana, April 10, 1949, *Letters*, 136.

103 "I hope some one told you": Letter from Robert Lowell to William Carlos Williams, April 10, 1949, *Letters*, 137.

104 "I'm going through another Yaddo": Letter from Robert Lowell to Jean Stafford, April 10, 1949, *Letters*, 136.

104 "My trouble was that": Frank Parker, interview with Ian Hamilton, 1980, Ian Hamilton Papers, British Library.

104 electroconvulsive therapy: For efficacy studies of electroconvulsive therapy, see, for example, S. Mukherjee, H. A. Sackeim, and D. B. Schnur, "Electroconvulsive Therapy of Acute Manic Episodes: A Review of 50 Years' Experience," *American Journal of Psychiatry* 151 (1994): 169–76; UK ECT Review Group, "Efficacy and Safety of Electroconvulsive Therapy in Depressive Disorders:

A Systematic Review and Meta-Analysis," *The Lancet* 361 (2003): 799–808; B. Dierckx, W. T. Heijnen, W. W. Van Den Broek, and T. K. Birkenhager, "Efficacy of Electroconvulsive Therapy in Bipolar Versus Unipolar Major Depression: A Meta-Analysis," *Bipolar Disorders* 12 (2012): 146–50.

105 "seemed like a prolonged dream": Letter from Robert Lowell to Dorothy Pound, August 13, 1949, *Collected Letters*, 145.

105 "I'm well and about to leave": Letter from Robert Lowell to Peter Taylor, July 7, 1949, *Letters*, 142.

105 "The hospital is still": Letter from Robert Lowell to T. S. Eliot, July 25, 1949, *Letters*, 143.

106 "I think it is much too soon": Letter from Robert T. S. Lowell to Robert Lowell, July 13, 1949, Houghton Library.

106 "All he could remember": Eileen Simpson, *Poets in Their Youth: A Memoir* (New York: Macmillan, 1982), 192.

106 "The curls, the infectious chuckles": Derek Walcott, "Elizabeth Hardwick (1916–2007)," *The New York Review of Books*, January 17, 2008.

107 "Oh my *Petite*": Robert Lowell, "Man and Wife," *Collected Poems*, 189.

107 "He liked women writers": Elizabeth Hardwick, interview with Darryl Pinckney, "The Art of Fiction No. 87," *Paris Review* 96 (Summer 1985).

107 "I didn't know what I was getting into": Elizabeth Hardwick, quoted in an obituary by Christopher Lehmann-Haupt in the *New York Times*, December 4, 2007.

107 "Certainly Cal had a great influence": Ibid.

107 "quite the most thrilling": Elizabeth Hardwick, interview with Darryl Pinckney, "The Art of Fiction No. 87."

108 "*Gosh*, your visit was wonderful": Letter from Robert Lowell to Elizabeth Hardwick, July 1, 1949, *Letters*, 141.

108 "Somehow, quite soon": Elizabeth Hardwick, interview with Ian Hamilton, 1979, Ian Hamilton Papers, British Library.

108 "Before receiving electric shocks": Letter from Robert Lowell to Peter Taylor, August 6, 1949, *Letters*, 144.

108 "My 'experiences' that led": Letter from Robert Lowell to Dorothy Pound, August 13, 1949, *Letters*, 145.

109 "Nothing I can say": Letter from Robert Lowell to Gertrude Buckman, August 16, 1949, *Letters*, 145–46.

109 Payne Whitney Psychiatric Clinic: Robert Lowell was hospitalized at the Payne Whitney Clinic from September 13, 1949, until January 3, 1950. His primary psychiatrist there was Dr. John Blitzer. The clinical observations in the text are from Lowell's hospital records.

110 "Dearest, dearest": Letter from Robert Lowell to Elizabeth Hardwick, n.d. September 1949, *Letters*, 147.

110 "O Lord, how empty I am": Letter from Robert Lowell to Elizabeth Hardwick, September 20–21, 1949, *Letters*, 148.

110 "After I'd told all": Letter from Robert Lowell to Elizabeth Hardwick, September 28, 1949, *Letters*, 148.

110 "beginning to really learn": Letter from Robert Lowell to Charlotte Lowell, November 5, 1949, *Letters*, 149.

111 In two pages of notes: Notes written by Robert Lowell while hospitalized at Payne Whitney, n.d. (probably September) 1949, Robert Lowell Papers, HRC.

111 "The *mystical* experiences": Letter from Robert Lowell to George Santayana, December 22, 1949, *Letters*, 151.

111 "Much against my will": Robert Lowell, "Beyond the Alps," *Collected Poems*, 113.

111 "I'm out of my dumps": Letter from Robert Lowell to George Santayana, n.d. August 1950, *Letters*, 157.

111 "inert, gloomy, aimless": Letter from Robert Lowell to George Santayana, December 22, 1949, *Letters*, 151.

114 "With what gratitude I look back": Elizabeth Hardwick, *Sleepless Nights* (1979; New York: New York Review Books, 2001), 87.

114 "It is quiet and still": Letter from Robert Lowell to Elizabeth Bishop, November 6, 1951, *Letters*, 179.

114 "got very wound up": Elizabeth Hardwick, interview with Ian Hamilton, 1979, Ian Hamilton Papers, British Library.

115 "All the faculty": Shepherd Brooks, interview with Ian Hamilton, 1980, Ian Hamilton Papers, British Library.

115 "It was extraordinary": Ibid.

115 "I pity Cal": Letter from Elizabeth Hardwick to Robie and Anne Macauley, August 24, 1952, HRC.

116 "terrified of such a thing": Letter from Elizabeth Hardwick to Robie and Anne Macauley, September 1952, HRC.

116 "'Oh mama, mama'": Robert Lowell, "A Mad Negro Soldier Confined at Munich," *Collected Poems*, 118.

116 "very mild repetition": Letter from Robert Lowell to Charlotte Lowell, October 19, 1952, *Letters*, 191–92.

116 "Cal's recuperative powers": Undated later from Elizabeth Hardwick to Ian Hamilton, Hardwick Papers, HRC.

118 "He was in the early stages": Blair Clark, interview with Ian Hamilton, 1980, Ian Hamilton Papers, British Library.

118 "I know you worry": Letter from Robert Lowell to Elizabeth Hardwick, February 17, 1954, *Letters*, 211.

119 Funeral mania: D. Lagache, "Deuil maniaque," *La Semaine des Hôpitaux de Paris*, January 15, 1938; G. A. Rickarby, "Four Cases of Mania Associated with Bereavement," *Journal of Nervous and Mental Disease* 165 (1977): 255–62; K. R. Krishnan, "Funeral Mania in Recurrent Bipolar Affective Disorders: Reports of Three Cases," *Journal of Clinical Psychiatry* 45 (1984): 310–11; R. M. Berlin, G. R. Donovan, and R. C. Guerette, "Funeral Mania and Lithium Prophylaxis," *Journal of Clinical Psychiatry* 46 (1985): 111.

119 "completely deranged": Elizabeth Hardwick to Blair Clark, n.d. March 1954, HRC.

119 "The blow will always fall": Letter from Elizabeth Hardwick to Blair and Holly Clark, April 6, 1954, HRC.

119 "I can't say": Letter from Elizabeth Hardwick to Blair Clark, April 1, 1954, HRC.

119 "tactless Yankee comments": Mary Jarrell, ed., *Randall Jarrell's Letters* (Boston: Houghton Mifflin, 1985), 395.

119 "So that's what it was": Ibid.

119 "Cal is definitely": Letter from Elizabeth Hardwick to Blair Clark, April 4, 1954, HRC.

119 "if he asked for a knife": Letter from Elizabeth Hardwick to Peter and Eleanor Taylor, April 11, 1954, Vanderbilt.

120 "One of the difficulties": Letter from Elizabeth Hardwick to Blair Clark, April 1, 1954, Elizabeth Hardwick Papers, HRC.

120 "His manic passion": Jonathan Raban interview with the author, June 20, 2012.

120 "encouraged by people": Letter from Robert Giroux to Charles Monteith, July 9, 1970, New York Public Library.

120 "Literary people": John Thompson, interview with Ian Hamilton, 1979, Ian Hamilton Papers, British Library.

121 "In his manic states": Letter from George Ford to Ian Hamilton, May 21, 1981, Ian Hamilton Papers, British Library.

121 "a tricky subject for Cal": Ibid.

121 "He came back to Cincinnati": Ibid.

121 "the strongest and biggest": Ibid.

121 "It seems": Letter from Flannery O'Connor to Sally Fitzgerald, December 26, 1954, in Flannery O'Connor, *The Habit of Being*, 74.

121 "is much more dangerous": Letter from Elizabeth Hardwick to Blair Clark, n.d. April 1954, HRC.

122 "Cal is badly deranged": Letter from Elizabeth Hardwick to Blair Clark, April 4, 1954, HRC.

122 "No one has the slightest idea": Ibid.

123 Cincinnati hospital: Robert Lowell was hospitalized at the Jewish Hospital from April 8, 1954, until September 15, 1954. His primary physician there was Dr. Philip Piker. He was then transferred to the Payne Whitney Clinic in New York. The clinical observations in the text are from the hospital summary of his history.

123 "more and more unruly": Letter from Elizabeth Hardwick to Blair and Holly Clark, May 1, 1954, HRC.

123 "I enjoyed him": Letter from Elizabeth Hardwick to Blair and Holly Clark, May 4, 1954, HRC.

123 "His wit, subtlety, variety": Letter from Elizabeth Hardwick to Harriet Winslow, May 4, 1954, Houghton Library.

123 "I know how much he means": Ibid.

124 "in which the patient": Letter from Elizabeth Hardwick to Blair and Holly Clark, May 1, 1954, HRC.

124 "You are so afraid": Ibid.

124 "I do not see any future": Ibid.

124 "I suppose that Mr. Lowell's wife": Letter from Philip Piker, M.D., to Merrill Moore, M.D., April 26, 1954, Houghton Library.

124 "One of the great troubles": Letter from Elizabeth Hardwick to Blair and Holly Clark, May 19, 1954, HRC.

125 "is not a pleasant thing to do": Ibid.

125 admitted to the Payne Whitney Clinic: Robert Lowell was hospitalized at the Payne Whitney Clinic in New York from May 21, 1954, until September 15, 1954. His primary physician was Dr. James Masterson. The clinical observations in the text are from Lowell's hospital records.

127 "Thank heaven [chlorpromazine] seems": Letter from Elizabeth Hardwick to Harriet Winslow, July 4, 1954, Houghton Library.

127 "I see more and more clearly": Letter from Robert Lowell to Giovanna Madonia, July 7, 1954, *Letters*, 237.

127 "I've really been quite sick": Letter from Robert Lowell to Giovanna Madonia, July 11, 1954, *Letters*, 238.

128 John Haslam, apothecary: John Haslam, *Observations on Madness and Melancholy* (London: J. Callow, 1809), title page. The quote from Dr. Samuel Johnson is from his book *The Prince of Abissinia: A Tale* (London: R. and J. Dodsley, 1759).

129 "I feel so sorry": Letter from Elizabeth Hardwick to Peter Taylor, April 20, 1954, Vanderbilt.

129 "They understand that a person": Ibid.

129 "Underneath, Cal feels dreadfully": Letter from Elizabeth Hardwick to Blair Clark, June 15, 1954, HRC.

129 "Cal will recover": Letter from Elizabeth Hardwick to Blair Clark, August 31, 1954, HRC.

129 "According to": Letter from Robert Lowell to Blair Clark, August 6, 1954, *Letters*, 239.

130 "I have been sick again": Letter from Robert Lowell to Elizabeth Bishop, November 14, 1954, *Letters*, 242.

130 "He just wanted to go back": Elizabeth Hardwick, interview with Ian Hamilton, 1979, Ian Hamilton Papers, British Library.

7. SNOW-SUGARED, UNRAVELING

131 "We feel the machine slipping from": Robert Lowell, "Since 1939," *Collected Poems*, 741.

131 "a block down Marlboro": Robert Lowell, Autobiographical Prose, Houghton Library.

131 "Here I am in Boston": Elizabeth Hardwick, *Sleepless Nights*, 4.

132 "His doctor is very": Letter from Elizabeth Hardwick to Blair and Holly Clark, November 29, 1954, Robert Lowell Papers, HRC.

132 "Together we have managed": Ibid.

132 "Cal is fine": Letter from Elizabeth Hardwick to Peter Taylor, February 10, 1955, Vanderbilt.

132 "This has been a funny": Letter from Robert Lowell to Ezra Pound, April 17, 1955, *Letters*, 246.

133 "Cal is feeling very well": Letter from Elizabeth Hardwick to Blair and Holly Clark, December 12, 1955, Robert Lowell Papers, HRC.

133 "It's soothing to be stopped": Letter from Robert Lowell to Harriet Winslow, December 27, 1955, Houghton Library.

133 "Cal is fine": Letter from Elizabeth Hardwick to Harriet Winslow, February 18, 1956, Robert Lowell Papers, Houghton Library.

133 "well and happy": Letter from Elizabeth Hardwick to Blair and Holly Clark, February 22, 1956, HRC.

133 "Already *we* are exhausted": Letter from Robert Lowell to Elizabeth Bishop, June 18, 1956, *Letters*, 257.

134 "It's terrible discovering": Letter from Robert Lowell to J. F. Powers, May 16, 1956, *Letters*, 256.

134 extended period of normal health: The findings underlying this pattern are extensively reviewed in F. K. Goodwin and K. R. Jamison, *Manic-Depressive Illness*.

135 "hardly passionate Marlborough Street": Robert Lowell, "Memories of West Street and Lepke," *Collected Poems*, 187.

135 "silken claith": Anonymous, "Sir Patrick Spens," in *The Oxford Book of English Verse: 1250–1900*, ed. Arthur Quiller-Couch (Oxford: Oxford University Press, 1919).

135 "I see clearly now": Letter from Robert Lowell to Elizabeth Bishop, August 9, 1957, *Letters*, 282.

136 "Today I feel certain": Ibid.

136 "Dear Cal, do please": Letter from Elizabeth Bishop to Robert Lowell, August 11, 1957, in *Words in Air: The Complete Correspondence Between Elizabeth Bishop and Robert Lowell*, ed. Thomas Travisano, with Saskia Hamilton (New York: Farrar, Straus and Giroux, 2008), 217.

136 "Cal is better than he has been": Letter from Elizabeth Hardwick to Susan Sontag, September 21, 1957, Robert Lowell Papers, HRC.

136 "nobody seemed to realize": Dido Merwin, interview with Ian Hamilton, 1980, Ian Hamilton Papers, British Library.

136 "So the police arrived": William Alfred, interview with Ian Hamilton, 1981, Ian Hamilton Papers, British Library.

137 Boston State Hospital: Robert Lowell was hospitalized at Boston State Hospital from December 12, 1957, until December 17, 1957. His primary physician was Robert Spitzer, M.D. The clinical observations in the text are from Lowell's hospital records, including the notes made by Dr. Robert Spitzer and Dr. David Blair.

138 Massachusetts Mental Health Center: Robert Lowell was hospitalized at the

Massachusetts Mental Health Center (formerly the Boston Psychopathic Hospital) from December 17, 1957, until January 14, 1958. His primary physician there was Marian Woolston, M.D. The clinical observations in the text are from Lowell's medical records.

139 More than fifty years later: Marian Woolston-Catlin, M.D., interview with the author, August 24 and 28, 2013.

140 "as active as electricity": Letter from Elizabeth Hardwick to Harriet Winslow, February 2, 1958, Houghton Library.

140 "are always like a Russian novel": Letter from Elizabeth Hardwick to Elizabeth Bishop, January 20, 1958, Vassar.

140 "begged to come home": Ibid.

140 "he would climb right back up": Ibid.

140 "I've just passed through": Letter from Robert Lowell to William Carlos Williams, January 22, 1958, Letters, 308.

140 "keeping up a front": Robert Lowell to Vernon Williams, M.D., n.d. 1950s, HRC.

140 "quieting down gradually": Letter from Elizabeth Hardwick to Harriet Winslow, January 24, 1958, Houghton Library.

141 "He has always loved": Ibid.

141 "just to sit tight": Ibid.

141 McLean Hospital: Robert Lowell was hospitalized at McLean Hospital in Boston from January 30/31, 1958, until May 22, 1958.

141 "I myself am hell": Robert Lowell, "Skunk Hour," Collected Poems, 192.

141 "within him Hell": John Milton, Paradise Lost, book 4, line 20.

141 "Which way I fly": Ibid., line 75.

142 "The Christ was killed": Letter from Robert Lowell to William Empson, January 29, 1958, Letters, 311.

142 "For the future": Letter from Elizabeth Hardwick to Harriet Winslow, February 15, 1958, Houghton Library.

143 "knowledge, fear and insecurity": Letter from Elizabeth Hardwick to Blair and Holly Clark, February 16, 1958, Robert Lowell Papers, HRC.

143 "There is in these manic things": Elizabeth Hardwick interview, with Ian Hamilton, 1979, Ian Hamilton Papers, British Library.

143 "He becomes furious": Letter from Elizabeth Hardwick to Blair and Holly Clark, February 16, 1958, Robert Lowell Papers, HRC.

143 "My mania has broken": Letter from Robert Lowell to Harriet Winslow, March 15, 1958, Letters, 318.

143 "It's not much fun writing": Letter from Robert Lowell to Peter Taylor, March 15, 1958, Letters, 317.

143 "What can you do after": Ibid.

143 "The man next to me": Letter from Robert Lowell to Elizabeth Bishop, March 15, 1958, Letters, 316.

144 "they tell me nothing's gone": Robert Lowell, "Home After Three Months Away," Collected Poems, 185–86.

144 "the kind that one wonders": F. Scott Fitzgerald, *The Crack-Up with Other Pieces and Stories* (1936; London: Penguin, 1965), 45.

144 "It can never again be": Ibid., 45.

145 "I feel rather like a character": Letter from Robert Lowell to Giovanna Madonia Erba, June 2, 1954, *Letters*, 236.

145 "We are both fine": Letter from Elizabeth Hardwick to Harriet Winslow, April 25, 1958, Houghton Library.

145 "My own things rise": Letter from Robert Lowell to Theodore Roethke, September 18, 1958, University of Washington Libraries.

145 rather like going to Mass: Elizabeth Hardwick, interview with Ian Hamilton, Ian Hamilton Papers, British Library.

145 readmitted to McLean: Robert Lowell was hospitalized at McLean Hospital from April 28, 1959, until July 22, 1959.

147 "it is distressing beyond words": Letter from Elizabeth Hardwick to Mary McCarthy, May 9, 1959, Vassar.

147 "flight into illness": Ibid.

147 "I feel particularly discouraged": Ibid.

147 "I feel rather creepy": Letter from Robert Lowell to Elizabeth Bishop, July 24, 1959, *Letters*, 351.

147 "an incredible formless time": Letter from Robert Lowell to Elizabeth Bishop, January 4, 1960, *Words in Air*, 308.

147 "I have been thinking much about you": Letter from Robert Lowell to John Berryman, September 19, 1959, *Letters*, 352–53.

148 "Boston's a pleasant place": Letter from Robert Lowell to Elizabeth Bishop, December 12, 1958, *Letters*, 333.

148 "We are awfully sick of Boston": Letter from Robert Lowell to Randall Jarrell, February 15, 1960, Berg Collection, New York Public Library.

148 "Boston had solved the universe": Henry Adams, *The Education of Henry Adams*, 34.

148 "had lost its seriousness": Robert Lowell interview with V. S. Naipaul, *Listener* 82 (September 4, 1969): 302.

148 "With Boston and its mysteriously enduring": Elizabeth Hardwick, "Boston: The Lost Ideal," *Harper's Magazine*, December 1959, 64.

148 "A simpler manner of life": Ibid., 65.

149 "The importance of Boston": Ibid.

149 "Boston is not a small New York": Ibid., 66.

149 "Boston is a winter city": Ibid., 68.

149 "What stands out": Letter from Robert Lowell to Harriet Winslow, October 12, 1959, *Letters*, 355.

150 "Harriet is terrific": Letter from Robert Lowell to Elizabeth Bishop, August 9, 1960, *Letters*, 368.

150 "Home from you": Robert Lowell, "Across Central Park," *Collected Poems*, 541.

150 "He leaves home": Letter from Elizabeth Hardwick to Mary McCarthy, April 3, 1961, Vassar.

150 a locked ward at Columbia-Presbyterian: Robert Lowell was hospitalized at Columbia-Presbyterian Hospital in New York from March 4, 1961, until the end of March 1961.

151 "No one predicts": Letter from William Meredith to Adrienne Rich and Philip Booth, March 17, 1961, Connecticut College.

151 an elated telegram: Telegram from Robert Lowell to Elizabeth Bishop, September 10, 1962, *Letters*, 409.

151 kept a record: Keith Botsford's records of Robert Lowell's 1962 trip to Buenos Aires and his interview with Ian Hamilton, 1981, Ian Hamilton Papers, British Library.

151 "became very fragmentary": Ibid.

152 Institute of Living: Robert Lowell was hospitalized at the Institute of Living in Hartford, Connecticut, from October 1, 1962, until November 7, 1962; early December 1963 through mid-January 1964; and early January 1965 through February 1965. Erik Linnolt, M.D., was his primary physician. Dr. Linnolt's clinical observations about Robert Lowell were made during an interview with the author, June 28, 2012.

152 "very warm, reserved": Erik Linnolt, M.D., interview with the author, June 28, 2012.

152 "This thing just came on him": Letter from Elizabeth Hardwick to Allen Tate, January 9, 1964, Princeton.

153 "How we miss you": Letter from Elizabeth Hardwick to Robert Lowell, December 12, 1963, Houghton Library.

153 "He said he had these periods": Correspondence from Harriet Winslow Lowell to the author, April 2012.

153 "It's a little painful": Letter from Robert Lowell to Mary McCarthy, February 20, 1964, *Letters*, 442.

154 "what a mess I've made": Letter from Robert Lowell to Elizabeth Hardwick, February 9, 1965, Robert Lowell Papers, HRC.

154 "full of irrational turbulence": Letter from Robert Lowell to Elizabeth Hardwick, February 5, 1965, Robert Lowell Papers, HRC.

154 "I am back from a month": Letter from Robert Lowell to Elizabeth Bishop, February 25, 1965, *Letters*, 456.

154 "I have a feeling": Letter from Elizabeth Bishop to Robert Lowell, March 11, 1965, *Words in Air*, 572.

154 "The cyclical beginning": Xandra Gowrie, interview with Ian Hamilton, 1980, Ian Hamilton Papers, British Library.

155 "I had never witnessed": James Atlas, "Robert Lowell in Cambridge: Lord Weary," 56–64.

155 "Cal was leaning back": Grey Gowrie, interview with Ian Hamilton, 1980, Ian Hamilton Papers, British Library.

155 "'You should go'": Ibid.

155 "and what is man?": Robert Lowell, "Christmas in Black Rock," *Collected Poems*, 12.

8. WRITING TAKES THE ACHE AWAY

156 "My great need of the moment": Robert Lowell, essay written for Vernon Williams, M.D., n.d. 1950s, Robert Lowell Papers, HRC.

156 doctors of antiquity: Many medical historians have written about how mania and melancholia were understood and treated at differing times and in different cultures, including J. R. Whitwell, *Historical Notes on Psychiatry: Early Times–End of 16th Century* (London: H. K. Lewis & Co., 1936); S. W. Jackson, *Melancholia and Depression: From Hippocratic Times to Modern Times* (New Haven: Yale University Press, 1986); and G. Roccatagliata, *A History of Ancient Psychiatry* (New York: Greenwood Press, 1986).

156 Its scarlet thread: S. E. Jelliffe, *Series of Research Publications 11, Manic-Depressive Psychosis, Research in Nervous and Mental Diseases Proceedings* (Baltimore: Williams & Wilkins, 1931).

156 The brain, Hippocrates said: Medical observations attributed to Hippocrates are generally believed to represent the writings and practice not only of Hippocrates but of his school: *Works of Hippocrates*, trans. and ed. W. H. S. Jones and E. T. Withington (Cambridge, MA: Harvard University Press, 1923–31).

157 "Mania," used by the early Greek physicians: See S. W. Jackson, *Melancholia and Depression*, and G. Roccatagliata, *A History of Ancient Psychiatry*, for detailed discussions of the ancient meanings of mania and the distinctions made between madness with or without fever.

157 "the modes of mania": Aretaeus, *The Extant Works of Aretaeus, the Cappadocian*, ed. Francis Adams (London: The New Sydenham Society, 1856), 301.

157 "laugh, play, dance": Ibid., 302.

157 "have madness attended with anger": Ibid.

157 "naturally passionate": Ibid., 301.

158 "truly from the muses": Ibid., 302.

158 "The painter keeps his brushes clean": J. R. Whitwell, *Historical Notes on Psychiatry*, 201–2.

158 "Melancholia is the commencement": Aretaeus, *The Extant Works*, 299.

158 more than sixty before 1750: O. Diethelm, "Mania: A Clinical Study of Dissertations Before 1750," *Confinia Psychiatrica* 13 (1970): 26–49.

159 "These Distempers often change": Thomas Willis, *Two Discourses on the Soul of Brutes*, trans. S. Pordage (London: Thomas Dring, 1683), 188.

159 "an open burning or flame": Ibid.

159 *la folie circulaire:* J. P. Falret, "Mémoire sur la folie circulaire," *Bulletin de l'Académie de Médecine* 19 (1854): 382–415. The clinical descriptions of Falret and Baillarger are translated and cited in Daniel Hack Tuke, "Circular Insanity," *A Dictionary of Psychological Medicine* (Philadelphia: P. Blakiston, Son & Co., 1892), 214–29.

159 *la folie à double forme:* J. Baillarger, "De la folie à double forme," *Annales Médico-psychologiques* 6 (1854): 369–91.

159 "The profusion of ideas": Ibid.

159 "compose and write prose and verse": Ibid.

159 His 1921 monograph: Emil Kraepelin, *Manic-Depressive Insanity and Paranoia* (Edinburgh: E. & S. Livingstone, 1921).

160 *Diagnostic and Statistical Manual*: Diagnostic and Statistical Manual: Mental Disorders (Washington, D.C.: American Psychiatric Association, 1952).

161 "The patient should be kept in bed": M. Ahonen, "Mental Disorders in Ancient Philosophy," in *Studies in the History of Philosophy of Mind* (Switzerland: Springer, 2014), 15–16.

161 leeches, fennel, and applying oil of roses: J. R. Whitwell, *Historical Notes on Psychiatry*, 93.

161 "curious compound of pharmacy": Daniel Hack Tuke, *Chapters in the History of the Insane in the British Isles* (London: Kegan Paul, 1882), 1.

161 "to be drunk out of a church-bell": Ibid., 2.

161 Medieval Persian treatments: N. Vakili and A. Gorji, "Psychiatry and Psychology in Medieval Persia," *Journal of Clinical Psychiatry* 67 (2006): 1862–69.

162 Ibn Sínà: Michael W. Dols, *Majnun: The Madman in Medieval Islamic Society*, ed. D. E. Immisch (Oxford: Clarendon Press, 1992).

162 the murder of Becket: John Guy, *Thomas Becket* (London: Viking, 2012).

162 marigold is "much approved": Robert Burton, *The Anatomy of Melancholy* (1620; New York: New York Review Books, 2001), 216.

162 "a ram's head": Ibid., 248.

162 "elixir made of dew": Letter from Sir Kenelm Digby to J. Winthrop, Jr., January 26, 1656, cited in James Russell Lowell, "New England Two Centuries Ago," 56.

163 The nineteenth-century asylum physicians: S. B. Woodward, "Observations of the Medical Treatment of Insanity," *American Journal of Insanity* 7 (July 1850): 1–34; S. B. Thielman, "Madness and Medicine: Trends in American Medical Therapeutics for Insanity, 1820–1860," *Bulletin of the History of Medicine* 61 (1987): 25–46.

163 "a medical fact": Rufus Wyman, quoted in "Evidences of Insanity," *Boston Medical and Surgical Journal* 11 (January 14, 1835): 364.

163 "I went off to the hospital": Letter from Robert Lowell to Adrienne Rich, February 25, 1964, *Letters*, 444.

164 "Then at last the books": Letter from Elizabeth Hardwick to Ian Hamilton, n.d., Robert Lowell Papers, HRC.

164 "I won't go into the boredom": Letter from Robert Lowell to Elizabeth Hardwick, January 30, 1965, *Letters*, 454.

165 "It was a sunny": Robert Lowell, "Near the Unbalanced Aquarium," *Collected Prose*, 357–58.

165 shielded his mania: William Styron spoke often about the underappreciated respite that came from being in a psychiatric hospital: "The hospital was my salvation, and it is something of a paradox that in this austere place with its locked and wired doors and desolate green hallways—ambulances screeching night and day ten floors below—I found the repose, the assuagement of the tempest in my

brain, that I was unable to find in my quiet farmhouse." William Styron, *Darkness Visible: A Memoir of Madness* (New York: Random House, 1990), 69.

165 electroconvulsive therapy: S. Mukherjee, H. A. Sackeim, and D. B. Schnur, "Electroconvulsive Therapy of Acute Manic Episodes: A Review of 50 Years' Experience," *American Journal of Psychiatry* 151 (1994): 169–76; H. K. Schoeyen, U. Kessler, O. E. Andreassen, et al., "Treatment-Resistant Bipolar Depression: A Randomized Controlled Trial of Electroconvulsive Therapy Versus Algorithm-Based Pharmacological Treatment," *American Journal of Psychiatry* 172 (2015): 41–51.

165 "All the late froth and delirium": Letter from Robert Lowell to Elizabeth Bishop, March 15, 1958, *Letters*, 315.

165 "Psycho-therapy is rather amazing": Letter from Robert Lowell to Elizabeth Bishop, November 18, 1949, *Letters*, 150.

165 "I have been seeing a psychiatrist": Letter from Robert Lowell to Charlotte Winslow Lowell, March 10, 1950, Houghton Library.

165 "I've been gulping Freud": Letter from Robert Lowell to Elizabeth Hardwick, September 10, 1953, *Letters*, 200.

166 "I get a funny thing": Robert Lowell interview with Al Alvarez, "A Talk with Robert Lowell," *Encounter* 24 (February 1965).

166 "All that human sort of color": Ibid.

166 "Were it not better": Sigmund Freud, "Reflections on War and Death," trans. A. A. Brill and A. B. Kruttner (New York: Moffat, Yard and Company, 1918).

166 "To bear life": Ibid.

166 "is not like Freudians": Letter from Robert Lowell to Giovanna Madonia Erba, March 13, 1954, *Letters*, 215.

166 "provides the conditions": Al Alvarez, "A Talk with Robert Lowell."

167 "He does me a lot of good": Letter from Robert Lowell to Elizabeth Bishop, November 19, 1958, *Letters*, 332.

167 "really doing great things": Letter from Robert Lowell to Elizabeth Bishop, March 30, 1959, *Letters*, 340.

167 "This was the first year": Richard Stern, "Extracts from a Journal," *TriQuarterly* 50 (Winter 1981).

167 "He felt very strongly": Peter Taylor, BBC program, "Robert Lowell," March 9, 1965.

167 "Once he was on lithium": Helen Vendler, e-mail correspondence with the author, February 9, 2011.

167 "Now coming back": Robert Lowell, essay written for Vernon Williams, M.D., n.d. 1950s, HRC.

168 "fairly well for long stretches": Ibid.

168 "largest thing I hope for": Ibid.

168 "I know you're all right": Letter from Elizabeth Hardwick to Robert Lowell, September 20, 1949, Houghton Library.

168 "there should not be": Letter from Elizabeth Hardwick to Peter and Eleanor Taylor, October 20, 1949, Vanderbilt.

168 "betrayed so often": Letter from Elizabeth Hardwick to Allen Tate, December 28, 1949, Princeton. Virgil wrote in *The Aeneid:*

> Aeneas felt his ship adrift, her pilot lost,
> and took command himself, at sea in the black night,
> moaning deeply, stunned by his comrade's fate:
> "You trusted—oh, Palinurus—
> far too much to a calm sky and sea.
> Your naked corpse will lie on an unknown shore.

Virgil, *The Aeneid*, trans. Robert Fagles (New York: Penguin, 2006), 181.

168 "it's all definitely over": Letter from Robert Lowell to Charlotte Lowell, October 19, 1952, *Letters*, 191.

169 "Cal takes this all with dead seriousness": Letter from Elizabeth Hardwick to Robie and Anne Macauley, September 1952, HRC.

169 "Over the noise of the band": Eileen Simpson, *Poets in Their Youth*, 193.

169 "out of the control of the will": Letter from Elizabeth Hardwick to Allen Tate, January 9, 1964, Princeton.

169 "Of course, he feared": Sidney Nolan, interview with Ian Hamilton, 1980, Ian Hamilton Papers, British Library.

169 "How often have my antics": Robert Lowell, "The Downlook," *Collected Poems*, 836.

169 "I am back from a month": Letter from Robert Lowell to Elizabeth Bishop, February 25, 1965, *Letters*, 456.

170 "'Remarkable breakdown'": Robert Lowell, "Home," *Collected Poems*, 824.

170 "before the metal shaving mirrors": Robert Lowell, "Waking in the Blue," *Collected Poems*, 184.

170 "now no one need": Robert Lowell, "Home After Three Months Away," *Collected Poems*, 185–86.

170 "'Waiting out the rain'": Robert Lowell, "Departure," *Collected Poems*, 726.

170 "After his first grave manic attack": Robert Fitzgerald, "Thinking of Robert Lowell: 1917–1977," Robert Fitzgerald Papers, Beinecke Rare Book and Manuscript Library, Yale University.

170 "with horror of his old mania": Letter from Mary McCarthy to Hannah Arendt, June 26, 1970, in *Between Friends: The Correspondence of Hannah Arendt and Mary McCarthy, 1949–1975*, ed. Carol Brightman (New York: Harcourt Brace, 1995), 257.

170 "I am back where I was": Letter from Robert Lowell to George Santayana, January 8, 1950, *Letters*, 153.

171 "Even now I feel as though": Robert Lowell, "The Puritan," ca. 1945, Miscellaneous Prose, Houghton Library, 2794.

171 "Cattle have guts": Robert Lowell, "Cattle," *Notebook 1967–68*, 143.

171 The image repeats: Robert Lowell, "Cow," *Collected Poems*, 458.

171 "We do not burn": Robert Lowell, "Andrei Voznesensky," *Collected Prose*, 120.

171 "If it's still": Elizabeth Bishop, "The Armadillo," *Poems* (New York: Farrar, Straus and Giroux, 2011), 101–2. The poem, dedicated to Robert Lowell, ends:

> *O falling fire and piercing cry*
> *and panic, and a weak mailed fist*
> *clinched ignorant against the sky!*

171 "I made men look": Robert Lowell, *Prometheus Bound* (New York: Farrar, Straus and Giroux, 1969), 23.

171 "can remake, or destroy": Ibid., 11.

171 "men had eyes": Ibid., 21–22.

172 The scars of madness: "Madness was like being in war," he told Richard Stern; "the humiliation and the increasing shame were terrible." Richard Stern, "Extracts from a Journal."

173 War, said Henry Adams: Henry Adams, *The Education of Henry Adams*, 249.

173 "a chance to gain": Robert Lowell, "War: A Justification," *The Vindex* (St. Mark's School), June 1935, Robert Lowell Papers, HRC.

173 In lectures given: W. H. R. Rivers, *Instinct and the Unconscious: A Contribution to a Biological Theory of the Psycho-Neuroses* (Cambridge: Cambridge University Press, 1924).

173 "banishing such experiences": Ibid., 188.

173 "was to find some aspect": Ibid., 191.

173 "It's bad to think of war": Siegfried Sassoon, "Repression of War Experience," in *Siegfried Sassoon: The War Poems* (London: Faber & Faber, 1983), 73.

173 "You're quiet and peaceful": Ibid., 74.

174 "I was on my Ghazala": T. E. Lawrence, *Seven Pillars of Wisdom* (1926, 1935; London: Penguin Classics, 2000), 561.

174 "If imagination is active": W. H. R. Rivers, *Instinct and the Unconscious*, 226.

175 "war's sordor, heroism": Letter from Robert Lowell to Richard Fein, March 13, 1960, *Letters*, 361.

175 "My definite approach": Siegfried Sassoon, *Sherston's Progress* (London: Faber & Faber, 1936), 28.

175 "fallen to pieces": Ibid., 149.

175 "unexpected and unannounced": Ibid.

175 "I undo the clotted lint": Walt Whitman, "The Wound-Dresser," *Leaves of Grass*, ed. Sculley Bradley and Harold Blodgett (New York: W. W. Norton, 2002), 310.

175 "I thread my way": Ibid., 311.

176 "I am weighed down": Letter from Robert Lowell to Frank Bidart, February 15, 1976, *Letters*, 644.

176 "I can't really function": Letter from Robert Lowell to Blair Clark, March 4, 1976, *Letters*, 645.

176 "I had a longish": Letter from Robert Lowell to Elizabeth Bishop, March 4, 1976, *Letters*, 644.

---

176 "terrified of being mad alone": Caroline Blackwood, interview with Ian Hamilton, 1979, Ian Hamilton Papers, British Library.

176 "if we see a light": Robert Lowell, "Since 1939," *Collected Poems*, 741.

176 "Lithium Salts in the Treatment": J. F. Cade, "Lithium Salts in the Treatment of Psychotic Excitement," *Medical Journal of Australia* 36 (1949): 349–52. The history of the use of lithium in mania and depression is extensively covered in F. N. Johnson, *The History of Lithium Therapy* (London: Macmillan, 1984). John Cade is quoted as asking why anyone should consider the use of lithium in manic episodes—"Why not potable pearl, or crocodile dung or unicorn horn?" Johnson discusses in detail lithium's long medicinal history going back to the ancient physicians and healing waters to its more systematic use in the treatment of depression in the nineteenth century.

176 "Experiences of Treatment": G. P. Hartigan, "Experiences of Treatment with Lithium Salts," in F. N. Johnson, *The History of Lithium Therapy*, 183–87.

177 "Some Australian physiologists": Ibid., 183.

177 "It is widely distributed": J. F. Cade, "Lithium Salts in the Treatment of Psychotic Excitement," 351.

177 Soranus of Ephesus: F. N. Johnson, *The History of Lithium Therapy*, 146. See S. W. Jackson, *Melancholia and Depression*, as well as G. Roccatagliata, *A History of Ancient Psychiatry*.

178 it treats and prevents mania: For reviews of lithium's efficacy, see J. R. Geddes, S. Burgess, K. Hawton, K. Jamison, and G. M. Goodwin, "Long-Term Lithium Therapy for Bipolar Disorder: Systematic Review and Meta-Analysis of Randomized Controlled Trials," *American Journal of Psychiatry* 161 (2004): 217–22; M. Bauer, P. Grof, and B. Müller-Oerlinghausen, eds., *Lithium in Neuropsychiatry: The Comprehensive Guide* (Abingdon: Informa UK, 2006); F. K. Goodwin and K. R. Jamison, *Manic-Depressive Illness*; J. R. Geddes, G. M. Goodwin, J. Rendell, et al., "Lithium Plus Valproate Combination Therapy Versus Monotherapy for Relapse Prevention in Bipolar I Disorder (BALANCE): A Randomised Open-Label Trial," *Lancet* 375 (2010): 385–95; E. Severus, M. J. Taylor, C. Sauer, et al., "Lithium for Prevention of Mood Episodes in Bipolar Disorders: Systematic Review and Meta-Analysis," *International Journal of Bipolar Disorders* 2 (2014): 1–17.

178 it acts to prevent suicide: For example, R. J. Baldessarini, L. Tondo, P. Davis, et al., "Decreased Risk of Suicides and Attempts During Long-Term Lithium Treatment: A Meta-Analytic Review," *Bipolar Disorders* 8 (2006): 625–39; A. Cipriani, K. Hawton, S. Stockton, and J. R. Geddes, "Lithium in the Prevention of Suicide in Mood Disorders: Updated Systematic Review and Meta-Analysis, *British Medical Journal* 346 (2013), DOI: 10.1136/bmj.f3646; U. Lewitzka, E. Severus, R. Bauer, et al., "The Suicide Prevention Effect of Lithium: More Than 20 Years of Evidence—A Narrative Review," *International Journal of Bipolar Disorders* (2015), DOI: 1186/s40345_015_0032_2; J. F. Hayes, A. Pitman, L. Marston, et al., "Self-Harm, Unintentional Injury, and Suicide in Bipolar Disorder During Maintenance Mood Stabilizer Treatment: A UK Population-

Based Electronic Health Records Study," *JAMA Psychiatry* (May 11, 2016): E1–E7.

178   protect and heal the brain: The potential neuroprotective and neurogenerative qualities of lithium have been studied extensively over the past several years. A small sampling of the studies includes H. K. Manji, G. J. Moore, and G. Chan, "Clinical and Preclinical Evidence for the Neurotropic Effects of Mood Stabilizers: Implications for the Pathophysiology and Treatment of Manic-Depressive Illness," *Biological Psychiatry* 61 (2000): 740–54; S. A. Johnson, J.-F. Wang, X. Sun, et al., "Lithium Treatment Prevents Stress-Induced Dendritic Remodeling in the Rodent Amygdala," *Neuroscience* 163 (2009): 34–39; C. I. Giakoumatos, P. Nanda, I. T. Mathew, et al., "Effects of Lithium on Cortical Thickness and Hippocampal Subfield Volumes in Psychotic Bipolar Disorder," *Journal of Psychiatric Research* 61 (2015): 180–87; T. Gerhard, D. P. Devan, C. Huang, et al., "Lithium Treatment and Risk for Dementia in Adults with Bipolar Disorder: Population-Based Cohort Study," *British Journal of Psychiatry* 207 (2015): 46–51; A. G. Gildengers, M. A. Butters, H. J. Aizenstein, et al., "Longer Lithium Exposure Is Associated with Better White Matter Integrity in Older Adults with Bipolar Disorder," *Bipolar Disorders* 17 (2015): 248–56; P.-M. Martin, R. E. Stanley, A. P. Ross, et al. "*DIXDC1* Contributes to Psychiatric Susceptibility by Regulating Dendritic Spine and Glutamatergic Synapse Density via GSK3 and Wnt/β-catenin Signaling," *Molecular Psychiatry* (2016), DOI: 10.1038/mp.2016.184.

178   "certain modest magical qualities": G. P. Hartigan, "Experiences of Treatment with Lithium Salts," 187.

179   "Nothing new worth writing about": Letter from Robert Lowell to Elizabeth Bishop, February 26, 1967, *Letters*, 483.

179   "I'm in terrific shape!": Letter from Robert Lowell to Peter Taylor, June 4, 1967, Vanderbilt.

179   "Yes, I'm well": Letter from Robert Lowell to Elizabeth Bishop, January 12, 1968, *Letters*, 494.

179   "These pills for my manic seizures": Letter from Robert Lowell to Al Alvarez, n.d. May 1968, *Letters*, 501.

180   his attacks of mania preceded: This clinical pattern of a more favorable response to lithium being associated with mania preceding depression rather than the other way around has been observed in many studies; they are reviewed in F. K. Goodwin and K. R. Jamison, *Manic-Depressive Illness*.

180   "He is taking some new drug": Letter from Mary McCarthy to Hannah Arendt, September 12, 1967, *Between Friends*, 204.

181   "became much more frazzled": Jonathan Miller, interview with Ian Hamilton, 1980, Ian Hamilton Papers, British Library.

181   "Lithium had made a terrible difference": Grey Gowrie, interview with Ian Hamilton, 1980, Ian Hamilton Papers, British Library.

181   "he appeared to be released": Esther Brooks, "Remembering Cal," 42–43.

181   His stepdaughter Ivana: Interview with the author, New York, April 16, 2014.

181 poet Kathleen Spivack agreed: Kathleen Spivack, *With Robert Lowell and His Circle* (Lebanon, NH: University Press of New England, 2012), 163; also, interview with the author, March 19, 2014, Cambridge, Massachusetts.

181 "I think it was a dampener": Sidney Nolan, interview with Ian Hamilton, 1980, Ian Hamilton Papers, British Library.

181 "I never wrote more": Robert Lowell, "A Conversation with Ian Hamilton," *Collected Prose*, 271–72.

182 "I guess the summer goes": Letter from Robert Lowell to Elizabeth Bishop, July 30, 1968, *Words in Air*, 643.

182 "This beautiful summer": Letter from Robert Lowell to Adrienne Rich, August 23, 1968, *Letters*, 506.

182 "Words came rapidly": Robert Lowell, "A Conversation with Ian Hamilton," *Collected Prose*, 271–72.

182 "He had a massive drive to write": Helen Vendler, correspondence with the author, February 9, 2011.

182 "different from the more pointed articulation": Ian Hamilton, "Robert Lowell," in *The Oxford Companion to Twentieth-Century Poetry in English* (Oxford and New York: Oxford University Press, 1996), 314.

182 Two small studies during the 1970s: M. H. Marshall, C. P. Neumann, and M. Robinson, "Lithium, Creativity, and Manic-Depressive Illness: Review and Prospectus," *Psychosomatics* 11 (1970): 406–8; M. Schou, "Artistic Productivity and Lithium Prophylaxis in Manic-Depressive Illness," *British Journal of Psychiatry* 135 (1979): 97–103.

182 A study of the impact: L. L. Judd, B. Hubbard, D. S. Janowsky, et al., "The Effect of Lithium Carbonate on the Cognitive Functions of Normal Subjects," *Archives of General Psychiatry* 34 (1977): 355–57. L. L. Judd, "Effect of Lithium on Mood, Cognition, and Personality Function in Normal Subjects," *Archives of General Psychiatry* 36 (1979): 860–65.

182 Other studies of patients: E. D. Shaw, J. J. Mann, P. E. Stokes, and A. Z. A. Manevitz, "Effects of Lithium Carbonate on Associative Productivity and Idiosyncrasy in Bipolar Outpatients," *American Journal of Psychiatry* 143 (1986): 1166–69; L. Pons, J. Nurnberger, D. Murphy, et al., "Mood-Independent Aberrancies of Word Responses and Action of Lithium on Their Repetition in Manic Depressive Illness," *Pharmacopsychiatry* 20 (1987): 227–29; J. H. Kocsis, E. D. Shaw, P. E. Stokes, et al., "Neuropsychologic Effects of Lithium Discontinuation," *Journal of Clinical Psychopharmacology* 13 (1993): 268–75.

183 "We'd all been to the opera": Robert Silvers, interview with Ian Hamilton, 1981, Ian Hamilton Papers, British Library.

183 "A week ago, you called": Letter from Curtis Prout, M.D., to Robert Lowell, May 13, 1975, Robert Lowell Papers, HRC.

184 Mania often comes back: T. Suppes, R. J. Baldessarini, G. L. Faedda, and M. Tohen, "Risk of Recurrence Following Discontinuation of Lithium Treatment in Bipolar Disorder," *Archives of General Psychiatry* 48 (1991): 1082–88; G. M. Goodwin, "Recurrence of Mania After Lithium Withdrawal: Implica-

tions for the Use of Lithium in the Treatment of Bipolar Affective Disorder," *British Journal of Psychiatry* 164 (1994): 149–52; R. J. Baldessarini, L. Tondo, and A. C. Viguera, "Discontinuing Lithium Maintenance Treatment in Bipolar Disorders: Risks and Implications," *Bipolar Disorders* (1999): 17–24.

184 risk of suicide increases: R. J. Baldessarini, L. Tondo, and J. Hennen, "Effects of Lithium Treatment and Its Discontinuation on Suicidal Behavior in Bipolar Manic-Depressive Disorder, *Journal of Clinical Psychiatry* 60 (1999): 77–84; L. Tondo and R. J. Baldessarini, "Reduced Suicide Risk During Lithium Maintenance Treatment," *Journal of Clinical Psychiatry* 61 (2000): suppl. 09, 97–104.

184 "I suppose it is back to the lithium": Letter from Elizabeth Hardwick to Mary McCarthy, January 29, 1976, Vassar.

184 He was taking lithium: Medical records of Robert Lowell, Massachusetts General Hospital. Lowell was admitted to the Boston hospital on February 1, 1977, and discharged on February 9, 1977. His medical history, including the findings from his hospitalization at Massachusetts General Hospital, is discussed in Appendix 3.

184 "Of all our conversations": Robert Giroux, in his introduction to *Collected Prose*, xiii–xiv.

184 "I am at the end of something": Letter from Robert Lowell to Elizabeth Bishop, January 23, 1963, *Letters*, 414.

185 "I have a formidable new doctor": Letter from Robert Lowell to Elizabeth Bishop, February 25, 1966, *Letters*, 468.

185 "Sickness, methinks": K. R. Eissler, *Goethe: A Psychoanalytic Study: 1775–1786*, vol. 2 (Detroit: Wayne State University, 1963), 1182.

185 "Sometimes nothing is so solid": Letter from Robert Lowell to Elizabeth Bishop, July 2, 1948, *Letters*, 103.

185 "If I don't write": Letter from Hannah Arendt to Mary McCarthy, October 17, 1969, *Between Friends*, 248.

185 "Directly I am not working": Virginia Woolf, diary entries, August 6, 1937, and December 18, 1928, in *The Diary of Virginia Woolf*, ed. Anne Olivier Bell (San Diego: Harcourt Brace, 1977), vol. 3 (1925–30) and vol. 5 (1936–41).

185 "For the last four months": Letter from Robert Lowell to Harriet Winslow, January 23, 1963, Houghton Library.

186 "I *fight* depression by work": George Mackay Brown, December 11, 1982, *George Mackay Brown: The Life* (London: John Murray, 2006), 38.

186 "All sorrows can be borne": Isak Dinesen, quoting a friend, in an interview with Bart Mohn, *New York Times Book Review*, November 3, 1957.

186 "To go through a terrible time": Apsley Cherry-Garrard, in *T. E. Lawrence: By His Friends*, ed. A. W. Lawrence (London: Jonathan Cape, 1937), 192.

186 "morbid self-introspection": Ibid.

186 "were worse than anything": Ibid.

186 "Then as th'earth's": John Donne, "The Triple Fool," in *John Donne*, ed. John Carey (Oxford: Oxford University Press, 1990), 96.

186 "Dejection of spirits": Letter from William Cowper to Lady Hesketh, Octo-

ber 12, 1785, in *The Correspondence of William Cowper*, vol. 2, ed. Thomas Wright (London: Hodder and Stoughton, 1904).

187 "Working, I sit groping": Robert Lowell, "15. Writing," draft manuscript, HRC.

187 "Writing fell to me": Robert Lowell, essay written for Vernon Williams, M.D., n.d. 1950s, HRC.

187 "The onionskin typing paper I bought": Robert Lowell, "Onionskin," *Collected Poems*, 589.

187 "But, for the unquiet heart": Alfred, Lord Tennyson, *In Memoriam*, ed. Erik Gray (New York: W. W. Norton, 2004), 9.

187 "No one has ever written": Antonin Artaud, "Van Gogh, the Man Suicided by Society (1947)," in *Antonin Artaud: Selected Writings*, ed. Susan Sontag (Berkeley and Los Angeles: University of California Press, 1988), 497.

187 "Sometimes I wonder": Graham Greene, *Ways of Escape* (New York: Simon and Schuster, 1980), 285.

187 "What it usually lights on": Letter from Robert Lowell to Elizabeth Bishop, June 15, 1964, *Words in Air*, 542.

188 "I think I am escaping": Letter from Robert Lowell to William Meredith, July 16, 1966, Connecticut College.

188 "I gather from your phone calls": Letter from Robert Lowell to Frank Bidart, September 4, 1976, *Letters*, 656.

189 "Is getting well ever an art": Robert Lowell, "Unwanted," *Collected Poems*, 834.

190 writing prose was less likely: Charlotte Lowell wrote to Jean Stafford on October 31, 1943, that she blamed the Tates for making Lowell more vulnerable to the "emotional excitement of poetry"; Blair Clark Papers, HRC. Elizabeth Hardwick wrote to Blair and Holly Clark on November 29, 1954, that prose writing was good for Lowell since prose, unlike poetry, "need not thrive . . . on bouts of enthusiasm"; Blair Clark Papers, HRC.

190 "I've just started messing around": Letter from Robert Lowell to John Berryman, October 6, 1954, *Letters*, 240.

190 "intolerable poetic darkness": Letter from Robert Lowell to J. F. Power, October 29, 1956, *Letters*, 264.

190 "I find it hard to be": Letter from Robert Lowell to Flannery O'Connor, January 16, 1956, *Letters*, 253.

190 "How different prose is": Letter from Robert Lowell to Elizabeth Bishop, April 15, 1976, *Letters*, 648.

190 "Near the Unbalanced Aquarium": Robert Lowell wrote many drafts of "Near the Unbalanced Aquarium." His editor Robert Giroux believes the final version was probably written in 1957 (*Collected Prose*, 377). It was published in the March 12, 1987, edition of the *New York Review of Books*. Quotations in the text are from *Collected Prose*, 346–63. Draft manuscripts are in Houghton Library.

191 "stirring up the bottom": Letter from Robert Lowell to Elizabeth Bishop, November 18, 1949, *Letters*, 150.

191 "a huge affair with snails": Robert Lowell, quoted in forthcoming book on Lowell's prose: *Memoirs*, ed. Steven Gould Axelrod and Grzegorz Kose (New York: Farrar, Straus and Giroux, 2018). Draft manuscripts in Houghton Library.

191 "remained in its recollections": Robert Lowell, "Near the Unbalanced Aquarium," *Collected Prose*, 348.

191 "trying as usual": Ibid., 346.

191 "the yeasty manic lift": Robert Lowell, draft 1, "The Balanced Aquarium," Houghton Library.

191 "seemed to change shape": Ibid., 346.

191 "purely and puritanically confined": Ibid.

192 "Tireless, madly sanguine": Ibid., 350.

192 "its own shuffle": Robert Lowell, draft 6, "The Balanced Aquarium," Houghton Library.

192 Dr. James Masterson: James Masterson, M.D., was Robert Lowell's psychiatrist during his hospital stay at Payne Whitney from May 21, 1954, until September 15, 1954. Dr. Masterson's clinical notes are in Robert Lowell's medical record.

192 "Was I paying Dr. Masterson": Robert Lowell's medical records, Payne Whitney Clinic, New York, 1954.

192 "Suddenly I felt": Robert Lowell, "Near the Unbalanced Aquarium," 352–53.

193 "For holding up my trousers": Ibid., 353.

194 "'Why don't I die'": Ibid., 354.

194 "I am writing my autobiography": Ibid., 362.

194 "symbolic and sacramental act": Robert Lowell, "On the Gettysburg Address," *Collected Prose*, 165.

194 "a symbolic significance": Ibid., 166.

IV. CHARACTER: HOW WILL THE HEART ENDURE?

197 "Your lacerations tell": Robert Lowell, "Mr. Edwards and the Spider," *Collected Poems*, 59.

9. WITH ALL MY LOVE, CAL

199 "Bringing ice out": Philip Booth, "Summers in Castine," 37–53.

200 "I think of my life": Letter from Robert Lowell to Elizabeth Bishop, November 16, 1964, *Words in Air*, 559.

200 "his life was once more broken": Henry Adams, *The Education of Henry Adams*, 209. Byron too wrote of reweaving the web of life:

> All suffering doth destroy, or is destroy'd,
> Even by the sufferer; and, in each event
> Ends:—Some, with hope replenish'd and rebuoy'd,
> Return to whence they came—with like intent,
> And weave their web again; some, bow'd and bent,
> Wax gray and ghastly, withering ere their time,
> And perish with the reed on which they leant.

NOTES TO PAGES 201–204

George Gordon, Lord Byron, *Childe Harold's Pilgrimage*, in *Lord Byron: The Complete Poetical Works*, vol. 2, ed. Jerome McGann (Oxford: Oxford University Press, 1980), 131.

201 "You play against a sickness": Robert Lowell, "Mr. Edwards and the Spider," *Collected Poems*, 59.

201 "The channel gripped our hull": Robert Lowell, "For Frank Parker 2," *Collected Poems*, 508.

202 "Cal was a big man": Derek Walcott interview, "The Art of Poetry, No. 37," *Paris Review* 101 (Winter 1986).

202 "attractive, rather feverish-faced": Joyce Carol Oates, *Salmagundi* (Winter–Spring 2004): 119.

202 "achingly well-mannered": James Atlas, "Robert Lowell in Cambridge: Lord Weary," 56–64.

202 "troubled blue eyes": Stanley Kunitz, "Talk with Robert Lowell."

202 "The ashtray was heaped": James Atlas, "Robert Lowell in Cambridge: Lord Weary," 62.

202 "At submanic velocity": Dudley Young, "Life with Lord Lowell at Essex U.," *PN Review* 28 (1982): 46.

203 "seemed to come out all in a heap": Jason Epstein, letter to Ian Hamilton, January 21, 1981, Ian Hamilton Papers, British Library.

203 "Lowell was the most engaging man": Peter Levi, in "Remembering Lowell," *Listener* 98 (September 22, 1977): 379.

203 "I feel almost too much": Letter from Flannery O'Connor to Betty Hester, April 21, 1956, in *Flannery O'Connor: Collected Works*, ed. Sally Fitzgerald (New York: Library of America, 1988), 992.

203 "really a kind": Letter from Donald Jenkins to Ian Hamilton, June 19, 1980, Ian Hamilton Papers, British Library.

203 "Everyone likes him": Letter from Isaiah Berlin to Noel Annan, May 1, 1964, in Isaiah Berlin, *Building*, 191.

203 "Until his arrival": W. D. Snodgrass, "A Liberal Education: Mentors, Fomenters and Tormentors," *Southern Review* (Summer 1992): 450.

203 "In the name of his art": William Phillips, *A Partisan View: Five Decades of the Literary Life* (New York: Stein and Day, 1983), 215.

203 Evgenia recollects: Evgenia Citkowitz, interview with the author, March 12, 2004.

203 "the last madness of child-gaiety": Robert Lowell, "Ivana," *Collected Poems*, 694.

204 The words used time and again: Ibid.; Evgenia Citkowitz, correspondence with the author, August 11, 2015; Harriet Lowell, correspondence with the author, April 2012; Ivana Lowell, interview with the author, April 16, 2014; Ivana Lowell, *Why Not Say What Happened?* (New York: Alfred A. Knopf, 2010), 27.

204 "I loved him at first sight": Elizabeth Bishop, "Elizabeth Bishop on Robert Lowell," *Words in Air*, 809, "Lowell Reminiscences," Bishop Papers, Vassar.

204 "Kindness has always been": Ibid., 810.

204 "There's no one else": Letter from Robert Lowell to Elizabeth Bishop, April 7, 1959, *Letters*, 344.

205 "I think of you daily": Letter from Robert Lowell to Elizabeth Bishop, March 10, 1963, *Letters*, 420.

205 "Please never stop writing": Letter from Elizabeth Bishop to Robert Lowell, July 27, 1960, *Words in Air*, 332.

205 "just the faintest glimmer": Letter from Elizabeth Bishop to Robert Lowell, February 27, 1970, *Words in Air*, 665.

205 "from thinking about your letter": Letter from Robert Lowell to Elizabeth Bishop, March 10, 1962, *Letters*, 397.

205 "It was a Maine lobster town": Robert Lowell, "Water," *Collected Poems*, 321–22.

206 "Swimming, or rather standing": Elizabeth Bishop, "Elizabeth Bishop on Robert Lowell," *Words in Air*, 811.

206 "inexhaustible pleasure": Alan Williamson, "Robert Lowell: A Reminiscence," *The Harvard Advocate* 113 (November 1979): 38.

207 "I know that he used": Elizabeth Bishop, statement for the English memorial service for Robert Lowell, London, October 12, 1977. Many writers noted Lowell's acts of kindness: unrequested financial help, unsolicited nominations for fellowships and awards, letters of support and understanding. Archibald MacLeish, one of these many, wrote to Lowell on May 10, 1960, that he was a "doer of good works. It seems to me that whenever I turn I see your hand held out to help somebody along." Quoted in *Words in Air*, 325.

207 "In my middle age": Letter from Donald Davie to Robert Lowell, June 24, 1967, Houghton Library.

207 "There was a kind of litmus quality": William Alfred, interview with Ian Hamilton, 1981, Ian Hamilton Papers, British Library.

207 "I have never had a more loyal friend": Frank Parker, "The Lively Arts: Robert Lowell: A Life Study," BBC Broadcast Archives, February 22, 1980.

207 "One of the most extraordinary things": Blair Clark, interview with Ian Hamilton, 1979, Ian Hamilton Papers, British Library.

207 "I think he never": William Alfred, interview with Ian Hamilton. Ian Hamilton Papers, British Library.

207 "was a supremely challenging": Diantha Parker, "Robert Lowell's Lightness," Poetry Foundation, November 25, 2010, www.poetryfoundation.org/features /articles/detail/69622.

207 "his gaiety, his love of life": Esther Brooks, "Remembering Cal," 42.

207 "modest and arrogant": Stanley Kunitz, "The Sense of a Life," *New York Times Book Review*, October 16, 1977, 3.

208 "You never felt quite safe": Seamus Heaney, "Gulliver in Lilliput: Remembering Robert Lowell," in *The Norton Book of Friendship*, ed. Eudora Welty and Ronald A. Sharp (New York: W. W. Norton, 1991), 547.

208 "All flaws considered": Norman Mailer, *The Armies of the Night*, 74.

208 "complex, tortured, and difficult": Kathleen Spivack, *With Robert Lowell and His Circle*.

208 "He was great fun": William Alfred, "The Lively Arts: Robert Lowell: A Life Study."

208 "The world became larger": Frank Parker, quoted by his daughter Diantha Parker in "Robert Lowell's Lightness," from remarks for "The Lively Arts: Robert Lowell: A Life Study."

208 "He had that quality": Caroline Blackwood, conversation with Kathleen Spivack, quoted in Kathleen Spivack, *With Robert Lowell and His Circle*, 150. Some of the comments about Robert Lowell are similar to those made about Virginia Woolf. "One would hand her a bit of information as dull as a lump of lead," said Nigel Nicolson. "She would hand it back glittering like diamonds. I always felt on leaving her that I had drunk two glasses of an excellent champagne." Joan Russell Noble ed., *Recollections of Virginia Woolf by Her Contemporaries* (Athens: Ohio University Press, 1972), 128.

208 "very sociable, curious": Elizabeth Hardwick, interview with Ian Hamilton, 1982, Ian Hamilton Papers, British Library.

209 "took up all the air": Correspondence from Wendy Lesser to the author, February 3, 2012.

209 "There was no point": Jonathan Raban, interview with Ian Hamilton, 1979, Ian Hamilton Papers, British Library.

209 Lowell staged a reenactment: Jonathan Raban, correspondence with the author, October 21, 2016.

209 "There were times toward the end": Ibid.

209 "I felt that I couldn't bear": Stephen Spender, interview with Ian Hamilton, Ian Hamilton Papers, British Library.

209 overwhelming, dominating, and draining: Jonathan Miller, interview with Ian Hamilton, 1980, Ian Hamilton Papers, British Library.

209 "I can remember being unable": Alan Brownjohn, interview with Ian Hamilton, 1981, Ian Hamilton Papers, British Library.

210 "We gossiped on the rocks of the millpond": Robert Lowell, "John Berryman," *Collected Prose*, 112.

210 "a bleak spot": Anne Sexton, "Classroom at Boston University," *The Harvard Advocate* 145 (November 1961): 13.

210 "with a cold chisel": Ibid.

210 "Week after week": W. D. Snodgrass, "A Liberal Education," 451.

211 "through uncharted galaxies": Ibid.

211 "I was disquieted": Robert B. Shaw, "Learning from Lowell," *Yale Review* 89 (January 2001): 78.

211 "once during class": Kathleen Spivack, interview with the author, March 19, 2014. Also in Kathleen Spivack, *With Robert Lowell and His Circle*, 26: "Lowell seemed agitated, we had the distinct fear he was going to throw himself out of the window."

211 "In the thin classroom": Anne Sexton, "Elegy in the Classroom," *To Bedlam and Part Way Back* (Boston: Houghton Mifflin, 1960), 45.

212 "Cal's bulk haunts my classes": Derek Walcott, "Midsummer XXXII," *Midsummer* (New York: Farrar, Straus and Giroux, 1984).

212 "incapable of dealing with": Kathleen Spivack, "Robert Lowell: A Memoir," *Antioch Review* 43 (Spring 1983): 183.

212 "I never was able to shake": Ibid., 185.

212 "altogether cowardice": Letter from William Meredith to Robert Lowell, September 16, 1959, Connecticut College.

212 "There was no point": Letter from Robert Lowell to William Meredith, September 18, 1959, *Letters*, 352.

213 "There's nothing wrong": Jonathan Raban, interview with the author, June 20, 2012.

213 "incredible flow of energy": Elizabeth Hardwick, interview with Ian Hamilton, 1982, Ian Hamilton Papers, British Library.

213 Empson did go: Meena Alexander, e-mail to Saskia Hamilton, August 28, 2016. Permission to cite from Meena Alexander.

213 "some grunt of commiseration": Anthony Hecht, *Robert Lowell: A Lecture Delivered at the Library of Congress on May 2, 1983* (Washington, D.C.: Library of Congress, 1983), 11.

213 "Your move, Cal": James Wolcott, "The Limits of Poetic License," *Harper's*, December 1982, 54.

213 "Not only death": Letter from William James to the daughter of Ned Hooper, brother of Clover Adams, after his (probable) suicide in 1901, May 10, 1901. Quoted in Natalie Dykstra, *Clover Adams: A Gilded and Heartbreaking Life* (New York: Houghton Mifflin Harcourt, 2012), 174.

214 "He cannot bear anything": Letter from Sophia Hawthorne to Nathaniel Hawthorne, 1861, Berg Collection, New York Public Library. Quoted in E. H. Miller, *Salem Is My Dwelling Place: A Life of Nathaniel Hawthorne* (Iowa City: University of Iowa Press, 1991), 468.

215 "We think it is nice to do well": Letter from Robert Lowell, Sr., to Robert Lowell, August 26, 1950, Houghton Library.

215 "All night I've held your hand": Robert Lowell, "Man and Wife," *Collected Poems*, 189.

215 "very beautiful, musical": Letter from Elizabeth Bishop to Robert Lowell, August 16, 1963, *Words in Air*, 481.

216 "Work-table, litter, books": Robert Lowell, "Night Sweat," *Collected Poems*, 375.

216 "He was the most extraordinary": Elizabeth Hardwick, quoted in Richard Locke, "Conversation on a Book," *New York Times*, April 29, 1979.

217 "If only these things of Cal's": Letter from Elizabeth Hardwick to Allen Tate, June 1, 1959, Princeton.

217 "I tire of my turmoil": Letter from Robert Lowell to Isabella Gardner, October 10, 1961, *Letters*, 389.

217 "Nothing! No oil": Robert Lowell, "Eye and Tooth," *Collected Poems*, 335.

217 "No doubt people did tire": Harriet Lowell, correspondence with the author, April 2012.

218 "He'd become a cartoonish version": Ibid.

220 "I wake to your cookout": Robert Lowell, "The Human Condition," *Collected Poems*, 632.

220 "Chaos grows like a snowball": Letter from Robert Lowell to J. F. Powers, February 6, 1957, provided to author by Katherine A. Powers.

220 "I've always suspected": Letter from Robert Lowell to Peter Taylor, June 27, 1960, Vanderbilt.

220 "Spring moved to summer": Robert Lowell, "Summer: 5. Harriet," *Collected Poems*, 609.

221 "Their sentiments and instincts": Daniel Hack Tuke, "Circular Insanity," 219.

221 Mania, Robert Lowell had said: "Mania is extremity for one's friends, depression for one's self. Both are chemical." Ian Hamilton, "A Conversation with Robert Lowell," 10–29.

222 "excessive involvement": *Diagnostic and Statistical Manual of Mental Disorders*, 5th ed. (Washington, D.C.: American Psychiatric Publishing, 2013), 124.

222 clinical studies of thousands: A review of studies of approximately two thousand patients found than 51 percent were hypersexual when they were manic. F. K. Goodwin and K. R. Jamison, *Manic-Depressive Illness*; D. H. Tuke *Dictionary of Psychological Medicine* (1892); Emil Kraepelin, Manic-Depressive Insanity (1921); Eugen Bleuler, *Textbook of Psychiatry*, 4th German ed., ed. A. A. Brill (New York: Macmillan, 1924); J. D. Campbell, *Manic-Depressive Disease* (1953); and Mayer-Gross, E. Slater, and M. Roth, *Clinical Psychiatry* (Baltimore: Williams and Wilkins, 1955) are among the many earlier clinicians who reported increased sexual desire and behavior during mania.

222 "lewdness and shamelessness": Arateus, *The Extant Works of Aretaeus*, 302, 304.

222 "Manic patients are very susceptible": John D. Campbell, *Manic-Depressive Disease* (Philadelphia: Lippincott, 1953), 156.

222 "the most powerful and important": John Custance, *Wisdom, Madness, and Folly: The Philosophy of a Lunatic* (New York: Farrar, Straus and Cudahy, 1952), 40–54.

222 "Chaucer's old January": Robert Lowell, "Morning," *Collected Poems*, 615.

223 "Spring's Lesson": Horace, *Odes and Epodes*, ed. and trans. Niall Rudd (Cambridge, MA: Harvard Univerity Press, 2004), 33.

223 "Now, now": Robert Lowell, "Spring," *Collected Poems*, 398.

223 "Cal's recuperative powers were almost": Elizabeth Hardwick letter to Ian Hamilton, n.d., HRC.

223 "it's only love": Letter from Robert Lowell to John Berryman, September 9, 1969, *Letters*, 525.

223 "The last pages of Pasternak's *Zhivago*": Letter from Robert Lowell to Harriet Winslow, September 16, 1958, *Letters*, 327.

223 "You must read the Pasternak": Letter from Robert Lowell to Elizabeth Bishop, September 18, 1958, *Words in Air*, 265.

223 "Did I write you about Pasternak": Letter from Robert Lowell to Elizabeth Bishop, October 16, 1958, *Words in Air*, 271.

224 "I'm shatteringly impressed": Letter from Robert Lowell to Peter Taylor, October 31, 1958, Vanderbilt.

224 unseverable emotional ties: "I am bound to Russia by my birth, my life, and my work. I cannot imagine my fate separated from and outside Russia." Letter from Boris Pasternak published in *Pravda*, November 1, 1958.

224 "the best by far": Peter Levi, *Boris Pasternak* (London: Hutchinson, 1990), 92.

224 "I have come to feel": Robert Lowell, *Imitations* (New York: Farrar, Straus and Giroux, 1961), xii.

224 "The Frosted Rowan": Boris Pasternak, *Doctor Zhivago*, trans. Richard Pevear and Larissa Volokhonsky (London: Vintage, 2011), 316–36.

224 "dense, impassable forest": Ibid., 316.

224 "solitary, beautiful, rusty-red-leafed": Ibid., 317.

224 "half covered with snow": Ibid., 336.

225 "a mad attempt to stop time with words": Ibid., 325.

225 "The rain falls": Robert Lowell, "The Heavenly Rain," *Collected Poems*, 559.

225 "I was in a hospital for five weeks": Letter from Robert Lowell to Elizabeth Bishop, June 27, 1961, *Words in Air*, 366.

225 "It has been as though": Letter from Robert Lowell to Giovanna Madonia Erba, February 22, 1954, *Letters*, 211.

226 "Away from you": Letter from Robert Lowell to Giovanna Madonia Erba, July 11, 1954, *Letters*, 238.

226 "Poor Giovanna": Letter from Elizabeth Hardwick to Blair and Holly Clark, April 16, 1954, HRC.

226 "Love is resurrection": Robert Lowell, "Mohammed," *Collected Poems*, 449.

226 "O to break loose": Robert Lowell, "Waking Early Sunday Morning," *Collected Poems*, 385.

226 "all that kept off death": Robert Lowell, "Three Poems: 1. Seal of the Fair Sex," *Collected Poems*, 519.

226 "Our town was blanketed": Robert Lowell, "William Carlos Williams," *Collected Prose*, 37.

226 "a slack of eternity": Ian Hamilton, "A Conversation with Robert Lowell," *The Review* 26 (Summer 1971): 12.

226 "in season to the tropical": Robert Lowell, "Circles: 6. The Hard Way," *Collected Poems*, 632.

226 "Tannish buds and green buds": Robert Lowell, "Return in March," *Collected Poems*, 806.

227 "I, fifty": Robert Lowell, "Mexico," *Collected Poems*, 624.

227 "I have lived without": Ibid., 627.

227 "I wanted to run over": Letter from Mary Keelan to Robert Lowell, January 9, 1967, Houghton Library.

227 "Poor Child": Robert Lowell, "Mexico," *Collected Poems*, 628.

227 "The flower I took away": Robert Lowell, "Eight Months Later," *Collected Poems*, 629.

228 "loves to fish in roiled waters": "Satan is now in his passions, he feels his passions approaching, he loves to fish in roiled waters." Nathaniel Ward, "The Simple Cobbler of Aggawan," 1647; reprinted in Perry Miller, *The American Puritans*, 95.

228 "are uniquely able": Frieda Fromm-Reichmann, "Intensive Psychotherapy of Manic-Depressives," *Confinia Neurologia* 9 (1949): 158–65.

228 documented in the clinical research: Donald Hack Tuke, "Circular Insan-

ity"; Emil Kraepelin, *Manic-Depressive Insanity and Paranoia*; D. S. Janowsky, M. Leff, and R. S. Epstein, "Playing the Manic Game: Interpersonal Maneuvers of the Acutely Manic Patient," *Archives of General Psychiatry* 22 (1970): 252–61; D. S. Janowsky, K. El-Yousef, and J. M. Davis, "Interpersonal Maneuvers of Manic Patients," *American Journal of Psychiatry* 131 (1974): 250–55; F. K. Goodwin and K. R. Jamison, *Manic-Depressive Illness*.

229 "I am God": John Custance, *Wisdom, Madness, and Folly*, 51.

229 Christopher Ricks has argued: Christopher Ricks, *The Force of Poetry* (Oxford: Clarendon Press, 1984), 256.

230 "The great design of moral management": Eli Todd, quoted in *The Institutional Case of the Insane in the United States and Canada*, ed. Henry Mills Hurd (Baltimore: Johns Hopkins Press, 1916), 81.

230 members of Johnson's staff: Jeffrey Meyers, "Ignorant Armies," *Times Literary Supplement*, May 21, 2015.

230 "Cal was perfectly analytic": Grey Gowrie, interview with the author, June 30, 2011.

230 "shattered by what he had done": Xandra Gowrie, interview with Ian Hamilton, 1980, Ian Hamilton Papers, British Library.

230 "he was blue": William Alfred, interview with Ian Hamilton, 1981, Ian Hamilton Papers, British Library.

230 "he could remember all": Esther Brooks, "Remembering Cal," 42.

231 "It's the most awful feeling": Caroline Blackwood, interview with Ian Hamilton, 1979, Ian Hamilton Papers, British Library.

231 "My Dolphin, you only guide": Robert Lowell, "Dolphin," *Collected Poems*, 708.

231 "I saw your eyes": Robert Lowell, "The Mills of the Kavanaughs," *Collected Poems*, 84.

231 "we know this": Robert Lowell, "Death of Alexander," *Collected Poems*, 437.

232 "His doom seemed": Robert Lowell, "Remarks to Trumbull Seniors at Yale," June 10, 1968, Yale Library.

232 "These attacks seem": Letter from Robert Lowell to Elizabeth Bishop, February 25, 1965, *Letters*, 456.

232 "impetuous driving force": Robert Lowell, "Remarks to Trumbull Seniors at Yale."

232 Frank Sinatra once said: Frank Sinatra, *Playboy* interview with Joe Hyams, February 1963.

232 "I'm for anything that gets you": Frank Sinatra, quoted in Bill Zehme, *The Way You Wear Your Hat: Frank Sinatra and the Lost Art of Livin'* (New York: HarperCollins, 1997).

10. AND WILL NOT SCARE

233 "The struck oak that lost": Robert Lowell, "We Took Our Paradise," *Collected Poems*, 767.

233 "All law, morals, and rewards": Letter from Robert Lowell to Anne Dick, n.d. summer 1936, *Letters*, 8.

234 "A man should stop his ears": Robert Louis Stevenson, *"Aes Triplex,"* in *Aes Triplex and Other Essays* (Portland, ME: J. B. Mosher, 1903), 16–17.

234 "What—beyond his poetry": Alan Williamson, "Robert Lowell: A Reminiscence," 38–39.

234 "Courage," Lord Moran said: Lord Moran, *The Anatomy of Courage* (1945; New York: Carroll & Graf, 2007), 67.

234 "exercise of mind over fear": Ibid., xvi.

235 "There are many reasons": Apsley Cherry-Garrard, *The Worst Journey in the World* (1922; New York: Penguin, 2005), 564.

235 "Much of that risk": Ibid., 532.

235 "in wind and drift": Ibid., 220.

235 "Oak and three layers of brass": Horace, "To Vergil Setting Out for Greece," *Horace: Odes and Epodes*, 29.

235 "The man with the nerves goes farthest": Apsley Cherry-Garrard, *The Worst Journey in the World*, 563–64.

236 "an overdraft on my vital capital": Ibid., 536.

236 "sheer good grain": Ibid.

236 "The man with nerves": Ibid.

236 "as fine a death": Ibid.

236 "Surely the greatest was": Ibid.

236 "We took risks": Robert Falcon Scott, *The Last Expedition* (1913; London: Vintage, 2012), 442.

237 "It fares, indeed": J. C. Bucknill and D. H. Tuke, *A Manual of Psychological Medicine* (London: John Churchill, 1858), 220–36.

238 "like prehistoric monsters dragged down": Robert Lowell, "On 'Skunk Hour,'" *Collected Prose*, 227.

238 "medieval armor's undermining": Letter from Robert Lowell to Elizabeth Bishop, December 3, 1957, *Letters*, 306.

238 "alive maybe, if anything can breathe": Letter from Robert Lowell to Elizabeth Bishop, February 26, 1967, *Letters*, 484.

238 "A poet can be intelligent": Robert Lowell, "Afterthought," *Notebook* (New York: Farrar, Straus and Giroux, 1970), 263.

238 "I too wore armor": Robert Lowell, "1930's 2," *Collected Poems*, 503.

238 "Lowell's poetry didn't attack": Seamus Heaney, "The Lively Arts: Robert Lowell."

239 "Don't keep me waiting": Letter from Robert Lowell to Giovanna Madonia Erba, March 6, 1954, *Letters*, 212.

239 "shedding one's costume": Letter from Robert Lowell to Ezra Pound, April 17, 1955, *Letters*, 246.

239 "The thought of going back": Letter from Robert Lowell to Elizabeth Bishop, July 16, 1955, *Letters*, 248.

239 "the shell breaks": Letter from Robert Lowell to Elizabeth Bishop, February 10, 1963, *Words in Air*, 445.

239 "great callousness": Ibid., 444.

239 "battle array against the fire": Robert Lowell, "Mr. Edwards and the Spider," *Collected Poems*, 59.

239 *"with one skin-layer missing"*: Robert Lowell, "Home," *Collected Poems*, 825.

239 "I pray for memory": Robert Lowell, "Turtle," *Collected Poems*, 809.

240 "'Of late they leave'": Robert Lowell, "Words for Muffin, A Guinea-Pig," *Collected Poems*, 633.

240 "I hear": Robert Lowell, "Skunk Hour," *Collected Poems*, 192.

240 "white stripes, moonstruck": Ibid.

240 "This is the dark night": Robert Lowell, "'On 'Skunk Hour,'" *Collected Prose*, 226.

241 "indomitable": Robert Lowell, Remarks on "Skunk Hour," Audio, Library of Congress, Washington, D.C., 1978.

241 "horrible blind energy": Letter from Robert Lowell to John Berryman, March 18, 1962, *Letters*, 400.

241 "freedom and an accomplishment": Letter from Robert Lowell to Richard Tillinghast, August 1969, *Letters*, 522.

241 "ruthless cutting edge": George Mackay Brown, "Hawkfall," in *Hawkfall and Other Stories* (1974; Edinburgh: Polygon, 2004), 128.

241 "A too-refined sensibility": Ibid.

241 "We must all live by taking": Letter from Robert Lowell to Philip Booth, October 10, 1966, Dartmouth College Library.

241 "I saw the spiders": Robert Lowell, "Mr. Edwards and the Spider," *Collected Poems*, 59–60.

244 "He was an ancestor": Letter from Robert Lowell to Richard Tillinghast, August 1969, *Letters*, 519.

244 "often threaten[ed] my Life": Ava Chamberlain, *The Notorious Elizabeth Tuttle: Marriage, Murder, and Madness in the Family of Jonathan Edwards* (New York: New York University Press, 2012), 86–87, 184–86.

244 "I have a constitution": Letter from Jonathan Edwards to the Trustees of the College of New Jersey, October 19, 1757, in *A Jonathan Edwards Reader*, ed. J. E. Smith, H. S. Stout, and K. P. Minkema (New Haven: Yale University Press, 1995), 321.

244 "The immense magnificence": Jonathan Edwards, "Images of Divine Things," *A Jonathan Edwards Reader*, 21.

245 "exuberant goodness": Jonathan Edwards, "The Spider Letter," October 31, 1723, *A Jonathan Edwards Reader*, 5.

245 "The Future Punishment": Jonathan Edwards, "The Future Punishment of the Wicked Unavoidable and Intolerable," *The Works of Jonathan Edwards*, vol. 2, ed. Edward Hickman (London: Westley and Davis, 1834), 78.

245 "What art thou": Ibid.

245 "shuts and no man opens": Ibid.

245 "trying to get a little prose piece": Letter from Robert Lowell to Babette Deutsch, February 24, 1955, *Letters*, 244.

245 "I have seen vast multitudes": Jonathan Edwards, "The Spider Letter," October 31, 1723, *A Jonathan Edwards Reader*, 2.

246 "As a boy": Robert Lowell, "Jonathan Edwards in Western Massachusetts," *Collected Poems*, 354.

246 "They purpose nothing": Robert Lowell, "Mr. Edwards and the Spider," *Collected Poems*, 59.

246 "the bowels of fierce fire": Ibid.

247 "How then will thine hands": Jonathan Edwards, "The Future Punishment of the Wicked Unavoidable and Intolerable."

247 "Your lacerations": Robert Lowell, "Mr. Edwards and the Spider," *Collected Poems*, 59.

V. ILLNESS AND ART: SOMETHING ALTOGETHER LIVED

251 "During this time": Letter from Robert Lowell to Chard Powers Smith, October 3, 1959, *Letters*, 354.

11. A MAGICAL ORANGE GROVE IN A NIGHTMARE

253 "There is personal anguish": Letter from Robert Lowell to Philip Booth, October 10, 1966, Dartmouth College Library.

253 "brilliant, mordant, and lighthearted": Robert Fitzgerald, "The Things of the Eye," *Poetry* 132 (May 1978): 108.

254 "I saw the best minds": Allen Ginsberg, *Howl and Other Poems* (San Francisco: City Lights, 1956).

254 "I'm cross with god": John Berryman, "153," in *The Dream Songs* (New York: Farrar, Straus and Giroux, 2014), 172.

254 "I feel the jagged gash": Robert Lowell, "John Berryman," *Collected Prose*, 114–15.

254 "Ah the swift vanishing": Robert Lowell, "Last Night," *Collected Poems*, 601.

254 "He seemed to throb": Robert Lowell, "John Berryman," *Collected Prose*, 104–5.

254 "Hyper-enthusiasms made him": Ibid., 112.

255 "I felt frightened": Letter from Robert Lowell to William Meredith, July 16, 1966, Connecticut College.

255 "the most hopeful": Ibid.

255 "some germ in the mind": Ibid.

255 "It seems there's been something curious": Letter from Robert Lowell to John Berryman, March 15, 1959, *Letters*, 338.

255 "What you said about the other poets": Letter from Robert Lowell to John Berryman, March 18, 1962, *Letters*, 400.

255 "all the best of life": Robert Lowell, "For John Berryman," *Collected Poems*, 737.

255 "I feel I know": Robert Lowell, "For John Berryman 1," *Collected Poems*, 600.

256 "a magical orange grove": Letter from Robert Lowell to Blair Clark, August 6, 1954, *Letters*, 239. Lowell was referring to his affair with Giovanna Madonia,

which began when he was manic. "The whole business was sincere enough," he wrote to Clark, "but a stupid pathological mirage, a magical orange grove in a nightmare. I feel like a son of a bitch." Ibid., 239.

256 "are a lot like yours": Letter from Elizabeth Bishop to Robert Lowell, January 8, 1963, *Words in Air,* 440.

256 "I have thought twice": Letter from Robert Lowell to Randall Jarrell, April 29, 1965, *Letters,* 458.

257 "the most heartbreaking": Robert Lowell, "Randall Jarrell," *Collected Prose,* 91.

257 "It was sad to hear": Letter from Robert Lowell to Ezra Pound, February 10, 1963, *Letters,* 419.

257 "I feel a great kinship": Letter from Robert Lowell to Theodore Roethke, June 8, 1958, University of Washington Libraries.

257 "What we share": Frederick Seidel, "The Art of Poetry: Robert Lowell," *Paris Review* 7 (Winter–Spring 1961): 56–95.

257 "Well, it's happened again": Letter from Theodore Roethke to Robert Lowell, October 8, 1957, Houghton Library.

257 "our dizzy explosions": Letter from Robert Lowell to Theodore Roethke, April 19, 1958, *Letters,* 320.

257 "Our troubles are a bond": Letter from Robert Lowell to Theodore Roethke, March 15, 1958, *Letters,* 318.

257 "For months (perhaps always)": Letter from Robert Lowell to Theodore Roethke, September 18, 1958, University of Washington Libraries.

258 "We couldn't be more different": Letter from Robert Lowell to Theodore Roethke, July 10, 1963, *Letters,* 428.

258 "the price one pays": Letter from Philip Larkin to Caroline Blackwood, February 4, 1976, HRC.

258 "Their senses are acute": Aretaeus, *The Extant Works of Aretaeus,* 303.

259 "advantages in disease": Ibid., 302.

259 "wrote poetry truly from the muses": Ibid.

259 "the senses of hearing and seeing": Benjamin Rush, *Medical Inquiries and Observations Upon the Diseases of the Mind* (Philadelphia: Kimber and Richardson, 1812), 765.

259 "Where is the hospital for mad people": Ibid., 152.

260 "cause surprise by the activity": J. P. Falret, "Memoire sur la folie circulaire," *Bulletin de l'Académie de Médecine* 19 (1854): 382–415.

260 "associates the ideas most unlike": J. E. D. Esquirol, *Des maladies mentales* (Paris: Balliere, 1838). Translated by E. K. Hunt, *Mental Maladies: A Treatise on Insanity* (Philadelphia: Lea and Blachard, 1845), 378.

260 "become unbridled": Emil Kraepelin, *Manic-Depressive Insanity and Paranoia,* 66.

260 "veritable passion for *writing*": Ibid.

260 "very fond of composing": Ibid., 68.

260 "often able to recall": John Macpherson, *Mental Affections: An Introduction to the Study of Insanity* (London: Macmillan, 1899), 175.

260 "mental brilliancy": Ibid.

260 "wonderful facility": Ibid.

260 "Urged on by the pressure": John D. Campbell, *Manic-Depressive Disease.*

263 Epidemiologic studies: The epidemiology of bipolar disorders is reviewed by M. Weissman in F. K. Goodwin and K. R. Jamison, *Manic-Depressive Illness,* 155–86; K. R. Merikangas, R. Jin, J. P. He, et al., "Prevalence and Correlates of Bipolar Spectrum Disorder in the World Mental Health Survey Initiative," *Archives of General Psychiatry* 68 (2011): 241–51; C. B. Pedersen, O. Mors, A. Bertelsen, et al., "A Comprehensive Nationwide Study of the Incidence Rate and Lifetime Risk for Treated Mental Disorders," *JAMA Psychiatry* 71 (2014): 573–81.

264 Biographical Studies of Depression: A. Juda, "The Relationship Between Highest Mental Capacity and Psychic Abnormalities," *American Journal of Psychiatry* 106 (1949): 296–307; C. Martindale, "Father's Absence, Psychopathology, and Poetic Eminence," *Psychological Reports* 31 (1972): 843–47; W. H. Trethowan, "Music and Mental Disorder," in M. Critchley and R. E. Henson, eds., *Music and the Brain* (London: Heinemann, 1977), 398–442; K. R. Jamison, *Touched with Fire: Manic-Depressive Illness and the Artistic Temperament* (New York: Free Press, 1993), 61–72; J. J. Schildkraut, A. J. Hirshfeld, and J. M. Murphy, "Mind and Mood in Modern Art, II: Depressive Disorders, Spirituality, and Early Deaths in the Abstract Expressionist Artists of the New York School," *American Journal of Psychiatry* 151 (1994): 482–88; A. M. Ludwig, *The Price of Greatness: Resolving the Creativity and Madness Controversy* (New York: Guilford, 1995); F. Post, "Verbal Creativity, Depression and Alcoholism: An Investigation of One Hundred American and British Writers," *British Journal of Psychiatry* 168 (1996): 545–55; A. Preti and P. Miotto, "Suicide Among Eminent Artists," *Psychological Reports* 84 (1999): 291–301; E. Czeizel, *Aki költö akar lenni, pokolra kell annak menni?* (Budapest: GMR Reklámügynökség, 2001); G. I. Wills, "Forty Lives in the Bebop Business: Mental Health in a Group of Eminent Jazz Musicians," *British Journal of Psychiatry* 183 (2003): 255–59; J. C. Kaufman, "The Door That Leads into Madness: Eastern European Poets and Mental Illness," *Creativity Research Journal* 17 (2005): 99–103.

266 In 1987, Nancy Andreasen: N. C. Andreasen, "Creativity and Mental Illness: Prevalence Rates in Writers and Their First-Degree Relatives," *American Journal of Psychiatry* 144 (1987): 1288–92.

266 eminent British artists and writers: K. R. Jamison, "Mood Disorders and Seasonal Patterns in British Writers and Artists," *Psychiatry* 52 (1989): 125–34.

267 Arnold Ludwig, a psychiatrist: A. M. Ludwig, "Mental Illness and Creative Activity in Female Writers," *American Journal of Psychiatry* 151 (1994): 1650–56.

268 Population Studies: S. Zammit, P. Allebeck, A. S. David, et al., "A Longitudinal Study of Premorbid IQ Score and Risk of Developing Schizophrenia, Bipolar Disorder, Severe Depression, and Other Nonaffective Psychoses," *Archives of General Psychiatry* 61 (2004): 354–60; K. C. Koenen, T. E. Moffitt, A. L. Roberts, et al., "Childhood IQ and Adult Mental Disorders: A Test of the Cognitive

Reserve Hypothesis," *American Journal of Psychiatry* 166 (2009): 50–57; J. H. MacCabe, M. P. Lambe, S. Cnattingius, et al., "Excellent School Performance at Age 16 and Risk of Adult Bipolar Disorder: National Cohort Study," *British Journal of Psychiatry* 196 (2010): 109–15; C. H. Tremblay, S. Grosskopf, and K. Yang, "Brainstorm: Occupational Choice, Bipolar Illness and Creativity," *Economic and Human Biology* 8 (2010): 233–41; S. Kyaga, P. Lichtenstein, M. Boman, et al., "Creativity and Mental Disorder: Family Study of 300,000 People with Severe Mental Disorder," *British Journal of Psychiatry* 199 (2011): 373–79; C. R. Gale, G. D. Batty, A. M. McIntosh, et al., "Is Bipolar Disorder More Common in Highly Intelligent People? A Cohort Study of a Million Men," *Molecular Psychiatry* 18 (2013): 190–94; S. Kyaga, M. Landen, M. Boman, et al., "Mental Illness, Suicide and Creativity: 40-Year Prospective Total Population Study," *Journal of Psychiatric Research* 47 (2013): 83–90; B. Biasi, M. S. Dahl, and P. Moser, "Career Effects of Mental Health," Social Science Research Network, September 21, 2015. Available at http://dx.doi.org/10.2139/ssrn.2544251; D. J. Smith, J. Anderson, S. Zammit, et al., "Childhood IQ and Risk of Bipolar Disorder in Adulthood: Prospective Birth Cohort Study," *British Journal of Psychiatry Open* 1 (2015): 74–80, DOI: 10.1192/bjpo.bp.115.000455.

270 A study of fifty thousand individuals: S. Zammit et al., "A Longitudinal Study of Premorbid IQ Score."

270 Two others: K. C. Koenen et al., "Childhood IQ and Adult Mental Disorders"; C. R. Gale et al., "Is Bipolar Disorder More Common in Highly Intelligent People?"

270 In a study of academic performance: J. H. MacCabe et al., "Excellent School Performance at Age 16."

270 A recent study from Stanford University: B. Biasi et al., "Career Effects of Mental Health."

270 A recent Swedish total population study: S. Kyaga et al., 2013.

271 marked deficits: See for example: F. K. Goodwin and K. R. Jamison, *Manic-Depressive Illness*, 273–322; I. Torres, V. Boudreau, and L. Yatham, "Neuropsychological Functioning in Euthymic Bipolar Disorder: A Meta-analysis," *Acta Psychiatrica Supplement* 434 (2007): 17–26; B. Arts, N. Jabben, L. Krabbendam, and J. van Os, "Meta-Analyses of Cognitive Functioning in Euthymic Bipolar Patients and Their First-Degree Relatives," *Psychological Medicine* 38 (2008): 771–85; M. J. Kempton, J. R. Geddes, U. Ettinger, et al., "Meta-Analysis, Database, and Meta-Regression of 98 Structural Imaging Studies in Bipolar Disorder," *Archives of General Psychiatry* 65 (2008): 1017–32.

271 prevailing mood during mania: T. A. Greenwood, Bipolar Genome Study (BiGS), and J. R. Kelsoe, "Genome-Wide Association Study of Irritable Versus Elated Mania Suggests Genetic Differences Between Clinical Subforms of Bipolar Disorder," 2013, *PLOS ONE* 8: e53804.PMC3542199; A. Stringaris, N. Ryan-Castellanos, T. Banaschewski, et al., "Dimensions of Manic Symptoms in Youth: Psychosocial Impairment and Cognitive Performance in the IMAGEN Sample," *Journal of Child Psychology and Psychiatry* 55 (2014): 1380–89.

272 An American study: Tremblay et al., "Brainstorm."

272 The first looked at three hundred thousand patients: S. Kyaga et al., "Creativity and Mental Disorder."

272 the second at more than one million: S. Kyaga et al., "Mental Illness, Suicide and Creativity."

273 a recent study from Yale University: R. G. Higier, A. M. Jimenez, C. M. Hultman, et al., "Enhanced Neurocognitive Functioning and Positive Temperament in Twins Discordant for Bipolar Disorder," *American Journal of Psychiatry* 171 (2014): 1191–98.

273 An investigation conducted in Iceland: J. L. Karlsson, "Genetic Basis of Intellectual Variation in Iceland," *Hereditas* 95 (1981): 283–88; J. L. Karlsson, "Creative Intelligence in Relatives of Mental Patients," *Hereditas* 100 (1984): 83–86.

273 Nancy Andreasen, in her study of writers: N. C. Andreasen, "Creativity and Mental Illness," 123–31.

273 In the late 1980s: R. L. Richards, D. K. Kinney, I. Lunde, et al., "Creativity in Manic-Depressives, Cyclothymes, Their Normal Relatives, and Control Subjects," *Journal of Abnormal Psychology* 97 (1988): 281–88.

273 family histories of eminent writers: K. R. Jamison, *Touched with Fire*, 149–237.

274 a study of nearly ninety thousand: R. A. Power, S. Steinberg, G. Bjornsdottir, et al., "Polygenic Risk Scores for Schizophrenia and Bipolar Disorder Predict Creativity," *Nature Neuroscience*, June 8, 2015, DOI: 10.1038/nn.4040.

275 "eugenic interest": B. Onuf, "The Problem of Eugenics in Connection with the Manic Depressive Temperament," *New York Medical Journal* 3 (March 13, 1920): 461–65.

275 Two decades later: A. Myerson and R. Boyle, "The Incidence of Manic-Depressive Psychosis in Certain Socially Important Families," *American Journal of Psychiatry* 98 (1941): 11–21.

275 "It does not necessarily follow": Ibid.

276 A study published in Germany: H. Luxenburger, "Berufsglied und soziale Schichtung in den Familien erblich Geisteskranker," *Eugenik* 3 (1933): 34–40.

277 If we purify: Robert Lowell, "River God," *Collected Poems*, 583.

277 "I think that your friends": Letter from Stephen Spender to Robert Lowell, December 13, 1965, British Library.

278 Manic speech is more pressured: See the review of sixteen studies (1,857 patients) of activity and behavior symptoms during mania in F. K. Goodwin and K. R. Jamison, *Manic-Depressive Illness*. Rapid or pressured speech was present in 88 percent of manic patients.

278 Manic patients use more adjectives: N. C. Andreasen and B. Pfohl, "Linguistic Analysis of Speech in Affective Disorders," *Archives of General Psychiatry* 33 (1976): 1361–67.

278 with more color, and greater urgency: J. Zimmerman and L. Garfinkle, "Preliminary Study of the Art Productions of the Adult Psychotic," *Psychiatric Quarterly* 16 (1942): 313–18; F. Reitman, *Psychotic Art* (London: Rutledge and Kegan Paul, 1950); E. C. Dax, *Experimental Studies in Psychiatric Art* (London:

Faber & Faber, 1953); C. Enâchescu, "Aspects of Pictorial Creation in Manic-Depressive Psychosis," *Confinia Psychiatrica* 14 (1971): 133–42.

278 "Bizarre associations": Vereen Bell, "Robert Lowell, 1917–1977," *Sewanee Review* 86 (January–March 1978): 103.

278 "talked almost without stopping": Leonard Woolf, *Beginning Again: An Autobiography of the Years 1911 to 1918* (New York: Harcourt, 1964), 172–73.

279 "Once the mind gets hot": Virginia Woolf, *Diary*, October 22, 1927, in *The Virginia Woolf Reader*, ed. Mitchell A. Leaska (Orlando: Harvest Book, 1984), 315.

279 "Apparently the only disorder": Emil Kraepelin, *Manic-Depressive Insanity and Paranoia*, 31–35.

279 "My thoughts bustle along": Samuel Taylor Coleridge, quoted in John Livingstone Lowes, *The Road to Xanadu: A Study in the Ways of the Imagination* (Princeton, NJ: Princeton University Press, 1986), 285.

279 The abnormal flow: Femi Oyebode, *Sims' Symptoms in the Mind* (Edinburgh: Saunders Elsevier, 2008), 157.

279 *Wisdom, Madness and Folly:* John Custance, *Wisdom, Madness and Folly*.

279 "Blue was the heavenly colour": Ibid., 35–36.

280 "In my mental or nervous fever": Letter from Vincent van Gogh to Paul Gaugin, January 21, 1889, *Vincent van Gogh—the Letters: The Complete Illustrated and Annotated Edition*, ed. Leon Jansen, Hans Luyten, and Nienke Bakker (Amsterdam, The Hague, and Brussels: Thames and Hudson, 2009), letter 739.

280 "especially poetical activity": Emil Kraepelin, *Manic-Depressive Insanity and Paranoia*, 17.

281 "rhyming, playing on words": B. Onuf, "The Milder Forms of Manic-Depressive Psychoses and the Manic-Depressive Constitution or Temperament," *Medical Record* 94 (1918): 969–70.

281 The Garden of Eden: Letter from Robert Lowell to William Empson, January 29, 1958, *Letters*, 310–11.

281 "'Come on, sir'": Robert Lowell, "Visitors," *Collected Poems*, 822.

282 "Because of the more rapid flow": E. Bleuler, *Textbook of Psychiatry*, trans. A. A. Brill (New York: Macmillan, 1924), 468.

282 "The molten stuff": Seamus Heaney, "Robert Lowell," a memorial address given at St. Luke's Church, Redcliffe Square, London, October 5, 1977. Reprinted in *Agenda* 18 (Autumn 1980): 26.

283 "so original, so perceptive": Esther Brooks, "Remembering Cal," 38.

283 "I more than envy": Letter from Stephen Spender to Robert Lowell, May 28, 1964, Houghton Library.

283 "not just a technical mastery": Al Alvarez, *Observer*, quoted on dust jacket of Robert Lowell, *The Dolphin* (London: Faber & Faber, 1973).

284 Creativity and intelligence: For a review of the relationship between intelligence and creativity, see E. Jauk, M. Benedek, B. Dunst, and A. C. Neubauer, "The Relationship Between Intelligence and Creativity," 212–21.

284 A review of forty-five brain-imaging studies: R. Arden, R. S. Chavez, R. Grazioplene, and R. E. Jung, "Neuroimaging Creativity: A Psychometric View," *Behavior Brain Research* 214 (2010): 143–56.

285 Early studies: Emil Kraepelin, in *Manic-Depressive Insanity* (1921), cites earlier studies by Aschaffenburg and Isserlin, as well as his own clinical observations; G. Murphy, "Types of Word-Association in Dementia Praecox, Manic-Depressives, and Normal Persons," *American Journal of Psychiatry* 79 (1923): 539–71; E. Bleuler, *Textbook of Psychiatry*.

285 symptoms associated with mania: See, for example, L. Welch, O. Diethelm, and L. Long, "Measurement of Hyper-Associative Activity During Elation," *Journal of Psychology* 21 (1946): 113–26; G. M. Henry, H. Weingartner, and D. L. Murphy, "Idiosyncratic Patterns of Learning and Word Association During Mania," *American Journal of Psychiatry* 128 (1971): 564–74; L. Pons, J. I. Nurnberger, and D. L. Murphy, "Mood-Independent Aberrancies in Associative Processes in Bipolar Affective Disorder: An Apparent Stabilizing Effect of Lithium," *Psychiatry Research* 14 (1985): 315–22; J. Levine, K. Schild, R. Kimhi, and G. Schreiber, "Word Associative Production in Affective Versus Schizophrenic Psychoses," *Psychopathology* 29 (1996): 7–13.

285 In studies of word fluency: See, for example, L. Pons et al., "Mood-Independent Aberrancies in Associative Processes in Bipolar Affective Disorder."

285 Lithium, presumably: L. L. Judd, B. Hubbard, D. S. Janowsky, et al., "The Effect of Lithium Carbonate on the Cognitive Functions of Normal Subjects," 355–57; L. Pons, J. I. Nurnberger, and D. L. Murphy, "Mood-Independent Aberrancies in Associative Processes in Bipolar Affective Disorder," 315–22; E. D. Shaw, J. J. Mann, P. E. Stokes, and A. Z. A. Manevitz, "Effects of Lithium Carbonate on Associative Productivity and Idiosyncrasy in Bipolar Outpatients," 1166–69; J. H. Kocsis, E. D. Shaw, P. E. Stokes, et al., "Neuropsychological Effects of Lithium Discontinuation," 268–76.

285 In 1858, Franz Richarz: Quoted in A. Koukopoulos and A. Koukopoulos, "Agitated Depression as a Mixed State and the Problem of Melancholia," *Psychiatric Clinics of North America* 22 (1999): 557–58.

286 one hundred acutely manic patients: G. Winokur and M. Tsuang, "Elation Versus Irritability in Mania," *Comprehensive Psychiatry* 16 (1975): 435–36.

286 In 1946, researchers: L. Welch, O. Diethelm, and L. Long, "Measurement of Hyper-Associative Activity During Elation," 113–26.

286 use broader conceptual categories: N. C. Andreasen and P. S. Powers, "Creativity and Psychosis: An Examination of Conceptual Style," *Archives of General Psychiatry* 32 (1975): 70–73; R. J. Larsen, E. Diener, and R. S. Cropanzano, "Cognitive Operations Associated with the Characteristic of Intense Emotional Responsiveness," *Journal of Personality and Social Psychology* 53 (1987): 767–74; M. R. Solovay, M. E. Shenton, and P. S. Holzman, "Comparative Studies of Thought Disorders: I. Mania and Schizophrenia," *Archives of General Psychiatry* 44 (1987): 13–20.

286 distractibility and attentional problems: For a review of attentional deficits in those at risk for or who have bipolar illness, see F. K. Goodwin and K. R. Jamison, *Manic-Depressive Illness*, 106–7, 289–91, 296–97. See also C. E. Bearden, K. M. Hoffman, and T. D. Cannon, "The Neuropsychology and Neuroanatomy of Bipolar Affective Disorder: A Critical Review," *Bipolar Disorders* 3 (2001):

106–50; U. S. Kolur, Y. C. J. Reddy, J. P. John, et al., "Sustained Attention and Executive Functions in Euthymic Young People with Bipolar Disorder," *British Journal of Psychiatry* 189 (2006): 453–58.

286 latent inhibition: S. H. Carson, J. B. Peterson, and D. M. Higgins, "Decreased Latent Inhibition Is Associated with Increased Creative Achievement in High-Functioning Individuals," *Journal of Personality and Social Psychology* 85 (2003): 499–506; S. H. Carson, "Creativity and Psychopathology: A Shared Vulnerability Model," *Canadian Journal of Psychiatry* 56 (2011): 144–53; A. Abraham, S. Bendt, D. Ott, and D. von Cramon, "Creative Cognition and the Brain: Dissociations Between Frontal, Parietal-Temporal, and Basal Ganglia Groups," *Brain Research* 1482 (2012): 55–70; A. Fink, M. Slamar-Halbedl, H. F. Unterrainer, and E. Weiss, "Creativity, Genius, Madness, or a Combination of Both?," *Psychology of Aesthetics, Creativity, and the Arts* 6 (2012): 11–18.

286 Lowell, in his essay: Robert Lowell, "Hawthorne's Pegasus," *Collected Prose*, 163.

287 The majority of the British writers and artists: K. R. Jamison, "Mood Disorders and Seasonal Patterns in British Writers and Artists," 125–34.

287 Researchers at Harvard University: R. Richards and D. K. Kinney, "Mood Swings and Creativity," *Creativity Research Journal* 3 (1990): 202–17; D. Schuldberg, "Six Subclinical Spectrum Traits in Normal Creativity," *Creativity Research Journal* 13 (2000–2001): 5–16.

287 "emotional excitement of poetry": Letter from Charlotte Winslow Lowell to Jean Stafford, October 31, 1943, Blair Clark Papers, HRC.

287 "need not thrive": Letter from Elizabeth Hardwick to Blair and Holly Clark, November 29, 1954, Blair Clark Papers, HRC.

287 "Men of genius": Thomas Middleton Stuart, *An Inaugural Essay on Genius and Its Diseases* (New York: Collins and Company, 1837). First written as a thesis for the degree of doctor of medicine, April 6, 1819.

288 He must sleep: Clinicians, patients and family members are well aware of the potential escalation into mania that can come from working and writing at too fevered a pitch; a lack of sleep is a common precipitant of mania: T. A. Wehr, D. A. Sack, and N. E. Rosenthal, "Sleep Reduction as a Final Common Pathway in the Genesis of Mania," *American Journal of Psychiatry* 144 (1987): 201–4; D. Lam and G. Wong, "Prodromes, Coping Strategies, Insight and Social Functioning in Bipolar Affective Disorders," *Psychological Medicine* 27 (1977): 1091–1100; G. Murray and S. L. Johnson, "The Clinical Significance of Creativity in Bipolar Disorder," *Clinical Psychology Review* 30 (2010): 721–32.

288 induce elevated mood: See, for example, a review of this literature in B. A. Hennessey and T. M. Amabile, "Creativity," *Annual Review of Psychology* 61 (2010): 569–98. A Dutch meta-analysis of sixty-six studies with more than seven thousand research participants found that positive moods, especially positive mood states that are activating, lead to more creativity than neutral moods: M. Baas, C. K. W. De Dreu, and B. A. Nijstad, "A Meta-Analysis of 25 Years of Mood-Creativity Research: Hedonic Tone, Activation, or Regulatory Focus?," *Psychological Bulletin* 134 (2008): 779–806.

288 scientists recently showed: S. Ramirez, X. Liu, C. J. MacDonald, et al., "Activat-

ing Positive Memory Engrams Suppresses Depression-like Behaviour," *Nature* 522 (2015): 335–39.

289 drugs that decrease dopamine: For a review of the pharmacological treatment of mania: F. K. Goodwin and K. R. Jamison, *Manic-Depressive Illness*; Stephen M. Stahl, *Stahl's Essential Psychopharmacology: Neuroscientific Basis and Practical Applications*, 3rd ed. (Cambridge: Cambridge University Press, 2011).

289 dopamine-enhancing drugs: R. Inzelberg reviewed more than twenty articles: R. Inzelberg, "The Awakening of Artistic Creativity and Parkinson's Disease," *Behavioral Neuroscience* 127 (2013): 256–61.

289 "is predominantly exalted": Emil Kraepelin, *Manic-Depressive Insanity and Paranoia*, 56.

289 Among adolescents: T. A. Greenwood et al., "Genome-Wide Association Study of Irritable Versus Elated Mania"; A. Stringaris et al., "Dimensions of Manic Symptoms in Youth."

289 The exuberant manic patients: A. Stringaris et al., "Dimensions of Manic Symptoms in Youth."

289 "Madmen are not as Melancholicks": Thomas Willis, *Two Discourses Concerning the Soul of Brutes Which Is That of the Vital and Sensitive of Man*, trans. S. Pordage (London: Thomas Dring, 1683), 255.

289 Mania is tied as well: D. Schuldberg, "Schizotypal and Hypomanic Traits, Creativity, and Psychological Health," *Creativity Research Journal* 3 (1990): 218–30; K. R. Jamison, *Touched with Fire*; G. Murray and S. L. Johnson, "The Clinical Significance of Creativity in Bipolar Disorder," 721–32.

289 Stanford researchers: C. M. Strong, C. Nowakowska, C. M. Santosa, et al., "Temperament-Creativity Relationships in Mood Disorder Patients, Healthy Controls and Highly Creative Individuals," *Journal of Affective Disorders* 100 (2007): 41–48; S. Srivastava and T. A. Ketter, "The Link Between Bipolar Disorders and Creativity: Evidence from Personality and Temperament Studies," *Current Psychiatry Research* 12 (2010): 522–30.

289 "of a fibre irritable and delicate": Ralph Waldo Emerson, "Fate," *Nature and Selected Essays*, 387.

290 an underlying hyperthymic temperament: S. Kesebir, S. Vahip, F. Akdeniz, et al., "Affective Temperaments as Measured by TEMPS-A in Patients with Bipolar I Disorder and Their First-Degree Relatives: A Controlled Study," *Journal of Affective Disorders* 85 (2005): 127–33; M. V. Mendlowicz, G. Jean-Louis, J. R. Kelsoe, and H. S. Akiskal, "A Comparison of Recovered Bipolar Patients, Healthy Relatives of Bipolar Probands, and Normal Controls Using the Short TEMPS-A," *Journal of Affective Disorders* 85 (2005): 147–51; T. A. Greenwood, H. S. Akiskal, K. K. Akiskal, and J. R. Kelsoe, "Genome-wide Association Study of Temperament in Bipolar Disorder Reveals Significant Associations to Three Novel Loci," *Biological Psychiatry* 72 (2012): 303–10.

290 "If I'm ill": John D. Campbell, *Manic-Depressive Disease*.

290 "Patient says he 'thinks'": Robert Lowell's medical record, Massachusetts Mental Health Center, December 1957.

290 half of those who have been manic: A review of 5,973 patients with a history

of mania (thirty-three studies) found that 53 percent had a history of delusions (31 percent had had grandiose delusions, 29 percent persecutory/paranoid delusions). F. K. Goodwin and K. R. Jamison, *Manic-Depressive Illness*, 53–60.

290 In children with bipolar I disorder: R. Tillman, B. Geller, T. Klages, et al., "Psychotic Phenomena in 257 Young Children and Adolescents with Bipolar I Disorder: Delusions and Hallucinations (Benign and Pathological)," *Bipolar Disorders* 10 (2008): 45–55.

290 Delusions during mania: E. Kraepelin, *Manic-Depressive Insanity*; G. Winokur, P. J. Clayton, and T. Reich, *Manic-Depressive Illness* (St. Louis: C. V. Mosby, 1969); Y. Lerner, "The Subjective Experience of Mania," in R. H. Belmaker and H. M. Van Praag, eds., *Mania: An Evolving Concept* (New York: Spectrum Publications, 1980), 77–88; F. K. Goodwin and K. R. Jamison, *Manic-Depressive Illness*.

291 "fulfill a divine mission": Emil Kraepelin, *Manic-Depressive Insanity and Paranoia*, 68–69.

291 progressive changes in the brain: See reviews of the literature in V. Maletic and C. Raison, "Integrated Neurobiology of Bipolar Disorder," *Frontiers in Psychiatry* 5 (2014): 1–24; C. Abé, C.-J. Ekman, C. Sellgren, et al., "Manic Episodes Are Related to Changes in Frontal Cortex: A Longitudinal Neuroimaging Study of Bipolar Disorder I," *Brain* 138 (2015): 1–9.

291 the broken plate: F. Scott Fitzgerald, "The Crack-Up," 45.

292 "It is hard to say": Interview with Jeanne Purcell, *Bangor Daily News*, August 8, 1967.

292 "What can you do after": Letter from Robert Lowell to Peter Taylor, March 15, 1958, *Letters*, 317.

293 "new and wonderful talents": Benjamin Rush, *Medical Inquiries and Observations Upon the Diseases of the Mind*, 153–54.

293 "The foundations of the earth": Isaiah 24:18.

293 "Life seemed to be there": Frederick Seidel, "The Art of Poetry: Robert Lowell," *Writers at Work: The "Paris Review" Interviews, Second Series*, ed. George Plimpton (New York: Viking, 1963), 336–68.

293 "He could have settled": Derek Walcott, *What the Twilight Says: Essays* (New York: Farrar, Straus and Giroux, 1998), 117.

12. WORDS MEAT-HOOKED FROM THE LIVING STEER

294 "The needle that prods": Al Alvarez, "Robert Lowell in Conversation," *Observer*, July 21, 1963.

294 "somehow lift the great sail": Letter from Robert Lowell to Elizabeth Bishop, April 14, 1962, *Letters*, 408.

294 "we walk the same sidewalks": Robert Lowell, "Hawthorne's Pegasus," *Collected Prose*, 162.

294 "Imagination catches us": Ibid.

294 "wanted to see things straight": Ibid., 163.

294 "even people of imagination": Ibid., 164.

295 "Let me warn you": Percival Lowell, *The Solar System: Six Lectures Delivered at the Massachusetts Institute of Technology in December 1902* (Boston: Houghton Mifflin, 1903), 71.

295 "The arts do not progress": Robert Lowell, "Robert Frost," *Collected Prose*, 9.

295 "There is something inside": Robert Lowell interview with Jonathan Miller, BBC program, "The Lively Arts: Robert Lowell," March 9, 1965.

295 "I think it must be sort of": Ibid.

295 "While you were playing your music": Letter from Robert Lowell to Harriet Lowell, July 30, 1968, Robert Lowell Papers, HRC.

296 "I see these winds": Robert Lowell, "These Winds," *Collected Poems*, 608. In "Soft Wood," ten years earlier, Lowell had described a wind that was without direction or inspiration: "there is no utility or inspiration," he wrote, "in the wind smashing without direction." *Collected Poems*, 370.

296 "how often": Robert Lowell, "These Winds," *Collected Poems*, 608.

296 "Tops of the midnight trees": Robert Lowell, "Redcliffe Square: 2. Window," *Collected Poems*, 646.

296 "groping for trout": Robert Lowell, "The Serpent," *Collected Poems*, 648.

297 "It is the future generation": The epigraph to "'To Speak of Woe That Is in Marriage,'" *Collected Poems*, 190, is a "spliced quotation from Schopenhauer's *The World as Will and Idea.*" Note by Frank Bidart in *Collected Poems*, 1045.

297 "It's not much fun": Letter from Robert Lowell to Peter Taylor, March 15, 1958, *Letters*, 317.

297 "Surely, there's some terrible flaw": Letter from Robert Lowell to Elizabeth Hardwick, February 5, 1965, Hardwick Papers, HRC.

298 "The patient has had": Robert Lowell's medical records, Massachusetts Mental Health Center, December 1957.

298 "Lowell felt that the early stages": Eric Linnolt, M.D., interview with the author, June 28, 2012.

298 "coincided with the patient's beginning": Robert Lowell's medical records, Payne Whitney Clinic, September 1949.

298 "a little too excited": Robert Lowell's medical records, Payne Whitney Clinic, 1954.

298 "might be having another manic episode": Robert Lowell's medical records, Boston State Hospital, December 1957.

299 "From February until April": Robert Lowell's medical records, Massachusetts Mental Health Center, December 1957.

299 "I write my best poetry": Robert Lowell to his London physician, Dr. Paul Brass. Dr. Brass was interviewed about Lowell's November 1975 hospitalization at the Priory by Nancy Schoenberger. Quoted in *Dangerous Muse: The Life of Lady Caroline Blackwood* (New York: Da Capo Press, 2001), 206.

299 "I noticed that at a certain point": Sidney Nolan, interview with Ian Hamilton, 1980, Ian Hamilton Papers, British Library.

300 "the particular hopped-up state": Allen Ginsberg, quoted in Jane Kramer, *Allen Ginsberg in America* (New York: International Publishing, 1969), 63.

300 "overborne by the fever": Robert Fitzgerald, "The Things of the Eye," 109.

300 "The affliction was so like the poetry": Jonathan Raban, interview with Ian Hamilton, 1980, Ian Hamilton Papers, British Library.

300 "I write in mania": Jonathan Raban, interview with the author, June 2012.

300 "In many ways": Jonathan Raban, interview with Ian Hamilton, 1980, Ian Hamilton Papers, British Library.

300 "I have always felt": Esther Brooks, "Remembering Cal," 39–40.

301 "unable to concentrate": Robert Lowell's medical records, Payne Whitney Clinic, September 1949.

301 "very depressed by how confused": Ibid.

301 "periodic *de profundis*": Letter from Robert Lowell to Peter Taylor, March 4, 1976, Vanderbilt.

301 "Only out of pain": Robert Lowell, "John Crowe Ransom," *Collected Prose*, 27.

301 "In truth I seem": Robert Lowell, "Afterthought" in *Notebook*, 263.

301 "On the great day": Robert Lowell, "Joy," *Notebook*, 246.

302 "Depression's no gift": Ian Hamilton, "A Conversation with Robert Lowell," 27. "Lost cake" is in the original transcript of Hamilton's interview, HRC.

302 John Berryman recalled: Robert Fitzgerald, "The Things of the Eye," 108.

302 When Frank Bidart pointed out: Frank Bidart, "Introduction: 'You Didn't Write, You *Rewrote*,'" in Robert Lowell, *Collected Poems*, xii.

302 "the mania for phrases": Robert Lowell, "Les Mots," *Notebook*, 38.

302 "I took 14 poems": Letter from Robert Lowell to Elizabeth Bishop, January 18, 1974, *Letters*, 618.

302 "I don't believe I've ever written": Robert Lowell, "An Interview with Frederick Seidel," *Collected Prose*, 248.

302 "was revising something": Elizabeth Hardwick, interview with Darryl Pinckney, "The Art of Fiction No. 87."

302 "I have observed that": Henry David Thoreau, *The Journal of Henry D. Thoreau*, January 1, 1852.

303 "madness does not give": Helen Vendler, correspondence with the author, February 9, 2011.

303 "One of the first things": Peter Taylor, "The Lively Arts: Robert Lowell."

305 "grinding labor": John Thompson, "Robert Lowell: 1917–1977."

305 "Lately, I've felt I was waking": Letter from Robert Lowell to Elizabeth Bishop, February 24, 1960, *Words in Air*, 313.

305 "It takes just a moment": Robert Lowell, "Balloon," *Collected Poems*, 987.

306 "skating the sheet": Robert Lowell, "While Hearing the Archduke Trio," *Collected Poems*, 477.

306 "I hang by a kitetail": Robert Lowell, "Leaving Home, Marshal Ney," *Collected Poems*, 476.

306 "window's sloping ledge": Robert Lowell, "Window-Ledge: 2. Gramsci in Prison," *Collected Poems*, 570.

306 "in flight without a ledge": Robert Lowell, "Morning Blue," *Collected Poems*, 657.

306 "foothold on the map": Robert Lowell, "Dropping South: Brazil," *Collected Poems*, 369.

306 "There is no foothold": Robert Lowell, *Prometheus Bound*, 60.

306 "We've reached the end of the road": Ibid., 66.

306 "When I finished *Life Studies*": Robert Lowell, acceptance speech for National Book Award, 1960.

306 "Have you seen an inchworm crawl": Robert Lowell, "For Elizabeth Bishop 4," *Collected Poems*, 595.

307 "Excellence had left": Robert Lowell, "Robert Frost," *Collected Prose*, 10.

307 "The subject throughout": Robert Lowell, "Wallace Stevens," *Collected Prose*, 12–13.

307 "makes a very different acquaintance": Robert Louis Stevenson, *Aes Triplex and Other Essays*, 18–19.

307 "just pride": Robert Lowell, "Reading Myself," *Collected Poems*, 591.

307 "The fires men build": Robert Lowell, "Long Summer," *Collected Poems*, 943.

307 "Fire will be the first absolute power": Robert Lowell, *Prometheus Bound*, 55.

308 "Like a plethoric burning martyr": Herman Melville, *Moby-Dick*, 462.

308 "For aught we know": William James, *The Varieties of Religious Experience* (1902; New York: Penguin, 1982), 15.

308 "it is only the wild": Henry David Thoreau, *The Journal of Henry D. Thoreau*, November 16, 1850.

308 "wild thinking": Ibid.

308 "marvelously expert" and "laboriously concocted": Robert Lowell acceptance speech, National Book Award, 1960.

308 "My mind's not right": Robert Lowell, "Skunk Hour," *Collected Poems*, 191–92.

308 "I watch my blood": Robert Lowell, "High Blood," *Notebook 1967–68*, 134.

309 "great days of sickness": Robert Lowell, "For Ann Adden 4. Coda," *Collected Poems*, 536.

309 "I have to brace my hand": Ibid.

309 "I so pray": Robert Lowell, "While Hearing the Archduke Trio," *Collected Poems*, 477.

309 "Stable equilibrium is death": Henry Adams, *A Letter to American Teachers of History* (Baltimore: J. H. Furst & Co., 1910).

309 "Life by definition breeds": Robert Lowell, "The Nihilist as Hero," *Collected Poems*, 590.

309 "each book of Lowell's": Al Alvarez, "A Talk with Robert Lowell," 39.

310 "not the first poet to undertake": Donald Hall, *The Weather for Poetry* (Ann Arbor: University of Michigan Press, 1982).

310 "a poet of great originality": Randall Jarrell, *No Other Book* (New York: Harper-Collins, 1999).

310 "To read Lowell in sequence": A. O. Scott, "A Life's Study: Why Robert Lowell Is America's Most Important Career Poet," *Slate*, June 20, 2003.

310 "There is an art of restraint": Adam Kirsch, *The Wounded Surgeon: Confession and Transformation in Six American Poets* (New York: W. W. Norton, 2005), 61.

310 "I was guided": Robert Lowell, *Prometheus Bound*, 50–51.

310 "It's been tough": Letter from Robert Lowell to Randall Jarrell, October 6, 1951, *Letters*, 177.

310 "I think I am going": Letter from Robert Lowell to Allen Tate, November 5, 1952, Princeton.

311 "It's hell finding a new style": Letter from Robert Lowell to Peter Taylor, December 7, 1952, Vanderbilt.

311 "It's only possible": Letter from Robert Lowell to Allen Tate, March 15, 1953, Princeton.

311 "seem to me a gift": Letter from Robert Lowell to Robert Frost, July 3, 1958, *Letters*, 325.

311 "old stuff": Letter from Robert Lowell to Chard Powers Smith, October 3, 1959, *Letters*, 354.

311 "One wants a whole new deck": Letter from Robert Lowell to Randall Jarrell, January 30, 1960, *Letters*, 359.

311 "Time to grub up": Robert Lowell, "Waking Early Sunday Morning," *New York Review of Books*, August 5, 1965; reprinted in *Collected Poems*, 933.

311 "a new tune": Letter from Robert Lowell to Elizabeth Hardwick, November 28, 1970, *Letters*, 560.

311 "owes all its onward impulses": Nathaniel Hawthorne, *The House of the Seven Gables*, 235.

312 "shows that every poet": Boris Pasternak quoted by Hilton Kramer in his obituary for Robert Lowell, "The Loss of a Poet," *New York Times*, October 16, 1977.

312 "have the courage to disregard": Ibid.

312 "Man is never happy": Letter from Robert Lowell to Elizabeth Hardwick, July 12, 1976, Robert Lowell Papers, HRC.

312 "continuing story": Robert Lowell, "After Enjoying Six or Seven Essays on Me," *Collected Poems*, 992.

312 "O to break loose": Robert Lowell, "Waking Early Sunday Morning," *Collected Poems*, 383, 386.

313 "about energy": Letter from Robert Lowell to Shozu Tokunago, June 26, 1967, *Letters*, 486.

313 "In the years I knew Lowell": Frank Bidart, "A Tribute to Robert Lowell," Academy of American Poets, October 14, 1987. Transcript of talk in the Robert Lowell Papers, HRC.

313 have compassion: Robert Lowell, "Yvor Winters," *Collected Prose*, 61.

314 "when one is dealing with horrors": Letter from Graham Greene to Lee Goerner, July 9, 1977, in *Graham Greene: A Life in Letters*, ed. Richard Greene (New York: Little, Brown, 2007), 345.

314 "Memory is not an end": Letter from Robert Lowell to Peter Taylor, July 1941, *Letters*, 33.

314 "No voice outsings": Robert Lowell, "Paradise Regained: June at McLean's Hospital," manuscript draft, Houghton Library, 2763.

314 "I can't see myself": Robert Lowell, "Summer Between Terms," *Collected Poems*, 658.

315 "Sometimes, my mind": Robert Lowell, "Fever," *Collected Poems*, 563.

315 "our hallucinator": Robert Lowell, "Moon-Landings," *Collected Poems*, 582.

315 "have my antics": Robert Lowell, "The Downlook," *Collected Poems*, 836.

315 "naming work of poetry": Helen Vendler, "Lowell's Persistence: The Forms Depression Makes," *Kenyon Review* 22 (Winter 2000): 233.

316 "admirably schooled in every grace": Edwin Arlington Robinson, "Richard Cory," *Collected Poems of Edwin Arlington Robinson* (New York: Macmillan, 1930).

317 "Waking in the Blue": Robert Lowell, "Waking in the Blue," *Collected Poems*, 183–84.

VI. MORTALITY: COME, I BELL THEE HOME

321 "Nothing will go again": Robert Lowell, "Mary Winslow," *Collected Poems*, 28.

13. LIFE BLOWN TOWARDS EVENING

323 "What shall I do": Robert Lowell, "New York Again," *Collected Poems*, 704.

323 "a bachelor world": Letter from Robert Lowell to Elizabeth Hardwick, April 25, 1970, *Letters*, 532.

324 "For all the horrors": *Life* magazine, February 19, 1965.

324 "I'll go back to America": Dudley Young, "Talk with Robert Lowell," *New York Times Book Review*, April 4, 1971, 33.

324 "hard to learn": Tim Mayer, *The Village Voice*, October 3, 1977.

325 "reckless blood": Steven Aronson, "Sophisticated Lady," *Town and Country*, September 1993, 144.

325 "thought alike": Kathleen Spivack, interview with the author, March 19, 2014.

325 "They were both drinkers": Xandra Gowrie, interview with Ian Hamilton, 1980, Ian Hamilton Papers, British Library. Lowell had written to Blackwood at the end of their relationship, "I do love you—two eggs colliding" (n.d. late May 1977, *Letters*, 668).

325 "Sufferer, how can you help me": Robert Lowell, "Seesaw," *Collected Poems*, 818.

325 "Will we always be": Ibid.

326 "had not seen him mad": Kathleen Spivack, interview with the author, March 19, 2014.

326 "someone he knew he had hurt": Ibid.

326 "dealt with consequences": Helen Vendler, correspondence with the author, February 9, 2011.

327 "more like the rest of us": Letter from Elizabeth Hardwick to Mary McCarthy, June 15, 1977, Vassar.

327 "I am a woman": Robert Lowell, "Mermaid Emerging," *Collected Poems*, 684.

327 "spotted the genius": Jonathan Raban, interview with Ian Hamilton, 1979, Ian Hamilton Papers, British Library.

327 They were close collaborators: Evgenia Citkowitz, interview with the author, March 12, 2014.

327 "Nobody gives me any credit": Steven Aronson, "Sophisticated Lady," 148.

327 "Writers can retaliate": Ibid.

327 "They were shy and nervous": Evgenia Citkowitz, interview with the author, March 12, 2014.

327 "took happiness where they could": Ibid.

327 "The golden summers": Ibid.

328 "who had her own afflictions": Ibid.

328 "She spoke of the dread": Ibid.

328 Always it was to be: Shakespeare, *King Lear*, act 1, scene 5.

329 "I didn't want him": Caroline Blackwood, interview with Ian Hamilton, 1979, Ian Hamilton Papers, British Library.

329 "Since you went": Robert Lowell, "Diagnosis: To Caroline in Scotland," *Collected Poems*, 649.

329 "He seemed a poor crazed creature": Letter from Philip Larkin to Monica Jones, May 1, 1970, *Letters to Monica*, ed. Anthony Thwaite (London: Faber & Faber, 2010), 408.

330 "I draw a card": Robert Lowell, "Doubt 1. Draw," *Collected Poems*, 672.

330 "All is as it was": Letter from Robert Lowell to Harriet Lowell, August 27, 1970, Robert Lowell Papers, HRC.

330 "left to make all the arrangements": Harriet Lowell, correspondence with the author, April 2012.

330 prescription for lithium: Letter from Elizabeth Hardwick to Robert Lowell, June 5, 1970, "Shouldn't I try to get a prescription from Dr. Platman?" (a psychiatrist at Columbia University), she asked Lowell; Harriet Lowell.

330 "more or less under control": Letter from Elizabeth Hardwick to Mary McCarthy, June 25, 1970, Vassar.

330 "Don't feel that the lithium": Letter from Elizabeth Hardwick to Robert Lowell, July 11, 1970, Harriet Lowell.

331 "brilliant, proud, dignified man": Blair Clark's notes taken before, during, and after Robert Lowell's hospitalization in London from June 9 to August 13, 1970, Blair Clark Papers, HRC.

331 "I realized when I got here": Letter from Elizabeth Hardwick to Mary McCarthy, August 4, 1970, Vassar.

331 "Sometimes a look": Ibid.

331 "Darling Cal": Letter from Caroline Blackwood to Robert Lowell, n.d. July 1970, Robert Lowell Papers, HRC.

331 "'I think of you every minute'": Robert Lowell, "Caroline 4. Marriage?" *Collected Poems*, 656.

332 Lowell struggled to convince: Letter from Robert Lowell to Caroline Blackwood, n.d. July 1970, *Letters*, 541.

332 "terrified of being mad alone": Caroline Blackwood, interview with Ian Hamilton, 1979, Ian Hamilton Papers, British Library.

332 "well and not depressed": Letter from Robert Lowell to Blair Clark, September 11, 1970, Robert Lowell Papers, HRC.

332 "I don't know whether I've said": Letter from Robert Lowell to Elizabeth Hardwick, October 18, 1970, *Letters*, 550–51.

333   "once annual depression": Letter from Robert Lowell to Elizabeth Hardwick, October 21, 1970, *Letters*, 551.

334   "I wonder if we": Letter from Robert Lowell to Elizabeth Hardwick, November 7, 1970, *Letters*, 556.

334   "Our love will not come back": Robert Lowell, "Obit," *Collected Poems*, 642.

334   "White clapboards": Robert Lowell, "No Hearing 3," *Collected Poems*, 638.

334   "This is almost the first time": Letter from Robert Lowell to Elizabeth Hardwick, June 14, 1970, *Letters*, 540–41.

334   "never wrote more": Robert Lowell, "A Conversation with Ian Hamilton," *Collected Prose*, 271–72.

334   "Ideas sprang from the bushes": Ibid., 272.

334   "The time is a summer": Robert Lowell, "Afterthought," *Notebook*, 262.

335   "beautiful and major work": William Meredith, "*Notebook 1967–68*," *New York Times Book Review*, June 15, 1969.

335   "the response of a racked": Ibid.

335   "so outrageously beautiful": Letter from Howard Nemerov to Robert Lowell, 1970.

335   "The prophecy has long been fulfilled": Douglas Dunn, "Snatching the Bays," *Encounter* 36 (1971): 65–70.

335   "preference for the large canvas": Ibid.

335   "sick in hospital": Letter from Robert Lowell to Peter Taylor, November 1, 1970, *Letters*, 555.

335   "baffling vacillation": Letter from Robert Lowell to Blair Clark, November 7, 1970, Robert Lowell Papers, HRC.

335   "I do not want Cal back": Letter from Elizabeth Hardwick to Blair Clark, October 23, 1970, Robert Lowell Papers, HRC.

335   "frantic affection": Letter from Robert Lowell to Blair Clark, November 21, 1970, *Letters*, 558.

335   "I increasingly fear": Ibid., 559.

336   "If I have had hysterical": Robert Lowell, "Flight to New York: 2. With Caroline at the Air-Terminal," *Collected Poems*, 702.

336   "Caroline and I": Letter from Robert Lowell to William Alfred, March 20, 1971, *Letters*, 564–65.

336   "I think I am happier": Letter from Robert Lowell to Peter Taylor, May 13, 1971, *Letters*, 572.

336   "Not a fight for seven months": Letter from Robert Lowell to Peter Taylor, June 24, 1971, Vanderbilt.

336   "Will the hailstones of the gods": Letter from Robert Lowell to Stanley Kunitz, April 25, 1971, *Letters*, 570.

336   "We breathe now": Ibid.

336   "We are never born again": Letter from Robert Lowell to Adrienne Rich, June 23, 1971, *Letters*, 574.

337   "The only important thing": Ibid.

337   "I think of Lizzie and Harriet hourly": Letter from Robert Lowell to Philip Booth, August 19, 1971, Dartmouth College Library.

337 "massively enthusiastic": Jonathan Raban, interview with Ian Hamilton, 1979, Ian Hamilton Papers, British Library.

337 "Lowell and Blackwood were both treating": Ibid.

337 "terrifically excited": Ibid.

338 "an animal in its own territory": Jonathan Raban, interview with author, February 2012.

338 "After 12 hours": Letter from Robert Lowell to Harriet Lowell, October 10, 1971, Robert Lowell Papers, HRC.

338 "too much blood is seeping": Robert Lowell, "Robert Sheridan Lowell," *Collected Poems*, 691.

338 "I have a doctor's and psychiatrist's statement": Letter from Robert Lowell to Peter Taylor, October 9, 1971, Vanderbilt.

339 "How unretentive we become": Robert Lowell, "Sheridan," *Collected Poems*, 779.

339 "Past fifty": Robert Lowell, "For Sheridan," *Collected Poems*, 793.

340 "Soft Wood": Robert Lowell, "Soft Wood," *Collected Poems*, 370–71.

342 "After fifty": Robert Lowell, "Flight to New York: 1. Plane-Ticket," *Collected Poems*, 702.

342 "a happiness so slow burning": Robert Lowell, "Marriage: 11. Ninth Month," *Collected Poems*, 690.

342 "when I open the window": Robert Lowell, "Morning Away from You," *Collected Poems*, 692.

342 "My hand": Robert Lowell, "Knowing," *Collected Poems*, 687.

343 "it's enough to wake without old fears": Robert Lowell, "Overhanging Cloud," *Collected Poems*, 691.

343 "None swims with her": Robert Lowell, "Mermaid 1," *Collected Poems*, 665.

343 "I see you as a baby killer whale": Robert Lowell, "Mermaid 4," *Collected Poems*, 666.

343 "I've searched the rough black ocean": Robert Lowell, "Mermaid 5," *Collected Poems*, 667.

344 "[W]e totter off the strewn stage": Robert Lowell, "Artist's Model," *Collected Poems*, 683.

344 *"Art just isn't worth that much"*: Letter from Elizabeth Bishop to Robert Lowell, March 21, 1972, *Words in Air*, 708.

345 "The writer's only responsibility": Jean Stein, "William Faulkner, The Art of Fiction No. 12," *Paris Review* 12 (Spring 1956).

345 "I couldn't bear": Letter from Robert Lowell to Elizabeth Bishop, April 4, 1972, *Letters*, 613.

345 "wonderful": Ibid. Elizabeth Bishop writes in the letter that the poems in *The Dolphin* are "wonderful poetry," "magnificent," "honest," "great poetry" (she emphasizes that she has never used the word "great" before).

345 "Lizzie is not dead": Letter from Elizabeth Bishop to Robert Lowell, March 21, 1972, *Words in Air*, 708.

345 "mixture of fact & fiction": Ibid.

345 "It is not being 'gentle'": Ibid.

346 "cruel invasion": Stanley Kunitz, "The Sense of a Life."

346 "tear Elizabeth apart": Letter from William Alfred to Robert Lowell, March 12, 1972, Houghton Library.

346 "DEAR WYSTAN": Quoted by Lowell in his letter to William Alfred, March 20, 1972, *Letters*, 587.

346 "cannibal-poet": Donald Hall, "Robert Lowell and the Literature Industry," *Georgia Review* 32 (1978): 7–12.

346 "What does one say": Adrienne Rich, "Carydid: A Column," *American Poetry Review* (September–October 1973): 42–43.

346 "I did not see them": Letter from Robert Lowell to Elizabeth Bishop, March 28, 1972, *Letters*, 590.

346 "The problem of making the poem": Letter from Robert Lowell to Elizabeth Bishop, April 4, 1972, *Letters*, 591.

347 "How can I want to hurt?": Ibid.

347 "a mixture of quotes": Letter from Robert Lowell to Robert Giroux, July 18, 1973, *Letters*, 614.

347 "Lizzie didn't come out badly": Steven Aronson, "Sophisticated Lady," 148.

347 "I don't know what": Letter from Elizabeth Hardwick to Robert Lowell, April 9, 1972, Harriet Lowell.

348 "the reality was disturbing": Letter from Elizabeth Hardwick to Robert Giroux, July 5, 1973, Harriet Lowell.

348 "He used and misquoted her letters": Harriet Lowell, correspondence with the author, April 2012 and December 2015.

348 "She minded his use": Ibid.

348 "I'm sorry I brought this on you": Letter from Robert Lowell to Elizabeth Hardwick, July 12, 1973, *Letters*, 612.

348 "On the evidence": Douglas Dunn, "Infinite Mischief—Lowell's Life," *Encounter* 6 (September–October 1983): 75.

348 "like no one else": Elizabeth Hardwick, quoted in Richard Locke, "Conversation on a Book."

349 "We had one hope": Caroline Blackwood, interview with Ian Hamilton, 1979, Ian Hamilton Papers, British Library.

349 "Cal was still walking around": Ibid.

349 "mad as the vexed sea": Shakespeare, *King Lear*, act 4, scene 3, Folger edition.

349 "adored English hardware stores": Caroline Blackwood, interview with Ian Hamilton, 1979, Ian Hamilton Papers, British Library.

350 "wandering out on the lawn": Jonathan Raban, correspondence with the author, October 21, 2016.

350 "They called him Professor": Seamus Heaney, "Gulliver in Lilliput: Remembering Robert Lowell," speech delivered at Harvard in 1987 on the tenth anniversary of Lowell's death, reprinted in *The Norton Book of Friendship*, ed. Eudora Welty and Ronald A. Sharp (New York: W. W. Norton, 1991), 547–48.

351 recalls the nightmare: John Julius Norwich, correspondence with the author, November 14, 2010.

351 "sad, mad event": Dennis O'Driscoll, *Stepping Stones: Interviews with Seamus Heaney* (London: Faber & Faber, 2008), 216.

351 "looking absolutely wild": Charles Monteith, interview with Ian Hamilton, 1980, Ian Hamilton Papers, British Library.

351 "[o]ur ears put us in touch": Robert Lowell, "Home," *Collected Poems*, 824–25.

352 "At visiting hours": Ibid., 825.

353 "I wish I could die": Robert Lowell's medical records, Payne Whitney Clinic, 1954.

353 "absolutely no future": Dido Merwin, quoted by Caroline Blackwood, interview with Ian Hamilton, 1979, Ian Hamilton Papers, British Library.

353 "I never know when": Caroline Blackwood, interview with Ian Hamilton, 1979, Ian Hamilton Papers, British Library.

353 "I did always worry": Ibid.

353 "I am weighed down": Letter from Robert Lowell to Frank Bidart, February 15, 1976, *Letters*, 644.

353 "I can't really function": Letter from Robert Lowell to Blair Clark, March 4, 1976, *Letters*, 645.

353 "I've been sixteen times": Sidney Nolan, interview with Ian Hamilton, 1980, Ian Hamilton Papers, British Library.

354 "I'd never drown myself": Jill Neville, *Fall-Girl* (London: Weidenfeld and Nicolson, 1966), 131–32.

354 effective in preventing suicide: See references in chapter 8 that document the efficacy of lithium in preventing suicide.

355 "Do I deserve credit": Robert Lowell, "Suicide," *Collected Poems*, 725.

355 "One light, two lights": Ibid., 724–25.

355 "At visiting hours": Robert Lowell, "Home," *Collected* Poems, 825.

355 "I don't need conversation": Robert Lowell, "The Withdrawal," *Collected Poems*, 783.

356 "I always felt it was my fault": Caroline Blackwood, interview with Ian Hamilton, Ian Hamilton Papers, 1979, British Library.

356 "It's like someone becoming an animal": Ibid.

356 "'Supposing I go mad'": Ibid.

356 "more wild, more destructive": Frank Bidart, interview with Ian Hamilton, Ian Hamilton Papers, 1981.

356 "At the sick times": Robert Lowell, "Runaway," *Collected Poems*, 814.

356 "And us?": Letter from Robert Lowell to Caroline Blackwood, April 22, 1977, *Letters*, 667.

357 "I don't know what to say": Letter from Robert Lowell to Caroline Blackwood, April 14, 1977, *Letters*, 667.

357 "Us? Aren't we too heady": Letter from Robert Lowell to Caroline Blackwood, April 19, 1977, *Letters*, 667.

357 "I am afraid of your visit": Letter from Robert Lowell to Caroline Blackwood, May 3, 1977, *Letters*, 668.

357 Lowell wanted peace: Blair Clark's notes, November 25, 1976, HRC.

357 He told Grey Gowrie: Grey Gowrie, interview with Ian Hamilton, 1980, Ian Hamilton Papers, British Library.

357 "He was very clear": Ibid.

357 "life with her was impossible": Helen Vendler, interview with Ian Hamilton, 1981, Ian Hamilton Papers, British Library.

357 "unbelievably grateful and relieved": Frank Bidart, interview with Ian Hamilton, 1981, Ian Hamilton Papers, British Library.

358 "There is no great renewed romance": Letter from Elizabeth Hardwick to Mary McCarthy, June 15, 1977, Vassar.

358 "She said she was unsure": Harriet Lowell, correspondence with the author, April 2012.

359 "faced the kingdom of the mad": Robert Lowell, "Man and Wife," *Collected Poems*, 189.

359 "I feel broken by all conversation": Letter from Robert Lowell to Caroline Blackwood, July 17, 1977, *Letters*, 671.

360 "bright as the morning star": Robert Lowell, "Mermaid 3," *Collected Poems*, 666.

360 "in the photo of you": Ibid.

360 "The passion and grief": Letter from Elizabeth Hardwick to Mary McCarthy, May 10, 1980, Vassar.

360 "I think there *was* more openness": Frank Bidart, interview with Ian Hamilton, 1982, Ian Hamilton Papers, British Library.

360 "Out of your wreckage": Robert Lowell, "Runaway," *Collected Poems*, 814.

14. BLEAK-BONED WITH SURVIVAL

361 "The line must terminate": Robert Lowell, "Fishnet," *Collected Poems*, 645.

361 "that of a man moving": Robert Lowell, "Robert Frost," *Collected Prose*, 10.

361 "Sing to me of the man": Homer, *The Odyssey*, trans. Robert Fagles, book 1 (New York: Penguin, 1996), 77.

361 "came piling on": Homer, *The Iliad*, trans. Robert Fagles, book 3, 136.

361 grace and sense: "What grace you give your words and what good sense within! / You have told your story with all a singer's skill, / the miseries you endured." Homer, *The Odyssey*, book 11, 261.

361 "life, energy, and enthusiasm": Robert Lowell, "War: A Justification."

361 "reach aesthetic perfection": Robert Lowell notes on *The Odyssey*, 1935 notebook, Houghton Library.

362 "grown bleak-boned": Robert Lowell, "Ulysses and Circe," *Collected Poems*, 717.

362 "contained a God": Letter from Robert Lowell to Ezra Pound, May 2, 1936, *Letters*, 4.

362 "It is hard for me to imagine": Stanley Kunitz, "Talk with Robert Lowell."

362 "grown wise in seafaring": Robert T. S. Lowell, "A Raft That No Man Made," in *Atlantic Tales: A Collection of Stories from the Atlantic Monthly* (Boston: Ticknor and Fields, 1867). Lowell's story was first published in 1862.

362 "Odysseus journeys home": Homer, *The Odyssey*, book 5, 153. See also book 1, "Odysseus journeys home—the exile must return!," 80.

362 "convoy of the gods": Homer, *The Odyssey*, book 5, 153.

362 "a lashed, makeshift raft": Ibid.

362 "She is a snipper-off'er": Robert Lowell, "Ulysses and Circe," *Collected Poems*, 716.

363 "Young / he made strategic choices": Ibid., 715.

363 "the cycle of Greek radiance": Robert Lowell, "Epics," *Collected Prose*, 214.

364 "England didn't have real summers": Letter from Robert Lowell to Elizabeth Bishop, July 12, 1976, *Letters*, 655.

364 "A big house in England": Robert Lowell, entry in his notebook for January 31, 1973, Harriet Lowell.

365 "this totally American man": Esther Brooks, "Remembering Cal," 43.

365 "I hope": Robert Lowell, "After Enjoying Six or Seven Essays on Me," *Collected Poems*, 993.

365 "I willed it": Homer, *The Odyssey*, book 13, 296.

365 "In silence": Ibid.

365 "He suddenly looked": Kathleen Spivack, *With Robert Lowell and His Circle*, 310.

365 His "erratic aloofness": Ibid., 211.

365 his suffering had made him: Peter Levi, "Remembering Lowell," *Listener* 98 (September 22, 1977): 380.

365 Blood smells of iron: Adam Nicolson, *Sea Room: An Island Life in the Hebrides*.

366 "Why don't they ever say": Helen Vendler, "Robert Lowell's Last Days and Last Poems," in *Robert Lowell: A Tribute*, 161.

366 "most heartbreaking": Robert Lowell, "Randall Jarrell," *Collected Prose*, 91.

366 "broken-hearted lions": Robert Lowell, "For George Santayana," *Collected Poems*, 156.

366 "heartbreaking": Letter from Robert Lowell to John Berryman, November 5, 1966, University of Minnesota.

366 "I expected him to choose Eliot": Grey Gowrie, "Robert Lowell: Image and Reflection," *Agni* 75 (2012): 190.

366 "Looking back now": Esther Brooks, "Remembering Cal," 43–44.

366 "America and teaching at Harvard": Ibid., 44.

366 "the pioneer going into": Dudley Young, "Talk with Robert Lowell."

367 "Keep Ithaka always": C. P. Cavafy, "Ithaka," in *Collected Poems*, trans. Edmund Keeley and Philip Sherrard, ed. George Savidis (Princeton, NJ: Princeton University Press, 1980).

367 "In the midst of life": The Burial Service, *The Book of Common Prayer* (Oxford: Oxford University Press, 1848).

367 "I miss the long roll of years": Letter from Robert Lowell to Elizabeth Bishop, July 30, 1968, *Words in Air*, 644.

367 "when I look inside": Letter from Robert Lowell to Elizabeth Bishop, September 5, 1968, *Letters*, 506.

367 "The things that cannot be done twice!": Ibid.

367 "I wake up thinking": Letter from Robert Lowell to Peter Taylor, June 27, 1960, Vanderbilt.

367 "It's hard to get used to knowing": Letter from Robert Lowell to Mary McCarthy, August 7, 1963, *Letters*, 430.

367 "Oh, oh, oh, how time": Letter from Robert Lowell to Elizabeth Bishop, October 27, 1963, *Letters*, 439.

368 "Each season we get older": Letter from Robert Lowell to William Meredith, December 6, 1969, Connecticut College.

368 "I still feel I can reach up": Letter from Robert Lowell to Elizabeth Bishop, September 11, 1970, *Letters*, 544.

368 "Is dying harder": Robert Lowell, "Last Night," *Collected Poems*, 601.

368 "It's the twinges of mortality": Letter from Robert Lowell to Elizabeth Bishop, May 3, 1973, *Words in Air*, 746.

368 "I climb the ladder, knowing": Robert Lowell, "Through the Night," *Notebook 1967–68*, 46.

369 "thing one writes for oneself": Robert Schumann, quoted in Waldo Selden Pratt and Charles Newell Boyd, eds., *Grove's Dictionary of Music and Musicians*, vol. 4 (Ann Arbor. MI: Macmillan, 1937).

369 "the more you realize": James Atlas, correspondence with the author, May 5, 2013.

369 "What we want to say": Al Alvarez, "A Talk with Robert Lowell," 41.

369 "His briefcase which he carried": Letter from Elizabeth Hardwick to Mary McCarthy [1980?], Vassar.

370 "isn't even that": Robert Lowell, notebook entry, January 11, 1973, Harriet Lowell.

370 "the hungry future": Robert Lowell, "The Withdrawal," *Collected Poems*, 784.

371 "I've been thinking": Letter from Robert Lowell to Peter and Eleanor Taylor, September 4, 1976, Vanderbilt.

371 "Those blessèd structures": Robert Lowell, "Epilogue," *Collected Poems*, 838.

372 "disarming openness": Helen Vendler, "Robert Lowell's Last Days and Last Poems," 157–58.

372 "without hysteria": Letter from Robert Lowell to Peter Taylor, September 11, 1975, Vanderbilt.

372 "to hold a shield": Letter from Robert Lowell to Elizabeth Bishop, March 4, 1976, *Letters*, 645.

372 "roles he played": Marjorie Perloff, "Robert Lowell: 'Fearlessly holding back nothing,'" *Washington Post*, September 25, 1977.

372 "Only when we read": William Pritchard, "*Collected Poems:* The Whole Lowell," *New York Times Book Review*, June 29, 2003.

372 "Ask for no Orphean lute": Robert Lowell, "The Quaker Graveyard in Nantucket," *Collected Poems*, 14.

372 "I ask for a natural death": Robert Lowell, "Death of a Critic," *Collected Poems*, 758.

372 "I have no hope": Robert Lowell, "Agamemnon," *The Oresteia of Aeschylus* (New York: Farrar, Straus, and Giroux, 1978), 31.

372 "Yet how much we carry away": Robert Lowell, notebook entry, January 28, 1973, Harriet Lowell.

373 "destroying her": Caroline Blackwood, interview with Ian Hamilton, 1979, Ian Hamilton Papers, British Library.

373 "The great circuit of the stars": Robert Lowell, "Leaving America for England: 4. No Telling," *Collected Poems*, 697.

373 He was in "awful" shape: Frank Bidart, interview with Ian Hamilton, 1981, Ian Hamilton Papers, British Library.

373 He was "just nervous": Ibid.

374 "After my cardiograph came out irregular": Letter from Robert Lowell to Caroline Blackwood, February 28, 1977, *Letters*, 665.

374 He told the attending physician: Robert Lowell was admitted to Massachusetts General Hospital on February 1, 1977, and discharged on February 9, 1977. Appendix 3 provides information on his medical condition at that time and a summary of the findings from his earlier medical records.

374 "A weak clamor": Robert Lowell, "Phillips House Revisited," *Collected Poems*, 798.

375 "very flat affect": Nursing notes from Robert Lowell's hospitalization at Massachusetts General Hospital, February 1 to February 9, 1977.

375 "Thank you for referring Mr. Lowell": Letter from Timothy Guiney, M.D., to Charles Weingarten, M.D., February 16, 1977, Massachusetts General Hospital medical records.

375 "Cal's tone was quite flat": Blair Clark, notes for an unpublished memoir, May 8, 1977, Blair Clark Papers, HRC.

375 "were quite nice to each other": Frank Bidart, interview with Ian Hamilton, 1981, Ian Hamilton Papers, British Library.

375 "tired and melancholy": Letter from William Styron to Ian Hamilton, July 1, 1981, Ian Hamilton Papers, British Library.

376 "He lived quietly": Elizabeth Hardwick, interview with Ian Hamilton, 1982, Ian Hamilton Papers, British Library.

376 "had been his life": Ibid.

376 "I would wish to live": Robert Lowell, "Loneliness," *Collected Poems*, 852.

376 "We were / so by ourselves": Ibid.

376 "It has been much more painful": Letter from Elizabeth Hardwick to Mary McCarthy, October 2, 1977, Vassar.

377 "Last year": Robert Lowell, "Summer Tides," *Collected Poems*, 853.

377 "My wooden beach-ladder": Ibid.

377 "He seemed a very lonely figure": Frank Bidart, interview with Ian Hamilton, 1981, Ian Hamilton Papers, British Library.

377 "That's how we're buried": Helen Vendler, interview with Ian Hamilton, 1981, Ian Hamilton Papers, British Library.

378 Lowell was extremely restless: Caroline Blackwood, interview with Ian Hamilton, 1979, Ian Hamilton Papers, British Library.

378 "sheer torture": Elizabeth Hardwick, interview with Ian Hamilton, 1982, Ian Hamilton Papers, British Library.

378 "drifts with the wild ice": Robert Lowell, "The Mouth of the Hudson," *Collected Poems*, 328.

378 "Christ, / may I die": Robert Lowell, "Fragment," *Collected Poems*, 988.

379 "My heart longs to be home": Homer, *The Odyssey*, book 10, 245–46.

379 "I remember once": Blair Clark, "On Robert Lowell," *Harvard Advocate* 113 (1979): 111.

381 "*The famous American poet*": Stanley Kunitz, "The Sense of a Life."

381 "Robert Lowell, who died": Anonymous, "Robert Lowell: Leading American Poet," *The Times* (London), September 14, 1977.

381 "He is dead now": Michael Ryan, "Lowell Cast Glow on Boston," *Boston Herald American*, September 14, 1977.

381 "Robert Lowell followed": Eugene McCarthy, "At the Moment of a Poet's Death, Stand Up and Be Quiet," *Washington Star*, September 18, 1977.

382 "A sense of loss": Hilton Kramer, "The Loss of a Poet."

382 "The Pulitzer Prize judges": Robert Taylor, "Lowell's Majesty," *Boston Globe*, September 14, 1977.

382 "Robert Lowell's painful": William McPherson, "Lowell: A Final Chapter," *Washington Post*, September 17, 1977.

383 "happy to report": Letter from the Reverend Whitney Hale to Robert Lowell, November 12, 1955, Houghton Library.

383 "After much irresolution": Letter from Robert Lowell to Elizabeth Bishop, May 5, 1955, *Words in Air*, 158.

383 "He appeared to be elated": Peter Taylor, "Robert Trail [*sic*] Spence Lowell 1917–1977," *Ploughshares* 5 (1979): 74–81.

384 Behold, I make all things: Revelation 21:5.

385 "I saw my city in the Scales": Robert Lowell, "Where the Rainbow Ends," *Complete Poems*, 69.

386 "The family graveyard": Elizabeth Hardwick to Mary McCarthy, October 2, 1977, Vassar.

386 "the black brook": Robert Lowell, "Near the Unbalanced Aquarium," *Collected Prose*, 348.

386 "Grandfather and I": Robert Lowell, "Dunbarton," *Collected Poems*, 169.

387 "THE IMMORTAL IS SCRAPED": Robert Lowell, "Endings," *Collected Poems*, 760.

387 "But there is": Linda Charlton, "Voznesensky's Elegy at Lowell's Grave," *New York Times*, October 15, 1977.

387 "I still hear you": Andrei Voznesensky, "Family Graveyard," trans. William Jay Smith and Fred Starr, *New York Times*, October 15, 1977.

387 "You were our night ferry": Seamus Heaney, "Elegy," in *Field Work* (New York: Farrar, Straus and Giroux, 1979), 24.

387 "Frank [Bidart] read me": Letter from Elizabeth Hardwick to Elizabeth Bishop, August 16, 1978, Vassar.

389 "*I can make out the rigging*": Elizabeth Bishop, "North Haven," in *The Complete Poems, 1927–1979* (New York: Farrar, Straus and Giroux, 1983), 188–89. Lowell had written in "Fall Weekend at *Milgate*" (*Collected Poems*, 659):

> Nature, like philosophers, has one plot,
> only good for repeating what it does well:
> life emerges from wood and life from life.

15. HE IS OUT OF BOUNDS NOW

390 "On a thousand": Robert Lowell, "For the Union Dead," *Collected Poems*, 377.

390 "The dead have no need": The Reverend Peter J. Gomes, the Plummer Professor of Christian Morals at Harvard Divinity School and Pusey Minister at Harvard Memorial Church, March 2, 1978, in *The Harvard Crimson*, March 3, 1978.

390 "exerted a giant's pressure": Robert Fitzgerald, "The Things of the Eye," 111.

391 He had written about only four places: Ian Hamilton, "A Conversation with Robert Lowell," *The Review* 26 (Summer 1971): 10.

392 "The old South Boston Aquarium stands": Robert Lowell, "For the Union Dead," *Collected Poems*, 376–78.

394 "childhood memories": Robert Lowell, introductory notes for his statement on "For the Union Dead," read at the Boston Arts Festival, June 1960, Robert Lowell Papers, Houghton Library, 2300, 2571.

394 "may be about a child maturing": Ibid.

394 "We're decaying": Robert Lowell, "In Bounds," *Newsweek*, October 12, 1964, 122.

395 "Perhaps because his own existence": Randall Jarrell, book jacket comments for Robert Lowell's *Life Studies*.

395 William Bradford had written: "I have been happy, in my first times, to see, and with much comfort to enjoy, the blessed fruits of this sweet communion, but it is now a part of my misery in old age, to find and feel the decay ... and with grief and sorrow of heart to lament and bewail the same." William Bradford, *Of Plymouth Plantation*, 33.

395 "was as crisp, bracing, and colorful": Robert Lowell, "New England and Further," *Collected Prose*, 181.

395 "I ponder on the railing": Robert Lowell, "At the Indian Killer's Grave," *Collected Poems*, 58.

396 "Here, also, are the veterans": Nathaniel Hawthorne, "The Gray Champion" in *Twice-Told Tales* (New York: Modern Library, 2001), 3–10. Lowell changed Hawthorne's wording in small ways.

396 "until every drop of blood": Abraham Lincoln, second inaugural address, March 4, 1865: "Fondly do we hope—fervently do we pray—that this mighty scourge of war may speedily pass away. Yet, if God wills that it continue, until all the wealth piled by the bond-man's two hundred and fifty years of unrequited toil shall be sunk, and until every drop of blood drawn with the lash, shall be paid by another drawn with the sword, as was said three thousand years ago, so still it must be said 'the judgments of the Lord, are true and righteous altogether.'" U.S. National Archives & Records Administration.

397 "Let justice be done": "We know the redemption must come," said John Quincy Adams, speaking to an audience of black citizens in Pittsburgh in 1843. "But whether in peace or blood, LET IT COME." Later, in the House of Repre-

sentatives, he added, "Though it cost the blood of millions of white men, let it come. Let justice be done, though the heavens fall." Joshua Reed Giddings, *History of the Rebellion: Its Authors and Causes* (New York: Follet, Foster & Co., 1864).

397 "The arm of the slave": Frederick Douglass, "Men of Color, to Arms!," speech at Rochester, New York, March 2, 1863, in Richard Benson and Lincoln Kirstein, *Lay This Laurel: An Album on the Saint-Gaudens Memorial on Boston Common Honoring Black and White Men Together Who Served the Union Cause with Robert Gould Shaw and Died with Him July 18, 1863* (New York: Eakins Press, 1973).

397 America, he believed: Letter from Robert Lowell to the editors, *The Village Voice*, November 19, 1964, *Letters*, 453.

397 "The more I think": Letter from Robert Gould Shaw to Annie Haggerty Shaw, June 1, 1863, in *Blue-Eyed Child of Fortune: The Civil War Letters of Colonel Robert Gould Shaw*, ed. Russell Duncan (Athens: University of Georgia Press, 1992).

398 "Col. Shaw, from the beginning": Letter from James Henry Gooding to the editors of the *New Bedford Mercury*, August 16, 1863 published on August 29, 1863.

398 "manner was more unbending": Ibid.

399 "A long line of phosphorescent light": Clara Barton quoted in Percy Harold Epler, *The Life of Clara Barton* (New York: Macmillan, 1915), 80.

399 "The dead and wounded": Lieutenant Iredell Jones, quoted in *Lay This Laurel*.

399 "The thousand little sand-hills": Letter from Clara Barton to Theodore Parker, December 9, 1863, in William E. Barton, *The Life of Clara Barton: Founder of the American Red Cross* (Boston: Houghton Mifflin, 1922), 261.

399 "We can imagine no holier place": Letter from Francis George Shaw to Lincoln Stone, the regimental surgeon of Robert Gould Shaw, 1863, in Lorien Foote, *Seeking the One Great Remedy: Francis George Shaw and Nineteenth-Century Reform* (Athens: Ohio University Press, 2003).

400 "There on horseback": Oration by William James, "Exercises at the Dedication of the Monument to Robert Gould Shaw and the Fifty-Fourth Regiment of Massachusetts Infantry, May 31, 1897" (Boston: Municipal Printing Office, 1897), 41.

400 "common and gregarious": Ibid., 50–51.

400 "Watchman, tell us": Booker T. Washington, "Exercises at the Declaration of the Monument," 60.

401 "You have immortalized": Quoted in Burke Wilkinson, *Uncommon Clay: The Life and Works of Augustus Saint Gaudens* (San Diego: Harcourt Brace Jovanovich, 1985), 286.

401 "You are a great American writer": Letter from Elizabeth Hardwick to Robert Lowell, June 26, 1970, Harriet Lowell.

401 "You drank America": Seamus Heaney, "Elegy," 24.

401 "I love my country": Letter from Robert Lowell to George Santayana, February 2, 1948, *Letters*, 93.

402 "Where is America?": Ian Hamilton, "A Conversation with Robert Lowell," 10–29. The published version of this interview quotes Lowell as saying "it streams through my eyes"; the original interview reads "seeps."

402 The color of his blood: Letter from Robert Lowell to Elizabeth Bishop, October 7, 1972, *Words in Air*, 729.

402 "I see now that": Letter from Charles Russell Lowell, Jr., to Josephine Shaw Lowell, July 28, 1863, in Edward W. Emerson, ed., *Life and Letters of Charles Russell Lowell* (Boston: Houghton Mifflin, 1907), 288–89.

403 "most like to have known": Jane Howard, "Applause for a Prize Poet," 58.

403 "Twelve horses killed under him": Robert Lowell, "Colonel Charles Russell Lowell 1835–64," *Collected Poems*, 485.

403 "He had, *gave*": Ibid.

403 Sixteen times and more: Sidney Nolan, interview with Ian Hamilton, 1980, Ian Hamilton Papers, British Library.

404 "the hum outliving": James Russell Lowell, "The Darkened Mind," 427.

404 "The bells cry": Robert Lowell, "Mary Winslow," *Collected Poems*, 28.

APPENDICES

406 "It was answered": William Bradford, *Of Plymouth Plantation*, 27.

408 "My relationship with Mr. Lowell": Letter from Viola Bernard to Ian Hamilton, July 2, 1980, Ian Hamilton Papers, British Library.

420 "I sleep sitting up": Letter from Robert Lowell to Caroline Blackwood, January 31, 1977, *Letters*, 663.

Index

Page numbers in *italics* refer to illustrations.

manic-depressive illness *(continued):*
diagnostic studies of, 262, 266, 267, 272, 277–83, 412–15
electroconvulsive therapy (ECT) in, 99–100, 104–5, 106, 108, 116, 123, 153, 163, 165, 169, 213, 281
"flight of ideas" in, 123, 127, 137–9, 141–2, 146–7, 160, 180, 221, 278–81, *280*, 285–6, 306, 412
folie circulaire (circular insanity) in, 159, 160, 221, 259–60
genetics and heredity in, 32, 36, *56*, 160, 163, 180, 262, 271, 274–6, 289, 325, 354, 415
intelligence as factor in, 267–70, 271, 272, 283–4
lithium toxicity in, 183–4, 349
lithium treatment for, 83, 127, 153, 167, 175, 176–84, *178*, *179*, 267, 269, 270, 285, 323, 326, 330, 334–5, 349, 353–4, 374–5, 419, 421–3, 468*n*, 469*n*
mania in, xv–xvi, 4–16, 19, 21, 23–4, 59, 62–3, 68, 83, 85, 88, 89, 97–100, 103–29, 132, 134–47, 152–94, 199–200, 212–13, 215, 221–41, 254–67, 271–310, 314–15, 323, 325–30, 333, 337, 344, 349–57, 367, 373, 379, 407–17, 422–3, 432*n*, 446*n*, 464*n*–5*n*, 468*n*, 469*n*, 478*n*, 490*n*, 491*n*–2*n*
memory in, 8, 18, 111, 125, 137, 172–5, 190, 259–61, 282, 292, 301, 314, 315, 344
moods in, 4–5, 6, 8, 18, 20, 31–2, 38–9, 41, 43, 48, 72, 75, 83, 97, 104, 124, 125, 126, 132, 135, 157–8, 160, 180–5, 208, 215, 235–7, 244, 261–7, 271–4, 277–8, 282, 285–91, 294, 295, 298, 301–7, 338, 350, 374–5, 407, 411–17, 490*n*
nomenclature of, 160, 416–17
population studies of, 262, 267–77
prognosis of, 104, 112, 124–5, 129–35, 139–40, 168–9, 221–5

recurrence of, 6, 115, 118, 124–5, 127, 132–5, 160, 165, 168–71, 175–6, *178*, 179–80, 183, 199–200, 221–5, 232, 264, 349, 359–60, 365–6, 367, 395, 416
as "salt deficiency," 153, 167, 179, 180, 184
suicide as risk in, 9, 109, 125, 137, 147, 163, 178, 184, 194, 199, 213, 230, 241, 253–4, 263, 264–5, 267, 269, 272, 273–4, 325, 352–5, 375, 411, 414, 423, 444*n*, 446*n*
Manic-Depressive Insanity and Paranoia (Kraepelin), 159–60, 260
Mann, Thomas, 223
Mariani, Paul, 9
"Marriage?" (Lowell), 331–2
Mars, 45–6, 47, 295
Mars as the Abode of Life (P. Lowell), 47
Marvell, Andrew, 16
"Mary Winslow" (Lowell), 321
Massachusetts Bay Colony, 54, 162
Massachusetts General Hospital (MGH), 113, 141, 184, 373–5, 419, 420, 421, 422
Masterson, James, 125–9, 192–4, 458*n*, 473*n*
Mather, Cotton, 55
Mattapoisett, Mass., 79
Mayflower, xiv, 17, 37, 48, 51, 316–17, 444*n*
McCarthy, Eugene, 323, 381–2
McCarthy, Mary, 147, 150, 153, 170, 180, 184, 253, 331, 345, 358, 369, 376
McLean Asylum for the Insane, *xv,* xiv–xvii, *41*, 43, 141, 163, *164*
McLean Hospital, *xv,* xiv–xvii, 3–4, *41*, 43, 112, 137, 141, *146*, 154, 163, *164*, 170, 211, 275, 314–15, 316, *316*, 358, 374–5, 433*n*
Mein Kampf (Hitler), 349–50
melancholia, 157, 162–3, 289
Melville, Herman, 14, 21, 31, 32, 36–7, 47, 85, 90, 153, 201, 273,

282, 308, 324, 345, 349–50, 376, 401, 403

"Memories of West Street and Lepke" (Lowell), 88

Meredith, William, 150–1, 212–13, 254

methyldopa, 180

Metropolitan Opera, 154

"Mexico" (Lowell), 226, 227

"Middle Age" (Lowell), 66, 74

Miller, Jonathan, 20, 33, 153–4, 181, 209, 295

Miller, Perry, 53

Mills of the Kavanaughs, The (Lowell), 78, 114, 354

"Mills of the Kavanaughs, The" (Lowell), 84, 98, 231

Milton, John, xix, 15, 20, 74, 81, 90, 141, 155, 201, 282, 292, 310

Mingus, Charles, 302

Moby-Dick (Melville), *xx*, 14, 90

Mont Saint Michel and Chartres (Adams), 14

Moore, Merrill, 56, 60–1, 62, 69, 70, 71, 72–3, 76–7, 408–9, 450*n*

Moran, Charles Wilson, Lord, 234, 236

Mount Sinai Hospital, 183

Mourt's Relation: A Journal of the Pilgrims at Plymouth (Winslow and Bradford), 51

"Mr. Edwards and the Spider" (Lowell), 134, 197, 241–7, *242*

Myers, Mordecai, 37, 49

"My Last Afternoon with Uncle Devereux Winslow" (Lowell), 67

Naipaul, V. S., 148, 441*n*

Nantucket Island, 12–13, 22, 25, 32, 85, 89, *89*, 97, 282

Napoleon I, Emperor of France, 7, 12, 23, 62–3, 64, 65, 79, 154, 172, 209, 292, 350

Narragansett Indians, 395

Nash, Bishop, 383

Nashville, Tenn., 81

National Institute of Mental Health, 415

Native Americans, 51, 102, 154, 395

Naturalis Historia (Pliny the Elder), 161

Nazism, 87–8, 276

"Near the Unbalanced Aquarium" (Lowell), 65, 75, 133, 164–5, 190, 191, 192, 194

Nemerov, Howard, 335

Neville, Jill, 353–4

New Bedford Whaling Museum, *xx*

"New England" (Lowell), 80

"New England and Further" (Lowell), 190, 369, 376

Newfoundland, 49

New Hampshire General Court, 42

Newman, John Henry, 86

"New York Again" (Lowell), 323

New York Drama Critics' Circle Award, 266

New York Medical Journal, 275

New York Psychoanalytic Society, 281

New York Review of Books, 106, 183, 323

New York Times, 381, 382

Nicolson, Adam, 32, 365–6

Nicolson, Nigel, 476*n*

"Night Sweat" (Lowell), 215–16

"91 Revere Street" (Lowell), 18–19, 37, 190

Nobel Prize, xviii

Nolan, Sidney, 169, 181, 299–300, 353

"North Haven" (Bishop), 387–9, *388*

Norwich, John Julius (Viscount Norwich), 351

Notebook (Lowell), 238, 301, 302, 333, 334–5, 344

Notebook 1967–68 (Lowell), 171, 181, 182, 334

"Notice" (Lowell), 3

Nunc Dimittis, 384

Oates, Joyce Carol, 202

"Obit" (Lowell), 334

O'Connor, Flannery, 99–100, 101, 121, 190, 203

PERMISSIONS ACKNOWLEDGMENTS

Grateful acknowledgment is made to the following for permission to reprint previously published material:

Carcanet Press Limited: Excerpt letter from D. Davie to R. Lowell, June 24, 1967, originally published in *Collected Poems* by Donald Davie. Reprinted by permission of Carcanet Press Limited, Manchester, UK.

Diane P. Cherot: Excerpts of a letter from Curtis Prout, M.D. addressed to Robert Lowell, dated May 13, 1975 (Harry Ransom Center, University of Texas). Reprinted by permission of Diane P. Cherot.

The Estate of George Sassoon: Excerpt from "Repression of War Experience" by Siegfried Sassoon, copyright © Siegfried Sassoon. Reprinted by permission of The Estate of George Sassoon.

The Estate of Stephen Spender: Excerpts from unpublished letters by Stephen Spender (British Library), copyright © Stephen Spender. Reprinted by permission of The Estate of Stephen Spender.

Farrar, Straus and Giroux, LLC: Excerpts from *Collected Poems* by Robert Lowell, copyright © 2003 by Harriet Lowell and Sheridan Lowell; excerpts from *Collected Prose* by Robert Lowell, copyright © 1987 by Caroline Lowell, Harriet Lowell, and Sheridan Lowell; excerpts from *The Letters of Robert Lowell* edited by Saskia Hamilton, copyright © 2005 by Harriet Lowell and Sheridan Lowell; excerpts from *Notebook: Revised and Expanded Edition* by Robert Lowell, copyright © 1967, 1968, 1969, 1970 by Robert Lowell, copyright renewed 1998 by Harriet Lowell; excerpts from *Prometheus Bound*, derived from Aeschylus by Robert Lowell, copyright © 1967, 1969 by Robert Lowell; excerpts from *Words in Air: The Complete Correspondence Between Elizabeth Bishop and Robert Lowell*, edited by Thomas Travisano with Saskia Hamilton. Writings of Elizabeth Bishop copyright © 2008 by Alice Helen Methfessel. Robert Lowell letters copyright © Harriet Lowell and Sheridan Lowell. Compilation copyright © 2008 by Thomas J. Travisano; excerpt of "North Haven" from *Poems* by Elizabeth Bishop, copyright © 2011 by The Alice H. Methfessel Trust, Publisher's Note and compilation copyright © 2011 by Farrar, Straus and Giroux, LLC. Reprinted by permission of Farrar, Straus and Giroux, LLC.

ILLUSTRATION CREDITS

242 Jonathan Edwards (1703–1758) letter, MS 2958.3107, The New-York Historical Society.

248 Photograph by Robert Gardner. First published in *AGNI* 75 (2012).

250 Illustration by Frank Parker. Courtesy of Judith Parker.

264–65 Table by the author (updated and revised by K. R. Jamison, in *Manic-Depressive Illness: Bipolar Disorders and Recurrent Depression* [New York: Oxford University Press, 2007]).

268–69 Table by the author.

280 Abnormal flow of thinking: flight of ideas. In *Sims' Symptoms in the Mind: An Introduction to Descriptive Psychopathology*, 4th ed., ed. Femi Oyebode (Saunders Elsevier, 2008), p. 157, figure 9.2. Copyright © Elsevier.

297 Photograph by Shoshannah White Studio.

303 Courtesy of the Harry Ransom Center, The University of Texas at Austin.

316 Courtesy of McLean Hospital Archives.

319 Stan Grossfeld/Getty Images.

320 Courtesy of King's Chapel.

326 © Walker Evans Archive, The Metropolitan Museum of Art.

328 Courtesy of Evgenia Citkowitz.

340 Photograph by Tom Traill. Used courtesy of the photographer.

358 Courtesy of Harriet Lowell.

359 Courtesy of Evgenia Citkowitz.

364 Courtesy of Harriet Lowell.

380 Courtesy of Harriet Lowell

388 Courtesy of Harriet Lowell.

391 Photograph by James T. Campen. Used courtesy of the photographer.

402 Photograph by James T. Campen. Used courtesy of the photographer.

405 Photo © Steve Schapiro (*Life* magazine, February 19, 1965).

It's amazing
the day is still here
like lightning on an open field,
terra firma and transient
swimming in variation,
fresh as when man first broke
like the crocus all over the earth.

—*From* "The Day"

NOTHING WAS THE SAME
A Memoir

Kay Redfield Jamison, award-winning professor and writer, changed the way we think about moods and madness. Jamison uses her characteristic honesty, wit, and eloquence to look back at her relationship with her husband, Richard Wyatt, a renowned scientist who died of cancer. *Nothing Was the Same* is a penetrating psychological study of grief viewed from deep inside the experience itself.

Memoir/Psychology

EXUBERANCE
The Passion for Life

With the same grace and breadth of learning she brought to her studies of the mind's pathologies, Kay Redfield Jamison examines one of its most exalted states: exuberance. This "abounding, ebullient, effervescent emotion" manifests itself everywhere, from child's play to scientific breakthrough, and is crucially important to learning, risk-taking, social cohesiveness, and survival itself. *Exuberance: The Passion for Life* introduces us to such notably irrepressible types as Teddy Roosevelt, John Muir, and Richard Feynman, as well as Peter Pan, dancing porcupines, and Charles Schulz's Snoopy. It explores whether exuberance can be inherited, parses its neurochemical grammar, and documents the methods people have used to stimulate it. The resulting book is an irresistible fusion of science and soul.

Psychology

AN UNQUIET MIND
A Memoir of Moods and Madness

Dr. Jamison examines bipolar illness from the dual perspectives of the healer and the healed, revealing both its terrors and the cruel allure that at times prompted her to resist taking medication. *An Unquiet Mind* is a memoir of enormous candor, vividness, and wisdom—a deeply powerful book that has both transformed and saved lives.

Psychology/Memoir

NIGHT FALLS FAST
Understanding Suicide

An internationally acknowledged authority on depressive illnesses, Dr. Jamison has also known suicide firsthand: after years of struggling with manic-depression, she tried at age twenty-eight to kill herself. Weaving together a historical and scientific exploration of the subject with personal essays on individual suicides, she brings not only her remarkable compassion and literary skill but also all of her knowledge and research to bear on this devastating problem. This is a book that helps us to understand the suicidal mind, to recognize and come to the aid of those at risk, and to comprehend the profound effects on those left behind. It is critical reading for parents, educators, and anyone wanting to understand this tragic epidemic.

Psychology